THE

OLD ENGLISH HERBARIUM

AND

MEDICINA
DE QUADRUPEDIBUS

———

EARLY ENGLISH TEXT SOCIETY

Original Series 286

1984

I. British Library MS Cotton Vitellius C III, f. 74

THE
OLD ENGLISH HERBARIUM
AND
MEDICINA
DE QUADRUPEDIBUS

EDITED BY

HUBERT JAN DE VRIEND

Published for
THE EARLY ENGLISH TEXT SOCIETY
by the
OXFORD UNIVERSITY PRESS
LONDON NEW YORK TORONTO
1984

Oxford University Press, Walton Street, Oxford OX2 6DP

London New York Toronto
Delhi Bombay Calcutta Madras Karachi
Kuala Lumpur Singapore Hong Kong Tokyo
Nairobi Dar es Salaam Cape Town
Melbourne Auckland
and associated companies in
Beirut Berlin Ibadan Mexico City Nicosia

Published in the United States by
Oxford University Press, New York

British Library Cataloguing in Publication Data
The Old English herbarium and medicina de
quadrupedibus.—(Early English Text Society.
Original series; 286)
1. Plants—Early works to 1800
I. Vriend, Hubert Jan de   II. Series 581
QK41
ISBN 0-19-722288-9

Printed in Great Britain
at the University Press, Oxford

PREFACE

MOST of the medical lore of Anglo-Saxon England is preserved in four texts, the *Læceboc*, in the tenth-century MS Royal 12 D XVII in the British Library (Ker, no. 264), the *Lacnunga*, in MS H, and the Old English versions of the *Herbarium* and the *Medicina de Quadrupedibus*, which are found together in MSS VBHO. All these texts were first printed by Cockayne in his *Leechdoms, Wortcunning and Starcraft of Early England* (1864–6). Subsequently, separate editions were published of each text; see the Bibliography for *Læceboc* and *Lacnunga*, and the descriptions of the OE manuscripts for the other texts.

The OE versions of the *Herbarium* and the *Medicina de Quadrupedibus* are translations of Latin compilations which date from the fourth and fifth centuries of the Christian era. The history of the ancestors of these compilations, in particular of the herbals, can be traced back over several centuries, beginning with the Greek rhizotomists of the fourth century BC, of whom Diokles of Karystos may be mentioned as the first known author of a systematic herbal. A discussion of the earliest texts containing materia medica falls outside the scope of this book; the subject has been dealt with in several authoritative works, among which the articles by Singer and by Talbot deserve to be mentioned in particular.

Pliny, in his *Naturalis Historia*, made extensive use of the knowledge that had been amassed by the writers of the early medical treatises. Since Pliny's main concern was to write down whatever information he could find, and since he recorded this information without any critical examination of the authenticity or plausibility of his sources, it is natural that his volumes on the medicinal use of plants and animals (books xx–xxxii) should consist of a very heterogeneous mixture of fact and fiction.

Both the Latin *Herbarium* and the *Medicina de Quadrupedibus* are compilations containing material from different sources, among which the *Naturalis Historia* occupies a prominent place.

Inevitably, the number of obvious inaccuracies and mistakes in the later Latin manuscripts is much larger than in the earlier texts, and, as will appear from a comparison of the OE and Latin texts in this edition, the proportion of corrupt and unintelligible cures in the OE version is even higher.

The present synoptical edition of the eleventh-century MS V and the twelfth-century MS O, with relevant variants from MSS B and H, and with Latin parallels, has been undertaken for two main reasons. In the first place the book may be seen as a somewhat belated reply to Cockayne's remark, in the Preface to his edition of MS V, that 'for the history of our language it may some day be required that [MS O] should be printed for comparison with [MS V]' (pp. lxxxiv f.). Secondly, it is hoped that this edition may facilitate and stimulate a comparative study of the Latin and OE versions of the two treatises.

My sincere thanks are due to the library staffs of the following institutes, who offered me hospitality, gave me their generous assistance, and granted me access to their priceless manuscripts: Archivio della Badia, Montecassino; Biblioteca Estense, Modena; Biblioteca Governativa, Lucca; Biblioteca Medicea Laurenziana, Firenze; Biblioteca Nazionale, Torino; Bibliotheek der Rijksuniversiteit, Leiden; Bodleian Library, Oxford; British Library, London; Burgerbibliothek, Bern; Engels Seminarium, Amsterdam; Koninklijke Bibliotheek, 's-Gravenhage; Museum Boerhaave, Leiden; Staats- und Stadtbibliothek, Augsburg; Universiteitsbibliotheek, Amsterdam; Wellcome Historical Medical Library, London.

The facsimiles are reproduced by courtesy of the Trustees of the British Library (Plates I, III, and IV) and of the Keeper of Western Manuscripts of the Bodleian Library (Plate II).

I also wish to thank the printer, who has carried out the difficult task of preparing this complicated text with admirable skill and care.

To mention all the friends and colleagues who in the past period have so generously given me their valuable advice and their moral support would make this preface too long; I shall therefore confine myself to naming two among them to whom I feel especially indebted: Professor Johan Gerritsen, of Groningen University, who inculcated in me the principles of good editorship, and Dr Pamela Gradon, Editorial Secretary of the Early English Text Society, who has been a true friend, always ready to discuss problems and answer queries with 'verray parfit gentilesse'.

Finally, I hope that this edition may not only throw some further light upon the history of the English language, but also prove to be useful to students of medical history and to those who are interested in 'wortcunning'.

CONTENTS

ILLUSTRATIONS

LIST OF ABBREVIATIONS

All book references are to the Bibliography.

Ack.	*see* Ackermann
Anm.	Anmerkung
Bi., Bi.¹, Bi.³	*see* Bierbaumer
b.m.	bottom margin
BT, BTS, BT(S), BTS(*Add*)	*see* Bosworth
Co.	*see* Cockayne
Cpb.	*see* Campbell
Dio.	*see* Sprengel
DP	*see* Lindheim
exp.	expunged
Fö.	*see* Förster
G. and S.	*see* Grattan
HA	*Herbarium Apulei*
H. and S.	*see* Howald
Hum.	*see* Humelberg
i.m.	inner margin
La	*see* Grattan
Lb	*see* Leonhardi
LHG	*see* Stracke
L. and S.	*see* Lewis
Li. and S.	*see* Liddell
M, MdQ	*Medicina de Quadrupedibus*
Ma.	*see* Niedermann
ME	Middle English
MED	*Middle English Dictionary*
note	explanatory note
OE	Old English
OED	*Oxford English Dictionary*
OEH	*Old English Herbarium*
o.m.	outer margin
Pl.	*see* Rackham
SB	*see* Sievers
t.m.	top margin
t.n.	textual note
WS	West Saxon

x LIST OF ABBREVIATIONS

SIGLA OF THE MANUSCRIPTS

A	London, British Library, Additional 8928
B	Oxford, Bodleian Library, Hatton 76
Ca	Montecassino, Archivio della Badia, V.97
H	London, British Library, Harley 585
Ha	London, British Library, Harley 4986
Har	London, British Library, Harley 5294
L	Lucca, Biblioteca Governativa, no. 296
O	London, British Library, Harley 6258 B
Slo	London, British Library, Sloane 1975
V	London, British Library, Cotton Vitellius C III
Vi	Wien, Nationalbibliothek, no. 93
Vo	Leiden, Bibliotheek der Rijksuniversiteit, Vossianus Latinus Q 9
W	London, Wellcome Historical Medical Library, no. 573

OFFICIAL ABBREVIATIONS OF NAMES OF BOTANISTS

Ait.	W. Aiton (1731–93)
Bak.	J. G. Baker (1834–1920)
Benth.	G. Bentham (1800–84)
Cyrill.	D. Cirillo (1739–99)
DC.	A. P. de Candolle (1778–1841)
Gilibert	J. E. Gilibert (1741–1814)
Hoffm.	F. G. Hoffmann (1761–1826)
Huds.	W. Hudson (1730–93)
Juss.	A. L. de Jussieu (1748–1836)
Koch	W. D. J. Koch (1771–1849)
L.	C. von Linné (1707–78)
Med.	F. K. Medicus (1736–1809)
Mill.	Ph. Miller (1691–1771)
Newm.	E. Newman (1801–76)
Pall.	P. S. Pallas (1741–1811)
P.B.	A. M. F. J. Palisot de Beauvais (1755–1820)
R.Br.	R. Brown (1773–1858)
Rehmann	A. Rehmann (1840–1917)
Schott	H. W. Schott (1794–1865)
Schreb.	J. C. D. von Schreber (1739–1810)
Sibth.	J. Sibthorp (1758–96)
Sm.	J. E. Smith (1759–1828)
Sprengel	C. Sprengel (1766–1833)
Sw.	O. Swartz (1760–1818)
Ten.	M. Tenore (1780–1861)
Trevir.	C. L. Treviranus (1779–1864)

INTRODUCTION

I. THE MANUSCRIPTS

In this edition of the two texts, three versions are printed on pp. 1–273; they are:

1. The OE version of MS V, with the relevant textual variants from MS B and MS H.
2. The OE version of MS O.
3. The parallel Latin version,[1] taken from the following manuscripts:

OEH	I–XXI	Vo
	XXII–CXXXII	Ca
	CXXXIII–CLXXXV	mainly A
MdQ	I–XIV	L.

Additional material has been taken from MSS Ha, Har, Slo, Vi, and W.

The OE manuscripts are described in the order in which they have been mentioned in this paragraph; the Latin manuscripts are briefly described in alphabetical order, except Slo and Vi, which are mentioned at the end.

1. THE OLD ENGLISH MANUSCRIPTS

MS V. London, British Library, Cotton Vitellius C III

Descriptions: MS Harley 6018, no. 168; Wanley, p. 217; Smith, p. 85; Planta, p. 423; Cockayne, pp. lxxv–lxxx; Flom, pp. 29–37; Beccaria, no. 74; Ker, nos. 218 and 219; Voigts, *OE Herbal*, ch. i.

In 1731 the codex was severely damaged by the fire in Ashburnham House: the edges of the leaves, especially the tops, were destroyed. Fortunately the text escaped destruction, but the top lines of many folios are slightly deformed on account of the shrinking of the vellum, and we must assume that the binding was

---

[1] The parallel Latin version of the table of contents of *OEH* is not included in this edition.

completely destroyed. In the nineteenth century[1] the leaves were
mounted separately in frames made of thick paper, and the codex
was placed in a new binding. It was rebound again in 1977.

The manuscript consists of six paper flyleaves, not numbered,
one paper folio numbered 1, 139 vellum folios numbered 3–141,
and five paper flyleaves, not numbered. The numbers used for
references are written in pencil in arabic numerals in the right-
hand top corners of the frames. On most of the original folios
there is still visible an earlier foliation in arabic numerals, often in
two places, running from 1 to 78, corresponding to our ff. 5 to 82.
As this foliation shows the same disarrangement of ff. 62–74 as
at present,[2] it is evident that it does not date back to the time when
the manuscript was still intact. In the top margin of both columns,
recto and verso, of the less damaged leaves of *OEH* there are in
roman numerals the numbers of the chapters corresponding with
the items in the table of contents on ff. 12–18. These two numberings do not correspond excactly with the numbering in this edition,
because five chapters (XI, LXXI, XCI, XCIX, and CLXXX in
this edition) were not included in the table of contents. As both
numberings show the same deviation from the actual arrangement
of the chapters, it must be assumed that the numbers in the text
were copied from the table of contents.[3] On the verso of the sixth
flyleaf preceding the texts is the note: 'Two flyleaves (ff. 2, 142)
taken out to be bound with 13 D I*, A psalter to which they
originally belonged. 16 Dec. 1912, J. Ph.'

Contents of the codex

f. 1r[4]	The book-plate of the Cottonian collection; at the bottom the signature *Robertus Cotton Bruceus*.
f. 1v	Blank.
f. 2	Removed (see above).
f. 3r	At the top in a late hand the title: *Macrobeus iii Saturnalibus*; under this in a different hand *Vitellius C III*.

---

[1] Planta (1802) refers to the older of the two foliations.
[2] See below, under *Ruling*.
[3] See pp. xxxix–xli for a collation of the numberings.
[4] Folio references: (*a*) folio number only: whole folio; (*b*) folio number with r
or with line number: recto; (*c*) folio number with v: verso.

f. 3v	Blank.
f. 4r	In a modern hand a list of contents of the codex.
f. 4v	Blank.
ff. 5r–10r	In Latin, the *Chronologia ab Adamo ad Apostolos*.[1]
f. 10v	In Latin, the titles of some chapters of *Macer Floridus de Viribus Herbarum*, some of them with glosses in OE.[2]
f. 11r	In an early modern hand the title *Herbal* (. . .) *Saxon* (. . .); at the bottom of the page in a sixteenth-century hand the name *elysabet colmore*; also some fragments of Latin herb cures.
f. 11v	A full-page coloured picture of a tall figure standing on a lion, dressed in amice, chasuble and stole, and flanked by a soldier and a monk.[3]
ff. 12r–18v/1a	A table of contents of *OEH* corresponding with the text contained in this manuscript; the names of the herbs in Latin[4] and OE, the cures in OE.[5]
f. 18v/2a–3b	Two recipes in OE in a hand later than that of *OEH*.[6]
f. 19r	A full-page coloured picture, explained by the inscription at the foot as representing Aesculapius, Plato, and a centaur.
f. 19v	A full-page coloured drawing showing a broad ornamental fillet surrounding the title of the book: (H)ERBARIU(M) APUL(EI P)LAT(ONIC)I QUOD AC(CE)PIT AB ESCOLAPIO ET (A) CH(I)RONE CENTAURO MAGISRO ACHILLIS.[7]

---

[1] Ker, no. 218: attributed to Peter of Poitiers, s. xii/xiii; Wanley, p. 217a: 'ante quadringentos annos'.

[2] For an English translation of this work, see G. Frisk (ed.), *A Middle English Translation of Macer Floridus de Viribus Herbarum* (Uppsala, 1949).

[3] Cockayne, p. lxxvii: 'It seems . . . to represent the church dignitary for whom the work was copied.' For a detailed discussion of the iconographic implications of this dedication page, see Voigts, 'A New Look', pp. 43 ff.

[4] In this book the terms 'Latin name', 'Latin title', etc., are used for all plant names which are not OE and which occur in one or more of the Latin manuscripts.

[5] Ed. Cockayne, pp. 2–68.

[6] Ibid., p. 378.

[7] In the manuscript the *S* of *MAGISRO* appears as a *Z* in mirror-writing.

ff. 20r–74v   An OE version of the enlarged[1] *Herbarium*:[2]

(1) Antonius Musa, *De herba vettonica liber* (f. 20/1a ÐEOS WYRT þe man betonican nemneð–f. 21v/4a ælteowe hælo);

(2) Apuleius Platonicus, *Herbarium* (f. 21v/14a Gif mannes heafod ace oððe sár sy–f. 58/11b ealle yfelu (heo) út anyd(eð));

(3) Dioscorides, *Liber medicinae ex herbis femininis* (f. 58/26b Ðeos wyrt ðe man lichanis stefanice–f. 74v/31b se sylfa drenc eac swylce on).[3]

ff. 75r–82v   The *Medicina de Quadrupedibus*,[4] an OE version of

(1) *De taxone liber* (f. 75/15a SAGAÐ ÐÆT ÆGYPta cyning–f. 75v/14b sona he bið gebeted);

(2) a treatise on the healing powers of the mulberry (f. 75v/15b Wið blodes flewsan–f. 76/8b þonne byþ heo geclænsod);

(3) the A-version of Sextus Placitus, *Liber medicinae ex animalibus* (f. 76/17b Wiþ nædran slite–f. 82v/20b hundas cene).

ff. 82v–83r   Four recipes in OE in three hands later than that of *OEH*.[5]

f. 83r–83v   In Latin, seven recipes in one hand and two charms in another hand.[6]

ff. 84r–85ra   In Latin, a tract on urines.

f. 85rb and 85v   Blank.

ff. 86r–138v   In Latin, the *Saturnalia* by Macrobius, book i and part of book ii.[7]

ff. 139r–141v   Recipes in English in different hands of the sixteenth or seventeenth century.

---

[1] The term 'enlarged *Herbarium*' is used to indicate the collocation in Latin manuscripts of the three texts mentioned in this item.

[2] Ed. Cockayne, pp. 70–324; Hilbelink (1 and 2 only).

[3] For the abrupt ending of the text at this point, see below under *Ruling*.

[4] Ed. Cockayne, pp. 326–72; de Vriend.

[5] Ed. Cockayne, pp. 374–6.

[6] Four of the recipes, ibid. p. 376.

[7] Wanley, p. 217: 'liber . . . eleganter (in Gallia ut videtur) octingentis abhinc annis exaratus'.

It is evident that the codex is made up of three major parts:

(A) The *Chronologia* (ff. 5–10).

(B) The *Herbarium*, the *Medicina de Quadrupedibus* and some minor texts (ff. 11–85).

(C) Macrobius' *Saturnalia* (ff. 86–138).

There is no reason to doubt that ff. 84 and 85 belong to part B: like the other folios of this part they are arranged in two columns of thirty-one lines.[1] As regards the three folios at the beginning of the codex, f. 1 was very probably prefixed to the volume when it was in the possession of Sir Robert Cotton, f. 3 must have been a flyleaf of part C, f. 4 may have been a flyleaf of any of the three parts. It may be assumed that parts A, B, and C were originally separate and were then bound in one volume.

In the *Catalogus Librorum Manuscriptorum in Bibliotheca Roberti Cottoni*, MS Harley 6018 (1621), we find this description of MS V:

168.

1. Chronologia ab Adamo ad Apostolos.
2. Herbarius Apulei Platonici quod accepit ab Aescolapio et a Chirone Centauro magistro et aliis.
3. Tractatus de urinis.
4. Exemplar vetus libri 1 Macrob. et partis 2.

As has been pointed out, items 2 and 3 of this description must have been parts of one original volume.

Folios 12–82 of the codex are in one hand of the eleventh century,[2] with the following exceptions:

(*a*) The OE plant names and nine Latin plant names (in XLIV, LXVI, LXVII, LXXVI, CX, CXIV, CXXXII, CXXXVI, and CLI) in the titles of the chapters in the text of *OEH*, also the animal names belonging to some of the additional drawings in *OEH*; according to Ker (p. 284) in a hand of s. xi med. (hand A);[3] it is certain that these

---

[1] Except ff. 12–18, which have two columns of thirty lines.

[2] Wanley, p. 217: 'liber est omnino similis et in Bibliotheca Bodleiana [i.e. MS B, which is "ante Conquisitionem Angliae"]'; Co, p. lxxv: between 1000 and 1066; Flom, p. 37: *c.*1040–50; G. and S., p. 28: *c.*950; Beccaria, no. 74: first half of eleventh century; Ker, no. 219: s. xi¹.

[3] This hand may also have written *wyrt* at the beginning of ch. I, and the instances of *w* and another sign indicating the places where plant names were to be added to the illustrations; these are clearly visible on ff. 53–56.

names were added after the illustrations were completed (see *omnimorbia* on Plate I, a typical example of the method followed); possibly they were added by the illustrator.[1]

(*b*) All the other Latin plant names in the titles of the chapters in the text of *OEH*, according to Ker (p. 284) in a hand of s. xv (hand B).[2]

(*c*) A note in a hand of s. xii on f. 17v.

(*d*) The recipes on f. 18v.

(*e*) Two imperfectly erased additions, probably in a hand of s. xvi, on ff. 35r and 38r.

(*f*) An addition in a hand of s. xvi on f. 76r.

(*g*) Some additional plant names in a clear hand of s. xiii–xiv on ff. 43r, 53v, and 54r (2×); see the textual notes.

(*h*) The plant name *beteyne* on f. 20r.

(*i*) The numberings of the chapters in table of contents and text.

The text is illustrated throughout with coloured drawings of plants and animals. There is a plant illustration at the beginning of each chapter, except XII and CLXXXV, in *OEH*,[3] an animal illustration at the beginning of each chapter, except II, in *MdQ*, and there are several additional drawings, mainly of snakes and scorpions.[4] Most of these drawings show a striking resemblance to the illustrations in MS Ca. That the illustrations in the OE manuscript are of Mediterranean origin becomes clear from

[1] Linda E. Voigts, 'A New Look', p. 41, points out that in a number of instances the same pigment was used for parts of the illustrations and for the OE titles.

[2] In several places earlier titles, or fragments of them, usually in Latin, occasionally in OE, written in a larger hand but otherwise resembling hand B, are vaguely visible; sometimes they occur in places where no title in hand B is added, as in IV, V, IX, XIV, etc., sometimes they are found in combination with a title in hand B, as in XX, XXXIX, LXIII, LXXII, etc., sometimes the title in hand B has been written on the earlier title or on part of it, as is the case in LXIX (f. 41/10a), where *nym* is visible on one side of the drawing, *f* on the other, and *ete* has been covered by the title in hand B. Since these titles, in as far as they are legible, do not differ substantially from the titles in hands A and B, they are not printed in the present edition.

[3] XII, *Mugwyrt tagantes*, is not a separate chapter in MS V; the space for CLXXXV, *colocynthisagria*, on f. 69v, was probably left open because the illustration of CLXXXIII, *milotis*, on f. 69r, is too clearly visible in this place.

[4] The additional drawings in the earlier chapters of *OEH* are provided with titles (*Nædre*, etc.) which are printed in this edition. The other drawings are found at pp. 72/1, 78/15, 82/8, 112/11, 146/9, 152/14, 160/5, 166/20, 174/6, 176/10, 244/1, 250/20, 256/7, 260/14, and 268/12.

drawings of such common English plants as henbane (f. 23v) and mugwort (f. 25v), which are of southern and not of English species, and from the accurate way in which the scorpion is drawn.[1]

One of the green pigments used, probably sulphate of copper, has frequently destroyed the vellum, causing great damage to several folios. This pigment was apparently not used for all the illustrations, for there are many places where the green colour has not caused any damage.

M. R. James (*The Ancient Libraries of Canterbury and Dover*, Cambridge, 1903) prints the list of English books belonging to the Library of Christ Church, Canterbury, which forms a separate section in the catalogue of Prior Henry Eastry (d. 1331); no. 308 is a 'Herbarius Anglice depictus'. About this text James (p. xxv) observes: 'Identified (correctly, as I think) by Wanley with the MS Vitellius C III.' Ker (p. 285) rejects the suggestion that the manuscript is from Canterbury, declaring that 'there is nothing to show that this is it', and that the twelfth-century writing in the manuscript is not of the Canterbury type.

It is possible that Elysabet Colmore, whose name appears on the title page of the *Herbarium* (f. 11r), was its owner for some period in the sixteenth century.

Description of the folios containing OEH and MdQ: *11–82*

Collation of the quires

Not possible because the leaves have been remounted.

Measurements[2]

Frames, 307 × 235 mm; what is left of the original leaves, 250–75 × 190 mm; written space, 225–30 × 155–65 mm; two columns (*a*, *b*) of thirty-one lines;[3] width of each column, 67–70 mm.

Pricking

No pricks; they were probably burnt away in the fire, or cut off when the volume was repaired.

---

[1] See G. and S., pp. 72 ff., for reproductions of parallel drawings in Ca and V.

[2] In all cases where measurements are given the qualification 'circa' should be added.

[3] Except ff. 12–18, which have two columns of thirty lines.

Ruling

By hard point; each sheet ruled separately on the hair side; hair facing hair, flesh facing flesh; the folios ruled are 11r, 12v/13r, 14v/15r, 16v/17r, 18v, 19v/20r, 21v/22r, etc., to 65v/66r, 67v, 68v/69r, 70r, 71v/72r, etc., to 81v/82r. After f. 18 a leaf was probably cut out; the irregularity after f. 67 is of more recent date. During the process of restoration of the manuscript ff. 62–74 were disarranged. Cockayne's explanation is that the person who repaired the manuscript probably possessed a model of the *Herbarium Apulei* to guide him accurately up to f. 59; he was then left on his own with the Dioscorides material, and not thinking of the table of contents or of the possibility of consulting parallel texts he was not able to determine the correct order. He adhered to the correct flesh–hair arrangement, except after f. 67, where he should have placed f. 70. The correct order between ff. 61 and 75 is: 64, 63, 74, 65, 66, 67, 62, 71, 70, 68, 72, 73, 69; this is in accordance with the hair–flesh arrangement. There are pairs of vertical lines to mark off the outer and inner margins; the space between the two vertical lines on the left is used for the initials of column a. The two columns are separated by three vertical lines which form two spaces of 10 mm each (x, y); space y is used for the initials of column b. The horizontal lines are not continuous: only the spaces for the text are ruled, with the exception of lines 1 and 31, which are extended into the margins. On most folios the ruling for line 1 is not visible, owing to the shrinking of the vellum.

Colour of the letters

Black; the initials are in different colours—red, green, blue, and brown.

Script

Late OE insular; very regular, and with a few exceptions, consistent. Some characteristics:

1. *a*: predominantly square. Cf. Flom (p. 34 n. 10), who prints a table giving the number of occurrences of round and square *a* on some folios of *OEH*, showing that round *a*

outnumbers square *a* only on ff. 20 and 21. After these first two folios the proportion changes rapidly: on the last folio in the table, 71, there are two instances of round *a* as against ninety-one of square *a*. The square *a* in this text is horned, i.e. the first stroke begins with a slight projection to the left of the top; this horn is also found in *c* and *e*. It is sometimes difficult to distinguish this *a* from *u*, because the top is not always completely closed.

2. *d*: both the low and the tall form are used, with many transitional varieties between these two. Tall *d* is smaller than *ð*. It is round-backed.

3. *ð*: nearly always tall, with a long crossbar which is tagged at the right end.

4. *e* is mostly found with a straight back. Round-backed *e* and tall *e* are used occasionally.

5. *ȝ* invariably has the flat insular head and a closed ring below the line.

6. *s* is usually the low type (deep-stroke and club); long *s* appears now and then, mostly in the combination *st*, but also before *m*, *w*, in pairs, and in final position; round *s* occurs very rarely.

7. *wynn* has a closed bowl and is easily distinguishable from *p*, whose bowl meets the main stroke at right angles.

8. *y* is mostly the straight-limbed type, the right stroke running through so far below the line that it cometimes touches the ascender of the letter in the next line. Rounded *y* is much less frequent. Both symbols are dotted.

9. Abbreviations: 'and' is invariably represented by the tironian sign *ȝ*; the swung dash is frequently used to indicate *e* in *ge-*, and final *-m*, *-(n)e*, *-er*; *þæt* is nearly always abbreviated to a crossed *þ*.

10. Accents: the long acute accent occurs fairly frequently; in most of the recorded instances it is on a long vowel in a stressed syllable. A striking feature is the frequent accentuation of the word *sar*.

11. Marks of punctuation: only the dot is used, the height ranging from the middle of the minuscules to the level of the line.[1]

---

[1] On f. 23/28b and f. 82v/20b there are two different signs not found elsewhere.

Printed editions of this version of *OEH* and *MdQ*: O. Cockayne[1] in vol. i, pp. 2–372 of *Leechdoms, Wortcunning and Starcraft of Early England* (London, 1864, repr. London, 1961), OE text of MS V with textual variants of MSS B and H and occasionally from MS O, and translation into Modern English with an Anglo-Saxon flavour; A. J. G. Hilbelink, *Cotton MS Vitellius C III of the Herbarium Apuleii* (diss.), (Amsterdam, 1930), only *OEH* chapters I–CXXXII, no table of contents; H. J. de Vriend, *The Old English Medicina de Quadrupedibus* (diss.) (Tilburg, 1972).

MS B. Oxford, Bodleian Library, Hatton 76

Descriptions: Bernard, I. i. 185, no. 4125.100; Wanley, pp. 71–6; Cockayne, p. lxxxiv; Madan II, part ii, 853–4, no. 4125 (100); Beccaria, no. 85; Ker, no. 328.

The codex consists of one paper flyleaf numbered I, 144 vellum folios numbered 1–65, 65a, 66–87, 87a, 87b, 88–110, 110a, 111–30, 130a, 131–9, and two paper flyleaves, the first of which is numbered 140 (ult.).

Contents of the codex

ff. 1r–54v	Fragments of an OE translation of Gregory's *Dialogi*.[2]
ff. 55r–67v	A fragment of an OE version of the *Monita* or *Admonitio* commonly ascribed to St. Basil.[3] It breaks off abruptly on f. 67v, where a later hand has written: 'Desunt folia circiter 12'.
ff. 68r–73v	A table of contents of the *Herbarium* which corresponds with the text contained in this manuscript; the names of the herbs in Latin and OE, the cures in OE.
ff. 74r–124r	An OE version of the enlarged *Herbarium*: (1) Antonius Musa, *De herba vettonica liber* (f. 74/16a ÐEOS WYRT ÐE MAN bettonican nemneð–f. 75v/8a æltæwe hælo);

[1] In the original edition of 1864–6 the editor's name appears as 'Rev. Oswald Cockayne, M.A. Cantab.', in the reprint of 1961 as 'Rev. Thomas Oswald Cockayne'.

[2] Ed. H. Hecht, *Bischofs Wærferth von Worcester Uebersetzung der Dialoge Gregors des Grossen* (Leipzig, 1900).

[3] Ed. H. W. Norman, *Hexameron of St. Basil* (London, 1848, 2nd impr. London, 1849).

(2) Apuleius Platonicus, *Herbarium* (f. 75v/20a
Gif mannes héafod ace oððe sar sy–f. 110a/5a
ealle yfelu heo út adeð);

(3) Dioscorides, *Liber medicinae ex herbis femininis*
(f. 110a/20a Ðeos wyrt þe man lichanis
stefanice–f. 124/29b hit astirað þone innoð).

ff. 124v–130ar The *Medicina de Quadrupedibus*, an OE version
of

(1) *De taxone liber* (f. 124v/2a SAGAÐ ÐÆT
ÆGYPTA cyninc–f. 125/30a sona he bið
gebeted);

(2) a treatise on the healing powers of the mulberry (f. 125/31a Wið blodes flewsan–
f. 125v/20a þonne bið heo geclænsod);

(3) the A-version of Sextus Placitus, *Liber
medicinae ex animalibus* (f. 125v/29a Wið
næddran slite–f. 130a/7a hundas cene).

ff. 131r–139v In Latin, two letters about precious stones; the
second letter is an alphabetical enumeration of
precious stones with healing powers.[1]

The codex, which in its present form was acquired by the
Bodleian Library in 1671, consists of two parts that were originally separate: part A (ff. 1–67) and part B (ff. 68–139). Part A was
at Worcester *c.*1200, as appears from a number of glosses in the
'tremulous' hand[2] (the first on f. 40v, the last on f. 67r). Of part
B, ff. 68–130a are in one hand of the eleventh century,[3] with the
following exceptions:

(*a*) The titles and the entire chapters CXX–CXXIII in the
table of contents, in a hand contemporary with the main
hand.

(*b*) The titles in the text, in a later hand, probably s. xii.

(*c*) The numberings of the chapters: one in the table of
contents and the text in a later hand; one early numbering,
faded, in the text, not always visible.

[1] Ed. Joan Evans, *Magical Jewels* (Oxford, 1922).

[2] Cf. W. Keller, 'Die litterarischen Bestrebungen von Worcester', *Quellen
und Forschungen zur Sprach- und Kulturgeschichte der germanischen Völker*, 84
(1900), 20.

[3] Wanley, p. 76: ante Conquisitionem Angliae; Cockayne, p. lxxxiv: the
same age nearly as MS V; Madan II, part ii, 853–4: first half eleventh century;
Beccaria, no. 85: first half eleventh century; Ker, no. 328B: s. xi med.

(*d*) Some additions in the text: in some places the plant names are also found in an early hand, much faded; in some spaces for illustrations in *OEH* a word, probably *bana*, is vaguely distinguishable; these additions are not printed.

There are faded stylus drawings in three places: a stylized flower on f. 76r, a dog sitting up on f. 95r, and a dragon on f. 126v. Both in *OEH* and in *MdQ* spaces have been left for illustrations, nearly always agreeing exactly in size with those in MS V, and in the same places.

Description of the folios containing OEH *and* MdQ: 68–130*a*

Collation of the quires

Starting from f. 68, regular eights, including ff. 87a, 87b, and 110a, with leaves cut out after ff. 72, 73, 114, 119, and 130, anterior to foliation; the leaf cut out after f. 73 was probably blank.

Measurements

Leaves, 295×208 mm; written space, 245×160–75 mm; two columns of thirty-one lines; width of each column, 73–6 mm. Folio 119 lacks a narrow strip at the bottom; f. 130a is a small fragment, measuring 80×75 mm and containing one column of seven lines; the verso is blank.

Pricking

Clearly visible in the top margin of most leaves and in the bottom margin of several leaves for all the vertical lines; no pricks visible in the side margins.

Ruling

By hard point; each leaf ruled separately on the hair side; hair facing hair, flesh facing flesh; the folios ruled are 68r, 69v/70r, 71v/72r, 73r, 74r, 75v/76r, etc., to 114v, 115 v/116r, 117v/118r, 119v, 120v/121r, etc., to 130v, 130av. The pattern of the lines is the same as that in MS V, but in this manuscript the top horizontal line, which runs from edge to edge, is clearly visible.

Colour of the letters

Black; the initials are green and red; in the table of contents the initials are alternately green and red.

DEOS PYRT ÐE MAN
bettonican nemneð.

II. Bodleian MS Hatton 76, f. 74

Script

Late OE insular; a very regular hand. Some characteristics:

1. *a* is round; occasionally the *a* with top is found.
2. *æ* is round; the '*e*' part is often so small that it is difficult to distinguish this symbol from *a*.
3. *c* is round-backed.
4. *d*: as in MS V.
5. *e* is mostly straight-backed, occasionally round-backed or tall. Final *e* has a long tongue.
6. *ʒ* has the flat insular head; the tail is always open.
7. *s* is mostly the low type; long *s* appears especially in the combinations *sm, st, sw*; round *s* is not found.
8. *wynn*: as in MS V.
9. *y* is always the straight-limbed type, dotted.
10. Abbreviations: as in MS V.
11. Accents: as in MS V, except that the accent is half-long.
12. Marks of punctuation: as in MS V.

There exists a transcript of this version of *OEH* and *MdQ* by Francis Junius: MS Junius 58 in the Bodleian Library. The copy is very accurate. It contains some marginal notes in Latin (see Notes to *MdQ* II, *MdQ* III. 7), and two emendations (see note to *MdQ* X. 5).

This version of *OEH* and *MdQ* has never been printed separately. Cockayne (pp. 2–372), in his edition of MS V, gives the textual variants of MS B.

MS H. London, British Library, Harley 585

Descriptions: Bernard, II. i. 359, no. 9164.3; Wanley, pp. 304–5; Cat. Harl. i. 353–5; Cockayne, p. lxxxiv; Wright, *Bald's Leechbook*, pp. 11–12; Beccaria, no. 75; Ker, no. 231.

The codex consists of two paper flyleaves, not numbered, two vellum flyleaves numbered 1* and 2*, 193 vellum folios numbered 1–193, and three paper flyleaves, not numbered. Two earlier foliations are still partly visible; f.1 has the old numbers xi and xiii. The first ten or twelve leaves of the original manuscript are apparently missing; f. 1 starts in cure 10 of ch. IV of *OEH*. The order of the chapters in *OEH* in this codex differs from that in V and B, as is shown in the following table:[1]

Numbering in this edition	Numbering in MS H
I, II, III, IV (part)	*om.* I, VI, VII, VIII (part)
IV (part), V	VIII (part),[2] IX
VI, VII, VIII, IX (intr. and cure 1)	*om.* II, III, IV, V (intr. and cure 1)
IX (cure 2)–LXXIV	XXXIV (cure 2)–XCVI[3]
LXXV–XCVII	X–XXXII
XCVIII	XXXIII (intr., cures 1, 2)[4] and XCVII (cure 3)
XCIX, C	XCVIII, XCIX
CI–CLXXXV	CI–CLXXXV

It may be observed that the part of the text which contains chs. IX. 2–LXXIV[5] is found on ff. 18–49, which constitute four regular quires of eight leaves. This part probably belonged to an earlier version of which the beginning was lost or discarded, and which was inserted in the existing codex, not after f. 9, at the end of our first quire, because this leaf ends in the middle of a long sentence (XC. 1), but after f. 17: the cure at the end of that quire (XCVIII. 2) was cut short by omission of the last four words. This would also account for the fact that on f. 2v ch. V is immediately followed by ch. LXXV. The lost fragment of the earlier version, in which the original order of chapters in the Latin texts was observed, must have consisted of approximately twelve folios containing chs. I–IX. 1.[6] This was followed by the four quires which in the existing manuscript begin at f. 18. The second version of the beginning of the text contained the chapters in the order I, VI–IX, II–V. Only the last part of this second version, containing chs. IV. 10 (part)–V, is extant; it is the beginning of the existing manuscript. The reference on f. 2v to *herba viperina* being *in v. folio huius libelli* confirms this: ch. I must have

---

[1] See also the collation of the numberings of the chapters in the printed text in VBH, pp. xxxix–xli.

[2] H begins on f. 1 at *genim ða ylcan wyrte*, in IV. 10.

[3] Numbers XXXVII, LXIV, LXV are used twice.

[4] The last four words of cure 2, *heo alyseþ þone man*, are omitted.

[5] All chapter numbers in this paragraph refer to the present edition.

[6] The space taken up by the missing parts can be easily estimated: one folio in H roughly corresponds to 36–8 half-lines in V.

taken up the first four folios. The missing part of this version consisted of approximately ten folios.

The double numbering of our chs. IX and XCVIII can be easily accounted for: our ch. IX is ch. V in the second version of the beginning of the text in H; it has this number in the table of contents. The last part of this chapter is at the beginning of the text in the inserted four quires, following the first part of H's ch. XXXIII; it has number XXXIV in the text.[1] The first part of our ch. XCVIII is at the end of the second quire of the extant manuscript; cure 2 is followed by the four inserted quires; cure 3 comes after the inserted part, which ends with H's ch. XCVI; it is therefore numbered XCVII in the text.

Contents of the codex

ff. 1*, 2*   Some doggerel verse in a seventeenth-century hand, signed *Barbara Crokker*.

ff. 1r–101v   An OE version of part of the enlarged *Herbarium*:
(1) Apuleius Platonicus, *Herbarium* (f. 1/1 genim ða ylcan wyrte–f. 66v/10 ealle yfelu heo ut anydeð);
(2) Dioscorides, *Liber medicinae ex herbis femininis* (f. 66v/11 Ðeos wyrt ðe man lichanis stæfanice–f. 101v/14 astyreð þone innoð).

ff. 101v–114v   An incomplete *Medicina de Quadrupedibus*, an OE version of
(1) *De taxone liber* (f. 101v/15 SAG'A'Ð ÐÆT EGYPta cyning–f. 104v/11 sona he bið gebeted);
(2) a treatise on the healing powers of the mulberry (f. 104v/11 Wið blodes flewsan–f. 106v/6 þonne bið heo geclænsod);
(3) part[2] of the A-version of Sextus Placitus, *Liber medicinae ex animalibus* (f. 106v/6 Wið nædrán slite–f. 114v/18 on gesmyred, hraðe hyt gelacnað).

ff. 115r–129v   An incomplete table of contents of the *Herbarium*, 'manu paullo recentiori' (Cat. Harl.).

---

[1] For the rest there is complete agreement between the text and the table of contents as regards the numbering of the chapters.

[2] From the beginning to ch. VI. 6 in this edition.

ff. 130r–151v⎫ *Lacnunga*, a collection of recipes, charms, etc.,
ff. 157r–193r⎭ mainly in OE.[1]
ff. 152r–157r In Latin, with continuous gloss in OE, the
                 Lorica of Gildas.[2]

Folios 1–114 of the codex are in one hand; about the date of
writing opinions range from early tenth century to mid-eleventh
century or a little later.[3] Wanley's estimate is demonstrably
incorrect: the language of H, like that of VB, is typical of the
period of Ælfric. A date earlier than *c*.975 is therefore highly
improbable. At the other end, there is no evidence which might
give support to Cockayne's suggestion.

Wanley's description of the manuscript in Cat. Harl. opens thus:
'Codex membranaceus in 8vo, diversis manibus (sed tamen per-
vetustis) exaratus; quondam peculium reverendi et doctissimi
viri Robert Bourscough; deinde meum: quem etiam in Catalogo
nostro Codicum Anglo-Saxonicorum descriptum, Domino Collec-
tori hujusque Bibliothecae, nuperrime vendidi.' Robert Bourscough
has been identified as rector of Totnes in the diocese of Exeter
(see Bernard II. i. 359). On f. 1 in the top margin appear the words:
'Liber Humfredi Wanley'.

In the *Herbarium* section the manuscript contains some rude
marginal sketches, mainly of serpents. Initials are sometimes
elaborated into serpents or 'biting beasts'. The Ð of the opening
of ch. CXXXIII is decorated in a special way, perhaps to mark the
beginning of the Dioscorides part; see Plate III.

Description of the folios containing OEH *and* MdQ: *1–129*

Collation of the quires

Folios 1–9 form an eight with one leaf inserted after f. 6, then
fourteen regular eights to f. 121, and an eight with one leaf
inserted after f. 123 and one leaf wanting after f. 129. The
incomplete text of *MdQ* ends at the bottom of f. 114v with the
sixth cure of ch. VI, and is immediately followed on f. 115r
by the table of contents of the *Herbarium*.

---

[1] Ed. G. and S., pp. 96–130 and 146–204, with a translation; Leonhardi,
pp. 121–55.

[2] Ed. G. and S., pp. 130–46, with a translation; Leonhardi, pp. 175–93.

[3] Wanley, p. 304: ante 800 annos; Cockayne, p. lxxxiv: a little later than MSS
V and B; Wright, *Bald's Leechbook*, p. 11: about 1000; Beccaria, no. 75: mid-
eleventh century; Ker, no. 231: s. x/xi.

ᵹepihte cnucato ⁊ piper mala án
dufte ᵹemænᵹe mid ele ⁊ mi þe
þon dǽ þ ſar ſone ⁊ þ þ ecean
uⁱhrum nyſſe habbað·

Ƿ iſ hraþ pylce heᵹᵹe yſelnyſſe·
on hiſ hꝛoſe ᵹeſeo ᵹenim edaꝛ
pyꝛte mand pæᵹo þam on mid
dan þam huⁱ ⁊ pa micel ⁊ pa he
þon hæbbe· eal la ⁊ ſelu heoꝛ
any ded·

Deoꝛpyꝛt de man lichamſ
ſtæ ꝼanice ⁊ oþ þun aman
læce pyꝛt o nemned· haꝼað lan
ᵹe leaſ· ⁊ ᵹe þuꝛe ⁊ hæpene ⁊ hyꝛe
ſtela biþ mid ᵹe þuꝛ um boᵹum
⁊ heo haꝛað· on uſ eþeaꝛonm
þam ſtelan ᵹeolupe bloſ
man· þyſſe pyꝛte ſæd on pine·

III. British Library MS Harley 585, f. 66v

Measurements

Leaves, 190×110 mm; written space, 145–50×75–85 mm; 17 or 18 lines per page.

Pricking

In the top and bottom margins pricks are visible for the vertical lines, and in the outer side margin there are two pricks for the top and bottom horizontal lines.

Ruling

By hard point; a whole quire taken at a time, ruled on the hair side; the ruling is clear and deep on the outer leaves and barely visible on the leaves in the middle of a quire; hair facing hair, flesh facing flesh. The vertical lines are single; only the top and bottom horizontal lines are extended into the margins.

Colour of the letters

Black (slightly faded). Originally some of the initials were coloured red; in most places the red colour has faded or has disappeared completely.

Script

Much less refined than the script in MSS V and B, with many erasures and corrections. Some characteristics:

1. *a* is round.
2. *æ* is round; the loop of the '*e*' part is higher than the top of the '*a*' part.
3. *c* is round-backed.
4. *d*: as in MS V.
5. *e*: tall; the height varies.
6. *ȝ* has the flat insular head; the tail is always open.
7. *s* is usually the low type. There are several instances of long *s* (mostly in the combination *st*) and round *s*.
8. *wynn*: as in MS V.
9. *y* is mostly straight-limbed; rounded *y* occurs a few times. Both are dotted.
10. Abbreviations: the same as in MSS V and B, but, apart from *7*, less frequent.

11. Accents: the half-long acute accent occurs frequently, also in non-root syllables and occasionally on consonants.

12. Marks of punctuation: only the dot is used, the height ranging from the middle of the minuscules to the level of the line. The scribe makes a liberal use of the dot in the middle of sentences, probably to lay emphasis on the word preceding it.[1]

This version of *OEH* and *MdQ* has never been printed separately. Cockayne (pp. 2–372), in his edition of MS V, gives the textual variants of MS H.

MS O. London, British Library, Harley 6258 B

Descriptions: Cat. Harl. iii. 347; Cockayne, pp. lxxxiv–lxxxv; Berberich, pp. 1–7; Delcourt, pp. xii–xiii; Wells, p. 428; (Ker, p. xix).

The codex consists of five paper flyleaves, not numbered, sixty-six vellum leaves numbered 1–66, and five paper flyleaves, not numbered. The vellum leaves also show an earlier numbering, running from 31 to 98. Collation of the two foliations:

Old:
31–3, 34–7, 38,   49,   54–5,   56–71, 71*, 72–98.
New:
1–3, 4,[2] 5–8, 9, 10, 11–18, 15=19, 20–1, 22, 23–38, 39, 40–66.

In this edition the new foliation is referred to, except where the qualification (*old*) is added. At the top of most of the folios containing *OEH* a letter is found, corresponding to the first letter of the Latin name of the herb mentioned there.

Contents of the codex

ff. 1r–44r   An OE herbal, based on the enlarged *Herbarium*;[3] the herbs from the three original texts are arranged in alphabetical order according to their Latin names;[4] the alphabetical order is observed only

---

[1] See C. G. Harlow, *The Punctuation of Six of Ælfric's Catholic Homilies* (Oxford diss., 1955), for this function of the dot.

[2] For the numbers in the new foliation which have no parallels in the old, see pp. xxxiv–xxxvi.

[3] Ed. Berberich, pp. 65–138.

[4] With three exceptions: *apium* (f. 22), probably a mistake of a later reviser, see p. xxxiv; *sion* (f. 23), see t.n. to p. 177/14; *temolum* (f. 39v), see t.n. to p. 95/9.

in respect of the first letter[1] (f. 1/1 Wið innoðes sar ȝením þa wirte–f. 44/26 ealne þane bíte þæs cancores heo afeormað).

ff. 44v–51r An OE version, with omissions, of the *Medicina de Quadrupedibus*:[2]

(1) *De taxone liber* (f. 44v/2 þe Egypta 'king' þe Idpartus wæs hatan–f. 45v/16 sona he byð ȝebeted);

(2) a treatise on the healing powers of the mulberry (f. 45v/16 Wid blodes flewsan–f. 46/20 þanne byð heo ȝeclænsod);

(3) the A-version of Sextus Placitus, *Liber medicinae ex animalibus* (f. 46/22 Wyþ nærdran slite– f. 51/23 swylas ȝedwæsceþ).

f. 51r In OE, a herb-cure[3] (f. 51/24 Wið eafodece pollege– f. 51/25 smyre þæt heafod mid).

f. 51v In OE, six herb-cures under the title *De Beta*;[4] in Latin, three herb-cures.[5]

ff. 51v–66v An incomplete English version of a collection of recipes called *Peri Didaxeon* (= 'about the schools', sc. of medicine), mainly based on the *Practica* by Petrocellus.[6]

Most of the cures in *OEH* and some in *MdQ* are provided with titles in the margin. In this edition the marginal titles are pre-fixed to the cures to which they belong; they are placed in round brackets. They are usually in Latin, but it is very unlikely that they were copied from a Latin original, first because the terms used

---

[1] For further details see pp. xxxvii–xxxviii.
[2] Ed. Delcourt, pp. 2–22; de Vriend.
[3] Ed. Cockayne, p. 380; Delcourt, p. 24.
[4] Ed. Cockayne, pp. 380–2.
[5] Ibid., p. 382.
[6] Ed. Cockayne, iii. 82–144; Löweneck. Although this part of the manuscript is in the same hand as the rest, its language appears to be further removed from late West Saxon than that of *OEH* and *MdQ* (see J. Schiessl, *Laut- und Flexions-verhältnisse der frühmittelenglischen Rezeptensammlung Peri Didaxeon* (Erlangen, 1905). Furthermore, Petrocellus produced his original text *c*.1035 (see Löwen-eck, p. viii), so that it is clear that the textual tradition of the English version is much later than that of the other texts. Therefore, although it is just possible to regard the text as belonging to the OE linguistic tradition, from the historical point of view it is certainly wrong to include it among the major texts contain-ing Anglo-Saxon medical lore.

are often very different from their parallels in the Latin manuscripts, secondly because OE mistranslations from the original Latin text are reflected in these titles; see I. 16, 21, 26, 27, II. 15, III. 1, etc.; a particularly interesting case is found in LXXXVI. 3, where the Latin texts have *renes*, the OE texts *æddran*, which means both 'kidneys' and 'veins', and the title in O has *vena*; for an instance in *MdQ* see t.n. to p. 237/17–19.

The text of the codex is in one hand; the titles of the chapters, the titles of the cures which were added in the margin, and most of the glosses are in a hand very similar to, and possibly identical with, that of the text. According to several authorities the manuscript dates from the middle of the twelfth century;[1] it is not described in Wanley's *Catalogus*; Cat. Harl. (iii. 347) merely states that 'the MS is evidently very old'; Beccaria does not include it in his catalogue because it is not pre-Salernitan. Ker does not include the manuscript in his *Catalogue* because he dates the codex after 1200 (p. xix). It is true that the text displays the two new features mentioned by him: biting of *d* with following *e* and *o* (but this is not done consistently; see Plate no. IV) and crossing of the downstroke of the sign for *and*. But these features are also found in some manuscripts written a dozen or more years before 1200 (Ker p. xix, n. 3). In addition it may be pointed out that there is an unmistakable resemblance between this codex and MS Harley 55, ff. 5–13 (Laws of Cnut), dated mid-twelfth century by Ker (no. 226). This part of MS Harley 55 has the same kind of 'prickly' script as MS O, although much neater and more regular; it is especially noteworthy that the *ð* is almost identical with the *ð* in MS O. It might therefore reasonably be proposed that it is possible, if not probable, that the manuscript was produced in the second half of the twelfth century at the latest.

Of this manuscript Cockayne (pp. lxxxiv f.) observes: 'MS O is a mean manuscript. . . . The language shows signs of change. . . . The collation of this manuscript was not carried through, it was not desirable. For the history of our language it may some day be required that the whole should be printed for comparison with our earlier text.'

---

[1] Berberich, p. 12: middle of the twelfth century; Wright, *Bald's Leechbook*, p. 29: probably about 1150; *MED, Plan and Bibliography*, p. 64: mid-twelfth century; G. and S., p. 75: *c.*1130.

As appears from the titles of their editions, both Berberich and Délcourt take pains to emphasize the ME character of the O-versions of *OEH* and *MdQ*. An examination of the grammatical introductions to these two books reveals that neither Berberich nor Delcourt presents a reliable description of the state of things in this manuscript: all the different spellings and inflexions are duly recorded, but whereas the picture presented of the 'Middle English' forms is fairly complete, the regular late West Saxon forms are merely given in a small number of examples followed by 'etc.', so that one can easily receive the impression that the language is ME. In the light of this evidence it is understandable that the O-versions of *OEH* and *MdQ* have been regarded as early ME texts by several scholars.[1] A statistical examination of the linguistic features displayed by O supplies abundant evidence that its language is not ME but late OE.[2]

Nothing is known of the earlier history of the manuscript. From the old foliation it may be assumed that the volume originally contained thirty more leaves which preceded the present contents; it suffered severe damage, probably through fire, as can be seen from the discoloration and deformation of parts of ff. 11–19. The leaves in the present volume have been remounted on fresh strips of vellum.

There are no illustrations in this manuscript.

Description of the folios containing OEH *and* MdQ: *1–51*

Collation of the quires

Not possible because the leaves have been remounted.

Measurements

Complete leaves, 184×145 mm; written space, $145–70 \times 95–110$ mm; the number of lines per page varies from 21 to 31.

Pricking

No pricks.

[1] The texts are ME according to Wells (X. 15, X. 4), Renwick and Orton (pp. 255, 257), and Ker (p. xix); Heusinkveld and Bashe, however, include them in their *Bibliographical Guide to Old English* (pp. 117, 124), and *MED*, which quotes instances from both texts, adds the parenthesis 'OE' after the titles.
[2] See pp. lxxv–lxxix.

Ruling

By pencil; the vertical lines marking the inner and outer margins are in pairs; the arrangement of the complete leaves is flesh facing flesh (ff. 1v/2r, etc.), hair facing hair (ff. 2v/3r, etc.)

Colour of the letters:

Black (sometimes slightly faded). The initials of most cures, the titles of most chapters, the marginal titles of some cures, and some of the glosses are in red;[1] in many places the red colour has faded or practically disappeared. Often the red initial of a chapter is accompanied by a corresponding black minuscule in the margin; it is probable that the minuscule was written when the text was copied and that the red initial was added afterwards.

Script

Very irregular and untidy; Ker (p. xix) qualifies it as a 'small ill-formed script'. On several folios the letters are not on the line, but above it, so that sometimes the descenders of the letters do not cross the line. Some characteristics:

1. *æ*: the size of the '*e*' part is variable, it is sometimes of the same size as the lobe of the '*a*' part, sometimes a very small loop at the top of the back of *a*. There are a few instances of *a* and *e* written separately: *þaes*, f. 5/14; *hael*, f. 27v/13; *ʒeneahlaech*, f. 28v/2; *dael*, f. 28v/3; *laecedon*, f. 46/4; *aeppes*, f. 48/21.
2. *ð* is less tall than in insular script. Instead of a crossbar it has a sort of comma, whose top is on the same level as the top of the back of *ð* and which touches, but does not cross the back.
3. *f*: caroline, with a top formed by a straight sloping line.
4. *ʒ/g*: the manuscript has *ʒ* with flat insular head and open tail, and caroline *g*, with a tail that is closed or nearly closed. For the different functions of these two symbols and the rendering of *ʒ* in this edition see pp. lxxvi f.
5. *r*: caroline; there are some instances of '2-shaped' *r* in the combination *-or-* (about one in ten).
6. *s*: caroline.

---

[1] If a chapter title is not in red, this is indicated in the apparatus.

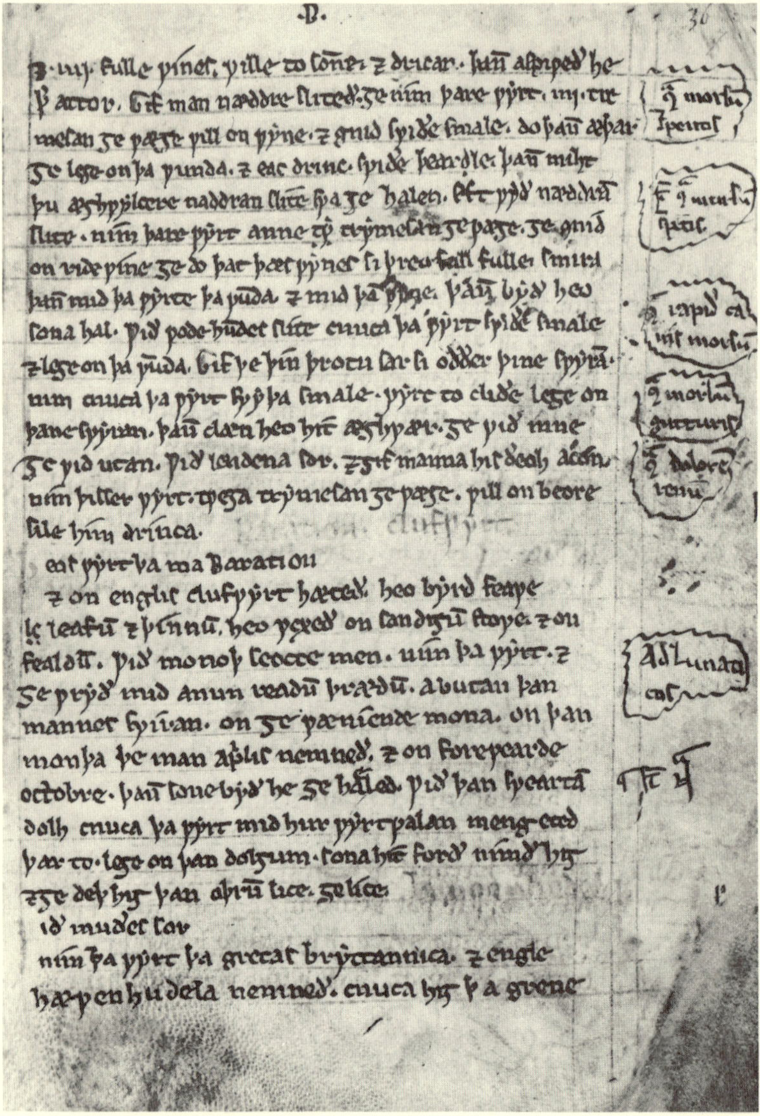

IV. British Library MS Harley 6258 B, f. 7

7. *wynn* is used; it is often found with a bowl that is not closed and a descender that slopes to the left, so that it is very much like *y*, from which it can only be distinguished by the absence of the dot. Capital *wynn* sometimes has a bowl about half-way up the stem, so that the symbol resembles capital *þ*. This occurs especially at the beginning of chapters.

8. *y*: a variety of rounded *y* is used: the left stroke forming the upper part is often vertical, and the lower part is longer than that of the earlier rounded *y*, and slopes to the left. The symbol is dotted.

9. Abbreviations: not so frequent as in MSS V and B; 'and' is nearly always represented by crossed *7*;[1] a straight horizontal line on one or two letters is used to indicate *-m-*, *-n-* (examples: frēmenne, wordū, nærdrā, wūderlice, þāne).[2] The word *þæt* (*þat*) is often abbreviated to *þ* with a sort of comma (see *ð*, point 2); the same device is used for *-er* in *æfter*, *oþþer*,[3] and *cetera*.

10. Accents: the half-long acute accent occurs frequently, both in stressed and in unstressed syllables; it is almost exclusively found on *i*, both long and short, and is probably intended to distinguish *i* from a letter of the same height on the line.

11. Marks of punctuation: the dot and the punctus elevatus are used, and once the colon (after *setlgange*, f. 45v/18).

The original version of the *OEH* section of MS O is shorter than the version of MSS VBH. Several chapters in MS O contain fewer cures than the other OE versions, and many of the cures in MS O are shorter than their parallels in MSS VBH. This part of the codex contains a number of leaves of smaller size, varying in measure (ff. 4, 9, 16, 17, 18, 21, 22, 29, 30, 33, 35, 41), all except f. 41 having text on one side only; they were presumably inserted after the completion of the original version, and contain chapters that were at first not included in the volume.

[1] *An* for 'and' is found in XXVI. 3, XXVII. 1, CVI. 1, and in the marginal title of CXXII. 1.

[2] This is the common mark of abbreviation in the twelfth century; see N. R. Ker, *English MSS in the Century after the Norman Conquest* (Oxford, 1960), p. 39.

[3] The expanded form of this word in the present edition is *oþþer*, because all the instances in the manuscript that are not abbreviated end in *-er*.

With one exception (f. 22) they are found in their correct alphabetical places, and they are all provided with corresponding numbers of the old system, except ff. 4, 9, and 22. Folio 22, which contains the chapter entitled *apium*, was probably originally inserted under *a* and afterwards moved to *m* on account of the OE name *merce*. This is our conclusion when we see that the old foliator began by numbering the complete leaves only, ignoring ff. 4, 22, and 9 (or 22, 4, and 9), and after that included the inserted leaves in his system.[1]

On the evidence of the alphabetical arrangement of the chapters, which was carefully observed, it may be reasonably assumed that in the undamaged part of the manuscript the following chapters were never included:

No.	Name in V	No.	Name in V
XIII	artemesia leptefilos	CXVII	ruta montana
LIV	papaver album	CXXVIII	sinfitus albus
LVIII	polion	CXXX	brassica silvatica
LXVIII	bryonia	CXLIV	trycnos manicos
LXXIX	gramen	CLI	omnimorbia
CV	porclaca	CLXXXII	gorgonion

The arrangement of ff. 11–19 requires some further remarks. These leaves are very badly damaged, and they are difficult to read, especially in those places where they are now covered with a protecting film of gauze. Folio 15 is a very small fragment; it is in fact the inner top corner of f. 19. This means that of the original eleven leaves (ff. 39–49 *old*) there remain eight. The table opposite shows the probable arrangement of these eleven leaves, with the corresponding numbers of the remaining folios.

From the flesh–hair arrangement of the remaining leaves and from the alphabetical order it appears that of the three lost folios one must have been after f. 10, and two after f. 11.

The text on one average page in MS O corresponds with approximately forty half-lines in MS V; the subjoined list shows that the space taken up by the chapters in V containing herbs whose Latin names begin with c[2] and d and which are not in O

---

[1] If in the printed text 'v' is added to the number of one of these inserted leaves, it indicates that the text is on a left-hand page in the manuscript.

[2] If *gallitricus* V/*callitricum* BH was originally in O, it must have had initial *c*; see the list on p. xxxvii.

Old	New	Flesh/Hair	
38v	10v	H	Last line: end of cure 1 of *centaurea maior* (XXXV)
39	—		One complete folio missing
40r	11r	F	First line: part of cure 2 of *celidonia* (LXXV)
40v	11v	H	Last line: part of cure 1 of *cucumis silvatica* (CXV)
41, 42	—		Two complete folios missing
43r	14r	H	First line: part of cure 2 of *dracontea* (XV)
43v	14v	F	Last line: end of *erusti* (LXXXIX)
44r	13r	F	First line: beginning of *erinion* (CIX)
44v	13v	H	Last line: part of cure 1 of *elleborum album* (CLIX)
45r	12r	H	First line: part of cure 1 of *elleborum album* (CLIX)
45v	12v	F	Last line: part of cure 1 of *feniculum* (CXXVI)
46	16 or 17	Inserted	*Filix* or *fraga* (LXXVIII or XXXVIII)
47	17 or 16	,,	*Fraga* or *filix* (XXXVIII or LXXVIII)
48	18	,,	*Gladiolus* (LXXX)
49r	15r = 19r	F	First line: part of cure 1 of *feniculum* (CXXVI)

is very nearly the equivalent of three leaves in O (we take into account the circumstance that V often has longer cures and sometimes more cures than O, and that there may have been one or more inserted leaves in this lost part of O).

Chapter no.	Name in V	No. of half-lines in V	
XV	dracontea (part)	22	
XXXV	centauria maior (part)	12	
XXXVI	centauria minor	46	
XLIV	cotiledon	10	
XLVIII	gallitricus	9	
LX	confirma	17	
LXX	crision	6	A total of 262 half-lines
CXVI	cannave silvatica	14	
CXLIII	coniza	34	
CLVI	camelleon alba	23	
CLXII	centimorbia	17	
CLXX	cynosbatus	25	
CLXXII	capparis	11	
CLXXXV	colocynthisagria	16	

With regard to the lacuna between f. 15 = 19 (49 *old*) and f. 20 (54 *old*), when we consider the old foliation, the flesh–hair arrangement (f. 15v = 19v is H, f. 20r is H), and the extent of the space taken up by the chapters in V containing herbs whose Latin names begin with the letters *h–m* and which are not in O (see the following list), it seems reasonable to conclude that there were four complete leaves here. Chapter XXII, *hieribulbum*, ends at the bottom of f. 15v = 19v, f. 20 begins with cure 9 of *millefolium* (XC).

Chapter no.	Name in V	No. of half-lines in V	
XIV	lapatium	13	
XXXI	lactuca silvatica	23	
XXXIV	lapatium	9	
XXXIX	hibiscus	15	
XL	ippirus	11	
XLI	malva erratica	29	
LXII	leporis pes	9	
LXXI	isatis	8	
LXXXIV	mercurialis	16	
XC	millefolium (part)	42	A total of 358 half-lines
XCVII	hinnula campana	14	
CXII	lupinum montanum	14	
CXIII	lactirida	9	
CXIV	lactuca leporina	15	
CXXI	hedera crysocantes	11	
CXXXIII	lycanis stefanice	15	
CLII	hypericon	27	
CLVIII	iris Illyrica	59	
CLXXX	litospermon	19	

Printed edition of this version of *OEH*: H. Berberich, *Das Herbarium Apuleii nach einer früh-mittelenglischen Fassung* (Anglistische Forschungen, Heft 5) (Heidelberg, 1901, repr. Amsterdam, 1966): introduction, mainly grammatical, and OE text with emendations from MSS VBH in apparatus; the arrangement of MS O is followed, with cross-references to the corresponding chapters in Cockayne.

Printed editions of this version of *MdQ*: J. Delcourt, *Medicina de Quadrupedibus, an early ME Version* (Anglistische Forschungen, Heft 40) (Heidelberg, 1914): introduction, mainly grammatical, emended OE text with manuscript readings in apparatus, translation, and glossary; H. J. de Vriend, *The Old English Medicina de Quadrupedibus* (diss.) (Tilburg, 1972).

Arrangement of the chapters in MS O (Latin titles)

Folio	
1	arthemisia,[1] astrologya (= aristolochia), apollinaria, agrimonia
2	astularegia, astularegia,[2] asterion, absinthium, anetum
3	abrotanus, aizos minor, aizos, acantaleace
4	acylleia (= achillea)
5	acanton, aini, ancura, aglafota, betonica
6	(betonica *continued*)
7	baration (= batracion), hæwen hudela,[3] buglosa
8	bulbus scilliticus, peristerion id est vervena,[4] basilica, bulbus
9	buoptalmon
10	camemelon, chamedris, cameelea, camepithis, chamedafne, centaurea maior
11	celidonia, caput canis, cynoglosa, coliandrum, cerefolia, cardium siluaticum, cucumis
14[5]	dracontea, dictanum, delfinion, eliotrophus, erusti
13	erinion, erifion, eliotropus, elleborum album, elleborum album[6]
12	ecios, eringius, ebulum, eptafilon, feniculum
16	filix
17	fraga
18	gladiolus
15 = 19	gentiana, gallicrus, grias, glicirida, hieribulbum
20	millefolium, mente, mandragora
21	mentastrum
22	apium[7]
23	sion,[8] melotis
24	nasturcium, narcisum, nymfete, nepta, orbicularis
25	ostriago, oenantes, oleastrum (= olisatrum), ocimum, origanum, plantago
26	pentafilon
27	pes leonis, proserpina, personacia
28	prassion, politricum, pionia, peristerion,[9] panastica (= pastinaca) siluatica, perdiculus, pollegium

[1] This chapter contains cures of XI and XII.
[2] These two identical titles correspond with XXXIII and LIII.
[3] In the text the Latin name *bryttannica*.
[4] In the text berbena.
[5] For the order of ff. 12–19 see pp. xxxiv–xxxv.
[6] These two identical titles correspond with CXL and CLIX.
[7] Inserted out of place; see p. xxxiv.
[8] Inserted out of place; see t.n. to p. 177/14.
[9] See t.n. to p. 111/3.

Arrangement of the chapters in MS O (Latin titles) (continued)

Folio	
29	peristerio[1]
30	peucedanum
31	psillios, philantropos
32	porrum = polloton, vica pervica = priaprissi, cimino (= qui-minon), rosemarino, radiolum
33	ruta
34	ricinum, symphoniaca, scelerata, saturion
35	saxifragia[2]
36	splenion, solago,[3] scordeon, solate, senecion
37	sparagia, sauina, saxifragia,[2] serpillum
38	sauina (= saluia), sisimbrium, semperviua, spreritis, struc-tium, samsuchon
39	stecas, scolinbos, scordios, stauisagria, temolum,[4] saxifragia[2]
40	titimallos calatites, petrosillinum = triannis, tribulus, tiapis
41	viola purpurea, viola
42	vermenaca, viperina
43	veneria, victoriole, verbascum,[5] urtica
44	xifion, zima lentition

2. INTERRELATIONSHIP OF THE OLD ENGLISH MANUSCRIPTS

From the description of the OE manuscripts it emerges that V, B, and H are identical in their organization of the texts; it is the same as that of the Latin originals from which they are ulti-mately derived. Only H has a slightly different arrangement of the chapters in *OEH*, but this is probably due to an unsuccessful attempt to incorporate part of an earlier copy in its proper place in the codex. A number of Latin cures has been left untranslated; in many cases this seems to be attributable to the translator's inability to render them in OE on account of his unfamiliarity with the meaning of one or more words, or on account of the obscurity of the Latin sentence; in some cases the translator may have decided that the cure was not worth including and left it out on that account.

---

[1] See t.n. to p. 111/3.
[2] See t.n. to p. 145/8.
[3] This chapter contains cures of LXIV and LXV.
[4] Inserted out of place; see t.n. to p. 95/9.
[5] This chapter contains cures of LXXIII and LXXIV.

The following table is a collation of the numbering of the chapters of *OEH* in the printed text and the numberings found in MSS VBH. The numbering of the chapters in the text of V is partly visible in the top margins; these numbers always correspond with those in the table of contents. In B and H the numberings in text and table of contents do not always run exactly parallel. For practical reasons the roman numerals of the manuscripts have been replaced by arabic numerals. A number placed in brackets corresponds to a number that is only partly legible, a dash indicates that there is no number in the manuscript or one that is completely illegible, *om.* signifies that the title does not occur in the manuscript.

Printed text	V (contents)	B (contents)	B (text)	H (contents)	H (text)
1	1	1	1	1	*om.*
2–3	—	2–3	2–3	6–7	*om.*
4	4	4	4	8	*om.*
5	—	5	5	9	9
6–8	6–8	6–8	6–8	2–4	*om.*
9	9	9	9	5	34
10	10	10	10	35	35
11	*om.*	11	11	36	36
12	11	12	12	37	37
13	12	13	13	37	37
14	13	14	13	38	38
15–20	14–19	15–20	15–20[1]	39–44	39–44
21–7	20–6	21–7	22–8[2]	45–51	45–51
28	27	28	—	52	52
29	(28)	29	30	53	53
30–1	—	30–1	31–2	54–5	54–5
32–3	(31–2)	32–3	32–3	56–7	56–7
34	33	34	34	58	58
35–6	(34–5)	35–6	35–6	59–60	59–60
37–41	36–40	37–41	37–41	61–5	61–5
42	41	42	(42)	64	64
43	42	43	43	65	65
44–53	43–52	44–53	44–53	66–75	66–75
54	—	54	54	76	76
55–70	54–69	55–70	55–70	77–92	77–92

[1] Numeral 15 altered from 14; the second title *dragance* (f. 81/7a), wrongly inserted in the space for a serpent-drawing, has numeral 15 struck out.

[2] Numeral 21 *karse* wrongly inserted in the space for a serpent-drawing, f. 82v/24a–25a.

Printed text	V (contents)	B (contents)	B (text)	H (contents)	H (text)
71	*om.*	71	71–2[1]	93	93
72	70	72	73	94[2]	94
73–4	71–2	73–4	73–4	95–6	95–6
75–7	73–5	75–7	75–7	10–12	10–12
78	76	78	79	13	13
79–90	77–88	79–90	79–90	14–25	14–25
91	*om.*	91	91	26	26
92–3	89–90	92–3	92–3	27–8	27–8
94	—	94	94	29	29
95–7	(92–4)	95–7	95–7	30–2	30–2
98	—	98	98	33, 97[3]	33, 97[3]
99	*om.*	*om.*	—	98	98
100	—	99	99	99	99
101–8	97–104	100–7	100–7	101–8	101–8
109	105	108	108	109	—
110	106	109	109	110	110
111	107	110	110	112	111
112	108	111	111	111	112
113	109	112	112	112	113
114–15	110–11	113–14	113–14	(113–14)	114–15
116–19	112–15	115–18	115–18	—	116–19
120	116	119	119	—	—
121	117	120	120	—	121
122	118	121	121	—	—
123–30	119–26	122–9	122–9	—	123–30
131	127	130	130	*om.*	131
132	128	131	131	—	132
133–4	129–30	132–3	132–3	*om.*	133–4
135	131	134	134	—	135
136	132	135	135	*om.*	136
137	133	136	136	—	137
138–9	134–5	137–8	137–8	*om.*	138–9
140	136	*om.*	—	—	140
141	137	*om.*	—	*om.*	141
142	138	*om.*	—	—	142
143	139	*om.*	—	*om.*	143
144	140	*om.*	—	—	144
145–7	141–3	*om.*	—	*om.*	145–7
148	144	*om.*	—	—	148

[1] Chapter 71 in B consists of title and introduction only; in the space for a serpent-drawing the title is repeated (f. 93v/7b) with numeral 72 and cure.

[2] The title *isatis* is repeated in ch. 94; probably because of *Eft* in cure 1 of this chapter.

[3] See description of MS H, p. xxv.

Printed text	V (contents)	B (contents)	B (text)	H (contents)	H (text)
149–51	145–7	om.	om.	om.	149–51
152–3	148–9	om.	—	om.	152–3
154–6	150–2	om.	—	—	154–6
157	(153)	om.	—	om.	157
158–64	154–60	om.	—	om.	158–64
165	161	164	164	—	165
166–8	162–4	165–7	165–7	om.	166–8
169–71	165–7	168–70	om.	om.	169–71
172	168	171	om.	—	172
173	169	172	—	om.	173
174–5	170–1	173–4	174–4	om.	174–5
176	172	175	—	om.	176
177	173	176	176	om.	177
178	174	177	177	—	178
179	175	178	178	om.	179
180	om.	179	179	om.	180
181–2	176–7	180–1	180–1	om.	181–2
183–4	178–9	182–3	132–3	om.	183–4
185	(180)	184	184	om.	185

In O the organization of *OEH* is different: the chapters are arranged alphabetically according to the Latin names of the herbs. Furthermore, O omits more cures than VBH, and in *OEH* a number of entire chapters was apparently never included.

With regard to the language of the three pre-Conquest manuscripts it can be said that apart from some minor differences, mainly in spelling, they are very similar to each other. MS O, although it displays some of the orthographical and inflexional changes that are typical of the early ME period, is practically identical with VBH in its vocabulary and sentence structure.[1]

In the extant OE versions *OEH* and *MdQ* are found together. But there are certain differences between the two treatises which give us sufficient grounds for concluding that this was not always the case. There is evidence that *MdQ* is closely connected with an earlier Anglian exemplar, as appears from the following characteristics:

(*a*) The treatment of the 3rd person sg. pres. indic. of strong verbs; see pp. lxx–lxxi.

[1] For grammatical details see pp. lxxv–lxxix.

(b) The occurrence of certain words typical of Anglian texts; see pp. lxxii–lxxxiii.

(c) The occurrence of a particular participial construction; see pp. lxxiii–lxxiv.

(d) The weight value of the *pening*; see p. lxxxii.

Of these features, only the first is also found in *OEH*, less frequently than in *MdQ*, but much more frequently than in Ælfric.

Although it is more difficult to prove that the original OE version of the *Herbarium* dates back any further than to the period of the revival of learning of the tenth century, there are some factors which seem to justify the theory that not only the OE *MdQ* but also *OEH* came into existence in the period of Northumbrian cultural ascendancy.

The study of herb medicine flourished throughout the post-classical and early medieval periods, as is abundantly proved by the survival of numerous Latin texts on the subject.[1] There can be little doubt that these Latin treatises were studied in the Northumbrian monasteries in the seventh and eighth centuries and that the medicinal herbs were grown in the monastery gardens. The undertaking of an OE translation of a herbal in that period might be seen as a circumstance which arose as the logical result of this interest in herb medicine.

The history of the Latin predecessors of the two treatises is another factor which may serve to confirm the theory that the original OE versions of the *Herbarium* and of *MdQ* are of the same period. There is no Latin text extant which has *MdQ* alone, whereas there are several which have the *Herbarium* and not *MdQ*.[2] Clearly the *Herbarium* was held in higher respect than *MdQ*, and the latter was treated as an appendix to the former. Accordingly it seems probable that in its earliest form the OE translation consisted of *OEH* and *MdQ* together, or of *OEH* alone.

It may be assumed that in Anglo-Saxon England, too, *OEH* was more popular than *MdQ*, and that consequently the two treatises, even though they may have been translated together, have different textual traditions. This theory finds some support

---

[1] See Beccaria's Index, pp. 439 ff., especially p. 453, 'Erbari medicinali'.
[2] See Beccaria, p. 441 and p. 485; H. and S., pp. v–xiv, xxiv.

in the treatment of Latin *stranguiria*[1] and *mel atticum*[2] in the two texts. In *OEH* the translation of *stranguiria* is an expression containing the verb *gemigan*, in *MdQ* the OE parallel is *stede*. The translation of *mel atticum* is *hunig* ($2 \times$) in *OEH*, *feldbeona hunig* ($3 \times$) and *doran hunig* ($1 \times$) in *MdQ*.

From what has been said in the preceding paragraphs, three conclusions may be formulated:

(*a*) Both the *Herbarium* and *MdQ* were translated into OE during an early period, probably the eighth century.

(*b*) The extant text of *OEH* is either directly descended from that early version, whose language, as a result of frequent copying and modernizing, was gradually adapted to the late West Saxon standard, or it is a new translation direct from Latin, which was subsequently supplemented by a pre-existing Anglian-coloured *MdQ*.

(*c*) The extant text of *MdQ* is closely connected with the early Anglian version.

The three eleventh-century manuscripts show so many points of resemblance that there can be no doubt about their descent from a common ancestor. This conclusion is supported by the occurrence of two conspicuous errors which the three versions have in common: in the introduction to LXXI the Latin caption *ad serpentis morsum* is wrongly inserted instead of the OE plant name *wad*, and in cure 1 of C the Latin verb *frangere* is mistranslated.[3]

A comparison of V, B, and H shows that there is a closer relation between V and B than between either of these two and H. Both V and B have the arrangement of the text in two columns of thirty-one lines, the spaces left open in B for illustrations are in the same places and nearly always on an equal number of lines as are the illustrations in V, and in most of the chapters where no OE equivalent is available for the Latin plant name, a space is found in the text following the phrase *7 oþrum naman*, both in V and in B.[4] The critical apparatus in this edition confirms the close relationship between V and B: for every instance of agreement of V

---

[1] *Stranguiria* occurs in XII. 1, LV. 1, CVII. 1, CVIII. 1; *M* III. 16, *M* IX. 11. See also note to *M* III. 16.

[2] *Mel atticum* occurs in LXXV. 1, LXXV. 2; *M* IV. 13, *M* VI. 2, *M* VI. 4, *M* XII. 3. See also note to *M* IV. 13.

[3] In H the second error was afterwards corrected.

[4] The two manuscripts have spaces in the same chapters, but B has six more instances, all but one in chapters preceding the first instance in V.

and H against B, or of B and H against V, there are at least four instances of agreement of V and B against H. But it is unlikely that V was copied from B or vice versa, as appears from the instances where either V or B has a better reading or shows a closer affinity with the Latin original.[1] It may be assumed, then, that from a common ancestor of V, B, and H at least two branches are descended, and that V and B belong to one branch, H belongs to another.[2]

In his edition of *OEH* and *MdQ* Cockayne takes V as the basic text, because its spelling 'is nearer to the customary manner [i.e. "the mode of Ælfric"] than that of MS B' (p. lxxvii). The present edition adheres to Cockayne's policy, though it must be admitted that the version of B also has very good claims to being taken as the basic text: apart from the loss of four folios B has not suffered any other damage, and it has several better readings than V.

With regard to the relationship between V, B, and H on the one hand and O on the other, there are several reasons to conclude that O, although it is about a century later and is totally different in its organization of *OEH*, is based upon an earlier OE manuscript that belongs to the same tradition as the three pre-Conquest codices. This becomes evident from an analysis of its language, and it can also be seen from the numerous instances where O is literally identical with V. In three places in *OEH*, O has a particular reading in common with B: in XLIII. 1 we find *sceattas* B, *sceattes* O, as against *scenceas* VH, in LXXIV. 1 we read *ænigre* B, *aniȝre* O, as against *ænigne* VH, and in CIX both B and O have the corrupted form *erinion* for *crinion*. O also resembles B in that it frequently, though less consistently, uses the spelling *i* for *y*. But this does not furnish sufficient evidence to claim a particularly close relationship between B and O, especially because in other respects, such as front mutation of *a/o* before nasals, O does not agree with B.

---

[1] Some examples: V is better than B in I. 3, VIII. 1, XCI. 1, XCII. 2, CLXV. 2, *M* III. 10, *M* VI. 12, *M* VII. 15; B is better than V in XXXII. 4, XLIII. 1, XLVI. 5, CXLVII. 1, CXLVII. 3, CLIII. 3, CLXXVIII. 1, *M* VII. 9, *M* IX. 11, *M* X. 2, *M* X. 6.

[2] V and H have one curious feature in common: in both manuscripts an unusual type of the letter *a*, with a lengthened back, is exclusively used in the same places: *amigdales* 58/6 and 80/3, *aristolochiam/arista-* 66/4, *acennede* 74/9. For other striking instances of peculiarities found in parallel places in two of the three manuscripts, see textual notes to V 18/3, V 56/11, B 184/10 and V 250/15.

3. THE LATIN MANUSCRIPTS USED FOR THIS EDITION

MS A. London, British Library, Additional 8928

Descriptions: *Catalogue of the Add. MSS*, p. 56; Beccaria, no. 84; Diels, ii, 31.

The codex is from *c*.1000;[1] it consists of seventy-six vellum folios; the outer half of f. 76 has been cut out. The Apuleius portion is partly illustrated with half-completed drawings.

The manuscript contains the following Latin parallels to the texts in this edition:

ff. 19r–23v	Table of contents of Musa and Apuleius.
ff. 26v–28r	Antonius Musa, *De herba vettonica liber*.
ff. 28r–50r	Apuleius Platonicus, *Herbarium* (class β).
f. 50r–50v	*De taxone liber*.
(ff. 50v–62v	Table of contents and text of the B-version of Sextus Placitus.)
ff. 62v–64r	Table of contents of Dioscorides.
ff. 64r–76v	Dioscorides, *Liber medicinae ex herbis femininis* (seventy-one chapters).

This manuscript has been used for the Latin parallels of most of the chapters in the Dioscorides part in *OEH*.

MS Ca. Montecassino, Archivio della Badia, V. 97

Descriptions: Inguanez, pp. 96–8; Beccaria, no. 95; H. and S., pp. v–vi; Hunger, pp. xxxv–xxxviii.

The codex is from the ninth or tenth century;[2] it consists of 226 vellum folios; the text is written in two columns; the numbering is per page (1–552).

The manuscript contains the following illustrated Latin parallels to the texts in this edition:

pp. 477a–522b	Apuleius Platonicus, *Herbarium* (class α), beginning at our ch. XXII.
pp. 476a–476b⎱	Dioscorides, *Liber medicinae ex herbis femininis*
pp. 523a–532b⎰	(forty-three chapters).
pp. 532b–533a	*De taxone liber*.
(pp. 533a–545a	The B-version of Sextus Placitus.)

---

[1] *Catalogue of the Add. MSS*, p. 56: s. xi; Beccaria, no. 84: s. x; Diels, ii. 31: s. xi; H. and S., p. xii: s. xi; Lawn, p. 7, p. 12 n. 4: s. x.

[2] Beccaria, no. 95: s. x in.; H. and S., p. v: s. ix; Hunger, p. xxxv: s. ix.

Pages 477–522 are printed in facsimile in Hunger's edition; here we also find a facsimile of the so-called *Editio Princeps*, which is the earliest known printed edition of the Latin *Herbarium*, by Ioannes Philippus de Lignamine, Rome 1481. The *Editio Princeps* shows strong affinities with Ca, but it is not a direct copy of this manuscript; it contains Musa and the complete Apuleius except ch. CV.

Ca has been used for the Latin parallels of the Apuleius part of *OEH*, beginning at ch. XXII, and of ch. CXLVII and part of ch. CLXV in the Dioscorides part.

MS Ha. London, British Library, Harley 4986

Descriptions: Cat. Harl. iii. 235; Cockayne, p. lxxxii; Beccaria, no. 77; H. and S., p. viii.

This is an illustrated codex consisting of eighty-four vellum folios; opinions about the date of writing are widely different, ranging from the tenth century to *c*.1200.[1] As regards the provenance of the manuscript, the occurrence of a number of German glosses in the *Herbarium* in hands of the twelfth and fourteenth centuries is an indication that the manuscript was in Germany during that period, and that it was probably written there, as is suggested by Beccaria. As appears from the description in Cat. Harl., Ha was bound in one volume with Har for some time.

The manuscript contains the following Latin parallels to the texts in this edition:

ff. 1*r–1r	Antonius Musa, *De herba vettonica liber*.
ff. 1r–44r	Apuleius Platonicus, *Herbarium* (class α, with interpolations).
ff. 44v–45r	*De taxone liber*.
ff. 45r–49v	The A-version of Sextus Placitus, *Liber medicinae ex animalibus*.

This manuscript has been used for most of the variants in the Musa and Apuleius parts of the *Herbarium* and in the *Medicina de Quadrupedibus*.

---

[1] Cat. Harl. iii. 235: s. x; Beccaria, no. 77: end s. xi or beginning s. xii; H. and S., p. viii: s. xii; Steinmeyer and Sievers, iv. 497, no. 279: s. xi; Gunther, p. 135: end s. xii; Singer, p. 35: end s. xii.

MS Har. London, British Library, Harley 5294

Descriptions: Cat. Harl. iii. 259; Cockayne, p. lxxxii; Singer, p. 35.

This illustrated codex is in a clear hand of the twelfth century;[1] it consists of sixty-eight vellum folios. It was bound in one volume with Ha for some time.

The manuscript contains the following Latin parallels to the texts in this edition:

ff. 1v–6v Table of contents of Antonius Musa and Apuleius.

ff. 7r–8v Antonius Musa, *De herba vettonica liber*.

ff. 8v–43v Apuleius Platonicus, *Herbarium* (class β).

ff. 43v–58r Dioscorides, *Liber medicinae ex herbis femininis* (seventy-one chapters).

(ff. 60r–62v First four chapters of the B-version of Sextus Placitus, *Liber medicinae ex animalibus*.)

This manuscript has been used for those Latin parallels of the chapters in the Dioscorides part in *OEH* which in MS A are on the damaged f. 76.

MS L. Lucca, Biblioteca Governativa, no. 296

Descriptions: Mancini, pp. 140–2; Giacosa, pp. 349–53 (no. 236, wrongly); Beccaria, no. 91; H. and S., p. vii (no. 236, wrongly).

The codex is in a hand which is assigned to dates ranging from the eighth to the tenth century by all authorities but one.[2] As regards the place where the manuscript was written, G. Muzzioli in *Mostra storica nazionale della miniatura*, 37, no. 51 (Firenze, 1953) points out that the drawings are characteristic of manuscripts composed in Northern Italy. It consists of 109 vellum folios, the rectos numbered in the top and bottom margins.[3]

---

[1] Cat. Harl. iii. 259: s. xii; Cockayne, p. lxxxii: s. xii; Singer, p. 35: a sister manuscript of MS Torino K IV 3, s. xi; H. and S., p. xii: s. xii.

[2] Mancini, p. 142: s. viii or s. ix; Giacosa, p. 349: end s. ix or beginning s. x; Beccaria, no. 91: end s. ix; H. and S., p. vii: s. ix; Thorndike, p. 597 n. 2: s. ix or s. x; ibid., p. 695: *c.*900; R. Simonini, 'Herbolarium et materia medica: cod. ms. no. 296 della Biblioteca Governativa di Lucca', *Atti e memorie della R. Acc. di sc. lett. ed arti di Modena*, s. 5a, i (1936), 188–90: s. xi or s. xii; R. P. Johnson 'Some Continental Manuscripts of the Mappae Clavicula', *Speculum* xii (1937), 90–1: s. viii or s. ix.

[3] The foliation in the top margin, which is older than the foliation in the bottom margin, is 1–6, 6 *bis*, 7–108, the other foliation is 1–109. In this edition the old foliation is quoted.

Four complete quires and several folios of the original volume are missing, so that of the *Herbarium* only the first and the last part are extant.

The manuscript contains the following illustrated Latin parallels to the texts in this edition:

ff. 1r–2r   Antonius Musa, *De herba vettonica liber*.
ff. 2r–17r   Apuleius Platonicus, *Herbarium* (class α, mutilated).
ff. 17v–18r   *De taxone liber*.
f. 18r–18v   A treatise on the healing powers of the mulberry.
ff. 18v–26v   The A-version of Sextus Placitus, *Liber medicinae ex animalibus*.
ff. 26v–45v   Dioscorides, *Liber medicinae ex herbis femininis* (forty-two chapters).

This manuscript has been used for the Latin parallels of seven chapters in the Dioscorides part in *OEH*, and of the entire *MdQ*.

MS Vo. Leiden, Bibliotheek der Rijksuniversiteit, Vossianus Latinus Q 9

Descriptions: De Meyier, pp. 20–5; H. and S., p. xiii; Singer, pp. 43–6.

This codex consists of three parts, of which ff. 1–81 are in one hand in half-uncial script of the sixth or seventh century,[1] with illustrations. It is by far the oldest extant Latin manuscript of the *Herbarium*.

The manuscript contains the following Latin parallels to the texts in this edition:

(ff. 6v–11v   Tituli morborum, i.e. a table of contents arranged according to the various diseases.)
ff. 13v–19r   Antonius Musa, *De herba vettonica liber*.
ff. 20r–81v   Apuleius Platonicus, *Herbarium* (class α), damaged and defective after f. 48, ending at *senecion* (ch. LXXVII).

The codex in its present form has two folios out of place; see the foliation of chs. IV–IX.

This manuscript has been used for the Latin parallels of chs. I–XXI in *OEH*.

----

[1] De Meyier, p. 20: s. vi second half–s. vii; H. and S., p. xiii: s. vii; Diepgen, p. 58: s. vii.

MS W. London, Wellcome Historical Medical Library, no. 573

Description: Moorat, i. 573 (pp. 446–8)

This illustrated codex of *c.*1250[1] shows strong affinities with MS L; it consists of 152 vellum folios.

The manuscript contains the following Latin parallels to the texts in this edition:

ff. 3v–6r	Antonius Musa, *De herba vettonica liber*.
ff. 6v–37r	Apuleius Platonicus, *Herbarium*, (class α, with omissions).
ff. 37v–38r	*De taxone liber*.
f. 38r–38v	A treatise on the healing powers of the mulberry.
ff. 38v–46v	The A-version of Sextus Placitus, *Liber medicinae ex animalibus*, with two long omissions.
ff. 46v–68v	Dioscorides, *Liber medicinae ex herbis femininis*.

This manuscript has been used for the Latin parallel, apparently much corrupted, of *gorgonion* (ch. CLXXXII).

Manuscripts used only for a number of variants in the text:

MS Slo.	London, British Library, Sloane 1975 (s. xii)
MS Vi.	Wien, Nationalbibliothek, no. 93 (s. xiii)

Of the other Latin manuscripts referred to in this edition, MS Bodley 130 deserves to be mentioned separately on account of the fact that its version of the *Medicina de Quadrupedibus* (except the part containing cures from the domestic goat) is clearly a Latin rendering of an OE text. For a detailed discussion, see de Vriend, pp. xlv–liii.

4. THE RELATIONS BETWEEN THE LATIN AND OE VERSIONS

In the choice of Latin parallels of the OE texts three criteria have been observed, wherever possible:

(*a*) An early date of composition or copying.

(*b*) A distinct textual resemblance between the Latin and OE versions.

(*c*) A close correspondence in the arrangement of the illustrations.

---

[1] Moorat, i. 446: s. xiii med.

The Latin version of the enlarged *Herbarium* is found in a considerable number of manuscripts;[1] there can be hardly any doubt that the text was immensely popular in the early Middle Ages. The extremely complicated textual tradition of the three Latin treatises which constitute the enlarged *Herbarium* has been the subject of a number of authoritative studies, among which special mention must be made of Howald and Sigerist, Singer ('Herbal in Antiquity'), Hunger, and Grattan and Singer. Many problems have remained unsolved, not only because at least three originally separate texts were combined, but also because from the earliest versions onwards the manuscripts were interpolated with new material, often consisting of lists of synonyms, charms, and prayers, or personal accounts of people who had successfully used some remedy or other. The interrelation of the most important manuscripts is discussed in detail in the *Praefatio* to H. and S., pp. v–xiv; here the manuscripts are divided into three classes: α, β, and γ. This division is based on the form in which the text of the *Herbarium Apulei* has been preserved. The manuscripts of class α contain a version which is supposed to be the most closely related to the archetype. Although there are many differences between the manuscripts of the three classes, the points of resemblance are numerous enough for the text of the *Herbarium* to be printed by H. and S. in one version with the relevant textual variants in the critical apparatus. It does not become clear why in this tripartite division MS Vo has been relegated to class γ: that part of it which it has in common with Ca runs almost exactly parallel with the latter manuscript, and there are also strong affinities with Ha; both Ca and Ha are placed in class α.

For the first part of *OEH*, chs. I–XXI, Latin parallels have been taken from Vo. This is the oldest extant text, and it may be regarded as a near relation of the exemplar used by the Anglo-Saxon translator. In several places V agrees more closely with Ha, a manuscript which is certainly later than the original OE version. From the following collations it can be seen that there

---

[1] It may be added that the terms 'scores of manuscripts' (Singer, *Introduction* to reprint of Cockayne, p. xxi), 'exceedingly numerous' (Singer, 'Herbal in Antiquity', p. 52), and 'paene innumerabiles' (H. and S., p. x) are exaggerations. In fact, H. and S. mention forty-seven manuscripts in their *Praefatio*, and many of these contain only fragments.

is no direct relationship between V and either Vo or Ha (references are to chapters and cures in this edition):

A. *Agreement of V and Vo against Ha*

	V	Vo	Ha
I. 20	iv trymesan	dragmas quattuor	dragmas iii
I. 22	feower ful	quiatos iv	ciatis iii
III. 4	bewrit þriwa	circumscribito ter	circumscriptam tenes
III. 5	Gif blod yrne to swiðe	ad sanguinem nimis profluentem	ad sanguinem fluentem
III. 9	gif ðu wille cancer ablendan	ad cancrum ex-caecandum	ad cancrum ex-(s)iccandum
V	wihst on (. . .) —	nascitur (. . .) —	nascitur (. . .) et in litoribus
V. 2	wið cneowa geswell oððe sceancena oððe swa hwær swa on lichoman geswell sy	ad tumorem genu-orum vel tibiarum aut crurium vel si tumor fuerit	ad omnem tumorem
VI	ðu scealt niman *etc. after cure* I	Legis *etc. after cure* I	Legis *etc. after introduction*
VI. 1	þone slyte	morsus	morsus vipperae
IX	fæstende	ieiunus	—
X	bið cenned (. . .) —	nascitur (. . .) —	nascitur (. . .) et aquosis
XI	heo awendeð yfelra manna eagan	evertit oculos malo-rum hominum	et erit oculus malo-rum hominum nihil
XIII. 1	do þonne on anne clænne clað 7 lege þærto	impones panno mundo et imponis	impones in panno
XX. 7	hunig	cum melle	—

B. *Agreement of V and Ha against Vo*

	V	Ha	Vo
II. 3	swyþe wundrum well	mirifice	—
III. 6	—	—	miraberis mire
IV	on smeþum landum 7 on wætum	in planis et aquosis locis	in aquosis et planis locis
IV. 1	þonne fremaþ hit healice	summe proficit	mirifice sanat
V. 6	7 þæt geswell óf animð	et tumorem aufert	—
IX. 2	7 þæt worsm út atyhð	et pus eiciet	discutit omnia malitia
XI	on stanigum stowum 7 on sandigum	locis lapidosis et sablosis	locis cultis, sablosis et lapidosis
XII. 1	7 wið þæt man ne mæge gemígan	et stranguiriam	—
XIV. 1	mid ealdum rysle buton sealte	cum axungia vetere sine sale	cum axungia (*MS* apsungia)
XVI. 1	gelycð	claudet	curat
XIX. 3	þe beoð melce	quae lac habent	qui lactem non habent

B. *Agreement of V and Ha against Vo* (*continued*)

	V	Ha	Vo
XIX. 6	ðe þince	tibi videbitur	tibi placet
XX. 1	heo oferswið ealle strenðe þæs attres	vim veneni vincit	venenum discutit
XXI. 2	hit þa hwitnesse þæs scurfes of þam heafde atyhð	albitionem furfuris ex capite eiciet	calvitionem furfures ex capite eiciet

The Latin parallels of the remaining chapters of the *Herbarium Apulei* section of *OEH*, XXII–CXXXII, have been taken from Ca, in which manuscript the *Herbarium* starts at our ch. XXII. As it happens, Vo begins to be defective very soon after ch. XXI. Not only is there a close textual resemblance between V and Ca, it has also been shown that there is a strong iconographic affinity between these two manuscripts.[1] As in the first twenty-one chapters of our text, there are several instances of closer agreement of V with Ha; the following collations show that there is no direct relationship between V and either Ca or Ha:

A. *Agreement of V and Ca against Ha*

	V	Ca	Ha
XXII. 1	*cure = Ca*	*cure = V*	*cure shorter than* VCa
XXIII	7 hy Esculapio þam læce syllan	et Asclepio dedisse	—
XXIII. 1	dó þærtó anne scenc ealdes wínes 7 þæt sy gehæt butan smice	et vinum vetus sine fumo ciatum i	—
XXIV. 1	7 wið (. . .) sare	vel dolorem	—
XXIX	þe wið duna standað	qui sunt circa montium radices	—
XXX	*cure 4, cure 5*	*cure 4, cure 5*	*cure 5, cure 4*
XXXI. 2	7 hunig	et mel	—
XXXII. 1	ofstlice	mature	maturat et
XXXII, 2, 3	*two cures*	*two cures*	*title of cure 2 followed by cure 3*
XXXII. 5	heo genimð þa weartan	tollet verrucas	mirifice sanat
XXXIV. 1	swynen smeru	axungia suilla	axungia ovilla
XXXVII. 1	wið ealle wunda	ad vulnera omnia	ad vulnera
XXXVII. 4	twegen (scenceas)	ciatis duobus	ciatos iii
XXXVIII. 2	—	—	Legis eam mundus
XL. 1	*cure = Ca*	*cure = V*	*cure different from VCa*
LV. 2	*cure = Ca*	*cure = V*	*om. cure*
LXXX. 1	þry (scenceas) wæteres	aquae cyatos tres	aquae calidae ciatos quattuor

[1] See G. and S., pp. 72–9.

A. *Agreement of V and Ca against Ha (continued)*

	V	Ca	Ha
XCIV	mid þam mæstan bleo	maximis coloribus	maximis (aestatis) caloribus
C. 6	—	—	emendat (*at end*)
CI. 1	to swyþe smalan duste	in pulvere mollissimo	in pulverem
CII. 2	on wine, lege tuwa oððe þriwa	in vino, bis aut ter positum	in vino austeri, positum
CXV. 1	—	—	sanabuntur (*at end*)
CXIX. 1	—	—	mire facit
CXX. 1	—	—	mire facit
CXXII. 1	cnuca eal tosomne	teris	—
CXXV. 1	—	—	mire facit
CXXVII. 1	þysse wyrte	eius	—

B. *Agreement of V and Ha against Ca*

	V	Ha	Ca
XXVI. 2	—	—	siccatam
XXXII. 7	Gif ðu hwylce þingc of ðam lichoman ceorfan wylle	ad ea quae secanda sunt	ad ea quae inmunda sunt
XXXIII. 1	wið sceancena sare oððe fota	ad dolorem tibiarum vel pedum	ad dolorem interiorem vel pedum
XXXVII. 5	—	—	mox sanat
XXXVIII. 1	wið miltan sare	ad splenis dolorem	ad splenis dolorem et colicis
XLII. 1	bogas ðæs sædes	tursos seminis	tursos similes
XLIII	*cures 1-2-3-4*	*cures 1-2-3-4*	*cures 1-3-4-2*
XLIII. 1	gedryge hy	torretur	tundetur
XLIV. 1	7 swinen smeru	axungia suilla	axungia ovilla
XLVI. 2	*cure = Ha*	*cure = V*	*cure longer than* VHa
XLIX	temolum	timola (*title*), temolum (*text*)	etmolum
XLIX	leaces	caepae	cerae
LV. 1	hyt fremað healice	summe facit	—
LXIII. 5	*cure = Ha*	*cure = V*	*om. cure*
LXXV. 2	weallende axan	cineri ferventi	cineri
LXXV. 3	*cure = Ha*	*cure = V*	*two cures telescoped*
LXXVII	onbutan wagum	circa parietes	circa parietinas
LXXVIII. 2	gewrið swa þæt he upweard sy gewend	fasciam sursum versus ligabis	ligabis
LXXXVI. 3, 4	*two cures = Ha*	*two cures = V*	*two cures telescoped*
XCVIII. 2	feower leaf	folia iv	folia tria
CXIII	byð cenned *etc.*	nascitur *etc.*	—
CXVIII	byþ cenned on beganum stowum 7 on sandigum landum	nascitur locis sablosis et cultis	—
CXXI. 1	of þam wine	ex eo vino	ex oleo et vino
CXXXII	swa mycel 7 swa mære	talis ac tanta	taiis sancta
CXXXII. 3	seofon dagas	per dies vii	per dies vi

Of the fifty-three chapters in the 'Dioscorides' section of *OEH*, thirty-six Latin parallels have been taken from A and Har.[1] These two codices, although less old than Ca and L, show the greatest affinity with the OE text, and they contain more 'Dioscorides' chapters than V, whereas Ca and L are shorter. It is unlikely that the 'Dioscorides' part of Ca is directly related to the OE version, as appears from a passage in CLII. 3, where in V we read *feowertigan*, in A and Har *xl*, in L and Slo *quadraginta*, while Ca has *undecim*. The recension of the 'Dioscorides' part of L can also be rejected as a possible exemplar of the OE text, because in most cases the cures in V are more closely related to the parallels in A/Har than to those in L.

Of the remaining seventeen chapters in V, seven parallels have been taken from L, one from Ca, and one from W. Four chapters describing herbs which are neither in the Latin manuscripts consulted for this edition nor in Kästner have been provided with parallels taken direct from the Latin translation of Dioscorides' *De materia medica*. Finally, there are four chapters for which no Latin parallels have been found.

The arrangement of the chapters in this part of *OEH* is totally different from that in any of the Latin versions. It may be assumed that, after having translated Apuleius, the Anglo-Saxon translator took the 'Dioscorides' material from various texts, selecting those herbs which he thought deserved to be included in his book.

The OE text of the *Medicina de Quadrupedibus* is a rendering of the A-version.[2] The text of the earliest known Latin manuscript containing the A-version, MS L, is printed in the present edition, with textual variants from the only other early Latin manuscript containing this version, MS Ha. These two Latin texts also stand apart from the other early manuscripts in that they contain the *Epistula ad Marcellinum*.[3]

There are some notable differences between L and Ha which give us good reasons to conclude that the OE version of *MdQ* was based upon a text which belonged to the same family as that of L. In the first place, only L and the OE texts contain the treatise on the healing properties of the mulberry. Secondly, several cures

---

[1] There are thirty-seven parallels in A/Har, but for ch. CXXXVII, *eliotropus*, the version of L has been taken, because it is closer to the OE text; the last three cures of ch. CLXV are not in A/Har and have been taken from Ca.

[2] For this term, see pp. lxiv–lxvi.

[3] See pp. lxii–lxiii.

are found in L and in the OE texts but not in Ha.[1] In the third place, whereas L and the OE texts are practically identical in their arrangement of the chapters containing cures of the wolf and the dog (X and XIV), Ha has a different arrangement.[2] Lastly, L and V have the same additional illustrations (see below). Nevertheless there is no direct relationship between L and the OE texts, as appears from the instances where in OE we find better readings which are also found in Ha.

At the same time it is clear that the version of L is further removed from the original than that of Ha: the treatise on the mulberry does not belong in this context; of the eight recipes that occur in L and not in Ha, only one (III. 13) has a parallel in the B-version, from which we may conclude that they were added later; the arrangement of chs. X and XIV is better in Ha than in L.

As regards the illustrations, V agrees with the illustrated Latin manuscripts in having one drawing for each chapter, both in *OEH* and in *MdQ*.[3] There are several additional drawings, mainly of snakes, as illustrations to cures prescribed against bites of these creatures. A comparison of V, Ca, L, and Vo brings to light the interesting circumstance that in the *Herbarium Apulei* section the four manuscripts usually have these additional drawings in exactly the same places. On f. 26v, in XV, V agrees with Vo in drawing a snake that is being attacked by a small animal, probably an ichneumon,[4] and on f. 40, in LXIV, V agrees with Ca in drawing a snake fighting with a scorpion. In *MdQ*, which has five additional drawings, there is complete agreement of V and L. In this respect Ha stands apart from the other Latin manuscripts mentioned: it has only two snake drawings in the *Herbarium* and none in *MdQ*.

II. THE SOURCES

I. THE OLD ENGLISH HERBARIUM AND ITS SOURCES

Titles

The title *Herbarium* is found in MS V, f. 19, and in most of the Latin texts. The *Old English Herbarium* in MSS V, B, and H,

---

[1] Cures III. 13, III. 14, VI. 11, IX. 8, X. 12, X. 13, X. 17, XII. 14.
[2] See note to *M* X. 5.
[3] There are no drawings for *OEH* XII, CLXXXV, and *M* II.
[4] Vo adds *aspis icneumon*.

which is written as one continuous text, is a translation of three originally separate Latin treatises:

1. *De herba vettonica liber* (ch. I).
2. *Herbarium Apulei* (chs. II–CXXXII).[1]
3. *Liber medicinae ex herbis femininis* (chs. CXXXIII–CLXXXV).

The combination of these three texts is usually referred to as the *enlarged Herbarium*.

De herba vettonica liber

In the older Latin manuscripts this treatise is a separate text with an incipit and an explicit; afterwards it is incorporated in the text as ch. I. In Vo we find the following dedication: 'Antonius Musa Marco Agrippae salutem. Caesari Augusto praestantissimo omnium mortalium . . . cum volueris uti, sic uteris.' It is not entirely unimaginable that this dedication is authentic. The fact that the physician Musa had cured Augustus but failed to cure Marcellus may have commended him to Agrippa;[2] that Musa enjoyed a high reputation may be inferred from the circumstance that he is often quoted by Galen.[3] There is further evidence that it was fashionable among prominent physicians in the period of the emperors to write treatises on single plants. Juba, king of Mauretania (c.50 BC–AD 23), was a man of learning and wrote many books, among them a treatise on the plant euphorbia, which he discovered and named after his physician Euphorbus, brother of Antonius Musa.[4] Another physician to the Emperor Augustus, Themison, who was a pupil of Asclepiades, wrote a treatise on the herb plantago.[5] Furthermore, the *De herba vettonica liber* differs markedly from the other two parts of the enlarged *Herbarium* in that many of the cures mention exact details concerning the quantities of the ingredients to be used, a practice which was generally followed by the earlier herbalists.

Nevertheless there are sufficient reasons to doubt the authenticity of the dedication. The custom of attaching great names from

---

[1] It is probable that in the earliest versions ch. CXXXII, *mandragora*, did not belong to the *Herbarium Apulei*: some Latin manuscripts contain a recipe entitled *Praesidium pastillorum* between chs. CXXXI and CXXXII, and the list of 'tituli morborum' does not include cures taken from the mandragora.

[2] See E. Cary, *Dio's Roman History, with an English Translation* (The Loeb Classical Library, 9 vols. (London, 1914–27, repr. 1954–5)), liii. 30–2.

[3] Galen, xii. 609, 636, 737, 740–1, 955–6, 989; xiii. 47, 57, 61, etc.

[4] See Pliny, xxv. 77.   [5] Ibid. xxv. 80.

the past to learned treatises in order to add prestige was popular
in the latter days of the Roman Empire, as can be seen in the
following paragraphs. Secondly, apart from the exactitude in
mentioning quantities, the phraseology of the cures in the *De
herba vettonica liber* is very similar to that in the *Herbarium
Apulei*, the most conspicuous feature being the opening formula
with *Ad*, which is heavily predominant in both texts. From this
we may conclude that, although the *De herba vettonica liber* is
originally a separate text, it belongs to the same tradition as the
Herbarium Apulei and is contemporaneous with it.

Herbarium Apulei

In the earliest extant manuscript of this work, MS Vo, we find
the title *Herbarium Apulei Platonici traditum a Chirone Centauro,
magistro Achillis*. In later Latin versions the words *et ab Aesculapio*
were often added. The author was formerly identified with
Lucius Apuleius of Madaura (born *c.*AD 125), Platonic philosopher
and author of a number of much-quoted works.[1] On the strength
of internal evidence to the effect that the *Herbarium* was not
composed until the fourth century it is now universally agreed
that Lucius Apuleius of Madaura was not the author of this book.[2]
For this reason modern editors sometimes use appellations like
Pseudo-Apuleius or Apuleius Barbarus.[3]

It has been suggested by some scholars that the compiler added
the name of Apuleius to his work to give it more authority.[4]
Others maintain that there was a conflation of names: Apuleius
may be a corruption of Peleus, the name of the father of Achilles,
whose great-grandfather Chiron, the inventor of medical botany,
was to instruct him in the art of healing,[5] or it could be a Christian
surrogate for Apollo.[6] The most recent explanation, which also
seems the most plausible, is that the compiler of the *Herbarium*
used the name of Apuleius for his work because Apuleius of

[1] See the article *Appuleius* (9) in Pauly–Wissowa, ii, cols. 246–58; Hunger,
p. xviii; Voigts, 'The Significance of the Name "Apuleius"', pp. 217–19.
[2] See H. and S., p. xx; Hunger, p. xviii; Pauly–Wissowa, ii, col. 257; Schanz–
Hosius, p. 131.
[3] The first in H. and S., Hunger; the second in Berendes, Gunther.
[4] So E. Bethe, *Buch und Bild im Altertum* (Leipzig, 1954), p. 33, and H. E.
Sigerist, 'The Medical Literature of the Early Middle Ages', *Bull. Hist. Med.*
2 (1934), 33–4.
[5] See Talbot, p. 29, who mentions Homer's *Iliad*, xi. 831.
[6] See G. and S., p. 78.

Madaura had repeatedly professed his worship of the god of medicine, Aesculapius.[1] This would mean that the compiler's choice of the name of Apuleius was motivated by the wish to declare that the ultimate source of the *Herbarium* was the god of medicine.

In the OE MS V the illustration on f. 19r shows three figures which according to the inscription at the foot represent Aesculapius, Plato, and Chiron the centaur. 'Plato' is probably a substitute for Apuleius Platonicus (cf. the title on f. 19v).[2] The picture shows 'Plato', the central figure, receiving a book from Aesculapius and Chiron.[3]

There are various motives, based upon palaeographic, iconographic, and botanical evidence, for locating the compilation of the Latin *Herbarium* in South Italy, Sicily, or North Africa.[4] With regard to the language, the prevailing opinion is that the work was originally composed in Latin.[5] It can be shown that a considerable number of cures are borrowings from similar cures in Pliny's *Naturalis Historia*,[6] and there is no linguistic evidence to support the theory that the text was translated from Greek.

Liber medicinae ex herbis femininis

Chapters CXXXIII–CLXXXV of the *Old English Herbarium* are purported to be an OE translation of a work which is known as the *Liber medicinae ex herbis femininis*[7] and whose authorship is

[1] For this theory, see Linda E. Voigts, 'The Significance of the Name "Apuleius" ', in particular the quotation from Apuleius' *Florida* (ch. 18), on p. 224: 'For I am well known as a frequenter of his [i.e., Aesculapius'] rites, my worship of him is no new thing, my priesthood has received the smile of his favour, and ere now I have expressed my veneration for him both in prose and in verse.'

[2] For a discussion of this substitution, see G. Swarzenski, 'Mittelalterliche Kopien einer antiken medizinischen Bilderhandschrift', *Jahrbuch des kaiserlich deutschen archäologischen Instituts*, 17 (1902), 50.

[3] For a discussion of the question who is giving the book to whom, see Linda E. Voigts, 'One Anglo-Saxon View of the Classical Gods', pp. 7 ff.; for two different views, see G. and S., p. 78, and Bonser, p. 315.

[4] See R. Simonini, *Medicinae varia in codice dell' viii secolo conservato nell' archivio capitolare della Metropolitana di Modena*, Apulei liber (Modena, 1929), pp. 25–6, 37; Singer, 'Herbal in Antiquity', pp. 37 ff.; Singer in G. and S., pp. 23 ff.; Talbot, p. 30.

[5] See H. E. Sigerist, 'Zum Herbarius Pseudo-Apulei', *Sudhoffs Archiv für Geschichte der Medizin*, 23 (1930), 200; Sigerist in H. and S., p. xix; Talbot, p. 30. For a different view, see Singer, 'Herbal in Antiquity', p. 37.

[6] For references, see Explanatory Notes (Preliminary Remarks, E2 (c)).

[7] The forms *feminis* and *femineis* are also found.

attributed to Dioscorides in most Latin manuscripts. The treatise
is usually found in combination with the *Herbarium Apulei*, but
always as an independent text with its own incipit and explicit.
It belongs to a different tradition, as can be seen from the phraseology of the cures: whereas most cures in the other two parts of the
enlarged *Herbarium* open with *Ad*, this formula is rarely found
in the *Liber medicinae ex herbis femininis*. The text comes after
Apuleius, as in Ca,[1] or after Sextus Placitus, as in L and Ha.

There is general agreement that the ascription of the book to
Pedanius Dioscorides of Anazarbos (*fl.* AD 40–65), the author of
the *De materia medica*, is fictitious. It is clearly a work from a later
period, and the only connection with Dioscorides is to be found
in the circumstance that there is a similarity between some of the
chapters in this work and the parallel chapters in the Latin
version of the *De materia medica*. The identity of the compiler is
unknown, and the ascription to Dioscorides is to be regarded as
another instance of adding prestige to the work in question.

The book must have been in existence in the sixth century,
as appears from the following quotation from Cassiodorus (490–
585), *De institutione divinarum et saecularium litterarum*, i. 31,
in which he addresses those among his monks in the Vivarium
at Squillace who were unable to read Greek: 'Quodsi vobis non
fuerit graecarum litterarum nota facundia, imprimis habetis
herbarium Dioscoridis qui herbas agrorum mirabili proprietate
disseruit atque depinxit.' Riddle (p. 126) remarks apropos this
quotation that the work referred to is probably the *Liber medicinae
ex herbis femininis* and not the Latin translation of the *De materia
medica*, first because Cassiodorus uses the word *herbarium*,
whereas the complete *De materia medica* discusses other subjects
besides herbs, and secondly because he refers to drawings of
wonderful likeness, which is certainly appropriate for most of the
manuscripts containing the *Liber medicinae*, whereas only one
copy of the Latin *De materia medica* (München, 337) has any
drawings, and they are crude ones. In addition Riddle points out
that the *Epistula ad Marcellinum* (sixth century)[2] contains a
passage which seems to apply to the *Liber medicinae*: '. . . libellum
botanicon ex Dioscoridis libris Latino sermone conversum cum

---

[1] Three chapters and the first part of *ciminum* are found on p. 476, preceding
Apuleius, the second part of *ciminum* and the remaining thirty-nine chapters
come after Apuleius.   [2] See also pp. lxii–lxiii.

depictis herbarum figuris ad te misi.' The use of the word *libellum* can be more easily associated with the *Liber medicinae* than with the much more voluminous *De materia medica*.

The *Liber medicinae* contains three categories of chapters:

1. Those that have been taken from Dioscorides' *De materia medica*.
2. Those that have parallel chapters in the *Herbarium Apulei*.
3. Those that are not found in any other extant text.

While the chapters in category 1 are clearly translated or adapted from the *De materia medica*, those in category 2 contain cures that are very different from the cures found in the *Herbarium Apulei*. According to Riddle (p. 126) the sources, if any, which the author or translator used in addition to Dioscorides are uncertain. He rejects both Pliny and Apuleius as possible sources and thinks that the work contains new material not found in any previous text.

The use of the adjective *feminine* presents a problem that has elicited many speculations.[1] The most plausible explanation is given by Saint-Lager: 'Le plus savant des botanistes grecs nous avertit lui-même que nous aurions tort de vouloir trouver toujours un sens précis aux mots "plantes mâles et femelles", car fréquemment ces expressions ont été employées sans autre intention que celle de distinguer entre elles, par une épithète banale, les espèces les plus voisines les unes des autres.'[2]

There are several versions of this work. The longest version consists of seventy-one chapters; it has been edited by Kästner.[3] Of the Latin manuscripts used for this edition, A and Har contain the long version; shorter versions, containing forty-three and forty-two chapters respectively, are found in Ca and L. The arrangement and the choice of chapters in L is very different from that in Ca, and some of the chapters in L are not found in the long version; L also stands apart from the other Latin manuscripts in that it does not mention the name of Dioscorides. For a full discussion regarding the textual tradition of this work, see Riddle, pp. 125-33.

[1] See Talbot, p. 30.

[2] J.-B. Saint-Lager, *Recherches historiques sur les mots* plantes mâles *et* plantes femelles (Paris, 1884), p. 36.

[3] Kästner's edition is based upon three manuscripts: Firenze, Bibl. Medicea Laurenziana LXXIII. 41 and LXXIII. 16, and Paris, Bibl. Nationale, Fonds latin 6862.

Editions of the Latin text

The earliest known printed edition of the *De herba vettonica liber* and the *Herbarium Apulei* is

1. The so-called *Editio Princeps* by Ioannes Philippus de Lignamine, which has no imprint, but must have been issued between 1480 and 1483, as appears from the dedication; de Lignamine states that he found a manuscript copy of the book in the library of Montecassino; a collation of the *Editio Princeps* and MS Ca shows that the *Editio Princeps* is not a direct copy of MS Ca.

Other printed editions containing the *De herba vettonica liber* and the *Herbarium Apulei* are

2. *Apuleji Madaurensis philosophi Platonici viri clarissimi de herbarum virtutibus . . . quam a Chirone Centauro praeceptore Achillis et ab Aesculapio accepit, hactenus nunquam in lucem edita*, by Albanus Torinus Vitodurensis (Basileae, 1528).

3. *Ant. Musae de Herba Vetonica Liber I, L. Apulei de Medicaminibus Herbarum Liber I, per Gabrielem Humelbergium Ravenspurgensem, Archiatrum Isinensem, recogniti & emendati, adiuncto Commentariolo eiusdem* (Isinae,[1] 1537).

4. *Parabilium Medicamentorum Scriptores Antiqui, Sexti Placiti Papyriensis de medicamentis ex animalibus liber, Lucii Apuleii de medicaminibus herbarum liber, ex recensione et cum notis Ioannis Christiani Gottlieb Ackermann, M.D. et prof. Altorf.* (Norimbergae et Altorfii, 1788).

5. E. Howald et H. E. Sigerist, *Antonii Musae de herba vettonica liber. Pseudoapulei herbarius. Anonymi de taxone liber. Sexti Placiti liber medicinae ex animalibus etc.* (Corpus Medicorum Latinorum, vol. iv) (Leipzig/Berlin, 1927).

The only printed edition of the *Liber medicinae de herbis femininis* is

H. F. Kästner, 'Pseudo-Dioscoridis de Herbis Femininis', *Hermes*, xxxi. 578–636, and xxxii. 160 (1896–7).

---

[1] Isina is Isny in Württemberg, where a Benedictine abbey was founded in 1090.

2. THE OLD ENGLISH MEDICINA DE QUADRUPEDIBUS AND ITS SOURCES

Titles, parts, date

The title *Medicina de Quadrupedibus*, by which the OE text in this edition has been known since Cockayne used it in 1864, is not found in any of the extant manuscripts. The word *medicina* occurs in the incipits and explicits of some of the Latin texts,[1] the word *quadrupes* is found in one manuscript only.[2] Francis Junius, in his transcript of MS B (Bodleian Library, MS Junius 58, p. 145), uses the title *Medicina ex quadrupedibus*, and Wanley indicates the text in the same way in his *Catalogus* (pp. 75, 217, 304). At the beginning of the text in MS O there is a marginal incipit; see the textual notes.

In the four OE manuscripts and in the Latin MS L, the *Medicina de Quadrupedibus*, which is written as one continuous text, consists of three originally separate parts:

1. *Liber de taxone* (ch. I).
2. A treatise dealing with the healing properties of the mulberry (ch. II).
3. The short or A-version[3] of the *Liber medicinae ex animalibus* (chs. III–XIV).

None of the other extant early manuscripts contains part 2.

In all four OE manuscripts the *Medicina de Quadrupedibus*, which comes immediately after the *Old English Herbarium*, is treated as a separate text, as appears from the way in which the opening phrase is written in VBH, and from the fact that in O a Latin incipit is added. In most Latin manuscripts the *Medicina de Quadrupedibus* comes immediately after the Apuleius part of the *Herbarium* and is followed by the *Liber medicinae ex herbis femininis*. In L and Ha the *Liber de taxone* is preceded by the so-called *Epistula ad Marcellinum*; this short text is clearly intended as an *epistula dedicatoria* to a copy of the *Liber medicinae ex herbis femininis*, but curiously enough this is not what follows. In both manuscripts the *Epistula* begins at the top of a page, and is directly followed on the same page by the *Liber de taxone*. This arrange-

---

[1] e.g. in MSS A, Slo, Harley 1585, Royal Appendix III.

[2] In Ca: 'Incipit de quadrupedibus', to introduce a text containing recipes obtained from quadrupeds and birds.

[3] See pp. lxv–lxvi.

ment, especially in Ha, where the initial *C* of the *Epistula* is of extravagant size and where the *Liber de taxone* follows without any interruption, makes it look like an introduction to that text, with which it has no relation whatever. In L the *Liber medicinae ex herbis femininis* comes after Sextus Placitus, in Ha it is not found at all.

The date of composition of the *Medicina de Quadrupedibus* in the form recorded in the earliest extant Latin manuscripts cannot have been much earlier than the fifth century.[1]

Liber de taxone

The title *Liber de taxone* does not occur in any of the extant manuscripts. One text, MS A, begins: 'Libellum Octaviani Augusti de mele bestiolo incipit'; in some other manuscripts (Slo, Harley 1585, Royal Appendix III) the word *epistola* occurs in the incipit.

Originally the *Liber de taxone* was a separate text. This becomes apparent from the following points:

1. It is clearly intended as a letter with a formal opening address, and, in the less corrupted B-version, a peroration at the end.[2]
2. The principle 'a capite ad calcem', which in Sextus Placitus is observed to a certain extent, is absent here.
3. In several Latin manuscripts there is a table of contents of Sextus Placitus between the *Liber de taxone* and Sextus Placitus.
4. There are some manuscripts which contain only Sextus Placitus.
5. In MS L and in the OE version the *Liber de taxone* and Sextus Placitus are separated by the treatise on the mulberry.

It seems therefore unlikely that the *Liber de taxone* is an *epistula dedicatoria* prefixed to his book by Sextus Placitus in a similar way as the treatise on the Herba Vettonica is prefixed to the *Herbarium*, as is suggested by H. and S. (p. xxii).

It is not possible to identify the author of this work. According to MSS L and Ha he is Idpartus/Iapartus rex Aegyptiorum. In Ca the name is Ypareus, in MS Bern 803, line 409,[3] it is Hibarcus.

---

[1] See H. Diller, *Placitus* (3), in Pauly–Wissowa, xx, cols. 1944–7.

[2] For some variant versions, see de Vriend, pp. xxxviii ff.

[3] MS Bern 803 is a scroll; there is a facsimile with numbered lines in the library (Burgerbibliothek, Bern).

None of these forms can be associated with the name of an Egyptian king. An interesting variant was found in MS K IV 3 of the Biblioteca Nazionale, Torino:[1] 'Regi Egyptiorum Octaviano Augusto salutem'. The same incipit occurs in the epitome of the work by Constantinus Africanus (ed. Ackermann, *Sextus Placitus*, p. 115). With the dative *regi* in the opening formula the interpretation might be thus: the alleged author, Idpartus, sends the treatise to the Emperor Augustus, whom he calls 'rex Aegyptiorum', to honour him for his victory at Actium. The dedication should be regarded as fictitious, because there is no evidence to show that the *Liber de taxone* was written earlier than the other texts with which it is usually combined, and which are all from the fourth or the fifth century.

The treatise on the mulberry

The second of the three texts, the treatise on the healing properties of the mulberry, has been inserted out of place: there is no mention in it of any four-footed animal. That the scribe of L regarded the treatise as part of the *Liber de taxone* is attested by his numbering: the original paragraph numbers of the *Liber* are continued in this text. Nor do the four OE manuscripts indicate that the treatise is a separate text, except that in O, where the scribe does not even take the trouble to begin a new paragraph (the scribe of H does not do this either), there is a sign referring to a marginal note that is no longer legible. It can hardly be doubted that the two texts were originally separate, as becomes evident from the subject-matter, and also from the fact that the only early manuscript containing a Latin version of the treatise is L.[2]

Liber medicinae ex animalibus

This text, attributed to Sextus Placitus, is found in two different forms:

(*a*) The short or A-version, also called α-version, which contains the cures taken from quadrupeds as they occur in the text of this edition.

---

[1] Beccaria, 110: late eleventh century; the manuscript was destroyed by fire in 1904.

[2] It is also found in at least one later manuscript: MS W, which on ff. 37v–46v has an almost exact copy of the version of the *Medicina de Quadrupedibus* in L, with two long omissions.

(*b*) The long or B-version, also called β-version, which contains
        cures taken from the same quadrupeds as in the A-version,
        moreover from the bear, the ass, the mule, the horse, the
        cat, the dormouse, the weasel, the mouse, from the boy and
        the girl, and from eleven birds.

With regard to the terms α-version and β-version it is necessary
to point out that this terminology,[1] as far as the *Medicina de
Quadrupedibus* is concerned, is misleading. The two versions
(there are no texts of class γ which contain the *Medicina de
Quadrupedibus*) are so different from each other that H. and S.
print them in two parallel columns. It becomes clear at once
that here the 'β-version' is more complete than the 'α-version',
and as Diller[2] demonstrates, is closer to the archetype than the
'α-version'. The only three early manuscripts containing both
the α-version of the *Herbarium* and a version of the *Medicina de
Quadrupedibus* are L, Ha, and Ca. The versions of the *Medicina
de Quadrupedibus* in L and Ha are very similar to each other;
they are the only two short versions found in the early manuscripts. In both codices the *Epistula ad Marcellinum*[3] is wrongly
prefixed to the text. H. and S. classify these versions of the
Medicina de Quadrupedibus as α, apparently because they are
found in texts containing the α-version of the *Herbarium*. The
third manuscript, Ca, has a version of the *Medicina de Quadrupedibus* which is much more closely related to the versions in
manuscripts of class β and which on that account is placed in class
β by H. and S.

It is a mistake to classify the texts of the *Medicina de Quadrupedibus* in the same manner as those of the *Herbarium*. The
Herbarium was presumably composed in the fourth century,[4] the
Medicina de Quadrupedibus in the fifth.[5] Consequently the textual
tradition of the one text is different from that of the other. It would
therefore seem more prudent not to apply the classification of the
texts of the *Herbarium* to the *Medicina de Quadrupedibus*, but to
employ a different terminology to distinguish between the short
and long versions, and call them A-version and B-version respectively.

---

[1] See p. l.   [2] See p. lxiii, n. 1.
[3] See pp. lxii–lxiii.
[4] See H. and S., p. xx.   [5] See p. lxiii, n. 1.

The two versions differ not only in length, but also in various other respects:

1. In the chapters which are found in both versions, some of the cures occur only in one of the two versions.
2. The order of the cures in the chapters is not always the same in the two versions.
3. In most cases there are considerable differences between the cures that occur in both versions as regards their wording.
4. In the A-version the fox precedes the hare, in the B-version the hare precedes the fox.
5. In the cures which are based upon parallels in Pliny's *Naturalis Historia* the differences from the original are smaller in the B-version.

As becomes evident in many places, the compiler of the *Liber medicinae ex animalibus* made a liberal use of the medical lore collected by Pliny in his *Naturalis Historia*, especially in book xxviii. The cures in Pliny which apparently served as models for Sextus Placitus are referred to in Appendix II.

Sextus Placitus probably produced his treatise as a supplement to the *Herbarium*, and organized it in the same manner: each of the chapters contains recipes taken from one species of animal. Some of the later copyists must have realized the disadvantages of this arrangement for physicians who seriously wanted to use the book: thus in MS Bern 803 the recipes are arranged more or less according to the diseases which they were intended to cure.

The name Sextus Placitus Papiriensis occurs in several Latin manuscripts;[1] the variant Placidus is also found.[2] MS Firenze Bibl. Med. Laur. LXXIII. 16, in which the explicit of this text contains the name Sextus Placitus, has some illustrations between the *Liber de taxone* and the table of contents of the *Liber medicinae ex animalibus*. On two of them we see the picture of an 'urbs': the one, on f. 151, is 'urbs Placiti Papiron', the other, on f. 152, is 'urbs Octaviani'. In this way the scribe honours the writer of the *Liber medicinae ex animalibus* and the addressee of the *Liber de taxone*. Some unsuccessful attempts have been made to demonstrate that there actually existed a man called Sextus Placitus.

[1] MSS A, Firenze Bibl. Med. Laur. LXXIII. 41, Wrocław III F 19, Bibl. Vat. Barb. Lat. 160.
[2] MSS Slo, Harley 1585, Royal Appendix III.

Both Humelberg (pp. 3–4) and Fabricius (Bibl. Graeca, xii. 613–14)[1] identify him with the philosopher Sextus Chaeronensis, of the second century, a nephew of Plutarch. Their evidence is so vague and unconvincing that this theory can be safely discarded. Moreover, the date of composition cannot have been so early, as appears from internal evidence. It seems therefore wiser to assume with Cockayne (p. lxxxix) that Sextus Placitus is 'a nominis umbra, a phantom name, a medieval bit of fun', just like that other creature of the imagination, Idpartus in the *Liber de taxone*.

Editions of the Latin text

The earliest known printed edition of Sextus Placitus is:

1. Franciscus Emericus, *Sextus Placitus Papyriensis De Medicamentis ex Animalibus Libellus* (Nürnberg, 1538).

Other printed editions are:

2. *Sextus philosophus Platonicus de medicina animalium bestiarum, pecorum, et avium, cum scholiis Gabrielis Humelbergi Ravenspurgensis medici* (Isinae,[2] 1539).

3. J. A. Fabricius, *Sexti Platonici Philosophi Liber de medicina ex animalibus*, in Bibliotheca Graeca, xiii. 395–423 (Hamburg, 1726).

4. *Parabilium Medicamentorum Scriptores Antiqui, Sexti Placiti Papyriensis de medicamentis ex animalibus liber, Lucii Apuleii de medicaminibus herbarum liber, ex recensione et cum notis Ioannis Christiani Gottlieb Ackermann, M.D. et prof. Altorf.* (Norimbergae et Altorfii, 1788).

All these editions contain the B-version of Sextus Placitus; the *Liber de taxone* and the treatise on the mulberry are not printed. Ackermann prints Sextus Placitus as well as the epitome which Constantinus Africanus, an eleventh-century scholar, made of the *Liber de taxone* and of Sextus Placitus. The first printed edition to appear after Ackermann's is

5. E. Howald and H. E. Sigerist, *Antonii Musae de herba vettonica liber. Pseudoapulei herbarius. Anonymi de taxone liber. Sexti Placiti liber medicinae ex animalibus etc.* (Corpus Medicorum Latinorum, vol. iv) (Leipzig/Berlin, 1927).

---

[1] See next section, item 3.
[2] See p. lxi, n. 1.

H. and S. print the text of the *Liber de taxone* and of the *Liber medicinae ex animalibus*, as found in the A-version and in the B-version, in two parallel columns on pp. 229–69, the rest of the B-version on pp. 270–86. The A-version of the *Medicina de Quadrupedibus*, as printed by H. and S., is mainly based on MS L, with numerous emendations.

III. THE LANGUAGE OF THE OLD ENGLISH MANUSCRIPTS

1. THE LANGUAGE OF MSS V, B, AND H[1]

In general the language of MSS V, B, and H displays with great regularity the features which are characteristic of late West Saxon. The following sections contain a discussion of the linguistic features which may throw some light upon the dialectal characteristics of these three texts.

Sounds and spellings

As regards the vowels in stressed syllables, all three manuscripts adhere closely to the system that is prevalent in late WS. The following details may be noted:

1. OE *æ* (fronted Gmc *a*). Predominant spelling: *æ*. For *a* in the adverbs *hraþe, smale*, see Cpb. 643 (1), SB 315 Anm. 2.

2. OE *e* (front mutated *a/o* before nasals). V has almost exclusively *e*, the predominant spelling in BH is *æ*. If one excludes *nemnan*, which is found only with *e*, and *fremian*, which is frequently found in VB but does not occur in H,[2] the distribution in percentages of *e/æ* in the three manuscripts is V 99:1, B 16:84, H 21:79. This *æ*-spelling is often found in late OE in a limited south-eastern area, including Essex, but not Kent; see Cpb. 193 (d).[3]

3. OE *e* (> *y*) in *hwylc, sylf, syllan*: in VH always *y*, except in V *sylf/self* (ratio 25:1); in B mostly *i*. See point 5, and Cpb. 325.

4. OE *ea* (from *æ* through fracture before *l*+consonant). Predominant spelling: *ea*. There are a few instances of

---

[1] In this chapter, for 'MS V', etc., read 'the part of MS V etc. containing *OEH* and *MdQ*'; when no further specification is given, the phenomenon discussed occurs in *OEH* as well as in *MdQ*.   [2] H uses the form *framian*.

[3] See also Sisam, *Psalter*, pp. 13 f., where a wide area of southern England is postulated for this phenomenon.

words containing Anglian *a*: *cald* VBH (1×, as against *ea* 2×), *halswyrt* VBH (always, except H *ea* 1×), *salf* V (1×, as against *ea* 11×), *scallan* B (always), *gewald* V (1×, as against *ea* 6×).

5. OE stable *y* and unstable *y*,[1] short and long. For all these sounds B has a far greater proportion of *i*-spellings than VH: in VH *i* is found mainly in words where the sound is followed by *x* < *hs* and by the palatal groups -*nc* and -*ng*, in B also in other positions. See Cpb. 316–17.

6. OE *ǣ*[1] (Wgmc *ā*) and *ǣ*[2] (Gmc *ai*, early OE *ā* by front mutation). Predominant spelling: *æ*, but B regularly has *a* for *ǣ*[1] in *þar* adv. and its compounds and in *þara* gpl., frequently in *þare* gdsgf., and in (*ge*)*hwar*. The form *þar* is late WS; see Cpb. 678 and Pope, p. 178, who records a preference for *þar* in the eleventh-century MS CCCC 178.

7. OE *ēa* before *g*, *h* is never smoothed, except in V 2×: *egena*, *þeh*, both in *OEH*. Smoothing of *ēa* to *ē* is frequent in Ælfric. See Bülbring, pp. 316–17.

8. Long *i* is often indicated by an additional *g* in B: *hig*, *gedriggan*, *þrig*, etc.

9. *a/o*, whether short or long, after *sc*, is always spelled without the diacritic *e* in B, mostly *ea/eo* in VH. Examples: *scafan*, *scallan*, *scanca*; *scolde*; *scadan*; *scoh*.

10. The late WS change *weor* > *wur* is represented, in *OEH* only, by the imp. (*ge*)*wurp* V (2×), BH (1×),[2] in all other instances we find *weor*-. In Ælfric the spelling *wur* in these words is predominant; see Pope, p. 178, Needham, p. 8.

Apart from the points just mentioned all three manuscripts contain a few instances of spellings which deviate from the usual late WS pattern and which can be regarded as isolated cases of analogy or as mistakes.

The spelling of vowels in terminations is mainly in accordance with the regular pattern of late WS. In endings which in early OE contained *a*, *o*, *u*, these vowels are usually still found. The only details worth mentioning are:

1. *æ* for *e* in *afeormungæ*, *doccæ*, *læssæ*, *þæræ*, *þissæ* V (all 1×), *hælæþ* H (1×).

---

[1] There are no instances of early WS *ie*.
[2] B also has *wyrp* (1×), which may be regarded as an inverted spelling.

2. -*gynde* for -*iende* in *wungynde* V (1×).
3. -*ud* for -*od* in past participles of weak verbs II, in VH.

On the whole the consonantal systems of MSS V, B, and H display the usual characteristics of late WS. A few instances of exceptional spellings may be mentioned:

1. Omission of initial *g* in *ealla* V (2×), B (2×), H (1×), *eornlice* VB (1×).
2. *c* for *g*: (*ge*)*cnid* V (3×), *stence* V (1×), *strencþ* V (1×).
3. *hg* for *g*: *dihglum* V (1×); see SB 214 Anm. 6.
4. *i/y* for *g*: *aleiþ* H (1×), *leyþ* H (1×).
5. *ch* for *h*: *elechtran* V (1×); this spelling for the fricative is found in early texts; see Cpb. 55, 57 (3).
6. *n* for *ng*: *s*(*t*)*renþ* V (3×), H (1×); see SB 184 Anm., 215 Anm. 1: apparently a Kentish spelling.
7. *ð* for *t*: *blosðman* VH (1×), *wundrasð* VH (1×).

There are the usual instances of omission and unetymological addition of consonants, especially of *h* and *t*: *raþe*, *toflyþ*; *ahrærþ*, *tophreoman*; *ongist*, *onsenst*, *ynsan*, etc.

Accidence

The inflexional system of late WS is observed very consistently in MSS V, B, and H. Most of the forms which contain inflexions deviating from the standard pattern are variants occurring regularly in late WS owing to the levelling of inflexional vowels. A few special features require our attention:

1. Personal pronoun, 3rd person npl. Always *hy/hi/hig*; VH have *hio* 1×. For an exhaustive treatment of *hio* in the npl., see Gericke and Greul.[1]
2. Simple demonstrative pronoun.
   asgm. *þone*, but *þæne* occurs a few times in VH; see Cpb. 380.
   gdsgf. *þære/þare*: VH mostly *æ*, B mostly *a*. V, in *MdQ*, has *þær* 1×: a regular Northumbrian form; see Cpb. 708 f. 1.
   gpl.: *þæra/þara*: VH mostly *a*, B always *a*.
3. Strong verbs, 2nd and 3rd sg. pres. indic. There is a marked deviation from the usual late WS pattern, especially so in

[1] B. Gericke and W. Greul, *Das Personalpronomen der 3. Person in spätangelsächsischen und frühmittelenglischen Texten*, Palaestra, 193 (Leipzig, 1934), pp. 66–9.

MdQ, as appears from the following tables, which are based on the relevant forms and which show the frequency of unmutated/mutated[1] and unsyncopated/syncopated forms in the 2nd and 3rd sg. pres. indic. of all the strong verbs in the two texts, except the forms of the verb *cuman*,[2] of the weak presents, and of the contracted *h*-roots.

	OEH			MdQ		
	V	B	H	V	B	H
Actual occurrences						
No mutation—no syncopation	23	20	22	15	14	8
No mutation—syncopation	—	—	—	—	—	1
Mutation—no syncopation	3	2	3	2	1	2
Mutation—syncopation	22	26	23	1	1	—
Primary *i*, *ǣ*[1], WS *ie*[3]—no syncopation	27	24	22	14	11	4
Primary *i*, *ǣ*[1], WS *ie*—syncopation	39	44	41	1	1	—
Frequency of unmutated and mutated forms in percentages[4]						
Unmutated forms	48	42	46	83	87	82
Mutated forms	52	58	54	17	13	18
Frequency of unsyncopated and syncopated forms in percentages						
Unsyncopated forms	47	40	42	94	93	93
Syncopated forms	53	60	58	6	7	7

The percentage of unmutated and unsyncopated forms in *MdQ* is much higher than in *OEH*; these forms are characteristic of Anglian texts; see Cpb. 733-4, SB 358, 371, Quirk and Wrenn 76, Hedberg, p. 298.[5] Although it must be admitted that there is an increasing occurrence of unsyncopated forms in non-Ælfrician late WS,[6] the striking predominance of these forms in *MdQ* may be regarded, in combination with some other features (see below), as an indication that this text is directly descended from an Anglian original.[7]

[1] In this context 'mutated' is used in the sense: showing early raising of *e* to *i* before *i*, or showing *i*-mutation.

[2] Mutation is regularly found in the 2nd and 3rd sg. pres. indic. of this verb, also in early texts; see Cpb. 742.

[3] Primary *i*: Gmc *e* before *m*, Gmc *e* before a covered nasal, Gmc *i*; WS *ie*: Gmc *e* > *ie* by front diphthongization.

[4] Roots containing primary *i*, etc., not included.

[5] Hedberg's conclusion: 'What is evident is this: the unsyncopated form was as typically Anglian as the syncopated form was West Saxon and Kentish.'

[6] See Hedberg, p. 290.

[7] It is interesting to compare the strong verbs of which forms of the 2nd and 3rd sg. pres. indic. occur in *OEH* and *MdQ* with the same verbs in the glossary

4. Strong verbs and weak verbs class I, 3rd sg. pres. indic. There are a few instances of forms in *-aþ*: *gedwæsc(e)aþ* VB (1×), *hataþ* V (1×), B (2×), *toscacaþ* B (1×). These forms may be regarded as examples showing the late OE confusion of inflexional vowels, but it must be added that *-aþ*-forms are already found in early Anglian; see Cpb. 735 (b).

5. Plural pres. subj. The ending *-en* is heavily predominant in all three manuscripts. Ælfric mostly has *-an*, sometimes *-on* in these forms, and very rarely *-en*; see Needham, p. 11, n. 1.

Vocabulary

Apart from the occurrence of a number of interesting names of plants and animals, there is not much that is remarkable about the vocabulary of the two texts. There is one difference between *OEH* and *MdQ* which may be regarded as significant: the occurrence, almost exclusively in *MdQ* (only the word *nænig* is found 1× in *OEH*), of a small number of words which are especially found in texts of Anglian provenance. Although the evidence is very modest, it may be an indication that there is a close relation between the extant text of *MdQ* and an earlier Anglian version. The subjoined list contains the words which may serve as evidence; the occurrences are those in the *MdQ* section of MS V.

1. *Beorþor* (2×). Most of the forms recorded in BT(S) are in texts of Anglian origin. See von Schaubert, p. 145. Jordan (*Eigent.*, pp. 106–7) gives other instances of nouns in *-or/-er* keeping *-r* in Anglian texts but generally losing *-r* in WS (*morþor*, *sigor*; *beger*, *stæner*).

2. *Nænig* (1×). General in OE in earlier times: found in the Prologue to Ine's laws, ed. Liebermann, i. 88. But very rare in Alfred and later WS texts; see Sisam, *Studies*, p. 294; Jost, pp. 159 ff.; Pope, p. 100.

3. *Sceþþan* (3×). In Anglian more usual than *derian* (1×; often in *OEH*); see Wildhagen, p. 185.

4. *Smyrenyss* (1×), as against *sealf* (11×). *Smyrenyss* is typically Anglian; see Rauh, p. 19.

5. *Snytro* (1×). In Anglian more usual than *wisdom*; see Jordan, *Eigent.*, pp. 91–2.

of Pope, all compounds included. The frequency in percentages of unmutated forms of these verbs in the homilies edited by Pope is ten, that of unsyncopated forms less than 0.5.

6. *Winnan* ($1 \times$), in the meaning 'labour, suffer', is typical of Anglian texts; see Wildhagen, p. 186, Scherer, p. 17.

7. *Wræc* ($9 \times$), as against *sar* ($50 \times$), *ece* ($3 \times$). *Wræc* is the metathesized form of Anglian *wærc*. The metathesis may be due to a non-Anglian scribe confronted with an unfamiliar word; see Jordan, *Eigent.*, pp. 51 ff.; G. and S., pp. 219–20. Both *OEH* and *MdQ* have *sar* far more frequently than either of the other two words. The two texts show a marked difference in their use of *wræc* and *ece*: *wræc* occurs in *OEH* $0 \times$, in *MdQ* $9 \times$; *ece* occurs in *OEH* $29 \times$, in *MdQ* $3 \times$.

Syntax

The texts of *OEH* and *MdQ* have little to show that is interesting in the field of syntax. The word order has the usual OE characteristics, and on the whole the sentence structure is extremely simple.

One syntactical feature, however, deserves to be mentioned. The participle group[1] which occurs throughout the Latin *Herbarium* and *MdQ*, and which is used in that part of the cure where directions for its preparation are given, is very frequently rendered by a similar construction in the OE *MdQ*; this is done only sporadically in *OEH*,[2] in which text the directions are nearly always introduced by the imperative or subjunctive singular of a verb, usually *(ge)niman*, a feature occurring in only one out of every four cures in *MdQ*.

Some examples of the participle group in the OE *MdQ*:

1. horn . . . gebeaten 7 drince on wine (III. 4).
2. se ytemæsta dæl . . . áhangen, þu gelyfest þæt þis sy . . . gedon (IV. 10).
3. lungen . . . gewriþen, . . . þa gongas beoþ gehælede (V. 3).
4. geallan . . . gemencged . . ., þa eagan gebeorhtigeaþ (V. 7).
5. brægen gesoden, gnid . . . mid þa toþreoman, hi beoþ clæne (V. 16).
6. horn . . . geled, weccan he on slæpe gecyrreþ (VII. 2).
7. niwe gate cyse þærto gewriþen, hyt hæleþ (VII. 6).

[1] The term *participle group* is used in the sense: word group consisting of a noun and one or more past participles. For a detailed discussion of the participle groups in *MdQ*, see de Vriend, pp. xcix ff.

[2] In MS V, *MdQ* has sixty-two instances, *OEH* seven. The length of *OEH* is more than five times that of *MdQ*; this puts the ratio *MdQ*:*OEH* at approximately 45:1.

The construction is often absolute, and its imperatival character is evident, especially in 1, where through the use of the conjunction *and* it is treated as a co-ordinate element in the sentence.[1]

The Latin parallels are:

1. cornus . . . tunsus, cum vino . . . bibat.
2. summa pars . . . suspensa, irritamentum . . . credat.
3. pulmo impositus . . . sanat.
4. fel . . . mixtum . . ., ad claritatem oculi perveniunt.
5. cerebrum . . . coctum, si ex eo gingivas . . . defrices, sanae efficiuntur.
6. cornu . . . suppositum vigilias in somnum convertit.
7. caseus [caprae recens] impositus . . . sanat.

The Latin construction is often a *participium coniunctum*, as in 3, 6, and 7, in other cases it is an absolute participle construction in which the noun and the participle are in the nominative or in the accusative, as in 1, 2, 4, and 5.

For the problems regarding the origin and history of the nominative/accusative absolute in OE, see von Schaubert, pp. 175 ff., who draws the interesting conclusion that the occurrence of an absolute nominative/accusative in OE texts is an indication of Anglian origin. The construction was not unusual in post-classical Latin;[2] it is a recognized fact that the Latin of the Irish missionaries who Christianized Northumbria had deviated more from the classical model than the Latin of the later missionaries from Rome who converted Kent and Wessex.[3] Without excluding the possibility that the construction is vernacular we may assume that this strong influence of post-classical Latin in the North of England favoured the use of the nominative/accusative absolute in Anglian texts.[4]

---

[1] The imperatival/adhortatory function of the past participle is also found in present-day Dutch and German; see E. Rijpma and F. G. Schuringa, *Nederlandse Spraakkunst*, 21st edn. (Groningen, 1968), p. 144, and J. Leopold, *Lehrbuch der deutschen Sprache*, ii, 10th edn. (Bussum, 1954), 151.

[2] See F. Horn, *Zur Geschichte der absoluten Partizipialkonstruktionen* (Lund/Leipzig, 1918); Y. M. Biese, 'Der spätlateinische Akkusativus Absolutus und Verwandtes', *Annales Academicae Scientiarum Fennicae*, ser. B. xxii (Helsinki, 1927/8); W. Havers, 'Zur Syntax des Nominativs', *Glotta*, 16 (1928), 121–7.

[3] See W. Hunt, *The English Church from its Foundation to the Norman Conquest* (London, 1899), pp. 1, 7; E. R. Curtius, *Europäische Literatur und lateinisches Mittelalter* (Bern, 2nd edn. 1954), pp. 55–8.

[4] For conclusions concerning the textual traditions of *OEH* and *MdQ*, see pp. xli ff.

2. THE LANGUAGE OF MS O

The language of MS O, which has many spellings and inflexions clearly showing that it was copied in the post-Conquest period, is a typical example of residual OE, that is late WS copied by a scribe who, though able to understand and copy texts in the late WS dialect, is so strongly influenced by the linguistic changes of his period that reflections of these changes are frequently found in the texts copied by him. With the evidence collected in this chapter it can be demonstrated that the characteristic features of late WS are still predominant in MS O, and that therefore it should be regarded as an OE, not a ME text.

Sounds and spellings

MS O displays most of the characteristics of late WS; the instances which may be called examples of standard late WS are always more numerous than the instances showing other forms. In this section those sounds and spellings are discussed of which there are variants in O which do not fit into the pattern of late WS and which occur too frequently for them to be explained as errors.

With regard to vowels in stressed syllables the following details are of importance:

1. OE *æ*, of whatever origin. Predominant spelling: *æ*. In a small number of words (*bæþ, bræȝen, fæst, hrædlice*) the instances with *a* are more frequent than those with *æ*; the spelling *a* for *æ* is to be regarded as ME; see Jordan, *MEG* 32. For *a* in the adverbs *hraþe, smale*, see Cpb. 643 (1), SB 315 Anm. 2.

2. OE *eo*, of whatever origin. Predominant spelling: *eo*. There are a few instances of forms with *o*: *hortclæfre, hortes*, but even in these words *eo* is found far more frequently. The spelling *o* for *eo* is ME; see Jordan, *MEG* 65.

3. OE stable and unstable *y*, short and long. Predominant spelling: *y*, except for long unstable *y*, which is mostly spelled *i*. The spelling *u* is found in approximately 15 per cent of all instances; it is a ME spelling; see Jordan, *MEG* 42, 70, 77, 83. In words like *wurm, wurt, wurtruma* the *u* is OE; see Cpb. 320–2.

4. OE *ā* (Gmc *ai*). The spelling *a* is strongly predominant in *OEH*, except in *sar/sor/sær*, of which there are 96/62/3

instances respectively. The only other *o*-forms in *OEH* are *gon, healso* (= *ealswa*), *more, on* (1× each). In *MdQ* there are no *o*-spellings. The spelling *o* for *a* is ME; see Jordan, *MEG* 44.

5. OE *ǣ*¹ (Wgmc *ā*) and *ǣ*² (Gmc *ai*, early OE *ā* by front mutation). Predominant spelling: *æ*, but mostly *a* in *þar* adv. and its compounds and in forms of the demonstrative pronoun, and also frequently, both for *ǣ*¹ and for *ǣ*², in other words: *lacedom, ondrade, yfeldade*; *alc, aniʒ, clane, dal, halan*.¹ The development of *ǣ*¹ and *ǣ*² into *ā* is especially found in the south-east in the twelfth century; see Schlemilch, pp. 18–20.

6. OE *ēo*, of whichever origin. Predominant spelling: *eo*. There are some instances of forms with *o*: *brost* (3×), *soþ* (1×), *ʒeþod* (1×). The spelling *o* for *eo* is ME; see Jordan, *MEG* 84. The forms *adeoþ* and *feot* show inverted ME spellings for OE *ē*.

The spelling of vowels in terminations is still predominantly in accordance with the regular late WS pattern. For evidence, see below in the section on Accidence.

The consonantal system of O is basically late WS, but an essential difference between O and VBH is that the functions of OE ʒ are divided between ʒ (in this edition printed ʒ) and *g*.

ʒ is generally found:

1. Initially before primary front vowels, and, followed by diacritic *e*, before back vowels: *ʒear, ʒifu; ʒeond* (occasionally *g*: *gealla, gyst*).

2. Medially after front and back vowels and after consonants: *bræʒen, ʒedriʒed; haʒol, toʒene; swelʒeþ* (occasionally *g*: *migþan, twigea; dagas, maga; halgusta*).

3. Finally after front vowels: *dæʒ, weʒ*; in the inverted spelling *hiʒ* (1× *g*: *papig*).

g is generally found:

1. Initially before back vowels, secondary front vowels, consonants: *gat, god; gyldene, gyrdels; gnid, grutta* (occasionally ʒ: *ʒeʒaderung, ʒoman; ʒreat, ʒrene*).

---

¹ In *alc* and *aniʒ* there may have been shortening and early development of *æ* to *a*; in *aniʒ* there may also have been influence of *an*.

2. Medially and finally in the combination -ng-, -ng, whether originally velar or palatal: *fingran*, *lungane*; *mengan*; *gang*, *wring*; *meng* (occasionally *nʒ*: *ʒepunʒen*; *ʒemenʒed*; *ʒeonʒ*; *sprenʒ*). In forms like *angynne*, *ongean*, *ongyst* the g is apparently treated as the second element of medial -ng-.

In all these cases the ratio rule:exception is more than 50:1, except in the combination *ng*, whether medial or final, where it is more than 20:1.

From the evidence found in O it appears that the palatal semi-vowel and the voiced velar fricative are generally written ʒ and that the voiced velar plosive is generally written g.

Of the numerous instances of omission or substitution of consonants, of intrusive consonants, of dittography, etc., no special mention will be made; it is quite clear that most of them are the result of careless copying. Three phenomena, however, require some further attention:

1. The spelling *d* for the dental fricative. In O there are several instances of *d* for *þ/ð*, especially in final position. This spelling does not reflect a sound-change: the examples are all found in forms where it is entirely impossible that the symbol was ever pronouned as a plosive. There are a few instances of this spelling in MS V; it occurs frequently in Alfred's *Blostman* in the twelfth-century part of MS Cotton Vitellius A XV; see Endter's edition: *æordlic* 12/13; *byd* 22/21, 22/24, 28/7, 29/2; *cwæd* 3/11, 3/13, 4/1; *deah* 41/5; *fordgefarenan* 68/5; *nytwyrde* 2/11; *wæordscipes* 36/13; *ydum* 22/23.

2. Confusion of *h* and *þ*. This phenomenon in O can hardly be attributed to the resemblance of the symbols *h* and *þ*, as Berberich (p. 8) and Delcourt (p. xvi) suggest. The vertical stroke of *h* is never extended downwards as far as that of *þ*, and the bowl of *þ* is always closed, whereas in *h*, even though the second limb is turned far inwards, there is no contact between the two parts. Some examples in O rather seem to suggest dittophony: *wiþ þreoflan*, *þurþ*, *þeopwrace*, *þreþ* (= *þweah*!); *hafa hara* (= *þære*) *hyde*. Pairs like *whack* and *thwack*, *whittle* and *thwittle* in Modern English (see *OED*, and Wright, *Dialect Dict.*) show that the confusion was not restricted to the written language. For instances of both

substitutions in other OE and ME texts and further literature, see Napier, pp. 80–1, notes 19 and 29.

3. *w* for *n* in the combination *cn-*: *ʒecwafan, cweo*. Substitution
cn- > cw- occurs in several late OE texts; see Sisam,
Psalter, pp. 31 f. for extensive evidence.

Accidence

MS O represents a much more advanced stage in the transitional levelling of inflexions than MSS VBH, but the regular late
WS endings are still predominant.[1] The following survey of the
inflexional endings of the strong verbs will confirm this. In this
list the occurrences are given in percentages in a descending
scale; the regular late WS ending is always given first. The numbers
at the end of the lines indicate the total number of occurrences.

Plain infinitive	*-an* 75, *-e* 12, *-en* 7, *-a* 5, rest 1	151
To+infinitive	*-enne* 33, *-anne* 33,[2] *-en* 17, *-ende* 17[3]	6
1 sg. pres. indic.	*-e* 83, rest (one corrupt form: *ofslean*) 17	6
2 sg. pres. indic.	*-(e)st* 100 (incl. *ongyst, fæst = færst*)	11
3 sg. pres. indic.	*-(e)þ* 77, *-(e)d* 10,[4] *-aþ* 9,[5] *-es* 1,[6] rest 3	152
Pl. pres. indic.	*-aþ* and contr. forms 79, *-eþ* 15, *-ad* 6[4]	33
Sg. pres. subj.	*-e* and contr. forms 76, *-an* 12, *-a* 10, *-en* 2	106
Pl. pres. subj.[7]	*-en* and contr. forms 19, *-on* 44, *-an* 19, *-e* 12, *-æn* 6	16
3 sg. pret. indic.	root with ablaut 100	7
Pl. pret. indic.	root with ablaut + *-on* 77, id. + *-an* 12, id. + *-o* 11	9
Sg. pret. subj.	root with ablaut + *-e* 100	1
Imp. sg.	root 100	426
Pres. part.	regular form 100	13
Past part.[8]	*-en* 69, *-an* 11, *-e* 9, *-on* 7, rest 4	100
Passive	*hatte* 100	1

[1] The ending *-un* occurs more frequently than *-um*, but mostly we find *-ŭ*, which can be a contraction of either *-um* or *-un*.

[2] For *-anne* in the inflected infinitive see Cpb. 735 (1).

[3] The inflected infinitive in *-ende* probably represents a phonetic tendency for *-nn-* to become *-nd-*; see Sisam, *Psalter*, p. 34 and notes 1, 3, where in-stances occurring in the *Psalter* ('the inflected infinitive *-enne* appears commonly as *-ende*') and in other late OE and early ME texts are mentioned.

[4] For *d* as a substitute for *ð* see the preceding section.

[5] For *-aþ* in the 3 sg. pres. indic., see p. lxxii.

[6] In *sceþþes* (2×, in *MdQ*).

[7] For the endings of the pl. pres. subj., see p. lxxii.

[8] In the great majority of cases O has the prefix *ʒe-*; there are four instances of past participles with the prefix *y-*.

Vocabulary, syntax

In its vocabulary and syntax MS O is practically identical with MSS VBH.[1]

IV. THE IDENTIFICATION OF PLANTS

According to the author of a recent treatise on the botanical vocabulary of OE the history of hardly any subject in the field of lexicography is as discouraging as the history of the semantics of plant names.[2] The problems confronting us have been summarized by Singer in a manner which deserves quoting: 'Scholars who have sought to identify plant-names have far too often treated the semantics of these words as though they were stable. They have never been stable. As in modern England, so in Anglo-Saxon England and in classical antiquity, the same species of plant is and was often known by different names in different regions, and different plants in different regions by the same name. Moreover, in any region the significance of plant-names changes with time. How labile then must have been the significance of the plant-names in the absence of any accurate standards, over a series of medieval centuries that had no idea of scientific standards.'[3]

We are now able to give exact descriptions and to make exact classifications of plants, thanks to the elaborate Linnaean system, which is based upon strictly scientific presuppositions. Neither the classical nor the Anglo-Saxon herbalists had knowledge of any of these presuppositions.

In the case of the *Old English Herbarium* there is another important factor which makes exact identification of the plants difficult, if not impossible: the text is a translation of a complex of herbals describing plants which were found in Mediterranean countries. Many of these plants, or of these particular varieties of plants, were not known in Anglo-Saxon England.

In the earliest pictorial herbal that is known to have existed, by Krateuas (*c.*100 BC), the plant drawings constituted the essential part: the book was composed in the first place to enable its users to recognize the plants from the drawings, the text served for

---

[1] See note to *M* I. 6 for the use of *to* as a conjunction and for the conjunction *fort*.   [2] Bi.[1], p. v.
[3] Introduction to reprint of Cockayne, p. xlii.

additional information. Krateuas' book is not extant, but the eleven illustrations which are found in that part of the *Codex Aniciae Julianae* that has been taken from Krateuas, and which are very probably first-hand copies of drawings in that early text, are sufficient evidence that the originals were remarkably accurate and true to nature.[1]

With regard to illustrations in herbals, Pliny remarks (xxv. 8): 'Crateuas, Dionysius and Metrodorus adopted a most attractive method [i.e., of describing plants]. . . . For they painted likenesses of the plants and then wrote under them their properties. But not only is a picture misleading when the colours are so many, particularly as the aim is to copy Nature, but besides this, much imperfection arises from the manifold hazards in the accuracy of copyists. In addition, it is not enough for each plant to be painted at one period only of its life, since it alters its appearance with the fourfold changes of the year.'[2]

Most of the later medical treatises of classical antiquity were merely copies of earlier works, or compilations from different sources; it can be reasonably assumed that each time a work was copied the illustrations went through one further stage of stylization and degeneration.[3] Therefore it is not surprising that the illustrations in the extant Latin and OE manuscripts of the *Herbarium*, which are copies many times removed from the original drawings, often give us little help in identifying the plants that are described. In many cases it is only possible to offer suggestions. Thanks to important research done by such scholars as Cockayne, Förster, Bonser, von Lindheim, Stracke, and Bierbaumer much progress has been made. Their work has clearly shown that the task of identifying plants described in medieval herbals is not entirely fruitless, as Singer believes it to be.[4] Nevertheless, much further research will be needed, not only by philologists, but more than anything else by specialized botanists, to disclose the secrets of the pre-Linnaean era.

[1] *Codex Aniciae Julianae picturis illustratus nunc Vindobonensis Med. I . . . moderante J. de Karabcek . . .* (Leiden, 1906). For a detailed discussion of Krateuas and further bibliography, see Singer, 'Herbal in Antiquity', pp. 5 ff. and his note 25.   [2] Jones's translation.

[3] See Bonser, pp. 312–14, for a discussion of the illustrations of betony and plantain in three different versions. What may happen when an animal is not drawn from nature can be seen from the illustration of an exotic creature like the elephant on f. 82 of MS V.

[4] See G. and S., p. 85.

The identification of the plants as presented in the Explanatory Notes of this book is based chiefly on the findings of the scholars mentioned in the preceding paragraph.

V. WEIGHTS AND MEASURES

The Roman system of weights and measures, which was introduced in Britain during the Roman occupation, was also the basis for the metrology of the Anglo-Saxons; it is easy to see that most of the OE terms are directly descended from their Latin equivalents. But this system, which had been developed to meet the needs of a highly organized society, where uniformity of weights and measures was an absolute necessity, began to disintegrate in the troubled and chaotic situation following the departure of the Roman legions and bureaucracy, and consequently the OE terms are frequently seen to indicate different values in different contexts, or even in one context. Therefore, when trying to determine the value of weights and measures in our OE texts, we are in the first place concerned with the terms used in the Latin manuscripts. As for the discrepancies between the Latin and the OE versions, we can only hope that the Anglo-Saxon constitution was able to cope with wrongly dosed drugs administered by physicians who took their prescriptions from the OE medical texts.

In the Latin version of our texts we find the following terms:[1]

(a) Weights:

    1 scripulus/scrupulus = 1.52 g.
    3 scripuli = 1 dragma = 1 denarius = 4.57 g.
    6 dragmae = 1 uncia = 27.41 g.
    12 unciae = 1 libra = 328.9 g.

(b) Measures of capacity:

    1 cochlear = 0.01 l.
    4 cochlearia = 1 cyat(h)us = 0.05 l.
    1½ cyathi = 1 acetabulum = 0.07 l.
    2 cyathi = 1 obolus = 0.10 l.
    2 acetabula = 1 quartarius = 0.14 l.
    2 quartarii = 1 (h)emina = 1 cotula = 0.29 l.
    2 heminae = 1 sextarius = 0.58 l.

[1] For documentation, see the *Oxford Classical Dictionary*.

6 sextarii = 1 congius = 3.48 l.
8 congii = 1 amphora = 27.84 l.

(c) Linear measures:

1 digitus = 18.5 mm.
16 digiti = 1 pes = 296 mm.
$1\frac{1}{2}$ pedes = 1 cubitus = 444 mm.

In the following list all the instances of OE terms indicating weights and measures which occur in the *Herbarium* and in the *Medicina de Quadrupedibus* are recorded, in as far as they can be compared with parallels in the Latin version.

(a) Weights:

1 pening = 1 dragma 3×: *M* V. 8 (1st and 3rd time), *M* V. 14
  ,,   = $\frac{1}{3}$ dragma 4×: *M* III. 11 (2×), *M* III. 15, *M* V. 8 (2nd time)
  ,,   = $\frac{1}{4}$ dragma 1×: CXXXIV. 1
  ,,   = $\frac{1}{5}$ dragma = $\frac{3}{5}$ scripulus 6×: CXLII. 4, CLVI. 2, CLXIII. 3, CLXV. 4, CLXXX. 1, *M* III. 2
  ,,   = $\frac{1}{6}$ dragma = $\frac{1}{2}$ scripulus 1×: CLXXXV. 1
  ,,   = $\frac{1}{3}$ scripulus 2×: CXXXII. 3, CXXXII. 4
  ,,   = $\frac{1}{10}$ denarius 2×: XX. 5, XXXVI. 5

The last equation seems to suggest that the translator regarded 1 *denarius* as equivalent to 10 *dragmae*.

It is remarkable that the ratios 1 *pening*:1 *dragma* and 1 *pening*:$\frac{1}{3}$ *dragma* occur in *MdQ* only. This may be seen as an indication that the text of *MdQ* is directly descended from an earlier Anglian version. In the earlier Anglo-Saxon period the *pening* was probably still often equated with the Roman *dragma*, whereas afterwards new values were attached to the *pening*, as can be seen from the quotation in BT: *an uncia stent on feower and twentig penegum*, which would explain the calculation 1 *pening* = $\frac{1}{4}$ *dragma*; see also Zupko, *W & M*, p. 11, who mentions the establishment by King Offa of Mercia (757–96) of a silver penny weighing 1.46 g.

1 pund = 1 libra 3×: XXII. 1, XXIII. 1, XLI. 1

For the instance occurring in CI. 3, see note.

1 scylling = 1 dragma 1×: CXXIX. 1

This is the only instance recorded in BT of the word used to indicate a weight. There are several quotations where *scilling* translates *dragma* or *denarius* indicating money.

1 trymes(s)(e), tremes(s) = 1 dragma 14×: I. 5, I. 9, I. 10, I. 13, I. 15, I. 17, I. 18, I. 19, I. 20, I. 22, I. 27, XVII. 1, XXXII. 4, LXXVIII. 1

,,   ,,   = ¼ uncia 1×: I. 16

,,   ,,   = ½ dragma 1×: I. 11

,,   ,,   = ¾ dragma 1×: I. 23

,,   ,,   = 6 dragmae 1×: I. 24

1 yndse, yntse = 1 uncia 8×: I. 19, XXII. 1 (2×), XLVII. 1 (2nd and 3rd time), CI. 3 (2×), CXXXII. 5

,,   ,,   = 2 unciae 1×: XLVII. 1 (1st time)

(b) Measures of capacity:

1 ambur = 1 congius 1×: XXXVI. 3

Clearly wrong; see note.

1 bolla = 1 cotula = 1 hemina 1×: CLXIX. 1

1 cuculer, cuceler = 1 cochlear 10×: III. 2, IV. 4, XXVI. 3 (3×), CVI. 1, CX. 1, CXXVIII. 2, CXLVI. 2, CLIII. 1

1 elefæt = 1 acetabulum 1×: CLXIX. 1

1 ful(l) = 1 cyathus 10×: I. 9, I. 10, I. 13, I. 17, I. 18, I. 19, I. 22, I. 24, II. 7, III. 6

,,   = ⅔ cyathus 1×: I. 20 (but see note)

1 scenc = 1 cyathus 20×: IV. 4, XVII. 1, XVIII. 3, XXIII. 1, XXX. 5, XXXII. 4, XXXVI. 5, XXXVII. 4, XLVII. 1, LV. 1, LIX. 1, LXXX. 1, XCIII. 3, XCIV. 10, CX. 1, CXII. 1, CXVII. 2 (2×), CXVII. 4, *M* VII. 8

,,   = 1 obolus 1×: XLIII. 1 (the translation does not run exactly parallel)

,,   = 1 hemina 1×: *M* XIV. 11

1 sester = 1 sextarius = 2 heminae 9×: XX. 5, XXXVI. 3, XCIII. 3, CXVII. 4, CXXI. 1, CXXVI. 2, CXXXVIII. 3, *M* I. 6, *M* III. 2

,,   = 1 hemina 1×: *M* IX. 10

1 sester = 6 heminae 1× : CXVII. 3

,, = less than 1 congius 1× : XLI. 1

1 sticca = 1 cochlear 1× : XVIII. 3

(c) Linear measures:

1 eln = 1 cubitus 2× : CXLVII. 1, CLIII intr.

There are ells of different lengths in Anglo-Saxon England. See Zupko, *Dict.* s.v. *eln*: 'a measure of length for cloth generally containing 45 inches (1.143 m) or $\frac{5}{4}$ yard of 36 inches, also some shorter variants'. In the context in which the *eln* is found in *OEH* it is very probably the equivalent of the Latin *cubitus*, as may be inferred from the descriptions of the plants in which the measure is mentioned.

1 fæþm = 1 digitus 1× : CXXXIV intr.

Here the Latin text is clearly wrong. The usual value of the *fæþm* is 6 feet (1.829 m); in BT(S) there are a few instances where the *fæþm* is equated with the *cubitus*, which means that the term was used as an alternative of *eln*. This would seem to be the most appropriate value in our text.

EDITORIAL NOTES

V has been taken as the basic OE text; it is printed on the left-hand pages, except in the table of contents of *OEH*, which appears on consecutive pages. The relevant variant readings of B and H are recorded in the apparatus. O is printed on the upper half of the right-hand pages; the marginal titles of the cures are prefixed to the cures to which they belong. For practical reasons the apparatus of O is printed at the bottom of the pages facing the text. The parallel Latin version is found on the lower half of the right-hand pages. The numbering of the chapters and cures in the printed text of V is also used for the other two texts.

I. THE OLD ENGLISH TEXTS

1. Foliation in V and O is indicated in the margin of the texts, foliation in B (both recto and verso) and H (recto only) is regularly indicated in the apparatus. Wherever the arrangement of either B or H deviates from that of V, this is indicated in the apparatus by an exclamation mark or by a special note.

2. The numbering of the chapters and cures, and of the paragraphs in *MdQ* I and II, is editorial; cures in *OEH* are numbered only when there is a corresponding title in the table of contents.

3. In the V-text of *OEH* the titles of the chapters in hand A are distinguishable from those in hand B by an initial capital.

4. In V, B, and H the OE symbol ᵹ is replaced by *g*, in O it is printed *ʒ*. For the different functions of *ʒ* and *g* in O see pp. lxxvi f.

5. The usual contractions and abbreviations in OE words are silently expanded, with the exception of the tironian sign for 'and'.

6. Punctuation and capitalization are modern.

7. Apart from the cases mentioned in 4, 5, and 6, and except for a small number of emendations which are explained in

the apparatus, the spelling of OE words has been left unchanged.

8. All the accents in V and O are recorded.

9. Interlinear and marginal insertions are enclosed in short slanting lines: ‘ ’. Unless stated otherwise in the textual notes, they are insertions added by the original scribe or by a contemporary corrector.

10. Word division has been regularized.

11. Brackets in the text of V:

(*a*) Round brackets for letters which owing to damage are only partly legible or completely missing; the words and letters in round brackets have been taken from B, or if B has no parallel, from H; round brackets are also used when in the opening paragraph of a chapter there is a space in V for the name of a herb, thus: (. . .); in such a case, if not stated otherwise in the apparatus, it is understood that this space is also found in B, but not in H.

(*b*) Square brackets for emendations of words which are evident corruptions, and for words, sentences, and spaces which have never been in V; wherever square brackets are used, they are accounted for in the apparatus.

12. Brackets in the text of O:

(*a*) Round brackets for marginal titles, and for letters which owing to damage are only partly legible, illegible, or missing; the letters in round brackets have been taken from the printed text of V; in Latin plant names the letters in round brackets are mostly editorial. In a few cases double dots are placed in round brackets; this indicates that there is no parallel in V; the number of double dots equals the presumable number of letters. Wherever one or more entire words are missing owing to damage or fading, this is indicated thus: (. . .); if the only word that is missing is *and*, the printed text has (7).

(*b*) Square brackets for emendations of words which are evident corruptions, and for words which have never been in O; wherever square brackets are used, they are accounted for in the apparatus.

13. The spelling of Latin words in the OE texts has been left unchanged, but all contractions and abbreviations are silently expanded.

14. All other particulars relating to the manuscript texts are given in the textual notes to VBHO.

2. THE APPARATUS TO THE OLD ENGLISH TEXTS

1. Variants marked BH are recorded in the spelling in which they occur in B.

2. If an emendation in V is marked 'from B' and if no separate variant in H is given, the term implies that H, if available, is identical with B, except for the spelling variants mentioned in 8.

3. Except in the apparatus to the table of contents, the names of the plants in the chapter titles in BH, if available, are always given, even when they have the same form as in V.

4. Only those glosses which are legible are mentioned.

5. Differences in accentuation are not recorded.

6. An oblique stroke in the middle of a word indicates that the second part is on the following line in the manuscript.

7. Expansions are silent.

8. Spelling variants not included in the apparatus:

    (*a*) Vowels in both stressed and unstressed syllables:

       1. *i* / *y*.
       2. *æ*+nasal / *e*+nasal.
       3. *ex* / *eax*.
       4. *eo* / *io* / *yo*.
       5. *a*+nasal / *o*+nasal.

    (*b*) Vowels in unstressed syllables:

       1. *a* / *æ* / *e* / *i* / *o* / *u* / *y*, except if V has a less usual variant than B and/or H.
       2. Vowel+*l, m, n, r* / zero+*l, m, n, r*.
       3. *c* or *g*+*e*+back vowel / *c* or *g*+back vowel.
       4. (In prefixes) *on-* / *a-*.
       5. (In suffixes) *-ig* / *-i* / *-eg*.
       6. (In suffixes) *-in(c)g* / *-un(c)g*.

    (*c*) Consonants:

       1. *ð* / *þ*.

2. Single consonants / double consonants, except where grammatically interesting.

3. -cg / -gc / -g / -c, except if V has a less usual variant than B and/or H.

(d) Inflexional (apart from those variants which are mentioned in (a), (b), and (c), and those which require special comment):

1. 2, 3 sg. pres. indic. -est, -eþ / -st, -þ.

2. (In nouns, adjectives, pronouns, adverbs) -um (if so in V) / -an, -on, -un in B and/or H, and -an, -on, -un (if so in V) / any of these in B and/or H.

3(a). Strong declension (if correct in V) / weak declension in B and/or H.

3(b). Weak declension (if correct in V) / strong declension in B and/or H.

(e) In individual words (apart from those variants which are mentioned in (a), (b), (c), and (d)):

1. *blostm-* / *blosm-.*

2. *-cnuc-* VH / *-cnoc-* B.

3. (Noun) *drænc* / *drenc* / *drinc* / *drync.*

4. *frem-* VB / *fram-* H.

5. *hwær, þær* / *hwar, þar.*

6. *hy, þy, þry* / *hig, þig, þrig.*

7. *penig-* / *pening-* / *peneg-.*

8. *sester* / *sister.*

9. *smyr-* / *smer-.*

10. Variants of *mearu, meolu, smeoru.*

3. THE LATIN TEXTS

1. Basic Latin texts:

OEH table of contents	no Latin parallel printed
I–XXI	Vo
XXII–CXXXII	Ca
CXXXIII–CLXXXV	mainly A
MdQ I–XIV	L.

2. Silent normalizations:

(a) Expansions.

(b) Inflexional endings.

(*c*) Correction of awkward errors in spelling and inflexion.

(*d*) Capitalization.

(*e*) The modern convention is followed for the spelling of *b | v*, *e | ae*, *h | zero*, *n*+labial / *m*+labial, *u | v*, etc.

3. Round brackets are used in two functions:

(*a*) (. . .) to indicate that part of a sentence has been omitted because it is irrelevant to the OE text; omission of entire sentences or cures is not indicated.

(*b*) (*word* or *words*) for words that are partly or completely illegible in the Latin texts consulted, as a result of damage or fading.

4. Additions and emendations are in square brackets. All additions and emendations in *Herbarium* I–CXXXII and in *MdQ* are from Ha, except the following (references are to chapters and cures):

From Vo:

XXX. 3 (2×)
XXXII. 6
XXXII. 7
XXXIII. 1
XXXIV. 1
XXXVII. 2
XXXVIII. 1
XL. 1
XL. 2
XLI. 3
XLII. 1
XLVII. 2
XLIX intr. (1st and 3rd emend.)
LXVII intr.
LXVIII. 1 (2×)
LXXIII. 2 (2nd emend.)
LXXV. 1
LXXV. 2
LXXV. 5
LXXVII intr.

From Ca:

M III. 19 (1st emend.)

From L:

XXX. 5

From Vi:

CXVII intr.

From *Editio Princeps*:

XC. 1

Editorial:

CIX. 1
M I. 7
M II title
M II. 1
M II. 2 (2×)
M II. 4 (2×)
M V. 14 (2nd emend.)
M X. 13
M XIV. 6 (2×)
M XIV. 9

Additions and emendations in *Herbarium* CXXXIII–CLXXXV:

From Ca:

CXLI. 1
CXLII. 6 (2×)
CXLIII. 4
CLII. 1
CLIII (5×)
CLXII. 1
CLXXIII. 4
CLXXV. 3
CLXXXV intr.

From L:

CXXXVIII intr.
CXLIII. 5
CXLV. 2, 3

From Har:

CLXVIII. 1
CLXXV. 2
CLXXXI. 3

From Slo:

CXLII. 4
CXLIII. 3
CXLVIII. 1
CLV. 4
CLVI intr.
CLXVI title
CLXX intr.
CLXXXIV. 1

From Dio.:

CXLVII. 1

From Kästner:

CXXXIII. 1 (2×)
CXXXV. 5

5. Synonyms of plant names in the titles of the Latin texts are mentioned only if they are relevant to the OE version.

INCIPIUNT CAPITA LIBRI ME(dici)nalis

I. NOMEN herb(e beto)nica þ(æt is biscopwy)rt

   1. (W)ið unh(yr)um nihtgengum 7 wið egeslicum gesyhþum
     7 swefnum.

   2. Gyf mannes heafod tobrocen sy.   5

   3. Wið eagena sare.

   4. Wið earena sare.

   5. Wið eagena dymnysse.

   6. Wið tyrende eagan.

   7. Wið swyðlicne blodryne of nosum.   10

   8. Wið toþece.

   9. Wið sídan sare.

  10. Wið lendenbrædena sare.

  11. Wið wambe sare.

  12. Wið þæt mannes innoð to fæst sy.   15

  13. Wið þæt men blod upp wealle þurh his muð.

  14. Wið þæt man nelle beon [druncen].

  15. Wið þæt man wille spring on gesittan.

  16. Wið þæt man sy innan abrocen.

  17. Wið þæt man on mycelre rade oþþe on myclum gangum 20
     weorþe geteored.

  18. Wið þæt man sy unhal oþþe hine wlatige.

  19. Wið þæt mannes mete eaþelice gemylte.

  20. Wið þæt man ne mæge his mete gehealdan.

  21. Wið [innoþes] sare oþþe gif he aþunden sy.   25

  22. Wið attorþigene.

---

1 CAPITA] capites B 68/1a, capituli H 115/1.   2 herbe] herba H.
3 egeslicum] egslicum B.   16 men] þe mon H   upp wealle] wealle up B
þurh] þur H.   17 druncen] *from* B, druc V (*see t.n.*).   18 man] þe
man H.   19 man] gif man H   abrocen] tobrocen BH.   20 man]
gif man H.   21 weorþe] wurðe B.   22 man] gif man H.   23 gemylte]
mylte B.   24 man] gif man H.   25 innoþes] *from* B, innoþe V.
26 attorþigene] -þige B.

23. Wið nædran slite.

24. Eft wið nædran slite.

25. Wið wodenhundes slite.

26. (W)ið þæt mannes þrotu sar sy oþþe his swyran hwylc dæl.

5   27. (W)ið l(e)ndena sare 7 gif his þeoh acen.

28. (W)ið þone hatan feofor.

29. Wið fotadle.

II. Herba arniglosa þæt ys wegbræd(e)

1. Wið heafodece.

10   2. Wiþ wambe sare.

3. Wiþ innoþes sare.

4. Eft wið þon þe man on wambe forweaxen sy.

5. Wiþ þon þe mon þurh his argang blode ut yrne.

6. Wið þæt man forwundud sy.

15   7. Wið þæt man wylle mannes wambeˋþw(æna)n.

8. Wið nædran slite.

9. Eft wið nædran slite.

10. Wiþ inwyrmas.

11. Wiþ þæt mannes lichoma sy aheardod.

20   12. Wið þæt men sy þæs feorþan dæges fefor.

13. Wiþ fotadle 7 wið syna sare.

14. Wið þam fefore þe þy þriddan dæge egleþ.

15. Wið þam fefore þe þy æftran dæge to c(y)mþ.

16. Wið wunda hatungæ.

25   17. Wið þæt mannes fet on syðe tydrien.

18. Wið þæt men weargebræde weaxe on þam nosum oððe on þam hleore.

19. Be æghwylcum uncuþum blædrum þe on mannes nebbe sittað.

30   20. Wið muðes wunde.

3 wodenhundes] wedehundes BH.   4 mannes] gif mannes H 116/1
sar sy] sy sar H   swyran] sweoran H.   6 feofor] fefor BH.   8 Herba
arniglosa þæt ys] *om.* H 116/17 (!)   wegbræde] -brade H.   13 blode]
blod B.   14 man] þe man B, gif man H   forwundud] gewundod/-ad BH.
15 man] gif man H   þwænan] þwinan H.   17 nædran] *gl.* scorpionis H.
19 mannes] gif mannes H.   20 men] gif man H.   22 þy] *om.* H.
24 hatungæ] hatunge BH.   25 mannes] gif mannes H 117/2.   26 men]
gif mæn H   27 on þam] oþam H.

21. Wið wedehundes slite.
22. [Wið] ælces dæges manes tyddernysse inneweardes. /

III. (Herba pent)afilon þæt is fif(leafe)   f. 12v

1. Wið þæt mannes lyþu acen oþþe ongeflogen sy.
2. (W)ið wambe sare.   5
3. Wiþ muþes ece 7 tungan 7 þrotan.
4. (W)iþ heafdes sare.
5. Wiþ þæt men blod ut of nosum yrne to swyþe.
6. (W)iþ þæt mannes midrif ace.
7. Wiþ nædran slite.   10
8. (W)iþ þæt man forbærned sy.
9. Gyf þu wylle cancer ablendan.

IV. (He)rba uermenaca þæt is æscþrotu

1. (W)ið wunda 7 deadspringas 7 cyrnlu.
2. Eft wið cyrnlu.   15
3. (W)ið þa þe habbað ætstandene ædran swa þæt þæt blod ne mæg his gecyndlican ryne habban 7 hyra þygne gehealdan ne magon.
4. Wið lifre sar.
5. (W)ið þa untrumnysse þe stanas weaxeþ on blædran.   20
6. Wið heafodsar.
7. (W)ið nædran slite.
8. Wið attorcoppan bite.
9. (W)ið wedehu'n′des slite.
10. Wið niwe wundela.   25
11. (W)ið nædran slite.

V. (He)rba [sinphoniaca] þæt is hennebelle

1. Wiþ earena sar.

2 Wið] *from* B, ið V   manes] mannes BH.   3 pentafilon] quinquefolium H.   4 mannes] gif mannes H.   8 men] gif mæn H. 9 mannes] gif mannes H   midrif] -hrif BH   ace] acen H.   11 man] gif man H.   16 Wið þa] Wið þæt þa H.   17 ne mæg] *om.* H   mæg] mæge B 68v/15a   hyra] heora BH   þygne] *gl.* mete H.   20 þa] *om.* B. 24 slite] *gl.* bite H.   25 wundela] wunda H.   26 slite] *gl.* bite H. 27 sinphoniaca] *from* B, sym(p)h(o)nia V, simphoniaca H.

2. Wið cneowa geswell oþþe sceancena oððe swa hwær swa on lichaman geswell sy.

3. Wiþ toþa sare.

4. (W)ið þæra gewealda sar oþþe ges(we)ll.

5. 5. Wiþ þæt wifes breost sare syn.

6. (W)iþ fota sar.

7. Wiþ lungenadle.

VI. Herba uiperina þæt is nædderwyrt

1. Wiþ nædran slite.

10 VII. [Herba] ueneria þæt ys beowyrt

1. Wiþ þæt beon ne ætfleon.

2. Wiþ þæt man gemigan ne mege.

VIII. Herba pes leonis þæt is leonfot

1. Wiþ þæt man sy cis.

15 IX. Herba scelerata þæt ys [clufþung]

1. Wið wundela 7 deadspringas.

2. Wiþ swylas 7 weartan.

X. Herba batracion þæt is clufwyrt

1. Wiþ monoðseoce.

20 2. Wiþ þa sweartan dolh.

XI. [Herba artemesia þæt is mugcwyrt

1. Wið innoðes sare.

2. Wið fota sare.]

XII. Herba artemesia tagantes þæt ys oþres cynnes mucgwyrt

25 1. Wið blædran sare.

---

5 wifes] gif wifes H   sare] sar H.   6 sar] sare B.   8 uiperina] *gl.*
venebula H 116/6 (!).   10 Herba] *from* B, Her bið V.   11 þæt
beon] þæt þæt beon H.   12 man] gif man H   mege] mæge BH.
13 pes] pedem H.   14 man] gif man H   cis] to cis H.   15 clufþung]
from B, cluðung V.   16 wundela] wunda H   deadspringas] *gl.* chironia
H.   17 weartan] wið weartan H.   18 batracion] batraci H 120v/20 (!).
19 monoðseoce] innoðseoce B, monaðseocne H.   21-3 *from* B, *om.* V.
21 artemesia] artenesia H.   23 sare] sar H.   24 Herba] Herbis B.

2. Wiþ þeona sare.

3. Wiþ sina sare 7 geswell.

4. Gyf hwa mid fotadle swyþe geswenced sy.

5. Gyf hwa sy mid feferum gedreht.

XIII. H(e)rba (arte)mesia lep(te)filos þæt ys þryddan (c)y(nne)s 5
mucgwyrt /

    1. Wiþ þæs magan sare.   f. 13

    2. Wiþ þæra sina bifunge.

XIV. Herba lapatium þæt ys docca

    1. Wið cyrnlu þe on wealde weaxeþ.   10

XV. Herba dracontea þæt ys dracentse

    1. Wiþ ealra nædrena slite.

    2. Wiþ banbryce.

XVI. Herba satyrion þæt ys refnes leac

    1. Wið earfoðlice wundela.   15

    2. Wiþ eagena sare.

XVII. Herba gentiana þæt ys feldwyrt

    1. Wið nædran slite.

XVIII. Herba orbicularis þæt ys slite

    1. Wið þæt mannes fex fealle.   20

    2. Wiþ in'n'oðes styrunga.

    3. Wiþ miltan sare.

XIX. Herba proserpinaca þæt ys unfortredde

    1. Wiþ þæt man blod spiwe.

    2. Wiþ sidan sare.   25

    3. Wiþ [breosta] sare.

---

2 geswell] geswelle H.   4 feferum] ferum B   gedreht] *gl.* nocitus H.
5 leptefilos] leptefilios B.   9 lapatium] lapatum H   docca] docce
B 69/3a, H = B.   10 wealde] gewealde BH.   14 satyrion] saturion H
refnes] hrefnes B, hræfnes H.   17 ys] i H.   20 þæt mannes] þæt þæt
mannes H.   21 innoðes] innoð B.   22 Wiþ] ið B.   23 proserpinaca]
second p *alt. from* b V.   24 man] gif man H.   26 breosta] *from* B,
bresta V.

4. Wiþ eagena sare.
5. Wiþ earena sare.
6. Wiþ utsihte.

XX. Herba aristolochia þæt ys smerowyrt

5　　1. Wið attres strencðe.
2. Wiþ þa stiþustan feforas.
3. Wiþ næsþurla sare.
4. Wiþ þæt hwa mid cyle gewæht sy.
5. Wiþ naedran slite.
10　6. Gyf hwylc cyld ahwæned sy.
7. Wiþ þæt wærhbræde on nosa wexe.

XXI. Herba nastur(ci)um (þæt i)s (cærse)

1. Wiþ ðæt mannes fex fealle.
2. Wiþ heafodsare þæt ys wið scurf 7 gicþan.
15　3. Wiþ lices sarnysse.
4. Wiþ swylas.
5. Wiþ weartan.

XXII. Herba hieribulbum þ(æt is gr)eate (wy)rt

1. Wiþ liþa sare.
20　2. Gif nebcorn on wifmannes nebbe wexen.

XXIII. Herba apollinaris þæt is glofwy(rt)

1. Wið handa sare.

XXIV. Herba camemelon þæt is mag(e)þe

1. Wið eagene sare.

25　XXV. Herba chamedris þæt is [heortclæfre]

1. Gyf hwa tobrysed sy.

6 stiþustan] stiþosstas H 122/7.　　　　7 næsþurla] -þyrla B, -þyrlu H.
8 hwa] gif hwa H.　　　10 hwylc cyld] cyld hwylc V, *marked for reversal.*
11 wærhbræde] wearh- B, gif werh- H.　　12 cærse] cerse H.　　13 mannes]
gif mannes H.　　14 gicþan] wið gicþan H.　　18 hieribulbum] geribulbum
H.　　20 on] of H.　　21 apollinaris] apollonaris H.　　22 handa] hada H.
23 camemelon] camemellon H.　　24 eagene] eagena BH.　　25 heort-
clæfre] *from* B, heortl(æfre) V.

2. [Wið] nædran slite.
3. Wiþ fotadle.

XXVI. Herba chameæleæ þæt is wulfes c(am)b

1. Wið liferseocnysse.
2. Wiþ attres drenc.　　　　　　　　　　　　　　　5
3. Wiþ wæterseocnysse.

XXVII. Herba chamepithys þæt is h(ene)p

1. Wiþ wundela.
2. Wiþ innoþes sare.

XXVIII. Herba chamedaf(ne) þæt is ræfnes fot　　　10

1. Wið innoþ to astyrigenne.

XXIX. Herba ostriago þæt is liðwyrt

1. Wiþ ealle þingc þe on men to sare innan acennede beoð. /

XXX. Herba br(it)tanica þæt is heawenhnydelu　　　f. 13v

1. Wiþ muðes sare.　　　　　　　　　　　　　　15
2. Eft wið muþes sare.
3. Wiþ toþa sare.
4. Wiþ fæstne innoð to astyrigenne.
5. Wið sidan sare.

XXXI. Herba lactuca siluatica þæt is wudulectric　　20

1. Wiþ eagena sare.
2. Eft wiþ eagene dymnysse.

XXXII. Herba argimonia þæt is garclife

1. Wið eagena sare.
2. Wið innoðes sare.　　　　　　　　　　　　　　25

---

1 Wið] *from* B, Gyf V.　　　3 chameæleæ] chameælete B.　　　5 drenc]
drynce H.　　　6 wæterseocnysse] *gl.* ydrops H.　　　7 henep] nepte B.
10 ræfnes] hrefnes B, hræfnes H.　　　14 brittanica] bryttannica BH　　heawen-
hnydelu] hæwenhnydele B, hæwenhydele H.　　　19 sidan sare] *gl.* paralisim
H 123/1.　　　21 sare] dymnesse BH.　　　22 eagene] eagena BH.
23 argimonia] acrimonia H.

3. Wiþ cancor 7 wið wundela.
4. Wiþ nædran slite
5. Wiþ weartan.
6. Wið miltan sare.
5   7. Gyf þu [hwilce] þingc on þam lichoman ceorfan wille.
8. Wiþ slege isernes.

XXXIII. Herba astularegia þæt is 'wudu'rofe

1. Wið sceancena sare.
2. Wiþ lifre sare.

10 XXXIV. Herba lapatium þæt is wududocce

1. Gyf hwylc stiþnes on lichoman becume.

XXXV. Herba [centauria] maior þæt is curmelle seo mare

1. Wið liferadîe.
2. Wið wunda 7 cancor.

15 XXXVI. Herba [centauria] minor þæt is curmelle seo læsse

1. Wið nædran slite.
2. Wið eagena sare.
3. Eft wið þon ylcon.
4. Wiþ sina togunge.
20   5. Wiþ attres onbyrginge.
6. Wiþ þæt wyrmas ymb nafolan derigen.

XXXVII. Herba personacia þæt i(s b)ete

1. Wið ealle wunda 7 wiþ nædran slitas.
2. II. 7 wiþ feforas.
25   3. Wið þæt cancor on wunde wexe.
4. Wiþ innoðes sare.
5. Wið wedehundes slite.
6. Wiþ niwe wunda.

---

1 wið] *om.* H.   5 hwilce] *thus* BH, 'h'wil e (*alt. from* wille, *no* c *inserted*) V   on] of B 69v/17a.   12, 15 centauria] *from* BH, centuria V curmelle] curmealle H.   15 minor] *om.* H.   17 eagena] egena H. 18 þon] þam H.   20 onbyrginge] tobyrgincge H.   21 wyrmas] gif wyrmas H.   25 cancor] gif cancor H.   28 H *om. this line.*

XXXVIII. Herba fraga þæt is streaberge
1. Wið miltan sare.
2a. Wiþ nyrwyt.
2b. Wiþ innoþes sare.

XXXIX. Herba hibiscus þæt is merscmealwe　　　5
1. Wið fotadle.
2. Wiþ ælce gegaderunga þe on þam lichoman acennede beoþ.

XL. Herba ippirus þæt is æquiseia
1. Wiþ utsiht.
2. Wiþ þæt man blod swyþe ræce.　　　10

XLI. Herba malfa erratica þæt is hocleaf
1. Wið blædran sare.
2. Wið sina sare.
3. Wið sidan sare.
4. Wið niwe wunda.　　　15

XLII. Herba buglossa þæt is hundes tunge
1. Gyf hwylcum men sy þæs þriddan dæges fefor oððe þæs feorþan.
2. Wiþ nyrwyt.

XLIII. Herba bulbiscillitica þæt is glædene /　　　20
1. Wið wæterseocnysse.　　　f. 14
2. Wiþ liða sare.
3. Wiþ þa adle þe Grecas paranichias nemneð.
4. Wiþ þæt man ne mæge wæterseoces mannes þurst ge(ce)lan.

XLIV. Herba cotiledon þæt ys umbilicus Veneris　　　25
1. Wið swylas.

---

1 fraga] fragra H　　　streaberge] strewberige B, streawberge H.　　　5 mersc-
mealwe] merc- H.　　　7 acennede] acænne H.　　　8 æquiseia] equisea H.
9 utsiht] gl. dissint(eria) H.　　　10 man] g:f man H　　　swyþe ræce] swy hræce
B, spiwe 7 hræce H, gl. emopt(ysis) H.　　　11 malfa] malua BH.　　　17 þriddan dæges] þriddæges H 124/5.　　　23 þa] om. B 70/5a　　　paranichias] paronichias BH　　　nemneð] -að H.　　　24 man] gif man H.　　　25 cotiledon]
om. H　　　umbilicus] umbiculus B, gl. þæt is penewort H.

XLV. Herba gallicrus þæt is attorlaðe

   1. Wið hundes slite.

XLVI. Herba prassion þæt [ys] harehune

   1. Wið geposu 7 wið þæt he hefelice hræce.

   2. Wið magan sare.

   3. Wið rengwyrmas abutan nafolan.

   4. Wiþ liþa sare 7 wið geþind.

   5. Wið attres þigne.

   6. Wiþ sceb 7 teter.

   7. Wið lungenadle.

   8. Wið ealle stiðnessa þæs lichoman.

XLVII. Herba xifion þæt is foxes fot

   1. Wiþ uncuðe springas þe on lichoman acennede beoð.

   2. Wiþ heafodbryce 7 ættrige ban.

XLVIII. Herba gallitricus þæt is wæterwyrt

   1. Gyf swylas fæmnum derien.

   2. Wiþ ðæt mannes fex fealle.

XLIX. Herba temolus þæt is singrene

   1. Wið cwiðan sare.

L. Herba æliotrophus þæt is sigelhweorfa

   1. Wiþ ealle attru.

   2. Wið flewsan.

LI. Herba gryas þæt is mæderu

   1. Wiþ banece 7 wiþ banbryce.

   2. Wið ælc sár þe þam lichoman dereþ.

---

3 ys] *from* B, *om.* V.   6 rengwyrmas] ryn- H   abutan] ymbutan þone
H.   12 Herba] Herbis H.   14 7 ættrige ban] *om.* H.   17 mannes]
gif mannes H.   19 cwiðan] cliþan H.   20 æliotrophus] elio- H   sigel-
hweorfa] f *alt. from high* s V.   22 *in* H *this cure is the first of the next chapter.*
23 gryas] gruas H   mæderu] mædere BH.   24 banbryce] -brece H.
25 ælc] æl H.

LII. Herba politricus þæt is hymele

   1. Wið innoðes sare 7 wið þæt fex wexe.

LIII. Herba malochinagria þæt is wudurofe

   1. Wiþ utsiht.

   2. Wiþ innoðes flewsan.   5

LIV. Herba metoria þæt is hwit popig

   2. Wiþ þunwonga sare.

   3. Wið slæpleaste.

LV. Herba oenantes

   1. Wið þæt man gemigan ne mæge.   10

   2. Gyf hwa swyþe ræce.

LVI. Herba na‘r′cisus þæt is halswyrt

   1. Wiþ þa wunda þe on men beoð acenned.

LVII. Herba splenion þæt is brunewyrt

   1. Wið miltan sare.   15

LVIII. Herba polion

   1. Wið monoðseoce.

LIX. Herba uictoriola þæt is cneowholen

   1. Wiþ ðone dropan 7 þæs magan sare.

LX. Herba confirma þæt is galluc   20

   1. Wiþ wifa flewsan.

   2. Gyf hwa innan toborsten sy.

   3. Wið magan sare.

---

1 politricus] pollitricus B   hymele] humele B.   2 wexe] fealle H.
3 wudurofe] -hrofe H.   4 utsiht] utsihte H.   6 metoria] uictoria H,
gl. papauer H.   7 *cure I om.* VBH.   8 slæpleaste] -lyste B, -leste
H 125/1.   9 oenantes] cenantes H.   10 man] gif man H.   11 ræce]
hræce BH.   12 na‘r′cisus] *the interlined black* r *in* V *is modern.*   13 þa]
om. H   men] mæn H   acenned]. acænnede H.   14 brunewyrt] brunt-
wyrt H.   22 toborsten] tobrocen H.

LXI. Herba asterion

   1. Wið fylleseocnysse.

LXII. Herba leporis pes þæt is haran hi(g)

   1. Wið innoðes fæstnysse.

f. 14v LXIII. Herba dictamnus

6   1. Wið þæt wif hæbbe on hyre innoðe deadborcn tuddur.

   2. Wiþ wunda.

   3. Wiþ nædran slite.

   4. Wiþ attorþigene.

10   5. Eft wið niwe wunda.

LXIV. Herba solago maior þæt is helioscorpion

   1. Eft wið nædran slite.

LXV. Herba solago minor þæt is æliotropion

   1. Wið rengwyrmas abutan nafolan.

15 LXVI. Herba peonia

   1. Wiþ monoðseocnysse.

   2. Wiþ [hypebanece].

LXVII. Herba peristereon þæt ys berbena

   1. Wiþ hundes beorc.

20   2. Wið ealle attru.

LXVIII. Herba bryonia þæt is hymele

   1. Wið miltan sare.

LXIX. Herba nymfete

   1. Wið utsiht; eft wið utsiht.

25   2. Eft wið innoþes sare.

---

2 fylleseocnysse] felle- H.   6 wif] gif 'wif' H   innoðe] om. B 70v/4a.
13 æliotropion] elio- B.   14 rengwyrmas] ryn- H.   16 monoðseoc-
nysse] innoð- B.   17 hypebanece] from B, ype- V.   19 beorc]
gebeorc BH.   21 hymele] humele B.   23 nymfete] nimphete H.

LXX. Herba crision þæt is clæfre

　1. Wiþ gomena sare.

LXXI. [Herba isatis

　1. Wið næddran slite.]

LXXII. Herba scordea　　　　　　　　　　5

　1. Eft wið nædran slite.
　2. Wið sina sare.
　3. Wiþ fefor.

LXXIII. Herba uerbascus þæt is [feltwyrt]
　　Be þam þe Mercurius þas wyrte Iulixe sealde.　　10

　1. Wið ealle yfele gencymas.
　2. Wið fotadle.

LXXIV. Herba heraclea

　1. Wið þæt man wylle ofer langne weg feran 7 him na sceaðan
　　ondrædan.　　　　　　　　　　　　　　15

LXXV. Herba cælidonia þæt is cyleþenie

　1. Wiþ eagen dymnysse 7 sarnysse.
　2. Eft wið dymgendum eagum.
　3. Wiþ cyrnlu.
　4. Wiþ heafudece.　　　　　　　　　　20
　5. Wiþ þæt man gebærned sy.

LXXVI. Herba solata þæt is solosece

　1. Wiþ geswel.
　2. Wiþ [earena] sare.
　3. Wiþ toðece.　　　　　　　　　　25
　4. Wiþ blodryne of nosum.

---

1 crision] crission H.　　　3, 4 *from* B, *om.* V.　　　5 scordea] isatis H.
9 feltwyrt] *emended from* feldwyrt VBH, *see note to* LXXIII.　　　10 Iulixe]
Ulixe BH.　　　11 gencymas] gean- H 126/6.　　　14 man] gif man H
sceaðan] scaþa H.　　　15 ondrædan] ondræde H.　　　16 cælidonia] celidonia H 118/1 (!)　　　cyleþenie] cyleþenige H, *gl.* Eliotropium i.e. solsece H.
17 eagen] eagena BH.　　　21 man] gif man H.　　　22 solosece] solasece B.
24 earena] *from* B, eagena V.　　　25 toðece] *gl.* dentium H.

LXXVII. Herba senecio þæt is grundeswylige

   1. Wið wunda þeah hy ealde syn.

   2. [Wið] isernes slege.

   3. Wiþ fotadle.

5   4. Wiþ lendena sare.

LXXVIII. Herba filix þæt is fearn

   1. Wiþ wunda.

   2. Wiþ þæt geong man healyde sy.

LXXIX. Herba gramen þæt is cwice

10   1. Wiþ miltan sare.

LXXX. Herba gladiolum þæt is glædene

   1. Wiþ blædran sare 7 gemigan ne mæge.

   2. Wiþ miltan sare.

   3. Wiþ innoðes sare 7 þæra breosta. /

f. 15 LXXXI. Herba rosmarinum þæt is boðen

16   1. Wið toðece.

   2, 3. Wið adligende 7 wið gicðan.

   4. Wiþ liferseocnysse 7 þæs innoðes.

   5. Wiþ niwe wunda.

20 LXXXII. Herba pastinaca siluatica þæt is feldmoru

   1. Wiþ þæt wifmen earfoðlice cennan.

   2. Wiþ wifa afeormunge.

LXXXIII. Herba perdicalis þæt is dolhrune

   1. Wiþ fotadle 7 wið cancor.

25 LXXXIV. Herba mercurialis þæt is cedelc

   1. Wið þæs innoðes heardnysse.

3 Wið] *from* B, iþ V.   4 Wiþ] ið B.   8 geong] gif geong H
healyde] healede BH.   11 glædene] *gl.* cum flore croceo H.   12 gemi-
gan] gif gemigan H.   17 adligende] adligendan B 71/5a.   21 wifmen]
gif wifmen H   earfoðlice] -lic H   cennan] cænnen H.   25 mercurialis]
id. H (ri *in black on erased red* li).

2. Wiþ eagena sare 7 geswelle.

3. Gyf wæter on earan swyþe gesigen sy.

LXXXV. Herba radiola þæt is eforfearn

1. Wið heafodece.

LXXXVI. Herba sparagiagrestis þæt is wuduceruille

1. Wiþ blædran sare oþþe geswelle.

2. Wiþ toðece.

3. Wiþ æddrena sare.

4. Wiþ þæt yfel man þurh [æfþancan] oþerne begale.

LXXXVII. Herba sabina þæt is safinæ

1. Wiþ togunga þæra sina 7 wiþ fota geswell.

2. Wiþ heafodece.

3. Wiþ deadspringas.

LXXXVIII. Herba canis caput þæt is hundes heafod

1. Wiþ eagena sare 7 geswel.

LXXXIX. Herba erusti þæt is bremel

1. Wiþ earena sare.

2. Wiþ wifes flewsan.

3. Wiþ heortece.

4. Wiþ niwe wunda.

5. Wiþ liþa sare.

6. Wiþ nædran slite.

XC. Herba millefolium þæt is gearwe

1. Wiþ isernes slege 7 þæt Achilles þas wyrte funde.

2. Wiþ toðece.

3. Wiþ wunda.

4. Wiþ geswell.

1 geswelle] geswel H.   2 gesigen] gesiged H.   3 radiola] radiolum H
eforfearn] euer- H.   5 sparagiagrestis] sparai agresstis H   wuduceruille]
-cerfille B, -cyrfille H.   9 yfel] gif yfel H 119/2   æfþancan] *from* B,
æfþacan V.   10 sabina] sauina H   safinæ] sauine BH.   11 togunga]
togunge BH.   14 caput] capuð H.   15 geswel] geswelle H.   16 bremel]
brembel H.   24 þas] þa B.

5. Wiþ þæt man [earfoðlice] gemigan mæge.

6. Gyf wund on men ácolod sy.

7. Gyf men þæt heafod berste oððe uncuð swyle on gesytte.

8. Eft wiþ þam ylcan.

9. Gyf hwylcum men ædran aheardode syn oþþe his mete gemyltan nylle.

10. Wiþ þæra þearma ece 7 þæs innoðes.

11. Wið þæt men sogoða eglige.

12. Wiþ heafodece.

13. Wiþ þam næddercynne þe man spalangius hateð.

14. Eft wið nædran slite.

15. Wiþ wedehundes slite.

16. Wiþ næddran slite.

XCI. [Herba ruta þæt ys rude

1. Wið þæt blod of nosum flowe.

2. Wið toþundennesse.

3. Wið þæs magan sare.

4. Wið eagena sare 7 geswelle.

5. Wið ofergitulnesse.

6. Wið eagena dymnesse.

7. Wið heafodece.]

XCII. Herba mentastrus [þæt is minte]

1. Wiþ earena sare.

2. Wiþ hreoflan.

XCIII. Herba ebulus þæt is wealwyrt

1. Wiþ þæt stanas on blædran wexen.

2. Wiþ nædran slite.

3. Wiþ wæterseocnysse.

---

1 man] gif man H   earfoðlice] *from* B, eafo῾ð´lice V.   3 berste]
toberste B.   6 nylle] nelle BH.   8 men] gif men H.   14–21 *from*
B, *om.* V.   15 blod] gif blod H.   22 mentastrus] mentastrum H 120/3
þæt is minte] *from* H, *om.* VB.   25 ebulus] ebulum H   wealwyrt] ellenwyrt H.   26 stanas] gif stanas H.

XCIV. Herba pollegion þæt is dweorgedwosle /

1. Wið þæs innoþes sare.   f. 15v
2. Wiþ þæs magan sare.
3. Wiþ gicþan þæra sceapa.
4. Eft wið þæs innoðes sare.   5
5. Wiþ þam fefore þe þy þriddan dæge egleþ.
6. Gif deadboren cild sy on wifes innoðe.
7. Gif hwa on scipe wlættan þolige.
8. Wiþ blædran sare 7 þæt stanas þæron wexen.
9. Gyf hwa onbutan his heortan oððe on his breostan sar   10
   þolige.
10. Gyf hwylcum men hramma derie.
11. Wiþ ðæs magan aðundenysse 7 þæs innoþes.
12. Wiþ miltan sare.
13. Wiþ lendenece 7 wið þeona sare.   15

XCV. Herba nepitamon þæt is nepte

1. Wiþ nædran slite.

XCVI. Herba peucedana þæt is cammoc

1. Eft wið nædran slite.
2. Wiþ gewitlæste þæs modes.   20

XCVII. Herba hinnula campana þæt ys sperewyrt

1. Wiþ blædran sare.
2. Wiþ toþa sare 7 wagunge.
3. Wiþ rengwyrmas ymb þone nafolan.

XCVIII. Herba cynoglossa þæt is ribbe   25

1. Wiþ nædran slite.

---

1 pollegion] pollegium H   dweorgedwosle] -dwæsle H.   4 sceapa]
gescapa B 71v/17a, gesceapa H.   6 þy] *om.* H   dæge] dæg H
10 breostan] breostum H.   13 aðundenysse] aðundennesse BH   7] *om.* H.
16 nepte] nefte H.   18 peucedana] peucena B, petuicedanum H
cammoc] cammuc H.   20 gewitlæste] -lyste BH.   21 hinnula] hinnila H.
22 blædran] bræddran H.   23 wagunge] gagunge H.   24 rengwyrmas
ymb] rynwyrmas ymbutan H.   25 Herba . . . mæge (p. 18/2)] *in* H *the title
and the second cure are on* 120v/16–19, *the title occurs again, with the three cures,
on* 126/11–15, H *then continues on* 126.

2. Wiþ þam fefore þe þy feorþan dæge on man becymeþ.

3. Wiþ þæt man well gehyran ne mæge.

XCIX. [Herba saxifragiam þæt is sundcorn]

1. Wiþ þæt stanas on blædran wexen.

5 C. Herba hedera nigra þæt is eorðifig

1. Eft wið þæt stanas on blædran wexen.

2. Wiþ heafodece.

3. Wiþ miltan sare.

4. Wiþ þæra wyrma slite þe man spalangiones nemneþ.

10   5. Eft wiþ þara wunda lacnunge.

6. Wiþ þæt næsðyrlu yfele stincen.

7. Wiþ þæt man ne mæge wel gehyran.

8. Wiþ þæt heafod ne ace for sunnan hætan.

CI. Herba serpillus þæt is organa

15   1. Wiþ heafdes sare.

2. Eft wið heafodece.

3. Gyf hwa forbærned sy.

CII. Herba absinthius þæt is wermod

1. Wiþ læla 7 wið oþre sar.

20   2. Wiþ rengwyrmas.

CIII. Herba salfia

1. Wiþ gicþan þæra gesceapa.

2. Eft wið gicþan þæs setles.

CIV. Herba coliandra þæt is [celendre]

25   1. Wið rengwyrmas.

2. Wiþ þæt wif hrædlice cennan mæge.

1 fefore] feuore H 120v; *gl.* febres H 126   þy] *om.* H 126   dæge] dæg H 120v.   2 man] gif man H.   3 *this title from* H, *om.* VB. 4 Wiþ þæt] ið þæt þe H   wexen] wexeð H.   6 þæt] *om.* B, þæt gif H. 7 heafodece] -ecce H.   11 næsðyrlu] gif næsþyrlu H.   12 man] gif man H   man ne mæge] mæge man ne V, *marked for reversal.*   13 heafod] þe heafod H.   14 organa] organe BH.   15 heafdes sare] heafodsare H. 18 absinthius] obsinthius B.   20 rengwyrmas] ryn- H.   21 salfia] saluia BH.   24 celendre] *supplied from text ch. CIV, a blank space here in* VBH.   25 rengwyrmas] ryn- H.   26 hrædlice cennan mæge] mæge hrædlice cennan H.

CV. Herba porclaca

1. Wiþ swyþlicne flewsan þæs sædes.

CVI. Herba cerefolia þæt is cerfille

1. Wiþ þæs magan sare.

CVII. Herba sisimbrius   5

1. Wiþ blædran sare 7 ne mæge gemigan.

CVIII. Herba olisatra

1. Eft wiþ blædran sare 7 þæs mi'c'gan.

CIX. Herba lilium þæt is lilie

1. Wiþ nædran slite. /   10
2. Wiþ geswell.   f. 16

CX. Herba tytymallus calatites þæt ys lacterida

1. Wiþ þæra innoþa sare.
2. Wiþ weartan.
3. Wiþ hreoflan.   15

CXI. Herba carduus siluaticus þæt is wuduþistel

1. Wiþ þæs magan sare.
2. Wiþ þæt þu nane yfele gencymas þe ne ondræde.

CXII. Herba lupinum montanum

1. Wiþ þæt wyrmas ymb þone nafolan dergen.   20
2. Wiþ þæt cildum þæt sylfe derige.

CXIII. Herba lactyrida þæt is giþcorn

1. Wiþ þæs innoðes heardnysse.

CXIV. Herba lactuca leporina þæt is lactuca

1. Wið feforgende.   25

---

3 cerefolia] cerefola H   cerfille] ceruille B 72/8a, cyruille H.   9 lilie]
lilige H 127/3.   10 slite] slite 7 geswel H.   11 Wiþ geswell] om. H.
12 tytymallus] -mallas BH   lacterida] lacteride H.   17 þæs] om. H.
18 gencymas] gean- BH.   21 cildum] gif cildum H.   22 lactyrida]
lacturide H.   25 feforgende] fefergendne H.

CXV. Herba cucumeris siluatica þæt is hwerhwette

1. Wiþ þæra sina sare 7 fotadle.
2. Gyf cild misboren sy.

CXVI. Herba cannaue silfatica

5   1. Wiþ þæra breosta sare.
2. Wiþ cile bærnettes.

CXVII. Herba ruta montana þæt is rude

1. Wiþ eagena dymnysse.
2. Eft wið breosta sare.
10   3. Wiþ lifersare.
4. Wiþ þæt man gemigan ne mæge.
5. Wiþ nædran slite.

CXVIII. Herba eptafilon þæt is seofonleafe

1. Wiþ fotadle.

15 CXIX. Herba ocimus þæt is mistel

1. Wiþ heafodece.
2. Eft wið eagena sare 7 geswelle.
3. Wiþ ædrena sare.

CXX. Herba apium þæt is merce

20   1. Wiþ eagena sare 7 geswelle.

CXXI. Herba hedera crysocantes þæt is ifig

1. Wiþ wæterseocnysse.

CXXII. Herba menta þæt ys minte

1. Wiþ teter 7 wið pypylgende lic.
25   2. Wiþ yfele dolh 7 wiþ wunda.

4 cannaue] canane H   silfatica] siluatica BH.   13 eptafilon] -philon H
seofonleafe] seofan- B.   17 geswelle] geswel H.   18 this line om. BH.
19 apium] apinum H.   20 this line om. H, cure CXX. 1 probably confused
with cure CXIX. 2.   21 crysocantes] crisso- H.   24 pypylgende]
pepelgende H.   25 this line om. B.

CXXIII. Herba anetum þæt is dile

   1. Wiþ gicþan 7 wið sar þæra gesceapa.

   2. Gyf þonne wifmen hwæt swilces derige.

   3. Wið heafodece.

CXXIV. Herba origanum þæt is organe   5

   1. Wiþ þone dropan 7 liferadle 7 nyrwytte.

   2. Wiþ gebræceo.

CXXV. Herba semperuiuus þæt ys sinfulle

   1. Wiþ ealle gegaderunga þæs yfelan wætan.

CXXVI. Herba fenuculus þæt [ys] finul   10

   1. Wiþ gebræceo 7 wið nyrwyt.

   2. Wiþ blædran sare.

CXXVII. Herba erifion þæt is lyþwyrt

   1. Wiþ lungenadle.

CXXVIII. Herba sinfitus albus   15

   1. Wiþ wifes flewsan.

CXXIX. Herba petroselinum þæt is petersilie

   1. Wiþ nædran slite.

   2. Wiþ þæra sina sare.

CXXX. Herba brassica [siluatica] þæt is [caul] /   20

   1. Wiþ ealle geswell.   f. 16v

   2. Wiþ sidan sare.

   3. Wiþ fotadle.

CXXXI. Herba basilisca þæt is nædderwyrt

   1. Wiþ eall næddercyn.   25

3 *this line om.* B   swilces] hwyllices H.   7 gebræceo] gebræce H 128/5.
10 ys] *from* B 72v/7a, *om.* V   finul] finol H.   11 gebræceo] gebræce H
wið] *om.* H.   15 sinfitus albus] sinfitum album H.   17 petro-
selinùm] triannem H   petersilie] petre- H.   20 brassica siluatica] brassicam siluaticam H   siluatica] *from* B, *om.* V   caul] *from* B, nædderwyrt V.
24–5 *chapter CXXXI om.* H.   25 eall] ealle B.

CXXXII. Herba mandragora

1. Wiþ heafodece.
2. Wiþ þæra earena sare.
3. Wið fotadle.
5   4. Wiþ gewitleaste.
5. Eft wiþ sina sare.
6. Gyf hwa hwylce hefige yfelnysse on his hofe geseo.

CXXXIII. Herba lychanis stephanice þæt is læcewyrt

1. Wiþ eal næddercyn.

10 CXXXIV. Herba action

1. Wiþ þæt man blod 7 worsm gemang hræce.
2. Wiþ þæra liða sare.

CXXXV. Herba abrotanus [þæt is suþernewuda]

1. Wyþ nyrwyt 7 banece 7 wið þæt man earfoþlice gemigan
15   mæge.
2. Wiþ sidan sare.
3. Wiþ attru 7 wið nædrena slite.
4. Eft wið nædrena slite.
5. Wiþ eagena sare.

20 CXXXVI. Herba sion þæt ys laber

1. Wiþ þæt stanas on blædran wexen.
2. Wiþ utsiht 7 innoðes styrungæ.

CXXXVII. Herba eliotropus [þæt ys] sigilhweorfa

1. Wiþ ealra næddercynn'a' slitas.
25   2. Wiþ þæt wyrmas ymb þone nafolan derigen.
3. Wiþ weartan.

5 gewitleaste] -lyste H.   6 Eft] *om.* H   sare] togunge H.   7 hefige
yfelnysse] hefignessa B   hofe] hrofe H.   8–12 *chapters CXXXIII,*
CXXXIV om. H.   8 lychanis] n *alt. from* m V.   11 worsm] worms B.
13 abrotanus] abrotanum H   þæt is suþernewuda] *from* H, *om.* VB.
14 banece] wið banece BH.   14–15 wið . . . mæge] *om.* H.   17 7
wið nædrena slite] *om.* H.   18 Eft] *om.* H   nædrena] næddran H.
20–2 *chapter CXXXVI om.* H.   22 styrungæ] stirunge B.   23 þæt ys]
from B, *om.* V   sigilhweorfa] sigel- H.   24 næddercynna] næddrena H.

CXXXVIII. Herba spreritis

1. Wiþ þone colan fefor.
2. Wiþ [wedehundes] slite.
3. Wiþ miltan sare.

CXXXIX. Herba aizos minor   5

1. Wiþ homan 7 eagena sare 7 fotadle.
2. Wiþ heafodece.
3. Wiþ þæra wyrma slite þe man spalangiones hateþ.
4. Wiþ utsiht 7 wiþ innoþes flewsan 7 wiþ wyrmas þe on þam
   innoðe deriaþ.   10
5. Eft wiþ gehwylce untrumnysse þæra eagena.

CXL. Herba elleborus albus þæt is tunsingwyrt

1. [Be] þysse wyrte mægenum.
2. Wiþ utsiht.
3. Wiþ adla 7 wið ealle yfelu.   15

CXLI. Herba buoptalmon

1. Wiþ gehwylce yfele springas.
2. Wiþ æwyrdlan þæs lichoman.

CXLII. Herba tribulus þæt is gorst

1. Wiþ mycele hætan [þæs lichaman].   20
2. Wiþ þæs muðes 7 þæra gomena fulnysse 7 forrotudnysse.
3. Wiþ þæt stanas on blædran wexen.
4. Wiþ nædran slite.
5. Wiþ attres drinc.
6. Wið flean.   25

CXLIII. Herba coniza /

1. Wiþ nædran slite 7 afligennysse 7 wið gnættas 7 micgeas   f. 17
   7 wið flean 7 wunda.

1–11 *chapters CXXXVIII, CXXXIX om.* H.   3 wedehundes] *from* B,
wædehudes V.   6 homan] oman B.   12 Herba . . . lichoman (p. 27/8)]
one folio missing B   elleborus albus] elebrum H   tunsingwyrt] tunsinc-
H.   13 Be] *emended from* SBe V, *this line om.* H.   15 *this line om.* H.
16–18 *chapter CXLI om.* H.   20 mycele] micelre H 129/2   þæs licha-
man] *from* H, *om.* V.   21 *this line om.* H.   22 wexen] wexað H.
26–p. 24/4 *chapter CXLIII om.* H.

2, 3. Wiþ wifes cwiþan to feormienne 7 wið þæt wif cennan ne mæge.

4. Wiþ þa colan feforas.

5. Wiþ heafodece.

CXLIV. Herba tricnos manicos þæt is foxes [glofa]

1. Wiþ homan.

2. Wiþ pypelgende lic.

3. Wiþ heafodes sare 7 þæs magan hætan 7 wið cyrnlu.

4. Wiþ earena sare.

CXLV. Herba glycyrida

1. Wiþ þone drigean fefor.

2. Wiþ breosta sare 7 þære lifre 7 þære blædra‘n'.

3. Wiþ leahtras þæs muþes.

CXLVI. Herba strutius

1. Wiþ þæt man gemigan ne mæge.

2. Wiþ liferseocnysse 7 nyrwytte 7 wiþ swyðlicne hracan 7 innoþes togotennysse.

3. Wiþ þæt stanas on blædran wexen.

4. Wiþ hreoflan.

5. Wiþ yfele gegadirunge.

CXLVII. Herba aizon

1. Wiþ tobo‘r'sten lic 7 forrotudnysse 7 wið eagena sare 7 hætan 7 forbærnednysse.

3. Wiþ nædran slite.

4. Wiþ utsiht 7 wið wyrmas on innoþe 7 wiþ swyðlicne cyle.

CXLVIII. Herba samsuchon þæt ys ellen

1. Wiþ wæterseocnysse 7 unmihtilicnysse þæs migðan 7 innoþa astyrunge.

---

5 glofa] *from* H, clofe V.   6 homan] oman H.   8 þæs . . . cyrnlu] *om.* H
10–25 *chapters* CXLV–CXLVII *om.* H.   20 gegadirunge] i *alt. from* u V.
24 V *om. one cure.*   27–8 unmihtilicnysse . . . astyrunge] *om.* H.

2. Wiþ springas 7 wið toborsten líc.

3. Wiþ scorpiones stincg.

4. Wiþ mycele hætan 7 geswel þæra eagena.

CXLIX. Herba stecas

1. Wiþ þæra breosta sare.   5

CL. Herba thyaspis

1. Wiþ ealle yfele gegaderunga þæs innoþes 7 wið wifa [monoð-
lican].

CLI. Herba polios þæt is omnimorbia

1. Wiþ nædran slite.   10

2. Wiþ wæterseocnysse.

3. Wiþ miltan sare 7 wið nædran to afligenne 7 wið niwe
wunda.

CLII. Herba hypericon þæt ys corion

1. Wiþ migþan 7 monoðlican astyringe.   15

2. Wiþ fefor þe þy feorþan dæge egleþ.

3. Wiþ þæra sceancena geswel 7 ece.

CLIII. Herba acantaleuca

1. Wiþ þæt man blode hræce 7 þæs magan sare.

2. Wiþ þæs migðan astyrunge.   20

3. Wiþ þæra toða sare 7 yfele læla.

4. Wiþ hramman 7 nædran slite.

CLIV. Herba acanton þæt is beowyrt

1. Wiþ innoþes astyrunge 7 þæs migðan.

2. Wiþ lungenadle 7 gehwylce yfelu.   25

CLV. Herba quiminon þæt is cymen

1. Wiþ þæs magan sare. /

2. Wiþ nyrwyt 7 n(ædr)an slite.   f. 17v

---

2 stincg] stenc H.   3 mycele] micelre H.   4–22 *chapters CXLIX–
CLIII om.* H.   7 ealle yfele] yfele ealle V, *marked for reversal.*
7–8 monoðlican] *emended from* noðlican V.   24 innoþes] þæs innoþes H.
25 7 gehwylce yfelu] *om.* H.   28 7 nædran slite] *om.* H.

3. Wiþ innoða toðundennysse 7 hætan.
4. Wiþ blodryne of næsþyrlon.

CLVI. Herba camelleon alba þæt is wulfes tæsl

1. Wiþ þæt wyrmas on þam innoðe ymb þone naflan dergen.
5　　2. Wiþ wæterseocnysse 7 þæs micðan earfoðlicnysse.

CLVII. Herba scolymbos

1. Wiþ fulne stenc þæra oxna 7 ealles þæs lichoman.
2. Wiþ fulstincendne migðan.

CLVIII. Herba iris Yllyrica

10　　1. Wiþ mycelne hracan 7 innoða astyrunge.
2a. Wiþ nædran slite.
2b. Wiþ wifa monoðlican to astyrigenne.
3. Wiþ cyrnlu 7 ealle yfelu cumlu.
4. Wiþ heafdes sare.

15 CLIX. Herba elleborus albus

1. Wiþ liferseocnysse 7 ealle attru.

CLX. Herba delfinion

1. Wiþ þam fefore þe þy feorþan dæge on man becymeþ.

CLXI. Herba acios

20　　1. Wiþ nædrena slitas 7 [lendena] sare.

CLXII. Herba centimorbia

1. Wiþ þæt hors on hrycge on þam bogum awyrd sy 7 hyt open
sy.

CLXIII. Herba scordios

25　　1, 2. Wiþ þæs migðan astyrunge 7 wið nædrena slitas 7 ealle
attru 7 magan sare.

---

1 innoða] þara innoþa H　　hætan] hæta H.　　　2 næsþyrlon] -þyrlum H.
4 innoðe ymb þone] *om.* H.　　　　5 wæterseocnysse 7] *om.* H　　micðan
earfoðlicnysse] migþan earfoþnesse (þn *alt. from* na) H.　　6–p. 27/8 *chapters*
CLVII–CLXIV om. H.　　　　13 yfelu] *above unexpunged* u, *in a later hand,*
a small e *interlined* V.　　　　20 lendena] *emended from* lendenena V.

3. Wiþ þa gerynnincge þæs wormses ym þa breost.
4. Wiþ fotadle.
5. Wiþ niwe wunda.

CLXIV. Herba ami þæt is miluium

1a. Wiþ þæs innoðes astyrunge 7 earfoðlicnysse þæs migðan 5
7 wildeora slitas.
1b. Wiþ wommas þæs lichoman.
2. Wiþ æblæcnysse 7 æhiwnysse þæs lichoman.

CLXV. Herba uiola þæt ys banwyrt

1. Wiþ þæs cwiðan sare 7 wið þone hætan.   10
2. Wiþ misenlice leahtras þæs bæcþearmes.
3. Wiþ cancor þæra toða.
4. Wiþ þa monoðlican to astyrigenne.
5. Wiþ miltan sare.

CLXVI. Herba uiola purpurea   15

1. Wið niwe wundela 7 eac wið ealde.
2. Wið þæs magan heardnysse.

CLXVII. Herba zamalentition

1. Wiþ ealle wundela.
2. Wiþ wunda cancor.   20

CLXVIII. Herba ancusa

1. Wiþ forbærnednysse.

CLXIX. Herba psillios

1. Wiþ cyrnlu 7 ealle yfelu gegaderunga.
2. Wiþ heafodes sare.   25

CLXX. Herba cynosbatus

1. Wiþ miltan sare.

---

9 uiola] uiolam H.   10 7 wið þone hætan] om. H.   11 misenlice]
misendlice B 73/3a, missenlice H.   12 þæra toða] on þam toþan H.
15–p. 28/5 chapters CLXVI–CLXXI om. H.   23 psillios] spillios B.
24 yfelu] ifele B.

CLXXI. Herba (ag)laofotis

1. Wiþ þone fefor þe þy þriddan dæge 7 þy feorþan on man becymeð. /

2. Gif hwa hreohnysse on rewytte þolige.

3. Wiþ hramman 7 wiþ bifunge.

CLXXII. Herba capparis þæt is wudubend

1. Wiþ miltan sare.

CLXXIII. Herba eryngius

1. Wiþ þæs migðan astyrunge 7 wið þa monoðlican 7 þæs innoþes astyrunge.

2. Wið mænigfealde leahtras þæs innoþes.

3. Wiþ þæra breosta geswell.

4a. Wiþ scorpiones styng 7 ealra næddercynna slitas 7 wið wedehundes slite.

4b. Wiþ oman 7 wið fotadle.

CLXXIV. Herba philantropos

1. Wiþ nædrena slitas 7 wið þæra wyrma þe man spalangiones hateþ.

2. Wiþ earena sare.

CLXXV. Herba achillea

1. Wiþ niwe wunda.

2. Gif wif of ðam gecyndelican limon þone flewsan þæs wætan ðolige.

3. Wið utsiht.

CLXXVI. Herba ricinus

1. Wiþ hagol 7 wið hreohnysse to awendenne.

CLXXVII. Herba polloten þæt ys porrum nigrum

1. Wiþ [hundes] slite.

2. Wiþ wunda.

CLXXVIII. Herba urtica þæt is [netele]

1. Wiþ forcillede wunda.

6 wudubend] -bed H.   8-29 *chapters CLXXIII-CLXXVII om.* H.
28 hundes] *from* B, hunde V.   30 netele] *from* B, ntele V.

2. Wið geswell.
3. Gyf (æn)ig dæl þæs lichoman geslegen s(y).
4. Wiþ lyþa sare.
5. Wiþ fule wunde 7 forrotude.
6. Wiþ wifes [flewsan].   5
7. Wiþ þæt ðu cile ne þolige.

CLXXIX. Herba priapisci þæt is uicaperuica
1. Wið deofulseocnyssa 7 wið nædran 7 wið wildeor 7 wið
   attru 7 wið gehwylce behatu 7 wið andan 7 wið ogan 7
   þæt þu gife hæbbe 7 wið þæt þu gesælig beo 7 gecweme.   10

CLXXX. [Herba litosperimon
1. Wið þæt stanas on blæddran wexen.]

CLXXXI. Herba stauisagria
1. Wiþ þone yfelan wætan þæs lichoman.
2. Wiþ scruf 7 wið sceab.   15
3. Wið toða sare 7 toðreomena.

CLXXXII. Herba gorgonion
1. Wiþ gehwylce yfele fotswaðu.

CLXXXIII. Herba milotis
1. Wiþ eagena dymnysse.   20
2. Wiþ sina togunge.

CLXXXIV. Herba bulbus
1. Wiþ geswel 7 wið fotadle 7 wið gehwylce gederednese.
2a. Wið wæterseocnesse.
2b. Wiþ hunda slitas 7 wið þæt man swæte 7 wið þæs magan 25
    sare.
3. Wiþ wundela 7 scurfe 7 nebcorne.
4. Wiþ þæra innoþa toðundennysse 7 toborstennysse.

CLXXXV. Herba colocynthisagria þæt is cucurbita /   29
1. Wið inno(þes a)styru(n)ge.   f. 18v

1 H *has after this one more cure*: Wiþ wunde, *and ends there.*   5 flewsan]
from B, slewsan V.   11, 12 *from* B 73v/4a, 5a, *om.* V.   15 scruf] scurf B
sceab] scæb B.   16 toðreomena] toða reomena B.   23 gederednese]
gedrecednesse B.   30 astyrunge] *in* B asti, *rest erased, there is a final stop.*

f. 20   I. [Betonica]

1. ÐEOS WYRT þe man betonican nemneð, heo biþ cenned on mædum 7 on clænum dunlandum 7 on gefriþedum stowum; seo deah gehwæþer ge þæs mannes sawle ge his lichoman, hio hyne

5   scyldeþ wið unhyrum nihtgengum 7 wið egeslicum gesihðum 7 swefnum; 7 seo wyrt byþ swyþe haligu, 7 þus þu hi scealt niman on Agustes monðe butan iserne; 7 þonne þu hi genumene hæbbe, ahryse þa moldan óf, þæt hyre nanwiht ón ne clyfie, 7 þonne drig hi on sceade swyþe þearle 7 mid wyrttruman mid ealle gewyrc to

10   duste, bruc hyre þonne 7 hyre byrig þonne ðu beþurfe.

2. Gif mannes heafod tobrocen sy genim þa ylcan wyrte betonican, scearfa hy þonne 7 gnid swyþe smale to duste, genim þonne twega trymessa wæge, þíge hit þonne on hatum beore, þonne halað þæt heafod swyðe hraðe æfter þam drince.

15   3. Wið eagena sár genim þære ylcan wyrte wyrttruman, seoð on wætere to þriddan dæle; 7 of þam wætere beþa þa [eagan]; 7 genim þæræ sylfan wyrte leaf 7 bryt hy 7 lege ofer þa eagan on þone an`d´wlatan.

4. Wið earena sár genim þære ylcan wyrte leaf þonne heo

20   grenost beo; wyl on wætere 7 wring þæt wos, 7 siþþan hyt gestanden beo do hit eft wearm 7 þurh wulle drype on þæt eare.

5. Wið egena dymnesse genim þære ylcan wyrte betonican anre tremesse wæge 7 wyl on wætere 7 syle dri`n´can fæstendum, þonne gewanað hit þone dæl þæs blodes ðe seo dymnys of cymð.

MS V

   1 *title: from* B 74/15a, beteyne (*in later hand*) V, *in* V *also* wyrt; *see textual note.*   2 þe man betonican] ÐE MAN bettonican B.   8 ahryse] ahrysa B.   14 hraðe] raðe B.   15 seoð] 7 seoð B.   16 to þriddan . . . wætere] *om.* B   eagan] *from* B, eaga V.   17 þæræ] þare B.   22 egena] eagena B.   23 tremesse] trymesse B.

MS O

10 si3 3ením] *between these words an erasure* of g.

I. De betonica

1. (Haec herba ualet contra timores nocturnos. contra sompnia. contra
uisiones nociuos) þeos wyrt þe man betonicam nemnað, heo deah
ʒehwæðer ʒe þas mannes sawle ʒi his lichaman. Heo hyne scyldeð wið
unhyrum nihtgengum 7 wyð eʒeslice ʒesihþum 7 swefenum; 7 seow wyrt 5
his swyðe haliʒu; 7 þus þu scealt hy níman on Augustus moðe butan
yserne; 7 þan þu hi ʒenuman hæbbe harise þa molda of, þæt hyre nan on
ne clíuiʒe; 7 þanne driʒ hiʒ on sceade swiðe þearlíce 7 mid wyrtuman
míd ealle ʒewyrc to duste; 7 bruc hyre þanne þu beðurfe.

2. (Ad capitis lesionem) Gif mannes heafod tobrocen siʒ ʒením þeos 10
wyrt, scearfa hiʒ þanne 7 gníd hi swiðe smale to duste; ʒením þanne
tweʒa trymesa ʒeweʒe, þeʒe hyt þanne on hatum beore; þanne halað þat
heafoð syðe raðe æfter þan drence.

3. (Ad morbum oculorum) Wið eaʒena sor ʒením þeos wyrt wurtruman
7 seoð on watere to þriddan dæle; 7 of þan watere beða eaʒan / 7 ʒením
þare wyrte leaf 7 byt hiʒ 7 leʒe ofer þa eaʒan on ðan anwítan.

4. (Ad aures) Wið earena sar ʒením þare ylcan wyrt leaf þanne hi
grenost beo, wel on watere 7 wríng þæt wos 7 læt stonden; do hit eft
wyrman 7 mid wulle drupe on þat eare.

5. (Ad oculos) Wið eaʒena dimnesse ʒením þare wyrte anre tremese 20
wæʒe, wil on watere, syle drincen fæstínden, þanne ʒewanað hit þonne
dael þæs blodes þeo seo dimnesse of cymð.

MS Vo

I. Herba vettonica

1. Haec herba vettonica nascitur in pratis et in montibus, locis mundis
et opacis circa frutices; animas hominum et corpora custodit, nocturnas
ambulationes et loca sancta et busta, etiam visus timendos et omni rei
sancta (. . .) et sic colligis mense Augusto [, cum ceterae herbae mature-
scere incipient, cum semine et radicibus sine ferro, eamque excussam,
nec terra ei inhaereat, et in umbra arefacias atque ita teres cum radicibus
suis cribro aromatico; mollissime in pulverem redactam cum volueris
uti, sic uteris].

2. Ad capitis fracturam. Herba vettonica contusa et super capitis ictu
imposita vulnus mira celeritate glutinatum sanabit (. . .).

3. Ad oculorum vitia vel dolores. Vettonicae herbae radices ex aqua
ad tertias coquito et ex ea aqua oculos foveto; ipsius autem folia trita
supra frontem et in oculos imponito.

4. Ad aurium vitia vel dolores. Herbae [vettonicae] recentis folia vel
per se aut in aqua madefacta perterito sucumque eorum excipito, deinde
adiecta rosa liquida tepefacta et in aure stillato lanamque superimponito,
mire proficit.

5. Ad caliginem oculorum. Vettonicae dragma una, aquae calidae
quiatos iv, ieiunus bibat, deducit ad inferiorem partem eum sanguinem
qui caliginem oculorum facit.

6. Wiþ tyrende eagan genim þa ylcan wyrte betonican 7 syle þigccean, heo gegódað 7 onliht þæra eagena scearpnysse.

7. Wiþ swyþlicne blodryne of nosum genim þa ylcan wyrte be-

f. 20v tonican 7 cnuca hy 7 gemeng þærto sum/ne dæl sealte(s) 7 genim
5 þonne swa mycel swa (þ)u mæge mid twam fingrum genima(n), wyrc hit sinewealt 7 do on þa næsþyrlu.

8. Wiþ toðece genim þa ylcan wyrte betonican 7 wyl on ealdan wine oþþe ón ecede to þriddan dæle, hit hælþ wundurlice þæra toða sár 7 geswell.

10 9. Wiþ sidan sare genim þære ylcan wyrte þreora trymessa wæge; seoð on ealdum wine 7 gnid þærto xxvii piporcornu, gedrinc his þonne on niht nistig þreo full fulle.

10. Wiþ lændenbrædena sare genim [þare] ylcan betonican þreora trymessa wæge, xvii piporcorn, gnid tósomne, wyll on
15 ealdum wine, syle hym swa wearm on niht nistig þreo full fulle.

11. Wið wambe sare genim þære ylcan wyrte twega trymessa wæge, wyl on wætere, syle hyt þonne him wearm drincan; ðonne bið þæs innoðes sar settende 7 liðigende þæt hit sona nænig lað ne bið.

20 12. Gif mannes innoð to fæst sy anbyrge þas ylcan wyrte on wearmum wætere on niht nistig; þonne bið se man hal on þreora nihte fyrste.

13. Wiþ þon ðe men blod upp wealle þu(rh h)is muð (ge)nim þær(e ylc)an wyrte þre(or)a tr(y)mess(a w)æge 7 cóle gate meolc
25 (þreo) f(ul) fulle; ðonne bið he swyþe raðe (h)al.

14. Gif man nelle be(o)n druncen nime þonne ærest, onb(y)rge betonican ðære wyrte.

2 þigccean] þicgan 7 B.   3 swyþlicne] swilcne B.   6 sinewealt] gl. rotundum B 74v/5a   næsþyrlu] nos- B.   11 piporcornu] u added later V, -corna B.   13 þare] from B, þæra V.   14 xvii] 7 seofontyne B. 20 mannes] ma'n'nes B.   22 nihte] nihta B.

MS O

12 ȝenim] ȝe (at end of line, no damage).

6. (Item ad idem) Wið tyrende eaȝene ȝením þa ylcan wyrte, syle þiȝean; 7 heo ȝegodeð 7 onliht eȝenan scearpnesse.

7. (Ad sanguinem de naribus) Wið swyðlícne blodrune of nosa ȝením þeos wyrt 7 cnuca hiȝ 7 meng þarto sum dal seltes, 7 ȝením þanne swa mícel swa ðu maȝe mid twa fingre, wyrc hit sinewealt 7 do on ða nosþyrle. 5

8. (Ad dolorem dentium) Wyð toðece ȝením þa ylcan wyrt 7 wyl on ealdan wíne oððer on ecede to ðriddan dale; hit hælþ wundorlica þara toða sor 7 ȝeswell.

9. Wið sidan sore ȝením þare wyrt þreo trymesan wæȝe, seoð on ealdan wíne, drinc hit þonne on níht níhstíȝ þreo ful fulle. 10

10. —

11. Wið wambe sor [ȝenim] þa wirt betonica tweȝa tremesa wæȝe, wyl on wætere 7 drincan hit wearm; þanne byð þas innoþas sar sentende 7 liðiȝende þæt sona nan lað ne byð.

12. (Ad soluendum uentrem) Gif mannes innoð to fast si drica þe wyrt 15 ȝesode on werma wætera on nih nichsiȝ; þanne byð se man hal on þreora nihte firsta.

13. (Ad sanguinem conspuentes) Wið þan þe man blod up welle þur hís muð ȝením þeos wyrt þreo tyrmesa wæȝe 7 cole gate meolc þreo ful fulle; / þanne byð he syyðe raðe hal. f. 6v

14. (Contra ebrietatem) Gif man nelle beon druncan níme þanne aryst, 21 onbyrȝe þeos wyrt betoneca.

MS Vo

6. Ad lacrimòsos oculos. Vettonicam manducet, (aciem oculorum) meliorem facit.

7. Ad sanguinem de naribus nimis (profluentem). Vettonicam tritam, paululum salis adicito digitis duobus, pollice et medio, quantum tolli potest sublata, rotundulam facis et naribus inseris.

8. Ad dentium vitia. Vettonica ex vino veteri aut aceto ad tertias decoque, gargarizet, dentium dolorem discutiet.

9. Ad lateris dolorem. Vettonicae dragmas iii cum vino veteri quiatos f. 16 iii et piperis grana xxvii, contritum et calefactum ieiunus bibat.

10. Ad lumborum dolorem. Vettonicae dragmas iii ex vino Amineo quiatos iii, piperis grana xvii, contritum calefactum ieiunus bibat, sanatur.

11. Ad ventris dolorem. Vettonicae dragma una in aqua calida quiatos duo bibendum dato. His autem dumtaxat haec apta erit compositio quorum non ex cruditate intestina (torquebuntur).

12. Ad alvum concitandum. Vettonicae dragmas iv, hydromelitos ix bibendum dato, ventrem mox movet.

13. Ad sanguinem qui per os reiciunt et purulentum. Vettonicae f. 17v dragmas tres ex vino veteri quiatos duo calefactum da [et lactis recentis caprini cyatos iii], bibat triduo continenti.

14. Ne ebrius fiat. Vettonicam prius sumat.

15. Gif men wylle spring on gesittan genime þonne anes trymeses gewæge, cnucige wið eald smeoru, lecge on ðone stede þe se spring on gesittan wolde; þonne byþ hit sona hal.

16. Gif mon sy innan gebrocen oþþe him se lichoma sár sy genime þonne betonican þære wyrte feower trymessan gewæge, wyll on wine swyþe; drince þonne on niht nistig; þonne leohtað him se lichoma.

17. Gif mon on mycelre rade oþþe on miclum gangum weorðe geteorad nime þonne betonican þære wyrte ane trymessan fulle, seoð on geswettum wine, drince þonne on niht nihstig þrec full fulle, þonne bið he sona unwerig.

18. Gif man sy innan unhal oþþe hyne wlatige þonne genim ðu betonican þære wyrte twa trymessan gewæge 7 huniges anre yndsan gewæge, wylle þonne on beore swyþe þearle, drince ðreo ful fulle on niht nistig; þonne / rumað him sona se innað.

19. Gif [þu] ðonne wylle þæt ðin mete eaðelice gemylte genim þonne betonican þære wyrte þreo trymessan gewæge 7 huniges ane yndsan, seoð þonne þa wyrte oðþæt heo heardige; drinc hy þonne on wætere twa full fulle.

20. Wiþ ðon þe man ne mæge his mete gehabban 7 he spiwe ðonne he hyne geðigedne hæbbe genim þonne betonican þære wyrte iiii trymesan gewæge 7 awylled hunig; wyrc þonne lytle poslingas feower þæróf; ete þonne ænne 7 ænne on hatum wætere 7 on wine tósomne, geðicge ðonne þæs wætan þreo full fulle.

21. Wið innoþes sare oððe gif he aþunden sy genim betonican þa wyrt, gnid on wíne swyðe smale, lege þonne abutan þa wambe 7 þyge hy; þonne eac hraðe cymeþ þæt to bote.

MS V

2 gewæge] wæge B. 8 weorðe] wurðe B. 10 nihstig] nistig B.
15 innað] innoð B 75/4a. 16 þu] *from* B, *om.* V. 27 hraðe] raðe B.

MS O

2 wæӡe] *preceded by exp.* ӡ. 3 ӡesittan] se ӡesittan (se *exp.*).
6 leo'h'tað] *betwen* o *and* t *an exp.* þ. 10 niht] nahue niht (nahue *exp.*).
17 trimesan] tw trimesan (tw *exp.*) 18 ӡeweӡe] ӡewe (*no damage*).
22 betoníca] *foll. by exp.* ӡ þa] þana (na *exp.*).

15. (Contra apostema) Gif men wylle spríncg on ȝesítte ȝením þanne anes trimesses wæȝe, cnuciȝe wið æld smeru, lecge on þan stede þe se spring on ȝesittan wolde; þanne byð hit þone hal.

16. (Contra internam rupturam) Gif man si innan ȝebrocen oð ðer him þe lichama sar si ȝením betonica feower trimesan wæȝe, welle on wine 5 swiþe, drince þanne on nih ni‘c′hstiȝ; þanne leo‘h′tað him se lichama.

17. —

18. (Contra nauseam) Gif man si ínnan unhal oð ðer him wlatie þanna níme betonica twa trimesan ȝewaiȝe 7 huniȝes anre yntsan ȝewæȝe, wille þanne on beore swiðe þearle, drinca þanne þreo ful fulle a niht 10 nihstiȝ; þanne rumeð hím ðat innoð sona.

19. (Ut cibus facile deratur) Gif þu wille þæt þín mete eaðelice ȝemulte ȝením betonica þa wírt þreo trymesan ȝewæȝe 7 huniȝes ane ynsan, seoð þanne þa wyrt forþat heo heardie, drinc hiȝ þanne on watere twa full fulle. 15

20. (Contra uomitum) Wið ðan þe man ne mæȝe his mete ȝehabban 7 he spiwe þanne he hyne ȝeðiȝedne habbe ȝením betonica iiii trimesan [ȝeweȝe] 7 awilled huniȝ, wyrc þanne lítle poslingas þarof, ete þanne ænne on hatum wætera 7 on wine tosomne, ȝeðicȝe þanne þæs wæte þreo full fulle. 20

21. (Pro dolore uiscerum) Wið ínnoðes sor oðer ȝif he aþunden si ȝením betonica, gnid on wíne swiþe smale, leȝe þanne abutan þa wambe 7 þiȝe hi, þanne eac raðe cumeþ þæt to bote.

MS Vo

15. Ad carbunculos. Vettonicae dragma una, aquae calidae quiatos duo f. 18 bibat. Idem: vettonicam cum axungia tritam plagae imponat.

16. Qui perfrictionibus laborant. Vettonica uncia una ex vino quiatis tribus, curat per triduum.

17. Lassis de via. Vettonicae dragma una, cum oximelli quiatis tribus potui dato.

18. Cibis fastidiosis ex aegritudine. Vettonicae dragmas ii ex aqua mulsa quiatos iii bibat, sanatur.

19. Ut facile concocat. Vettonicae dragmas iii, mellis unciam i, cocito melle donec indurescat, ex aqua calida quiatos ii bibat.

20. Ad eos qui cibum continere non possunt et reiciunt. Vettonicae dragmas quattuor, mellis decocti uncia, pastillos ex eo facito iv, ex quibus pastillum unum gluttiat et aquae calidae quiatos duo bibat.

21. Ad veretri tumorem vel dolorem. Vettonica ex vino trita tumores foveto ipsamque tritam opponito, potenter facit.

22. Gif þonne hwylc man attor geþycge genime ðonne þære ylcan wyrte þreo trymessan gewæge 7 feower ful fulle wines, wylle tosomne 7 drince; þonne aspiweð he þæt attor.

23. Gif hwylcne man nædre toslite genime þære wyrte iiii trymesan gewæge, wyll on wine 7 gnid swyþe smale, do þonne gehwæþer, ge on ða wunde lege 7 eac drinc swyþe þearle; ðonne meaht ðu æghwylcere nædran slite swa (g)ehælan.

24. Ef(t w)ið nædran slite genim þære ylcan wyrte a(ne) tr(ym)esan g(e)wæge, gecnid on r(e)ad w(ín), gedo þonne ðæt þæs wines syn þre(o) ful fulle, smyre ðonne mid (þ)am wyrtum ða wunde 7 mid þy wíne, þo(nne) byð hio sona hal.

25. Wið wedehundes sli(t)e genim betonican ða wyrte, gecnuca hy swyþe smale 7 lege on þa wunde.

26. Gif þe ðin þrotu sar sy oððe þines swyran hwylc dæl genim þa ilcan wyrte 7 gecnuca swyðe smale, wyrc to clyþan, lege on þone swyran, ðonne clænsað heo hit æghwær, ge innan ge utan.

27. Wiþ lendena sare 7 gif men his ðeoh acen genim [þare] ylcan wyrte twega trymessa gewæge, wyll on beore, syle him drincan.

28. Gif he ðonne sy febrig 7 he sy mycelre hætan ðrowiende syle ðonne þa wyrte on wearmum wætere, nalæs on beore; ðonne godiað þæra lendena sár 7 þæra ðeona swyðe hræðe.

29. Wiþ fotadle genim þa ylcan wyrte, seoð on wætere oþðæt þæs wæteres sy ðriddan dæl on besoden, / cnuca ðonne þa wyrte 7 lege on þa fet 7 smire þærmid 7 drinc þæt wos, þonne findest ðu þæræt bot(e) 7 ælteowe hælo.

f. 21v

26

7 meaht] miht B.   9 gecnid] gegnid B   10 syn þreo] syndrig iii B.
18 þare] *from* B, þæra V.   22 syle] syle him B.   23 hræðe] raðe B
75v/1a.   27 ælteowe] æltæwe B.

MS O

6 þearle] þeardle (d *exp.*).   9 trymesan] ty trymesan (ty *exp.*).
16 clænsað] clæn (*no damage*).

22. (Contra venenum sumptum) Gif aní man attor ȝeþícȝe nim þare wyrt þreo trimesan wæȝe / 7 iiii fulle wínes, wille tosomne 7 drican; þanne aspiweð he þæt attor. f. 7

23. (Contra morsum serpentis) Gif man næddre sliteð ȝením þare wyrt iiii tremesan ȝewæȝe, will on wyne 7 gnid swiðe smale, do þanne æþar, ȝeleȝe on þa wunda 7 eac drinc swiðe þearle; þanne miht þu æȝhwylcere naddran slíte swa ȝehalen. 5

24. (Iterum contra morsum serpentis) Eft wyð næddran slite ním þare wyrt anne trymesan ȝewæȝe, ȝegníd on ride wíne, ȝedo þat þæs wynes si þreo full fulle, smira þanne mid þa wyrte þa wunda 7 mid þam wyne; þanne byð heo sona hal. 10

25. (Contra rapidi canis morsum) Wið wodehundes slíte cnuca þa wyrt swiðe smale 7 leȝe on þa wunda.

26. (Contra morbum gutturis) Gif þe þín þrotu sar si oðð er þine swyran nim cnuca þa wyrt swyþa smale, wyrc to cliðe, leȝe on þane swyran; þanne [clænsað] heo hít æȝhwær ȝe wiðinne ȝe widutan. 15

27. (Contra dolorem renum) Wið lendena sor 7 ȝif manna his ðeoh acon ním þisser wyrt tweȝa trymesan ȝewæȝe, will on beore, sile hím drínca.

28, 29. — 20

MS Vo

22. Ad venenum si quis sumpserit. Vettonicae dragmas iii ex vini quiatos iv statim dato, dum biberit reiciet venenum.

23. Ad serpentium morsus. Vettonicae dragmas iii in vini eminis tribus diluito, potui dato, omnium serpentium morsus sanat.

24. Idem ad serpentium morsus. Vettonicae dragmas vi, vini nigri quiatos iii trito, illinito super vulnus, sanatur.

25. Ad canis rabidi morsum. Vettonica contusa morsui imponitur.

26. Ad fistulas. Vettonica contrita, turundulas facito et paululum salis inserito, obligat et expurgat. f. 19

27. Ad lumborum et coxarum dolorem. Vettonicae dragmas ii, ex mulso potui datum,

28. febricitanti ex aqua calida, lumborum dolorem sanare creditur.

29. Ad podagram. Vettonica decocta ad tertias, aqua potui data, ipsamque tritam et impositam mire dolorem lenire experti affirmant.

II. Wægbræde   plantago

1. Gif mannes heafod ace oððe sár sy genime wegbrædan wyrtwalan 7 binde him on swyran; ðonne gewiteð þæt sar of þam heafde.

5   2. Gif men his wamb sar sy genime wegbrædan seaw ðære wyrte, gedo þæt hio blacu sy 7 þyge hy, ðonne mid mycelre wlatunge gewiteþ þæt sár onweg; gif hyt þonne sy þæt sio wamb sy aþundeno, scearfa ðonne þa wyrte 7 lege on þa wambe, ðonne fordwineð heo sona.

10   3. Wið þæs innoðes sare genim wegbrædan seaw, do on sumes cynnes ealo 7 þycge hyt swyðe; þonne bataþ he inneweard 7 clæn(sa)ð þone magan 7 þa smælþ(ea)rmas swyþe wundrum well.

4. Eft wið þon þe man on wambe forweaxen sy seoð þonne þa wegbrædan swyþe 7 éte þonne swyþe, ðonne dwineþ seo wamb 15 sona.

5. Eft wið þon þe man þurh hys árgang blode ut yrne genim wegbrædan seaw, syle him drincan, þonne bið hit sona oðstilled.

6. Gif man gewundud sy genim wegbrædan sæd, gnid to duste 7 scead on þa wunde, heo bið sona hal; gif se lichoma hwær mid 20 hefiglicre hæto sy gebysgod gecnuca ða sylfan wyrte 7 lege þærón, ðonne colað se lichoma 7 halað.

7. Gif ðu þonne wylle mannes wambe þwænan þonne nim ðu þa wyrte, wyll ón ecede, do þonne þæt wos 7 þa wyrte swá awýllede on wín, drince þonne on niht nihstig symle an ful to fylles.

25   Nædre

8. Wið nædran slite genim wegbrædan ða wyrt, gnid on wíne 7 ete hy.

Scorpio /

f. 22   9. Wiþ scorpiones slite genim wegbrædan wyrtwalan, bind [on] 30 þone man; þonne ys to gelyfenne þæt hyt cume him to godre are.

MS V

1 *title*: weibrode B.   2 wegbrædan] a *alt. from* e V.   5 seaw] *gl.*
ius B.   7–8 aþundeno] aþunden B.   24 nihstig] nistig B.   25 Nædre]
om. B.   26 slite] geslite B 76/4a.   28 Scorpio] *om.* B.   29–30 on þone
from B, oþone V.

MS O

6 blacu] *a signe de renvoi on this word refers to* brocen, i.e. fracta *in o.m.*
12 þurh] his þurh (his *exp.*).

II. De plantagine

1. (Ad dolorem capitis) Gif mannes heafod ace oðöer sar si níma
weȝbrædan wyrtwalam 7 bindan him on swuran, 'þanne' ȝewiteð þat sor
of þan heafeden.

2. (Ad morbum uentris) Gif mannes wambe sor si níme weȝbrædan 5
seaw, ȝedo þæt heo blacu si 7 þiȝe hiȝ; þanne mid micelre wlatunge
ȝewiteð þæt sar onweȝ. Gif hít þanne si þæt seo wambe siȝ aþundene
scearfa þane þa wyrt 7 leȝe on (þ)a wambe; þane fordwineð heo sona.

3. —

4. (Ad dissinteriam) Eft wyd þæt þe man on wamba forwexen si seoð 10
þane (we)ȝebrade swiðe 7 ete swiðe, þane dwineþ / seo wambe sona.   f. 26

5. Eft wið ðat man þurh his arsgange blod ut ryne ním web'r'ade seaþ,
sile hym drinca; þanne byð hit sona oðstilled.

6. (Ad plagam) Gif man yyundod sy ním webræde sæd, gnít to duste
7 scead on ða wunde, heo byð sona hal.   15

7. —

8. (Contra morsum serpentis) Wið næddran slite ním þa wyrt, gníd on
wíne 7 ete hiȝ.

9. —

MS Vo

II. Herba arnoglossa

1. Ad capitis dolorem. Herbae plantaginis radix in collo suspensa
capitis dolorem tollit.

2. Ad ventris dolorem. Herbae plantaginis sucum tepefacito, fomentando ventris dolorem tollet, et si tumores fuerint tunsa et imposita f. 21
tollit tumorem.

3. Ad dolorem interiorum. Herbae plantaginis sucus potui datur et
interiora sanat et toracem hominis purgat [mirifice].

4. Ad disintericos. Herbam plantaginem cum lenticula coquito et da,
manducet, stringet ventrem,

5. qui purulentum excreant cum sanguine, herbae plantaginis sucum
dato eis bibere, sanabuntur.

6. Ad vulnera. Herbae plantaginis semen tunsum, in vulnus asparsum
vulnera cito sanat et ipsa [tunsa et] imposita refrigerat ea loca quae nimio
calore uruntur et persanat.

7. Ad ventrem stringendum. Herba plantago ex aceto cocta in mero
bibitur mensura quiati unius.

8. Ad morsum serpentis. Herba plantago tunsa, ex vino sumpta
commoda erit.

9. Ad scorpionum percutionem. Herbae plantaginis radicem alligatam,
mire prodesse creditur.

10. Gif men innan wyrmas eglen genim wægbrædan seaw, cnuca 7 wring 7 syle him supan 7 nim ða sylfan wyrte, gecnuca, lege on þone naflan 7 wrið þærto swyðe fæste.

11. Gif hwylces mannes lichoma sy aheardod nim þonne weg-
5 brædan þa wyrte 7 gecnuca wið smeru butan sealte 7 wyrc swa to clame, lege þonne on þær hit heardige, hnescaþ hyt sona 7 bataþ.

12. Gif hwylcum men sy þæs feorðan dæges fefer getenge genim ðonne þære wyrte seaw, cnid on wætere, syle him drincan twam tidum ær [he] hym þæs feferes wene, þonne ys wén þæt hyt him
10 cume to mycelre freme.

13. Wið fotadle 7 wið sina sare genim þonne wægbrædan leaf, gnid wið sealt, sete ðonne on þa fet 7 on þa syna; þonne ys þæt gewisslice læcedom.

14. Wið þam fefore þe ðy þriddan dæge on man becymeð
15 genim wegbrædan þry cyðas, cnid on wætere oþþe on wine, syle him drincan ær þon se fefor him tó cume on niht nihstig.

15. Wiþ ðy fefore þe ðy æftran dæge to cymeð, gecnuca þas ylcan wyrte swyþe smale, syle him on ealoð drincan, þæt ys to gelyfenne þæt hit dyge.

20 16. Wið wunda hatunge nim þonne wegbrædan þa wyrt, cnuc(a) on sm(er)we butan sealte, lege on þa wunde, þonne bið he sona hal.

17. Gif mannes fet on syþe tydrien genim þonne wegbrædan ða wyrt, gnid on écede, beþe ða fet þærmid 7 smyre; ðonne þwineþ
25 hy sona.

18. Gif hwylcum weargbræde weaxe on þam nosum oððe on þam hleore genim ðonne wegbrædan seaw, wring on hnesce wulle, lege þærón; læt licgan nigon niht, þonne halaþ hyt hraðe æfter ðam.

MS V

1 eglen] eglian B   wægbrædan] weg- B.   8 wyrte] wyrtan B   cnid]
gnid B   twam] id. B (a alt. from u).   9 he] from B, om. V   feferes]
feres B.   11 wægbrædan] weg- B.   15 cnid] gnid B.   24 þwineþ]
þwinað B.   26 weargbræde] wearh- B.   28 hraðe] raðe B.

MS O

2 wyrt 7 wring] wyrt 7 / 7 wring.   4 lichama] lichama hany (no expunction).
11 þriddan] first d alt. from n.   15 on ealoþ] between these words two exp.
letters, of which the first is e.

10. (Contra uermes in uentre) Gif manne inne wurmes eȝlian cnuca sa wyrt 7 wring 7 sile hím supen þat seaw, 7 cnuca þa sulfe wyrt 7 leȝe on þæne næfelen 7 wrið þarto swyðe fæste.

11. (Si aliquid membrum sit induratum) Gif manne lichama si ahearded nim webræde 7 cnuca wyð smera botan scealte, wyrc to clame, leȝe on dær 5 hit headíe; þanne hnescað hit sona 7 batað.

12. —

13. (Ad morbum pedum) Wið fotadle 7 wið sína sore gníd þisse wy`r´te leaf wið sealte, sete þanne on ða feot 7 on ða sína; þanne ys þæt ȝewíslice lacedom.   10

14. (Ad febres tertianas) Wið ða fefore þe ði þriddan dæȝe on man becumed ȝenim webræde þry ciðas on wætere oððe on wíne, sile him drincan ær þan se fefor him to cume on niht nichstiȝ.

15. (Item ad febrim) Wið fefore þe ði æf`t´ran dæȝe to cumeð cnuca þeos wirt swiðe smæle, sile hím on ealoþ drincan, þæt him diȝe.   15

16. Wið wunda hatuga cnuca webræde mid smerere butan sealte, leȝe on þa wunda; þanne byð heo sona hal.

17. —

18. Gif hwilcum manne werȝbrædan wexe on nosum oððer on ðan hleore nim webrade seaw, wyrng on hnesce wulle, leȝe þæron, læt ligge 20 neoȝon nih, þanne / halað hit raðe after þan.   f. 26v

---

MS Vo

10. Ad lumbricos. Herbam plantaginem contundis et sucos eius de cocliario vel de ligula dabis bibere, ipsam quoque herbam tunsam in umbilico impone.

11. Si qua duritia in corpora (fuerit). Herba plantago pisata cum axungia sine sale et factum quasi malagma, imponis in duritiam et discutit.

12. Ad quartanas. Herba plantago, sucus in aqua mulsa ante duas horas accessionis potui datur, miraberis effectum.   f. 22

13. Ad podagram et omnium nervorum dolorem vel tumorem. Herbae plantaginis folia contusa vel pisata cum salis modico et pisata optime facere certum est.

14. Ad tertianas. Herbae plantaginis radices tres conterito et sub accessionem cum vino aut ex aqua ieiuno da, bibat.

15. Ad secundarum dolorem. Herbae plantaginis semen contritum et potui datum prodesse creditur.

16. Ad [recentia] vulnera. Herba plantago contrita, cum axungia vetere sine sale imponat, sanus fit.

17. Si pedes tumuerint ab itinere. Herba plantago contrita, cum aceto imposita tumorem tollit.

18. Si cui vulnus secus oculum vel secus nares natum fuerit. Herbae plantaginis sucos expressos contusos et lanam mollem suco madefactam imponat per dies ix, sanus fiet.

19. Be æghwylcum uncuþum blædrum ðe on mannes nebbe sittað nim wegbrædan sæd, drig tó duste 7 gnid, meng wið smeoru, do lytel sealtes to, wes‘c′ mid wine, smyre þæt neb mid; þonne smeþað hyt 7 halað.

5 20. Wiþ muþes wunde genim wegbrædan leaf 7 hyre seaw, gnid tosomne, hafa ðonne swiþe lange on þinum muðe 7 et ðone wyrtwalan.

21. Gif wedehund man toslite genim þas ylcan wyrte 7 gegnid 7 lege on; ðonne bið hit sona hal.

10 22. Wiþ ælces dæges mannes tyddernysse inneweardes nime
f. 22v þonne / wegbræda(n), do o(n) win 7 sup þæt wos 7 et ða wegbr(æ)dan, ðonne deah hit wið æghwylcre innancundre ‘un′hælo.

III. Fifleafe   pentafolium

1. Gif men his leoðu acen oððe ongeflogen sy genim fifleafe
15 ða wyrt, cnuca on smeorwe swyþe smale, lege ðæron butan sealte; ðonne halað hyt sona.

2. Wiþ wambe sare genim fifleafan seaw þære wyrte, gewring twegen cuculeras fulle, syle him supan; þonne clænsaþ hit onweg þæt sar eall.

20 3. Wiþ muðes ece 7 wið tungan 7 wið þrotan genim fifleafan wyrtwalan, wyll on wætere; syle him supan; ðonne clænsað hit ðone muð innan 7 bið se éce litliende.

4. Wiþ heafdes sare genim fifleafan ða wyrt; bewrit þriwa mid þam læstan fingre 7 mid þam ðuman, ahefe þonne upp of
25 ðær(e e)orþan 7 gegnid swyþe smal(e 7) bind on þæt heafod, ðonne biþ se ece lytliende.

5. Gif men blod ut of nosum yrne to swiðe syle him drincan fifleafan on wine 7 smyre þæt heafud mid þam, ðonne oðstandeþ se blodgyte sona.

MS V

3 wes‘c′] wes B 76v/2a.   8 Gif] Gi‘f′ B   wyrte] wyrt B.   13 *title*: fifleaue B.   14 fifleafe] -leafan B.

MS O

2 webræde] ȝe webræde (ȝe *exp.*).   12 *title: first two words in black.*
18 aweȝ] aȝ aweȝ (a *exp.*).

19. (Ad omnem uesicam surgentem in facie hominis) Be æʒhwylcum
uncuðun bladdran þe on mannes nebbe sittaþ ním webræde sæd, driʒ to
duste 7 gnid, meng wid smere, do litel sealtes to, wes mid wine, smure
þat nebb mid; þanne smeðad hit 7 hæled.

20. Wid muþes wunde ním webræde leaf 7 híre seaw, gnid, hafa 5
þanne swiðe lange on þine muðe 7 et þane wyrtwalan.

21. ——

22. (Contra omnem morbum cotitianum in homine) Wið ælces
dæʒes mannes tidderenesse ínnewerdes níme þanne webræden, don on
wín 7 sup þæt wos 7 ete þa web'r'æden, þanne deah hit wyd æʒhwylære 10
ínnancundra unhælo.

III. Herba pentafilon   v folia   f. 26v/10

1. (Ad neruum) Gif man his liðu acen oþþer onʒefloʒen si ním fifleauen
þa wurt, cnuca mid smerewe swiðe smale, leʒe þaron butan sealte,
þanna hæled hít sona.   15

2. (Ad morbum uentris) Wið wambe sare ním fifleauen þa wurt, wring
tweʒen cuculeres fulle þes seawes, sule hím suppe, þanne clansað hít
aweʒ þæt sar.

3. (Ad dolorem oris et linguae et gutturis) Wið muðes ece 7 wid tungan
7 wið þrotan ním þeos wurtewalan, will on wætere, sile him suppan; 20
þanne clænsað hit þane muð innan 7 byð þe ece lytlende.

4. ——

5. (Ad fluxum sanguinis ex naribus) Gif man blod ut of nosum yrne to
swiþe sule hím drincan fifleafan wyrt on wíne 7 smure þæt heafod mid
þan; þanne onstandeð se blodgyte sona.   25

MS Vo

19. Ad parotidas. Herba plantago cum axungia vetere pisata et imposita persanat.

20. Ad ulcera oris. Herbae plantaginis sucus in ore teneatur vel folia
eius [et radix] commanducantur.

21. Ad canis rabidi morsum. Herba plantago contusa ac imposita
facillime sanabit.

22. *A different cure.*

III. Herba pentafilos   f. 23

1. Ad vitia articulorum sive si percussa fuerint. Herba quinquefolium f. 24
tunsa cum axungia vetere sine sale imposita, sanatur.

2. Ad ventris dolorem. Herba quinquefolium tunsa, sucum eius
dabis bibere, dolorem tollit sine mora, cocliaria duo dabis.

3. Ad oris vitia aut linguae aut gulae. [Herbae quinquefolii radices ex
aqua coctas dabis, gargarizet;] etiam arteria purgat.

4. Ad capitis dolorem. Quinquefolium cirsumscribito ter digito medio
et pollice, sublata et trita et capiti illita efficaciter sanat et peracto remedio loco puro reponi convenit.

5. Ad sanguinem de naribus nimis profluentem. Sucus quinquefolii
potus vel illitus restringit sanguinem.

6. Gif mannes midrife áce genime fifleafan seaw, mencg to wine 7 drince ðonne þreo ful fulle þry morgenas 7 on niht nihstig.

7. Wiþ nædran slite genim fifleafan þa wyrte, gnid on wine 7 drince swiðe; ðonne cymeð him þæt to bote.

5   8. Gif man forbærned sy genime fifleafan þa wyrt, bere on him, ðonne cweþað cræftige men þæt him [þæt] to 'gode' cume.

9. Gif ðu wille cancer ablendan genim ðonne fifleafan ða wyrte, seoð on wine 7 on ealdes bearges rysle butan sealte, mencg eall tósomne, wyrc to clyðan 7 lege ðonne on þa wunde, þonne 10 halað heo sona.

Ðu scealt ðonne eac gewyrcean þa wyrt on Agustus monðe.

Nædre /

f. 23 **IV. Æscþrote**

Ðeos wyrt þe man uermenacam 7 oðrum naman æscþrote 15 nemneð bið cenned gehwær on smeþum landum 7 on wætum.

1. Wiþ wunda 7 wið deadspringas 7 wið cyrnlu genim þære ylcan wyrte wyrtwalan 7 gewrið abútan ðone swyran, þonne fremað hit healice.

2. Eft wið cyrnlu genim ða sylfan wyrte uermenacam, gecnuca 20 hy 7 lege ðærto, heo hælð wundorlice.

3. Wiþ ða þe habbað ætstandene ædran swa þæt þæt blod ne mæg hys gecyndelican ryne habban 7 heora þigne gehealdan ne magon nim þære ylcan wyrte seaw 7 syle drincan, 7 syððan genim win 7 hunig 7 wæter, mencg tosomne 7 hyt sona hælð þa untrum- 25 nysse.

4. Wið lifre sar genim on middesumeres dæg þa ylcan wyrte 7 gegnid to duste, nim þonne fif cuculeras fulle ðæs dustes 7 þry scenceas godes wines, mencg tosomne, syle drincan, hyt fremað miclum, eac swa same manegum oðrum untrumnyssum.

MS V

2 nihstig] nistig B.   3 wyrte] wyrt B.   6 þæt²] *from* B 77/2a, ð V 'gode'] bote B.   9 eall] 'eal' B   ðonne] *om.* B.   11 wyrt] *om.* B. 12 Nædre] *om.* B.   13 *title*: beowurt B.   14 æscþrote] -þrotu B. 15 cenned] acænned B.   18 fremað] fremat B.

MS O

7 crafti3e men] crafti3e men crafti3e men (*last two words exp.*).   9 buton] botu buton (botu *underl.*).   12 uerm'e'nacam] *second* e *interl. above exp.* a.

6. (Wys mannes midhrif ace) Gif mannes midhríf ace nim fifleafwan seaw, meng to wine 7 drincan þanne þreo fulle fulle þry morȝenes 7 on niht nihtiȝ.

7. Wið næddran slite ním fifleafwan wyrt, gnid on wine 7 drican swiðe, þanne cimeð him þæt to bote. /   5

8. (Ad exules) Gif man forbæned sy níme fifleafan wyrt, bere on hím; f. 27 þane cweþað craftiȝe men þæt hit to gode cume.

9. (Ad crancram) Gif þu wille cancer ablendan ním þeos wyrt, seod on wine 7 on ealdes berches risele buton sealte, meg eal tosomne, wyrc to cliðam, leȝe þanne on þa wunda; þana hæled heo sona.   10

IV. Vermenaca ascþrota   f. 42/1

þeos wyrt þæt man uermˈeˊnacam 7 Engle ascþrotu nemneð.

1. (Wyd wunda 7 deadspringas 7 curnles) Wið wunda 7 wið dead-springas 7 wið cyrnlu ním þissa wyrte wales 7 ȝewrið abutan þane swuran; þanne fremað hit healíce.   15

2. (Wyd curnles) Eft wid crunle cnuca þa wyrt 7 leȝe þarto; heo haleð wunderlice.

3. —

4. (Wyd lifersor) Wið líuersar ním on middes sumere mæssedæȝ þa wyrt 7 gníd to duste, ním þanne fif cuculeres fulle ðæs dustes 7 þru 20 scencas godes wínes, meg tosomne, syle dríncan, hít fremeð 7 eac swa to maneȝum oðrum untrumnesse.

MS Vo

6. Ad anguenae remedium ad synancis. Quinquefolii sucus quiatis tribus potui datur, miraberis mire.

7. Ad morsum serpentis. Quinquefolium contrita et sucus expressus cum vino potui datus remediat mirifice.

8. Ad combustum. Herbam quinquefolium portatam prodesse plures auctores affirmant.

9. Ad cancrum excaecandum. Quinquefolium cum vino et cum adipe suilla vetere sine sale pisata de ligno in ligno, vino sane veteri aspargis et sic imponis, [rem] unicam experieris.

[Leges eam mense Augusto.]

IV. Herba hierabotana   f. 26(!)

Nascitur ubique in aquosis et planis locis.

1. Ad ulcera et parotidas. Herbae verminacae radix in collo ligata mirifice sanat.

2. Ad strumas et parotidas. Herba verminacia tunsa et imposita mirifice sanat.

3. Ad eos qui induratas venas habent et cibos non recipiunt. Herbae f. 27 verminacae sucus datur bibere, sed coctum, postea miscetur cum vino, melle et aqua, statim sanat.

4. Ad eparis dolorem. Herba verminaca solistitio lecta, in pulverem red-acta, robusto dabis cocliaria quinque, ex vino quam optimo quiatis tribus, potui sumpta mire proficere dicitur et ceteris pro cuiusque viribus sic dabis.

5. Wiþ þa untrumnysse þe stanas weaxað on blædran genim
þære ylcan wyrte wyrtwalan 7 cnuca hy, wyll þonne on hatan
wine, syle drincan, hyt hælð þa untrumnysse wundorlicum gemete;
7 na þæt án, eac swa hwæt swa þæne migðan gelet hyt hrædlice
5 gerymð 7 forð gelædeþ.

6. Wið heafodsar genim þa ylcan wyrte 7 gebind to þam hefde
7 heo gewanað þæt sar ðæs heafdes.

Nædre /

f. 23v   7. Wið nædran s(li)te swa hwylc man swa þas wyrt uermenacam
10 mid hyre leafum 7 wyr(t)trumum on him hæfð, wið eallum nædrum
he bið trum.

Attorcoppe

8. Wiþ attorcoppan bite genim þære ylcan wyrte leaf, seoð on
wine gecnucode; gif hyt mid geswelle on forboren byð, gelege
15 þærtó, seo wund sceal sona beon geopenud, 7 syððan heo geopenud
beo, þonne gecnuca þa wyrt mid hunige 7 lege þærto oþðæt hyt
hal sy, þæt bið swiðe hrædlice.

9. Wiþ wedehundes slite genim þa ylcan wyrte uermenacam 7
hwætene corn swa gehale 7 lege to þære wunde swa oþþæt ða
20 corn þurh ðone wætan gehnehsode syn 7 swa toðundene; nim
þonne ða corn 7 gewurp to sumum henfugule; gif he hy þonne
etan nelle, ðonne nim ðu oþre corn 7 mencg to þære wyrte þam
gemete þe þu ær dydest 7 lege to ðære wunde swa oþðæt þu
ongite þæt seo frecnys óf ánumen sy 7 ut atogen.

25   10. Wiþ niwe wundela genim þa ylcan wyrte 7 cnuca mid
buteran 7 lege to þære wunde.

Nædre

MS V

2 hatan] hatum B.   4 eac] ac eac B 77v/2a   þæne] þone B
hrædlice] rædlice B.   6 hefde] heafde B.   8 Nædre] om. B.
10 on him] him mid B.   12 Attorcoppe] om. B.   17 hrædlice]
rædlice B.   18 þa ylcan wyrte] þare ylcan wyrte leaf B.   23 oþðæt]
þæt B.   24 frecnys] fræc- B.   25 genim] H begins here 1/1.
27 Nædre] om. BH.

5. (Wyd stanes on bladren) Wið stanes þæt wexaþ on bladren cnuca
þisse wyrtwalan 7 will hiȝ on hate wine, syle drícan, hit haleð þa untrumnesse; 7 na þat, ac eac þane míȝan hit hrædlíce ȝehrymð 7 forð ȝeladeð.
6. (Ad capitis dolorem) Wið heafodsore bind þa wyrt to ðan heafede 7
heo ȝewanaþ þæt sar.   5
7. (Ad morsum serpentis) Wið nardra slíte hwylc man mid ʽhymʼ
hæfd þeos wyrt mid hure leafa 7 wyrtruma, wið eallan nædran heo
byð trum.
8. (Contra morsum aranee) Wið attorcoppan bite seoð þare wyrte leaf
on wíne 7 ȝecnucode; ȝif hít mid ȝswelle on forbore byð, leȝe þarto; seo   10
wunde sceal sona beon ȝeopenod, 7 sydðe heo ȝeopenod beo, þanne
cnuca þa wyrt / mid huníȝe 7 leȝe þarto forð þæt hít hæl siȝ; þæt byð   f. 42v
swyðe hrædlice.
9. (Ad morsum rapidi canis) Wið wodehundes slíte ním þeos wyrt 7
hwætecorm swa ȝehale 7 leȝe to þare wunde swa oðþat þa corn ȝehnescode   15
sín þur þane wæten 7 swa toþundene; ním þanne ða corn 7 ȝewurp to
sume hennefuȝulum; ȝif he hiȝ þanne etan nelle, þanne ním þu oðre
corn 7 meng to þare wyrt þan ȝemete þe ðu ær dydest 7 leȝe to þare
wude swa oðþæt ðu onȝyte þæt seo frecnis of anumen síȝ 7 ut atoȝen.
10. —   20

MS Vo

5. Ad cauculos. Herbae verminacae radix contusa, ex mulso optimo
tepido dato, incredibiliter calculos pellit, non solum ipsis calculosis, sed
et quidquid esset, quod urinam impediret, celeriter reducit.
6. Ad capitis dolorem. Herbae verminacae coronam facito, in capite
impone, dolorem capitis tollit.
7. Ad serpentium morsus. Herba verminacia cum [foliis] suis [et]
radicibus, quisquis offultam incinctam secum portaverit ab omnibus
serpentibus erit tutus.
8. Ad morsum araneorum quos Graeci spalangiones vocant. Herbae
verminacae ramulos ex vino decoctos, deinde contritos quo adcaecaverit,
plagae imponis et aperit, postea crudam cum melle contritam in ulcus
mature ad sanitatem perducit, certus auctor affirmat.
9. Ad canis rabidi morsum et hidrofobiam. Herba verminacia, ad
vulnus imponito, tritici quoque [grana] integra apposita vulneribus,
donec humore mollita expleant, tumida tollito et proicito illa gallinae;
si non appetit, simili modo alia grana coicito; si sic esse coeperit, peri-   f. 28
culosum signum erit.
10. Ad vulnera recentia. Herba verminacia contrita cum butyro
vulneri imponitur.

11. Wið nædran slite genim [þære] ylcan (w)yrte twigu 7 seoð on wine 7 cnuca syþþ(a)n, gyf sé slyte blind bið 7 mid þam ge(swelle) ungeheaf`d´ud, þonne lege ðu þa w(y)rte þærto, sona hyt sceal openian; 7 syððan hyt geopenud beo, þonne nim ðu ða 5 ylcan wyrte ungesodene 7 cnuca mid hunige, lege to þære wunde oðþæt heo hal sy, þæt [is] swyþe hrædlice gyf man hy þyssum gemete þærto alegð.

V. Hennebelle /

f. 24 Ðeos wyrt þe man symphoniacam (ne)mneð 7 oðrum naman 10 belone 7 eac (su)me (me)n henne(be)lle hat(a)þ (wi)hst on be-(g)anum (l)andum (7 on) sandigum l(an)dum (7 o)n wyr(tun)um. þonne ys oð(e)r þ(is)se ylcan wyr(t)e sweart on h(iw)e 7 stiðran le(afum) 7 eac ætrigum; þonne ys seo aerre hwitr(e) 7 heo hæfð þas mægnu.

15 1. Wið earena sár genim þysse ylcan wyrte seaw 7 wyrm hit, drype on þæt eare, hyt wundorlicum gemete þæra earena sár afligð; 7 eac swa same, þeah þær wyrmas on beon, hyt hy ácwelleð.

2. Wið cneowa geswell oððe sceancena oððe swa hwær swa on lichoman geswell sy nim þa ylcan wyrte simphoniacan 7 cnuca hy, 20 lege þærto, þæt geswell heo óf animeð.

3. Wiþ toða sare genim þære ylcan wyrte wyrtwalan, seoð on strangum wine, supe hit swa wearm 7 healde on his muðe, sona hit gehælð þara toða sár.

MS V

1 þære] *from* H, þa VB   twigu] twiga H, *gl.* bowes H   7] *om.* H. 3 þa wyrte] *om.* H.   4 7] *om.* H.   6 is] *from* H, *where it is interlined,* *om.* VB   hrædlice] rædlice B.   7 alegð] leyð H (y *undotted*).   8 *title*: hennebelle B 78/13a, *om.* H.   9 symphoniacam] symfoniacam BH, *gl.* id est jusquiamum V   oðrum] on oþrum H.   11 landum[1]] lande B. 12 oðer] *om.* H   þissre] ðæe H.   13 leafum] leafu H.   18 geswell oððe] geswelle oððæ H.   19 simphoniacan] symphoniacam BH, *in* H *followed by a sign referring to* beþe þarmid, *in a later hand, in b.m.*   20 þærto] þæron (to *interl. above on*) H   animeð] hanymeð H 2/1.   21 sare] sar H. 22 supe] sup H   healde] heald H.

MS O

8 ylcan] ylcan ylican (*no expunction*).

11. (Ad morsum serpentis) Wið nadren slite seoð þisse wyrt twiʒu on wine; 7 ʒif slite blynd byð 7 mid þan ʒeswelle unʒeheafod, þanne leʒe þa wyrt þarto; sona hit seal opínien; 7 sydðan hit ʒeopened byð, þannením þa wyrt unʒesodene 7 cnuca mid huníʒe, leʒe to þara wunde oðþæt heo hal síʒ; þæt swiðe hradlice hælþ ʒif hi man þissen ʒemete þarto leʒð. 5

V. Symphoniaca   hennebelle 7 belone   f. 34/17

þeos wyrt þæt man symphoniacan 7 oþrum náma belone 7 sume men hennebelle hatað, þanne is oþer þisse ylcan wyrt sweart on hiwe 7 stiþran leaf 7 eac etriʒum; þanne is seo ærre hwittere 7 heo hafad þas mæʒenu.

1. (Ad aurium morbum) Wid earane sare ním þisse wirt seaw 7 wyrm 10 hít, drupe hyt, wunderlicen ʒemete ðæra earena sar afliʒþ; 7 eac swa same, þeah þar wirmaþ on beon, hit hi acwelleð.

2. (Ad inflationem genuum et tibiarum) Wið cneowa ʒeswel oþþer sceancena oþþer swa hwær swa on lichama bid ʒeswell heo of aním`e´ð.

3. (Ad dolorem dentium) Wið toða sare ním þara wyrte walan, seoð on 15 strange wine, sup hít swa wearm 7 healde hit on þine muðe; sona hyt ʒehaleð þara toðe sar.

MS Vo

11. Ad serpentium morsus. Herbae verminacae ramulos ex vino decoctos et contritos si caecaverit plaga cum tumore, impositi adaperiunt primum, exulcerant deinde, postea [crudi] cum melle contrita et ulceribus inserta, donec ad sanitatem, quod celeriter fit, perducant, imponuntur.

V. Herba yosciamus

Nascitur locis cultis et sablosis et hortis. Est et altera subnigro colore, f. 25(!) sordidis et venenosis foliis. His ergo candidior has vires habet.

1. Ad aurium dolorem. Herbae symfoniacae sucos tepefactos auribus instillato, aurium dolorem mire tollet; etiam si vermes habuerit, necat.

2. Ad tumorem genuorum vel tibiarum aut crurium vel si tumor fuerit. Herba symfoniaca tunsa et imposita tumorem tollit.

3. Ad dentium dolorem. Herbae symfoniacae radix cocta cum vino austero, sorbeat, teneat eam in dente qui dolet, mox sanat dentium dolorem.

4. Wið þæra gewealda gesar oððe geswell genim þæ῾re´ ylcan wyrte wyrtwalan 7 gewrið to ðam þeo, ge þæt sár ge þæt geswell þara gewalda hio of animeð.

5. Gif wifes breost sáre sien genim ðonne þære ylcan wyrte 5 seaw, wyrc to drence 7 syle hyre drincan 7 smyre ða breost þærmid, þonne byð hyre sona þe sel.

6. Wið fota sar genim þa ylcan wyrte mid hyre wyrtruman 7 cnuca tosomne, lege ofer ða fet 7 þærto gebind, hyt hælþ wundurlice 7 þæt geswell óf animð.

10 7. Wiþ lungenadle genim þære sylfan wyrte seaw, syle drincan, mid healicre wundrunge he við ῾ge´hæled.

VI. Nædrewyrt

Ðeos wyrt þe man uiperinam 7 oðrum naman nædderwyrt nemneð bið cenned on wætere 7 on æcerum, heo bið hnesceum 15 leafum 7 bitterre on byrgingce.

Nædre /

f. 24v   1. Wið næddran slit(e) genim ðas sylfan uiperinam, cnu(ca) hy, mengc mid wine, syle drincan, heo hælð wundorlice þone slyte 7 þæt attor todrifð; 7 þas wyrte ðu scealt niman on ðam monðe þe 20 man Aprelis nemneð.

VII. Beowyrt

Ðeos wyrt þe man on Leden ueneriam 7 on ure geþeode beowyrt nemneð, heo bið cenned on beganum stowum 7 on wyrtbeddum 7 on mædum; 7 þas wyrte þu scealt niman on þam (m)onðe þe man 25 Augustum nemneð.

MS V

1 ylcan] sylfan BH.   3 gewalda] gewealda BH   of animeð] fornimeð
H.   4 sien] syn BH.   5 drence] *gl.* cum croco H.   6 þe] *om.* H.
7 wyrte] wyrt-/te H.   8 tosomne] *gl.* cum polenta H   hælþ] hylpð H.
10 þære] *id.* B (æ *alt. from* a, *darker ink*).   12 Nædrewyrt . . . unbindan
(p. 52/18)] *om.* H   *title*: neddrewurt B 78v/14a.   15 bitterre] biter B.
16 Nædre] *om.* B.   21 *title*: beowurt B.   22 Leden] Læden B.
25 Augustum] Agustum B.

MS O

14 syle] se syle (se *exp.*).   18 wyrt] t *alt. from* ð.

4. —

5. (Ad morbum pectoris mulierum) Gif wiwes breost sar si ȝenim þisse wyrt / seaw, wyrc to drincan 7 sile hire drincan 7 smyre þa brost þarmid, f. 34v þanne byð hure sona hale.

6. (Ad morbum pedum) Wið fota sora nim þeos wyrt mid hure 5 wyrtrume, cnuca tosomne, leȝe ofer þa fet 7 þarto ȝebind, hit wunderlice þat ȝeswell of animð.

7. (Ad morbum pulmonis) Wið lungunadle nim þa sylfan wyrt, sile drincan; mid healicre wundrunge he byð sona ȝehæled.

VI. Viperina naddrawyrt   f. 42v/19

þeos wyrt þæt man on Ledene viperina 7 Engle nadrawyrt nemneð, 11 'heo byþ' on wæte cenned; heo byð hnescum leafun 7 bite're' on birȝinȝe.

1. (Ad morsum serpentis) Wið nadran slita þeos wyrt cnuca 7 meng wið win, syle drincan; heo / hæleð wunderlice þane slite 7 þæt attor f. 43 todrifð; 7 þeos wyrt þu s'c'ealt nime on þan monþe þæt man Aprilis 15 nemneð.

VII. De veneria id est beowyrt   f. 43/3

þeos wyrt þæt man on Ledene veneriam 7 Engle beowyrt hæteð þu scealt nime on þan monþa þæt man Augustes nemneð.

MS Vo

4. Ad inguinum dolorem. Herbae symfoniacae radix alligata in femore nimium dolorem [et tumorem] tollit.

5. Ad pectinem mulierum. Herbae symfoniacae sucum mixtum cum croco dabis potionem [et] miraberis effectum.

6. Ad pedum dolorem. Herba symfoniaca alligata pedum dolorem tollit [et tunsa omnis cum sua radice et super pedes imposita mire dolorem et tumorem aufert].

7. Ad iocineris vel pulmonum dolorem. Herbae symfoniacae sucos da bibere, summa admiratione sanabitur.

VI. Herba viperina   f. 32(!)

Nascitur iuxta flumina aut segetes, foliis mollibus, gustatu aspero.

1. Ad viperae morsum. Herba viperina cum vino potui data mirifice morsus sanat et venenum discutit. Legis eam mense Aprile.

VII. Herba acorum   f. 29(!)

Nascitur locis cultis et hortis aratis. Legis eam mense Augusto.

1. Wiþ ðæt beon ne ætfleon genim þas ylcan wyrte þe we ueneriam nemdon 7 gehoh hy to ðære hyfe, þonne beoð hy wungynde 7
næfre ne swicað ác hym gelicað. þeos wyrt byð seldon funden ne
hy man gecnawan ne mæg buton ðonne heo grewð 7 blewð.

5   2. Gif hwa ne mæge gemígan 7 se micgða ætstanden sy nime
þysse ylcan wyrte wyrtwalan 7 seoþe on wætere to þriddan dæle,
sylle drincan; þonne binnan þrym dagum he mæg þone migþan
forð asendan, hyt hælð wundorlice þa untrumnysse.

VIII. Leonfot

10   Ðeos wyrt þe man pedem leonis 7 oðrum naman leonfot nemneð,
heo bið cenned on feldon 7 on dicon 7 on hreodbeddon.

1. Gyf hwa on þære untrumnysse sy þæt he sy cis, þonne meaht
ðu hine unbindan, genim þysse wyrte þe we leonfot nemdon fif
ðyfelas butan wyrttruman, seoð ón wætere on wanwægendum
15 monan 7 ðweah hine þærmid 7 læd út of þam huse onforan nihte 7
stér hyne mid þære wyrte þe man aristolochiam nemneð, 7 þonne
f. 25 he út ga ne beseo he hyne ná onbæc; þus / ðu hine meaht of þære
untrumnysse unbindan.

IX. Clufþunge

20   Ðeos wyrt þe man sceleratam 7 oðrum naman clufþunge nemneð, heo bið cenned on fuhtum 7 on wæteregum stowum, swa
hwylc man swa þas wyrte fæstende þigð, hlihhende he ðæt lif
forlæteð.

1. Wið wundela 7 wið deadspringas genim þas ylcan wyrte 7
25 gecnuca hy mid [smeruwe] butan sealte, lege to þære wunde, ðonne

MS V

    1 ne ætfleon] æt ne fleon V, *marked for reversal.*   2 wungynde] wuni-
gende B.   5 gemígan] migan B   micgða] migþa B.   9 *title*: ꝉeones fot B
79/t.m.a.   11 hreodbeddon] reod- B.   12 meaht] miht B.   16 stér]
styr B.   17 meaht] miht B.   19 *title*: clofþung B, clufþung H 18/1(!).
20 Ðeos . . . lichaman (p. 54/5)] *om.* H.   20 clufþunge] clofþunce B.
25 smeruwe] *from* B, swmeruwe V.

MS O

    1 hoh] hoh to (to *exp.*).   2 heom] eo heom (eo *exp.*).   3 hi ꝟecwafan]
man hi ꝟecnawen cwafan (man *and* cnawen *exp.*).   12 fot] fot fot (*first word
stained and exp.*).   13 huse] hus huse (hus *stained and exp.*).   18 cluf-
þunca] cluþ clufþunca (cluþ *struck out*).   21 yt] *a signe de renvoi to* comedit
in o.m.

1. (Ne apes auolant) Wið þæt beon ne atfleon hoh hi to þare hufe; þanne beoð hi þar wuniende 7 næfre ne atfleoþ ac þar heom ȝelicað; þeos wyrt man finden ne hi ȝecwafan ne mæȝ buto þan heo grepð 7 blewð.

2. (Ad vrinam) Gif hwa ne miȝan ne maeȝen 7 se migga ætstanden si seoðe þisse wyrte walen on wætere to þriddan dæle, sille drince; bínnan 5 þrim daȝum he mæȝ þane miggan forð asenden; hit hælð wunderlice þa untrunnesse.

VIII. Pes leonis   f. 27/7
Introduction om. O.

1. (Gif man si cis) Gif man on þære untrumnysse si þæt he si cís, 10 þanne miht þu hine unbínde; ním þysse wyrt þæt man pedem leonís 7 Engle leones fot nemned fif þyfeles butan wyrtetrume, seoð on wætere on waniende monan, þreþ híne þærmíd 7 læd ut of þan huse onfore nihte 7 ster hine mid þara wyrt þa man aristologiam nemneð; 7 þanne he ut ga ne beseo he hine na onbæc; þus þu miht híne of þare untrum- 15 nasse unbíndan.

IX. Scelerata   clufþunca   f. 34v/8

þeos wyrt þæt man sceleratam 7 Engle clufþunca nemned, þe man þæt þeos wyrt fæstende þiȝð, he byð sona unhal.

1. (Ad plagam 7 wid deadspirngas) Wið wundela 7 wið deadspringas 20 cnuca þa wurt mid smerewe butan sealte, leȝe to þare wunde, yt heo 7

MS Vo

1. Ne apes examinent vel ne effugiant. Herbam veneriam in vaso apium suspensam habeto, numquam se ducent. Haec herba raro invenitur nec eam scire poteris nisi cum flosculum emiserit.

2. Ad duritiam urinae, si quis facere non potuerit et stranguiriam patitur. Herbae veneriae radicem ex aqua decoctam ad tertias dabis bibere per triduum, urinam mirifice deducet et stranguiriam sanat.

VIII. Herba leontipodium   f. 30

Nascitur campis et circa fossas et arundineta.

1. Si quis devotus defixusque fuerit, sic eum resolvis. Herbae pede- leonis frutices septem sine radicibus coquito ex aqua nimfale luna decrescente, lavato eum et te ipsum qui facis ante limen prima nocte et herbam incendis aristolociam et fumigato eum et revertere in domum et ne post vos respiciatis, resolvisti eum.

IX. Herba [scelerata]   f. 31

Nascitur locis humidis et aquosis. Si quis homo eam ieiunus gusta- verit ridendo exanimatur, est enim caustica.

1. Ad ulcera chironia. Herba scelerata tunsa cum axungia sine sale, imponis in vulnere, excomedet, et si qua fuerit sordes, expurgat, sed non

yt heo 7 feormað gyf ðær hwæt horwes on bið; ác ne geþafa þæt
heo lengc þæræt licge þonne hyt þearf sy þy læs heo þone halan
lichoman fornime, gyf þonne mid orþance þisses ðinges fandian
wille gecnuca ða wyr(te) 7 wrið hy tó þinre halan handa, sona
5 heo yt þone lichaman.

2. Wið swylas 7 wið weartan genim þa sylfan wyrte 7 gecnuca
hy mid swinenum gore, lege to þam swylum 7 to þam weartum,
binnan feagum tidum heo drifð þæt y(f)el (7) þæt worsm út
atyhð.

10 X. Clufwyrt

Ðeos wyrt þe man batracion 7 oþrum naman clufwyrt nemneð
bið cenned on sandigum landum 7 on feldum, heo bið feawum
leafum 7 þynnum.

1. Wið monoðseoce genim þas wyrte 7 gewrið mid anum
15 readum þræde onbutan þæs monnes swyran on wanwegendum
monan on þam monþe ðe man Aprelis nemneð 7 on Octobre
foreweardum, sona he bið gehæled.

f. 25v   2. Wiþ ða sweartan dolh genim þas ylcan / wyrte myd hyre
wyrtwalan 7 gecnuca hy, (m)engc éced þærto, lege to ðam dolchum,
20 sona hyt fornimð hy 7 gedeð þam oþrum lice gelice.

XI. Mugcwyrt   artemesia

Ðeos wyrt þe man artemesiam 7 oðrum naman mucgwyrt
nemneð bið cenned on s˙t˙anigum stowum 7 on sandigum; þonne

MS V

6 þa] þas B.   7 swylum] u alt. from e V.   8 feagum] feawum B
worsm] worms BH.   10 title: clofwurt B 79v/t.m.a, clufwyrt H.   11 batra-
cion] batraci.on H.   12 landum] stowum BH.   14 monoðseoce]
m˙o˙noðseocne H   7] om. H.   15 readum] readan H   wanwegendum]
-wægendum BH.   18 sweartan] gl. nigras H   hyre] id. H (between y and
r an imperfectly erased s).   19 gecnuca] gecnucuca H   dolchum] dolgum
B, dolhum H.   20 gedeð] gedeð hig B.   21 title: mugwurt B, mucgwyrt
H.   22 artemesiam] arcenesiam H   oðrum] ˙o˙þrum H   mucgwyrt]
mugwyrt B.   23 s˙t˙anigum] alt. from sandigum V   sandigum] san˙d˙igum
(between s and a an erasure of t) H.

MS O

1 þaræt] þar beo æt (beo exp.).   4 hyt] a signe de renvoi to comedit in
o.m.   7 atyhð] atyd atyhð (atyd exp.).   10 leafum] lc leafum (lc exp.).
14 ʒehæled] æ alt. from a.   18 title in a modern hand (black) in t.m. of f. 1.

feormed ȝif þar wæt horíes on byð. Ac ne þafa ðæt heo leng þaræt lícȝe
þanne hít þearf sí þi læs heo þane hælne lichame forníme. Gif þu þanne
mid orðance þises þinges fondian wille cnuca þa wyrt 7 wrið hi to
þinre hæle handa; sona heo hyt þane lichame.

    2. (Ad apostema et ad uerrucas) Wið swylas 7 wið wírtan cnuca þa wyrt 5
mid swinenum gore, leȝe to þan swilan 7 to þan weartan; bínnan feawen
tide heo drif þæt wyrms 7 þæt yuel ut atyhð.

X. Baration   clufwyrt   f. 7/15

    þeos wyrt þa ma baration 7 on Englis clufwyrt hæteð, heo byrd feawe
leafum 7 þínnum, heo wexeð on sandiȝum stowe 7 on fealdum.   10
    1. (Ad lunaticos) Wið monoþseocce men ním þa wyrt 7 ȝewryð mid
anun readum þrædum abutan þan mannes swíran on ȝewæníende mona
on þan monþa þe man Aprilis nemneð 7 on forewearde Octobre; þanne
sone byð he ȝehæled.
    2. Wið þan sweartan dolh cnuca þa wyrt mid hur wyrtwalan, meng 15
eced þarto, leȝe on þan dolȝum; sona hít forð nímð hiȝ 7 ȝedeþ hiȝ þan
oþrum lice ȝelíce.

XI. Arthemisia

    (Ne quis fatigetur in itinere) Gif man on weiȝe gon wille, ðanne f. 1/5
ȝenime he him on hande þas wirte artemesiam 7 habbe mid him; þanne 20
ne beþ he weri on ȝeíe.

MS Vo

diutius patiaris quam necesse est, ne et corpus sanum exedat. Si argumen- f. 33(!)
tum [rei] experiri volueris, tunde eam et super manum sanam impone et
alligato, statim rodet corpus.
    2. Ad strumas et furunculos. Herba scelerata tunsa, subacta cum fimo
porcino, impone strumis vel furunculis, intra paucas horas discutit omnia
malitia.

X. Herba botracion statice

    Nascitur locis sablosis et campis arenosis. Radix eius verticulo est
similis, radiculas paucas et tenuissimas habet.
    1. Ad lunaticos. Herba botracion statice si lunatico in collo ligetur lino
rubro luna decrescente cum erit signum tauri vel scorpionis parte prima, f. 34
mox sanabitur.
    2. Ad cicatrices nigras. Herba botracion tunsa cum sua radice, mixta
cum aceto imponis [his] qui habent cicatrices nigras, eximit eas et similem
corpori [reliquo] facit colorem.

XI. Herba artemisia monoclonos

    Nascitur locis cultis, sablosis et lapidosis. Ad iter faciendum. Herba f. 35
artemisia monoclonos, si quis iter faciens eam secum in manu portaverit

hwa siðfæt onginnan wille ðonne genime he him on hand þas wyrte
artemesiam 7 hæbbe mid him, ðonne ne ongyt he na mycel to
geswynce þæs siðes; 7 eac heo afligð deofulseo(c)nyssa 7 on þam
huse þe he h(y i)nne (hæ)fð heo for(byt y)fele lacnunga (7) eac heo
5 awendeð yfelra manna eagan.

1. Wiþ innoðes sár genim þas ylcan wyrte 7 gecnuca hy to
duste 7 gemengc hy wið niwe beor, syle drincan, sona heo geliðegað þæs in(no)þes sár.

2. Wiþ fota sár genim þas ylcan wyrte 7 gecnuca hy mid smeruwe,
10 lege to þam fotum, heo þæt sár ðæra fota of genimð.

XII. [Mugwurt tagantes]

1. Wið blædran sár 7 wið þæt man ne mæge gemígan genim
þyssæ wyrte seaw þe man eac mugwyrt nemneð, seo ys swaþeah
oþres cynnes, 7 gewyll hy on hatan wætere oððe on wine 7 syle
15 drincan.

2. Wið þeona sár genim þas ylcan wyrte 7 gecnuca hy mid smeruwe 7 gewæsc hy wel mid ecede, gebind syþþan to ðam sare, ðy
þriddan dæge him bið sel.

3. Wið sina sare 7 wið geswel genim þa ylcan wyrte artemesiam,
20 cnuca hy mid ele wel gewylde, lege þærto, hyt hælð wundorlice.

4. Gyf hwa mid fotadle swyþe 7 hefelice geswenced sy, þonne
f. 26 genim ðu / þysse ylcan wyrte wyrtwalan, syle etan on hunige,
7 eftsona he bið gehæled 7 aclænsod swa þæt ðu ne wenst þæt
heo mæge swa mycel mægen habban.

25   5. Gyf hwa sy mid feferum gédreht genime þonne ðysse ylcan
wyrte seaw mid ele 7 smyre hyt, sona heo þone fefer fram adeþ.

1 he] *om.* H.   2 artemesiam] arcemesiam H.   3 afligð] fligð H.
5 eagan] egan H.   10 ðæra] 'of' þæra H 19/5.   11 *title: from* B, *om.*
V, herba artemesia tagantes þæt is mucgwyrt H (*see also t.n. to* VB 56/11).
12 þæt] þæ H.   13 þyssæ] æ *alt. from* e V, þisse BH   mugwyrt] mucg- H.
14 gewyll] wyl H.   17 gewæsc] gewes BH.   19 geswel] *id.* H (w *alt.*
from e)   artemesiam] arcemesiam H.   22 on] o'n' H.   23 7 eftsona]
sona *preceded by erasure of* 7 eft H   aclænsod] geclænsod B 80/9a.   26 mid
ele] *gl.* oleo rosaceo H.

MS O
11 hi on] hi mid on (mid *exp.*).

(Contra demoniacos et contra alia quaedam) And eac heo afliȝh deoful-
seocnesse. And on þan huse se he hinne hæfð heo forbyt yfele lacnunga
7 eac heo awendeþ yfelra manna eaȝan.

   1. (Ad dolorem uiscerum) Wið innoðes sar ȝením þa wirte þe man   f. 1/1
artemesiam 7 oðrum naman mugwyrt nenneð 7 ȝecnuca hiȝ to duste 7   5
ȝemeng hi wið beor, syle drincan; sona he ȝeliðeȝaþ þas innoðes sar.

   2. —

XII. (*No separate chapter in* O)

   1. (Ad eum qui non potest mingere) Wið blædran sare 7 wið þan man   f. 1/10
ȝemiȝan ne mæȝe ȝením þa ylcan wyrt 7 ȝecnuca hi mid smeruwe 7   10
ȝewylle hi on hatan watere oþðer on wine 7 syle drincan.

   2. (Ad dolorem tibiarum) Wið þeona sore ȝením þas ylcan wyrt 7
ȝecnuca hi mid smerewe 7 wes hiȝ mid ecede, ȝebind syðþan to ðan sare,
þi þriddan dæȝe him byð sel.

   3. (Ad tumorem neruorum) Wið sina sare 7 wið ȝeswell ȝemín þa   15
ylcan wyrt artemesiam, cnuca hi mid ele wel ȝewyllede, leȝe þarto; hit
hælð wundorlice.

   4. —

   5. (Ad febrim) Gif hwa si mid feferan ȝedreht ȝením þanne ðysse wyrt
seaw mid ele 7 smire hit, sona heo þan fefer fram adeþ.   20

MS Vo

non sentiet itineris laborem. Fugat et daemonia et in domo posita prohibet
mala medicamenta; evertit oculos malorum hominum.

   1. Ad interaneorum dolorem. Herba artemisia pisata et in pulverem
redacta, cum aqua mulsa potui data intestinorum dolorem tollit.

   2. Ad pedum dolorem. Herba artemisia monoclonos tunsa cum axungia
et imposita pedum dolorem tollit.

XII. Herba artemisia tagantes

   1. Ad vesicae dolorem [et stranguiriam]. Herba artemisia tagantes,
sucus, scripula duo ex vino, febricitanti in aqua calida quiatos duo potui   f. 36
dabis.

   2. Ad coxarum dolorem. Herba artemisia, tundis eam cum axungia et
aceto, [bene] subiges et imponens alligabis, tertia die sanabitur.

   3. Ad nervorum [dolorem] vel tumorem. Herba artemisia tagantes
tunsa cum oleo bene subacta, impone, mirifice sanat.

   4. Ad pedum dolorem, si quis graviter vexabitur. Herbam artemisiam
cum melle dabis manducare; item cenato, purgabitur, ut vix credi possit
tantam virtutem eam habere.

   5. Si quis febribus vexatur. Herbae artemisiae sucum cum oleo
rosacio perungue, febres tollet (. . .).

XIII. Mugwyrt

Ðeos þridde wyrt þe we artemesiam leptefilos 7 oðrum naman mucgwyrt nemdon, heo bið cenned abuton dicum 7 on ealdum beorgum, gyf ðu hyre blosðman brytest he hæfð swæc swylce ellen.

5   1. Wið þæs magan sáre ge'nim' þas wyrte 7 cnuca hy 7 gewyll hy wel mid ámigdales ele þam gemete ðe þu clypan wyrce, do þonne on anne clænne clað 7 lege þærto, binnan fif dagum he bið hal; 7 gif þysse wyrte wyrttruma byð ahangen ofer hwylces huses duru, þonne ne mæg ænig man þam huse derian.

10   2. Wið þara sina bifunge genim þysse ylcan wyrte seaw gemencged mid ele, smyre hy ðonne þærmid, hy geswicað þære bifunge 7 hyt ealne ðone leahtor genimeð.

Witodlice þas þreo wyrta þe we arte(m)esias nemdon ys sæd þæt Diana hy f(in)dan scolde 7 heora mæ(g)en(u) 7 læcedo(m) 15 Chironi centauro s(y)ll(an) se ærest o(f) þyssum wyrtum l(acnunge) gesette 7 (he) þas wyrta o(f naman) ðære Dianan þæt is artemesia(s) [genemnede].

XIV. Doccæ /

f.26v   Ðeos wy(rt) þe man lapatium 7 oðrum naman docce nemneð 20 bið cenned on sandigum stowum 7 on ealdum myxenum.

  1. Wið cyrnlu þe on gewealde wexeð genim þas wyrte lapatium 7 cnuca hy mid ealdum rysle buton sealte swa þæt ðæs smeruwes sy twam dælum mare þonne þære wyrte, swyþe wel gemenged do hyt þonne sinetrundæl 7 befeald on caules leafe 7 berec on hatum 25 ahsum, 7 þonne hit hat sy lege ofer þa cyrnlu 7 gewrið ðærtó; þys is selest wið cyrnlu.

MS V

1 title: mugwurt leptefilios B, mucgwyrt H, in V an erasure between u and g. 2 þridde wyrt] wyrt þridde V, marked for reversal   artemesiam] arcemesiam H   leptefilos] -filios B, lepitefilos H.   3 mucgwyrt] mug- B   nemdon] nemneð BH.   4 blosðman] blosman B   swæc] gl. smac H.   8 hwylces] swylces H 20/7.   11 gemencged] gemæŋgc H.   13 artemesias] arcemesias H.   14 heora] hyre H.   15 lacnunge] læcnunge H.   17 genemnede] emended from genemned VBH.   18 title: docke B 80v/16a, om. H. 21 þe on gewealde] gl. inguinem H   wexeð] weaxað H.   22 rysle] smeruwe H.   24 sinetrundæl] syntrændel B, sinetrum del H   caules] cawles H   berec] beræc H.   25 ahsum] axsum B (xsum expunged, m also underlined).   26 selest] id. H (second e alt. from o).

XIII, XIV *om.* O.

MS Vo

XIII. Artemisia leptafillos

Nascitur circa fossas et aggeres. Flosculum eius si contriveris, samsuci odorem habet.

1. Ad stomachi dolorem. Herba artemisia cum oleo amigdalino tunsa, f. 37 bene subacta, more malagmatis impones panno mundo et imponis, quinto die sanabit; et si fuerit eius artemisiae radix super limen aedificii suspensa, domui nemo nocebit.

2. Ad nervorum tremorem. Herbae artemisiae sucum cum oleo rosacio mixto perungues eo desinentes tremuli et omne vitium tollet.

Nam has tres artemisias Diana dicitur invenisse et virtutes earum et medicamina Cironi centauro tradidit, qui primus de his herbis medicinam instituit. Has autem herbas ex nomine Dianae, hoc est artemisia nuncupavit.

XIV. Herba lapatium

Nascitur locis sablosis et aggeribus et pratis.   f. 38

1. Ad paniculam quae in inguine nascitur. Herba lapatium, contundes eam cum axungia [vetere sine sale], ut duplo sit quam herba, et bene mixtum facies turundulam et involvis in folium caulis et mittis eam herbam sub cinerem calidum, et cum caluerit, tunc imponis super paniculam et ligabis. Hoc eximium remedium est (. . .).

XV. Dracentse

Ðeos wyrt þe man dracontea 7 oðrum naman dracentse nemneð
ys sæd þæt heo of dracan blode acenned beon sceolde; he'o' bið
cenned on ufeweardum muntum þær bærwas beoð, swyþost on
5 haligum stowum 7 on þam lande þe man Apulia nemneð; heo
on stanigum lande wyxð, heo ys hnesce on æthrine 7 weredre
on byrincge 7 on swæce swylce grene cystel, 7 se wyrtruma
neoðeweard swylce dracan heafod.

Nædre

10   1. Wið ealra nædrena slite genim þysse wyrte dracontea wyrttruman, cnuca mid wine 7 wyrm hyt, syle [drincan], eall þæt
áttor hyt toféreð.

   2. Wið bánbry'c'e genim þysse ylcan wyrte wyrtruman 7
cnuca mid smerwe þam gelice þe ðu clyþan wyrce, ðonne átyhð
15 hyt of þam lichoman þa tobrocenan bán; ðas wyrte þu scealt
niman on þam monðe þe man Iulium nemneð. /

f. 27   XVI. Hreafnes leac

Ðeos wyrt ðe man satyrion 7 oðrum naman hræfnes leac nemneð, heo bið cenned on hean dunum 7 on heardum stowum 7
20 swa some on mædum 7 on beganum landun 7 on sandigum.

   1. Wið earfoðlice wundela genim þysse wyrte wyrtruman þe
we satyrion nemdon 7 eac sume men priapisci hatað 7 cnuca
tosomne, hyt þa wunda aclænsað 7 ða dolh gelycð.

MS V

1 *title*: dragance B, dracen't'se H.   2 oðrum] 'o'þrum H 21/2.
4 bærwas] bearwas BH.   5 heo] he H.   6 wyxð] wixst B.
7 byrincge] biriginge B, byrigincge H   cystel] cysten H.   8 neoðeweard]
nyðe- B   dracan] dra'ca'n H.   9 Nædre] *om.* BH, B 81/7a *has*
title dragance.   10 nædrena] nædran H   dracontea] dracontean BH.
11 drincan] *from* B, drinc/can V, drican H.   13 bánbry'c'e] c *interl. above*
exp. n V   wyrtruman] *gl.* radix H   7] *om.* H.   15 hyt] *om.* H.
16 niman] 'ni'man H   nemneð] 'nem'neþ H.   17 *title*: refneslec B,
hræfnes leac H.   18 hræfnes] ræfnes B.   19 on hean] 7 h'e'an H.
20 landun] landum BH.   21 earfoðlice] 'ear'foðlice H   wyrte] wyrtan B.
23 ða dolh] *gl.* cicatrices H.

XV. *Only the end of this chapter is in* O.

2. ðu wyrt þu (. . .) on þan moþa þe `man´ (. . .).

f. 14/1

XVI. Saturion   hrefnes leac

f. 34v/23

þeos wyrt þæt man satirion 7 oþrum nama hrefnes leac nemneþ.

1. (Wyd earforðlice wundele) Wið earfoðlice wundela ním þisse wyrt 5 wyrtrumen þæt we saturion nemdon 7 eac sume men priaprisci hataþ 7 cnuca tosomne; hyt þa wunda afermaþ 7 clansað 7 þa dolh ӡelícð.

MS Vo

XV. Herba dracontea

De draconis sanguine fertur nata esse dracontea. Nascitur in montibus f. 39 [summis, ubi] sunt luci, maxime locis sanctis, terra Apulia super saxis, tactu molli, gustu dulci, tamquam castanea (viridis) saporem habens, radix eius ima caput draconis habens.

1. Ad omnium aspidum morsus. Herbae draconteae radix ex vino trita, tepefactam dabis potionem, venena discutit.

2. Ad ossa fracta in homine. Herbae draconteae radix cum axungia pisata, factum quasi malagma, mox ossa fracta de corpore educit et lapides extrahit. Legis eam mense Iulio.

XVI. Herba satyrion

f. 40

Nascitur in montibus, locis solidis et pratis et maritimis.

1. Ad vulnera difficilia vel cicatrices. Herbae priapisci radices tundis et imponis, expurgat et cicatricem curat.

2. Wiþ eagena sár þæt is þonne þæt hwa tornige sy genim þysse ylcan wyrte seaw 7 smyre ða eagan þærmid, butan y'l'dincge hyt of genimð þæt sár.

XVII. Feldwyrt

5 Ðeos wyrt þe man gentianam 7 oðrum naman feldwyrt nemneþ, heo bið cenned on dunum 7 heo framað to eallum drenceom, heo bið hnesce on æthrine 7 bittere on byrgingce.

Nædre

1. Wið nædran slite genim þysse ylcan wyrte gentianam wyrt-

f. 27v truman 7 gedrige hine, cnuca / ðonne to duste anre tremese

11 gewihte, syle drincan on wine þry scenceas, hit fremað miclum.

XVIII. Sl(it)e   herba orbicul(aris)

Ðeos wyrt ðe man orbicularis 7 oþrum naman slíte nemneð, heo bið cenned on beganum stowum 7 on dunlandum.

15   1. Wiþ þæt ðæt mannes fex fealle genim þas ylcan wyrte 7 do on þa næsþyrlu.

2. Wið innoþes styrunga genim þas ylcan wyrte, wyrc to salfe, lege to ðæs innoðes sare; eac heo wið heortece well fremað.

3. Wið miltan sare genim þysse ylcan wyrte seaw anne scenc

20 7 fif sticcan fulle ecedes, syle drincan ix dagas, þu wundrasð ðære gefremmincge, genim eac ðære ylcan wyrte wyrtruman 7 áhoh abutan þæs mannes swyran swa þæt he hangie forne gean ða miltan, hrædlice he bið gehæled; 7 swa hwylc man þysse wyrte seaw þigeð, wu(n)d(orlic)re hrædnysse he ongi(t þ)æs innoðe(s)

25 liðunge; þas wyrte (man mæg nim)an on ælcne sæl.

MS V

1 tornige] toran eage (*first a alt. from* n) B   genim] nim H.   2 wyrte seaw] wyrt seaw 7 hunig H   y'l'dincge] yldin'c'ge H.   4 *title*: feld-wurt B, feldwyrt H 22/1.   6 framað] fremað B 81v/1a   drenceom] dryncum B.   7 bittere] biter B   byrgingce] birigingce H.   8 Nædre] *om.* BH.   10 hine] hig B.   11 gewihte] gewæge H.   12 *title*: slite BH.   15 ðæt] þe B.   16 on] 'on' H   næsþyrlu] nos- B.   17 salfe] sealfe BH.   20 ix] nigon B, syx (*alt. from* ix) H   wundrasð] wundrast B.   21 gefremmincge] -icge H.   22 abutan] buton B   swyran] sweoran H   he] heo (o *added later*) H   gean] 'ge'an H.   23 hrædlice] rædlice B   he bið] hit bið H.   24 wundorlicre] wundorlice B   hrædnysse] ræd- B.

MS O

1 earane] *this word made out of two mutilated words in MS.*   2 toreneȝe sí] *above these words, in a different hand,* to toreniȝen.   18 scenc] scea scenc (scea *exp.*).   20 he hangian] he he hangian (*second* he *exp.*).

2. (Wyd ea`ʒ´ne sor 7 earane) Wið eaʒene sare, þæt is þanne ʒif / hwa   f. 36
toreneʒe sí, ním þisse wirte seaw 7 smere þa eaʒene þarmid, buten
yldinʒe hit of ʒenímð þæt sar.

XVII. (. . .)   f. 19/10

þeos wyr(t) þe man (ʒenti)anam 7 sume men feldwyrt hatad, heo 5
fremeþ to eallum drencum.

1. Wið naddran slite nim þisse wyrt wutrume (7) ʒedriʒe híne, cnucan
þanne to duste anre trumesan ʒewihte, sile drincan on wíne þ(ry) scencas
fulle, hit fremes micel.

XVIII. De orbiculari   f. 24v/14

þeos wyrt þæt man orbicularis 7 oþrum naman slite nemneþ.   11

1. (Ad capillos si cadunt) Wið þæt manes fex fealle ním þeos wyrt, do
on þa nosþurlu.

2. (Contra fluxum uentris et dolorem cordis) Wið innoþes stirunga
ním þeos wyrt, wyrc to sealue, leʒe to þan innoþes sare; heo eac wið 15
heorte ece wel fremeð.

3. (Ad morbum splenis) Wið milte sare ním þisse wyrte seaw anne
scenc 7 fif sticcan fullu ecedes, syle drincan ix dæʒes; þu wundrast þære
fremunʒa. Ahoh eac þare wurte wurtume abutan þas man/nes swuran   f. 25
þa þæt he hangian aforne ʒean þa miltan, hrælice he byð ʒehæled; 7 swa 20
hwlc man swa þisse wyrte ðiʒþ, wundorlice hradnysse he onʒit þæs innoþes
liþunge; þeos wyrt man mæʒ niman o alce tíma.

MS Vo

2. Ad lippitudines oculorum. (Herbae priapisci suco oculos inunguis
et lippitudines) et dolores tollit sine mora.

XVII. Herba gentiana   f. 41

Nascitur Gemellis montibus. Haec herba facit ad omnia antidota, tactu
molli, gusto amaro, [scapo] solido.

1. Ad serpentium morsus. Herbae gentianae radicem siccam et in
pulverem redactam, pondus dragmam unam dabis in vini quiatos iii,
sumptum validissime proderit.

XVIII. Herba cyclaminos   f. 42

Nascitur locis cultis et montuosis.

1. Ad caput deplendum. Herbae orbicularis sucum quiatum unum et
acetum optimum in naribus mittitur.

2. Ad alveum concitandum. Herba orbicularis collurio facta et iniecta
catarticum est.

3. Ad splenis dolorem. Herba orbicularis, sucum quiatum unum et
aceti optimi cocliaria v, diebus continuis ix potui dato, miraberis. Item
radix eius in collo suspensa, ut contra splenem pendeat, efficaciter
medetur. Nam et ciclaminis suco quisquis anum tetigerit, mire celeriter   f. 43
alvei solutionem significat. Legis eam omni tempore.

XIX. Unfortrædde herba proserpinaca

Ðeos wyrt ðe man proserpinacam 7 oðrum naman unfortre`d´de nemneð, heo bið cenned gehwær on begánum stowum 7 on beorgum; ðas wyrte ðu scealt on sumera nimen. /

f. 28 1. Wið þæt man blod spiwe genim þysse wyrte seaw proser-
6 p(in)ace 7 b(ut)an smice ge(wyl) on swi(ðe go)dum (7) strangum wi(ne), drince (þ)onne fæstende n(igon da)gas, (bin)nan (þ)am fæce þu on(gyt)st on þam wun(d)orlic ðingc.

2. Wiþ sydan sare genim þysse ylcan wyrte seaw mid ele 7
10 smyre gelomlice, hit genimð þæt sár.

3. Wið titta sár wifa þe be(o)ð melce 7 toðundene genim ða ylcan wyrte 7 cnuca hy 7 mid buteran geliðga, lege ðonne þærto, heo todrifð wundorlice ða toðundennysse 7 þæt sár.

4. Wið eagena sare ær sunnan upgange oððe hwene ǽr heo
15 fullice gesigan onginne ga to ðære ylcan wyrte proserpinacam 7 bewrit hy abutan mid anum gyldenan hringe 7 cweð þæt þu hy to eagena læcedome niman wylle; 7 æfter ðrim dagum gá eft þærtó ær sunnan úpgange 7 genim hy 7 hoh onbutan þæs mannes swyran, heo fremað wel.

20 5. Wið earena sár genim þysse ylcan wyrte seaw gewlæht, drype on þæt eare, wundorlice hit þæt sar tófereð; 7 eac we sylfe efenlice 7 glæwlice onfunden habbað [þæt hit fremað] 7 eac witodlice utene þæra earena sar gehælð.

6. Wið utsihte genim þysse ylcan wyrte leafa seaw 7 wyll on
25 wætere, syle drincan þam gemete þe ðe þince, he bið hal geworden.

MS V

1 *title*: unfortredde B 82/t.m. a, H = B.   3 gehwær] gehwær 7 H
4 wyrte] wyrt B   nimen] niman B, niman H 23/1.   5 man] þe man B
wyrte] ilcan wyrte B.   6 on] on `on´ H   7 strangum] strangum H.
12 7 mid] mid H   geliðga] geliðega (a *alt. from* e) B.   16 hy²]
alt. from ni, *followed by erasure* V.   17 to eagena læcedome niman wylle]
in V *these words in b.m. referred to by a signe de renvoi in text*   7] *om.* H.
11 úpgange] gancge H.   20 gewlæht] gewleht BH.   22 glæwlice]
gleawlice B   þæt hit fremað] *from* B, *om.* V.

MS O

9 hít] hin hít (hin *exp.*).   16 eft] est eft (est *exp.*).   21 hael] he b ȝe
hael (he b ȝe *exp.*).

XIX. Proserpina   fortredde   f. 27/17

þeos wyrt þat man proserpinam 7 Engle fortredde nemned þu scelt on
sumere níme.

1. (Si homo sanguinem per os nimis conspuit) Gif man blod spiwe
ním þisse wyrt seaw 7 bute smice wyll on swiþe gode wine 7 strange; 5
drinca þanne fastínde ix dæзes; bínnan þan fæce þu onзyst on ðam
wunderlice þíngc.

2. (Ad dolorem lateris) Wið sidan sora ním þisse wyrte seaw mid ele 7
smíre зelomlice; hít benímþ þæt sar.

3. (Ad mammas mulierum) Wið tytta sare wiwa þe beoþ mycele 7 10
toðundene cnuca þeos wyrt 7 mid bu/tera зeliðeзe, leзe þanne þarto, f. 27v
heo todrifð wunderlice þa toþundnysse 7 þæt sær.

4. Wið eæзena sore ær sunna upgange oððe heo fullice síзan ongínne,
ga to þara wyrt proserpinam 7 bewyrt hi abutan mid an gildene hrínge
7 cweþ þæt þu wylle hi nímen to eaзene læcedome; 7 æfter þrim dæзen 15
ga eft þarto ær sunne upgange 7 ním hi 7 hoh hi abutan þis mannes swuran;
heo fremeð wel.

5. Wid earena sor ním þisse wyrte seaþ зewleht, drupe on þæt eare,
wunderlice hit þæt sor tofereþ, 7 þis we silfe gleawlice yfunden habbeð.

6. Wið utsihte nim þisse wyrte leaf seaw 7 wil on wætere, sile drince 20
þan зemete þe þince; he byð hael зeworden.

MS Vo

XIX. Herba poligonus

Nascitur ubique locis cultis et aggeribus. Legis eam aestivo tempore.

1. Ad eos qui sanguinem reiciunt. Herbae proserpinacae sucum cum
vino optimo austero potui sine fumo tepefactum ieiunus bibat per dies
ix, miram rem experieris.

2. Ad lateris dolorem. Herbae (proserpinacae sucus cum oleo) rosaceo f. 44
saepius (perunguendus est, dolorem tollit).

3. Ad mammillarum mulierum dolorem [quae lac] habent et tument.
Herba proserpinaca tunsa, cum butyro subacta et imposita, mire discutit
dolorem et tumorem tollit.

4. Ad oculorum vitia vel dolores. Herba proserpina, vadis ad herbam
ante solis ortum vel occasum et circumscribis eam cum anulo aureo et
dicis tollere te eam ad remedium oculorum; vadis ibi postero die ante
solis ortum, sublatam circumdabis collo, proficiet diligenter.

5. Ad aurium dolorem. Herbae proserpinacae sucus tepefactus et
auribus instillatus [dolorem] mirifice discutit, etiam ipsi experti sumus.
Potenter proficit, ut et ulcera quoque aurium sanet.

6. (Ad disentericos. Herbae proserpinacae sucos) foliorum, cum aqua
calida potui dabis quantum tibi placet, sanus efficitur.

XX. Smerowyrt herba aristolochia

Ðeos wyrt þe man aristolochiam 7 oðrum naman smerowyrt nemneð, heo bið ce`n´ned on dunlandum 7 on fæstum stowum.

1. Wið attres strenðe genim þas wyrte aristolochiam 7 cnuca, 5 syle drincan on wine, heo oferswið ealle strenðe þæs attres.

2. Wiþ þa stiþustan feferas genim ðas sylfan wyrte 7 gedrige hy, smoca þonne þærmid, heo afligð nalæs þone fefer, eac swylce / f. 28v deofulseocnyssa.

3. Wið næsðyrla sare genim þysse ylcan wyrte wyrtruman 7 do 10 (on) þa næsðyrlu, hr(ædl)ice hyt hi áfeormeð 7 to (h)æle gelædeð. Wito(d)lice ne magon læceas naht mycel hæla(n b)utan þisse wyrte.

4. Wið þæt hwa mid cyle gewæht sy genim þ(a)s ylcan wyrte 7 ele 7 swinen smero, dó tósomne, þonne hæfð hit ða st(ren)gðe hyne to gewyrmenne.

15 Nædran

5. Wið nædran slite genim þysse ylcan wyrte wyrttruman tyn penega gewæge 7 healfne sester wines, gewesc tosomne, syle drincan gelomlice, þonne tofereð hit þæt attor.

6. Gyf hwylc cyld ahwæned sy þonne genim þu þas ylcan wyrte 20 7 smoca hit mid, þonne gedest ðu hit ðe glædre.

7. Wið þæt wærhbræde hwam on nosa wexe genim þa ylcan wyrte 7 cypressum 7 dracentsan 7 hunig, cnuca tosomne, lege þærto, ðonne bið hit sona gebet.

MS V

1 *title*: smeorewurt B, smerowyrt H. 2 aristolochiam] -lichiam H. 3 on²] `on´ H 24/1. 4 strenðe] strengðe B 82v/1a, stræroðe H aristo-lochiam] arista- H. 5 oferswið ealle] `o´fer`s´wið eale H strenðe] strengþe B, strængðe H. 6 ðas sylfan] þæsylfan H. gedrige] gedrig B. 6–7 7 gedrige hy, smoca] `7 gedrige hy´ 7 mængc hy, smoca hy H. 7 afligð] afli`g´ð H nalæs] nælæs B, nalas H. 10 næsðyrlu] nosþyrla B áfeormeð] afeormað BH. 11 hælan] *id.* H (æ *imperfectly alt. from* a). 13 swinen] swynes H. 15 Nædran] *om.* BH, B *has title* karsc. 16 tyn] ten B. 17 gewesc] gewes BH. 19 þas ylcan] ða sylfan H. 20 mid] *om.* B ðe] *id.* H (ð *alt. from* g). 21 wærhbræde] wearh- BH nosa] nosan B, nosa`n´ H. 22 dracentsan] *id.* B (*second* a *alt. from* e). 23 ðonne bið] *om.* H.

MS O

8 strenȝþe] þ *alt. from* d, *or from incomplete* ð.

XX. De astrologya   f. 1/20

þes wyrt byð cenned on dunlandun 7 on faste stowun.   f. 1v/3
    1. (Contra uenenum) Ið attres strenȝe ȝením þa wyrt þe man aristo- f. 1/20
liam 7 oþru nama smeriewyrt nemneð, ním þas wyrt 7 cnuca hi 7 sile
drencan on wine; heo oferswið ealle strenȝ`þ´e þæs attres.   5
    2, 3. —
    4. (Contra f(rigus)) Wið þæt ȝif hwa mid cyle ȝeweht si nime þas ylcan
wirt 7 ele 7 swynen smere, do tosomne; þanne hæfð (. . .) strenȝþe hyne
to ȝewurmenne.
    5, 6. —   10
    7. Wið (. . .) / hwam on nosa wexe ȝením þa ylcan wirte 7 cipressum 7 f. 1v
dracentsan 7 huniȝ, cnuca tosomna, leȝe þarto; þanne byð hit sona hal.

MS Vo

XX. Herba aristolacia rotunda

Nascitur locis montuosis et lapidosis et cultis.
    1. Ad vim veneni. Herba aristolacia trita vel pisata, cum mero potui f. 45
data [vim veneni vincit].
    2. Ad febres acerrimas. Herba aristolacia sicca, suffumigabis, tunc
hilariorem facies; fugat et daemonia.
    3. Ad fistulas. Herbae aristolaciae radix purgata et factum medica-
mentum [expurgat et ad sanitatem perducit]. Medici quoque sine ea
nihil faciunt.
    4. Ad frigore exustos. Herba aristolacia ex oleo cocta calefactoriam
vim habet, et cum axungia porcina.
    5. Contra serpentis morsum et hominum. Herbae aristolaciae radicem
pondus denarii unius, vinum eminam, saepius bibitur, discutit venenum.
    6. Si infans contristatus fuerit. Herba aristolacia, suffumigabis, tunc
hilariorem facis infantem.
    7. Ad cancrinomata quae in naribus nascuntur. Herba aristolacia cum
cypero et draconteae semen cum melle impositum emendat.

XXI. Cærse   herba narstucium

1. Wið þæt mannes fex fealle genim þære wyrte seaw þe man nasturcium 7 oðrum naman cærse nemneð, do on þa nosa, þæt fex s`c´eal wexen.

5   Ðeos wyrt ne bið sáwen ac heo of hyre sylfre cenned bið on wyllon 7 on brocen, eac hit awriten ys þæt heo on sumum landon wið wagas weaxen wylle.

2. Wið heafodsár, þæt ys wið scurf 7 wið gicðan, genim þysse

f. 29 ylcan wyrte sǽd 7 gose smeru, cnuca tosomne, / hit þa (h)witnesse
10 þ(æs s)curfes of ðam hea(f)de atyh(ð).

3. Wið lices sarnysse ge(nim) þas y(lcan) wyr(t)e nasturcium 7 polleian, seoð on w(æte)re, syle drincan, þonne gebetst ðu þæ(s l)ichoman sarnysse 7 þæt yfel tofærð.

4. Wið swylas genim þas ylcan wyrte 7 cnuca hy mid ele, lege
15 ofer þa swylas, [nim] ðonne þære ylcan wyrte leaf 7 lege þærtó.

5. Wið weartan genim þas ylcan wyrte 7 gyst, cnuca tosomne, lege þærto, hy beoð sona fornumene.

XXII. Greate wyrt   hieribulbum

Ðeos wyrt þe man hieribulbum 7 oðrum naman greate wyrt
20 nemneþ, heo biþ cenned abutan heogan 7 on fulum stowum.

1. Wið liþa sare genim þysse ylcan wyrte þe we hieribulbum nemdun syx yntsan 7 gǽtenes smeruwes ðam `be´ gelicon 7 of cypresso þam treowcynne anes pundes gewihte eles 7 twegea yntsa, cnuca tosomne wel gemeng`c´ed, hit genimð þæt sar ge
25 þæs innoðes ge þæra liða.

MS V

1 title: karse B, cærse H.   2 þæt] þæt þe H.   3 cærse] cerse B.
4 wexen] weaxan B, wexan H.   5 heo] om. H. 25/1   bið] om. H.
6 brocen] brocon BH   eac] ac H   landon] lande H.   7 weaxen]
wexan H   wylle] id. H (alt. from wyllað).   9 sǽd] sece H.   10 þæs
scurfes] þæscurfes H   heafde] he`a´fde H.       12 drincan] dri`n´can H
þonne gebetst ðu] þone gebetstu H.   13 tofærð] tofereð H.   15 nim]
from B 83/10a, nin V   þære] æ alt. from a V.   18 title: greatwurt B,
greate wyrt H.   20 heogan] hegon BH.   21 hieribulbum] hierbulbum H.
22 syx yntsan] i libra H (added twice to expunged syx ensan).   23 cypresso]
cypressa H   eles] 7 eles H.

XXI. De narsturcio   f. 24/1

1. (Ad capillos si fluunt et cadunt) Gif manes feax fealle ním þisse wirte seaw þe man narsturcium 7 oðrum naman cærse nemned; do on þa nosa, þat feax sceal weaxan.

þeos wyrt wexaþ on wylle 7 on wætere 7 eac on landum 7 by waȝas 7   5 by stanes.

2. (Ad scabiem) Wið 'h´eafodsar, þæt ys scurf, 7 wið ȝicþan ním þisse wyrt sæd 7 gose smere, cnuca tosomne, hit þa hwitnysse þæs scurfes of þan heafode atyhð.

3. (Wis lices sor sare) Wid lices sare ním þa wyrt narsturtium 7   10 pollegian, seoð on wætere, sile drincan; þanne ȝebetst þu þæs licames sarnísse 7 þæt yfel tofærð.

4. (Ad apostema) Wið swylas ȝením þeos wyrt 7 cnuca hi míd ele, leȝe ofer þa swylas, nim þanne þara ylcan wyrt leaf 7 leȝe þarto.

5. (Ad dertas) Wið weartan ním þisse wyrte leaf 7 gyst, cnuca togadere,   15 leȝe þarto, hi beod son fornumene.

XXII. (. . .)   f. 19v/14

Introduction om. O.

1. Wið liþa sare nim þeos wyrt, hieribulbum hated, síx ynt(sa)n 7 gætenes smer(u)wes be þan ȝelicon 7 of cypres(s)o (. . .) treow(cy)nne   20 annes pundes ȝewi(hte) (. . .) (twe)ȝra ynsena, cnuca tosomna (. . .), hit benímð þæt sor ȝe ðæs innoþ(e)s (. . .) (þæ)ra (li)ða.

MSS Vo, Ca

XXI. Herba nasturcium   f. 46

1. Ad caput deplendum. Herba nasturcium, sucum in naribus inicis, caput deplet.

Hoc nasturcium non seritur, sed ipse nascitur ubique [circa ima parietum].

2. Ad capitis vitia vel porrigines vel furfures. Herba nasturcium, semen mixtum, cum adipe anserina tritum [albitionem furfuris] ex capite eiciet.

3. Ad cruditatem. Herbam nasturcium et puleium ex aqua decoctum bibere dato, emendabis, et discutit cruditatem.

4. Ad strumas. (Herba nasturcium), cum lomento tritum, (super strumas) imponis cum folio oleris.

5. Ad furunculos sanandos. (Herba nasturcium) cum fermento imponitur, coctum mire sanat.

XXII. Herba hierobulbus   Ca p. 477

Nascitur ubique circa saepibus, locis sordidis.

1. Ad articulorum dolorem. Herba hierobulbum uncias vi, sebum caprinum uncias vi, cyprinum oleum libram i et uncias ii in se pisatum et commixtum uteris, dolorem articulorum tollit.

2. Gif nebcorn on wifmannes nebbe wexen genim þysse sylfan wyrte wyrtruman 7 gemengc wið ele, þwea syððan þærmid, hyt afeormað of ealle þa nebcorn.

XXIII. Glofwyrt

5 Ðeos wyrt þe man apollinarem 7 oðrum naman glofwyrt nemneþ, ys sǽd þæt Apollo hy ærest findan sceolde 7 hy Esculapio f. 29v þam læce / syllan; þanon he hyre þæne naman ón ásette.

1. Wið handa sare genim þas ylcan wyrte apollinarem, cnuca hy mid ealdum smerwe butan sealte, dó þærtó anne scænc ealdes 10 wínes, 7 þæt sy gehæt butan smice, 7 þæs smerwes sy ánes pundes gewihte, cnuca tosomne þam gemete þe ðu clyþan wyrce 7 lege to þære handa.

XXIV. Mageþe

1. Wið eagena sare genime man ǽr sunnan upgange ðas wyrte 15 þe man camemelon 7 oðrum naman mageþe nemneð, 7 þonne hy man nime cweþe þæt he hy wille wið flean 7 wið eagena sare niman; nyme syððan þæt wós 7 smyrige ða eagan ðærmid.

XXV. Heortclæfre

Ðeos wyrt þe man chamedris 7 oðrum naman heortclæfre 20 nemneð, heo bið cenned on dunum 7 on fæstum landum.

1. Gyf hwa tobrysed sy genim þas wyrte þe we camedris nemdon, cnuca hy on trywenum fæte, syle drincan on wine, eac swylce to slite heo gehæleð.

MS V

1 sylfan] ilcan B, sylffan H 26/1.   4 *title*: clofwurt B, glofwyrt H. 6 nemneþ] nem/nemneð H.   7 þæne] þone B.   13 *title*: meiðe B 83v/19a, mageþe H.   14 sare] sar H.   16 hy] *om.* H   eagena] eagana H (*above the second* a *a vague* e).   17 smyrige] smyrge H.   18 *title*: heortcloure B, heortclæfre H.

MS O

10 þæs] þæ / þæs (þæ *struck out*).   14 odrum] oþer odrum (oþer *exp.*). 20 tob'r'ysed] *a signe de renvoi to* brused sy i.e. quassatus *in o.m.*   21 treowenum] tre / treowenum (tre *exp.*)   Eac] Eac to (to *exp.*).

2. Gif nebcorn on wifm(annes) nebbe (wex)an (n)ím þisse wyrte wurtruman (. . .) wið ele, (þ)wea sidðan þ(æ)rmid, (. . .) (a)feormaþ ealle þa nebcorn.

XXIII. De apollinaria   f. 1v/4

þeos wyrt þe man apollinarem 7 oþrum namam glofwyrt nemneð, ys 5 sæd þæt Apollo hi arest finden (sc)eolde 7 hi Esculapio þan læce sellan; þa he hyre þannan naman on asette.

 1. (Ad cyrragram) Wið handan sara ӡením þas ilcan wyrt, cnuca híӡ míd ealde smerewe buton sealte, do þarto anne senc ældes wínes 7 þat si ӡehæt butan smíce, 7 þæs smerewes si anes pundes ӡewhite, cnuca tosomne 10 þam ӡemete ðe þu clíðan wyrce 7 leӡe to ðare handa.

XXIV. De camemelon id est mæӡeðe   f. 10/17

 1. (Ad oculorum morbum) Wið eaӡena sare ӡením ær sunna upgange þeos wyrt þe man camemelon 7 odrum naman mæӡeðe nemneþ, 7 þanne hi man nimen cweðe þæt he hi wyle wið flean 7 eaӡena sore níme, 15 níme syððan þæt wos, smyre þa eaӡen þærmid.

XXV. De chamedris id est heortclæfe   f. 10/22

þeos wyrt þa man chamedris 7 oþrum naman heortclæfre nemneð, heo byð cenned on dune 7 on fæstum landum.

 1. (Contra corporis conquassuram) Gif hwa tob'r'ysed si níme þas 20 wyrt camedris, cnuca hi on treowenum fæte, syle drincan on wíne. Eac swylce to slíte heo ӡehæled.

MS Ca

2. Ad lentigines si in facie mulierum fuerint. Herbam hierobulbum, radicem cum lumento lupinacio commixtum mulier si faciem laverit lentiginosam, statim purgat.

XXIII. Herba apollinaris

Apollo hanc herbam fertur invenisse et Asclepio dedisse, unde nomen ei imposuit apollinaris.

 1. Ad vulnera cyronia et ad ranatum. Herbam apollinarem cum axungia vetere sine sale teris et vinum vetus sine fumo cyatum i, axungia libram simul pisabis et facies tamquam malagma et imponis.

XXIV. Herba camemelon

 1. Ad oculorum vitia vel dolorem. Herba camemelon, si quis ante p. 478 solis ortum eam herbam carpuerit, dicit albuginem vel dolorem oculorum se carpere, eamque alligatam secum gestet.

XXV. Herba camedris

Nascitur locis montuosis et solidis.

 1. Ad convulsos. Herbam camedrim contunsam de ligno in ligno et adiecto vino potui dato, etiam ruptos sanare assignat.

2. Wið nædran slite genim þas ylcan wyrte, cnuca hy swyþe smæl on duste, syle drincan on ealdum wine, þearle hyt þæt attor [todræfð].

3. Wið fotadle genim þas ylcan wyrte, syle drincan on wearmum
f. 30 wine þam / gemete þe we ʻhʹær beforan cwæ(d)on, wundorlice hyt
6 þæt sár geliþegað 7 þa hæle gegearwað; þas wyrte þu scealt niman on þam monðe þe man Augustus nemneð.

XXVI. Wulfes camb

1. Wið liferseocnysse genim þysse wyrte seaw þe man chameae-
10 leæ 7 oðrum naman wulfes camb nemneð, syle drincan on wine, 7 fefergindum mid wearmum wætere, wundurlice hyt fremað.

2. Wið attres drinc genim þas ylcan wyrte, cnuca hy to duste, syle drincan on wine, eal þæt attor tofærð.

3. Wið wæterseocnysse genim þas ylcan wyrte 7 hræfnes fot 7
15 heortclæfran 7 henep, ealra ðissa wyrta (gelice m)ycel be gewihte, cnuca (h)y to smalon duste, syle þy(c)gean on wíne geongum men (fíf) cuceleras f(ull)e 7 gingrum 7 un(t)ru(m)rum 7 wi(fum) þry cuculeras, litlum cildum áne; wundurlice he þæt wæter þurh micgðan forlæteð.

20 ## XXVII. Henep

1. Wið wundela genim þas wyrte (þ)e man chamepithys 7 oðrum n(am)an henep nemneð, cnuca 7 lege to ðære wunde; gyf þonne seo wund swyþe deop sy genim þæt wos 7 wring on ða wunda.

2. Wiþ innoðes sare genim þas ylcan wyrte, syle drincan, heo
25 þæt sár [genimð]. /

MS V

2 smæl on] smalon B, ʻsʹmalan H 27/1.   3 todræfð] *from* B 84/1a, todref V,
H = B.   4 drincan] driʻnʹcan H.   5 ʻhʹær] her BH.   7 monðe]
monʻðʹe H   Augustus] Agustus B, Aʻuʹgustus H.   8 *title*: wuluescomb
B, wulfes camb H.   9–10 chameaeleæ] ʻcʹhameaeleæ H.   10 drincan]
drican H.   11 fefergindum] *id.* B (um *alt. from* an).   14 hræfnes]
ræfnes B.   18 litlum] *id.* H (*first* l *alt. from* h)   áne] ænne BH.   18–19 he
. . . micgðan] *om.* H.   19 micgðan] migðan B.   20 *title*: nepte B,
hænep H.   21 chamepithys] chamepiþys H.   23 7] *om.* H   wunda]
id. B (a *alt. from* e), wunde H.   25 genimð] *from* B 84v/1a, genmð V.

MS O

8 seow] þe seow (þe *exp.*).   9 camb] ca camb (ca *exp., then hole in parch-
ment*).   10 wyrmc watere] watere wyrme, *marked for reversal*.   14 hrefnes]
href/fnes (*second* f *exp.*).

2. (Contra venenum sumptum) Wyð næddran slite ȝenim þas wyrt, cnuca hi to swyðe smale duste, syle drincan on ældan wyne; æl þæt attor todrewf.

3. Wið fotadle / ním þeos wyrt, syle drincan on wyrme wine þan f. 10v
ȝemete þe we her beforan cwædon; wunderlice hít sor liðeȝað 7 hælað; 5
þes wyrt þu sceal níme on Auguste monþe.

XXVI. De camee(le)a   Anglice wulfes camb   f. 10v/3

1. (Ad morbum epatis) Wið liferseocnysse ním þeos wyrt seow þe man chameelee 7 oðun nama wulfes camb nemneþ, syle drincan on wine, 7 feferȝindum manna mid wyrme watere; wunderlice hit fremað.   10

2. Wið attres dryng nim þeos wyrt, cnuca hi to·dust, sile drincan on wíne; æl þæt attor tofærð.

3. (Ad morbum epatis et contra uenenum et ydropias) Wið wæter-seocnysse nim þeos wyrt an hrefnes fot 7 hortclæfran 7 henep, ealle þisse wyrte ȝelice ; mycel be ȝewihte, cnuca hi to smale duste, syle dicȝan on 15
wíne, ȝeongum menn fif cuceleras fulle 7 untrumum 7 wifun iiii cuceleras fulle, litle cyldum anne; wundelice he þæt wæter þur míngþan forlæt.

XXVII. Camepithis   Anglice h(e)nep   f. 10v/15

1. (Ad plagam) Wið wundela nim þas wyrt ða man chamepithis 7 on Eglis henep hæteð, cnuca an leȝe to þære wunda. Gif þanne þe wunda 20
swiðe deop si ȝením þat wos 7 wring on ða wunda.

2. (Ad dolorem uiscerum) Wið innoðes sare ȝením þas ylcan wyrt, syle drincan, heo þæt sor benimð.

MS Ca

2. Ad viperae morsum. Herba camedris in pulvere mollissimo redacta, in vino veteri potui data venenum vehementer discutit.

3. Ad podagram. Herba camedris idem dabis ut supra calidam, mire paragoriam praestat. Legis eam mense Augusto.

XXVI. Herba camelea

1. Ad epaticos. Herbae cameleae sucus, potui dato cum vino, febri-citanti cum aqua calida, mire proficit.

2. Contra venenum si quis acceperit. Herbam cameleam siccatam in pulverem redactam ex vino potui datam, discutit venenum.

3. Ad ydropicos. Herbam cameleam et camedafne et camedris et camepithis aequali pondere tunsas et mollissime cribratas in potione vini mixti, iuvenibus coclearia v, item minoribus et mulieribus coclearia p. 479
iii, pueris coclear i, mirifice aquam omnem per urinam digerit.

XXVII. Herba camepytium

1. Ad vulnera. Herba camepytis contusa et imposita, si autem altum vulnus fuerit sucum eius in vulnere mittis.

2. Ad strofi dolorem, hoc est interaneorum. Herba camepitis potui data dolorem strophi tollit.

f. 30v XXVIII. Hrefnes fot

1. Wið innoð to astyrigenne genim ðas wyrte ðe Grecas chamedafne 7 Engle hræfnes fot nemnað, cnuca to smælon duste, syle
drincan on wearmum wætere, hit ðone innoð astyreð.

5 XXIX. Lyðwyrt

Ðeos wyrt þe man ostriago 7 oðrum naman lyðwyrt nemneð
bið cenned abutan byrgenne 7 on beorgum 7 on wagum þæra husa
þe wið duna standað.

1. Wiþ ealle ðingc ðe on men to sare acennede beoð genim þas
10 wyrte þe we ostriago nemdon 7 cnuca h(y), lege to ðam sare, ealle
þa þincg, swa we ær cwædon, þe on ðæs mannes lichoman to laðe
ácennede beoð, heo ðurhhæleð.

Gif ðu þas wyrte niman wylle ðu scealt clæne beon 7 eac ær
sunnan upgange þu hy scealt niman on ðam monðe þe man Iulius
15 nemneð.

XXX. Hæwenhydele /

f. 31 1. Wið muðes sare genim þas wyrte þe Grecas brittanice 7
Engle hæwenhydele nemneð, cnuca hy swa gréne 7 wring þæt wos,
syle drincan 7 healde swa on his muðe; 7 þeah man hwylcne dæl
20 þærof swelge, gelice hit fremað.

2. Eft wið muþes sare genim þa ylcan wyrte bryttanicam; gyf
ðu hy grene næbbe genim hy dryge, cnuca mid wine on huniges
þicnysse; nim ðonne þam sylfan gemete þe we ær cwædon, heo
hæfð þa sylfan gefremmincge.

MS V

1 *title*: refnes fot B, hræfnes fot H.   3 hræfnes] ræfnes B   smælon]
smalan B.   4 drincan] drican H 28/3.   5 *title*: liðwurt B, lyðwyrt H.
7 byrgenne] byrginum B, byrgenum H   on¹] abuton B.   8 duna] dunum
B.   9 Wiþ] ið B   sare] sare sy '7´ H.   11 þincg] þingc (g *alt. from* c) H
mannes] mon'n´es H   to laðe] bið 7 (7 *crowded in*) H.   12 ácennede]
acænned H.   13 ðu¹] 'þu´ H.   16 *title*: hævenhydele B 85/t.m. a,
hæwe'ne´nhydele H.   17 muðes sare] innoþes sar H   brittanice]
britanice B   18 hæwenhydele] hæwe'ne´nhydele H   nemneð] nemnað
B.   19 drincan] supan BH.   21 þa] þas H.   22 cnuca] 7 cnoca hig
B, cnuca hy H   wine] wine 7 H   23 þicnysse] -'n´ysse H.   24 gefrem-
mincge] ge'f´remuncge H.

MS O

3 hrefnes] re hrefnes (re *exp.*).   17 bryttanican] by bryttanican (by
exp.).

XXVIII. Chamedafne id est hre(f)nes fot

f. 10v/21

1. (Ad constipationem) Wið innoþ to astirȝenne ȝením þas wyrt þe Grecas chamedafne 7 Engle hrefnes fot nennað, cnuca to smale duste, syle drinca on werme wætere; hit þane innoþ astyreþ.

XXIX. De ostriago id est liþewyrt

f. 25/5
6

þeos wyrt þæt man ostriago 7 oþrum naman liþwyrt nemneð.

1. (Ad omnem corporis morbum) Wið ealle þa þing ðe on manne to sore acenned byð ním þa wyrt 7 cnuca hi, leȝe to ðan sora. Ealla þa þing þe on mannes lichame to laðe acenned byð heo þurhæleð.

Gif þu þeos wyrt nime wulle þu scealt clæne beon 7 ar sunne upgange 10 þu scealt hy nimen on þan monða þæt man Iulius nemneð.

XXX. Hæwenhudela

f. 7/26

1. (Ad morbum oris) Wið muðes sor ním þa wyrt þa Grecas bryttannica 7 Engle hæwenhudela nemneð, cnuca hiȝ þa grene, / wryng þat f. 7v wos, syle supan 7 healde swa on his muþe; 7 þeah man hylcne dæl þarof 15 swelȝe, ȝelice hít fremað.

2. Eft wyð muðes sore ním þa ylcan wyrt bryttanican; ȝif þu hiȝ grene nabbe ȝením 'hi' driȝe 7 cnuca mid wíne on huniȝes þicnesse; ním þanne þam sylfan ȝemete þe we ær cwædon; heo hæfð þe sylfan ȝefremunge.

MS Ca

XXVIII. Herba chamedafne

1. Ad alveum concitandum. Herba camedafne in pulverem redacta mollissime in aqua calida potui data alveum concitat.

XXIX. Herba hostriago

Nascitur circa monumenta aut in monumentis aut parietibus qui sunt circa montium radices.

1. Facit ad eas res quae in homine nascuntur. Herba ostriago tunsa et p. 480 imposita omnes res quae in corpore nascuntur persanat.

Hanc herbam si volueris evellere, mundus et ante solis ortum legis eam mense Iulio.

XXX. Herba brittanica

1. Ad vitia quae in ore nascuntur. Herba brittanica sumpta viridis in modum lactucae sanat et per se trita atque expressa; sucus in ore contineatur et aliquid ex ea devoretur, adaeque proficit.

2. Ad oscidinem. Herbam brittanicam si viridem non habueris, etiam arida contusa cum vino ut mellis crassitudo fiat, eodem modo sumpta eundem effectum habet.

3. Wið toþa sare 7 gyf hy wagegen genim þas ylcan wyrte,
heo of sumre wundurlicre mihte helpeð; hyre wos 7 hyre dust
ys to gehealdenne on wintre for ðam þe heo ælcon timan ne
atýweð; hyre wos þu scealt on [rammes] horne gehealdan, drige
5   eac þæt dust 7 geheald; witodlice eac hyt scearplice fremað
to ðam sylfan bryce mid wine onbyrged.

4. Wið fæstne innoð to styrigenne genim þisse ylcan wyrte
seaw, syle drincan be þære mihte þe hwa mæge þurh hit self;
butan frecnesse hit áfeormað wundurlice ðone innoð.

10   5. Wið sidan sare þæt Grecas paralisís nemnað genim þas ylcan
wyrte swa grene mid wyrttrum(um), cnuca hy, syle drinca'n' on
wine twegen scenceas oððe ðry; hyt is gelyfed þæt heo wundurlice
fremige.

XXXI. Wudulectric

15   Ðeos wyrt þe man lactucan silfaticam 7 oðrum naman wudulectric nemneð bið cenned on beganum stowum 7 on sandigum.

1. Wið eagena dymnesse ys sæd þæt se earn, þonne he up fleon
wille to þy þæt he þy [beorhtor] geseon mæg(e), þæt he wylle mid
f. 31v   þam seawe his eagan hreppan 7 wætan, 7 he / þurh þæt onfehð
20   þa mæstan beor'h'tnesse.

2. Eft wið eagena dymnysse genim þysse ylcan wyrte seaw þe
we lactucam silfaticam nemdon mid ealdon wi(n)e 7 mid hunige
gemencged, 7 þi(s s)y butan smice gesomnud; þæt bi(ð s)elust
þæt man þysse wyrte seaw s(wa w)e ǽr cwædon 7 win 7 hunig

MS V

    2 heo of] heof H   sumre] *id.* H (*alt. from* sumum).   3 gehealdenne]
healdenne B   wintre] wintra B, wintra H 29/2.   4 atýweð] ætywð B
rammes] *from* H, ramnes V, hrammes (h *alt. from* r) B   drige] 7 drigge B.
4–5 drige . . . geheald] *om.* H.   5 eac²] *om.* BH.   7 styrigenne] astirigenne
B, astyrgenne H   wyrte] wyr`t´e H.   8 self] silf BH.   9 frecnesse]
fræc- BH.   11 wyrttrumum] -truman BH   syle] `sy´le H.   12 oððe ðry]
oþþry H, *later alt. to* `o´ðþ`e´ þry.   14 *title*: wudelestric B, wudulectric *gl.*
scariole H.   15 silfaticam] siluaticam BH.   15–16 wudulectric] -lectrix
B, *gl.* scariole H.   17–18 fleon wille] wille fleon H.   18 beorhtor] *from* B,
beortur V.   22 lactucam] lactucan BH   silfaticam] siluaticam B 85v/1a,
om. H.

MS O

    1 Wyð] Wd Wyð (Wd *exp.*).

3. (Ad dolorem dentium) Wyð toða sare 7 ʒif hi waʒion ʒením þas wyrt, 'heo' hæfþ sume wundorlicre mihte helpeð. Hire dust 7 hure wos is to ʒehealdenne on wyntra forþan þe heo on ælcon tyman ne ætywð; hure wos þu scealt on rammes horne ʒehealdan. Driʒe eac þæt dust 7 ʒeheald; witodlice hit scearplice fremæð to ðan sylfe brice mid wíne 5 onʒebyrʒeð.

4. (Ad constipationem uentris) Wið fæstne innoþ to astyrʒenne min seaw þisse wyrte, syle dríncen be þare mihte þa hwa mæʒe surþ hit sylf, butan frecnesse hit afermaþ wundorlice þane ínnoð.

5. (Contra paralisin) Wið sidan sore þæt Grecas paralisím nemnað 10 þeos wyrt grene mid hire wurtruman, cnuca hiʒ, sile dríncan on wine tweʒen scences odðir ðry; hit his ʒelyfed ðæt heo wundorlice fremeð.

XXXI *om.* O.

MS Ca

3. Ad dentium dolorem [vel si laxi fuerint]. Herba brittanica mira quadam potentia succurrit; reponenda autem est in hieme suco vel pulvere eius, nam non semper apparet; sucum eiusdem herbae servabis in vaso arietino; arefacito vel pulverem eius reponito, nam ad eiusdem usus cum vino sumpta [aeque] efficaciter prodest.

4. Ad alveum concitandum. Herbae brittanicae sucus pro viribus cuiusque potui sumptus per se sine periculo purgat.

5. Ad paralysin. Herba brittanica viridis cum radicibus contusa, vini meri optimi cyati ii vel iii, potui sumpta mire [proficere creditur].

XXXI. Herba lactuca silvatica

Nascitur locis cultis et sablosis.

1. Ad caliginem oculorum. Dicitur, cum aquila altum vult volare ut p. 481 prospiciat rerum naturam, lactucae silvaticae folium evellere et de suco sibi tangere oculos et accipere maximam claritatem.

2. Herbae ergo lactucae silvaticae sucum mixtum cum vino veteri et melle acapno quod sine fumo collectum est, optimum sucum herbae,

(gem)engce tosomne 7 on a(nr)e glæ(senr)e ampullan gelo(gige,
bruce þonne h)im þearf sy; of ða(m þu healicne) læcedom ongitst.

XXXII. Garclife   agrimonia

1. Wið e‛a′gena sare genim þas wyrte þe man argimoniam 7
5 oðrum naman garclife nemneð, cnuca hy swa grene þurh hy
selfe; gyf ðu hy þonne grene næbbe genim hy drige 7 dype on
wearmum wætere swa þu eaþelicost hy brytan mæge; smyra
þonne þærmid, ofstlice heo ða tale 7 þæt sár of þam eagan adrifð.

2. Wið innoðes sare genim þysse ylcan wyrte wyrtruman þe we
10 argimoniam nemdon, syle drincan, hyt fremað wundorlice.

3. Wið cancor 7 wið wundela genim þas ylcan wyrte swa grene,
cnuca hy, lege to þam sare, gecwemlice heo þone leahtor gehælan
mæg; gyf ðonne seo wyrt drigge sy dype hy on wearmum wætere;
hyt ys gelyfed þæt heo to ðam ylcan fremige.

15 4. Wið nædran slite genim þysse ylcan wyrte [twegra trymesa
gewihte 7] twegen scenceas wines, syle drincan, wundurlice hyt
þæt attor tofereð.

5. Wið weartan genim þas ylcan wyrte, cnuca on ecede, lege
þærtó, heo genimð þa weartan.

20 6. Wið miltan sare genim þas ylcan wyrte, syle þicgean on
wine, heo þæt sar fornimð þære miltan. /

f. 32   7. (Gif) ðu hwylce þingc of ðam lichoma(n) ceorfan wylle 7 ðe
þonne þince þæt ðu ne mæge, genim þas ylcan wyrte gecnucude,
lege (þ)ærto, [heo] hyt geopenað 7 gehæleð.

25 8. Wið slege isernes oððe stenges þeos ylce wyrt gecnucud 7
to gelæd, heo wundurlice gehæleþ.

MS V
   1 glæsenre] glæsenne (*second* n *alt. from* r) H   ampullan] anpullan H.
2 bruce] broce H   þearf] þea‛r′f H.   3 *title*: gorfclif B, garclife H 30/1.
4 argimoniam] a‛c′rimoniam H.   6 selfe] silfe BH   genim] nim H
dype] drype H.   8 7] *om.* H.   9 genim] *id.* H (*preceded by erasure
of* genim).   10 argimoniam] a‛c′ri- (i *alt. from* r) H.   14 ylcan]
mi‛c′clan H.   15–16 twegra . . . 7] *from* B, *om.* V.   22 hwylce] ‛h′wyll′c′e H.
24 heo] *from* B, he (*between* h *and* e *an erased* y) V.   26 gelæd] gelegd
B 86/2a, geled H.

MS O
   3 garclife] gr garclife (gr *exp.*).   11 seo] þ seo (þ *exp.*).

XXXII. De agrimonia   f. 1v/13

   1. (Ad oculos) Wið eaჳena sare ჳením þas wyrte þa man agrimoníam 7
oðrum naman garclife nemneð, cnuca hi swa ჳre(ne) þur hi sylfe; ჳif þu
hi þanne grene nabbe ჳením hi driჳe 7 dípe on wermun watere swa ðu
eaðelicost hy brytan mæჳe; smyra þanne þarmíd, ofstlice heo þa tale 5
þæt sar of ðan e`a´ჳan adrifð.

   2. (Ad dolorem uiscerum) Wið innoþes sare ჳením þysse ylcan
wyrtruma þe we agriminiam nemde, syle drican, hyt fremad wundelice.

   3. (Ad plagam et ad cancrum) Wið cancre 7 wið wundela ჳením ðas
ylcan wírt swa grene, cnuca hi, leჳe to þan sore; ჳecwemlice heo þanne 10
leahtre ჳehalan mæჳ. Gif þan seo wyrt driჳen si dype hi on wearmun
wætere; hit ys ჳelife þæt heo to ðan ylcan fremíჳe.

   4. —

   5. (Ad dertes) Wid weartan ჳením þas ylcan wyrte, cnuca on ecede,
leჳe þarto; he benímd þa weartan.   15

   6. (Ad dolorem splenis) Wið milte sare ჳenim ðas wyrt, syle dicჳan on
wíne; heo þæt sor benímð þare miltan.

   7. (Ad vulnera clausa aperienda vel aliud aliquid) Gif ðu hwylce
(. . .) (o)f þan lic`h´aman ceorfan wílle 7 þe þanne / ðínce þæt ðu ne f. 2
mæჳe, ჳenim ðas ylcan wirt ჳecnucode, leჳe ðarto; heo hit ჳeopeneð 7 20
ჳehælð.

   8. (Item ad plagas sanandas) Wið sleჳe isernes oþþe stenges þeos
ylcan wyrte ჳecnucod 7 to ჳeled, heo wunderlice ჳehælð.

MS Ca

vinum et mel in se commisce et tere et in ampulla vitrea conde et ex eo
uteris, summam medicinam experieris.

XXXII. Herba argimonia

   1. Ad oculorum vitia vel dolorem. Herba argimonia viridis per se
trita, si arida fuerit in calida aqua intincta ut facillime teri possit, illinita
suggellationes et livores in oculis mature discutit.

   2. Ad ventris dolorem. Herbae argimoniae radicem bibere dato, mire
prodest.

   3. Ad vulnera et ulcera canceromata. Herba argimonia viridis contusa et apposita vitia sanare apta est; si autem arida fuerit aqua tepida
remissa idem proficere creditur.

   4. Ad morsum serpentis. Herbae argimoniae dragmas ii cum vini
cyatis ii potui dato, discutit venenum mirifice.

   5. Ad verrucas tollendas. Herba argimonia cum aceto imposita tollet
verrucas.

   6. Ad splenis vitia vel dolorem. Herba argimonia in cibo sumpta
splenem [consumet].

   7. Ad ea quae [secanda] sunt. Herba argimonia imposita et contrita
aperit et persanat.

   8. Ad percussum de ferro vel sude. Herba argimonia contusa et
imposita mirifice sanat.

XXXIII. Wudurofe   astularegia

1. Wið sceancena sare oððe fota genim þysse wyrte seaw þe
man astularegia 7 oðrum naman wudurofe nemneð mid amigdales
ele, smyre þær þæt sár sy, hyt bið wundorlice gehæled, 7 gyf
5 hyt geswell sy cnuca hy 7 wel geliðegode lege þærto.

2. Wið lifre sare genim þysse sylfan wyrte wyrtruman, syle
drincan on geswetton wætere, hit þæt sar wundorlice of genimð.

XXXIV. Wududocce

1. Gyf hwylc [stiðnes] on lichoman becume genim þas wyrte þe
10 man lapatium 7 oðrum naman wududocce nemneð 7 eald swynen
smeru 7 ðone cruman of ofenbacenum hlafe, cnuca tosomne þam
gemete ðe ðu clyðan wyrce, lege to ðam sare, hyt gehælð wundorlice. /

f. 32v XXXV. Eor(ð)gealla [oððe] curmelle   centauria maior

15 1. Wið liferadle genim þas wyrte þe Grecas centauria maior 7
Angle curmelle seo mare nemnað 7 eac sume men eorðgeallan
hatað, seoð on wine, syle drincan; wundorlice heo gestrangað;
7 wið miltan sare do þis sylfe.

2. Wið wunda 7 wið cancor genim þas [ilcan] wyrte, cnuca hy,
20 lege to þam sare, ne geþafað heo þæt ðæt sár furður wexe.

Ðeos sylfe wyrt centauria ys swyþe scearpnumul niwe wunda
7 wide to gehælenne swa þæt þa wunda hrædlice tógædere gað; 7
eac swa some heo gedeþ þæt flæ(sc) togædere geclifað gyf hyt
m(an) on þam wætere gesygð þe heo on bið.

MS V

1 title: wuderoua B, wudurofe H 31/1.   2 wyrte] wyrtan B.   5 geliðe-
gode] geliðe H.   6 sylfan] ilcan B.   8 title: wudedocce B, wududocce
H.   9 stiðnes] from B, stiðres (r exp.) V   lichoman] man B.
10 lapatium] lap`a´tium H.    12 lege] le`ge´ H.   12–13 wundorlice]
wurdorlice H.   14 title: centauria maior B 86v/14a, om. H   oððe] in V
the Latin nota for vel.   16 Angle] Engle B, Ængle H   curmelle] curmealle B.
19 ilcan] from B, illan V.   20 ðæt] om. H   furður] fuþur H.
22 gehælenne] gehealdenne H.

MS O

11 sume] sume / sume.

XXXIII. (. . .) (as)tula(re)gia   f. 2/5

1. (Ad infirmitatem pedum uel tibiarum) Wið sceancena sare oðer
fota ȝením þissera wyrte seaw þa man astularegia 7 oðrum nam`a´n
wuderofe nemneð mid amígdales ele, smere þar þat sor si; hit byð wundelice ȝehaled; 7 ȝif hít ȝeswelleð si cnuca hi 7 wel ȝeliðegode leȝe þarto. 5

2. (Ad dolorem epatis) Wið lifre sore ȝenim þisser wurte wirtrume,
sele drincan on ȝeswetun watere; hit þat sor wundelice of ȝenínð.

XXXIV *om.* O.

XXXV. Centaurea maior   f. 10v/25

1. (Ad dolorem epatis) Wið liferadle þeos wyrt centaurea maior 7 10
Engle curmelle seo mære nenneð 7 eac sume menn eorðȝelle hatað, seod
on wine, syle drincan; wundorlice heo ȝest`r´angad seo lifer, 7 wið miltan
sare do þis sylfe.

2. —

MS Ca

XXXIII. Herba asfodulus (*gl.* id est astula regia)

1. Ad dolorem [tibiarum] vel pedum. Herbae asfoduli sucus cum oleo
amygdalino, ungues quod dolet, mirifice sanabitur, etiam si tumores
fuerint ipsam tunsam et subactam imponis.

2. Ad eparis dolorem. Herbae asfoduli radicem discoque et ex aqua
mulsa da potui, eparis dolorem mire tollit.   p. 482

XXXIV. Herba oxilapatium

1. Si qua duritia in corpore fuerit. Herba oxilapatium [cum] axungia
vetere suilla pisata et ex pane domestico facta ut malagma imposita
mirifice sanat.

XXXV. Herba centauria maior

1a. Ad eparis dolorem. Herba centauria maior in vino decocta ac
potui data mirifice auxiliatur.

1b. Ad spleneticos. Herba centauria maior item ex vino decocta et
potui data splenem persanat.

2a. Ad ulcerosa vulnera et canceromata. Herba centauria maior
contrita imposita tumorem fieri non patitur.

2b. Ad vulnera recentia. Herba centauria efficax est ad plagas glut
tinandas, ut etiam carnes cohaerescant, quae ex aqua eius coquuntur.

XXXVI. Curmelle Feferfuge centauria minor

Ðeos wyrt þe man centauriam minorem 7 oðrum naman curmelle seo læssæ nemneð 7 eac sume men febrifugam hatað, heo
bið cenned on fæstum landum 7 on strangum; eac ys sæd þæt
5 Chyron centaurus findan sceolde þas wyrta þe we ǽr centauriam
maiorem 7 nú centauriam minorem [nemdon], ðanun hy eac
þone naman healdað centaurias. /

f. 33 1. Wið nædran slite genim þysse ylcan wyrte dust oððe hy
sylfe gecnucude, syle drincan on ealdum wine, hyt fremað
10 swyðlice.

2. Wið eagena sare genim þysse ylcan wyrte seaw, smyra ða
eagan þærmid, hyt gehælð þa þynnysse þære gesihðe; gem(e)ncg
eac hunig þærtó; hyt fremað swa some witodlice dimgendum
eagum to þy þæt seo beorh`t´nys agyfen sy.

15 3. Gyf hwa þonne on þas frecnysse befealle genim þysse ylcan
wyrte godne gripan, seoð on wine oððe on ealoð swa þæt þæs
wines sý an ambur full, læt standan þry dagas, nim þonne æghwylce dæge þonne ðearf sy healfne sester, mengc mid hunige,
drince ðonne fæstende.

20 4. Wið sina togunge genim þas ylcan wyrte, seoð on wætere to
þriddan dæle, syle drincan swa mycel swa he þonne mæge 7
þearf sy, he bið gehæled.

5. Wið attres onbyrgingce genim þas [ilcan] wyrte, cnuca on
ecede, syle drincan, sona hit þæt attor todrefð; eac þære sylfan
25 wyrte wyrtruman genim tyn penega gewihte, do on wine, syle
drincan þry scenceas.

6. Wið þæt wyrmas ymb nafolan dergen do ealswa we her
beforan cwædon; wið syna togunge þæt ys ðonne þæt ðu [genime]
þas ylcan wyrte, seoð on wætere to ðriddan dæle, heo ða wyrmas
30 út [awyrpð].

MS V

1 *title*: centauria minor B, curmelle H. 3 læssæ] læsse B, læsse H
32/3. 6 maiorem . . . centauriam] *om.* H nemdon] *from* B, nendun V.
9 ealdum] cealdan H. 10 swyðlice] `s´wiðlice H. 12 þynnysse] dymnesse
H. 14 agyfen] agyfe H. 15 frecnysse] fræc- B 87/8a, fræc- H.
16 on²] o`n´ H. 20 ylcan] ylca H. 22 he] heo H. 23 ilcan]
from B, illcan V on] o`n´ H. 24 todrefð] todræfð BH. 25 tyn] ten B.
27 her] hær H 33/5. 28 genime] *from* H, genim VB. 30 awyrpð] *from* B,
aweorð V.

XXXVI *om.* O.

MS Ca

XXXVI. Herba centauria minor

Nascuntur locis solidis et fortibus. Cyro centaurus has herbas fertur   p. 483
invenisse, unde tenent nomen centauriae.

1. Ad viperae morsum vel dolorem. Herbae centauriae minoris
[pulverem in vino dato, vel pisata in vino vetere et da, bibat, mire prodest].

2. Ad oculorum aciem deponendam. Herbae centuriae minoris sucus
oculis inunctus aciem extenuat, sanantur, adiecto etiam melle idem
proficit, caliginantibus quoque oculis ut claritas restituatur.

3. Centauriae minoris manipulos in vini congio coquito ac triduo
macerato, mox eximito, inde cotidie ad eminam mixtum melle adiecto
ieiunus bibat.

4. Ad auriginem. Herbam centauriam minorem decoque in aqua ad
tertias et ex ea dabis bibere quantum potuerit, sanabitur.

5. Ad venenum qui sumpserit. Herbam centauriam minorem ex aceto
tritam dato, bibat, mox discutit venenum; item centauriae minoris
radices pondus denarii unius in cyatis tribus vini bibatur.

6. Ad lumbricos et tineas. Herbam centauriam minorem dabis ut
supra, eiciet tineas.

XXXVII. Bete   personacia

1. Wið ealle wunda (7 wi)ð næddran slitas genim þysse wyrte seaw þe (ma)n personaciam 7 oðrum n(am)an boete ne(m)neð, syle drincan on ealdon win(e), ealle nædran slitas hyt wundurlice
5 gehæleð.

2. Wið feferas genim þysse ylcan wyrte leaf, begyrd to þam fefergendan; sona hyt wundorlice ðone fefer afligeð.

3. Wið cancor [þe] on wunde wexe genim þas wyrte, wyll on wætere, beþe þa wunde ðærmid, syððan genim þa wyrte 7 sapan 7
f. 33v smeru, cnuca mid ecede, / do þonne on cla(ð), lege to ðære wunde.

11 4. Wið innoðes sare genim þysse ylcan wyrte seawes anne scenc 7 huniges twegen, syle drincan fæstendum.

5. Wið wedehunde(s) slite genim þysse [ilcan] wyrte (wy)rtru-man, cnuca mid (greatan se)alte, le(ge to) ðam slite.

15 6. Wið niwe (wunda þ)a þe þon(e) wætan (gewy)rce(aþ gen)im þisse ylcan wyrt(e) wy(rttruman 7 hæ)gðornes leaf, ægþres e(fen)-mycel, cnuca tosomne, lege to ðam w(u)ndum.

XXXVIII. Streowberian wise   fraga

Ðeos wyrt ðe man fraga 7 oðrum naman streawbergean nemneð
20 bið cenned on dihglum stowum 7 on clænum 7 eac on dunum.

1. Wið miltan sare genim þysse ylcan wyrte seaw þe we fragan nemdon 7 hunig, syle drincan, hyt fremað wundurlice.

2. Ðysse ylcan wyrte seaw wið hunig gemengced mid pipere, hit fremað myclum gedruncen wið nyrwyt 7 wið innoðes sare.

MS V

1 *title*: bete BH.   2 wyrte] ilcan wyrte B.   3 boete] bete BH.
7 sona] *om*. H.   8 þe] *from* O, *om*. VBH   wexe] weaxað H.   9 þa²]
þas H.   10 wunde] wu'n'de H.   12 fæstendum] *id*. H (æ *alt. from* a).
13 ilcan] *from* B 87v/3a, illan V, ylca H.   15 niwe] 'ni'we H   gewyrceaþ]
wyrcað B.   18 *title*: streaberie B, streawberge H.   20 dihglum] diglum B,
diglum H 34/3.   21 ylcan] *om*. BH.   23 Ðysse] isse B   pipere]
pipopore B.   24 hit] *om*. BH.

MS O

3 persinacam] *in o.m.* personaciam.

XXXVII. Personaciam bete　　　　　　　　　　　　　　　　f. 27v/14

1. Wið ealle wunde 7 naddran slite nim þisse wyrte seaw þæt man persinacam 7 Engle bete nemneð, sile drincan on ealdon wyne; ealle naddre slite hit wundorlice ȝehaled.

2. Wið feferes nim þisse wyrte leaf, bigyrd to þan feferȝendan, sone 5 hít wunderlice þane fefer afliȝð.

3. Wið cancor þe on wunde wexe ním þas wyrt 7 sapan 7 smeru, cnuca mid ecede, do þane on cla� 7 leȝe to þare wunda.

4. Wid innoþes sor nim þisse wyrte seawes anne scenc 7 huníes tweȝen, sele drínca fæstende.　　　　　　　　　　　　　　　　10

5. Wid wodehundes slite ním þisse wyrt wurtruman, cnuca mid greaton sealte, leȝe to þan slite.

6. Wið níue wunda ním þisse wyrte wurtrume 7 hæȝþornes leaf, æȝþres / efenmicel, cnuca tosomne, leȝe to ðan wunda.　　　　f. 28

XXXVIII. (. . .)　　　　　　　　　　　　　　　　　　　　f. 17/1

þeos wyr(t) þe man fragra 7 Engle streowberie nemned.　　16

1. (Ad infirmitatem spenis) Wið miltan sare ním þisse wyrte seaw 7 huniȝ, syle dríncan, hyt fremeþ wunderlice.

2. (Ad constrictum pectus vel nirwet) þisse wyrte seaw wyð huniȝe ȝemenged 7 mid pipere fremeð mycel ȝedruncen wyð nirwet 7 wið 20 innoþes sare.

MS Ca

XXXVII. Herba prosepis (gl. id est personacia)

1. Ad vulnera omnia. Herbae personaciae sucus cum vino vetere, potione data, omnes morsus serpentium vel colubri mirifice sanat.

2. Ad febres. Herbae personaciae foliis [cingis] febricitantem, statim mirifice effugat febrem.

3. Ad vulnus si canceraverit. Herbam personaciam aqua foveto, deinde ipsam cum nitro et axungia et picula cum aceto tere et in panno induc et pone.

4. Ad intestinorum dolorem. Herbae personaciae sucus, cyatus i, ex melle cyatis duobus, ieiunus bibat.

5. Ad canis rabiosi morsum. Herbae personaciae radicem cum sale marino tritam morsui impone, mox sanat.

6. Ad vulnera vetera quae satis humorem praestant. Herbae personaciae radicem et spinam quae in locis siccis nascitur aequali pondere conteris et imponis.

XXXVIII. Herba fraga

Nascitur locis opacis et mundis et collibus.　　　　　　　　p. 484

1. [Ad splenis dolorem. Herbae fragae sucus, ex melle potui dato mire facit.]

2. Ad suspiriosos et colicos. Herbae fragae sucum cum pipere albo et melle mixtum potui datum, mirificum est.

XXXIX. Merscmealuwe   hibiscus

Ðeos wyrt þe man hibiscum 7 oðrum naman merscmealwe nemneð bið cenned on fuhtum stowum 7 on feldum.

1. Wið fotadle genim þas wyrte þe we hibiscum nemdon, cnuca
5 mid ealdum rysle, lege to ðam sare, þy þryddan dæge heo hit
gehælð; þysse wyrte onfundelnysse manega ealdras geseðað.

f. 34   2. Wiþ æghwylce gegaderunga þe on þam / lichoman acenned
beoð genim þas ylcan wyrte, seoð mid wyllecærsan 7 mid linsæde 7
mid melwe, lege to þam sare, hit tofereð ealle þa stiðnyssa.

10 ### XL. ipirus

1. Wið þæt mon on wambe forwexen sy genim þysse wyrte
seaw þe Grecas ippirum 7 Itali æquiseiam nemnað on geswettum
wine, syle drincan twegen scenceas; wel ys gelyfed þæt hyt þæt
yfel gehæle.

15   2. Gyf hwa blod swiþe hræce genime ðysse ylcan wyrte seaw,
seoðe on strangum wi(n)e butan smice, drince þonne fæstende,
sona hyt þæt blod gewrið.

XLI. Hocleaf   malua eratica

Ðeos wyrt þe man malue erratice 7 oðrum naman hocleaf
20 nemneð byð cenned æghwær on beganum stowum.

1. Wið blædran sare genim þysse wyrte þe we maluam erraticam
nemdon mid hyre wyrtruman anes pundes gewihte, seoð on
wætere þearle to healfan d(æle, 7) ðæs wæteres sy sester ful oððe
mare, 7 þæt sy binnan þrim dagum gewylled, swa we ǽr cwædon,
25 to healfan dæle, syle drincan fæstendum, hyt hyne gehæleð.

2. Wið sina sare genim þas ilcan wyrte, cnuca mid ealdun rysle,
f. 34v   / hyt þæra si(na) sár wundorlice gehæleð.

3. Wið sidan sar(e) genim þas ylcan wyrte, seo(ð on) ele 7
syððan þu hy gesoden hæb(b)e 7 togædere gedón (genim) þo(nne
30 þ)a lea(f, c)nuca on ánum (m)or(ter)e, (do ð)onne ón anne (cla ð),

MS V

1 title: mercmealuwe B, merscmealwe H.   4 genim þas] gem þæs H.
8 wyllecærsan] willecersan B, wy'l'lecærsan H.   10 title: aquiseiam
B 87a/15a,om. H.   11 mon] þe man B.   12 geswettum] ge's'wettum H.
18 title: hocleaf B, hocleaf H 35/3.   23 þearle to] 'to' þeare (followed by
crasure of to) H.

XXXIX, XL, XLI *om.* O.

MS Ca

XXXIX. Herba altea (*gl.* id est malva viscum)

Nascitur locis humidis et campis.

1. Ad podagram. Herba ibiscum pisata cum axungia vetere imposita tertia die sanat; eius herbae experimentum auctores plures affirmant.

2. Ad collectiones quae in corpore nascuntur. Herba ibiscum decocta cum feno Graeco et lini seminis polline imposita duritias omnes discutit.

XL. Herba hyppirum (*gl.* id est equiseia)

1. Ad dysintericos. Herba [equiseta], sucus eius ex vino dulci cyatis ii potui datus dysinteriam sanare creditur.

2. Ad eos qui sanguinem per os reiciunt. [Herbae equisetae sucum ex vino austerissimo sine fumo ieiunus bibat, mox restringit sanguinem.]

XLI. Herba malva erratica

Nascitur ubique in locis cultis.   p. 485

1. Ad vesicae dolorem. Malva erratica, cum totis radicibus suis libram pensatam, hanc libram in congio aquae coctam ad dimidias per triduo ieiuno dabis bibere, sanabis eum.

2. Ad nervorum dolorem. Malva erratica cum axungia vetere pisata et imposita nervorum dolorem mirifice sanat (. . .).

3. Ad lateris dolorem. Malvam erraticam decoques cum oleo et

leg(e þær)to s(wa) þæt ðu hyt þri(m d)ag(um n)e (unbi)nde, þu
þæt sár gebetst.

4. Wið niwe wunda genim þysse ylcan wyrte wyrttruman, bærn
to duste, do on þa wunda.

5 XLII. Hundes tunge buglossa

Ðeos wyrt þe Grecas buglossam 7 Romane lingua bubula nemnað 7 eac Engle glofwyrt 7 oðrum naman hundes tunge hatað, heo
bið cenned on beganum stowum 7 on sandigum landum.

1. Gif hwylcum men sy þæs þriddan dæges fefer oððe þæs
10 feorðan genim þone wyrttruman þysse wyrte ðonne heo hæbbe þry
bogas ðæs sædes, seoð þone wyrttruman on wætere, syle drincan,
þu hyne gelacnast.

Seo eac ðe hæfð þæs sædes feower bogas fremað þam gelice
þe we her beforan cwædon.

15 Ðonne ys oþer wyrt þysse gelic, seo hæfð sume dæle læssan
leaf ðonne doccoe; þære wyrte wyrttruma on wætere geðyged
wiðræð iceom 7 næddrum.

2. Wið nyrwyt genim þas ylcan wyrte 7 hunig 7 hlaf þe sy mid
smeruwe gebacen þam gelice þe þu clyðan wyrce, wundorlice hyt
20 þæt sár toslít.

XLIII. Glædene bulbiscilittica /

f. 35　1. Wið wæterseocnysse genim þas wyrte þe man bulbiscillitici
7 oðrum naman glædene nemneð 7 gedryge hy syððan eal onbutan,
genim [þonne innewearde, seoð on wætere], ðonne hyt wearm sy
25 gemengc eac þærto hunig 7 éced, syle þry scenceas fulle, swyðe
hraðe sceal seo seocnys beon ut átogen þurh migðan.

MS V

1 lege] 'le'ge H.　　2 gebetst] gebest H.　　5 *title*: hundes tunge
B 87av/27a, hundes tunge H.　　7 Engle] on Ænglisc H.　　8 landum]
lande H.　　9 oððe þæs] oððes H 36/1.　　15 dæle] dælan B.
16 doccoe] docce BH　　wyrttruma] *id.* B (*followed by an erased* n), -truman H.
17 næddrum] næd`d´rum H.　　18 hlaf] hlæf H.　　21 *title*: gledene B
87b/t.m.a, glædene H.　　23 oðrum] þrum H　　7²] '7' H　　syððan]
sy'þ'þan H.　　24 þonne . . . wætere] *from* B, *om.* V.　　25 scenceas]
sceattas B.　　26 hraðe] raðe BH.

MS O

3 glowyrt] s glowyrt (s *exp.*).　　　　16 onbutan] *this word preceded and
followed by erasure of one letter*　　ðanne] *in MS a horizontal line on the first* n.

XLII. De buglosa　　　　　　　　　　　　　　　　　f. 7v/20

þeos wyrt þa Grecas buglosam 7 Romane lingua bubula 7 Engle
glowyrt 7 oþrun nama hundes tunge hataþ.

1. (Contra febrem tertianam vel quartanam) Gif man si þæs ðrindan
dæȝes fefer oþþar þas feorðan ȝením þane wyrttrume ðisse wyrte þanne 5
heo habbe þry boȝes þæs sædes, seoð þane wyrttruman on / wætere, syle f. 8
drincan; þu hine ȝelæcnest.

þanne is oðer wyrt þysse ȝelic, seo haueð sume dale lassan leaf þanne
docce; þara wyrt wyrtruman on wætere ȝeþiȝed wyðreð iceom 7 næddran.

2. (Ad strictum pectus) Wyð nyrwyt ȝením þeos ylca wyrt 7 huniȝ 7　10
hlaf þe si mid smeru'we' ȝebaccen þam ȝelice þe ðu clyðan wyrce;
wunderlice hit þat sor toslit.

XLIII. De bulbo scillitico　Anglice gladene　　　　　f. 8/7

1. (Contra ydropisim) Wyð wæterseocnesse ȝením þas wyrte þe man
bulbiscillitici 7 odrum naman gladene nemneð 7 ȝedriȝe hiȝ seððan eal　15
onbutan, ȝením ðanne innewerde, seod on wæte, þanne hit wearm si
ȝemeng eac þarto huniȝ 7 ecede, syle þri sceattes fulle; syyðe raðe sceal
þeo sceonesse beon ut atoȝen þur micȝþan.

MS Ca

postquam [destringis] folia in mortario teres, in panno inducis et imponis, triduo non solvis, emendasti dolorem.

4. Ad vulnera recentia. Malvae erraticae radicem in cinerem coctam
tere et impone.

XLII. Herba buglossa

Nascitur locis cultis et sablosis (. . .).

1. Ad tertianas sive quartanas. Herba bovis lingua quae tres tursos
[seminis] mittit, eius radicem totam ex aqua decoques, potum dabis,
remediabis.

Quae autem quattuor tursos habet facit ad quartanas, dabis ut supra.

Alia item herba similis est quae folia lapatii fert minuta, eius radix
potata ex aqua ranis et serpentibus adversatur.

2. Ad suspirationes in corpore. Herba bovis lingua ex melle et pane
spissata vice malagmatis mirifice rumpit.

XLIII. Herba bulbiscillitici

1. Ad ydropicam. Herba bulbiscillitici [torretur], deinde circum-
purgetur et medium eius in aqua coquatur, cum madidum fuerit eximito
ex eo tres obolos, dentur potui ex melle et aceto et evacuatur per urinam.　p. 486

2. Wið liþa sare genim þas ylcan wyrte swa we ǽr cwædan innewearde, wyll on ele, smyra þæt sár ðærmid, sona hyt fremað.

3. Wið þa adle þe Grecas paronichias nemnað genim þysse ylcan wyrte wyrttruman, cnuca mid ecede 7 mid hlafe, lege to þam
5 sare, wundorlice hyt hy gehæleð.

4. Wið þæt man ne mæge wæterseoces mannes þurst gecelan genim þysse sylfan wyrte leaf, lege under þa tungan, sona heo þone þurst forbyt.

XLIV. Umbilicum   herba cotulidonus

10   Ðeos wyrt ðe Grecas cotiledon 7 Romane umbilicum ueneris nemnað byð cenned on hrofum 7 on beorgum.

1. Wið swylas geni(m) þas wyrte 7 swinen smeru, wi(f)um swaðeah unges(yl)t, ægþres gelic(e) micel be wihte, c(nuc)a tosomne, (leg)e to þam swyl(um), hy(t hy) tofereð; þ(as w)yrte
15 þu sc(ealt) nima(n) on winter(tid)e.

XLV. Attorla(ðe)   gallicrus

Ðeos wyrt þe man gallicrus 7 oðrum naman attorlaðe nemneð bið cenned on fæstum stowum 7 wið wegas.

1. Wiþ hundes slite genim þas wyrte, cnuca mid [rysle] 7
f. 35v mid heorð/bacenum hlafe, lege to ðam slite, sona hyt bið gehæled;
21 eac þys sylfe fremað wið heard geswell 7 hyt eal tofereð.

XLVI. Harehune   marabium

1. Wið geposu 7 wið þæt man hefelice hræce genim ðas wyrte ðe Grecas prassion 7 Romane marubium nemnað 7 eac Angle
25 harehune hatað, seoð on wætere, syle drincan þam ðe hefelice hræcen, heo hine gehæleð wundorlice.

MS V

3 þa] þam B.   4 lege] gele H.   6 wæterseoces] -seocnes H.
7 sylfan] ylcan H.   9 title: vmbilicum ueneris B, om. H 37/2.
10 cotiledon] cotilidon B   umbilicum] unibilicum B.   13 wihte] gewihte
H.   16 title: atterloðe B 87bv/15a, atorlaðe H.   19 rysle] from B,
hrysle V.   20 heorðbacenum] heo'r'ðbacenan H.   22 title: horhune
B, harehune H.   24 Angle] on Ænglisc H.   26 hræcen] hræca'n' H.

MS O

1 swa] þe swa (þe exp.).

2. (Contra morbum neruorum) Wið liða sare ȝenim þa wyrt swa we ær cwædon innewerde, wel on ele, smíra þat sar þarmid; sona hit fremað.

3. (Ad morbum quem Graeci paro(nic)hiam uocat) Wyð þa adle þe Grecas paronichias nemnað ȝenym þisse ylcan wyrte wyrtruman, cnuca mid ecede 7 myd hlafe, leȝe to ðan sore; wunderlice hit ȝehæled.   5

4. (Contra sitim ydropicorum) Wyð þat man ne mæȝe wæterseoces mannes þurst ȝecelan ním þisse wyrte leaf, leȝe under þa tungan; sona heo þane þurst forbit.

XLIV *om.* O.

XLV. (. . .)   f. 19/16

þeos wyrt þe man gallicrus 7 oþrum naman attorlaþe nemnað, he 11 wexeþ on fastum stowum 7 wid weiȝeas.

1. Wið hundes slite cnuca þas wyrt mid res(e)le 7 he(orþb)acenum hlafe, leȝe to þan slíte, hit byd ȝe(hæled), ea(c) þis sylfe fremeð wið heard ȝeswel (7) hit æl tofereð.   15

XLVI. Prassion   marubium   harehune   f. 28/2

1. þeos wyrt þæt man prassion Grecas 7 alii marubium 7 Engle harehune hataþ, seoþ on wætere, sile drincan þane heafalice hrace, heo híne wunderlice hæled.

MS Ca

2. Ad perniones. Herbae scillae quod est in medio eius cum oleo ferve-factum atque ea quae dolorem exhibebunt ter unguendo sedabuntur.

3. Ad paronychiam. Herbae scillae radix pisata cum aceto et pane imposita paronychiae mire facit.

4. Item ydropicis ut sitis extinguatur. Herbae scillae folium subiectum sub lingua sitim compescit.

XLIV. Herba cotuledon

Nascitur in tectis aut in monumentis.

1. Ad strumas discutiendas. Herba cotulidon pisata cum axungia [suilla], feminis sine sale, aequis ponderibus calidum imponito, strumas discutit; legis eam hiemis tempore.

XLV. Herba gallicrus

Nascitur locis solidis circa vias.

1. Ad morsum canis. Herbam gallicrus teris cum axungia et pane domestico et ponis, mox sanabitur; idem et duritias discutit (. . .).

XLVI. Herba prassion (*gl.* id est marrubium)

1. Ad tussem gravem. Herbam marrubium coques ex aqua et dabis   p. 487
bibere his qui graviter tussiunt, sanabuntur mirifice.

2. Wið magan sare genim þysse ylcan wyrte seaw, syle drincan, hyt þæs magan sár fram adeð; 7 gif him fefer derige syle him þas ylcan wyrte wel drincan on wætere, heo hyne [arærð].

3. (W)ið rengwyrmas abutan nafolan genim þas ylcan wyrte
5 marubium 7 wermod 7 elehtran, ealra þyssa wyrta gelice fela be gewihte, seoð on geswetton wætere 7 mid wine twie oððe þriwa lege to þam nafolan, hit cwelð þa wyrmas.

4. Wið liþa sare 7 wið geþind genim þas ylcan wyrte, bærn to ahsan, do to þam sare, sona hit gehælð.

10 5. Wið attres ðigne genim þysse ylcan wyrte wos, syle [on ealdum wine] drincan, sona þæt attor tofærð.

6. Wið sceb 7 wið teter genim þas ylcan wyrte, seoð on wætere, ðweh þone lichoman þærmid þær þæt sár sy; heo of genimð þone scruf 7 þone teter.

15 7. Wið lungenadle genim þas ylcan wyrte, seoð on hunige, syle þiggean, he bið wundorlice gehæled.

8. Wið ealle stiðnessa þæs lichoman genim þas ylcan wyrte, cnuca mid rysle, lege to þam sare, heo hælð wundorlice. /

f. 36 XLVII. [Foxes fot]

20 1. Wið uncuðe springas þe on lichoman acennede beoð genim þysse wyrte wyrttruman þe man xifion 7 oðrum naman foxes fot nemneð þreora yntsena gewihte 7 smedman six yntsena gewihte, ecedes twegean scenceas 7 foxes smeoruwes ðreora yntsena ge-wihte, cnuca tosómne on wine, déc þonne anne claðþ ærof, lege
25 to ðam sare, þu wundrast þære lacnunge.

MS V

1 sare] *om.* H.　　　3 arærð] *from* B, ahrærð V.　　　4 abutan] abuto B
nafolan] neafelan H　ylcan] *om.* H.　　5 ealra] ealru H 38/1.　　6 twie]
tuwa B 88/1a, twigea H.　　9 ahsan] axsan B, duste H.　　10–11 on ealdum
wine] *from* B, *om.* V.　　12 sceb] scæb BH.　　13 ðweh] þweah B.
14 scruf] scurf BH.　　16 þiggean] þicgan B, þiggcan H.　　17 ylcan]
ylca H.　　19 *title*: *from* B, H = B, *om.* V (*folio damaged*).　　22 smedman
six yntsena gewihte] *om.* H.　　23 twegean] twegen BH　7] *om.* H
yntsena] yntsa H.　　24 déc] do H.　　25 lacnunge] lacnugge H.

MS O

7 þat] sa þat (sa *exp.*).　　　8 seoh] seaw seoh (seaw *exp.*).　　　15 six]
f six (f *exp.*).

2. Wið mæჳen sore ním þisse wyrt seaw, sile hím ðas wyrte wel drincan on wætere, heo hine areerh.

3, 4. —

5. Wið attres ðyჳene nim þisse wyrte wos, sile on ealdan wine drincan; sona þat attor toferð.

6. Wið sceb 7 wið teter ním þeos wyrt, seoð on wætere, þweh þane lichama þarmíd þar þat sar si, heo ჳenímð þane scurf 7 þane teter.

7. Wið lungenadle nim þisse wyrt, seoh on huniჳe, sile þicჳan, he byð wunderlice ჳehæled.

8. Wið ealle stiþnysse þæs lichamen ním þas wyrt, cnuca mid risele, leჳe to þan sore, heo hæl wunderlice.

XLVII. Xifion   foxes fot

1. (Wyd uncuþe springe) Wið uncuþe springas þe on lichama acenned byð ním þisse wyrte wurtruma þæt man xifion 7 Engle foxes fot nemned þreora entwa ჳewihte 7 smedma six entsan ჳewihte, ecedes tweჳen scencas 7 foxes smerewes þreora entsan ჳewihte, cnuca tosomne on wíne, dec þanne anne clað þarof, leჳe to þan sore; þu wundrast þare lacnunge.

MS Ca

2. Ad stomachi dolorem. Herbae marrubii sucus potatus stomachi dolorem tollit, et si febricat ex aqua potatum satisque elevat (. . .).

3. Ad lumbricos. Herbae marrubii, absynthii et lupinorum paria pondera in aqua mulsa cocta cum vino bis aut ter in umbilico posita, necat lumbricos.

4. Ad condolomata. Herbam marrubium combure, eius cinerem infrica, sanabitur.

5. Ad venenum si quis biberit. Herbae marrubii sucum dabis ex vino veteri, discutit venenum.

6. Ad scabiem vel impetiginem. Herbam marrubium discoque et ex aqua corpus lavato, scabiem discutit et impetiginem.

7. Ad pulmonum extensionem. Herbam marrubium ex melle coctam sumat, mire curat.

8. Ad omnem duritiam. Marrubium tunsum cum axungia et impositum mire sanat.

XLVII. Herba xyfion

1. Ad fistulas quae in corpore nascuntur. Herbae xifion radix uncias vi, amuli uncias vi, aceti cyatos ii, adipis vulpini uncias iii ex vino pisabis, in panno linis et imponis, miraberis.

2. Wið heafodbryce genim þas ylcan wyrte ufewerde, gedryge hy 7 cnuca, genim þonne be gewihte efenmycel wines, meng tósomne, lege to þam sare, hyt ðonne þa forbrocenan bán út atyhð; eac gif hwæt on þam lichoman dergende byð hyt wel wið
5 þæt fremað; oððe gif hwa mid his fet (ofs)tepð ættrig (ban snacan) oð(ðe næ)dd(ran), ðeos s(ylfe) wyrt is swy(þe) sce(arp)nu(mul) wið (þæt att)or.

XLVIII. W(æ)ter(wyrt)   gallitricus

1. Gyf swylas fæmnum derigen genim ðas wyrte þe man galli-
10 tricum 7 oðrum naman wæterwyrt nemneð, cnuca hy syndrige, lege to þam sare, heo hyt hælð.

2. Gif mannes fex fealle genim þas ylcan wyrte, cnuca on ele, smyra ðonne þæt fex þærmid, hyt sona bið fæst. /

f. 36v ## XLIX. Syngrene

15 Ðeos wyrt þe man temolum 7 oðrum naman singrene nemneð þæs þe Omerus sægð ys wyrta beorhtust 7 þæt Mercurius hy findan sceolde, ðysse wyrte wós ys swyðe fremful 7 hyre wyrttruma ys synewealt 7 sweart, eac on ðære mycele þe leaces.

1. Wiþ cwiþan sare genim þas wyrte, cnuca 7 lege þærto, heo
20 geliþegað þæt sár.

L. Sigelwéarfa   (uertam)nus

(Ðeos wyrt þe Grecas æliotr)ophus 7 (Romane uertamnum n)emn(að 7 eac Angle sigelhweorf)a ha(tað byþ) c(enned gehwar on began)um st(owum) 7 on cl(ænum 7 eac on mædum).

MS V

1 heafodbryce] -brece H   ufewerde] -wearde B, -wear`de´ H 39/1.
1–2 gedryge hy 7 cnuca] gedrigede 7 cnuca hy H.   5 ofstepð] -stæpð B,
-stapð H.   6 scearpnumul] teart- B.   8 title: waterwurt
B 88v/14a, wæterwyrt H.   9–10 gallitricum] calli- BH.   11 hælð] gehælð
H.   13 sona bið] bið sona BH.   14 title: singrene B, syngrene H.
16 sægð] segð B   beorhtust] beorht/tost H.   21 title: sielhweorfa B,
sigelhweorfa, gl. cyrmela H.   22 æliotrophus] id. H (between h and
u an erased i).   23 Angle] on Ænglisc H.

MS O

4 ȝewihte] ȝewiȝe   ihte (wiȝe exp.).   11 þisse] þe þisse (þe exp.).

2. (Wyd hoferfodbrice. ad ossa fracta extrahenda a corpore. si quis calcauit supra ossa uenata vel supra serpentem vel buffonem) Wið heafodbrice ním þeos wyrt ufenwerde, ʒedríʒe hi 7 cnuca, nim þane be ʒewihte efenmucel wines, meng tosomne, leʒe to þan sare, hit þane ða forbrocan ban ut atihþ. Eac ʒif hwæt on þa lichaman deriʒende byð hit 5 wel wyð þæt fremeð; oþþar ʒif hwa mid hys fest ofstæpð ætriʒ ban snacan oððer nadran, þeos wyrt is swiðe scearpnímol wið þæt attor.

XLVIII *om.* O.

XLIX. Temolum   singrene   f. 39v/17

þeos wyrt þæt man temolum 7 oþrum nanman singrene nemneð, 10 þisse wyrte wos is swiþe fremful, 7 þæs þa Omerus sehʒ his wyrte beohtust 7 þæt Mercurius hi scolde finde.

1. (Wyd cwiþan sore) Wið cwiþan sare cnuca þeos wyrt 7 leʒe to þan sora, heo ʒeliþegad þat sar.

L. *The beginning of this chapter is missing; see t.n.*   15

MS Ca

2. Ad capitis fracturam. Herbae xyfionis superiorem partem conteris et trita sicca aequis ponderibus mixta vino capitis ossa fracta extrahit; aut si quid in corpore suppuratum fuerit vel si pedibus calcata sint ossa serpentis, [eadem] contra venena similiter efficax est.

XLVIII. Herba gallitricum

1. Ad strumas virginum. Herba gallitricum pisata per se imposita p. 488 virginibus strumas sanat.

2. Ad capillos tingendos. Herba gallitricum in oleo trita et in caput perunctum capillos inficit.

XLIX. Herba etmolum

Clarissima herbarum [est] Homero teste et inventionem eius Mercurio assignat, contra [quaevis] sucus beneficia demonstrat, radice rotunda nigraque magnitudine [caepae].

1. Ad dolorem matricis. Herba etmolum contusa et imposita dolorem matricis sedat.

L. Herba eliotropis

Nascitur ubique in locis cultis et mundis et in pratis.

þ(eos) w(yrt hæfð mid hyre sume wundorlice) go(dcundnysse,
þæt is) þonne þæt hyr(e) blostm(an [hig æfter þare sunnan
[ryne] wændað, swa þæt þa blosman], þonne seo) sunne gesihð,
hy sylfe (be)clysað, 7 eft þonne heo up gangeð, hy selfe geopeniað
5 7 tobrædaþ; 7 heo fremað to þyssum læcedomum þe we her
wiðæftan awryten habbað.

 1. Wið ealle attru genim þas sylfan wyrte, cnuca to swiðe
smalon duste, oððe hyre wos syle drincan on godum wine, wundorlice heo þæt attor tofereð.

10 2. Wiþ flewsan genim ðysse ylcan wyrte leaf, cnuca 7 lege to
ðam sare, hyt [is] gelyfed þæt heo scearplice gehæle.

LI. Mædere gryas

 Ðeos wyrt þe man gryas 7 oðrum naman mædere nemneð byð
f. 37 cenned / fyrmust in Lucania, heo hæfð hwites marman bleoh 7
15 heo bið gefrætewud mid feower readum stælum.

 1. Wi(ð b)anece 7 (w)ið banbryce genim (þas) ylcan wyr(te),
cnuca hy, lege to þam ba(ne), þy þriddan dæge him bið sel swylce
þær clyþa to gelæd wære.

 2. Eac þysse wyr(t)e wyrttruma fremað wið ælc sár þe þam
20 lichoman dereð, þæt ys ðonne þæt man þone wyrttruman cnucige
7 to ðam sare gelecge, eal þæt sár he gehælð.

LII. Hymele herba politricus

 Ðeos wyrt ðe man politricum 7 oðrum naman hymele nemneð
byþ cenned on ealdum husstedum 7 eac on fuhtum stowum.

MS V

 1 þeos] eos B. 2–3 hig . . . blosman] *from* B 89/1a, *om.* V. 3 ryne]
from H 40/4, hryne B. 4 selfe] silfe BH. 6 awryten] y *alt. from* i V.
7 þas] þa B swiðe] swiþan H. 10 wyrte] *om.* H. 11 is] *from* B, hys V.
12 *title*: mædere BH. 13 mædere] mæd`e´re H. 14 Lucania]
Lucana H marman] mar`br´an (br *in a later hand above expunged* m) H.
15 stælum] stelum BH. 16 genim] geniim H. 18 to] þærto H gelæd]
geled BH. 19 wyrttruma] wyrtruman H. 20 cnucige] cnuca hy H.
22 *title*: humele B, hymele H. 23 man] ma B.

MS O

4 duste] d / duste (d *exp.*). 6 fwesan] we fwesan (we *exp.*). 16 poli-
tricum] poltricum politricum (poltricum *exp.*).

forþ þeos (w)yrt h(æfð) (. . .) hure rune wendaþ, (h)y sylfe hi clusað   f. 14v/1
þanne seo sunne ʒesyhð, 7 þanne heo eft up gangeð, heo ʒeopenað.

   1. ((Contra) omne uenenum) Wið ealle attor (ni)m sio (::)le wyrt,
cnuca to syðe smale duste, oþþe hure wos sile dríncan on gode wíne;
ell þat attor hu tofereþ.   5

   2. Wið fwesan ʒením þisse wyrt leaf, cnuca 7 leʒe to þan sore, hit his
lifed þæt heo s(cea)rplice hæleð.

LI. (. . .)   f. 19/22

   (Ð)eos wyrt þe man grias 7 (::)me mænn mædere hatad.

   1. Wið (ban)ece 7 wið banbryce ʒecnu(ca) (. . .) (ba)ne, ði ðrid(dan) 10
dæʒe (. . .) (þ)ær cliþa to ʒel(ed) (. . .). /

   2. Eac þisse wyrte wurtru(m)e fre(m)ad wið æc sor þe þan lichamann ff. 15v, 19v
deriað, þæt is (þon)ne þæt man þone wurtruma cnucie 7 to þan sor(e
ʒe)lecge, heall þat sor he ʒehælð.

LII. Politricum   f. 28/15

   þeos wyrt þæt man politricum 7 Engle hymele nemnað.   16

MS Ca

   Huius herbae divinae ad solis cursum flores se vertunt, et cum sol
occidit flores se cludunt, rursum cum sol oritur flores se aperiunt; facit ad
remedia multa.

   1. Facit ad omne venenum. Herbae eliotropis pulverem mollissimum
ex ea aut sucum eius cum vino veteri optimo potui datum, mire venena
discutit.

   2. Ad luxum. Herba eliotropum, folia contusa et apposita, efficaciter
sanare dicitur.

LI. Herba grias

   Nascitur in Lucania, marmoris albi colorem habet, quattuor rubicundis
ornata coliculis.

   1. Ad sciaticos sanandos. Herba grias, radix pisata et imposita sciaticos
tertia die sanat, quasi malagmae genus imponatur.

   2. Ad omnes dolores in corpore. Herba grias, radix pisata et imposita, p. 489
ubi dolet sanat.

LII. Herba politricum

   Nascitur in parietinis et humorosis locis.

1. Wið innoðes sare genim þysse wyrte leaf þe we politricum nemdon, hyre twigu beoð swylce swinen byrst, cnuca ðonne þa leaf 7 nigon pipercorn 7 coliandran sædes nigon corn eall tosomne, syle drincan on godum win(e), 7 þys sý ðonne he gange tó bæðe;

5 eac þeos ylce wyrt gedeþ þæt ægþer ge wera ge wifa fea(x w)exeþ.

LIII. Wuduhrofe   malochinagrea astularegia

1. Wið þæt man on wombe forwexen sy genim þysse wyrte wyrttruman ðe Grecas malochinagria 7 Romane astularegia
f. 37v nemnað 7 eac Ængle wudurofe hatað, cnuca mid wine, / syle
10 drincan, sona þu ongi`t´st þysses fremfulnysse.

2. Wið innoðes flewsan genim þysse wyrte sǽd þe we astula-regia nemdun gemencged mid stiþum ecede, syle drincan, hyt gewrið þone innoð.

LIV. Popig   papauer album

15   1. W(ið) eagena (sare) þæt ys þæt we cweðað tornige geni(m) þysse wyrte wos ðe Grecas moe(t)orias 7 Romane papauer albu(m) nemnað 7 Engle hwit popig hatað, oððe þone stelan mid þam wæstme, lege to þam eagan.

2. Wið þunwonga sare oððe þæs heafdes genim þysse sylfan
20 wyrte wos, cnuca mid ecede, lege ofer þone andwlatan, hyt geliþegað þæt sár.

3. Wið slæpleaste genym þysse ylcan wyrte wos, smyre þone man mid, sona þu him þone slep onsenst.

MS V

2 twigu] twiga H 41/2.   3 7 ²] *om.* H   nigon corn] *om.* H.   4 þys sý] þysse H.   5 wexeþ] wexeð (w *erased between* x *and* e) H.   6 *title*: wuderoue B 89v/21a, wuduhrofe H.   8 malochinagria] malochimagria B. 9 Ængle] on Ænglisc H.   13 gewrið] gew`r´ið H.      14 *title*: hwit popi B, popig H.      16 Grecas] G`r´ecas (*caroline* r) H.   17 Engle] on Ænglisc H. 18 wæstme] *gl.* i.e. fructus H.   19 þunwonga] þanwongan B, *gl.* i.e. emigranea H   sylfan] *om.* H.   20 andwlatan] 7wlatan BH.   23 slep] slæp BH.

MS O

7, 8 malochinagría *and* wuderofe *struck out in red ink.*   10 flewsan] *pre-ceded by an erased* w.   11 drincan] a (*marked for expansion*) *followed by partly erased* n.

1. Wið innoþes sare nim þisse wyrte leaf, politricum hateð, hyre twíȝu beoð swilce swinenne byrst, cnuca þa leaf tosomne, sile drincan on gode wíne, 7 þys si þane gange to baðe. Eac þeos sylue wyrt deð þæt æȝþer ȝe wifa ȝe wera feax wexeð.

LIII. Item astularegia   f. 2/12

1. (Ad uentrem et stomachum) Wyð þæt man on wambe forwexi si 6 ȝením þisse wyrtrunan þe Grecas malochinagría 7 Romane astularegia nemneð 7 Englisc wuderofe hatað, cnuca mid wíne, sile drincan; sona þu onȝist þisse wurte frenfulnesse.

2. (Ad fluxum uentris) Wið innoþes flewsan ȝením þisse wurte sæd, 10 ȝemencg to stiþun drenche, drincan hit; hít ȝewriþ þane innoþ.

LIV *om.* O.

MS Ca

1. Ad coli dolorem. Herba polytricum quae habet ramulos quasi seta porcina, eius folia contrita cum piperis granis ix et seminis coliandri granis ix, contrita cum vino optimo, dabis bibere introeunti in balneo; facit et ad capillos mulierum nutriendos.

LIII. Herba astula regia

1. Ad dysintericos. Herbae astulae regiae radix cum vino trita potui datur dysintericis, statim sentiunt beneficium.

2. Ad ventris fluxum ut restringat. Herbae astulae regiae semen mixtum cum aceto acerrimo potui datum ventrem restringet.

LIV. Herba papaver

1. Ad epyforas oculorum. Herbae papaveris sucum vel caliculum, p. 490 fructu suo oculis imponitur.

2. Ad emigraneum vel capitis dolorem. Herbam papaver silvaticum teres cum aceto et imponis super frontem, sedabit dolorem.

3. Ad somnum, qui non dormit. Herbae papaveris suco si quem perungueas somnum cum sopore obicit.

LV. [Oenantes]

1. Gyf hwa gemigan ne mæge genim þysse wyrte wyrttruman þe man oennantes 7 oðrum naman [. . .] nemneð tó duste gecnucude, syle drincan on wíne twegean scenceas fulle, hyt fremað
5 healice.

2. Gyf hwa swyþe hræce genime þysse ylcan wyrte wyrttruman, þicge þam gemete þe we nu hér beforan cwædun, hyt geliðigað þone hracan.

LVI. Halswyrt   narcisus /

f. 38   1. Wið þa wunda þe on þam men beoð acenned genim þysse
11 wyrte wyrttruma(n) ðe ma(n) narcisum (7) oþrum n(am)an (hals)wy(rt n)emne(ð mi)d ele 7 (mid meluwe gecnu)cud(ne þa)m gelice (þe þu clyðan wyrce, lege) to (þa)re wun(de, hit hælð wundorlice).

15 ## LVII. Brunewyrt   teuerion

1. Wið miltan sare genim þysse wyrte wyrttruman þe Grecas splenion 7 Romane teuerion nemnað 7 eac Engle brunewyrt hatað, cnuca to swiðe smalan duste, syle drincan on liþum wine, healic þingc ðu þærmid ongitst, eac ys sæd þæt heo þus funden wære:
20 þæt is ðonne þæt hyt gelamp hwilon þæt man þearmas mid þære miltan uppan þas wyrte gewearp, þa sona geclyfude seo milte to þysse wyrte 7 heo hrædlice þa miltan fornam, for ðy heo eac fram sumum mannum splenion geciged ys, þæt ys on ure geðeode milte nemned, for þam, þæs þe man sægð, þa swin þe hyre
25 wyrttruman etað þæt hy beon butan milten gemette.

MS V

1 title: from B 90/9a, om. VH.   2 gemigan] migan B.   3 oennantes] oenantes BH   space in B only   tó] tu B.   3–4 tó duste gecnucude] cnuca to duste H 42/1.   4 twegean] twegen BH.   6 hræce] ræce B.   9 title: halswurt B, healswyrt H.   11 narcisum] narcissum H.   12 gecnucudne] gecnucud H.   15 title: brunewurt B, brunewyrt H.   17 splenion] s'p'lenion H   Romane] id. H (r alt. from o)   Engle] on Ænglisc H. 19 þingc] þin`g´c H.   23 mannum] om. H   þæt ys] þæt H.   24 nemned] nemnemned H   sægð] segð B 90v/8a.   25 wyrttruman] -truma B milten] miltan BH.

MS O

7 hracan] ra hracan (ra exp.).   21 wurtrumme] wrurtrumme (first r exp.).

LV. Oenantes herba   f. 25/13

1. (Si homo mingere nequit) Gif man miȝan ne maȝe nín þisse wyrt wyrtrume þa man oenantes, cnuca to duste, syle drinca on wine tweȝen scencas fulle, hit fremeð heahlice.

2. (Si quis nimis conspuit) Gif hwa swiðe hrǽce ním þisse wyrt wyrtrume, þicȝe þan ȝemete þe we nu her beforen cwedon, hit ȝeliþegað þane hracan.

LVI. De narciso   id est halswyrt   f. 24/17

1. (Ad ulcera corporis id est ulcus) Wið wunda þa on þa mana byð cenned nim þisse wurte wurtrume þæt man narcisum 7 oþrum nama halswyrt nemnaþ mid ele 7 mid melewe ȝecnucodne þam ȝelice þe cliþan wyrce, leȝe to þare wunde, hit hæleð wunderlice.

LVII. Splenion   verio   brunewyrt   f. 36/3

1. (Ad morbum spenis) Wid miltan sare ním þisse wyrte wyrtrume þæt Grecas splenion 7 Romane uerion 7 Engle brunewyrt hatað, cnuca to swiðe smale duste, syle drincan on lyþum wíne; healice ðincȝ þarmid onȝist; eac ys sæd þæt heo þus ȝefunde ware: þæt is þanne þæt hít ȝelamp þæt man þearmes mid þara miltan uppan þeos wyrt ȝewearp, þeo sona clifode þa milta to þisse wylt 7 heo hradlice þa miltan fornam; forþi heo ys ȝehateð spenío 7 þæs þe man seȝþ þæt þa swín þe hire wurtrumme etað þæt hi beon botan miltan.

MS Ca

LV. Herba oenantes

1. Ad stranguiriam. Herbae oenantis radicem in pulverem redactam, ad stranguiriam in vini ciatis duobus detur[, summe facit].

2. Ad tussem. Herbae oenantis radicem dabis ut supra, tussem sedat.

LVI. Herba narcissus

1. Ad vulnera quae ab se nascuntur. Herbae narcissi radix contusa cum oleo et farina vice cataplasmae imponitur in vulnere et sanat mirifice.

LVII. Herba splenion

1. Ad splenis dolorem. Herbae splenion radix in pulvere mollissimo redacta, in vino [leniore] potui dato, summam rem experieris, constatque sic inventam: cum exta super eam proiecta essent, adhaesisse lieni   p. 491 eumque exinanisse, propter hoc a quibusdam splenion vocatur; narrant etiam sues qui radicem eius edunt sine splene inveniri.

Sume eac sæcgeað þæt heo stelan mid twigum hysopan gelicne
hæbbe 7 leaf beanum gelice, þanon hy sume men þam s(ylfum)
naman nemnað hysopan; þa wyrte man nimeð þonne heo [blewð];
swiðust heo ys gehered on þam muntlandum þe man Cilicia 7
5   Pisidia nemneð.

LVIII. polion /

f. 38v   Ðeos wyrt þe man polion 7 oðrum naman [. . .] nemneð bið
cenned on unsmeþum stowum.

1. Wið [monoðseoce] genim þysse wyrte seaw þe we polion
10   nemdun, gemengc wið eced, smyra þærmid þa ðe þæt yfel þoligen
toforan þam þe hyt hym to wylle, 7 þeh þu hyre leaf 7 hyre
wyrttruman dó on ánne clænne cla∂ 7 gewriðe onbutan þæs
mannes swyran þe þæt yfel ðolað, hyt deþ onfundelnysse þæs
sylfan þinges.

15   ## LIX. (C)neowholen   (vi)ctoriole

1. Wið þone dropan 7 wið þone magan genim twegen scenceas
fulle woses ðysse wyrte þe man uictoriole 7 oðrum naman cneowholen nemneð, syle drincan fæstendum wið hunig gemenged, sona
hyt ðone dropan gewæceð.

20   ## LX. Galluc   confirma

Ðeos wyrt þe man confirman 7 oðrum naman galluc nemneð
bið cenned on morum 7 on feldum 7 eac on mædum.

1. Wið wifa flewsan genim þas wyrte confirmam, cnuca to swyþe
smalon duste, syle drincan on wine, sona se flewsa ætstandeþ.

MS V

1 sæcgeað] secgað B, secgeað H 43/1.   2 gelice] gelicne (n *exp.*) V.
3 hysopan] *id.* H (i *erased between* p *and* a)   blewð] *from* B, bleþ V.   6 *title*:
polion B, *om.* H.   7 *space in* B *only.*   9 monoðseoce] *from* B, innoð-
V.   11 þeh] þeah BH   7²] 7 / 7 H.   15 *title*: cneowholen BH.
16 þone magan] þæs magan sare BH.   17–18 cneowholen] ceow- H.
18 fæstendum] fæstende H.   20 *title*: galluc B 91/15a, galluc H.
23 swyþe] swiþan H 44/2.

MS O
7 fulle] f *alt. from* w.

Sume men eac secgað þæt heo stelan habbe mid twiȝum ysopan
ȝelicne 7 leaf beanum ȝelice; þanne hy sume menn þam sylfan naman
ysopa nemneð.

LVIII *om.* O.

LIX. De victoriola id est cneowholem Anglice   f. 43/15

1. (Wyd þan dropan; wyd þan maȝan sore) Wyð þan dropan 7 wið þas   6
maȝan sare ním tweȝen scencas fulle woses þisse wyrte þe man uíctoriole
nemneð 7 Engle cneowholem nemneð, sele drince fæstinde wyð huniȝ
ȝemenȝed; sona hit þane dropan ȝewæceð.

LX *om.* O.   10

MS Ca

Quidam eam dicunt ramis ysopi, surculos vel folia oblonga fabae
eodem nomine appellant; legunt [autem eam cum floret, maxime] ex
Ciliciae et Pisydiae montibus laudant.

LVIII. Herba polion

Nascitur locis asperis.
1. Ad lunaticos. Herbae polion sucum commisces cum aceto scillente
et perungues eos qui patiuntur antequam accedat eis; item pilulas eius et
radicem in linteolo mundo circa collum eius qui patitur ligabis, experimentum factum est.

LIX. Herba victoriola

1. Ad flegmata intercidenda. Herbae victoriolae foliorum sucus, cyatis
duobus vel tribus dabis cum melle bibere ieiuno, mox flegmata intercidet.

LX. Herba symphitum

Nascitur locis paludis vel hortis.
1. Ad profluvium mulieris. Herbae confirmae pulverem mollissime
tritum potui dabis in vino, mox restringit.

2. Gyf hwa innan toborsten sy genime þysse ylc
truman, gebræde on hatan axan, þicge þonne on h
he bið gehæled, 7 eac hyt þone magan ealne afeorma

f. 39   3. Wið magan sare genim þas ylcan wyrte 7 gemeng
5   7 wið eced, þu ongitst mycele fremfulnysse.

LXI. asterion

Ðeos wyrt þe man asterion 7 oðrum naman [. . .] nemneð byð
cenned betweoh stanum 7 on unsmeþum stowum.

Ðeos wyrt scineð on nihte swilce steorra on heofone, 7 se
10 ðe hy [nytende] gesihð, he sægð þæt he scinlac geseo, 7 swa afæred
he bið tæled fram hyrdum 7 fram swylcum mannum swylce
þære wyrte miht`a´ cunnun.

1. Wið fylleseocnysse genim þysse wyrte bergean þe we asterion
nemdon, syle etan on wa`ni´gendum monan, 7 sy þæt ðonne
15 þære sunnan ryne beo on þam tacne þe man Virgo nemneð,
þæt bið on þam monðe þe man Augustus hateð, 7 hæbbe ðas
sylfan (w)yrte (o)n h(i)s swyran (ahange)ne, h(e b)ið (ge)lac(n)ud.

LXII. Haran [hyge]   pes leporis

1. Wið innoþes fæstnysse genim ðas wyrte þe man leporis pes
20 7 oðrum naman haran hige nemneð, gedryge hy, cnuca þonne to
duste, syle drincan on wine gif he unfeferig sy, gyf he þonne on
fefere sy syle drincan him on wætere, sona seo fæstnys toslypeð. /

MS V

1 toborsten] tobrocen H   genime] genim H.   2 hatan] om. H   þicge]
þingce H   fæstende] fænstende wið hunige gemænged, sona H.   5 mycele]
miccle B   fremfulnysse] frym- H.   6 title: asterion B, om. H.   7 space
in B only.   8 unsmeþum] unsmyðum B, smeþum H.   9 wyrt]
wyrte B.   10 nytende] from O, nytente VBH   sægð] segð B, `ad´rætð H.
11 tæled] tæ/dæled (first d alt. from t) H.   12 þære wyrte] þara wyrta B
miht`a´] a interlined above exp. e V, nihta H.    14 wa`ni´gendum] wangendum H
sy þæt] þæt sy BH.   15 þære] `ær´ þære H.   17 swyran] sweoran H.
18 title: auence leporis pes B 91v/16a, haran hyge H, haran hyne V.   20 ge-
dryge] drige H 45/3   cnuca] cnuca hy H.   22 drincan] om. BH.

MS O

9 sunne . . . Virgo] gl. sol in (vi)rgine.   10 Augustus monþeȝð] gl. in
mense Augusto.   11 ȝelacnod] ȝela`c´nod (la`c´nod struck out), lacnod
written in t.m. above this.

LXI. De asterion vel sauina   f. 2/20

þeos wurt þe mam asteˋriˊon 7 oþrum naman sauíne nemneð, he byð cenned betweoh stanum 7 on smeþum stowun.

Ðeos wyrt scíneþ on nihte swylce sterre on heuena, 7 þe þe hi nytende ȝesihþ, he seȝh þæt he scinlac ȝeseo, 7 swa afæred he byð tæled fram 5 hyrdum 7 fram swicum mannum swylcum ðære wyrte myhte ne cunnun.

1. (Ad morbum caducum) Wyð fylleseocnysse ȝením þisse wyrte berȝean ðe asterion nendon, syle etan on waniȝendum monan, 7 þæt si þanne sunne ryne beo on þan tacne þe man Virgo nemneþ, þat byð on Augustus monþeȝð, 7 habbe / ðas sylfan wyrte on his swíran ahange; he   f. 2v byð ȝelacnod.   11

LXII *om.* O.

MS Ca

2. Ad convulsos vel qui ab intus ruperunt. Herbae confirmae radicem in cinere tepido coquito, ex melle ieiuno dabis ut edat, sanabitur, et thoracem totum purgat.   p. 492

3. Ad stomachi languorem. Herbae confirmae sucus cum oxigaro, idem et dolorem tollit, et magnum beneficium sentit.

LXI. Herba asterion

Nascitur inter petras et loca aspera.

Haec herba nocte tamquam stella in caelo lucet ut qui videt ignorans dicit fantasma se videre et metu [plenus] irridetur, maxime autem pastoribus.

1. Ad caducos. Herba asterion, bacas eius si dederis manducare luna decrescente, cum erit signum virginis, et ipsam herbam in collo habeat suspensam, remediabitur.

LXII. Herba leporis pes

1. Ad ventrem solvendum. Herba leporis pes siccata et in pulverem redacta, dabis potionem in vino si sine febre est, si autem febricitat in aqua calida, mox solvet ventrem.

f. 39v   LXIII. herba dictamnus

Ðeos wyrt 'þe man' dictamnum 7 oðrum naman [. . .] nemneð
byþ cenned on ðam iglande þe man [Crete] hateð 7 on þam munte
þe man Ida nemneð.

5   1. Gyf hwylc wif hæbbe on hyre innoðe deadboren tuddur
genim þysse wyrte wós þe we dictamnum nemdun, gif heo butan
fefere sy syle drincan on wine, gif hyre þonne fefer derige syle
drincan on wearmum wætere, sona hit þæt tuddur ut asendeþ
butan frecnysse.

10   2. Eft wið wunda, som hy syn of iser(ne som hi s)yn of stence
oððe (f)ram (næ)dran, genim þys(s)e yl(c)an wy(rt)e wos, do on þa
wunda 7 syl(e) dr(in)can, sona he byð hal.

3. Eft soðlice wið næddran slite genim þysse ylcan wyrte seaw,
syle drincan on wine, sona hyt þæt attor tofereð.

15   4. Gyf hwa attor þicge genime þysse ylcan wyrte wós, drince
on wine, witodlice swa mycel ys þysse wyrte [strengð] swa na
þæt án þæt heo mid hyre andweardnysse næddran ofslyhð swa
hwær swa hy hyre gehende beoð, ac forþon of hyre stence,
þonne he mid winde ahafen bið, swa hwær swa hy beoð 7 hy
20 þone swæc gestincað, hy [sculon] sweltan.

Eac ys sæd be þysse sylfan wyrte gyf man on huntuþe rán
oððe rægean mid flane oððe oðrum wæp'ne' gewæceþ þæt hy
wyllon þas wyrte etan swa hy hraþost to cuman mægen, 7 heo
sona þa flane ut adeð 7 ða wunde gehæleþ.

MS V

   1 *title*: dictannum B, *om.* H.   2 *space in* B *only.*   3 cenned on]
cenned H   Crete] *from* B, Grete V   þam munte] þem munte H.
5 hwylc] h'w'ylc H   innoðe] *om.* H   deadboren] deað- (ð *has the form of* d
with cross-bar added) H.   9 frecnysse] fræc- B, fræce- H.   10 stence]
stenge B, stæn'c'ge H.   11 on] o'n' H.   12 7] *om.* B 92/1a.   15 þicge]
ðigcgce H.   16 strengð] *from* B, srenð V, strængð H.   17 and-
weardnysse] 7weard- BH.   18 hy hyre] hy B.   20 sculon] *from* B,
scealon V, sceolon H 46/2   sweltan] swyltan B, swyltá (*erasure after* á) H.
21 sylfan] ilcan B   rán] hran B.   23 etan] eácan H   hraþost] raðost BH.

MS O

   11 ahafen] ef ahafen (ef *exp.*).

LXIII. (. . .)

(*No introduction*)

1. Gif wyf h(æ)bbe on hure ínnoþ dead(bo)ren trudor ӡeni(m
þyss)e wurte wos þe man dictanu(m 7 oþrum na)man ditanie nemneþ;
ӡif heo butan (. . .) sy sile dri(n)can on wíne, ӡif hyre fefere derian sile 5
d(ri)ncan on wy(r)me watere; sone hi(t) þæt tuddor ut (a)sendeð butan
(fre)cnysse.

2, 3. —

4. (Contra venenum) Gif h(wa) (. . .) þisse wyrt wos, drince on wine,
witodlice swa micel his þisse wyrt st(re)nӡþe s(wa) þ(æt) (. . .) swa hi 10
h(y)re ӡehende beoð, ac (. . .) of (. . .) þan he mid winde ahafen byð
(. . .) (s)wa hi þane stence ӡest(inc)að hi scylon (swelt)an.

Eac ys sæd þæt ӡyf (ma)n on huntoð ran (oðð)er ræӡan mid flane
(oðð)er oþrum wæpne ӡe(wæc)eð þæt hi willad ðas wurt eta(n) (. . .) hi
raðost (. . .), 7 heo sona þa flane ut adeoþ 7 (. . .) wun(de) hælað. 15

MS Ca

LXIII. Herba diptamnum

Nascitur in insula Creta in monte Ida.

1. Si qua mulier in utero pecus mortuum habuerit. Herbae diptamni
sucum si sine febre fuerit cum vino dabis, si autem febricitat cum aqua
calida, mox eiciet pecus sine periculo.

2. Ad plagas sive a ferro sive a sude sive a serpente inflictas. Herbae
diptamni sucum in plaga infundet aliquis et bibet, mox sanus erit.

3. Ad serpentium autem morsus sucum eius cum vino bibat, mox
discutit venenum.

4. Si quis venenum biberit. Herbae diptamni sucus item cum vino
potui datur; nam tanta vis est diptamni ut non solum interficiat serpentes ubicumque fuerint praesentia sui, sed et si odor eius vento
deferente pervenerit, mox occidit.

Fertur et hoc exemplum: si caprea in venatione telo percussa fuerit,
si cum sagitta pervenit ad herbam diptamnum, mox pascitur et telum a
se eicitur et plaga sanatur.

5. Wið niwe wunda genim þas ylcan wyrte 7 æþelferðincwyrte 7 hindehæleþan, cnuca mid buteran, lege to þære wunde, þu wundrast on eallum þingum ðysse wyrte gefremincge. /

f. 40　LXIV. s(o)lago maior

5　　1. Wið næddran slite 7 wið scorpiones stincg genim þas wyrte þe man solago maior 7 helioscorpion nemneð, dryge hy þonne 7 cnuca to swyþe smalon duste, syle drincan on wine 7 genim þa wyrte gecnucude, lege to þære wunde.

　　Nædran

10　LXV. solago minor

　　1. Wiþ ðæt rængcwyrmas dergen ymb nafolan genim þas wyrte þe man solágo minor 7 oþrum naman [æliotropion] nemneð gedrigede, cnuca to duste, syle (dr)incan on wearmum wætere; (heo þa wyrm)as ofsli(h)ð.

15　LXVI. Pionia

　　Ðeos wyrt ðe man peonian nemneð wæs funden fram Peonio þam ealdre 7 heo þone naman of him hæfð; heo bið cenned fyrmest in Greca; þa eac se mæ(ra) ealdor Homerus on hys bocum amearcode; heo bið funden swyþost fram hyrdum 7 heo hæfð
20　corn þære mycelnysse þe maligranati 7 heo on nihte scineð swa leohtfæt 7 eac hyre corn beoð gelice coccele 7 heo byð, swa we ǽr cwædon, oftust fram hyrdum on nihte gemet 7 gegaderod.

　　1. Wið monoðseocnysse gyf man þas wyrte peoniam þam monoð-/
f. 40v　seocan ligcgendon ofer aleg(ð), sona he hyne sylfne halne up (ah)ef(ð,
25　7 gy)f he (hig mid him hafað næ)fre seo adl h(im) eft ge(nealæceð.
　　MS V

1 æþelferðincwyrte] ælþelferþingc- (g alt. from c) H.　　2 hindehæleþan] a alt. from e V, -heleþan B.　　3 gefremincge] gefremminge B, gefræmmincge H.　　4 title: helioscorpion B, om. H.　　7 swyþe] swiþan H.　　9 Nædran] om. BH.　　10 title: eliotropion B 92v/t.m.a, om. H.　　11 rængcwyrmas] ryn- H, gl. lumbrici H.　　12 æliotropion] from B, celio- V.　　15 title: pionia B, peonia H.　　16 peonian] peoniam H.　　18 Greca] Creca B, Creaca H　　mæra] om. H.　　20 on] an H 47/4.　　21 heo] he B.　　23 peoniam] pioniam H.　　24 ligcgendon] licgendon/-an BH　　alegð] aleið H.　　25 genealæceð] ne genealæceð B, nealæceð H.

MS O
　　2 title: the last three words in black.　　4 helyoscorpion] this word in o.m.　　in text helyoscorpion (scorpion exp.).　　13 scineþ] sii scineþ (sii exp.).　　16 aleʒð] ahe aleʒð (ahe exp.).

5. —

LXIV. Solago id est solsequium

1. (Ad morsum serpentis et scorpionis) Wið nadran slite 7 wið scor-   f. 36/17
piones stíng ním þeos þæt man solago maior helyoscorpion nemneð,
driȝe hiȝ 7 cnuca to duste, sile drincan on wíne 7 cnuca þa wyrt eac 7   5
leȝe to þara wunde.

LXV. (*No separate chapter in* O)

1. (Ad uermes circa umbilicum) Wið þat re`n´gcwyrmas derian ymbe   f. 36/21
þa nafolen ním þa wyrt solago mínor 7 oþrum namen elyotropion nemneð
ȝedriȝede, cnuca to duste, sile drinca on wearma wætere; heo þa wyrmas   10
ofslíhþ.

LXVI. Pionia   f. 28/22

þeos wyrt þæt man peoníam 7 oþrum pionia hateð, heo on niht scineþ
seo leohtfæt.

1. Wið moneðseocnesse ȝif man þeos wyrt þam monaðseoccan licgen-   15
dan ofer aleȝð, sone he hine halne ahefh; / 7 ȝis he hy mid him hafed   f. 28v
næfre þe adle hym eft ne ȝeneahlaech.

MS Ca

5. [Ad vulnera recentia. Herbam diptamni et agrimoniam et ambrosiam
contritas cum butiro, imponito plagae, miraberis in omnibus diptamni
effectum.]

LXIV. Herba solago maior

1. Ad serpentium morsus et scorpionis ictum. Herba solago maior
siccata et in pulvere mollissimo redacta, in vino potui data et ipsa contusa,
plagae imponito.

LXV. Herba solago minor

1. Ad lumbricos necandos. Herba solago minor siccata et in pulverem   p. 494
redacta et in aqua calida potui data lumbricos occidit.

LXVI. Herba peonia

Inventa peonia nomen auctoris retinet; nascitur Cretae, quam Homerus
sacerdos auctor libris suis inseruit; invenitur plurimum a pastoribus; haec
in extrema regula bacula habet mali granati magnitudine quae nocte
sic lucet tamquam lucerna; quod est grano cocci simile; plurimum noctu
a pastoribus invenitur et colligitur.

1. Ad lunaticos. Herba peonia si lunatico iacenti imposita fuerit,
statim se levat ut sanus, et si eam secum habuerit nunquam ei accedit.

2. W(i)þ hy(pe)banece geni(m þy)sse ylcan w(y)rte sumne d(æ)l wy(rt)truman 7 mid linenan (claðe) gewrið (to) þam (sa)re; hyt geh(ælð).

LXVII. Berbena

5 Ðeos wyrt þe man peristereon 7 oðrum naman berbenam nem-neð, heo ys culfron swiðe hiwcuð, þanun hy eac sum þeodscipe columbinam hateð.

1. Gyf hwa þas wyrte mid him hafað þe we peristereon nemdon, ne mæg he fram hundum beon borcen.

10 2. (Wi)ð e(alle) attru genim (þysse sylfa)n wyrte dust, (sile drincan, ea)lle a(tr)u heo to(drifð), e(ac mo)n sægð þæt (d)ryas (to heora) cræf(tum h)y(r)e br(u)cen.

LXVIII. Hymele brionia

1. Wið miltan sare genim þas wyrte ðe man bryonia 7 oþrum 15 naman hymele nemneð, syle þycgean gemang mete, þonne sceal þæt sár liþelice þurh þone micgþan forð gan; ðeos wyrt is to þam herigindlic þæt hy man wið gewune drenceas gemencgeað. /

f. 41 ## LXIX. nymfete

1a. Wið þæt man on wambe forwexen sy genim þysse wyrte sæd 20 þe man nymfete 7 oðrum naman [. . .] nemneð, cnuca mid wine, syle drincan.

1b. Eft þæt sylfe be ðam wyrttruman, syle hyne þam seocan þicgean x dagas.

MS V

2 linenan] linenum B.   4 *title*: berbena B, berbene H.   5 oðrum naman berbenam] oþrumman berbena (*foll. by erasure of* 7 oðrum) H.   7 colum-binam] columbinan B 93/1a, columbinam (i *alt. from* a) H.   8 hwa] h'w'a H.   9 he] *om.* H   borcen] brocen H.   11 atru] attru BH sægð] segð B.   12 brucen] bruca H.   13 *title*: brionia wildemep B, hymele H.   14 bryonia] breonia H.   15 þonne] þon H 48/1.   16 micgþan] micgan B, mi'c'gan H   forð gan] *om.* B   to] *om.* H.   17 herigindlic] hergendlic BH   gewune] wune H.   18 *title*: *om.* BH.   19 forwexen] forwex H.   20 *space in* B *only*.   22 ðam] ðam ylcan H.

MS O

10 þrias] d (*modern*) *interlined above unexpunged* þ.   15 þíczan] þíczan þíczan (*first word exp.*).

2. Wið hipesbanes ece nim þeos wyrt sum dael wrítrumen 7 mid linnen clæþa ȝewyrþ to þan sare; hit ȝehaled.

LXVII. Peristerion   id est veruena   f. 8/22

þeos wyrt þe man perísteríon hoc est berbenan uel ueruenam, hanc quidam columbinam uocant propter colorem columbinam.   5

1. Gif hwa þas wyrt mid hím hafað ne mæȝ he fram / hundes beon f. 8v borcen.

2. (Contra omnia incommoda et uenenum) Wið ealle attre ȝením þisse wirte dust, sile dríncan; ealle attra heo todrifd; eac man seȝð þæt þrias to hyra crafte hira brucon.   10

LXVIII om. O.

LXIX. Haec herba est nymfete   f. 24v/1

1a. (Ad morbum uentris) Wið þæt man on wambe forwexen sy nim þisse wyrte sæd þæt man nymfete nemneð, cnuca mid wíne, syle drincan.

1b. Eft for þan sylfe ním þane wyrtrume, syle hine þan seocan þícȝan 15 tyn daȝas.

MS Ca

2. Ad sciaticos. Herbae peoniae radicem, partem alligabis lino, eum qui patitur circumcinges, res est saluberrima.

LXVII. Herba peristereon

[Haec herba admodum columbis est familiaris, unde hoc nomen habet.]

1. Ne quis a canibus latretur. Herbam peristereon si quis secum habuerit negat a canibus latrari.

2. Ad omnia venena. Herbae peristereon pulverem si quis potui dederit omnia venena discutit; nam dicunt quod et magi eam arte sua utuntur (. . .).

LXVIII. Herba brionia   p. 495

1. Ad splenem. Herba brionia in cibo data et per urinam [lien] digeritur; haec herba tam laudabilis est ut [et in tyriacis] potionibus mittatur.

LXIX. Herba nymfea

1a. Ad dysentericos. Herbae nymfeae semen cum vino tritum potui datur.

1b. Item radicem eius radis, dabis manducare dysenterico diebus decem.

2. Eft gyf þu þas wyrte sylst þicgean on strangon wine heo þæs [innoðes] unryne gewrið.

LXX. Clæfre crisyon

1. Wið þæra (gom)ena (sare), gyf hwa þysse wyrt(e w)yrt(tru-
5 m)an þe ma(n) crision 7 o(ð)rum (naman clæ)fre nemneð mid h(im h)a(fað) 7 on his swyran byrð, n(æ)fre him his gom(a)n ne deriað.

LXXI. ysatis

Ðas wyrte Grecas isatis 7 Románe alutam nemnaþ 7 eac Angle hateð ad serpentis morsum.

10   1. Wið næddran slite genim þysse wyrte leaf þe Grecas issatis nemnað, cnuca on wætere, lege to þære wunde, heo fremað 7 þæt sár of genimð. /

f. 41v ## LXXII. sc(or)dea

1. Wið nædran slite genim þas wyrte þe man scordean 7
15 oðrum naman (. . .) nemneð, seoð on wine, syle drincan, cnuca þonne þa wyrte 7 lege to þære wunde.

2. Wið sina sare genim þas sylfan wyrt, cnuca hy, 7 gewyld mid ðam ele ðe sy of lawertreowe gewrungan hyt þæt sár of animð.

3. Wið þam fefore þe dæghwamlice oþþe ðy þriddan on man be-
20 cymð, genim þas ylcan wyrte 7 gewrið hy onbutan þæs mannes lichoman, heo of animð þone dæghwamlican 7 [þæs] þriddan [dæges] fefor.

MS V

1 strangon] strangum B.   2 innoðes] *from* B, innodes V   unryne]
sar H.   3 *title*: clæfre B 93v/12a, clære H.   6 hafað] hafæð H   ne
deriað] nedriað H.   7 *title*: isatis alutam B, *om.* H.   8 Angle] on
Ænglisc H.   9 hateð ad] hatað 'wad´ ad (*last* d *alt. from* ð) B.   10 *here*
B *has a new chapter, title* isatis   issatis] isatis BH.   13 *title*: scordeon
wildegorlec B, *om.* H.   16 7 lege] lege þonne H.   18 lawertreowe]
-trywe H 49/1   gewrungan] gewrungen B 94/2a, H = B.   19 þriddan]
þriddan dæg H.   21 þæs] *emended from* þy VBH   þriddan] þryddan (y
alt. from e) H.   22 dæges] *from* B, dæge V   fefor] *id.* (*erased*) H.

MS O

1 dicȝean] ðe dicȝean (ðe *exp.*).   10 dæȝehwanlice] de dæȝehwanlice (de
exp.).   11 ðriddan] *first* d *imperfectly alt. from* n.

2. Eft ȝif þu ðas wyrte sylst dicȝean on stange wíne þas innoþ unryne ȝewyð.

LXX, LXXI *om.* O.

LXXII. Scordeon album (. . .) Anglice   f. 36/26

1. (Ad morsum serpentis) Wið nadran slite þa wyrt þæt man scordeon 5 hateð, seoh on wíne, sile dríncan 7 cnuca eac þa wurt 7 leȝe to þara wunda.

2. Wið sína sare / cnuca þa wyrt, 7 ȝewild mid þan ele þe si of lawer- f. 36v berietreowe 7 ȝewrungen hit þæt sær of anymð.

3. (Contra febres cotidianas et tertianas) Wið ða fifere þe dæȝehwanlice 10 oþþer ðe ðriddan dæȝe on man becumð ním þa wyrt 7 ȝewrið hy onbutan þæs mannes lichame, heo of anímd þane dæȝehwanlice 7 þane ðriddan dæȝes fefere.

MS Ca

2. Item sucum in vino austeri si datum fuerit ventris cursum re-stringit.

LXX. Herba crysion

1. Ad faucium dolorem. Herbae crysion radicem si quis in collo eam p. 496 portaverit suspensam, fauces ei nunquam dolebunt.

LXXI. Herba ysatis

1. Ad morsum serpentis. Herbae ysatis folia contrita cum aqua, in plaga imposita, adiuvat et dolorem tollit.

LXXII. Herba scordeon

1. Ad morsum serpentis. Herba scordeon, coquito et dato ius eius potui cum vino; ipsa autem contusa in plaga imponito.

2. Ad nervorum dolorem ex aegritudine. Herba scordeon trita, cum oleo laurino subacta tollit dolorem.

3. Ad cotidianas vel tertianas. Herba scordeon alligata circa corpus hominis cotidianas et tertianas tollit.

LXXIII. Feltwyrt verbascus

Ðeos wyrt þe man uerbascum 7 oðrum naman [feltwyrt]
nemneð bið cenned on sandigum stowum 7 on myxenum, þas
wyrte ys sæd þæt Mercurius sceolde Iulixe þam ealdormen syllan
5 þa he com to Circean 7 he na syþþan ænige hyre yfelan weorc
ondred.

1. Gyf hwa mid hym þysse wyrte ane tealgre byrð ne bið he
breged mid ænigum ogan, ne him wildeor ne dereþ, ne ænig yfel
geancyme.

10 2. Wiþ fotadle genim þas ylcan wyrte uerbascum gecnucude,
lege to þam sare, binnan feawum tidum heo gehælþ þæt sár to
f. 42 ðam scearplice þæt he eac gan dyrre 7 mæge; eac / ure ealdras
cwædon 7 sædun þæt ðeos gesetednys healicost fremade.

LXXIV. heraclea

15 1. Se þe wylle ofer langne weg féran hæbbe mid him on þam
wege þas wyrte þe man heraclean 7 oðrum naman [. . .] nemneþ,
þonne ne ondrædeþ he hym ænigne sceaþan, ac heo hy aflygeþ.

LXXV. Cyleþenie celidonia

1. Wiþ eagena dymnysse 7 sarnysse 7 ofertogennysse genim
20 þysse wyrte seaw þe (ma)n celidoniam 7 oðru(m n)am(an) þam
gelice cyleþenie (nem)neð (ge)cnucud of þam wyrttru(man m)id
ealdum wine 7 hunige 7 (p)i(pore), 7 s(y) þæt wel tosomne gepu-
nud, smyre þon(ne) þa eagan inna(n).

Eac we onfundun þæt sume men of ðære meolc(e) þysse ylcan
25 wyrte heora e(ag)an (sm)yred(on) 7 him þy sel wæ(s).

MS V

1 *title*: feldwurt filtrumterre B, feldwyrt H.   2 7] 7 / 7 B   feltwyrt]
from B, feldwyrd V, feldwyrt H.   3 þas] þeos H.   4 Mercurius]
Mærcurius H   Iulixe] Ulixe BH.   5 Circean] Circan B.   6 ondred] ondræd
H.   10 gecnucude] gepunode / -ude BH.   13 sædun] seðdon B, sædun (ð *erased
between* æ *and* d) H.   14 *title*: heracleam B, *om.* H.   16 *space in* B *only*.
17 ænigne] ænigre B.   18 *title*: celidonia B 94v/16a, cyleþenige H 2v/5(!).
19 ofertogennysse] -togenysse H.   20 man] *om.* H   celidoniam]
cælidoniam B   oðrum] on oðrum H.   21 gecnucud] gecnud H.
22 7 sy] sy H.   23 smyre] 7 smere H   innan] wiðinnan B.   25 þy] ðe H.

MS O

3 sceolde] sceolde sceolde (*first word stained and exp.*).   5 malum]
followed by an illegible word, underlined.   11 lagne] g *alt. from* n.

LXXIII. De verbascum   id est feldwurt   f. 43/21

(þ)eos wyrt þæt man verbascum 7 Engle feldwurt, ðas wyrt ys sæd þæt Mercuríus sceolde Vluxe þan aldermen syllem ða he com to Cyrcean 7 he na syþþan aniȝe hyre yfelen weorc ondræde.

   1. (Ne quis lassetur in uia et ne fera nec aliquid malum occurrat in uia)   5
Gif / hwa mid hím þisse wyrt anne telȝre byrð ne byð he breȝed mid   f. 43v
aniȝum ongange, ne hym wilde deor ne dereð, ne aní yfel aȝean cyme ne
mæȝ.

   2. —

LXXIV. (*No separate chapter in* O)   10

   1. (Habentem hanc herbam omnia mala fugiunt) þe þe wille ofer lagne   f. 43v/4
faren habben mid hym on þan weȝe þeos wurt þæt man herecleam nemneð;
þanne ne drædeð he hym aníȝre sceaþan, ac heo hi aflyȝeð.

LXXV. (*Title, cure 1, and beginning of cure 2 om.* O)

MS Ca

LXXIII. Herba verbascum

Nascitur locis sablosis et aggeribus; hanc herbam dicitur Mercurius   p. 497
Ulixi dedisse cum devenisset ad Circen et nulla facta eius timuisset.

   1. Adversus concursos malos. Herbae verbasci virgulam qui secum
portaverit nullo metu terrebitur neque beluae neque malorum incursio
molestabit eum.

   2. Ad podagram. Herba verbascum contusa atque imposita intra
paucas horas dolorem [adeo] efficaciter sedabit ut etiam [ambulare
audeat]; hanc compositionem praecipue auctores proficere affirmant.

LXXIV. Herba heraclea

   1. Ut in via tutus ambules. Herbam heracleam si tecum in via por-
taveris latrones non timebis, [quin] etiam fugat eos.

LXXV. Herba celidonia

   1. Ad caliginem oculorum et qui ulcera in oculis et scabritudinem habet
et albuginem oculorum tollit. Herbae celidoniae sucum de radice eius
conteris cum vino veteri et melle attico, et piper album simul bene
contritum misces et ungues de intus.

Hoc experti sumus: aliqui de suco eius, [id est] lacte, oculos sibi ungent.

2. Eft wið dymgendum e(ag)um g(en)im þysse ylcan wyrte wós oþþ(e) ða blostman (g)ewrungene 7 gemengced mid hunige, gemengc þonne liþelice weallende axan þærto 7 seoð þær tosomne on ærenum fæte; ðys is synderlic læcedom wið eagena dymnysse.

5   Eac is gewis þæt sume men, swa we ær cwædon, þæs woses synderlice brucað.

3. Wið cyrnlu genim þas ylcan wyrte, cnuca mid rysle, lege to þam cyrnlun swa þæt hi ærest syn mid wætere gebeþode.

4. Wiþ heafodece genim þas sylfan wyrte, cnuca mid ecede,
10 smyre þone andwlatan 7 þæt heafod. /

f. 42v   5. Wið þæt man forbærned sy genim þas ylcan wyrte, cnuca mid gætena smerwe 7 lege þærto.

LXXVI. Solsequia

1. Wið geswel genim þas wyrte þe man solate 7 oðrum naman
15 solosece nemneð gecnucude 7 mid ele gemengcede, lege þærto, hyt fremað.

2. Wiþ earena sare genim ðysse ylcan wyrte wos, gemengc mid þam ele of cypro 7 'ge'wyrm hyt 7 swa wlæc drype on þæt eare.

20   3. Wið toðece syle etan ðysse sylfan wyrte croppas.

4. Wið blodryne of nosum genim þysse ylcan wyrte w(os) 7 dype anne lin(en)ne clað 7 (forsete þa næ)sðy(r)lu þærmi(d, sona þæt blod ætstent).

LXXVII. Grundeswylige   senecio

25   Ðeos wyrt ðe man senecio 7 oðrum naman grundeswylige nemneð byþ cenned on hrofum 7 onbutan wagum.

MS V

2 oþþe] oð H 3/1.   4 synderlic] wislic H.   5 cwædon] sædan H.
8 cyrnlun] cyrnlum H.   11 forbærned] gebærned BH.   12 gætena]
gætenum BH, gl. gotene H.   13 title: solocece B 95/t.m.a, om. H.
14 solate] solatæ B   oðrum] on oðrum H.   17 gemengc] gemænged B,
gemængc do H.   18 7 swa] swa H.   22 7 dype] drype ðurh H
linenne] gl. oþþe wolle H   næsðyrlu] -þyrla H.   23 ætstent]
oðstænt H.   24 title: grundeswilie B, om. H.

MS O

13 solosece] followed by three illegible symbols, underlined, and solosece, unexpunged.   14 cypro] this word repeated in o.m.

2. wellenden axan þarto 7 seoð þær tosomne o(n) æren fæte, þis is f. 11/1
wunderlic lacedom wið eæȝene dimnesse.

Eac is ȝewys þæt sume mænn, swa we ær cwaðo, þæs woses wundelice brucað.

3. Wið cyrnlu ȝením þa wyrt, cnuca mid rysele, leȝe to þe cirnle swa 5
þæt hi ærest mid wætere sinde ȝe(beþo)de.

4. ((. . .) (do)lorem (ca)pitis) Wið heafodece nim (. . .), (c)nuca þa wyrt
mid ecede, smire þan andwlitan 7 þat heæfod.

5. Wið þat man ȝebærned si cnuc(a) (. . .) gætene smereȝe 7 leȝe þarto,
hit haleð wel. 10

LXXVI. Solosece solate f. 36v/7

1. (Contra inflaturam) Wið ȝewel ním þa wyrt þæt man solate 7 oþrum
nama solosece 7 cnuca 7 mid ele ȝemenged leȝe þarto, hít fremed.

2. Wið earan sare ním þisse wyrte wos, meng mid þam ele of cypro
7 ȝewirm hít 7 swa wlæc do on þat eara. 15

3. (Ad dolorem dentium) Wið toðece sile ete þisse wyrte croppes.

4. (Ad fluxum sanguinis de naribus) Wið blodríne of nose ním þisse
wirte wos 7 drupe anne linnene claþ 7 forsete þa nosþyrlles þarmíd;
sone byð þat blod ætstonde.

LXXVII. Senecion grundesswulie f. 36v/18

þeos wyrt þat man senecíon 7 Engle grundeswulíe hateð. 21

MS Ca

2. Ad caliginem oculorum. Herbae celidoniae sucus vel flos eius
expressus et mixtus cum melle attico in vaso aereo, leniter cineri [fer- p. 498
venti] commixtus decoctusque singulare remedium contra caliginem
oculorum.

Quidam suco tantum utuntur.

3. Ad parotidas. [Celidonia cum axungia trita imponatur, sed ante
aqua foveto.]

4. Ad capitis dolorem. Herba celidonia ex aceto contrita, illinito fronti
et capiti.

5. Ad combustum. Herbam celidoniam cum [sebo] caprino conteris
et imponis.

LXXVI. Herba solata

1. Ad tumorem corporis. Herbam solatam tunsam cum oleo subactam
impone, prodest.

2. Ad auricularum dolorem. Herbae solatae sucum cum oleo cyprino
misce et tepefacito, stilla in auriculas.

3. Ad dentium dolorem. Herbae solatae bacas commanducet.

4. Ad sanguinem si de naribus fluit. Herbae solatae suco madido
linteolo nares obturet, mox restringit.

LXXVII. Herba senecion

Nascitur in tectis et circa [parietes].

1. Wið wunda, þeah hy syn swyþe ealde, genim þas wyrte þe we
senecio nemdun, cnuca mid ealdum rysle, lege to þam wundum,
hyt hæleþ sona.

2. Gyf hwa mid iserne geslegen sy genim þas ylcan wyrte on
f. 43 ærne/mergen oððe to middan dæge, cnuca hy, swa we ǽr cwædon,
6   mid ealdum rysle, lege to þære wunde, sona heo þa wunde geopenað 7 afeormað.

3. Wið fotadle genim þas ilcan wyrte, cnuca mid rysle, lege to
þam fotum, hyt geliþegað þæt sár; eac hit fremað mycelum wið
10 þæra sina sáre.

4. Wiþ lendena sare genim þas ylcan wyrte, cnuca mid sealte
þam gemete ðe þu clyþan wyrce, lege to ðam lendenum; þam
gelice hyt fremað eac wið þæra fota sare.

LXXVIII. Fern   ffelix

15   1. Wið wunda genim þysse wyrte wyrttruman þe man filicem 7
oðrum naman fearn nemneþ gecnucudne, lege to þære wunde, 7
æþelferþincgwyrte twegea trymessa gewæge syle drincan on wine.

2. Wið þæt geong man healyde sy genim þas ylcan wyrte þær
heo on bécenan treowes wyrttruman gewexen sy, cnuca mid rysle
20 7 gedéc anne cla ð þærmid 7 gewrið to ðam sare swa þæt he þa
hwyle upweard sy gewend; þy fifta(n d)æge he bið gehæled.

LXXIX. Cwice   gramen

1. Wið miltan sare genym þysse wyrte leaf þe man gramen /
f. 43v 7 oðrum naman cwice nemneð 7 geseoð hy, smyre þonne anne
25 cla ð þærmid, lege to þære miltan; þu ongytest fremfulnysse þæróf.

MS V

1 syn] synd H.   2 to] þær to H 4/1.   5 cwædon] sædon H.
7 afeormað] feormað H.   9 þæt] þa H   fremað] frymað H.
14 *title*: filix fearn B 95v/16a, *om.* H.   16 gecnucudne] gecnucude H.
18 healyde] healede BH.   19 bécenan] becænnan H   treowes
wyrttruman] *om.* H.   21 fiftan] fiftan (tan *crossed out*) H.   22 *title*:
cwice BH. 25 lege] 7 lege H.

MS O

12 *title*: *in black, in addition to a faded title in red.*

1. (Ad plagam) Wið wunda, þeah hi sín swiþe ealde, cnuca þa wyrt mid ealde risele, leʒe to þa wunda, hit hæleð sona.

2. (Ad plagam per ferrum factam) Gif hwa mid iserne ʒesleeʒen sy nim þa wyrt on ærne morʒen oþþer to middæʒe, cnuca hi mid ealden / risele,   f. 37 leʒe to þare wunda; sona heo þa wunda anopenað 7 afermað.   5

3. (Ad dolorem pedum) Wið fotadle cnuca þa wyrt mid risele, leʒe to ðan fote, hit ʒeliþegað þæt sær. Eac hít fremeð miclum wyð þara sina sare.

4. (Ad dolorem renum) Wið lendenna cnuca þa wyrt mid sealte þan ʒemete þe ðu clyðan wyrche, leʒe to þan lendane, þan ʒelice hit fremeþ   10 wid þara fote sare eac.

LXXVIII. De felice   Anglice fer(n)   f. 16/1

1. Wið wund(a) nim þisse wyrt wyrttrume (þæ)t man fel(ix) 7 Engle fearn nemneð ʒecnucode, 7 æðelferþinʒcwyrt twea trimesa ʒewaʒe sile drincan on wine.   15

2. Wið þat ʒeong man healyde si ním þeos wyrt þare heo on becenu(m) treow(es) wurtrume wexen si, cnuca mid risele 7 ʒedec anne clað þæ(r)mid 7 ʒewrið to þan sara swa þat he þa hwile uppe(weard) ʒewend si; þi fiftan dæʒe (. . .).

LXXIX *om.* O.   20

MS Ca

1. Ad vulnera quamvis vetustissima. Herba senecion tunsa et subacta cum axungia vetere in plaga imposita sanat vulnera.   p. 499

2. Si quis ferro percussus fuerit. Herba senecion si mane, ad hora sexta collecta fuerit et tunsa cum axungia vetere et in plaga imposita plagam aperit et expurgat (. . .).

3. Ad pedum tumorem vel dolorem aut idem nervorum. Herba senecion tunsa cum axungia et imposita pedum dolorem sedat vel nervorum potentissime.

4a. Ad lumborum et coxarum dolorem. Herba senecion per se ieiuno potui data validissime prodest.

4b. Ad podagram. Herba senecion trita cum sale ut sive sit genus malagmae, opposita pedibus prodesse dicitur.

LXXVIII. Herba filix

1. Ad vulnera. Herbae filicis radicem contritam, vulneri appositam, argimonitidis dragmas ii cum vino potui si dederis, mox sedat dolorem.

2. Ad ramicem pueris. Herbam filicem quam in radice aesculi arboris inveneris, tunde eam cum axungia et panno induc; cum imposueris, [fasciam sursum versus] ligabis; sanabitur quinto die.

LXXIX. Herba gramen

1. Ad splenis dolorem. Herbae graminis decoquis eius florem et in panno linis et imponis in splenem, sentiet beneficium.

LXXX. Glædene gladiolus

1. Wið blædran sare 7 wið þæt man gemigan ne mæge genim þysse wyrte wyrttruman utewearde ðe man gladiol'u'm 7 oþrum naman glædene nemneþ, drige hyne þonne 7 cnuca 7 gemengc 5 ðærto twegean scenceas wines 7 þry wæteres, syle drincan.

2. Wið miltan sare genim þas [ilcan] wyrte gladiolum þonne heo geong sy, drige hy 7 cnuca to swyþe smalan duste, syle þicgean on liþum wine; hyt is gelyfed þæt hit wundorlice þa miltan (g)e-hæleþ.

10 3. Wiþ innoþes sare 7 þæra breosta genim þysse sylfan wyrte bergean gecnucude 7 on gætenre meolce oððe gyt selre on wine gewlehte syle drincan, þæt sár geswiceþ.

LXXXI. Boðen rosmarinum

Ðeos wyrt þe man rosmarim 7 oðrum naman boþen nemneþ 15 byþ cenned on sandigum landum 7 on wyrtbeddum.

1. Wið toþece genim þysse wyrte wyrtwalan þe we rosmarim nemdun, syle etan, butan yldincge he genimð þæra toða sár, 7 f. 44 healde þæt wos on his muþe, / sona hyt gehælþ þa teð.

2. Wið adligende genim þas wyrte rosmarinum, cnuca mid ele, 20 smyre ðone adligendan, wundorlice þu hine gehælest.

3. Wið gicþan genim þas ylcan wyrte, gecnuca hy 7 gemengc hyre wos wið eald win 7 wið wearm wæter, syle drincan þry dagas.

MS V

1 title: gledene B 96/t.m.a, glædene H. 2 genim] genime H 5/1. 3 wyrttruman] gl. rote H gladiol'u'm] u interlined above exp. i V. 4 hyne] hy (followed by erasure of two letters) H. 5 twegean] twegen B. 6 ilcan] from B, illan V. 7 smalan] id. H (second a alt. from u). 8 þæt] ð H. 10 innoþes sare] gl. colica past(i) H genim] genime H þysse] þa H. 11 gætenre] gætenne H. 13 title: rosmarinum boðen B, boðen H. 14 rosmarim] id. H (i alt. from u). 15 cenned] cænned (alt. from nemned) H. 16 wyrte wyrtwalan] wirt wirttruman B we] me H rosmarim] id. H (i alt. from u). 17 yldincge] gl. swolewinge H. 18 sona hyt] sona hit sona hit (first two words struck out and exp.) H gehælþ] gehæl H. 19 adligende] gl. bedrede H rosmarinum] rosmarum H. 22 drincan] drin H.

MS O

10 oþþer] oþer (þ marked for doubling), unexpunged a. 13 boȝan] e interlined above

LXXX. (. . .)   f. 18/1

1. ((. . .) (dolo)rem ues(ic)ae) þeos wyrt þat men gladiolum(. . .) gladen(e)
nemneð. Wið bl(ædran) sara 7 wið man miȝan ne mæȝe þisse wyrt
wyrtrume utewearde 7 driȝe hine þane 7 cnuca þarto tweȝen scences
wines 7 þru wæteres, sile drínc(an).   5

2. (Ad dolorem splenis) (Wi)ð miltan sare ním þeos wurt þane heo
ȝeonȝ si, driȝe hy 7 cnuca (. . .) smalum duste, sile drincan on liþum wíne,
hit is ȝelyfed þat hit (. . .) miltan wunderlice ȝehæleð.

3. (Ad dolorem uiscerum) Wið þas innoþes sare 7 þæra (breo)sta
cnuca þisse wyrt beriȝean 7 on gætene meolce oþþer selra on wine   10
ȝewlehte syle drincan, þat sar ȝes(wiceþ).

LXXXI. De rosemarino   f. 32v/17

þeos wyrt þæt man rosmaríni 7 oþrum naman boȝan nemneð byð
cenned on sandiȝum lænde 7 on wyrtbedde.

1. (Ad dolorem dentium) Wið toðece ním þisse wyrt walan 7 sile   15
etan; butan yldyncge he binimð þara toða sar; 7 healde þæt wos on his
muþe; sona hit hæleð þa teð.

2. Wið adliȝende cnuca þas wyrt mid ele, smere þane adliȝenda,
wunderlice þu hine ȝehælest.

3. (Wyd ȝycþan) Wid ȝycþan cnuca þeos wyrt 7 hire wos meng wiþ   20
eald wín 7 wyd wearm wæter, sile drincan þri daȝas.

MS Ca

LXXX. Herba gladiolum   p. 500

1. Ad vesicae dolorem et ad eos qui urinam non faciunt. Herbam
gladiolum effodies et siccato cortice radicis eius conterito et addito in
vino cyatis duobus, aquae cyatos tres coniunges et sic potabis.

2. Ad splenis dolorem. Herbam gladiolum maturissimam lectam,
siccatam et pisatam et in pulvere mollissimo redactam et vino [lenissimo],
id est inerticio, mixto pulvere potui datum, mire creditur splenem siccare.

3. Ad coli et praecordiarum dolorem. Herbae gladioli bacas tritas
[ex] lacte caprino, melius si asinino, tepefactum dato bibere, desinet dolor.

LXXXI. Herba rosmarinum

Nascitur locis marinis et hortis (. . .).

1. Ad dentium dolorem. Herbae rosmarini radix commanducata
dentium dolorem sine mora tollet; sucum eius super dentem si tenueris,
mox sanat.

2. Ad languentes. Herba rosmarinum trita cum oleo languidum perungues, mire sanabis.

3. Ad pruriginem. Herbam rosmarinum conteris et sucum eius cum
vino veteri et aqua calida per triduum bibat.

4. Wið liferseocnysse 7 þæs innoðes genim þysse sylfan wyrte sumne gripan, scearfl(a) on (wæ)ter 7 gemencg þærto nar(d)is twá handfulla 7 rudan su(m)ne stelan, seoð tosomne on wætere, syle drincan, he bið hal.

5. 5. Wið niwe wunda genim þas ylcan wyrte þe we rosmarim nemdun, cnuca mid rysle, lege to þam wundum.

LXXXII. Feldmoru   pastinaca siluatica

þeos wyrt þe man pastinace siluatice 7 oðrum naman feldmoru nemneþ bið cenned on sandigum stowum 7 on beorgum.

10 1. Wið þæt wifmen earfuðlice cennen genim þas wyrte þe we pastinacam siluaticam nemdun, seoð on wætere, syle þonne þæt se man hyne þær(m)id beð(i)ge, he bið gehæled.

2. Wið wifa afeormungæ genim þas ylcan wyrte pastinacam, seoð on wætere, 7 þonne heo ge(sod)en beo mengc hy wel 7 syle 15 drinc(an), hy beoð afeormud(e).

LXXXIII. Dolhrune   perdicalis

Ðeos wyrt þe man perdicalis 7 oðrum naman dolhrune nemneð byþ cened wið wegas 7 wið weallas 7 on beorgum. /

f. 44v   1. Wið fotadle 7 wið cancor genim þas wyrte þe we perdicalis 20 nemdun, seoð on wætere, beþe þonne þa fet 7 þa cnewu, cnuca syððan þa wyrte mid rysle, dó on ænne clað 7 lege to þam fotum 7 to þam cneowum, þu hy wel gehælst.

MS V

1 sylfan] ilcan B.   2 sumne] *gl.* i.e. litel H 6/2.   3 handfulla] -fulle (a *interlined above unexpunged* e) H   wætere] wæter H.   5 rosmarim] rosmarinum BH.   7 *title*: feldmore B 96v/15a, feldmoru H.   8 þeos] Ðeo H   pastinace] pastimace H.   9 stowum] lande H.   10 cennen] cænnen (c *and left part of* æ *alt. from* n) B.   11 pastinacam] pastimacam H.   13 afeormungæ] afeormunge B, feormunge (f *preceded by erasure of* a) H.   14 7[1]] *om.* H   syle] syle hy H.   16 *title*: dolhrune B, *om.* H.   18 cened] cænned BH.   19 cancor] cneowu (n *alt. from* a) H   perdicalis] *gl.* halmerwet H.   20 beþe] beða B   cnewu] cneowa B, cneowu H.

MS O

2 *no title, see textual note.*   4 earfoþlice] eaf earfoþlice (eaf *exp.*). 13 cneowe] cnu cneowe (cnu *exp.*).   14 ȝehælst] *the symbol between* l *and* t *is unidentifiable.*

4, 5. —

LXXXII. (*No title in* O)

þeos wyrt þæt man panastica siluatica.　　　　　　　　　　f. 28v/8

1. (Ut mulier concipiat citu) Wið þæt wifmen earfoþlice cennen nim
þeos wyrt, seoþ on wætere, sile þanne þat se man hine þarmid beþie; 5
he byð ȝehæled.

2. Wið wifa afeormunge nim þeos wyrt pastinacam, seoð on wætera,
7 þanne heo ysode beod meng hi wel 7 sile drincan, heo byð afeorm`o´d.

LXXXIII. Perdiculus　dolhrune　　　　　　　　　　　f. 28v/15

þeos wyrt þat man perdiculis 7 Engle dolhrune hæteð.　　　　10

1. (Ad morbum pedum et ad cancram et ad genua) Wið feotadle 7
wið cancor nim þeos wyrt perdicalis, seoð on wætere, beðe þanne þa fet
7 þa cneowe, cnuca þissa þa wyrt mid risle, don on anne clað 7 leȝe to
þan fote 7 to þan cneowum; þu hi wel [ȝehælst].

MS Ca

4. Ad eparis dolorem vel interaneorum. Herbae rosmarini fasciculum
concidis ex aqua, adicies illi amomum pusillum aut spicam nardi et
palmulas duas, rutae caliculum, in se coque et aquam earum dabis bibere,
sanus fiet.

5. Ad vulnera recentia. Herba rosmarinum contusa vel cocta cum　p. 501
axungia imposita optime facit.

LXXXII. Herba pastinaca silvatica

Nascitur locis saxosis et aggeribus.

1. Ad mulieres quae a partu laborant et non purgantur. Herba pastinaca silvatica cocta et de aqua eius se fomentet, sanabitur.

2. Ad purgationem mulieris. Herba pastinaca silvatica cocta, cum
eadem aqua ubi cocta est commisce et dato ei bibere, purgabitur.

LXXXIII. Herba perdicalis

Nascitur per parietibus aut maceriis aut aggeribus.

1. Ad podagram aut onogram. Herba perdicalis coquitur in aqua, et
ex ea aqua fovebis pedes vel genua, deinde ipsam tunsam cum axungia
impones panno, inductam in pedes vel in genua, sanabis mire.

LXXXIV. Cedelc mercurialis

1. Wið þæs innoðes heardnysse genim þas wyrte þe man mercurialis 7 oðrum naman cedelc nemneð on wætere gegnidene, syle þam ðolegendum, sona heo ða heardnysse ut atyhð 7 ðone magan afeormað, þam gelice þæt sæd fremað.

2. Wið eagena sár 7 geswel genim ðysse sylfan wyrte leaf gecnucude on ealdum wine, lege to þam sare.

3. Gif wæter on earan swiðe gesigen sy genim þysse ylcan wyrte seaw wlæc, drype on þæt eare, sona hyt toflyð.

LXXXV. Eforfearn radiola

Ðeos wyrt þe man radiolum 7 oðrum naman eforfearn nemneð ys gelic fearne 7 heo byð cenned on stanigum stowum 7 on ealdum husstedum, 7 heo hæfð on æghwylcum leafe twa endebyrdnyssa fægerra pricena, 7 þa scinað swa gold.

f. 45

1. Wið heafodece genim þas wyrte / þe we radiolum nemdun swiðe clæne áfeormude, seoð on ecede þearle, smy(re) þonne þæt heafud [þærmid], hyt geliðe(ga)ð þæt sár.

LXXXVI. Wuduceruille spurgia agrestis

1. Wið blædran sare oððe geswelle genim þysse wyrte wyrttruman þe man sparagiagrestis 7 oðrum naman wuducerfilla nemneð, seoð on wætere to feorðan dæle, drince ðonne fæstende seofan dagas, 7 he manegum dagum bæþes bruce 7 na on caldum wætere cume ne he cealdne wætan ne þicge, wundorlice he hæle ongyt.

MS V

1 *title*: mercurialis cedelc B 97/16a, *om.* H.   2 heardnysse] nearunesse H.   7 gecnucude] 'ge'cnucade H. 7/9.   9 toflyð] toflihð BH. 10 *title*: euerfearn radiolum B, *om.* H.   11 eforfearn] euorfearn BH. 12 stowum] lande H.   13–14 endebyrdnyssa] ændebyrdnysse (a *interlined above unexpunged final* e) H.   17 þærmid] *emended from* þær/þar VBH. 18 *title*: wudecearuilla B 97v/11a, *om.* H.   19 geswelle] geswe'l'le H. 20 sparagiagrestis] sparagiægrestis H   wuducerfilla] -cearuilla B, -cyrfille H. 22 bæþes] beþæs H   caldum] *alt. from* ealdum V.   23 cume] 'he' cume H   cealdne] *id.* H (n *alt. from* r).

MS O

9–10 wudacæruílla] æ *alt. from* a.

LXXXIV *om.* O.

LXXXV. De radiolo id est pollipodio   f. 32v/27

þeos wyrt þat man radiolum 7 oþer nama eaforfirn nemniað.

1. (Ad dolorem capitis) Wið heafodece nim þeos wyrt radiolum swiþe clane afermede, þeos on ecede þearle, smire þanne þæt heafod, hit ȝeli- 5 þegað þat sar.

LXXXVI. Sparagia   wudeceruilla   f. 37/8

1. (Ad dolorem et inflationem uesice) Wið bladra sare oþþer ȝeswelle ním þissa wyrt wurtruman þæt man sparagiagrestis 7 Engle wuda- cæruílla hatað, seoð on wætere to feorþan dæle, drinca þanne fæstende 10 seofan dæȝes, 7 he maneȝum dæȝun bæþas ne bruca 7 he on cælda wætere ne cume ne he cealdne wæte ne þicȝe; wunderlice he hæle onȝyt.

MS Ca

LXXXIV. Herba mercurialis

1. Ad ventris duritiam. Herbam mercurialem coques et tritam ex p. 502 passo dabis, statim detrahet et stomachum purgat; nam semen eius tritum cum passo dabis, idem detrahet.

2. Ad oculorum epiforas. Herbae mercurialis folia cum vino albo veteri imponantur.

3. Si aqua in aures introierit. Herbae mercurialis sucum tepidum in aure stillatum, mox liberabitur.

LXXXV. Herba radiolum

Similis est filici quae fere in lapidetis nascitur vel in parietinis, habens in foliis singulis binos ordines punctorum aureorum.

1. Ad capitis dolorem. Herbam radiolum contusam, ante curiose depurgatam, cum aceto scillitico usque adeo decoctam donec non pareat, perunguendo capitis dolorem sedat.

LXXXVI. Herba sparagi agrestis

1. Ad vesicae dolorem vel tumorem. Herbae sparagi agrestis radicem coque in aquae sextario in pultario novo ad quartas, et ieiunus diebus vii sumat potui, plurimis diebus balneum utatur, in frigida non descendat neque frigida bibat, mirifice experietur.

2. Wið toðece genim þysse sylfan wyrte seaw þe we sparagi nemdun, syle supan, 7 healde hyt swa on hys muðe.

3. Wið æddrena sare genim þysse ylcan wyrte wyrtwalan gecnucude on wine, syle drincan, hyt fremað.

5 4. Gyf hwylc yfeldæde man þurh ænigne æfþancan oþerne begaleþ genim þysse sylfan wyrte wyrttruman gedrigide, syle þicgean mid wyllewætere 7 besprengc hyne mid þam wætere, he bið unbunden.

LXXXVII. Sauine   sauina

10 1. Wið þa cynelican adle þe man aurignem nemneð, þæt ys on ure geþeode þæra syna getoh 7 fota geswel, genim þas wyrte þe man sabinam 7 oðrum naman wel þam gelice sauinam hateþ, syle drincan mid hunige, heo tofereþ þæt sár, þæt sylfe heo deþ

f. 45v mid wine / gecnucud.

15 2. Wiþ heafodece genim þas ylcan wyrte sabinam eornlice gecnucude mid ecede 7 mid ele gemencgede, smyra þonne þæt heafud 7 þa þunwonga, healice hyt fremað.

3. Wiþ deadspringas genim þas wyrte sabinam mid hunige gecnucude, smyre þonne þæt sár.

20 ## LXXXVIII. Hundes heafod   canis capud

1. Wið eagena sár 7 geswel genim þysse wyrte wyrtwalan þe man canis caput 7 on ure geþeode hundes heafod hatað, seoð on wætere, 7 syþþan mid þam wætere þa eagan gebeþa, hrædlice hyt þæt sár geliþigað.

MS V

6 wyrttruman] gl. rote H 8/12   gedrigide] gedrigede BH.   7 wyllewætere] wyllwætere H.   9 title: sabinam sauinam B, om. H.
10 cynelican] gl. kinkes H   aurignem] auprignnem H.   11 geþeode]
ðeode H.   12 sauinam] sauinan H.   15 genim] gen'i'm H   sabinam]
sabinan BH   eornlice] eorðlice H.   16 gemencgede] gemænged B.
17 fremað] frymað H.   18 deadspringas] -spryn'c'gas, gl. ad morbum
regium, in o.m. (. . .)iginem H   sabinam] sabinan H.   20 title: hundes
heafod B 98/19a, om. H.   22 caput] capuð B   hatað] hateð B, hateð
H 9/2.

MS O

2 muþe] moðe muþe (moðe exp.).   4 sele] sele / le.   6 æníȝne]
aníne æníȝne (aníne exp., æ alt. from a).   16 ele] gl. oleo.

2. (Ad dolorem dentium) Wið toðece sule suppe þisse wyrt seaw, 7 healde hyt swa on his muþe.

3. (Ad dolorem uene) Wið æddrana sara cnuca þissa wyrt walan 7 on wine sele drinca; hít fremaþ.

4. (Si quis maleficus aliquem per incantationem noceat sic curabitur) 5 Gif hwylc yfeldade man þurh æníȝne ærþancan oþerne begaleð ním þisse wyrt wurtruman ȝedriȝede, sile ðícȝan mid willewætere 7 bespenȝ híne mið þan wætere, he byð unbunde.

LXXXVII. Sauina siue sabina   f. 37v/1

1. (Ad regiam morbum hoc est Anglice þara sina ȝetoh 7 fota ȝeswel) 10 Wið þa cunelican adle þæt man aurignem nemneð, þæt ys on ure ȝeþode þara sína ȝetoh 7 fota ȝewel, ním þa wyrt þæt man sabinan 7 oþþer nama sauínam nemneð, syle drincan mid huníȝe; heo tofereþ þæt sar. Ðat silue heo deþ mid wíne ȝecnucod.

2. (Ad dolorem capitis) Wið heafodhece cnuca þa wyrt mid ecede 7 mid 15 ele ȝemengede, smyra þanne þæt heafod mid 7 þa þunwunga; healice hit fremeþ.

3. —

LXXXVIII. (. . .)   f. 11/10

1. (Ad inflationem et infirmitatem oculorum) Wið eaȝene sar 7 ȝeswel 20 þisse wyrt 'wurt'trumen þe man capð canis 7 Engle hundes hæfod (n)ennað, seoð wætere, 7 siþþan mid þan wætere þa eaȝene ȝebeða; hrædlice hit þat sar (ȝ)eliþeȝeð.

MS Ca

2. Ad dentium dolorem. Herbae sparagi sucum in ore contineri oportet.

3. Ad renum dolorem. [Herbae sparagi radix trita, cum vino potata proficit.

4. Si quis malevolus devotaverit hominem.] Herbae sparagi agrestis radicem siccam cum aqua fontana, lustrabis eum et solutus erit.

LXXXVII. Herba savina   p. 503

1. Ad morbum regium quod est auriginem. Herba savina cum melle et vino potata auriginem discutit, cum vino trita idem facit.

2. Ad capitis dolorem. Herba savina diligenter trita, cum aceto et oleo rosaceo mixta, capiti et temporibus illinita valde prodest.

3. Ad carbunculum. Herba savina, cum melle illinito.

LXXXVIII. Herba canis caput

1. Ad epiforas oculorum. Herba canis cerebrum, radicem cum aqua decoctam, de ea aqua [subinde] oculos foveat, epiforas celeriter lenit.

LXXXIX. Bremel   herba erusti

1. Wið earena sár genim þas wyrte þe man erusti 7 oþrum naman bremel nemneð, swa mearwe, gecnuca, nim þonne þæt wós gewleht, drype on þæt eare, hyt þæt gewanað 7 gewislice gehæleþ.

5   2. Wið wifes flewsan genim þysse ylcan wyrte croppas swa mearwe, 7 þæra syn þriwa seofeone, seoð on wætere to þriddan dæle, syle drincan fæstende þry dagas swa þæt ðu þeah æghwylce dæg þone drenc niwie.

3. Wið heortece genim þysse ylcan wyrte leaf gecnucude þurh f. 46 hy sylfe, lege ofer þone wynstran / tit; þæt sár tofærð.

11   4. Wið niwe wunda genim þysse sylfan wyrte blostman, lege to ðam wundum, butan ælcre yldincge 7 frecenysse hy þa wunda gehælað.

5. Wiþ liþa sare genim þysse ylcan wyrte sumne dæl, seoð on 15 wine to þriddan dæle, 7 of þam wine syn þonne þa lyþu gebeðede, ealle þæra liða untrumnysse hyt geliðigaþ.

6. Wið næddran slite genim þysse ilcan wyrte leaf þe we erusti nemdun swa niwe gecnucude, lege to ðam sare.

XC. Gearwe   millifolium

20   1. Ðas wyrte þe man [millefolium] 7 on ure geþeode gearwe nemneþ, ys sæd þæt Achilles se ealdorman hy findan scolde, 7 he mid þysse sylfan wyrte gehælde þa þe mid iserne geslegene 7 gewundude wæran. Eac heo of sumum mannum for þy genemned ys achylleos, mid þære wyrte ys sæd þæt he eac sumne man ge- 25 hælan sceolde þam wæs Thelephon nama.

MS V

1 *title*: bremel B, *om.* H.   3 bremel] bræmbel H.   6 seofeone] seofone B, syfone H.   8 dæg] *id.* H (æ *alt. from* e).   9 heortece] *gl.* ad cardiacos H.   11 lege] gele`g´e H.        12 frecenysse] frecen/nysse B 98v/1a. 19 *title*: garuwe B, *om.* H.        20 Ðas wyrte] Ðeos wyrt B        millefolium] *from* B, millefoliu V.        21 Achilles] Ahchilles H.        22 he] *om.* H 10/2. 24 sumne] sume H.        25 Thelephon] Thelefon B, þelefo`n´ (þ *alt. from* th, *between second* e *and* f *an imperfectly erased* o) H.

MS O

3 `earena´] *interlined above* eaȝean (*exp.*).   19 de millefolio (*black*) *also in* t.m.; *see t.n. for beginning of this chapter.*

LXXXIX. (. . .)　　　　　　　　　　　　　　　　f. 14v/8

1. (Ad surditatem) (þ)eos wyrt þæt man (e)rusti 7 oþer nama bremel
nemneð. Wið ˋearenaˊ sar ȝením þa wyrt (s)wa mearwe, ˋȝeˊcnuca, nim
þanne þat wos ȝewleht, drupe on þat eare, hit þat ifel ȝewanað 7 ȝewislice
ȝehælð.　　　　　　　　　　　　　　　　　　　　　　　5

2. (Contra fluxum mulierum) Wið wifes flewsan nim þisse wyrt
croppes swa meˋaˊrwe, 7 þara sín ðriwa seofne, seod (. . .) wætere to
ðriddan dæle, sile drincan fæstende þ(ry) dagas swa þæt þu ðeah æȝhwilce
dæȝ þane drenc ni(wie).

3. (Contra dolorem cordis) Wið heortece nim þisse wyrt leaf ȝe-　10
cnucode þurþ hi silfe, leȝe ofer þone wynstran tæt, þat sor tofærð.

4. (Ad plagam recentam) Wyð niwa wunda ním þissan sylfan wyrt
blost(ma)n, leȝe to ðara wunda, butan alcera yldincge (7) (frecen)nysse
þa wunda ȝehæleð.

5. (Ad dolorem memb(rorum)) Wið lyþa sore ním þisse wyrt su(mne)　15
dæl, seoð (o)n wine to ðridda(n dæ)le, 7 of (þa)m wíne sy þa(nne) (. . .)
liþu (. . .) þæra (. . .).

6. (Ad punctum (ser)pentium) (. . .) (næ)dr(an) (. . .).

XC. De millefoli(o) (. . .) gearwe Anglice　　　　　f. 20/1

　1–8. —　　　　　　　　　　　　　　　　　　　　20

MS Ca

LXXXIX. Herba erustum

1. Ad aurium dolorem. Herbae rusti teneri cimas, sucus expressus,　p. 504
tepefactum et stillatum, aurium dolorem liberat et persanat, certum est.

2. Ad profluvium mulieris. Herbae rusti cimas teneras ter septenas
coque in aqua usque ad tertias et triduo ieiuno potum dabis, ita ut cotidie
renoves potionem.

3. Ad cardiacos. Herbae rusti folia per se trita imponuntur mamillae
sinistrae, dolori resistit.

4. Ad vulnera recentia. Herbae rubi aut flos aut mora imponitur, sine
collectionis periculo sanat.

5. Ad condolomata. Herba rubus de vino coquitur ad tertias eoque
vino foventur condolomata et omnia vitia sedat.

6. Contra serpentium et hominum morsus. Herbae [rubi] folia recentia
trita imponantur.

XC. Herba millefolium

1. Hanc herbam Achilles invenit, unde vulnera ferro percussa sanavit;
quae ob id achillea vocatur, de hac sanasse [Telephon] dicitur.

2. Wið toðece genim þysse wyrte wyrtwalan ðe we millefolium nemdun, syle etan fæstendum.

3. Wiþ wunda þe mid iserne syn geworhte genim þas ylcan
wyrte mid rysle gecnucude, lege to þam wundum, heo þa wunda
5 afeormaþ 7 gehæleð.

4. Wiþ geswell genim þas ylcan wyrte myllefolium mid buteran
gecnucude, lege to þam geswelle.

5. Wið þæt hwylc man earfoðlice gemigan mæge genim þysse
ylcan wyrte wos mid ecede, syle drincan, wundurlice heo hæleþ.

10 6. Gif wund on men acolod sy genim þonne ða sylfan wyrte
millefolium 7 gnid swyþe smale 7 mengc wið buteran, lege ðonne
on ða wunda, heo cwicaþ sona 7 wearmað. /

f. 46v   7. Gif men þæt heafod berste oððe uncuð swyle on gesitte
nime þysse ylcan wyrte wyrtwalan, binde on þone swyran, ðonne
15 cymeð hym þæt to godre freme.

8. Eft wið þam ylcan genim þas ylcan wyrte, wyrc to duste,
do on ða wunde, þonne byþ heo sona hatigende.

9. Gyf hwylcum men ædran aheardode syn oððe his mete gemyltan nelle nym þysse ylcan wyrte seaw, mengc ðonne win 7
20 wæter 7 hunig 7 'þæt' seaw eall tosomne, syle hyt him ðonne
wearm drincan, ðonne byþ him sona bet.

10. Eft wið þæra ðearma ece 7 wið ealles þæs innoðes nim þas
ylcan wyrte, dryg hy þonne 7 gegnid to duste swyþe smale, do
ðonne þæs dustes fif cuculeras fulle 7 ðreo full godes wines, syle
25 hym ðonne drincan þæt; ðonne deah hyt him wið swa hwylcum
earfoðum swa him on innan bið.

MS V

1 millefolium] mile- H.   3 geworhte] ge / geworhte (geworhte *preceded
by erasure of* worhte) H.   10 ða] þas BH.   11 millefolium] mile- H.
12 wunda] wunde B   cwicaþ sona 7] *om.* H   wearmað] gewearmað H.
14 swyran] sweoran H.   15 freme] fryme H.   18 aheardode]
heardode H   oððe] oðð B 99/2a.   20 7²] *om.* B.   22 innoðes] innoþes
'sares' H 11/5.

MS O

2 7 þat seaw] seaw *preceded by erasure of one symbol.*   3 's'one] s *interlined above unexpunged* þ.

9. Gif hwylcum men ædran ahe`a´rdode sín oþþer his mete ӡemilten nelle nime þisse wyrt seaw, meng to wín 7 wæter 7 huniӡ 7 þat seaw eal togadere, syle hít hím þane wearm drincan; þane byð `s´one bet.

10. Eft wið þara ðearma eca 7 wid ealle þas innoþes ním þeos wyrt, driӡ hi 7 ӡegnid to duste swuþe smale, do þane þæs dustes fif cuceleras 5 fulle 7 þreo fulle godes wínes, sile drican þæt, þone deah hit hím wið hyylcum earfuðum swa hym innan byð.

MS Ca

2. Ad dentium dolorem. Herbae millefolium radicem ieiunus com- p. 505 manducet.

3. Ad vulnera de ferro facta. Herba millefolium cum axungia pisata et imposita vulnera purgat et sanat.

4. Ad tumores. Herba millefolium contusa, cum butyro impone.

5. Ad urinae difficultatem. Herbae millefolium sucus cum aceto bibitur, mire sanat.

6–16. —

11. Gyf ðonne æfter ðam men sy sogoþa getenge oððe hwylc innan gundbryne genim ðonne þysse wyrte wyrtwalan 7 gecnuca swyþe wel; do ðonne on swyþe god beor, syle hyt him þonne wlacu supan; ðonne wene ic þæt hyt him wel fremie ge wið
5 sogoðan ge wið æghwylcum incundum earfoðnyssum.

12. Wið heafodece genim þas ylcan wyrte, wyrc clyþan þærof, lege ðonne on þæt heafod, ðonne genimð hyt sona þæt sár onweg.

13. Wiþ þan næddercynne ðe man spalangius hateð genim þysse ylcan wyrte twigo 7 þa leaf, seoð on wine, gnid þonne swiþe
10 smale 7 lege on wunde gyf heo tosomne hleapan wolde, 7 ðonne æfter þam genim ða wyrte 7 hunig, mengc tosomne, smyre þa wunde ðærmid, þonne hatað heo sona.

14. Wið næddran slite, gyf hwylc man hyne begyrdeþ mid þysse wyrte 7 hy on wege mid him bereþ, he bið gescylded fram
15 æghwylcum næddercynne.

15. Wið wedehundes slite genim ðas ylcan wyrte, gnid, 7 hwæten corn lege on þa wunde, ðonne halað heo sona.

16. Eft wið nædran slite, gyf seo wund forþunden sy, genim þysse sylfan wyrte telgran, seoð on wætere, gnid þonne swyþe
20 smale, gesodene lege þonne on ða wunde, ðonne þæt dolh open
f. 47 sy genim þa ylcan / wyrte unsodene, gnid swyþe smale, mengc wið hunig, lacna þonne þa wunde þærmid, ðonne byð heo sona hal.

XCI. Rude   ruta

1. Gif blod of nosum flowe genim ðas wyrte þe man rutam 7
25 þam gelice oðrum naman rudan nemneþ, do gelomlice on þa næsðyrlu, wundorlice heo þæt blod of ðam næsðyrlun gewrið.

MS V

1 Gyf] Eft H.   2 gundbryne] cund- B.   4 wlacu] swa wlacu H.
6 clyþan] to clyðan H.   8 þan] þam BH.   9 þonne] om. H.
10 wunde] ða wunde H.   14 he] 'he' H   fram] wið B.   19 sylfan]
ilcan B   telgran]·telgan B.   23 title: ruta B 99v/13a, om. H 12/13.
25 oðrum] 7 oðrum H.   26 næsðyrlu . . . ðam] om. BH.

MS O

. 1 soӡoða ӡetenge] also syӡoþa ӡetenge in o.m.   2 wyrte] followed by
wyrtetruma, struck out and framed   cnuca] preceded by cnu(s), struck out.
4 soӡeþan] preceded by soþe, exp.   'uncunda'] in text iucunda, with a signe
de renvoi to uncunda in o.m.   7 aweӡ] aӡe aweӡ (aӡe exp.).   14 þissan]
si þissan (si exp.).   15 telӡran] telӡra(n) telӡran (first word exp.).   18 title:
in black, framed in red.   20 do] followed by unexpunged h.

11. Gif þanne æfter þam man sy soʒoða ʒetenge oþþer hwylc innan cundbríne ním þane þisse wyrte wurtewalan 7 cnuca swyðe wel; do ðane on swiþe god beor, sile hit hím þanne wlacu supan; þanne wene ic þæt hít hím wel fremia ʒe wyð soʒeþan ʒe wyð æʒhwylcum 'uncunda' earfadnysse.   5

12. Wið heæfodece ním þeos wyrt, wyrc cliðan þarof, leʒe þane on þat heafod; þanne binímð hyt sona þæt sor aweʒ.

13. —

14. Wið naddran slite, ʒif hwylc man hine begyrdeþ mid þisse wyrt 7 hi on weʒe mid him bereð, he byð ʒescylded fram æʒ'h'wylcen nædd-   10 drecunne.

15. Wið wodes hundes slite ním þeos wyrt, gnid, 7 hwæten corn leʒe on wunde; heo haleð sona.

16. Eft wið næddra slíte, ʒif se wunde forþundon si, ním þissan wyrt telʒran, seoþ on wætere, gnid þane swyðe smale, ʒeso/tone leʒe on þa   f. 20v wunda; 7 þanne ðæt dolʒ open si ním þa wyrt ʒeesodone, gnid swyde   16 smale, meng wyd huníʒ, læcna þa wunda þarmid; héo byd þona hæl.

XCI. De ruta   f. 33v/1

1. (Ad sanguinem de naribus) Gif blod of noþe flowe ním rutam, 7 on þa nosðyrlu do ʒelomlice; wunderlice heo þæt blod of þan nosþurle   20 ʒewrið.

MS Ca

XCI. Herba ruta hortensis

1. Ad sanguinem fluentem de naribus. Herba ruta hortensis frequentius odorata sanguinem de naribus mire restringit.

2. Wið toðundennysse genim þas ylcan wyrte rutam, syle hy
dælmelum swa grene etan oððe on drince þicgean.

3. Wið þæs magan sare genim þysse ylcan wyrte sæd 7 swefel
7 eced, syle þicgean fæstendum.

5　　4. Wið eagena sare 7 geswel genim þas ylcan [wyrte] rutan wel
gecnucude, lege to ðam sare, eac sé wyrttruma gecnucud 7
ðærmid gesmyred, þæt sár hyt wel gebet.

5. Wið þa adle ðe man litargum hateð, þæt ys on ure geþeode
ofergytulnys cweden, genim þas ylcan wyrte rutam mid ecede
10　gewesede, begeot þonne ðæne andwlatan ðærmid.

6. Wiþ eagena dymnysse genim ðysse sylfan wyrte leaf, syl(e)
etan fæstendum 7 syle hy drinc(an) on wine.

7. Wið heafodece ge(nim) ðas (ylcan) wyrte, syle drincan on
(wine), cnuca eft þas sylfan wy(rte) 7 wring þæt wos on eced,
15　sm(yre) ðonne þæt heafod þærmid; ea(c þeos) wyrt fremað wið
deadsp(ringas).

XCII. [Mentastrum horsminte]　mentastrus /

f. 47v　　1. Wið earena sáre genim þysse wyrte wos þe man mentastrum
7 oðrum naman (. . .) hateþ mid strangon wine gemengced, dó
20　on þæt eare, þeah ðær beon wyrmas on acennede hi þurh ðis
sceolon beon ácwealde.

2. Wið hreoflan genim þysse ylcan wyrte leaf, syle etan,
gewislice he bið gehæled.

MS V

2 dælmelum] -mælum BH　　　drince] drincan H.　　　　　3 sæd] sed H
swefel] *gl.* i.e. cum sulphure uiuo H.　　4 syle] 7 syle H.　　　5 wyrte]
from B, *om.* V.　　　6 wyrttruma] wyr`t´truma H.　　　10 ðæne] þone B.
11 sylfan wyrte] silfe wyrtan B.　　　14 cnuca] *om.* H 13/3　　þas] þa H
eced] `e´cede 7 H.　　　15 fremað] frymað H.　　　17 *first title: from* B,
om. VH.　　18 mentastrum] myntastrum H.　　　19 oðrum] on oþrum H.
20 acennede] `a´cænnede H.　　21 sceolon] sculon B 100/2a.　　23 gewislice]
om. B.

MS O

1 dælmæle] dæl male mæle (male *exp.*).　　　2 þicʒean] si þicʒean (si *exp.*).
3 þicʒen] drincan þicʒen (drincan *exp.*).　　　9 beʒeot] be li ʒeot (li *exp.*).
10 anw`l´itan] *gl.* faciem.　　11 eta] eta 7 drica (7 drica *exp.*).　　14 title: *the*
last word in black.　　18 etan] etan etan (*first word stained and exp.*).

2. Wið toðundunnysse ním ruta, sile hy dælmæle swa grene to etan oþþer on drincan þicȝean.

3. Wið þas mæȝe sara nim rute sæd 7 swewel 7 ecede 7 sile þicȝen fastinde.

4. (Ad occulos inflatos) Wið eæȝe sare 7 ȝeswelle cnuca ruta, leȝe to 5 þan sare, eac se wrutrume ȝecnucod 7 þarmid ȝesmired, þæt sar hit ȝebet.

5. (Ad mo(rbum) (. . .)) Wið þa adle þæt man litargum hateð, þæt on Englis oferȝyttolnysse cwedan, ním ruta mid ecede bewesede, beȝeot þane anw'l'itan mid.   10

6. Wið eæȝena dimnysse rute leaf eta fastínde 7 drinca on wíne.

7. Wið heæfedece drinca rue on wine. Eaft cnuca rue 7 wring þat wos on ecede, smyra þæt heæfod þarmid. Eac rue fremeð wyd deade sprícas.

XCII. De mentastro   menstrastrum   f. 21v/1

1. Wið earan sare ním þara wurte wos þæt man mentastrum 7 Engle 15 brocminte nemneð mid strange wíne ȝemenged, do on þæt eare; þeah þar beon wurmas acenned hi þur þis sceolon beon awealde.

2. Wið hreoflan ním þisse wyrte leaf 7 syle etan, ȝewislice he byd ȝehaled.

MS Ca

2. Ad inflationes. Herba ruta hortensis cruda, paululum edito vel in potione sumito.

3. Ad stomachi dolorem. Herbae rutae semen cum sulfure vivo et aceto ieiunus gustato.

4. Ad epiforas oculorum. Herba ruta cum polenta bene trita et posita lenit epiforas; nam et radix contusa et illinita emendat.

5. Ad litargos excitandos. Herba ruta ex aceto infunditur fronti.

6. Ad aciem oculorum. Herbae rutae folia eius subinde manducet ieiunus, cum vino contrita potui data antidotum est.

7. Ad capitis dolorem. Herba ruta ex vino potui data et trita, stillato capiti cum aceto et rosaceo.

XCII. Herba mentastrum

1. Ad aurium vitia vel dolores. Herbae mentastri sucus cum vino p. 506 austero mixtus, etiam auriculae coniectus vermes natos necare creditur.

2. Ad elefantiosos. Herba mentastrum, folia eius adhibentes commanducant, sanare certum est.

XCIII. Wælwyrt [oððe] ellenwyrt   ebulus

1. (W)ið þæt stanas on blædran wexen genim þas wyrte þe man
ebulum 7 oðrum naman ellenwyrte nemneþ 7 eac sume men wealwyrt hatǎ, gecnuca hy þonne swa mearwe mid hyre leafum, syle
5 drincan on wine, heo út anydeþ ða untrumnysse.

2. Wið næddran slite genim þas ylcan wyrte þe we ebulum
nemdun, 7 ǽr þam ðe þu hy forceorfe heald hy on þinre handa
7 cweð þriwa nigon siþan: Omnes malas bestias canto, þæt ys
þonne on ure geþeode: Besing 7 ofercum ealle yfele wilddeor;
10 forceorf hy ðonne mid swyþe scearpon sexe on þry dælas; 7 þa
hwile þe þu ðis dó þenc be þam men þe þu ðærmid þencst to
gelacnienne, 7 þonne þu þanon wende ne beseoh þu þe ná; nim
ðonne þa wyrte 7 cnuca hy, lege to þam slite, sona he bið hal.

3. Wiþ wæterseocnysse genim þysse ylcan wyrte wyrtwalan
15 gecnucude, wring þonne þærof swa þæt þu. hæbbe þærof feower
scenceas 7 wines healfne sester, syle drincan [æne] on dæg,
hyt fremað myclum þam wæterseocan.

Eac hyt bynnan healfon geare ealne þone wætan ut atyhþ. /

f. 48 XCIV. Dweorgedweosle   pollegion

20 Ðeos wyrt þe man pollegium 7 oþrum naman dweorgedwosle
nemneþ hæfð mid hyre manega læcedomas þeah hy fela manna né
cunne; þonne ys þeos wyrt twegea cynn'a', þæt is wer 7 wif. Se
wer hafaþ hwite blostman 7 þæt wif hafaþ reade oþþe brune,
æghwæþer ys nytlic 7 wundorlic, 7 hi on him habbaþ wundorlice
25 mihte, mid þam mæstan bleo hy blowaþ ðonne nealice oþre
wyrta scrincaþ 7 weorniað.

MS V

1 title: walwurt B, om. H   oððe] in V the Latin nota for vel.   2 wexen]
weaxaþ H.   3 ellenwyrte] -wyrt H   sume men] sumæn H.   9 wild-
deor] wildeor BH.   10 forceorf hy] forceorfe 'hy' H.   11 þenc] 7
þænc H.   13 lege] le'ge' H 14/1.   14 wyrtwalan] gl. rote H.
15 gecnucude] gecnude H   þærof²] id. H (þær alt. from feo).   16 healfne
sester] gl. i.e. libram H   æne] from B, ænne V.   19 title: dweorgedwosle B 100v/t.m.a, om. H.   22 wer] wær H.   23 wer] wær H.
24 nytlic] netlic H.

MS O

2 wexon] wehes wexon (wehes exp.).   13 feower] iiii interlined.
20 æȝhwæðer] æȝhhwæðer (first h written on w and exp.).

MS O

XCIII. Ebulum (. . .)   f. 12/24

1. (. . .) stanes on blandre wexon (. . .) þeos wyrt þe man (ebu)lum 7
oþrum / naman ellenwyrt 7 eac suma men wealwyrt hæteð, cnuca hi swa f. 12v
mearwe mid hire leafe, sule drincan on wíne, heo ut adeð þa untrumnesse.

2. (Contra omnes malas bestias) Wið naddran slite ȝením þeos wyrt 5
ebulum, 7 ær þam ðe þu hi forcerfe hea(ld) hi on þinre handa 7 cweð
þrywa niȝan siþan: Omnes bestias malas canto, þæt is on Englis: Besing
7 oforcum ealle wide yfele deor; forcearf hi þanne mid swyþe sceape
sexe on ð'r'y dæles; 7 þa wile ðe ðu þis do ðenc be þan men þe þu
þarmid ðencst to læcniende; 7 þanne þu þanne wende ne beseoh þu þe 10
na. Ním þanne þe wyrt, cnuca hi, leȝe to þam slite, sona hit byð hal.

3. (Ad ydropicos) Wið wæterseocnysse nim þisse wyrte wurtewalan
ȝecnucod, wríng þat þu habbe ðærof feower scencas 7 wines heafne serter,
syle drincan æne on dæȝ; hit fremeð miclum þam wæterseocan.

Eac binnan healfan ȝeare ealne þane wæten ut atihð.   15

XCIV. Pollegium   dwerorȝedwosle   f. 28v/21

þeos wyrt þæt man pollegium 7 oþrum naman dweorȝedwosle nemneð
hæfed mid hire læcedomes þeah hi feala man ne cunna. Ðanne hys
þeos wyrt tweȝra cunna, þæt his wer 7 wyf; þe were hafað hwíte blostman
7 þæt wyf reade oþþer brune, æȝhwæðer nítlic, hi / blofað þanne oþer f. 31(!)
wyrt scríncað 7 weorniað.   21

MS Ca

XCIII. Herba ebulum

1. Ad cauculosos. Herba ebulum tenerum cum foliis tritum ex vino
potui datum cauculum expellit.

2. Ad colubri morsum. Herba ebulum, antequam succidas eam, tenes
eam et ter novies dicis: Omnes malas bestias canto, atque eam ferro quam
acutissimo (. . .) trifariam praecidito et id faciens de eo cogitato cui
medeberis, reversus ita ne respicias et ipsam herbam contritam imponito,
continuo sanabitur.

3. Ad ydropicos. Herbae ebuli radicis sucus expressus ciatos iv ex
vino sextario semis potui semel in die datus ydropicis validissime prodest.
Per anum enim humor omnis detrahitur.

XCIV. Herba puleium   p. 507

Puleium quam vim medicamenti secum habeat, multi ignorant; duo
enim genera sunt, masculus et femina. Masculus florem album habet,
femina rubeum sive purpureum; utrique utiles sunt et mirabiles, mirabile
autem in se habent, cum maximis coloribus floreant, cum fere aliae
herbae arescunt.

1. Wiþ ðæs innoþes sare genim þas ylcan wyrte pollegium 7 cymen, cnuca tosomne mid w(æte)re 7 lege to þam nafolan, sona he bið gehæled.

2. Eft wið þæs magan sare genim þas sylfan wyrte pollegium, cnuca hy 7 mid wætere gewæsc, syle drincan on ecede, hyt þone wlættan þæs magan wel geliþigaþ.

3. Wið gicþan þæra gesceapa genim þas ylcan wyrte, seoð on weallendon wætere, let þonne colian swa oðþæt hyt man drincan mæge, 7 hyt þonne drince, hyt geliþegaþ þone gicþan.

4. Eft wið þæs innoðes sare þeos sylfe wyrt fremaþ wel geetan 7 to þam nafolan gewriþen, swa þæt heo fra(m) þam nafolan feallan ne mæge, sona heo þæt sár tofereþ.

5. Wið þam fefore þe þy ðryddan dæge on man becymeþ genim þysse ylcan wyrte twigu, befeald on wulle, ster hyne þærmid toforan þam timan þe se fefor hym to wylle; 7 gyf hwa hys heafod mid þysse wyrte onbutan bewindeþ heo þæt sár þæs heafodes geliðigaþ.

6. Gyf deadboren cyld sy on wifes innoðe genim þysse ylcan wyrte þry cyþas, 7 þa syn niwe swa hy swyþost stincen, cnuca on f. 48v ealdon / win(e, s)yle drincan.

7. Gyf hwa on scipe wlættan þolige genime þas ylcan wyrte polleian 7 [wermod], cnucie tosomne mid ele 7 mid ecede, smyrige hyne þærmid gelomlice.

8. Wið blædran sare 7 wið þæt stanas þaron wexen genim þas ylcan wyrte polleian wel gecnucude 7 twegen scenceas wines, gemencg tosomne, syle drincan, sona seo blædder to selran gehwyrfeð, 7 binnan feawum dagum heo þa untrumnysse gehæleþ 7 þa stanas þe þæron weaxeþ út anydeð.

MS V

5 gewæsc] gewes BH   on] o H.   7 Wið gicþan] gl. contra pruritum H gesceapa] gesc`e´apa H.   8 let] læt BH   hyt] hi B.   9 drince] gedrince H.   10 geetan] geeten H 15/3.   11 heo] he B.   14 twigu] twiga H   ster] stýr B, gl. crune H.   19 cnuca] cuca H.   21 genime] genim H.   22 polleian] po'l´leian H   wermod] from B, wærmo V cnucie] cnuca H   smyrige] smera B, smyre, gl. i.e. nosþerls H.   24 wexen] weaxað H.   25 gecnucude] gecnu`cu´de H.   27 gehwyrfeð] gehweorfeð H   heo] 7 heo H.   28 weaxeþ] weaxað BH.

MS O

10 swa] sa swa (sa exp.).   13 befeald] befealdon on tu (on on tu exp.).

1. (Ad morbum uiscerum) Wið innoþes sare nim þeos wyrt 7 cumin'
cnuca togadere mid watere, leʒe to þan nafelon, sona he byð ʒehæled.

2. (Ad stomacum) Eaf wið þas maʒan sare cnuca seos wyrt 7 mid
wætere wes, sile drinca on ecede, hit þane w`l´ættan þæs mæʒan wel
ʒeliþegað.   5

3. (Ad manguam membri) Wið ʒycþan ʒesceapu seos þas wyrt on
wellende wætere, lat þanne colian swa þæt hyt man drincan maʒen, 7
hyt þanne drincan; hít ʒeliþegað þane ʒycþan.

4. (Ad morbum uiscerum) Eft wið þas innoþes sore þeos wyrt fremeð
wel ʒeeten 7 to þan nafelan ʒewriðen, swa þæt heo fram nafolan ne feallan 10
ne maʒa, sona heo þæt sor toferað.

5. (Ad febrem tertianam; ad dolorem capitis) Wið þriddan dæʒe
fefere ním þisse wyrt twiʒu, befeald on wulle, ster þanne man þe feferes
þarmid toforan þan tyme þe se fefer him to wylle. 7 hwa his heafod mid
þisse wirt onbutan bebíndeð, heo þat sar þæs heafedes ʒeliþegad.   15

6. (Ad puerum mortuum in utero) Gif deadboren cild sy on wiwes
ínnoþe ním þeos wyrte dri ciþas, 7 ða sin niwe swa hi swyðust stincon,
cnuca on eade wíne, sile drincan.

7. (Contra nause(am) in naui) (G)if hwa on scipe wlæ`t´tan þolie
cnuca þeos wyrt 7 weremod togadere mid ele 7 ecede, smyre híne þarmid 20
ʒelomlice.

8. (Ad vesicam et lapides in uesicam) Wid blæddran sore 7 wið þæt
stænes þæron wexæn cnuca þeos wyrt wel 7 ním tweʒen scencas wínes,
meng togadere, sele drincan, sona þa blædræ to selran ʒefyrfeð; 7 binnan
feawum dæʒe heo ða untrumnysse ʒehæleð 7 þa stanes þe þaron wexeþ ut 25
anydeð.

MS Ca

1. Ad dolorem intestinorum infantium. Herbam puleium et ciminum
tritum ex aqua et super umbilicum imponito, continuo sanus fiet.

2. Ad stomachi nausiam. Herbam puleium tritam vel in aqua macera-
tam cum aceto potui dabis, nausiam stomachi sedat.

3. Ad veretri pruriginem. Herba puleium in aqua fervente maceratum,
tamdiu donec bibi possit aqua, optimum est et pruriginem sedat.

4. Ad ventris dolorem. Herba puleium commanducatum et in umbilico
positum religatum ne excidat, continuo dolorem discutit.

5. Ad tertianas. Herbae puleium ramulos lana involutos odoret ante
accessionem; quod si coronam exinde in capite habuerit, capitis dolorem
sedat.

6. Si infans mulieri in utero mortuus fuerit. Herbae puleium codas
tres recentes, quod olet suaviter, tritum in vino veteri optimo quartario
da, bibat.

7. Ne in nave nausieris. Herbam puleium et absynthium simul tere et
ex oleo et aceto nares frequenter frica.

8. Ad vesicae dolorem et cauculum. Herbam puleium in vino cyatis
ii bene contritum ieiunus bibat et continuo in solium descendat, intra
paucos dies sanat et cauculum expellet.

9. Gyf hwa onbutan his heortan oþþe on his breoston sar þolie, þonne ete he þas ylcan wyrte polleium 7 drince hy fæstende.

10. Gyf hwylcum men hramma derige genim þas ylcan wyrte, twegen scenceas ecedes, drince fæstende.

5   11. Wið þæs magan toþundennysse 7 þæra innoþa genim þas ylcan wyrte pollegium gecnucude 7 on wætere oððe on wine gewyllede, oþþe þurh hy sylfe syle þicgean, sona byþ seo untrumnys forlæten.

12. [Wið] miltan sare genim þas ylcan wyr(te) polleium, se(oð) 10 on ecede, syle dri(n)can swa wea(r)m.

13. Wiþ l(ende)na ece 7 wið [þara] þeona sare genim þa(s) ylcan wyrte poll(ei)um 7 pipo(r, ægþ)res (gelic)e mycel be gewihte, cnuca tosomne, 7 þon(ne) þu on (b)æþe sy smy(re þ)ærmid þær hyt swyþost derige.

15   XCV. Nepte   neptamnus

Ðas wyrte man nepitamon 7 oþrum naman nepte nemneþ 7 eac Grecas hy mente orinon hataþ.

Neddre

1. Wiþ nædran slite genim þas wyrte ðe we nepitamon nendun, f. 49 cnuca mid wine, wring þonne þæt wos 7 syle / drincan on wine, 21 genim eac þa leaf þysse sylfan wyrte [gecnocode], lege to þære wunde.

MS V

2 ete he] ece þe H, *gl.* ciatis ii ieiunus bibat (*see cure 10*) H.   3 men] Men H 16/2.   4 twegen] 7 twegen BH.   5 toþundennysse] toþúndenesse B 101/1a.   6 pollegium] polleium H.   7 þicgean] þyngcan H   untrumnys] -nesse H.   9 Wið] *from* B, iþ V.   11 þara] *from* B, þera V, þæra H.   13 7] *om.* H.   15 *title*: nepte B, *om.* H. 16 Ðas] Ðeos H   wyrte] wyrt `þ´e B, wyrte ðe H   7 oþrum] on urum H.   18 Neddre] *om.* BH.   19 nendun] nemdon/-un BH. 20 7] *om.* B.   21 gecnocode] *from* B, gecnude V, gecnucude H.

MS O

14 nenterion] nenterion hæteð nym nenterion (*first three words exp.*). 16 wryng] wyr wryng (wyr *exp.*).   þat] þæt (*abbreviated, not exp.*) þat.

9. (Ad morbum cordis et pectoris) Gif hwa / on his heorten oþþer on   f. 31v
breoste sor þolia, þanne etan he þa wyrt pollegiam 7 drincan hi fæstende.

10. (Wið hramma) Gif manne hramma deriʒe ním þeos wyrt 7 tweʒen
scencas ecedes, drinca fastinde.

11. (Ad morbum stomachi et uiscerum) Wið þas mæʒe sare toþun-   5
ʒennysse 7 þara innoþa cnuc(a) þeos wirt 7 on wætere oððer on wíne
ʒewillede oþþer sur hy silue sile ðicʒan; sona byð þa untrumnesse forlæte.

12. (Ad morbum splenis) Wið miltan sare

13. 7 wið þar(a) þeona sare ním þa wírt 7 piper, æʒþres ʒelice micel be
ʒewyhta, cnuca tosomne, 7 þanne þu on baþe sy smire þarmid hit swiðust   10
dersize.

XCV. De nepta   f. 24v/7

þeos wyrt þæt man nepitamnon 7 oþrum nama nepte 7 Grecas hy
nenterion hæteð.

1. (Ad punctionem serpentis) Wið næddran slite cnuca þa wyrt níd   15
wine, wryng 7 þat wos sule drincan mid 'þan' wine, ním eac þa leaf,
cnuca, leʒe to þare wunda.

MS Ca

9. Si quis circa cor et pectus dolet. Herbam puleium gluttiat ieiunus.

10. Si spasmus fuerit. Herbam puleium in aceto cyatis ii ieiunus bibat.

11. Ad stomachi inflationem aut intestinorum. Herbam puleium ex
aqua calida contritum vel ex vino aut per se dato, remitteris cito.

12. Ad splenis dolorem. Herbam puleium decoque ex aceto et idem
acetum calidum permixtum potui dabis; ne quid puleium praegnanti
dederis.

13. Ad [isciam] vel coxarum dolorem. Herbam puleium et piper
aequis ponderibus tritum in balneo fricabis ubi dolet frequenter, sanus
erit.

XCV. Herba nepeta   p. 508

1. Ad serpentium morsus. Herba nepeta montana ex vino trita, sucus
eius expressus cum vino potui datur, cuius etiam folia contrita plagae
utiliter imponuntur.

XCVI. Cammoc

Ðas wyrte man peucedanum 7 oðrum naman cammoc nemneþ. Neddre

Ðeos wyrt þe we peucedanum nemdun mæg nædran mid hyre
5 swæce aflian.

1. Wið nædran slite genim þas ylcan wyrte peucedanum 7 betonican 7 heortes smeoruw oððe þæt mearh 7 eced, dó tosomne, lege þonne to þære wunde, he bið gehæled.

2. Wið þa adle þe Grecas frenesis nemnað, þæt is on ure ge-
10 þeode gewitlest þæs modes, þæt byþ ðonne þæt heafod áweallen byþ, genim þonne þas ylcan wyrte peucedanum, cnuca on ecede, begeot þonne þæt heafod þærmid, hyt (fr)e(m)a(þ) healice.

XCVII. Sperewyrt   hinnula campana

1. Wið blædran sare genim þas wyrte þe man hinnula campana
15 7 oþrum naman sperewyrte nemneþ 7 merces sæd 7 eorðnaflan 7 finules wyrtwalan, cnuca tosomne, syle þonne wlæc drincan, scearplice hyt fremað.

2. Wið toþa sare 7 wagunge genim þas ylcan wyrte, syle etan fæstendum, heo þa teþ getrymeð.

20 3. Wið þæt ymb þæne nafolan syn rengwyrmas genim þas
f. 49v ylcan wyrte hinnulan, cnuca on wíne, / lege to þam innoðe.

XCVIII. Ribbe   arnoglossa

Ðas wyrte þe man cynoglossam 7 oðrum naman ribbe nemneþ 7 hy eac sume men linguam canis hateþ.

MS V

1 *title*: cammoc B, *om*. H.   2 Ðas] þeos H   wyrte] wyrt 'þ'e B, wyrt þe H   peucedanum] petuicedamum H.   3 Neddre] *om*. BH. 4 peucedanum] pencedanum H.   5 aflian] aflígan B 101v/1a.   6 wyrte peucedanum] wyrt peucedamum H 17/1.   8 gehæled] gelacnod/-ud BH. 10 gewitlest] -least B.   11 ecede] 'e'cede H.   13 *title*: sperewurt B, *om*. H.   14 wyrte þe man] ylcan wyrte H   hinnula] himmila H. 15 oþrum] 'o'þrum H   sperewyrte] -wyrt B   merces sæd] mercesæd H. 18 wagunge] wugunge H   genim . . . wyrte] *om*. B   19 getrymeð] ge't'ry-með H.   20 þæne] þone BH.   22 *title*: ribbe B, *om*. H (*see also t.n. to* 144/7 H).   23 wyrte] wyrt B   þe man] *om*. H.

MS O

5 ʒelacnud] le ʒelacnud (le *exp*.).   10 *no trace of a title in red.*

XCVI. Peucedanum   cammoc   f. 30v/1

(Ad fugam serpentium) þeos wyrt þæt man peucedanum 7 Engle cammoc nemneð mæȝ nædran mid hure swæcce afliȝan.

1. Wið nærdran slíte ním þas wyrt 7 bettanícan 7 hortes smere oþ þat marh 7 ecede tosomne 7 leȝe to þara wunda; he byð ȝelacnud.   5

2. (Contra frenesim) Wið þa adle þæt Grecas frenesis nemneð, þat his on Englis ȝewítlest ðæs modes, þæt byð þanne þat heafod awellen byð, cnuca þas wurt on ecede, beȝeat þæt heafod þarmid; hit fremeð healice.

XCVII *om.* O.

XCVIII.   f. 11/14

(. . .) (w)yr(t) þe man (cy)noglosam (7) oþrum naman (ri)bbe nemned   11
7 (. . .) linguam canis (ha)tað.

MS Ca

XCVI. Herba peucedanum

Herba peucedanum arcet enim serpentes odore suo.

1. Ad serpentes effugandos. Peucedanum cum vettonica et adipe cervina aut medulla, aceto mixto, eademque morsui imposita medetur.

2. Ad freneticos. Herba peucedanum cum aceto capiti infusa summe facit.

XCVII. Herba innula campana

1. Ad vesicae dolorem. Herba innula campana et appii semen et   p. 509
sparagi et feniculi quoque radices in unum tritae, et in tepida potui data efficaciter prodest.

2. Ad dentium remedia. Herba innula campana, ieiunus commanducet, dentes confirmat.

3. Ad lumbricos. Herbae innulae folia ex vino trita supra ventrem ponantur.

XCVIII. Herba cynoglossa

Nædre

1. Wið nædran slite þeos wyrt þe we cynoglossam nemdun wel fremað gecnucud 7 on wine geþiged.

2. Wið þam fefore ðe þy feorþan dæge on man becymeþ
5 genim þas ylcan wyrte cynoglossam, ða þe feower 'leaf' hæbbe, cnuca hy, syle drincan on wætere, heo alyseþ þone man.

3. Wiþ ðæra eare(na u)nnyttlicnysse 7 wi(ð) þæt man wel gehyran ne mæge genim þas ylcan wyrte cynoglossam gecnucude 7 on ele gewlæhte, drype on þæt eare, wundorlice hyt hæleþ.

10 XCIX. Sundcorn   saxifragia

Ðeos wyrt ðe man saxifragam 7 oþrum naman sundcorn nemneð byþ cenned on dunum 7 on stænihtum stowum.

1. Wið þæt stanas on blædran wexen genim þas wyrte þe we saxifragam nemdun, cnuca on wine, syle drincan þam þoligendan
15 7 ðam fefergendan on wearmum wætere, swa andweard heo ys þæs þe is sæd of ðam þe his afandedon þæt heo þy ylcan dæge þa stanas forbrycð 7 hy ut atyhð 7 þone man to hys hæle gelædeþ.

f. 50 C. Eorðyfig   hedera terrestris

1. Wið þæt stanas on blæddran wexen genim þysse wyrte þe
20 man hederan nigran 7 oþrum naman eorðifig nemneþ seofon berian oððe endlufon on wætere gegnidene, syle drincan, wundorlice heo stanas on þære blædran gegaderað 7 hy [tobricð] 7 þurh migþan út atyhð.

2. Wið heafodsár genim þas ylcan wyrte hederam 7 rosan wos
25 on wine gewesed, smyre þonne þa ðunwonga 7 þone andwlatan, þæt sár geliðigaþ.

1 Nædre] om. BH.   2 cynoglossam] cynoglosam H.   3 fremað]
fram'mað' H.   6 heo . . . man] om. H.   9 gewlæhte] gewlehte
B 102/11a, gewlehte H 50/5(!).   on²] o B.   10 title: saxifragia B,
sundcorn H.   12 stænihtum] stænigum BH.   14 syle] sele H.
15 fefergendan] fefrigendan B, 'fe'fergendum H   andweard] anræde (on an
erasure) H.   16 his] 'h'is H.   18 title: eorðíuí B, eorðyfig H.
20 nemneþ] 'nem'neþ H.   21 endlufon] endlifene B, ænlufan H.
22 stanas] þa stanas BH   gegaderað] gegæderað H   tobricð] from H (erasure
of n between i and c), to brincð V, tó bringð B.   23 atyhð] aty'h'ð H.
24 heafodsár] -ece B 102v/1a, H = B.

1. (Contra morsum serpentium) Wið naddre slite þes wy(rt) (. . .) ȝec(n)ucod 7 on (. . .) (ȝe)þiȝed wel fremað.

2. Wið fe(orþa)n dæȝe fefore (cy)noglosam þe ðe fefor leaf h(æb)be, cnuca hy, drincan on wætere, heo alyseð þa(ne ma)n.

3. ((Ad) surditatem) Wið (. . .) (unnytl)icnysse 7 wið þæt man ȝehyran 5 n(e) (. . .) þeos w(yr)t ȝecnucod 7 mid ele ȝewlehte, (dryp)e on þæt e(are, w)undelice hit hæleð.

XCIX. Saxifragia   sundcorn

þeos wyrt þæt man saxifragam 7 oþer naman sundcorn nemneð.

1. (Ad lapides in uesica) Wið stanes þe on blædran wexan cnuca þeos 10 wyrt on wine, sile drincan 7 ȝef haueþ fefere ȝif on wætere; swa anwerd heo ys þæs þe ys sæd of þan þe his afonded þæt heo þi ylcan dæȝe þa stanes forbricð 7 hi ut atyhð 7 þane man ȝehaleð.

C *om.* O.

MS Ca

1. Ad morsum serpentis. Herba lingua canis trita ex vino sumpta prodest.

2. Ad quartanas. Herba cynoglossa quae folia [iv] habet pisata et potui data ex aqua liberat.

3. Ad aurium inutilitatem et qui minus audiunt. Herbae cynoglossae sucum ex passo et oleo tepefactum in aure stilla, mire sanat.

XCIX. Herba saxifraga

Nascitur in montibus, locis saxosis.

1. Ad cauculosos. Herbam saxifragam contritam in vino bibendum dato, febricitanti in aqua calida; tam praesens effectus ab expertis traditur, ut eodem die perfractis eiectisque cauculis ad sanitatem perducat.

C. Herba hedera nigra

1. Ad cauculos expellendos. Herbae hederae nigrae bacas aut vii aut xi contritas ex aqua potui sumptas, mire cauculos in vesica congregatos frangere et extrahere per urinam certum est.

2. Ad capitis dolorem. Herba hedera nigra, cum oleo rosaceo et cum suco eius mixto vino tempora et frontem perfricabis, sedat dolorem.

3. Wið miltan sare genim þysse [ilcan] wyrte croppas, ærest
þry, æt oþrum sæle fif; æt þam þryddan sæle seofone, æt þam
feorþan cyrre nigon, æt þam fiftan cyrre endlufon, æt þam sixtan
cyrre þreotyne, 7 æt þam seofoþam cyrre fiftyne, 7 æt þam
5 ehte'o'þan cyrre seofontyne, 7 æt þam nigoþan cyrre nigontyne,
æt þam teoþan sæle án 7 twentig; syle drincan dæghwamlice on
wíne, gyf he þonne on fefore sy s(yl)e drincan on wearmum
wætere, myc(el)on he byþ geb(et) 7 gestrangod.

4. Wið þæra wyrma slite þe man spalangiones nemneð genim
10 þysse sylfan wyrte seaw þæs wyrtwalan þe we hederam nemdun,
syle drincan.

5. Eft wið þæra wunda lacnunge genim þas ylcan wyrte, seoð
on wine, lege to þam wundun.

6. Wiþ þæt næsþyrlu yfele stincen genim þysse sylfan wyrte
15 seaw, wel ahlytred geot on þa næsþyrlu.

7. Wið þæra earena unnytlicnysse 7 wið þæt man ne mæge
well gehyran genim þysse ylcan wyrte seaw swyþe clæne mid wine,
drype on þa earan, he bið gelacnud.

f. 50v   8. Wiþ þæt heafod ne ace for sunnan / hætan genim þysse
20 sylfan wyrte leaf swyþe hnesce, cnuca on ecede, smyre þonne
þone andwlatan þærmid, eac hyt fremaþ ongean ælc sár þe þam
heafode dereþ.

CI. Organe   serpillum

1. Wið þæs heafodes sare genim þysse wyrte seaw þe man ser-
25 pillum 7 oþrum naman organe nemneþ 7 ele 7 gebærned sealt,
to swyþe smalan duste gebryt, gemengc ealle tosomne, smyre
þæt heafod þærmid, hyt byþ hal.

2. Eft wið heafodece genim þas ylcan wyrte serpillum gesodene,
cnuca on ecede, smyre þærmid þa ðunwonga 7 þone andwlatan.

1 ilcan] *from* B, ylan V.   2 æt¹] 7 H.   3 nigon] nygone H 51/1
endlufon] endlifon B.   4 seofoþam] seofoðan BH   fiftyne] -tene B.
5 ehte'o'þan] eahtoþan BH   7] *om.* BH.   6 twentig] twenti B.
10 sylfan] *om.* H.   13 wundun] wundum BH.   18 þa earan] þæt
eare BH.   21 ongean] ongen H.   23 *title*: serpillum id est organe
B 103/t.m.a, organe H.   25 gebærned] gebærnet B.   26 swyþe]
swiþan H.   26–7 smyre . . . þærmid] smyra þonne þarmid þæt heafod B.

CI. Serpillum   organa

1. (Ad dolorem capitis) Wið þæs heafodes særením þisse wyrte seaw þe man serpillum 7 oþrum name organe hatað 7 ele 7 ʒeberned seaht, to swile smale duste ʒebryt 7 meng eal tosomne, smíre þat heafod þarmíd, hyt byð hal. 5

2. ──

MS Ca

3. Ad splenis dolorem. Herbae hederae nigrae grana primo iii, secundo v, tertio vii, quarto ix, quinto xi, sexto xiii, septimo xv, octavo xvii, nono xix, decimo xxi in vino bibantur diurnis diebus, si cum febre in aqua calida, maximo auxilio lienosis auxiliatur.

4. Ad spalangionum morsus. Herbae hederae radicis sucus bibitur.

5. Ad ulcerum remedia. Herba hedera ex vino decocta imponitur.

6. Ad nares male olentes. Herbae hederae sucus bene colatus, in nares infundito.

7. Ad aurium inutilitatem et qui minus audiunt. Herbae hederae sucus mundissimus cum vino stillatus medetur.

8. Ad caput, ne a sole doleat. Herbae hederae folia mollissime trita in aceto et rosaceo, adversus omnem dolorem fronti illinitur.

CI. Herba serpullum

1. Ad capitis dolorem. Herbae serpulli sucum cum oleo et sale frictum et in pulvere mollissimo redactum, omnia commixta, caput perunctum sanatur.

2. Item serpullum decoctum, in aceto tritum linitur temporibus et p. 511 fronti.

3. Gif hwa forbærned sy genim þas ylcan wyrte serpillum 7
æscþrote anne wrid 7 anre yntsan gewihte ges(wyrfes) of seolfre
7 r(osan þ)reora yn(t)sena gewihte, gepuna þonne eall (to)somne on
(a)num mo(rtere), do þo(nne ðærto wex) 7 healfes pundes gewihte
5 beran smeruwes 7 heortenes, seoð ealle tosomne, feor(m)a (hyt)
7 lege to þam bærnette.

CII. Wermod   absynthius

Ðeos wyrt þe man absinthium 7 oþrum naman wermod nemneð
byþ cenned on beganum stowum 7 on dunum 7 on stænihtum
10 stowum.

1. Wið þæt man læla 7 oðre sár of lichaman gedó genim þas
wyrte absinthium, seoð on wætere, do þonne on anne cla ð, lege
to þam sare, gyf þonne se lichoma mearu sy, seoð on hunige,
lege to þam sare. /

f. 51   2. Wið þæt rengwyrmas ymbe þone nafolan derigen genim þas
16 ylcan wyrte absinthium 7 harehunan 7 elechtran, ealra gelice
mycel, seoð on geswettum wætere oþþe on wine, lege tuwa oððe
þriwa to þam nafolan, hyt cwelþ þa wyrmas.

CIII. Saluie   saluia

20 1. Wið gicþan þæra [gescapa] genim þas wyrte ðe man saluian
nemneð, seoð on wætere, 7 mid þam wætere smyre þa gesceapu.
2. Eft wið gicþan þæs setles genim þas ylcan wyrte salfian,
seoð on wætere, [7 mid ðam wætere] beþa þæt setl, hyt geliðigað
ðone gicþan healice.

MS V

2 yntsan] yndsan B, yntsena (n *alt. from* d) H 52/10.   3 yntsena] yndsa
B, yndsena H.   4 healfes] 'h´ealfes H.   5 heortenes] hyrtenes H
ealle] eal B, eall H.   7 *title*: wermod BH.   9 stænihtum] stænigum B,
stænigum (li *erased between* i *and* g) H.   12 absinthium] absin't´hium H.
13 hunige] hunig B.   15 ymbe] ymb (m *alt. from* b) H   nafolan]
naf'o´lan H   genim] genin H.   16 harehunan] *second* a *alt. from* e V
elechtran] elehtran BH.   17 tuwa] tua H.   19 *title*: saluia B 103v/t.m.a,
saluie H 53/2.   20 gescapa] *from* B, gesceapena V, gesceapa H.
21 7 . . . wætere] *om.* H.   22 salfian] saluian BH.   23 7 . . . wætere]
from B, *om.* V   beþa] beðe H   geliðigað] liðigað H.

MS O

8 'þas´] *in text* þisse (*exp.*), þas *in o.m.*   11 absinthium] absin /
sinthium   elehtran] h *alt. from* t.   15 þara] *foll. by erasure of* (sc)eap(an).

3. (Ad arsuram) Gif hwa forbærned sy ním þeos wyrt 7 æscþrote anne wrid 7 anre untsa ȝewyhte ȝesweorfes of seolfre 7 rosan þreora untsa ȝewihta, ȝepuna þanne eal tosomne on ane mortere, do þanne þarto wexs 7 healfes pundes ȝewihte beran seruwes 7 heo`r´tes, seoð eal tosomne,   4 feorma / hit 7 leȝe to þan bærnette; sona hít byð hal.   f. 38

CII. De absinthio   f. 2v/2

þeos wyrt þæt man absinthium 7 oþrum nama weremod nemned.

1. Wid þæt man læla 7 oþre sar of lichaman ȝedon ȝením `þas´ wyrt; ȝif þanne þe lichama mearuw si seoð on huniȝe, leȝe to þan sore.

2. (Ad uermes intus circa umbilicum) Wið þat rencgwírmas embe þone   10 nafelan derian ȝením þas ylcan wyrt absinthium 7 harahuna 7 elehtran, ealra ȝelíce micel, seoð on swetum watere odðer on wíne, leȝe tuwa odðer ðrywa to þan nafolan; hit cwelð þa wyrmas.

CIII. Savína   f. 38/2

1. (Ad membra) Wið ȝycþan þara sceapan ním þa wyrt þæt man   15 saluíam nemneð, seoð on wætere, 7 mid þan wætera smyre þa ȝesceapan.

2. (A mangua ad membrum) Eft wið ȝicþan þæs setles seod þa wyrt saluiam on wætere, 7 mid þa wætere beþe þat setl; hit ȝeliþecget þane ȝicþan healice.

MS Ca

3. Ad combustum. Herbam serpullum et ancusae surculum unciam, spuma argenti uncias iii et rosas, haec in mortario teres, ceram pumicam, adipem ursinam et cervinam semunciam, simul decoques, colabis et impones.

CII. Herba absynthium

Nascitur locis cultis et montuosis et saxis.

1. Ad livores tollendos. Herbam absynthium in aqua decoctum et inductum panno imponis in corpus; tenerum si fuerit, ex melle impone.

2. Ad lumbricos. Herbae absynthii et marrubii et lupinorum paria pondera in aqua mulsa cocta vel vino, bis aut ter positum in umbilico necat lumbricos.

CIII. Herba salvia

1. Ad veretri pruriginem. Herba salvia, decoquito et de ea aqua infricas veretrum.

2. Ad pruriginem circa anum. Herba salvia, decoquito et de ea aqua inferiores partes fomententur et sedat pruriginem summe.

CIV. Celendre   coliandrum

1. Wið þæt rengwyrmas ymb ðone nafolan wexen genim þas wyrte þe man coliandrum 7 oðrum naman þam gelice cellendre nemneð, seoð on ele to þryddan dæle, do to þam sare 7 eac to ðam
5 heafode.

2. Wið þæt wif hrædlice cennan (m)æg(e) genim þysse ylcan coliandran sæd, endlufon corn oððe þreottyne, cnyte mid anum ðræde on anum clænan linenan claþe, nime ðonne an man þe sy mægðhades man, cnapa oþþe mægden, 7 healde æt þam wynstran
10 þeo neah þam gewealde, 7 sona swa eall seo geeacnung gedón
f. 51v beo, dó sona þone læcedom aweg, þy læs / þæs in(noðes d)æl þæ(ræ)fter (filige).

CV. [Porclaca]

1. Wið swiðlicne flewsan þæs sædes fremað wel þeos wyrt þe
15 man porclaca 7 oðrum naman (. . .) nemneþ, ægþer ge þurh hy sylfe geþiged ge eac mid oþrum drenceon.

CVI. Cearfille   cerefolium

1. Wið þæs magan sare genim þysse wyrte þe man cerefolium 7 oþrum naman þam gelice cerfille nemneþ ðry croppas swa grene
20 7 dweorgedwoslan, cnuca on anum trywenan mortere, 7 anne cuculere fulne améredes huniges 7 grene popig, wyll tosomne, syle ðicgean; hyt þone magan hrædlice gestrangaþ.

MS V

1 *title*: coliandrum B, celendre H.   2 ymb] yb H.   3 coliandrum] *id*. H (r *alt. from* u)   cellendre] celendre H.   4 7 eac] eac H. 6 mæge] 'ne' mæg H   þysse] þas H.   7 endlufon] endlifan B þreottyne] þreottene B.   8 ðræde] ðræðe H   clænan] a *alt. from* e V linenan] *om*. H.   10 ʒeeacnung] eácnung H.   11 dó] do 'man' H. 12 þæræfter] æfter H.   13 *title*: *from* B, *om*. VH.   14 wyrt] wyrte H. 15 porclaca] *id*. H (*erasure of* c *between* a *and* c)   þurh] ðu'r' H.   16 ge eac] eac H.   17 *title*: cerofolium cerfille B 104/13a, cearfille H. 19 cerfille] cearfille H 54/4.   21 améredes] aneredes (*erasure of* n *between* a *and* n) H.

MS O

6 dreotyne] ðe dreotyne (ðe *exp*.).   7 nime] ním / nime   cnapa] cwen cnapa (cwen *exp*.).   9 aweʒ] aʒe aweʒ (aʒe *exp*.).   12 sisse wyrt] wyrt sisse (*no marks for reversal visible*).

CIV. De colian(dro)

1. (Contra (. . .)) (. . .) reng(wyrmas y)mbe (. . .) (nafol)an wexe, þa wyrt þe man coliandrum 7 Engle (. . .) (ʒel)ice cellendre nemnað, seoð on ele to þrid(dan dæ)le, do to þan sore 7 eac to þan heafde, hit helped. /

2. Wið þæt wif hrædlice cenned maga ním þisse wyr(te) sæd endlufan corn odðer dreotyne, cnyte mid ane ðrade on ane clæne linnene clæþe, nime þan a man þe sy mæʒþehades man, cnapa oðder mæden, 7 healdan at þan wynstran ðeo neah þan ʒewealdan, 7 sona swa eal seo eacun(g) (. . .) do sona þone læcedom aweʒ, þi læs þæs innoþes (þ)æræfter fyliʒe.

CV om. O.

CVI. D(e) (. . .)

1. (W)ið þæs magan sare nim sisse wyrt (. . .) croppas grene þa man cerefoliam 7 Engle cerfille nemnað 7 dweorʒedwoslan, cnuca on anum tr(y)w(enan) mortere, 7 anne cuculere fulne amerede huníʒ(es) (7) grene papig, wyl tosomne, sile ðicgan; hit þane maʒan hradlice ʒehælð an 15 ʒestra(ng)eð.

MS Ca

CIV. Herba coliandrum

1. Ad lumbricos. Herba coliandrum, coquito ad tertias in oleo et in capite mittatur.

2. Mulier ut cito pariat. Herbae coliandri semen grana xi aut xiii in linteolo mundo de tela alligato, puer aut puella virgo ad femur sinistrum prope inguen teneat, et mox ut omnis partus fuerit peractus, remedium cito solvat, ne intestina sequantur.

CV. Herba porcacla

1. Ad semen nimium profluentem. Herba porcacla sumpta bene facit per se et cum oxigaro.

CVI. Herba [cerifolium]

1. Ad stomachi dolorem. Herbae cerefolium viridis cimas iii colligis et puleium in ligno teres, mellis coclear malaxas, bulliat [cum] papavere viridi, et inducis in stomachum.

CVII. Brocminte   sisimbrium

1. Wið þære blæddran sare 7 wið þæt man gemigan ne mæge genim þysse wyrte wos þe man sisimbrium 7 oþrum naman brocminte nemneþ, syle þam þoligendan on wearmum wætere ðicgean
5 gyf he feforgende sy, gyf he þonne ne sy syle him on wine drincan, ðu hine gelacnust wundorlice. /

f. 52   ## CVIII. olisatra

1. Eft wið þære blædran sare 7 wið þæt man gemigan ne mæge genim þas wyrte þe man olisatrum 7 oþrum naman (. . .) nemneþ,
10 cnuca on gewylledan wine, syle drincan, heo ðone migðan mihtelice gebet.

CIX. Lilie   lilium

Ðas wyr(te þe man erinion 7 oðrum) naman lili(um) nemneþ.
1. Wið nædran slite ge(nim) þas wyrte þe we lilium nemdu(n)
15 7 bulbum þa wyrte ða man (e)ac oþrum naman halswyrt hateþ, cnuca tósomne, syle drincan, nim þonne bulbum þa wyrte gecnucude, lege to ðam slite, he byð gehæled.
2. Wið geswel genim lilian leaf gecnucude, lege to þam geswelle, scearplice hyt hæleþ 7 þæt geswel geliðigaþ.

20 ## CX. Lacterida   titimallus calatites

f. 52v   Ðeos wyrt þe man titymallos calatites 7 oþrum naman / (lacteridam nemneþ biþ) cenned (on w)ætum stowum 7 on ofrum.

MS V

1 *title*: brocmínten B, brocminte H.   2 gemigan] migan B.   5 fefor-gende] fefrigende B.   6 gelacnust] gelacnast B, -ost H   wundorlice] wundo'r´- H.   7 *title*: olisatrum B 104v/t.m.a, *om.* H.   9 olisatrum] olistratum H.   10 gewylledan] gewylledum H.   10–11 mihtelice] mihtiglice B.   12 *title*: lilium B, lilie H.   13 Ðas wyrte þe] Ðeos wyrt 'ð´e H (*see textual note to* V)   erinion 7] *om.* H.   14 genim] genimm H.   15 ða] þe BH   hateþ] nemneð B.   17 gecnucude] gecnude H.   20 *title*: lacteridam B, lacterida H 55/4.   21 naman] n`a´man H.

MS O

3 blocminte] l *later alt. to* r (*pale red ink*).

CVII. Sisímbrium   brocminte   f. 38/7

1. Wið bladran sare 7 wið þæt man miȝæn ne maȝe nim þisse wyrte wos þæt man sísímbríum 7 E`n´gle blocminte hateð, sile ðicȝan on wearme wætere ȝif he haueþ fifere; 7 ȝif na haueþ fifere sili him on wíne drincan, þu hine læcnest wunderlíce.   5

CVIII. De oleastro   f. 25/19

1. (Ad morbum uesicae et si homo nequit mingere) Wid þara blædran sare 7 ȝif man míȝan ne mæȝe ním þa wyrt þæt man oliastrum nemnað, cnuca on ȝewylledum wyne, sele drincan; heo þane miȝeþan míhtelice ȝebet.   10

CIX. (. . .)   f. 13/1

þeos wyrt þ(æt) man eri(nion) (. . .).

1. (Ad serpentis punctionem) Wyð næ(dran) slite ȝe(nim) þeos w(yr)t þe we lilium nemdun 7 bul(b)um þa wy(rt)e ða man eac oþrum nama halswyrt hateð, cnuca tosomne, syle drincan; nim þanne bulbum ða wyrt, ȝecnuca, leȝe to þam slíte, he byd ȝehaleð.   15

2. (Contra inflaturam) Wið ȝewel ním lilian leaf, ȝecnuca, leȝe to þam ȝewelle; scearplice hit haleð 7 þæt ȝe`s´wel (w)el ȝeli(þiȝad).

CX. Titimallos calatites vel lacterídam   f. 40/3

þeos wyrt þæt man titimallos calatíces 7 oþrum nama lacteridam   20 nemnad.

MS Ca

CVII. Herba sisimbrum

1. Ad vesicae dolorem et stranguiriam. Herbam sisimbrum contritum excepto suco scripulos ii, febricitanti ex aqua calida, non febricitanti ex vino potui dabis, remediabis mire.

CVIII. Herba olixatrum

1. Ad vesicae dolorem et stranguiriam. Herba olixatrum trita, ex passo potui sumpta stranguiriam potenter emendat.

CIX. Herba lilium

1. Ad percussum serpentis. Herbae lilii bulbum conterito et potui   p. 514 dabis, [aut] ipsum bulbum tritum morsui apponas, sanabitur.

2. Ad luxum. Herbae lilii folia tunsa et posita, efficaciter sanat, et si tumor fuerit, sedat.

CX. Herba titimallo salatite

Nascitur locis humidis et ripis.

1. (W)i(ð þ)æra innoða sare genim þysse wyrte wrid titymalli, (cnuca on) wine swa þæt þæs wines syn twegen scenceas, do þonne of þære wyrte þæs woses þærto twegen cuculeras fulle, drince ðonne fæstende, he byþ gehæled.

5   2. Wið weartan genim þysse ylcan wyrte meolc 7 clufþungan wos, do to þære weartan, þy þriddan dæge hyt þa weartan gehæleþ.

3. Wið hreoflan genim ðysse sylfan wyrte croppas mid tyrwan gesodene, smyre þærmid.

10   CXI. Wud(u)þistel   (cardu)um silu(aticum)

(Ð)eos wyr(t ðe man carduum sy)lfaticu(m 7 oð)rum naman wuduþis)tel (n)em(neð bið cænned on mædum 7 w)ið we(g)as.

1. W(ið þæ)s magan sare ge(nim þy)ss(e) wyrte þe we cardu(um silu)aticum (ne)mdum ðone (cro)p ufeweard(ne) swa mearune 7 15 swa grenne, syl(e) þicgean on geswetton ecede, hyt geliðigað þa sarnysse.

2. Wiþ þæt ðu nane yfel(e gean)cymas ðe ne ondræde genim þas ylcan wyrte carduum silfaticum on ærnemergen þonne seo sunne ærest up gange, 7 þæt sy þonne sé mona sy in Capricornu, 7 20 heald hy mid þe, swa lange swa ðu hy mid þe byrst nanwiht yfeles þe ongean cymeð.

CXII. lapinum montanum /

f. 53   Ðeos wyrt þe man lupinum montanum 7 oþrum naman (. . .) (ne)m(n)eþ byþ cenned (wi)ð hegas 7 on sa(ndig)um stowum.

MS V

2 þonne] ðonne (o *alt. from* u) H.   5 meolc] meolúc H   clufþungan] clofþuncan B.   10 *title*: wudeðistel B, wuduðistel H.   11 sylfaticum] syluaticum BH.   13 þysse] þas ylcan H.   14 nemdum] nemdon/-un BH mearune 7] mearuwne H.   15 geswetton] geswettum BH   geliðigað] liðigað H.   18 silfaticum] siluaticum B, siluaticum H 56/1.   21 cymeð] 'ne' cymeð H.   22 *title*: lupinum B, *om.* H.

MS O

2 wríd] wyi wríd (wyi *exp.*).   3 fastende] si fastende (si *exp.*). 6 wearte] a *alt. from* r.   7 'hreoflem'] *this word very pale in o.m.* tyrwan] tyrfe tyrwan (tyrfe *exp.*).

1. (Ad morbum uiscerum) Wið þara innoþa sare cnuca þisse wyrte
wríd on wine, sile drican swa þæt þas wínes si tweȝen scences, do þane
þare wyrte wos þarto tweȝe cuceleres fulle, drican fastende, he byð
ȝehæleð.

2. (Ad dertas) Wið wirte ním þisse wyrte meoluc 7 clufþuncan wos, 5
do to þare wearte; þi ðriddan dæȝe hit þa wyrte ȝehæled.

3. (Ad lepram) Wið 'hreoflem' ním þisse wyrte croppas mid tyrwan
ȝesode, smire þarmid.

CXI. (. . .)   f. 11v/14

(Ðe)os wyrt þe man cardium siluaticum 7 Engle wudeþistel nemnað. 10
þeos wyrt byð cenned on mædum 7 onȝean (. . .).

1. W(ið) þæs mæȝe sare nim þisse wyrt (c)rop ufewerdne s(wa)
mearew`n´e 7 swa grene, sile þicȝan on ȝesweto(n) (. . .) (ȝe)liþeȝ(a)ð ða
sornisse.

2. Wið þæt þe nane y(fele ȝeancym)es þe ne ondrade nim þas wyrt on 15
ærn(e) (. . .) þanne þa sunne (ær)est up gange, (7) þæt si ðonne se m(ona) si
in Capricornu, 7 heald hi mid þ(e), s(wa) la(ng)e s(wa) (. . .) hi mid þe
byrst nanwyht y(fele)s (. . .) ongea(n) (. . .).

CXII *om.* O.

MS Ca

1. Ad interaneorum dolorem. Herbae titimalli fruticem teres et in
vino cyatis ii ex eadem mittes sucos coclearia ii, dato ieiuno bibere,
sanabitur.

2. Ad verrucas tollendas. Herbae titimalli lactem mixtum cum botrachi
herbae suco si in verruca posueris, tertio die sanabitur.

3. Ad licenas id est lepras. Herbae titimalli flos cum resina decoctus,
illinito.

CXI. Herba cardum silvaticum

Nascitur in pratis et secus vias.

1. Ad infirmitatem stomachi. Herbae cardi silvatici quod habet in
capite in summo, medullam viridem dato ex oxygaro, edat.

2. Ad occursus malos, ut non timeas. Herbam cardum silvaticum, si
sole novo fuerit luna in Capricorno, tollis eam, et quamdiu tecum por-
taveris nihil mali tibi occurrit.

CXII. Herba lupinum montanum

Nascitur secus saepibus aut locis sablosis.   p. 515

1. Wið þæt w(y)r(m)a(s) ymb ðon(e na)fola(n der)igen genym (þ)as wyr(te) lupi(n)um m(o)nt(anu)m gecnucu(d)e, syle drincan on ece(d)e anne scenc fulne; butan yldingce heo ða wyrmas ut awyrpeð.

5   2. Gyf þonne cildun þæt sylfe derige genim ðas ylcan wyrte lupinum 7 wermod, cnuca tosomne, lege to ðam nafolan.

CXIII. Gyðcorn   lactirida

þeos wyrt þe man lactyridem 7 oþrum naman giðcorn nemneð byð cenned on beganum stowum 7 on sandigum.

10   1. Wið þæs innoþes heardnysse genim þysse wyrte sæd, þæt syndon ða corn, wel afeormude, syle drincan on wearmum wætere, (s)ona hyt þone innoð astyreþ.

CXIV. Lactuca   lactuca leporina

Ðeos wyrt þe man lactucam leporinam 7 oþrum naman þam
15   gelice lactucam nemneþ bið cenned on beganum stowum 7 on sandigum; be ðysse wyrte ys sæd þæt se hara, ðonne he on sumura for swiðlicre hætan geteorud byþ, mid þysse wyrte hyne sylfne
f. 53v   gelacnað; for þy heo ys lactuca leporinam / genemned.

1. Wið feforgende genim þas wyrte lactucam leporinam, lege
20   him nytendum under his pyle, he byþ gehæled.

CXV. Hwerhwette   (c)ucumeris siluatica

Ðeos wyrt þe man cucumerem siluaticum 7 oþrum naman hwerhwette nemneþ byþ cenned neah sǽ 7 on hatum stowum.

1. Wið þæra sina sare 7 wið fotadle genim wyrtwalan þysse
25   wyrte þe we cucumerem silfaticum nemdun, seoð on ele to þriddan dæle, smyre þærmid.

MS V

1 derigen] dergen B, de'ri'gen H.   7 title: guðcorn B 105v/15a, giðcorn H.
8 lactyridem] lactiride B, lacteride H.   10 innoþes] 'innoþes' H   þysse
þy's's'e' (y alt. from u) H.   13 title: lactuca BH.   14 leporinam]
lepori'n'am H.   16 sandigum] sandigu H.   18 gelacnað] lácnoð H
57/3   þy] þon H   leporinam] leporina BH.   19 feforgende] fefrigende
B, fefórgendne H.   20 pyle] pele H.   21 title: cucumerem B 106/12a,
hwerhwette H.   22 man] ma B.   23 neah sǽ] neahre H.   25 silfaticum]
siluaticum BH.

CXIII, CXIV *om.* O.

CXV. De c(ucumere) (. . .) f. 11v/25

Introduction om. O.

1. (W)ið sy(na) sore 7 (. . .) (fot)adlením þa wyrtwalum þe man cu(cu-
merem) / (. . .). 5

MS Ca

1. Ad lumbricos et tineas. Herbam lupinum montanum tere (. .) et
dato ex aceto cyatum unum bibere, sine mora eiciet.
2. Idem infanti cum absinthio trito in umbilico imponitur.

CXIII. Herba laterida

[Nascitur locis cultis et sablosis.]
1. Ad duritiam ventris. Herbae latyridae semen quod est granum,
dabis ipsum granum purgatum potui in aqua calida, mox alveum excitat.

CXIV. Herba lactuca leporina

Nascitur locis cultis et sablosis. Lepus aestate cum animo deficit
aestu, haec herba remediat, ideo lactuca leporina dicitur.
1. Ad febricitantes. Herba lactuca leporina opponitur sub pulvino
nescienti, remediabitur.

CXV. Herba siciden agria (*gl.* id est cucumis silvaticus)

Nascitur locis maritimis et calidis. p. 516
1. Ad nervorum dolorem et podagram. Herbae cucumeris silvatici
radices ex oleo cibario pondo iii [decoques ad tertias et exinde perungues].

2. Gif cild misboren sy genim ðysse ylcan wyrte wyrttruman to þriddan dæle gesodenne, þweah ðonne þæt cild þærmid; 7 gyf hwa þysse wyrte wæstm fæstende þygeð hyt him becymð to fre(cn)ysse, for ði gehwa (hine) forh(æbb)e þæt he hi na fæ(stende) ete.

CXVI. Henep   id est canuere

Ðeos wyrt þe man cannane silfatica 7 oþrum naman henep nemneþ byþ cenned on wiþerrædum stowum 7 wið wegas [7 hegas].

1. Wið þæra breosta sare genim þas wyrte cannauem siluaticam gecnucude mid rysle, lege to þam breostan, heo tofereþ þæt geswel; 7 gyf þær hwylc gegaderung biþ heo þa afeormaþ.

2. Wið cile bærnettes genim þysse ylcan wyrte wæs't'm mid netelan sæde gecnucud'n'e, 7 mid ecede gewesed lege to þam sare. /

f. 54 CXVII. Rude   ruta montana

Ðeos wyrt þe man rutam montanam 7 oþrum naman þam gelice rudan nemneþ byþ cenned on dunum 7 on unbeganum stowum.

1. Wið eagena dymnysse 7 wið yfele dolh genim þysse wyrte leaf þe we rutam montanam nendun on ealdum wine gesodene, dó þonne on an glæsen fæt, smyre syþþan þærmid.

2. Wiþ ðæra breosta sare genim þas ylcan wyrte rutam siluaticam, cnuca on trywenan fæte, nim þonne swa mycel swa ðu mid ðrim fingron gegripan mæge, do on an fæt 7 þærto anne scenc wines 7 twegen wæteres, syle drincan, gereste hyne þonne sume hwile, sona he byð hal.

3. Wið lifersare genim þysse ylcan wyrte anne gripan 7 oþerne healfne sester wæteres 7 ealswa mycel huniges, wyll tosomne, syle drincan þry dagas, ma gyf him þearf sy, þu hine miht gehælan.

MS V

2 þriddan dæle] þriddæle B.   4 frecnysse] fræc- B, frea- H.
6 *title*: hænep B, wilde henep (*later hand*) H.   7 cannane silfatica]
cannaue siluatica BH   henep] *added later* V, *om.* H.   8 7 hegas] *from* B,
om. V.   10 breostan] breostum BH.   13 gecnucud'n'e] gecnucude
H 58/2.   14 *title*: ruta B 106v/12a, rude H.   15 rutam] ruta B.
18 nendun] nemdon/-un BH.   20 rutam] rutan B.   21 trywenan]
trywenum H.   25 oþerne] oðer B.   26 healfne] hea'l'fne H.

2. —

CXVI, CXVII *om.* O.

MS Ca

2. Ad abortum. Herbae cucumeris silvatici, radicem eius ad tertias coquat et inde se sublavet; si quis autem ieiunus fructum eius ederit, periclitabitur, ideoque abstineat ne manducet.

CXVI. Herba cannabum silvaticum

Nascitur locis asperis et secus vias et saepes.
1. Ad mamillarum dolorem. Herbam cannabem silvaticam tunsam cum axungia imponat, discutit tumorem, et si collectio fuerit, expurgat.
2. Ad frigore exustos. Herbae cannabis silvaticae fructum tritum cum urticae semine subiges aceto et eis impones.

CXVII. Herba piganum agrion (*gl.* id est ruta montana)

[Nascitur in montibus, locis asperis.]
1. Ad caliginem oculorum et qui ulcera habent. Herbae rutae montanae [roscidae], folia eius cocta et in vasculo vitreo mitte, vinum vetus admisce et sic inungues.
2. Ad praecordiorum dolorem. Herbam rutam silvaticam contunde in vaso ligneo, deinde adde tribus digitis quod prendere potueris, mitte in calicem et vini cyatum i et aquae cyatos ii, da ut bibat, et contineat se in lecto modicum, mox sanus erit.
3. Ad eparis dolorem. Herbae rutae montanae manipulum in ollam et aquae eminas iii, mellis eodem adicito exempta ruta, et facis ut fervescat aqua cum melle, et per triduum facis bibere et plures poteris sanare.

4. Wið þæt man gemigan ne mæge genim þysse ylcan wyrte rute
siluatice nigon stelan 7 wæteres ðry scenc(ea)s, cnuca tosomne, 7
e(ce)de(s heal)fne sester, wyll e(al) tosomne, syle drincan singal-
lice n(igon) dagas, he byð geh(æ)led.

5   5. Wið þære nædran sli(t)e þ(e man) scorpius hateþ gen(i)m
þysse ylcan wyrte sæd rut(e silua)tice, cnuca on wine, syle drincan,
hyt geliðigaþ þæt sár.

CXVIII. Seofenleafe   septifolium /

f. 54v   Ðeos wyrt þe man eptafilon 7 oðrum naman septifolium nemneð,
10   7 eac sume men seofonleafe hatað, byþ cenned on beganum
stowum 7 on sandigum landum.

1. Wið fotadle genim þas wyrte septifolium gecnucude 7 wið
croh gemengcgede, smyre ðonne þa fét mid þam wose, þy ðryddan dæge hyt þæt sár genimeþ.

15 ## CXIX. Mistel   ocimus

1. Wið heafodece genim þas wyrte þe man ocimum 7 oðrum
naman mistel nemneþ, cnuca ʽmidʼ rosan (wo)se oððe wyrtriwes
oððe mid ecede, lege to ðam andwlatan.

2. Eft wið eagena sare 7 geswel cnuca ðas sylfan wyrte on
20   godu(m) wine, s(m)yre þa ea(g)an þær(mi)d, þu hy (ge)hæls(t).

3. Wið (ædre)na sa(re) do þæt syl(fe, sy)le drin(can) on (rinde
þ)æs (æples) þe man malum (gran)at(um nemn)eþ.

CXX. Merce   herba apium

1. Wið eagena sare 7 wið geswel nim ðas wyrte þe man appium
25   7 oðrum naman merce nemneþ wel gecnucude mid hlafe, lege to
þam eagon. /

MS V

1 gemigan] migan B.   2–4 7 ecedes . . . tosomne, syle . . . gehæled] syle
. . . gehæled, 7 ecedes . . . tosomne V, *marked for reversal.*   3 drincan]
drican H.   7 geliðigaþ] liðigað H 59/1.   8 *title:* septem folia B
107/14a, seofonleafe H.   13 gemengcgede] gemængede B, gemænʽcʼgede
H.   15 *title:* mistel BH.   17 oððe] oððe mid BH.   22 granatum]
gramatum H.   23 *title:* apium merc B 107v/12a, merce H.

CXVIII. (Epta)f(ilo)n

þeos wirt þa man eptafilon 7 sume men septifolium 7 eac su(m)e men seofanleafe hatað.

1. (Ad infirmitatem pedum) Wid fotadle þeos wyrt ȝecnucod 7 wiþ cro(h) ȝemengede, smíre þa fet míd þam wose, þi ðriddan dæȝe hit þar 5 sor binímeð 7 æl wo ȝehæleð.

CXIX. De ocimo   Anglice mistel

1. þeos wurt þæt man ocímum 7 oþrum nama místel nemned, cnuca / mid rose wose oððer mid wyrtreowes oððer ecede, leȝe to þan anwlitan.

2. Eaft wið eaȝena sor 7 ȝeswel cnuca þas wyrt on godon wyne, smera 10 þa eaȝena ðærmid, þu hi ȝehælst.

3. Wyð ædrena sore do þæt silfe, syle dríncan on rinde þas æpples ðe man malum granatum nemneð.

CXX. De apio

1. Wid eaȝene sare 7 ȝeswel cnuca þa wyrt þæt man merce hatað 15 swiþe wel mid hlafe, leȝe to þan eaȝon.

MS Ca

4. Ad eos qui urinam facere non possunt. Herbae rutae silvaticae caliculos ix conterito, addito aquae cyatos iii et aceti eminam, sufferveat, et [da; bibat continuo] dies ix, sanus fiet.

5. Si quem scorpio percusserit. Herbae rutae silvaticae semen contritum ex vino dabis potui, dolorem sedat.

CXVIII. Herba eptafillon

[Nascitur locis sablosis et cultis.]

1. Ad pedum dolorem vel auriginosos. Herba septemfolium trita cum luteo mixto suco, pedes perungues, tertio die dolorem tollit.

CXIX. Herba ocimum

1. Ad capitis dolorem. Herba ocimum tritum cum oleo roseo aut myrtino vel aceto fronti imponitur.

2. Ad epiforas oculorum. Herba ocimum ex vino optimo tritum oculis illinatur.

3. Item ad renes in mali granati cortice bibito.

CXX. Herba appium

1. Ad epiforas oculorum. Herba appium tritum bene cum pane,
oculi teguntur.

f. 55   CXXI. Yfig   hedera

Ðeos wyrt þe man hedera crysocantes 7 oðrum naman ifig nemneþ is gecweden crysocantes for ðy þe heo byrð corn golde gelice.

5   1. Wið wæterseocnysse genim þysse wyrte twentig corna, gnid on anne sester wines, 7 of þam wine syle drincan þry scenceas seofon dagas, seo untrumnys ðurh þone migðan byð aidlud.

CXXII. Minte   menta

1. Wið teter 7 pypylgende lic genim ðysse wyrte seaw þe man
10 mentam 7 þam gelice oþrum naman mintan nemneð, do þonne þærtó swefel 7 eced, cnuca eal tosomne, smyre mid anre feþere, sona þæt sár geliðigað.

2. Gyf yfele dolh oððe wund(a o)n heafde sýn genim þas ylcan wy(r)te mentam gecnucude, lege to þam wundum, heo hy
15 gehæleþ.

CXXIII. Dile   annetum /

f. 55v   1. Wið gicða(n) 7 wið sár þæ(r)a (ge)scea(pa) genim þ(as) wy(rt)e ðe man a(n)etum 7 oþr(um n)aman dyle (n)emneþ, bæ(r)n to duste, nim þon(ne) þæt dust 7 hu(n)ig, men(gc) tosomne, beþa
20 ærest þæt sa(r) mid wætere, þwe(a)h syþþan (m)id wearmum wyrtrywenum wose, lege þonne ða lacnunge þærto.

2. Gyf þonne wifmen hwæt swylces derige do hyre man fram hyre byrþþinene þone sylfan læcedom þære wyrte þe we nu her beforan cwædon.

25 3. Wið heafodece genim þysse ylcan wyrte blostman, seoð mid ele, smyre ða þunwonga 7 gewrið þæt heafod.

MS V

  1 title: ivi B, yfig H.   3–5 corn . . . twentig] om. H (see t.n.).
7 ðurh] ður H.   8 title: mentam B, minte H.   9 teter 7] teter 7 wið BH
ðysse] ðys`se´ H 60/2.   11 swefel] gl. bremston H   eal] om. H   feþere]
fyðere B.   13 sýn] synd H.   14 ylcan] om. H   mentam] ðe man
mentan H.   16 title: anetum dile B 108/18a, dile H.   17 þæra gesceapa]
gl. píntel H.   26 þunwonga] -wongan H.

MS O

  7 hyfele] y alt. from u.   11 anetum] anetum a (a exp.).   13 wer-
mamum] followed by watere, struck out and underlined.   15 Gyf] Gif Gyf
(Gif exp.).

CXXI *om.* O.

CXXII. De menta   f. 20v/5

1. (Wyd teter an pipellinde lic 7 wunda 7 sor on efede) þeos wyrt þæt
man mentam 7 Engle minte hæteð. Wyð teter 7 wið pipilȝende lic ním
þisse wyrt seaw, do þanne þarto swewel 7 eced, cnuca togadera ell, smere 5
mid ane feðere; sona þæt sor liþeȝað.

2. Gif hyfele dolh oþþer wunda on heafedon sy ȝením þeos wyrt
ȝecnucada, leȝe to þan wunda; heo hi ȝehæleð.

CXXIII. De aneto   Anglice dile   f. 2v/11

1. (Contra (. . .) et infirmitatem membri) Wyð ȝicðan 7 wyð sar þara 10
sceapa ȝením þas wyrt ða man anetum 7 oþrum naman nemneð dile,
bærn to duste, ním þæt dust 7 huniȝ, meg tosomne, beða ærest þæt sar
mid watere, hreaw sedðan mid wermamum wyrtreowenum wose, leȝe
þona þa lacninge þarto.

2. (Idem ad feminas) Gyf þanan wyfmen hwæt swilces deríe do hyre 15
man fram hyre byrððinene þone sylfan læcedom þara wyrte þe we nu
her before cwædon.

3. (Ad dolorem capitis) Wið heafodhece ȝením þisse ylcan wyrte
blostman, seoð mid ele, smire þanne ða þunwonga þarmid 7 ȝewyrð þæt
heafod.   20

MS Ca

CXXI. Herba hedera crisocantes

1. Ad ydropicos. Herba hedera crisocantes, ideo quia grana fert
coloris aurei, haec grana xx in vini sextario contrita et ex oleo et vino
terni cyati bibantur per dies vii, qui per urinam exinaniuntur.

CXXII. Herba menta

1. Ad ignem sacrum. Herbae mentae sucus expressus, adiecto sulphure
et aceto, teris et de penna inunctus sine dolore sanat.

2. Ad ulcera in capite manantia. Herba menta contrita et imposita
ulcera siccat.

CXXIII. Herba anetum

1. Ad veretri pruriginem. Herbam anetum combure et cinerem eius
commisce cum melle, deinde vulnus foves ex aqua, deinde ex myrtino
oleo calido lavas et sic medicamen impone.

2. Loca mulierum si dolent. Herbae aneti medicamen suprascriptum
[pessum] factum iniciatur ab obstetrice.

3. Ad capitis dolorem. Herbae aneti flos, cum oleo decoque, temporibus
linito et ligato.

CXXIV. Organe   origanum

1. Ðeos wyrt þe man origanum 7 oðrum naman þam gelice organan nemneþ is hattre (g)ecynde 7 swyðlicre 7 heo gebr(æceo u)t (atyh)ð 7 h(eo) ælc yfe(l bl)od 7 ðone dr(o)pan gewyldeþ 7 5 heo wyþ ny(r)w(et) 7 liferseocum wel fremað.

2. Wið gebræceo genim þas ylcan wy(r)te organan, syle etan, þu wundr(ast) hyre fremfulnysse.

CXXV. Sinfulle   semperuiuus

1. Wið ealle gegaderunga þæs yfelan wætan of þam lichoman 10 genim þas wyrte þe man semperuiuum 7 oðrum naman sinfulle nemneþ 7 rysle 7 hlaf 7 coliandran, cnuca eal tosomne þam gelice þe ðu clyþan wyrce, lege to þam sare.

CXXVI. Finol   ffeniculus /

f. 56   1. Wið gebræceo 7 wyð nyrwyt genim þysse wyrte wyrttruman 15 þe man fenuculum 7 oðrum naman finul nemneþ, cnuca on wine, drince fæstende nigon dagas.

2. Wið blædran sare genim þysse ylcan wyrte þe we (f)enuculum nemdun anne gripa(n) swa grene 7 merces wyrttru(m)a(n) grenne 7 eorðnafolan wyrtruman grene, dó on anne niwne croccan 20 7 wæteres anne sester fulne, wyl tosomne to feorðan dæle; drince þonne fæstende seofon dagas oþþe ma, 7 he bæþes bruce, na swaþeah coles, ne he colne wætan þicge, butan yldincge þære blæddran sar byð geliðigod.

MS V

1 *title*: origanum B, organe H.   4 ðone] þæne H.   6 gebræceo] gebræced, *gl.* host H.   7 fremfulnysse] fram- H 61/2.   8 *title*: synful B 108v/7a, sinfulle H.   13 *title*: feniculum B, finol H.   14 gebræceo] gebræced, *gl.* host H.   16 drince] drice B.   18 grene] grenne BH merces] myrces BH.   19 7 eorðnafolan wyrtruman grene] *om.* B   grene] grenne H   anne] anne clænne H.   21 bæþes] beðæs H.

MS O

10 risel] risel 7 risel (risel 7 *exp.*).   15 neoʒan] niʒa neoʒan (niʒa *exp.*). 17 wyrt] þ wyrt.   18 eorðnafelan] eornafela eorðnafelan.   21 þaræ] ðare þaræ (ðare *exp.*).

CXXIV. De origano f. 25v/7

1. (Ad malum sanguinem et ydroposim et ad strictum pectus et ad pulmonem) þeos wyrt þæt man origanum 7 oþrum namen organe nemneð his hattre ȝecunde 7 heo bræco ut atyhd 7 heo ælc yfel blod 7 þane dropan ȝewyldeð 7 heo wyd nyrwít 7 liferseocum wel fremeð. 5

2. Wið ȝebræco ȝením þeos wert, sele etan, þu wundrast hyre fremfulnesse 7 hure læcecrafte.

CXXV. Sempervíua synfulle 7 syngrene Iouis barba f. 38/13

1. (Ad apostema) Wið ȝegaderunga þas yfelen wæte of þan lichama nim þa wyrt þæt man semperuíua nemneð 7 Engle synfulle hateð 7 risel 10 7 hlaf 7 coliandram, cnuca ealle tosomne ða ȝelice þa þu clyðan wyrce, leȝe to þan sare.

CXXVI. (. . .) f. 12v/24

1. Wyð ȝebræce 7 wyð nirwyt nim þisse wyrte wyrtrume þ(e) / man ff. 15, 19 feniculum 7 sume men fenel hataþ, cnuca on wíne, drinca fastinde neoȝan 15 daȝeð.

2. (Contra malum uesicae) Wyd blæddra sore ním þisse wyrt feniculum anne gr(i)pe swa grene 7 merces wyrtrume gren(e) 7 eorðnafelan 7 wæteres anne sesterne fulle, wyl tosomne to feorðe dale; (dri)ncan þanne fastinde seofon dæȝeþ oþer ma, 7 (he) bæðes brucan, na swaþeaþ 20 coles, ne he colne wætes þicge; bute yldincge þaræ sar bladdran byð aliðeȝed.

CXXIV. Herba origanum p. 519

1. See Note.

2. Ad tussem. Herbam origanum commanducet, miraberis effectum eius.

CXXV. Herba sempervivum

1. Ad apostema. Herbam sempervivum cum axungia et pane et coliandro simul contritum vice malagmae impone.

CXXVI. Herba fenuculum

1. Ad tussem. Herbae fenuculi radicem tunsam in mero ieiunus bibat per dies novem.

2. Ad vesicae dolorem. Herbae fenuculi viridis fascem et appii viridis radicem, sparagi agrestis radicem, in pultario novo mittis et aquae sextarium, et simul ferveat ad quartas, et ieiunus bibat diebus vii vel pluribus, balneum utatur, in recente non descendat, frigida non bibat, vesicae dolorem sedat sine mora.

CXXVII. Liðwyrt　erifion

Ðeos [wyrt] þe man erifion 7 oþrum naman liðwyrt nemneþ
byþ cenned fyrmest in Gallia, þæt is on Franclande, on þam munte
þe man Soractis hateþ; heo hæfð merces gelicnysse 7 heo hafað
5 blost(man rea)dne swylce cærse (7) heo hafaþ s(e)ofon wyrttruman
7 swa fel(a) st(e)l(ena) 7 heo hy sylfe tobræd(eð o)n unbeganum
stowum 7 na on wætum; heo byþ ælcon timan blowen(de 7 heo)
hafað sæd swylce beana.

1. Wiþ lungenadle genim þas wyrte erifion gecnucude þam
10 gelice þe þu clyþan wyrce, lege to þam sare, heo hit gehæleþ;
nim þonne þæt wos þisse sylfan wyrte, syle drincan, þu wundrast
þæs mægenes þysse wyrte.

CXXVIII. Halswyrt　sinfitus albus /

f. 56v　1. Wið wifes flewsan genim þas wyrte þe man sinfitum album 7
15 oþrum naman halswyr't' nemneþ, gedrige hy 7 cnuca to swiþe
smalan duste, syle drincan on wine, sona heo þa flewsan gewrið.

CXXIX. Petersilie　petrosilinum

Ðas wyrte man triannem 7 oþrum naman petroselinum nemneþ,
7 eac hy sume men þam gelice petersilie hateþ.

20 1. Wið næddran slite genim of ðysse wyrte petroselini swyþe
smæl dust anes scyllincges gewihte, syle drincan on wine, nim
ðonne þa wyrte gecnucude, lege to þære wunde.

2. Wiþ ðæra sina sare genim þas ylcan wyrte petroselinum
gepunude, lege to þam sare, heo geliþigað þæt sár þæra sina.

25 ## CXXX. Cawel　brassica

1. Wið ealle geswel genim þysse wyrte croppas þe man brassicam siluaticam 7 oðrum naman caul nemneþ, cnuca mid ealdon
rysle, gemencg ðonne swylce ðu clyðan wyrce, do on anne þicne
linenne cla ð, lege to þam sare.

MS V

1 title: liðwurt B 109/t.m.a, liðwyrt H.　　2 wyrt] from B, wyr V.　　5 cærse]
cerse B, cerse H 62/2.　　7 na] om. H (see also t.n.).　　9 gecnucude] gecnode B.
13 title: halswurt B, om. H.　　15 halswyr't'] om. H　　hy] 'hy' H
swiþe] wiðe H.　　16 þa] þone BH.　　17 title: petrosilinum B, petersilie H.
18 Ðas wyrte man] Ðeos wyrt ðe man H　　naman] nan H.　　25 title: wilde
cawul B 109v/20a, cawel H 63/1.　　26–7 brassicam] brasicam B.　　27 caul]
cawel BH　　ealdon] ealdum H.　　28 þicne] þynne H.　　29 lege] l'e'ge H.

CXXVII. Erif(ion)   f. 13/8

þeos wyrt þe man erifion 7 oþrum nama liðewyrt hateð, heo byd ælcon timan 7 heo hafad sæd swylce beana.

1. (Ad morbum pulmonis) Wið lungenadle ȝením þas wyrt erifion, ȝecnuca ðam ȝelice þe þu clyþan wyrce, leȝe to þan sore, heo hit hæleð; 5 nim þonne þat wos þisse wyrte, sile drincan, ðu wundrast þæs mæȝenes ðisse wyrte.

CXXVIII *om.* O.

CXXIX. Petrosillinum   triannem   f. 40/13

þeos wyrt þæt man triannem 7 oþrum nama petroselínum hataỗ 7 10
Engle wætersylie hateð.

1. (Ad morsum serpentis) Wið nadran slite ním of þisse wyrt swiðe smale dust anes scínlinges ȝewihte, sile drícan on wine, cnuca þanne þa wyrt, leȝe to þare wunda.

2. (Ad morbum neruorum) Wið þara sína sare ním þa wyrt ȝepunode, 15
leȝe to ðan sare, heo liþegað þare sina sar.

CXXX *om.* O.

MS Ca

CXXVII. Herba erifion

Nascitur in Gallia, in monte Syracti; figuram habet appii, florem habet p. 520
purpureum similem nasturcii, septem radicibus, totidemque ramulis;
ipsa autem patula humo [locis] asperis, minimeque irriguis, omni florens
tempore, semen habet tamquam faba.

1. Ad tysicos. Herba erifion pisata, malagmae genus imposita sanat;
sucum eius potui datum, miraberis virtutem eius.

CXXVIII. Herba symfitum album

1. Ad profluvium mulieris. Herba symfitum siccata, pisata, et in
pulvere mollissimo redacta, in vino potui data, et mox restringit.

CXXIX. Herba petroselinum

1. Ad morsum serpentis. Herbae petroselini pulverem mollissimum
dragmam i ex vino potui dabis, ipsa contrita plagae imponitur.

2. Ad nervorum dolorem. Herba petroselinum tunsa, imposita nervorum dolorem sedat.

CXXX. Herba brassica silvatica

1. Ad tumores omnes. Herbae brassicae silvaticae cinis, cum axungia p. 521
vetere pisata et commixta quasi malagma, inducis in linteolo grosso aut
in aluta, imponis.

2. Wið sidan sare genim þas ylcan wyrte brassicam siluaticam, lege to þam sare swa gemencged swa we her beforan cwædon. /

f. 57　　3. Wið fotadle genim þas sylfan wyrte brassicam on þa ylcan wisan þe we ær cwædon, 7 swa se læcedom yldra byþ swa he
5　scearpnumulra 7 halwendra byþ.

CXXXI. Nædderwyrt　basilisca

1. Ðeos wyrt þe man basilisca 7 oðrum naman nædderwyrt nemneþ byð cenned on ðam stowum þær seo nædre byþ þe man þam ylcan naman nemneð basiliscus; witodlice nys heora cyn án
10　ác hi sindon þreora cynna, án ys olocryseis, þæt is on ure geðeode gecweden þæt heo eall golde scine; ðonne is oðer cyn stillatus, þæt is on ure geþeode dropfah, seo ys swylce heo gyldenum heafde sy; þæt ðridde cyn ys sanguineus, þæt is blodread, eac swilce heo gylden on heafde sy; ealle ðas cyn þeos wyrt basilisca h(æ)fð
15　(þ)o(nne) gyf hwa þas wyrte (mid) h(im h)a(fað) þonne ne mæg (him nan ðyssa næ)ddercynna derian; (se)o forme næddre olo-cryssus is genemned eriseos, seo swa hwæt swa heo gesihð heo toblæwð 7 anæleþ; ðonne seo oþer stillatus is soðlice gecweden crysocefalus asterites, þeos swa hwæt swa heo gesyhð hyt for-
20　scrincð 7 gewiteþ; þonne is seo ðridde genemned hematites 7 crysocefalus, swa hwæt swa ðeos gesyhð oþþe hrepeð hyt to-flewð swa ðæt þær nanwiht belifeþ buton þa ban; þonne hæfð þeos wyrt basilisca ealle heora stren'g'ða; gyf hwylc man þas wyrte mid him hafað wið eall næddercyn he biþ trum.

MS V

4 se] we H.　　　　5 scearpnumulra] sceárp/pra numulra H　　　7 halwendra]
bið 7 halwyndrá H.　　　　　　　　　　6 title: neddrewurt B, nædderwyrt H.
10 olocryseis] olocris/seis B.　　　　　12 swylce] swilce/swilce B 110/1a.
14 ealle] eall H.　　　　　　　19 crysocefalus] chryso- B, chryso- H 64/6.
21 crysocefalus] chriso- BH.

MS O

4 'olocryseis'] in text olocresis (exp.), olocryseis in o.m.　　　　7 Ealla]
Ealla / ealla.　　　11 forsormð] could also be read forsorinð.　　　14 'hwylc']
in text hyf (exp.), hwylc in o.m.

CXXXI. De basilica id est n(ædder)wy(rt)   f. 8v/3

1. (Basillica contra omne genus serpentium ualet) þeos wyrt þe man
basillicam an oþrum naman næddrewyrt nemnað, hira cun is þreora
cynna. An is 'olocryseis', þæt is þæt heo ealþa gold scineþ; þanne is
oðer cyn stillatus, þæt on ure þeode dropfah, seo ys swycce heo gildenun 5
heafde si; þæt þrínde cyn ys sanguineus, þat is blodread, eac swy'l'ce
gylden on heafedan si. Ealla ðas cynne wirt basillica hæfð. Gif hwa þas
wyrt on him hæfð na mæʒ him nan ðysra næddrecynna derian. Seo
forme næddre olocrissus ʒenemdeð eriseos; hel þat heo ʒesyhð heo
toblæwð 7 onælð. Seo oþer stillatus is soðlice ʒecweden chrisocefalus 10
asterítes; þeos el þæt heo ʒesyhþ hit forsormð 7 forwyteð. þeo þriddan
is ʒenemned hematites 7 chrisocefalus; eal þat seo ʒesihð hit toflewð
swa þæt þar nanwyht ne belifð butan þa ban; þanna hæfeð þeos wyrt
basilica ealla hyra strengþa. Gif 'hwylc' man þas wyrt mid hym hafad
ealle næddrecún he byð trum.   15

MS Ca

2. Ad lateris dolorem. Herba brassica silvatica, imponis ut supra.

3. Ad podagram. Herba brassica silvatica, idem conficies ut supra,
quod si vetustissimum fuerit eo magis efficacior erit.

CXXXI. Herba basilisca

1. Haec herba basilisca illis locis nascitur ubi fuerit serpens basiliscus;
non enim unum genus est eorum, sed genera sunt tria: unus est olocrissus,
alius est stillatus capite aureo, tertius est sanguineus capite aureo. Hos
omnes haec herba basilisca obtinet facile. Si quis eam secum portaverit,
hos obtinet nec visa mala nocere possunt. Olocrissus autem qui dicitur
criseos, quod viderit insufflat et incendit. Stellatus autem qui est criso-
cephalus asterites hic est qui quod viderit arescit et occidet. Tertius
autem qui est ematites crisocefalus, quod viderit vel percusserit, defluescet
et ossua per se remanent. Omnes violentias eorum haec herba regula
obtinet. Si quis homo eam secum habuerit, ab omne generatione serpentium tutus erit.

þeos wyrt ys rudan gelic 7 heo hæfð meolc reade swylce celidonie 7 heo hæfð wolcenreade blostman; 7 se þe hy niman wylle, he hyne sylfne clænsie 7 hy bewrite mid golde 7 mid seolfre f. 57v 7 mid heortes / horne 7 mid ylpenbane 7 mid bares tuxe 7 mid 5 fearres horne, 7 mid hunige geswette wæstmas þær onbutan gelecge.

CXXXII. Mandragora   mandregara

Ðeos wyrt þe man mandragoram nemneþ ys mycel 7 mære on gesihþe 7 heo ys fremful; ða þu scealt þyssum gemete niman,
10 þonne þu to hyre cymst, þonne ongist þu hy be þam þe heo on nihte scineð ealswa leohtfæt, þonne ðu hyre heafod ærest geseo, þonne bewrit þu hy wel hraþe mid iserne þy læs heo þe ætfleo, hyre mægen ys swa mycel 7 swa mære þæt heo unclænne man, þonne he to hyre cymeþ, wel hraþe forfleon wyle, for ðy þu hy
15 bewrit, swa wé ǽr cwædon, mid iserne, 7 swa þu scealt onbutan hy delfan swa ðu hyre mid þam iserne ná æthrine; ác þu geornlice scealt mid ylpenbanenon stæfe ða eorðan delfan; 7 þonne þu hyre handa 7 hyre fet geseo, þonne gewrið þu hy; nim þonne þæne oþerne ende 7 gewrið to anes hundes swyran swa þæt se
20 hund hungrig sy, wurp him syþþan mete toforan swa þæt he hyne [aræcan] ne mæge buton he mid him þa wyrte up abrede; be þysse wyrte ys sæd þæt heo swa mycele mihte hæbbe þæt swa hwylc þincg swa hy up atyhð þæt hyt sona scyle þam sylfan gemete beon beswycen; for þy sona swa þu geséo þæt heo up abroden sy

MS V

2 celidonie] celidon'i'e H   wolcenreade] wolcreade H.   3 clænsie] clænne H.   4 horne] 'hor/ne' H   bares] bearges H   tuxe] tuxle BH.   5 geswette] gewætte H.   7 *title*: mandragoram BH. 8 mandragoram] -goran B.   9 heo] he'o' H.   10 ongist] ongitst BH. 10 ongist] ongitst BH.   16 hyre mid þam iserne] mid þam iserne hyre B 110v/4a   æthrine] ætríne B.   17 ylpenbanenon] -bænenan B, -bænenon H 65/5.   19 þæne] þone B   swyran] sweoran H.   20 syþþan] þonne H.   21 aræcan] *from* B, áhræcan V.   22 mycele] mic'e'le H.   23 hyt] he H.

MS O

1 'hys'] *this word in o.m., referred to by a signe de renvoi in text.*   9 þat] þat þat.   10 he] he(o) (o *incomplete and exp.*).   12–13 mid ylpenbænenan stæfe] *gl.* cum eburneo baculo.

Ðeos wynt ‘hys᾽rudan ȝelíc 7 heo hæfd meoluc reade swilce cilidoníe 7
heo hæfð wolenreadan blosmam; 7 þe þe hi níme wille, he clæne sie 7 hi
bewriþe mid golde 7 mid seolfre 7 mid heortes horne 7 mid hilpenbane
7 mid bares twuxe 7 mid fearres horne; 7 mid huniȝe ȝeswete wæsmas
ðær onbutan ȝelecge.   5

CXXXII. De mandragora f. 20v/13

þeos wyrt mandragora hys fremful; heo on niht scíneð healso leohfæt;
þanne þu hure heafod ærest ȝeseo þanne bywyrt þu hy wel raðe mid
ysene þe læs heo þe attfleo. Hure maenȝen ys sa mycel 7 swa mere þat heo
unclænne man, þanne he to hyre cymeð, wel raðe forlæte wile; forþi þu 10
hi bewyrst mid ysene swa we ær cwadan; 7 þanne þu scealt onbute hy
delfan swa þæt þu hy na mid þan ysene athryne. Ac þu ȝeorn/lice mid f. 23(!)
ylpenbænenan stæfe ðe eorðan delfan; 7 þane þu hyre hænde 7 hyre fet
yseo, þane ȝewyrt þu hy; ním þanne þane oðerne ende 7 ȝewyrt to anes
hundes swyran ða þæt þe hund hungri sy; wyrp hím seððam mete   15
toforen þa þæt he hyne aracen ne mæȝe bute he míd hym þa wyrt habbe;
for yt ys ysæd be þisse wyrt þæt heo habbe swa micele myhte þæt hwylce
þing hi up atihð þæt hit sona scyle beon beswicen. Ac þane heo up

---

MS Ca

Est autem herba talis similis rutae, lactem habens aurosum subsimilem
celidoniae, florem autem crisococcum; et qui eam leget mundus sit,
circumscribat eam auro, argento, cornu cervino, ebore, dente apruno,
cornu taurino, et fruges mellitos in vestigio ponat.

CXXXII. Herba mandragora

Effectus herbae mandragorae quam sic colligi oportet, quia magna est
visio ac beneficia eius. Ad quam cum perveneris ita eam intellegis: nocte p. 522
tamquam lucerna sic lucet. Caput eius cum videris, cito circumducis eam
ferro, ne tibi fugiat. Talis [ac tanta] est virtus eius, ut venientem ad se
hominem immundum cito ante eum fugit, ideo circumducis eam ferro et
ita circum eam effodies, ne eam de ferro tangas, et diligentissime de palo
eburneo amoves ab ante eam terram. Et cum videris pedem eius mandragorae et manus eius, tunc demum et herbam alligabis fune novo, et
postquam alligasti herbam, tunc et cani alligabis in collo antequam
canem esurientem facis et mitte paulo longius illi escam canis, quo
tendens possit herbam evellere. Quod si nolueris canem decipere quia
tantam fertur ipsa herba habere divinitatem, ut qui eam evellet, eodem modo illum decipiat (. . .). Mox vero cum tibi fuerit data herba in

7 þu hyre geweald hæbbe, genim hy sona on hand swa, andwealc
hi 7 gewring þæt wos of hyre leafon on ane glæsene ampullan; 7
þonne ðe neod becume þæt þu hwylcon men þærmid helpan
scyle, þonne help þu him ðyssum gemete. /

f. 58   1. Wið heafodece 7 wið þæt man slapan ne mæge genim þæt
6   wós, smyre þone andwlatan; 7 seo wyrt swa some þam sylfan
gemete þone heafodece geliðigaþ; 7 eac þu wundrast hu hrædlice
se slæp becymeþ.

     2. Wið þæra earena sare genim þysse ylcan wyrte wós [gemæn-
10   ged] mid ele þe sy of nardo, geot on ða earan, þu wundrast hu
hrædlice he byþ gehæled.

     3. Wið fotadle, þeah ðe heo hefegust sy, genim of þære swyþran
handa þysse wyrte 7 of þære wynstran, of ægþerre handa þreora
penega gewihte, wyrc to duste, syle drincan on wine seofon dagas,
15   he byþ gehæled, na þæt án þæt þæt geswel geset, ác eac þæra
sina togunge to hæle gelædeþ 7 þa sár butu wundurlice gehæleþ.

     4. Wið gewitleaste, þæt is wið deofulseocnysse, genim of þam
lichoman þysse ylcan wyrte mandragore þreora penega gewihte,
syle drincan on wearmum wætere swa hé eaðelicost mæge, sona
20   he byþ gehæled.

     5. Eft wið sina togunge genim of ðam lichoman þysse wyrte
anre ynsan gewihte, cnuca to swyþe smalan duste, gemencg mid
ele, smyre þonne þa þe ðas foresprecenan untrumnysse habbað.

     6. Gyf hwa hwylce hefige yfelnysse on his hofe geseo genime
25   þas wyrte mandragoram onmiddan þam huse, swa mycel (sw)a he
þonne h(æbbe), ealle yfelu (heo) út anyd(eð).

MS V

1–2 andwealc hi] anwealche H.   4 scyle] scule B, sceole H.   5 hea-
fodece] hea'fod´ece H.   6 sylfan] om. H.   8 se] him B.
9–10 gemænged] from B, gemencg/ged V, gemæn'c´ged H.   10 wundrast]
wundranst H.   13 7] om. H 66/2   wynstran, of] wynstran hánd 7 of H.
16 butu] buta BH.   18 mandragore] mandragora H.   22 ynsan]
yndsan B, yntsan H.   24 hofe] hrofe H.   25 mandragoram] mandra-
goran B 110a/2a.   26 anydeð] adeð B.

MS O

4 þissum ȝemete] gl. i.e. ita auxilium   7 ȝemete] ȝeme (no damage).
9 of nardo] gl. de nardo.   11 swyrðr'a´n] alt. from swyrðarn.
17 wætera] wíne wætera (wíne exp.).

abroden sy 7 þu hyre ȝeweald hæbbe, ȝením hy sona on handa swa,
anwelce 7 ȝewyr`n´g þæt wos of hure leafen on ane glæsene ampulle, 7
þanne þe neod beo þæt þu hwylcon men þarmíd helpen wylle, þane do
hím þissum ȝemete.

1. (Ad dolorem capitis et sompnum) Wið heafodece 7 wið þæt man 5
slapen ne mæȝe ním þæt wos, smire þane anwlitan; 7 seo wirt swa some
san silfan [ȝemete] þane heafodece ȝeliþeȝað `7 hrædlice slapeþ´.

2. (Ad morbum aurium) Wið earena sare ním þisse wyrt wos, meng
mid ele þe si of nardo, ȝeot on þa earan, hrædlice he byð ȝehæled.

3. (Ad morbum pedum) Wið fotadle, ðeah heo hefigust si, ním of þare 10
swyrðr`a´n handa 7 of þara wynstran hænde þysse wyrt, of æȝre handan
ðreora peneȝa ȝewyhta, wyrc to dust, sile drincan / on wine seofan dæȝas, f. 23v
heo byð ȝehaled; na þæt þat an þæt ȝeswel ȝeset, ac eac sara sína toȝunge
to hæle ȝelædeð 7 þæt sar þara abuta wunderlice ȝehæled.

4. (Ad demoniacos) Wið ȝewitleaste, þæt is wið deofolseocnesse, 15
ȝením of þan lichama þisse wyrt ðreora peneȝa ȝewihte, syle drincan on
wyrme wætera swa he eaðelicost mæȝe, sona he bið ȝehæled.

5. 6. —

MS Ca

potestate, hoc est in manibus, integra herba, statim de foliis eius sucum in
ampullam vitream repones, et cum advenerint in necessitate homines sic
facies.

1. Ad capitis dolorem et cui somnus non venit. Herbae mandragorae
proanacollima in frontem inducis, sucus eius eodem modo capitis
dolorem sedat, etiam somnus ei cito veniet mira celeritate.

2. Ad aurium dolorem. Herbae mandragorae sucus eius cum oleo
nardino solutus, mixturas suffundis auribus, statim mire sanat.

3. Ad podagram quamvis gravissimam. Herbae mandragorae dextram
manum et pedem dextrum tollis scripula singula et facies pulverem et
dabis potui in mero per dies [vii], mira celeritate sanat. Non solum
tumorem, sed et contractionem nervorum utrique ad se revocat et
dolores utrique [mire] sanatur (. . .).

4. Ad epilempticos, hoc est daemoniacos et qui spasmum patiuntur
sic facies: Herbae mandragorae, de corpore eius tribulis scripulum i
et dabis bibere in aqua calida quantum merus continet, statim mirifice
sanantur.

5. Ad strictionem et nervorum contractionem. Herbae mandragorae,
de corpore ipsius herbae unciam i, tribulas pulverem tenuissimum,
commisce cum oleo suave et perungues eos qui supradictas curas habent.

6. Si qua gravis cuiusque malitia in domo visa fuerit. Herbae mandragorae quantumcumque in media domo habeat, omnia mala expellit.

CXXXIII. Læcewyrt lycanis stefanice

1. Ðeos wyrt ðe man lichanis stefanice 7 oðrum naman læcewyrt nemneþ hafað lange leaf 7 geþufe 7 hæwene, 7 hyre stela byð mid
f. 58v geþufum bogum, 7 heo hafað on ufeweardum þam stelan /
5 geoluwe blostman; þysse wyrte sæd on wine geseald fremað wel ongean eal næddercyn 7 wið scorpiones stincg to ðam swyþe þæs ðe sume men secgeað þæt gyf hy man ofer þa scorpiones gelegð þæt heo him (un)mihtignesse 7 untrumnysse on gebri(n)cge.

CXXXIV. [Action]

10 Ðeos wyrt ðe man action 7 oðrum naman (. . .) nemneð hafað gelice leaf cyrfættan, ac hy beoð maran 7 heardran, 7 heo hafað wið þone wyrttruman greatne stelan 7 twegea fæðma lange, 7 heo hafað on ufeweardon þam stelan sæd ðistele gelic, ac hyt byð smælre 7 read on bleo.

15 1. Wið þæt man blod 7 worsm gemang hræce genim þysse wyrte feower penega gewiht sædes 7 cyrnlu of [pintrywenum] hnutum, cnuca tosomne þam gelice þe þu anne æppel wyrce, syle þicgean þam untruman, hyt hyne gehæleð.

2. Wið þæra liða sare genim þas ylcan wyrte gecnucude 7 to
20 clyþan geworhte, lege to ðam sare, heo hyt geliðigað. Eac þam sylfan gemete heo ealde wunda gehæleþ.

CXXXV. Suþernewuda

Ðeos wyrt þe man abrotanum 7 oðrum naman suðernewuda nemneþ ys twegea cynna; þonne is þæt oðer cyn greaton bogum
25 7 swyþe smælon leafon swylce heo má fexede gesewen sy, 7 heo
f. 59 hafað / blostman 7 sæd swyþe gehwæde, 7 heo is godes swæces 7 myceles 7 biterre on byrgynge.

MS V

1 *title*: lechewurt B, *eras*. H. 2 stefanice] stæf- H. 5 fremað] hit frámað H 67/1. 6 scorpiones] scopiones B. 9 *title*: *from* B, *om*. VH. 10 oðrum] oðru H. 11 gelice leaf] lange leáf gelic H cyrfættan] cyfettan B, cyrfettan H ac] 7 B. 14 read] hread B. 15 worsm] worms BH hræce] hræ'ce' H. 16 gewiht] gewihte BH pintrywenum] *from* B, win- V. 18 þicgean] *id*. H (*alt. from* þicgcan) hyne gehæleð] bið gehæled H. 19 sare] *om*. H. 22 *title*: suðerwude B 110av/20a, suðerne wuda H. 23 suðernewuda] *space* B, *om*. H. 25 smælon] smalon B. 27 biterre] biter B.

MS O

3 actíon] *also* action *in o.m.* 8 wyrms] *alt. from* wyrmet.

CXXXIII *om.* O.

CXXXIV. De action

þeos wyrt þe man actíon nemned hafeð ȝelice leaf cyrfættan, 7 hi beoð
maran 7 herdran, 7 heo hæfd wyð þane wyrtruman greatne stelan 7
tweȝra feðma lagne, 7 heo hæfed on ufewear/don þam stelan sæd þistele
ȝelice, 7 hit byð smælre 7 read on bleo.

1. (Ad eos qui sanguinem et tabem mixtum conspuunt) Wið þæt man
blod 7 wyrms ȝemang hracce ȝením þisse wyrte iiii peneȝa ȝewihte sædis
7 cyrnlu of pintreowenum hnutum, cnuca tosomne ðan ȝelice þe ðu
anne appel, syle ðingan; ða untrumnysse hit hine ȝehælð.

2. —

(margin: f. 2v/22 · f. 3 6 · 10)

CXXXV. De abrotano

þeos wyrt þe man abrotanum 7 on Englisse nemneð suþernewudu is
tweȝra cynna, þanne is þæt oðer cyn ȝreatum bogum 7 swiðe smala
leafon swilce heo ma fexede si, 7 heo hafað sæd swiðe ȝehwede, 7 heo his
godes swæcces 7 míceles 7 biter on bírȝincȝe.

(margin: f. 3/6 · 15)

CXXXIII. Herba licanis

(margin: Har f. 57v/18)

1. Licanis stefanotice folia habet oblonga, angusta, lanuginosa,
[caulem cum ramis lanuginosis, in] summo capite cauliculos e quibus
flos violae prominens; huius semen cum vino datum adversus omnium
serpentium et scorpionum ictum prodest adeo [ut quidam affirment eam]
scorpionibus superpositam stuporem isdem languoremque incutere.

CXXXIV. Herba actionum

(margin: L f. 27/1)

Folia habet similia cucurbitae sed maiora et duriora et prope radicem
densam caulem longum duobus digitis, in capite caliculos in quibus
semen cardis simile et angustius, colore rufo.

1. Ad eos qui sanguinem reiciunt herbae action dragma una (. . .) cum
pineis nucleis (. . .), facto pastillo cum vino potui dato, mire sanat.

2. —

CXXXV. Herba abrotanum

(margin: Har f. 57v/26)

Huius genera sunt duo: femina et masculus; femina ramosa, minutis-
sima folia ut potius capillamentum videatur, flores vel semina minu-
tissima et aurosa, boni odoris et gravis, gustu amara.

1. Wyð nyrwyt 7 wið banece 7 wið þæt man earfoðlice gemigan mæge, þysse wyrte sæd wel fremað gecnucud 7 on wætere geðiged.

2. Wið sidan sare genim ðas ylcan wyrte 7 betonican, cnuca tosomne, syle drincan.

3. Wið attru 7 wið nædrena slite genim ðas ylcan wyrte abrotanum, syle drincan on wine, heo helpeð wel; cnuca hy eac mid ele 7 smyre ðone lichoman þærmid; eac heo wið þone colan fefor wel fremað; eac þæt sæd þysse wyrte stranglice afligeþ gindstred oððe onæled.

4. Wið þæra nædrena slite þe man spalangiones 7 scorpiones nemneð þeos sylfe wyrt wel fremað.

5. Wið eagena sáre genim þas ylcan wyrte abrotanum gesodene mid ðære wyrte þe man melacidoniam 7 oðrum naman codoniam hateþ, 7 ðonne mid hlafe gecnucude, þam gelice þe þu clyþan wyrce, lege to þ(am) sare, hyt byð geliðigod.

þeo(s) wyrt is, swa we her b(ef)or(an) cwædon, twegea (c)ynna, (oð)er (y)s wif, oðer wer, 7 hy habbað on eall(um) þingo(n g)elice m(iht)e ongean (þa) ðincg ðe we her beforan s(ædon).

CXXXVI. Laber

Ðeos wyrt þe man [sion] 7 oðrum naman [laber] nemneþ byð cenned on wætum stowum.

1. Wið þæt stanas on blædran wexen genim ðas wyrte, syle etan oððe gesodene oððe hræwe, heo þa stanas [þurh] migþan ut atyhð.

2. Eac ðeos sylfe wyrt wel fremað wið utsiht 7 wið þæs innoþes astyrunge. /

f. 59v ## CXXXVII. [Sigilhweorfa]

Ðeos wy(r)t þe man eliotropus 7 oðrum naman sigilhweorfa nemneð byþ cenned on fættum landum 7 on beganum 7 heo hafað

1 man] *om.* H 68/5.   8 gindstred] gnid- H.   10 þæra nædrena] nædrán H   spalangiones] spalánguio'ne's H.   11 þeos sylfe] þeos B, ðeosylfe H.   17 on] of H   þingon] *om.* B 111/3a.   19 *title:* lawer B, sion / laber / agrimonia / id. (*these words in later hand in b.m.*) H.   20 sion] *from* H, son V, s'i'on B   oðrum] þrum H   laber] *from* H, lader V, lawer B. 23 hræwe] hreawe B, hreawe H 69/2   þurh] *from* B, þurð V.   25 sylfe] *om.* H.   27 *title: from* B, (sigil)hweorwa V, H = B.   28 man]ma'n' B.

1. (Ad strictum pectus et ad eos qui mingere nequeunt) Wið nyrwet 7 wiþ banece 7 wyþ þæt man earfðlice ȝemiȝan mæȝe þisse wyrte sæd wel fremeð ȝecnucod 7 on wateran ȝeþiȝed.

2. (Ad dolorem lateris) Wið sidan sare ȝením þas wyrt 7 betonícan, cnuca tosomne, syle dríncan.   5

3. 4. —

5. (Ad dolorem oculorum) Wid eaȝena sare ȝením þas wyrt ȝesodena mid þare wyrt þa man melacedoniam 7 oþrum naman eodoniam, 7 þonne mid hlafe ȝecnucode þam ȝelican ðe þu cliðam wyrce, leȝe þarto; hít byd ȝeliþeȝod.   10

Ðeos wyrt is, swa we her beforan cwædon, tweȝra cinna, oðer his wif, oþer his were, 7 hi habbeð on ælcum þinga ȝelice mihta onȝean þa þinga ðe ȝe her beforan sæden.

CXXXVI. De sion   id est lafere   f. 23v/8

þeos wyrt þæt man síon 7 oþþer name laber nemneð byþ cenned on   15 wætere stowe.

1. (Ad lapides in uesica) Wið stanes on bladdra ním þeos wyrt, sile etan ȝesodone oþþer hreawe; hu þa stanes sur mihþan ut atihð.

2. (Contra fluxum uentris) Eac þeos wyrt wel fremað wid utsiht 7 wið þas innoþes astirunge.   20

CXXXVII. (. . .)   f. 13/15

þeos wyrt þe man eliotropus 7 oþrum naman siȝelhweofa.

---

1. Semen eius cum aqua tritum et potum suspiriosis, sciaticis et qui urinam difficiliter emittunt prodest,

2. et paraliticis cum betonica in condito datum (. . .).

3. Adversus venena et morsus serpentium in vino pota subvenit; cum oleo tritum et corpori superlinitum adversus febres frigidas prodest, serpentes etiam vel sparsum vel incensum fugat,

4. principaliter ad spalangionum et scorpionum ictus prodest.

5. Oculorum fervores cum malis cidonicis cocta et cum pane trita vice cataplasmatis mitigat (. . .).

Eandem vim in [omnibus] etiam masculus habet.

CXXXVI. Herba syon   Har
                                    f. 57v/11
Nascitur locis aquosis (. . .).

1. Quae manducata vel elixa vel cruda cauculosis prodest, quia cauculos defricat et per urinam foris eicit (. . .),

2. et disentericis subvenit mirabiliter.

CXXXVII. Herba eliotropus masculus   L f. 28/20

Nascitur in agris pinguibus et cultis, folia habet ocimo similia, lanuginosa et latiora, semen rotundum (. . .).

leaf neah swylce mistel, þa beoð ruge 7 brade, 7 heo hafað sæd
sinewealt 7 þæt byð þreora cynna bleos.

1. Wið ealra næddercynna slitas 7 wið scorpiones genim þysse
wyrte wyrttruman eliotropos, syle drincan on wine, 7 gecnucude
5 lege to þære wunde, heo fremað mycelon.

2. Wyð þæt wyrmas ymb ðone nafolan on þam innoðe derigen
genim ðas ylcan wyrte 7 ysopan 7 nytrum 7 cærsan, cnuca tosomne
ealle, syle drincan on wætere, heo ácwelleþ ða wyrmas.

3. Wið weartan genim þas ylcan wyrte 7 sealt, cnuca tosomne,
10 lege to þam weartun, heo hy fornimeþ, þanon heo eac uerrucaria
genemned is.

CXXXVIII. [Speritis]

Ðeos wyrt ðe man spreritis 7 oðrum naman (. . .) nemneþ
hæfð gehwæde leaf 7 geðufe, 7 heo of anum wyrttruman manega
15 bogas asendeþ, 7 þa beoð neah ðære eorðan alede, 7 heo hafað
geoluwe blostman; 7 gyf þu hy betweonan þinum fingrum gebry-
test, þonne hafað heo swæc swylce myrre.

1. Wið þone colan fefor genim þas wyrte spreritis, seoð on
f. 60 ele; 7 to ðam timam ðe se fefor to ðam men genealæcean / wylle
20 smyre hyne þærmid.

2. Wyð wedehundes slite genim þas ylcan wyrte, cnuca to
duste, nim ðonne anne cuculere fulne, syle drincan on wearmum
wætere, he byð hal.

3. Wyþ miltan sare genim þysse sylfan wyrte anne godne gripan
25 7 anne sester fulne meolce, wyll tósomne, syle drincan healf on
mergen [healf] on æfen þa hwyle þe him þearf sy, seo milte byð
gelacnud.

MS V

1 leaf] om. H. 2 sinewealt] -weal B. 3 ealra] ealle H. 4 syle]
syle / syle (first word erased) V. 7 cærsan] cersan B 111v/1a. 7–8 tosomne ealle] ealle tosomne B, eal tosomne H. 10 weartun] weartum BH.
12 title: from B, om. VH. 13 spreritis] sp'r'eritis H 16 betweonan]
betweonum B. 19 timam] timan B, timan H 70/4. 22 drincan]
drican H. 26 mergen] ærnemergen H healf] from B, heal V.

MS O

3 cnu(ca)] cnuca cnu(ca) (first word underlined). 12 swæc] sma swæc
(sma exp.). 13 nim] four minims, swung dash on last two.

1. —

2. (Contra vermis circa umbilicum) Wið wyr(mas þe) embe þa nafolan
on þan innoþ derion (. . .) (þ)as wyrt 7 ysopum 7 nítrum 7 cærsan, cnu(ca
ea)ll tosomne, sile drican on wætere, heo awelleð ða wyrmas.

3. (Ad ver(ru)cas) Wið wyrtan ním þas wyrt 7 sealt, cnuca tosomna, 5
leȝe to þan wyrte; heo hi fornimeð, þanon heo heac uerrucaría ȝenemneð
his.

CXXXVIII. Spreritis   f. 38/19

þeos wirt þæt man spreritís nemnað haueð ȝehwæde 7 þufe leaf, 7 of
ane wyrtruma maníȝe boȝas, 7 þa beoþ neah þare eorða alede, 7 heo 10
hafaþ ȝeoluwe blostma; 7 ȝif þu hi bitwínan þínum fíngrum ȝebritest,
þanne hafeþ heo swæc swylce mirra.

1. (Ad (. . .)rinas) Wið þæt cole fefere nim þa wyrt, soð / on ele; 7 to   f. 38v
þan time þæt þe fefor to þan manna wyle neahlæcan smyre híne þarmid.

2. (Ad rapidis canis morsum) Wið wodehundas slíte cnuca þeos wyrt 15
to duste, ním þanne anne cucelere fulne, sile drincan on wearme wætere.

3. —

---

1. Ad scorpionum et serpentium morsus herbae eliotropi radix cum
vino pota et vulneri imposita mire sanat.

2. Ad lumbricos herba eliotropion cum ysopo et nitro et nasturtio et
aqua pota lumbricos (. . .) necat.

3. Ad verrucas heliotropion cum sale si in modum cataplasmatis
imponis, abstergit verrucas, unde etiam verrucaria nominatur.

CXXXVIII. Herba spreritis   A f. 69v/1

Habet folia minuta, lanuginosa, ex una radice multos ramos emittit
per terram fusos, florem croceum (. . .), odorem [mirrae] si digitis conteratur.

1. Haec herba si in oleo decoquatur et ex eo his qui cum rigore febri-
citant sub initio accessionis ungatur, sanus fiet.

2. Haec tunsa et cribrata pleno cocleario ex aqua calida pota hydro-
fobas et canis rabidi morsus sanat.

3. Huius fasciculum si in sextario lactis decoquatur, dimidium vespere
acceptum spleni medetur (. . .).

CXXXIX. [Aizos]

Ðeos wyrt þe man ayzos minor 7 oðrum naman (. . .) nemneþ
byð cenned on wagum 7 on stænigum stowum 7 on dunum 7 on
ealdum byrgenum, 7 heo of anum wyrttruman manega gehwæde
5 (bo)g(as) asen(d)eþ 7 þa b(eo)ð f(ulle of geh)wæ(d)um le(af)um 7
la(n)gum 7 sc(e)a(rpum) 7 fæ(ttum 7) w(el) wo(si)gum; 7 þysse
w(yrt)e wyrtt(ruma ys un)nyt(lic).

1. W(ið oman 7 w)ið e(agena sare 7) wið (fotadle genim þas
wyrte bútan) wyrttru(man, cnoca mid smed)man ðam (gelice þe þu
10 cliða)n wyrce, lege (to þisum) untrumnyssum, hit hy geliðiga(ð).

2. Wyð heafodece genim þysse ylcan wyrte wos 7 rosan wos,
mængc tósomne, smyre þæt heafod þærmid, þæt sár byð geliðigud.

3. Wyð þæra wyrma slite þe man spalangiones hateþ genim þas
ylcan wyrte aizos on wine gecnucude, syle drincan, hyt fremað
15 nytlice.

4. Wið utsiht 7 wið innoðes flewsan 7 wyð wyrmas þe on ðam
innoþe deriað þeos sylfe wyrt wel fremað.

5. Eft wyð gewhylce untrumnysse þæra eagena genim þysse
ylcan wyrte wos, smyra ðonne þa eagan þærmid, nytlice hyt
20 fremað. /

f. 60v ## CXL. Tunsingwyrt

1. Ðeos wyrt þe man elleborum album 7 oðrum naman tunsincg-
wyrt nemneð 7 eac sume men wedeberge hatað byð cenned on
dunum, 7 heo hafað leaf leace gelice; þysse wyrte wyrttruman
25 man sceal niman onbutan midne sumur 7 eac swa some þa wyrt
ealle for ðy heo is to læcedomum wel gecweme; þæt ís to lufigenne

---

MS V

1 *title*: *from* B, *om.* VH.   2 oðrum] 'o'þrum H   3 stænigum]
stanigum H.   6 7⁴] *om.* B 112/6a.   12 þæt heafod] *om.* H   þærmid]
þæ'r'mid (m *alt. from* t) H.   13 spalangiones] spálongiones H 71/2.
18 gewhylce] gehwilce B, geswylce H   untrumnysse] -nyse H.   19 ðonne]
om. BH.   21 *title*: clucþunge tunsingwurt B, *om.* H.   22 elleborum
album] eleborum H.

MS O

1 *in addition to title, in o.m.* aizos / vel aiz / aizos ð (aiz *exp.*).   2 aizos]
above this word w.s.   8 smedeman] *alt. from* smedenan.

CXXXIX. Aizos mínor f. 3/21

þeos wyrt þe man aizos minor nemneð byð cenneð on waȝum 7 on
staniȝum stowum 7 on dunum 7 o(n) ealden byrȝen, 7 heo of anum
wyrtruman maneȝa ȝehwitede leafun 7 langum 7 scearpum 7 fattum 7
wel ȝewosiȝum; 7 þisse wyrt wyrtrume is unnetlic. 5
   1. (Ad oman ad oculos et pedes; ad morbum qui dicitur Anglice
oman) Wid oman 7 wið eaȝena sare 7 wið fotadle ȝením þas wyrt butan /
wyrtruman, cnuca mid smedeman þam ȝelice ðe þu cliþem wyrce, leȝe f. 3v
to þissum untrumnesse, hit ȝeliðeȝað.
   2. (Ad dolorem capitis) Wid heafodece ȝenim þisse ylcan wyrte wos 7 10
rosan wos, meng tosomne, smyre þat heafod ðarmid, þæt byð ȝeliþeȝod.
   3. —
   4. (Contra fluxum uentris et lumbricos) Wið utsiht 7 wið innoðes
flewsan 7 wiþ wyrman þe on wambe 7 on þan innoþe deriað seos silfe
wyrt wel fremað. 15
   5. (Contra morbum oculorum) Eft wiþ ȝehylce untrumnesse ðara
eaȝena ním þisse wirte wos, smyra þa eaȝena þarmid, nitlice hit fremaþ.

CXL. (Elle)bor(um album) f. 13/23

   1. (þ)eos wyrt þæt man elleborum album 7 oþrum nama tunsingwyrt
7 sume men wedeberȝe h(atað), (he)o hafah leaf swilce leac; þisse (w)yrte 20
wyrtru(m)e man seal nime onb(u)ten (m)idde su(mer) / (. . .) wurtruma f. 13v

---

CXXXIX. Herba aizos minor A f. 69v/27

Nascitur in parietibus et petris et locis montuosis et umbrosis et in
sepulcris, ramulos ex una radice plurimos et inflexos mittens, foliis plenos
parvis vel longis et acutis et pinguibus et sucosis (. . .); huius radix
inutilis.
   1. Ipsa vero herba trita cum polenta in modum cataplasmatis imposita
ignem sacrum sanat, herpetas et oculorum fervores et combusturas et
dolorem podagrae sedat.
   2. Sucus eius cum oleo roseo dolorem capitis mitigat.
   3. Eadem herba contrita cum vino adversus spalangionum morsus
bibitur.
   4. Disentericis quoque et ventris fluxum et tormina et lumbricosos
sanat (. . .).
   5. Sucus eius etiam dolentibus oculis utiliter unguetur.

CXL. Herba elleborum album L f. 30/11

   1. Albumque est in similitudinem caepae, folia angustiora habet;
nascitur in montuosis locis; radices eius colligi debent circa aestiva
solstitia. Non tamen passim omni elleborum medicinae aptum est, nam

on ðysse wyrte þæt heo hafað gehwædne wyrttruman 7 na swa
rihtne þæt he be sumum dæle gebyged ne sy; he byþ breaþ 7
tidre þonne he gedriged byð, 7 þonne he tobrocen byþ (h)e rycþ
eal swylce he smic of him asende, 7 he byð hwonlice bitterre on
5 byrgincge; þon(ne) beoð þa maran wyrttruman lange 7 hearde 7
swyþe bittere on byrgincge, 7 hy habbaþ to ðam swyþlice mihte
7 frecenfulle þæt hy foroft hrædlice þone man forþilmiaþ; ðonne
sceal man þysne wyrttruman swa we ær cwædon gedrigean 7
þa lan`g´nysse toceorfan on pysena gelicnysse; mycel læcedom is tó
10 gehwylcum þingum þæt man ðonne þysses wyrttruman genime
tyn penega gewihte, swaðeah ne mæg man æfre for his strengðe
hyne syllan þicgean onsundrum ac mid sumum oðrum mete
gemencgedne be þære swylcnysse þe seo untrumnys þonne byð,
þæt is gyf seo untrumnes swa stið beo syle þicgean on beore oððe
15 on blacan briwe.

    2. Gyf he þonne on utsihte sy syle þicgean on pysena wose
oððe mid þære wyrte ðe man oriza hateþ mid smedeman, þa ealle
swaþeah s`c´eolon beon ærost on liðon beore gesodene 7 geliðigode.

    3. Ðeos wyrt soðlice ealle ealde 7 hefige 7 unlacnigendlice
20 adlu tofereþ, swa þæt he byþ gelacnud þeah he ær his hæle on
tolætenesse wære. /

CXLI.

f. 61   1. Ðeos wyrt þe man buoptalmon 7 oðrum naman (. . .)
nemneþ hafað hnesc`n´e stelan 7 leaf gelice finule, 7 heo hafað
25 geoluwe blostman eal swylce eage, þanon heo eac þone naman
onfeng; heo byþ cenned fyrmest wið Meoniam ða ceastre;
þysse wyrte leaf gecnucude 7 to clyþan geworhte tolysað gehwylce
yfele springas 7 heardnyssa.

MS V

    1 gehwædne] gehwæde H.   4 7 he byð] 7 he bið / 7 he bið B 112v/1a
bitterre] biter B.   5–6 þonne . . . byrgincge] om. H.   7 frecenfulle]
fræcen- BH.   9 toceorfan] toceofan H.   12 onsundrum] onsundran
B   sumum] sum H 72/6.   13 gemencgedne] gemæn`c´ged H.
14, 16 þicgean (2 ×)] drincan (2 ×) H.   18 s`c´eolon] sculon B.   20 þeah]
ðæh H.   21 tolætenesse] tolætennesse BH.   22 title om. VBH.
24 hnesc`n´e] hnesce B, hnesne H.   26 Meoniam] Meonian B, Meoniam
(a alt. from u) H.   27 geworhte] geworht H.

(. . .). þeos wyrt ȝedriȝed þa(nne h)e to(b)rocen byð he ric(þ) ealswa he
smic of hym asenda, 7 he byð biter on ȝebirȝyncȝe; 7 he habbað mihte
þæt hi hradlice þana man forþilmíað; þanne sceal man þisne wyrtrume
ȝedriȝ`e´an 7 langnisse toceorfan on pisena ȝelicnysse; mucel læcedom is
to ȝehwilcum þínge þæt man þanne þisse wyrtrume ȝenima tyn peneȝa　5
ȝewh(ihte), swaþeah ne mæȝ man afre for his strenȝe hine sylne ȝeþicȝean
asundrum, ac mid sumum oðrum mete ȝemenȝcedne be þare swilnesse
ðe seo untrumnesse þone byð, þæt is ȝif þa untrumnesse swa stiþ byð sile
ðicȝe(a)n on beore oþer on blacan briwe.

　　2. Gif he þanne on utsyhte sy syle (ð)icȝean on pisena wosa oþer mid　10
þara wyrte þa man oriza h(ate)ð mid smedeman, þa ealla swaþeah scylon
beon ærest on liðe beore ȝesodena 7 ȝeliþeg(ode).

　　3. Ðeos wyrt soðlice eall ealde 7 hefia 7 unlæcniende adlu tofereð,
swa þæt he byð ȝelæcned þeah he ær his hæle un tolætenysse ware.

CXLI. De buoptalmon

　　1. þeos wyrt þe man buoptalmon, heo hafad hnescne stelan 7 leaf　16
ȝelice finule, 7 heo hafað ȝeoluwe blosman eal swylce eaȝe, þanne heo
eac þane naman onseng; þisse wyrt leaf ȝecnucada 7 to cliðan ȝeworehte
tolisaþ ȝehwylce yfele springas 7 hearnysra.

---

iam maxime diligendum est quod radices mediocres habeat et non ita
directa sunt non aliquantum flexae sint; eadem cum siccata fuerint,
fragiles esse debent, et cum fractae fuerint fumum exemittunt, gustatu
autem mediocres sunt, mordaces ceterum maiores sunt, in longitudinem
rectae et durae, gustatu mordaces, nimiam vim et periculosam habent,
statim plerumque provocant. Huius radicem colligis, siccas et per longitudinem media dividant(. . .); hoc propter vim sui numquam solum dari
debet, sed cum aliqua commixtum prout morbi qualitas fuerit (. . .).

　　2. Ad fluxum ventris cum lenticulae suco dari debet vel cum oriza
sive polenta, quae utraque ex aqua pura cocta, deinde ex aqua mulsa
quae prius decocta fuerit, temperat.

　　3. Haec autem herba omnes morbos inveteratos, graves, insanabiles
destruet, ita ut (. . .).

CXLI. Herba buotthalmon

　　1. Haec herba caulem habet mollem, folia feniculo similia, florem
habet [croceum], oculo similem, unde nomen accepit; nascitur iuxta
moenia civitatum; huius folia trita cum ceroto imposita livores et duritias solvunt.

2. Wyþ æwyrdlan þæs lichoman þe cymeþ óf tógotennysse þæs
eallan genim þysse wyrte wos, syle drincan, heo agyfð þæt gecyndelice hiw; 7 he byð gehywlæht swylce he of swiðe haton
bæþe geode.

5 CXLII. Gorst

Ðeos wyrt ðe man tribulus 7 oðrum naman gorst nemneþ is
twegea cynna, oþer byþ cenned on wyrtunum, (o)ðer út on felda.

1. Wið mycelne hætan þæs lichaman genim þas wyrte tribulum
gecnucude, lege þærtó.

10 2. Wyð þæs muþes 7 þæra gomena fulnysse 7 forrotudnysse
genim þas wyrte tribulum gesodene, cnuca mid hunige, heo
hæleþ ðone muð 7 þa goman.

3. Wiþ þæt stanas on blædran wexen genim þysse ylcan wyrte
sæd swa grene gecnucud, syle drincan; wel hyt fremað. /

f. 61v　4. Wyþ (n)æddra(n slite genim) þys(se ylc)an wyrte (sæd swa
16　grén)e (ge)cnucud fif pene(ga gewihte, sile) drincan; e(ac s)wyl(c)e
(nim þ)a (wy)rte (mid h)yre (sæ)de gecnucude, lege (to þæ)re
'wunde', heo alyseþ hyne of þære (fræce)nysse.

5. (Þisse sy)lfan wyrte s(æ)d eac swyl(ce on wine) gedrun(c)en
20 is halwende ongean (a)ttres drync.

6. Wiþ flean genim þas ylcan wyrte mid hyre sæde gesodene,
sprengc into þam huse, heo cwelð þa flean.

CXLIII.

1. Ðeos wyrt þe man conize 7 oðrum naman (. . .) nemneþ
25 ys twegea cynna, þeah þe oðer sy mare, oþer læsse, þonne hafað

MS V

1 þe] se BH.　　　　3 swylce] swyl`c´e H　　　haton] hátum B.　　　　4 geode]
eode B.　　　　5 title: om. B 113, gorst H 73/1.　　　　6 gorst] go`r´st H.
10 Wyð] yð B, ið H.　　　16 gewihte] gewæge H.　　　18 alyseþ] alesyð H
fræcenysse] fræcennysse BH.　　　22 cwelð] acwelð B.　　　　23 title
om. VBH.　　　　24 wyrt] wyr`t´ H　　　conize] onizæ B, gl. papauer H.
25 læsse] læssa B　　hafað] hæfð H.

————

MS O

1 'of toȝeotenysse'] in text of toȝeonenysse (second word exp.), with signes de
renvoi to of toȝeotenysse in b.m.　　2 sile] þi sile (þi exp.)　　aȝifð] af aȝifð
(af exp.).　　　3 ȝehiwlæht] ȝe hiwe hiwlæht (hiwe struck out and underlined)
hæte] baþeðe hæte (baþeðe exp.).　　　9 þara] þas þara (þas exp.).

2. Wið æwyrdlan þas lichamas se cymeð 'of toȝeotenysse' þæs ȝeallan ním þisse wyrte wos, sile drincan; he aȝifð þæt ȝecundelice hif; 7 he byð ȝehiwlæht swylce he of hæte baþe eode.

CXLII. Tribulus   gorst   f. 40/22

þeos wyrt þæt man tribulus 7 oþrum nama gorst nemned ys tweȝra 5
cunna, oþer byð cenned on wurtunum, oþer on fealde.

1. (Ad magnum calorem) Wid mucele hæte / þas lichamas cnuca þeos f. 40v
wyrt tribulum þæt hated, leȝe þarto.

2. (Ad fetorem et putredinem oris) Wis þas muþes 7 þara gomena
fulnesse 7 forrotednysse ním þa wyrt ȝesodene, cnuca mid huniȝe; heo 10
hæled þana muð 7 þa goman.

3, 4. —

5. (Contra uenenum) þisse sylfe wyrte sæd eac swylce on wíne ȝedrucen
halwende onȝean attres drinc.

6. (Ad pulices et ad muscas) Wyþ flean ȝením þeos wyrt mid hure 15
sæde ȝesodone, sprenȝ into þan husa, heo cwelleð þa fleam.

CXLIII om. O.

---

2. Sucus eius expressus et potus ictericis naturalem colorem reddet,
si priusquam de balneo calidissimo exeant, hauriant, perfecte medentur.

CXLII. Herba tribulosa   A f. 68v/15

Huius genera sunt duo: unum quod in hortis nascitur, aliud agreste
est, cuius maior est efficacia.

1. Haec herba trita et corpori apposita fervores mulcat.

2. Elixa et trita cum melle omnes oris putredines et faucium curat.

3. Semen eius viride tritum et potum cauculosis prodest.

4. Si quem vipera momorderit, seminis huius viridis triti dragmam
[unam], hoc est scripulos tres, bibat, et praeterea herba ipsa cum semine
contrita vulneri imponatur et a periculo liberat.

5. Cuius seminis cum vino potio etiam contra potionem veneni salu-
taris est.

6. Eadem herba cum semine decocta [pulices necat], si [aqua ipsius]
domus aspergatur.

CXLIII. Herba coniza   A f. 68v/32

1. Duae sunt: una maior, altera minor est; minor odorem gratissimum

seo læsse smæle leaf 7 gehwæde 7 swyþe gecwe(m)ne swæc 7
seo (o)ðer hafað mar(a)n (l)eaf 7 f(ætt)e 7 hefigne swæc, 7 þy(s)sa
wyrta w(y)rttruman [syndon] unnytlice; ac þysse wyrte stela
mid þam leafum gindstred 7 onæled nædran afligeþ; 7 eac heo
5 gecnucud 7 to clyþan geworht þæra nædrena slite gehæleþ, 7
heo gnættas 7 micgeas 7 flean ácwelleþ, 7 heo eac swylce ealle
wunda gelacnað 7 heo earfoðlicnysse þæs migþan astyreþ, 7
heo þa cynelican adle gehæleþ, 7 heo on ecede geseald fylleseocum
helpeþ.

10   2. þeos wyrt conize on wætere gesoden 7 sittendum wife under
[geléd], heo ðone cwiþan afeormaþ.

   3. Gyf wif cennan ne mæge nime þysse ylcan wyrte wos mid
wulle, dó on þa gecyndelican; sona heo þa cennincge gefremeþ.

   4. Wyþ ða colan feforas genim þas ylcan wyrte, seoð on ele,
15 nim þonne þone ele, smyre þone lichaman; ða feforas beoð
fram anydde.

   5. Wiþ heafodece þyssa wyrta genim ða læssan, wyrc to clyþan,
lege to ðam sare, heo hyt geliðigaþ. /

f. 64(!) **CXLIV. Foxes glofa**

20   1. Wið oman genim þysse wyrte leaf þe man trycnos manicos 7
oðrum naman foxes [glofa] nemneþ, wyrc to clyþan, lege to þam
sare, hyt geliðigaþ.

   2. Wiþ pypelgende lic þæt Grecas erpinam nemnað, genim þas
ylcan wyrte ðe we trycnos manicos nemdun 7 smedeman, wyrc to
25 clyþan, lege to þam sare, hyt byþ gehæled.

   3. Wið heafdes sare 7 wið þæs magan hætan 7 wið cyrnlu genim
þas ylcan wyrte mid ele gecnucude, smyre þa sár, hy toslupað.

   4. Wiþ ðæra earena sare genim (þisse) sylfan wyrte seaw mid
r(ósan) se(a)we, (d)rype on þæt eare.

MS V

1 smæle] smale BH.   3 syndon] *from* B 113v/2a, synson V, synson H 74/1
unnytlice] unnyttlice (*alt. from* unnytte) B, ῾u῾nnytlice H   stela] stelan H.
4 gindstred] gnid 7 stred H.   6 micgeas] m῾i῾cgeas H.   9 helpeþ]
om. H.   11 geléd] *from* B, *om.* V.   12 ylcan] *om.* H.   13 cennincge]
cænnicge H   gefremeþ] gefremað B.   19 *title*: *om.* BH.   21 glofa]
from B, clofa V, glofa (g *alt. from* c) H.   23 pypelgende] pipligende B.
29 seawe] se῾a῾we H 75/6.

CXLIV *om*. O.

---

habet, folia angustiora et minutiora; alia maiora et pinguia, odorem gravem (. . .); harum radices inutiles. Nam minor cum foliis sparsa et incensa serpentes fugat, pulices et culices interficit, contusa et pro cataplasmate imposita morsus serpentium sanat, vulneribus etiam cunctis medetur (. . .), difficultatem urinae movet, torminosos et morbum regium sanat, cum aceto data epilepticis id est caducis subvenit.

2. Eadem herba decocta in aqua et supersessa matricem purgat.

3. Sucus earum [cum] lana genitalibus iniectus abortionem praegnantibus facit.

4. Oleo [in quo] decoctae fuerint, si corpus unguatur, febres frigidae expelluntur.

5. Capitis etiam dolorem [minor earum] pro cataplasmate imposita sedat.

A f. 69/12

CXLIV. Herba strignos, alii manicos dicunt

1. Huius folia pro cataplasmate imposita ignem sacrum sanant.

2. Herpeta quoque, quae se papulis rubris per corpus ostendit cum polentae cataplasmate imposita sanat (. . .).

3. Dolorem quoque capitis et ardorem stomachi et parotides cum oleo contrita dissolvit.

4. Dolores aurium sucus eius cum oleo rosaceo sanat.

CXLV.

1. Wið þone drigean fefor genim þas wyrte ðe man glycyridam 7 oðrum naman (. . .) nemneþ, wyl on wearmum wætere, syle drincan, hyt fremaþ nytlice.

5   2. Eac swylce þeos sylfe wyrte ðæra breosta sár 7 þære lifre 7 þære blædran 7 þæra ædrena mid gesodenan wine gehæleþ. Eac heo þyrstendon þone þurst geliþigað.

3. Wið leahtras ðæs muþes þysse ylcan wyrte wyrttruma ge-/ f. 64v (et)en oððe gedruncen wel fre(m)að 7 þa leahtras gehæleþ; eac 10 (he)o wunda (ge)hæleþ ðærmid ge(w)esede; 7 se (w)yrttruma swa (sam)e þæt syl(fe geg)earwað a(c na swa)þeah s(wa sce)arplice.

CXLVI.

1. Wið þæt man gemigan ne mæge genim ðysse wyrte wyrttruman ðe man strutium 7 oþrum naman (. . .) nemneþ, syle 15 ðicgean, he þone migðan astyreð.

2. Wið liferseocnysse 7 wið nyrwyt 7 wið swiðlicne hracan genim þysse wyrte to duste gecnucudre anne cuculere fulne, syle drincan on liþan beore, hyt framað; 7 eac hyt þone innoð wið þæs eall(an) togotenysse gegladað 7 þæt y(fel forð) gelædeþ.

20   3. W(iþ) þæt stan(as) on blæd(r)æn wex(en) g(e)nim ðas sylf(a)n wyrte str(utium) 7 lub(as)tica(n) wyrttruma(n 7) ðære wy(rte) ðe m(an) capparis hateð, cnuc(a) tosomne, syle drincan on liðon beore, hyt (to)lyseþ ða blædran 7 ða stanas forð gelædeþ 7 eac þære miltan sár hyt tolyseþ.

25   4. Wið hreoflan genim þas ylcan wyrte 7 meluw 7 eced, cnuca togædre, lege to þam hreoflan, he bið gelacnud.

5. Eft ðeos sylfe wyrt mid berenum meluwe on wine gesoden, ealle yfele heardnyssa 7 gegaderunga heo tofereþ. /

---

1 *title om.* VBH.   12 *title om.* VBH.   17 to] 'to' H.   18 fra-
mað] fremað B 114/9b.   19 eallan] geallan H   togotenysse]
togotennesse B, togotennysse H 76/1.   20 blædræn] blædran BH.
22 hateð] hæteð H.

MS O

19 þreoflan] h (*modern*) *interl. above unexpunged* þ.   22 heardnesse] a *alt. from* r.

CXLV. (. . .)

f. 19v/4,

1. (W)ið þone driȝan fefor nim þa wy(rte) (. . .) (ma)n gliciridam, wel f. 15v
on wearme w(æt)era, sile drincan, hít fremeð nítlíce.

2. Eac ðe(os) (. . .) (wy)rt þæra breosta sar 7 þara lifra 7 þara blæd(ran)
7 þaræ ederana mid wine ȝesodenum ȝeh(æ)leð.   5

3. Wið leahtres þæs muðes (þy)sse wurte wurtruma ȝeetan odðer
ȝedrucan (. . .) leahtres ȝ(e)hæleð. Eac heo wunda ȝe(hæleþ) (. . .) ȝewe-
sede; (7) se wurtruma swa same þæt sylfe ȝeȝearwað ac na swa scearp(lice).

CXLVI. Structium   byscupwyrt

f. 38v/5

1. (Ad urinam) Wið þæt man ne maȝen míȝam ním þisse wyrt 10
wurtruman þæt man strutium 7 Engle byscupwýrt nemneð, sile þícȝan;
heo þanne miggan þon astíreþ.

2. (Ad morbum epatis 7 wyd nirwet 7 þinca hrocan et uiscera) Wið
liferseocnysse 7 wyð nírwet 7 wið swyþlice hracan cnuca þeos wyrt to
duste, sile anne cuculere fulne drincan on liþe beore, hit fremað; 7 eac 15
hit þane innoþ wið þas ȝeallan toȝotenysse ȝegladað 7 þæt yfel for
ȝelædeð.

3. —

4. (Ad lepram) Wið þreoflan ním þeos wyrt 7 melu 7 ecede, cnuca
togadere, leȝe to þan þreoflan, he byð ȝelæcnud.   20

5. (Ad omnem malam collectionem et duriciam) Eac þa sulfe wyrt mid
berene melewe ‘7’ on wíne ȝesoden, ealle yfele heardnesse 7 ȝegaderunga
heo tofereð.

CXLV. Herba glycyriza

A f. 71v/7

1. Sucus idem decoctus febrem aridam patientibus cum aqua calida
utiliter datur.

2, 3. Vitia etiam pectoris et iocineris et ulcera vesicae et renum cum
careno et passo curat; sitientibus sitim sedat radix comesta vel sucus
haustus, etiam vitia oris curat, vulnera quoque illinitus sanat; eadem
praestat etiam radicis decoctio, sed [minus] efficaciter medetur.

CXLVI. Herba strutios

A f. 74v/27

1. Radix eius amara est et diuretica, urinam movens.

2. Huius tunsae pulvis, coclearium plenum, cum aqua mulsa potus
prodest hepaticis, tussientibus, suspiriosis, ictericis, ventrem quoque
deducit.

3. Eadem cum panacis radice et capparis ex aqua mulsa pota cauculos
vesicae solvit et provocat, splenis duritiam solvit.

4. Cum polenta et aceto trita leprosis imposita medetur.

5. Cum polenta hordeacia et vino cocta omnes duritias et collectiones
spargit.

CXLVII.

f. 63(!)   1. Ðeos wyrt ðe is aizon 7 oðrum naman (. . .) gecweden, seo
is swylce heo symle cwycu sy, 7 heo hafað elne langne stelan
on fincres greatn(ys)se, 7 heo [is wel wosig 7 heo] (h)a(f)að fætte
5 leaf (i)n f(in)ge(res leng)e; h(eo) bið cenn(e)d on du(num) 7 (h)e(o
eac b)yþ hwilon on wealle geseted, ðeos wyrt mid meoluwe
gecnucud gehæleþ mænigfealde untrumnyssa ðæs lichoman, þæt
is berstende lic 7 forrotudnysse þæs lices 7 eagena sarnysse 7 hætan
7 forbærnednysse, ealle þas þing heo gehæleþ.

10   2. Wið heafodece genim þysse ylcan wyrte wos aizon mid rosan
wose gemenged, begeot þæt heafod þærmid, hyt geliðigaþ þæt sár.

3. Wið þære nædran slite þe man spalangionem nemneþ genim
þas ylcan wyrte aizon, syle drincan [on háton wine].

4. Eft do þæt sylfe wið utsiht 7 wið wyrmas on innoðe 7 wið
15 swiðlicne cyle, hyt fremað.

CXLVIII. Ellen

1. Wið wæterseocnysse genim þas wyrte þe man samsu(c)hon 7
oðrum naman ellen h(at)eþ, syle drincan gewyllede, heo gehnæceþ
ða anginnu þam wæterseocum; eac swylce heo fremaþ wið þa
20 unmihticnysse þæs migðan 7 wið þæra innoða ástyrunga.

2. Wið springas 7 wið toborsten lic genim þysse ylcan wyrte
leaf samsuchon gedrigede 7 gecnucude 7 mid hunige gemencgede,
lege to þam sare, hyt sceal berstan 7 halian.

3. Wið scorpiones stincg genim þas ylcan wyrte 7 sealt 7 eced, /
f. 63v (cnuca) tosomne 7 to plastre (gewyr)c, lege to ðam stinge, he (bið
26 gehæ)led.

MS V

1 *title om.* V, *for* BH *see textual notes.*   3 cwycu] cuca B 114v/17a,
cwice (e *alt. from* u) H.   4 fincres] fingres BH   is . . . heo] *from* B,
om. V.   5 lenge] længe H.   6 wealle] weallon B.   7 mænigfealde]
manigfealdu H.   12 þære] ðara B, þæra H 77/1.   13 on háton
wine] *from* B, *om.* V.   16 *title*: *om.* BH.   18 gewyllede] geswylede H.
19 heo] he B.   20 unmihticnysse] unmihtignessa B   ástyrunga . . .
fornimeþ (p. 194/13)] *one folio missing* B.   22 gecnucude] gecnu/de H.
24 stincg] stencg H.

MS O

1 *in addition to title* barba Iovis *in o.m.*   6 ȝehæleð] æ *alt. from* a.
8 ȝihæleð] li ȝihæleð (li *exp.*).   18 7 wið] *between these words an erasure of*
two symbols.   21 samsuchon] sansucan samsuchon.

CXLVII. Item de aizon   singrene   Jovis barba   f. 3v/9

1. (Ad pistulas corporis et putredinem et morbum oculorum et
contra feruorem et ustionem et contra uarios corporis morbos et dolorem
capítis) þeos wyrt þe man aizon 7 oþrum naman singrenan nemneð, seo
is swilce heo symle cwicu si, 7 heo ys wel wosi; þeos wyrt mid melewe   5
ȝecnucod ȝehæleð maniȝfealde untrumnesse þæs lichaman, þæt ys
bertende lic 7 forrotudnysse þas lices 7 eaȝena sarnesse 7 hætan 7 for-
bernednysse; ealle þas þing heo ȝihæleð.

2. Wið heafoðece ȝením ðisse wyrte aizon mid rosan wosan þemenged,
beȝeot þæt heafod þarmíd; hit leðegað þæt sor.   10

3. —

4. Eft do þæt sylfe wiþ utsiht 7 wið wyrmað on innoðe 7 wiþ swydline
cyle, hit fremað.

CXLVIII. Samsuchon   elle   f. 38v/19

1. (Ad ydropisim; ad urinam ad fluxum uentris) Wið wæterseocnysse   15
ním þeos wyrt þæt man samsuchon nemneð 7 oþrum naman elle, sile
dríncan ȝewilled, heo ȝehnesceð þa angynnu þam wætereseocum. Eac
swylce heo fremað wið þa unmíhtinísse þæs micþan 7 wið innoþa astí-
runga. /

2. (Wyd springes 7 tobrochene liches) Wið springas 7 wið toborstene f. 39
lice ním þisse wyrte leaf samsuchon ȝedriȝede 7 ȝecnucade mid huníȝe, 21
leȝe to ðan sare, hit seal berstan 7 hala.

3. —

CXLVII. Herba aizonos   Ca p. 524

1. Aizonos dicta quasi sempervivus, [caules] cubitales in crassitudine 16a
digiti, suculentos, folia pinguia in longitudine digitorum (. . .); nascitur
in locis montuosis vel in maceris (. . .); trita vel sola vel cum polenta ignem
sacrum, putredines corporis, oculorum fervores, corporis fusturas, im-
petum podagrae placat.

2. Sucus eius cum oleo rosaceo mixtus capiti infusus dolorem eius
sedat.

3. Incipiente frigido dolore calido cum vino cum potat, contra morsus
spalangionum facit.

4. Idem disintericis et lumbricosis prodest.

CXLVIII. Herba samsucum   A f. 65v/26

1. Decoctio eius pota principia hydropicis reprimit, [urinae] difficul-
tati et intestinorum tortionibus prodest.

2. Cuius folia sicca et trita, melli mixta collectionibus imponuntur, ut
rumpant (. . .).

3. Ictum scorpionis cum sale et aceto trita et pro implastro apposita
sanat (. . .).

4. (Wið micele hætan 7 wið geswel ðæra eagena genim ðas
syl)fan (wyrte mid meluwe gem)encgede (7 to cliðan geworhte,
leg)e to þam (eagon, [hit] bið) geliþigad.

CXLIX.

5   þeos wyrt ðe man stecas 7 oþrum naman (. . .) nemneþ hæfð
sæd mycel, 7 þæt ys smæl 7 gehwæde, 7 heo sylf ys boþene gelic,
buton þæt heo hafað sumon dæle maran leaf 7 stiðeran.

     1. [Genim] þas wyrte gesodene, syle drincan, heo þæra breosta
sár gehæleþ.

10   Eac hyt is gewunelic þæt hy man to manegum godum drenceon
gemencge.

CL.

     Ðeos wyrte ðe man thyaspis 7 oþrum naman (. . .) nemneþ
hafaþ smæle leaf on fingres lencge 7 todælede 7 nyþer wið þa
15 eorþan ahyldende, 7 heo hafað [ðynne stelan 7 langne, 7 heo hafað]
on ufeweardum hæwene blostman, 7 þæt sæd byþ cenned gind
ealne þone stelan; eal ðeos wyrt is strangre gecynde 7 bitterre;
ðysse wyrte wos wel gewrungen 7 an scenc ful gedruncen, ealle
þa biternysse ðe of þam geallan cymeþ heo ðurh ða gemænelican /
f. 74(!)   neode 7 ðurh spiwðan ut anýdeþ.

21   1. Ðeos sylfe wyrt, ealle þa yfelan gegaderunge þæs innoþes
heo fornimeþ, 7 eac swylce heo wifa monoðlican astyreð.

MS V

    3 hit *from* O, hy H.   4 *title om.* VH.   5 7 oþrum naman] *om.* H.
8 Genim] *from* H, Ðenim V.   10 drenceon] *om.* H.   12 *title om.* VH.
13 wyrte] 'wyrt' H 78/5   7 oþrum naman] *om.* H.   14 hafaþ smæle]
hæfað smale H   lencge] længe H.   15 ðynne . . . hafað] *from* H, *om.* V.
19 biternysse] biterternysse H.   22 monoðlican] innoð (in *alt. from* m,
after this o *erased*) H.

MS O

    12 lagne] g *alt. from* n   hafað on] hafað o(n) on (o(n) *exp.*).   13 ðone]
dan ðone (dan *exp.*).

4. (Ad nímiam calorem et inflationem occulorum) Wið micele hæten 7 ʒeswel þara eaʒene ním þeos wyrt mid meluwe ʒemengede 7 to clydan ʒeworrhte, leʒe to þan eaʒene, hit byd ʒeliþegod 7 ʒehaled.

CXLIX. Stecas
f. 39/8

1. (Ad morbum pectoris) þeos wyrt þæt man stecas, heo ys boþele 5 lelic, botan þæt heo hafad sumon dale more leaf 7 stiþran, 7 heo hafaþ mucel sæd; syle drincan þeos wyrt ʒesodene, heo þara brosta sar ʒehæled; 7 hít hys ʒewunelíc þæt hi man to maniʒe gode drencan ʒemenge.

CL. Tiapis
f. 40v/9

(De felle) þeos wyrt þæt man tiapis hatað hafað smale leaf on fingres 10 lenge 7 todælede 7 niþer wið þa earþan ahyldende 7 hafeð þínne stele 7 lagne 7 heo hafað on ufewerde hæwene blosme, 7 þæt sæd byþ ʒeond ælne ðone stelen cenned; þeos wyrt ys strangre ʒecynde 7 bytere; þisse wyrt wos wel ʒew`r´ungen 7 ane scenc ful ʒedruncen, ealle ða byternysse þe of ðan ʒe`a´llan cumeð heo þuruh ða ʒemænelican neode 7 þurh 15 spywþan ut anydeð.

1. (Ad uiscera) Ðeos sylfe wyrt, ealle þa yfele ʒegaderunge þæs innoþes heo fornimeð 7 eac heo wyfa manoðlican astirað.

---

4. Fervores etiam et tumores oculorum cum polentis mixta et pro cataplasmate imposita mitigat.

CXLIX. Herba sticas
A f. 66v/3

Semen habet plurimum et minutum, ipsa thymo similis, nisi quod foliis aliquanto maioribus et austerioribus.

1. Decoctio eius pota vitia pectoris sanat.

Antidotis quoque plurimis admisceri solet.

CL. Herba thlaspi
A f. 67/3

Folia habet angusta et admodum digiti longa et scissa, in terra fluentia, caulem tenuem, longum (. . .), flores in capite subalbidos; per caulem totum semen nascitur; est autem tota herba naturae thermanticae et amari saporis; cuius sucus expressus et admodum ciati potus fella per stercus et vomitum expellit (. . .).

1. Menstrua etiam mulierum potus movet, collectionem quoque internorum viscerum rumpit (. . .).

CLI. Omnimorbia

Ðeos wyrt þe man polios 7 oþrum naman omnimorbia nemneþ
7 eac sume men (. . .) hataþ byþ cenned on dunum, 7 heo of anum
wyrttruman manega telgran ásendeþ, 7 heo on ufewerdum hafaþ
5   sæd swylce croppas, 7 heo is hefegon swæce 7 hwon weredre on
byrgincge.

1. Wið nædran slite genim þysse wyrte wós polios on wætere
gesoden, syle drincan, hyt gehæleþ ðone slite.

2. Wið wæterseocnysse do þæt sylfe, hyt þone innoð alyseþ.

10   3. Wið miltan sare genim þas ylcan wyrte polios, seoð on
ecede, syle drincan, nytlice heo þone miltseocan gehæleþ; ðeos
sylfe wyrt on huse gestred oþþe onæled nædran aflígeþ, 7 eac
swylce heo niwe wunda fornimeþ.

CLII.

15   1. Ðeos wyrt þe man hypericon 7 oþrum naman corion nemneþ
for gelicnysse cymenes, heo hafaþ leaf rudan gelice, 7 of anum
stelan manega telgran weaxaþ, 7 þa reade, 7 heo hafaþ blostman
f. 74v   swylce banwyrt, 7 heo hafað berian synewealte / 7 hwon lange on
beres mycelnysse on þam ys sæd, 7 þæt sweart, 7 on swæce
20   swylce tyrwe, 7 heo bið cenned on beganum stowum; ðeos wyrt
gecnucud 7 gedruncen þone migþan astyreþ, 7 heo þa monoðlican
wundorlice deþ gyf hy man ðam gecyndelican lime under gelegeþ.

2. Wið þone fefor þe þy feorðan dæge on man becymeþ genim
þas ylcan wyrte gecnucude, syle drincan on wine.

25   3. Wiþ ðæra sceancena geswel 7 ece (genim) þysse ylcan wyrte
sæd, s(y)le drincan on wine, binnan f(eo)wertigan dagon he byð
gehæled.

1 *title om.* H.   3 7 . . . hataþ] *om.* H   byþ] heo bið H.   4 on
ufewerdum] of ufeweardum H.   9 Wið . . . alyseþ] *om.* H.   14 *title
om.* VBH.   17 weaxaþ] weaxeð B 115/5a, wexeð H 79/10.   20 tyrwe]
cyrse H.   21 monoðlican] mo'no'þlican (*one letter erased between* þ *and* l)
H.   22 gelegeþ] geleið H.

CLI. De polio   Dio. 3.114

Eius species montana (. . .) usitata est (. . .), graveolens cum quadam
suavitate.
   1. Earum decoctum epotum succurrit venenatorum morsibus,
   2. hydropicis et ictericis;
   3. spleneticis autem ex aceto propinatur. Ceterum substratum suffi-
tumve venenatas bestias abigit; impositum vero vulnera conglutinat.

CLII. Herba hypericon sive corion propter similitudinem cimicis dicta   A f. 72v/31

   1. Folia habet rutae similia, de uno caespite multae virgultae russeae
prosurgunt, florem violae aurosae similem affert, bacas habet teretes et
oblongas in hordei magnitudinem, in his semen est nigrum, odore
resinae; nascitur in locis asperis sed cultis. Trita haec herba et pota
urinam movet [et] menstrua, si verendis subiciatur.
   2. Cum vino pota quartanam fugat.
   3. Semen autem eius cum vino xl diebus potum ciliacos vel sciaticos
curat.

CLIII.

Ðeos wyrt þe man acantaleuce 7 oðrum naman (. . .) nemneþ
byð cenned on stænigum stowum 7 on dunum, 7 heo hafaþ
leaf swylce wulfes camb, ac hi beoþ [mearwran] 7 hwittran 7 eac
5 geþufran, 7 heo hafað twegea elne lancne stelan on fingres greatnysse oððe sumon dæle maran.

1. Wið þæt man blode hræce 7 wið þæs magan sare genim ðas
ylcan wyrte [acantaleuce], cnuca to duste, syle drincan on wætere
anne cuculere fulne, hyt fremað wel.

10 2. Wið þæs migðan astyrunge genim þas ylcan wyrte swa
wosige gecnucude, syle drincan, heo ðone migðan forð gelædeþ.

3. Wið yfele læla genim 'þas' ylcan wyrte, wyrc to clyþan,
lege to þam sare, heo hyt afyrmeþ; þysse sylfan wyrte syde
þæra toþa sar geliðigað gyf hyne man swa wearmne on þam
15 muþe gehealdeþ.

4. Wið hramman genim þysse ylcan wyrte sæd gecnucud,
syle drincan on wætere, hyt helpeþ, se sylfa drenc eac swylce
f. 65(!) on/gean næddrena slite wel fremað.

Ec swylce gyf mon þas wyrte on mannes swyran ahehð heo
20 næddran aflygeþ.

CLIV. [Beowurt]

Ðeos wyrt þe man acanton 7 oþrum naman beowyrt nemneð
byþ cenned on wynsumon stowum 7 on wætum 7 eac swylce on
stænigum.

MS V

1 title om. VBH.   2 7 oðrum naman] om. H.   3 stænigum] stenigum
H.   4 mearwran] from B, mealuwran V, mearuwrán H 80/1.
5 geþufran] þufran H   elne lancne] elna langne BH.   7 þæt] om. H.
8 ylcan] exp. V, silfan B   acantaleuce] from H, acataleuce VB.   10 þæs]
om. H.   11 forð gelædeþ] út alædeð B 115v/2a.   13 afyrmeþ]
afyrreð BH.   19 Ec] Eac B, Eác H   swyran ahehð] sweorán aheð H.
21 title: from B, om. VH.   23 wynsumon] winsumum B   stowum]
lande H.

MS O

3 ac] 7 ac (7 exp.)   hwítran] h interl. above unexpunged s.   4 great-
nysse] a alt. from t.

CLIII. De acantaleace f. 3v/19

þeos wyrt þe man acantaleace nemneð, heo hafað leaf swylces wulfes camb, ac hi beoð mearuwran 7 hwítran 7 eac ȝeþufran, 7 heo hafeð tweȝra elna langne stelan an of fingres greatnysse oþþer sum dale maran.

1. (Ad sanguinem conspuentes et ad stomachi morbum) Wið þæt man 5 blod hræce 7 wiþ þæs maȝen sara ȝením þeos wyrte acantaleuce, cnuca to duste, sile dríncan on watere an cucelerne / fulne, hit fremeð wel. f. 5(!)

2, 3. —

4. (Ad crampam; ad serpentis morsum) Wið hramman ȝením þisse sæd ȝecnucad, syle drincan on wateran; hit helpeð. Se sylfa drenc eac 10 swylce onȝean nædrena slíte wel fremað.

Eac swylce man þas wyrte on mannes swyran ahehd, heo nædre aflyȝð.

CLIV. Acanto beowurt f. 5/5

þeos wyrt þa man acanton 7 oðrum naman beowurt nemneð.

CLIII. Herba hecinum quam Afri efram vocant A f. 64/1b

Nascitur in montuosis et lapidosis locis (. . .), folia habet similia cameleonti albo et teneriora [et albidiora] et spissa et spinosa, caulem duobus cubitis longum, digiti crassitudinem habet vel aliquo amplius (. . .).

1. Huius radix tunsa et cribrata ad modum cocleari [i] cum aqua pota emopticis, ciliacis[, stomachicis] prodest.

2. Urinam etiam provocat, si suculenta tundatur.

3. Vice cataplasmae composita livores aufert; decoctio eius dolores dentium sedat, si in ore teneatur.

4. Infantibus qui spasmum patiuntur semen eius tritum et cum aqua potatum subvenit; eadem potio etiam adversus morsus serpentium prodest.

Quam etiam volunt [eandem] homines suspensam serpentes [fugare].

CLIV. Herba acantum A f. 64v/1

Nascitur locis amoenis et aquosis nec non et in petrosis.

1. Wið þæs innoþes astyrunge 7 þæs migþan genim þysse ylcan wyrte wyrttruman gedrigedne 7 to duste gecnucedne, syle drincan on wearmum wætere.

2. Wiþ lungenadle 7 wið gehwylce yfelu þe on þam innoðe
5   dereþ ðeos sylfe wyrt wel fremað geþiged þam gelice þe we her beforan cwædon.

CLV. Cymen

1. Wyð þæs magan sare genim þysse wyrte sæd þe man quim-minon & oþru(m) naman cymen nemneþ on ele gesodene 7 mid
10 syfeðon gemencged 7 swa togædere gewylled, wyrc þonne to clyþan, lege to ðam innoþe.

2. Wyþ nyrwyt genim þas ylcan wyrte quiminon 7 wæter 7 eced, meng tósomne, syle drincan, hyt fremað nytlice; 7 eac on wine geþiged heo næddran slite wel gehæleþ.

15   3. Wiþ ðæra innoþˈaˊ toðundennysse 7 hætan genim þas ylcan
f. 65v   wyrte / mid (w)inberian gecnucede (oððe m)id (b)e(anenon m)eo-luwe, (wyrc t)o clyþan, (he)o ge(h)æle(þ ða t)ˈoˊðun(d)ennysse.

4. (Eac) swylce blodryne of næsþy(rlon h)eo gewrið mid ecede gem(æng)edum.

20 ## CLVI.

Ðeos wyrt þe man camelleon alba 7 oþrum naman wulfes tæsl nemneþ hafað leaf wiþerræde 7 þyrnyhte, 7 heo hafaþ on middan sumne sinewealtne crop 7 þyrnyhtne, 7 se biþ brunon blostmun behæfd, 7 he hafað hwit sæd 7 hwitne wyrtruman 7 swyðe
25 gestencne.

MS V

2 gedrigedne] gedrigede H 81/1   gecnucedne] gecnocode B, gecnucude H.
7 title: om. BH.   8–9 quimminon] quiminon BH.   9 nemneþ] ˈnemˊneð B.
10 gemencged] gemængde H.   16 winberian] -bergan B 116/10a, -beriúm H
oððe] om. H.   19 gemængedum] gemængˈcˊedum H.   20 title om. VBH.
21 Ðeos] eos B   camelleon] camellæon (between æ and o an erased n) B.
22 wiþerræde 7] wiðerˈræde 7ˊ H.   23 þyrnyhtne, 7] þyrnihte H.
24 he] heo H.

MS O

3 wearmum] a alt. from r.   10 clyþan] alt. from clysan.   11 cymín]
7 wa cymín (7 wa exp.).   18 ȝewryð] ȝewyr wryð (wyr exp.).

1. (Contra motum intestinorum et urinam) Wið innoþes astyrunge 7
þæs migðan ʒením þisse wyrt wurtrumen ʒedriʒede to duste, sile dríncan
on wearmum wætere.

2. (Ad pulmonem et contra omnem morbum interiorem) Wið lungenadle 7 wið ʒehwilce yfele ðe on ðan innoþe dereð þeos silfe wyrt wel 5
fremeð ʒeþiʒed ðam ʒelíce þe we her beforem cwæðon.

CLV. De címíno

f. 32v/5

1. (Ad stomachi dolorem) Wið þas mæʒen sore ním þisse wyrte sæd
þæt man químínon 7 oþrum cymín nemned on ele sodene 7 mid syfeþon
ʒemenged 7 þa togædere wyrc to clyþan, leʒe to þan innoþe. 10

2. (Wyd nirwt) Wið nírwyt ním þeos wyrt cymín 7 wæter 7 ecede,
meng tosomne, syle drincan, hít fremeð nytlice; 7 eac on wíne ʒeþiʒed
heo nadran slite wel ʒehælað.

3. (Wyd þat innesþes toþungenesse) Wið þara innoþes toþunʒenísse
7 hætan cnuca þeos wirt mid winberie oþþer mid beanenan meluwe, 15
wyrc to clyðan; heo ʒehæleð þa toþundennysse.

4. (Ad sanguinem de naribus) Eac swilce blodrune of nosþurlen heo
ʒewryð mid ecede ʒemenged.

CLVI om. O.

---

1. Radix eius sicca et tunsa et cribrata cum aqua calida pota ventrem et
urinam movet.

2. Phthisicos quoque et eos qui spasmum patiuntur vel quibus aliquae
intrinsecus venae crepuerint similiter hausta sanat.

CLV. Herba cyminum

A f. 64v/27

1. Cyminum, quod Latine quiminum vocant, stomacho valde utile
est (. . .); semen ipsum, quod in oleo coctum est, furfuribus admixtum
et cum hisdem calefactum pro cataplasmate ventri superponatur.

2. Suspiriosis autem cum posca bibendum utiliter datur; cum vino
autem ictum serpentium sanat.

3. Tumores quoque et fervores testium cum uva passa tritum vel cum
fabae polline vel cum ceroto curat.

4. (. . .) [sanguinem de naribus fluentem ipsa herba] cum aceto mixta
sistit.

CLVI. Herba camelleon alba

A f. 65/5

Habet folia aspera et spinosa (. . .), et medio quasi [quendam echinum]
rotundum et spinosum generat, qui purpureis floribus vestitus est; semen
habet album, radicem albam et odoriferam.

1. Wiþ þæt wyrmas on þam innoþe ymb þone nafolan dergen genim ðisse ylcan wyrte wyrttruman seaw oððe dust, syle drincan on wine oððe on wætere þe ǽr wære organe oððe dweorg(e)dwosle on gewylled, hyt rume þa wyrmas forð (g)elædeþ.

5　2. þysse sylfan w(yr)te wyrtruma(n) fif pene(ga) gewihte on wine geþiged þa w(æt)erseocan ge(dr)igeþ, ðas sylfan stre(ng)þe h(eo ha)f(a)þ gewylled 7 gedruncen (w)ið þæs migþan earfoðlic-nyssa.

CLVII.

10　1. Ðeos wyrt þe man scolimbos 7 oþrum naman (. . .) nemneþ on wine gewylled 7 gedruncen, heo þone fulan stenc ðæra oxna 7 ealles þæs lichaman afyrreþ.

2. Eac swylce ðeos sylfe wyrt ðone fulstincendan migþan /
f. 66　forð gelædeþ 7 eac halwendne mete mannum 'ge'gearwaþ.

15　CLVIII.

Ðeos wyrt þe man iris Illyricam 7 oðrum naman (. . .) nemneþ is gecweden iris Illyrica of ðære misenlicnysse hyre blostmena, for þy þe ys geðuht þæt heo þone heofonlican bogan mid hyre bleo geefenlæce se is on Leden iris gecweden; 7 heo on Illyrico
20　þam lande swiðost 7 strengost wexeþ, 7 heo hafað leaf glædenan gelice þa Grecas xifian hataþ, 7 heo hafað trumne wyrtruman 7 swyþe gestencne; 7 þone man sceal mid linenan claþe befealdan 7 on sceade ahon oððet he gedriged beon mæge, for ðy h(ys ge)cynde is swiþe hát 7 slæ(pbæ)re.

MS V

　　2 ðisse] ðas H 82/2　　oððe] odde H.　　　9 *title om.* VBH.　　　10 scolim-
bos] scolymbon H　　　7 . . . nemneþ] *om.* H.　　　　　15 *title om.* VBH.
16 Illyricam] Iliricam B 116v/14b　　7 . . . nemneþ] *om.* H.　　　19 se] seo
H　Leden] Læden BH.　　20 swiðost] swiðos B.　　　22 þone] þon H.
23 oððet] oðþæt BH.

———

MS O

　　2 on] on / on.　　　4 afyrȝed] afermaþ afyrȝed (*first word exp.*).

CLVII. Scolinbos   f. 39/14

1. (Ad fetorem corporis) þeos wyrt þæt man scolínbos on wine
ȝewillad 7 ȝedruncan, heo þana fulne stenc þara oxna 7 ealle þas lichama
afyrȝed.

2. (Ad urinam fetententem) Eac þeos sulfe wyrt þane fulestincenden 5
migþan for ȝelædeþ 7 eac halwende mete mannum ȝeȝearfað.

CLVIII *om.* O.

---

1. Sucus radicis eius vel pulvis cum vino et aqua, in quo origanum decoctum fuerit, lumbricos latos deducit.

2. Cuius idem dragma una cum vino data hydropicum siccat; eandem
vim theriacae habet; decoctio ipsius pota difficultatem urinae solvit.

CLVII. Herba scolimos   A f. 70/26

1. Haec namque in vino decocta et pota fetorem ascellarum et totius
corporis putida aufert.

2. Praeterea urinas putidas deducit, nec non et salubrem cibum rusticis
praestat (. . .).

CLVIII. De iride   Dio. 1.1

Iris Illyrica a coelestis arcus similitudine nomen accepit. Folia habet
gladiolo similia (. . .). Radices subsunt geniculatae, solidae, suaveolentes,
quae concisae siccantur in umbra et lino traiectae conduntur. Praestantior
est Illyrica et Macedonica (. . .).

1. Gyf hwa (m)ycelne hracan þolige 7 he þone him 'e'aþelice fram bringan ne mæge for ðycnysse 7 to hnesce, genime of þysse wyrte wyrtruman ðæs dustes smæle gecnucudes tyn penega gewihte, sylle drincan fæstende on liþon beore feower scenceas

5 þry dagas oþðæt he sy gehæled.

Ðam gelice þæt dust þysse sylfan wyrte on liþon beore geþiged ðone slep on gelædeþ 7 eac þæra innoþa astyrunge geliþigað.

2. Eac swylce þæt dust þysse ylcan wyrte næddrena slitas ge-

10 lacnaþ; þæt sylfe gemet þæt we her beforan cwædon þæs dustes ðysse ylcan wyrte iris Illyrice foran mid ecede gemencged 7 gedruncen, hyt fremað þam þe his gecyndelice sæd him sylfwylles fram gewiteþ, þone leahtor Grecas gonorhoeam nemneþ; gyf hit þonne soðlice þam ylcan gemete mid wine gemetegud /

f. 66v byþ, hit þæra wifa (m)onoðlican astyreð þeah hy (ær la)ngæ

16 forlætene wæron.

3. Wið cyrnlu 7 wið ealle yfele cumulu genim ðysse ylcan wyrte wyrttruman swa anwealhne wel gedrigedne 7 siððan gesodenne, cnuca hyne ðonne swa hnes'c'ne, wyrc to clyþan,

20 lege to ðam sare, hyt tofereþ.

4. Eac swa some hyt fremað wið ðæs heafodes sare mid ecede 7 mid rosan wose gemencged.

CLIX. [Elleborum]

1. Wið liferseocnysse genim þas wyrte þe man elleborum

25 album 7 oðrum naman (. . .) nemneþ gedrigede 7 to duste gecnucude, syle drincan on wearmum wætere, þæs dustes syx

2 ne] om. H 83/5   hnesce] hnese (between s and e an erasure) H.
4 feower] seofon H.   6 þæt] þæs H   sylfan] ylcan H.   7 slep] slæp
B 117/12a, H = B.   8 geliþigað] geli'ði'gað H.   9 næddrena] næd-/
redrena H.   11 ylcan] om. H.   12–13 sylfwylles]
id. H (wy alt. from um).   13 gonorhoeam] gonorheam H.
14 gemetegud] gemænged B.   15 langæ] lange BH.   16 forlætene]
forlæde H.   17 yfele] yfelu B, ylfele H   ðysse] ðas H.   18 wel] 'to'
wel H   gedrigedne] gedrigede H.   19 gesodenne] gesodene BH.   20 ðam]
om. H   hyt] 'hyt' H 84/1.   23 title: from B, om. VH.   25 7 . . .
nemneþ] om. H.

CLIX. Ellebo(rum album)   tunsig(wyrt)   f. 13v/23

1. Wið liferseocnysse nim þas wyrt þe man elleborum album 7 oþrum naman tunsingwyrt nemneð ӡedriӡede to duste ӡecnucode, sile drincan on wyrme wætere, þas d(uste)s sýx cu(cule)res fulle, hit ӡelac/nad þa   f. 12(!)

---

1. Dum tunditur, sternutationem ciet.
2. Ex aceto potae eos iuvant qui a venenatis animalibus morsi sunt (. . .) aut quibus genitura effluit. Ex vino potae menstruum cursum promovent (. . .).
3. Molliunt etiam strumas scirrhosque inveteratos, dum coctis (partes) foventur.
4. Conferunt et ad capitis dolores ex aceto et rosaceo appositae (. . .).

CLIX. (*See Note*)

cucu(leras) fulle, (hit gela)cnað þa lifre; (þæt silf)e is f(ramigendlic
l)æcedom (on w)ine (g)eþiged (on)gean ealle attru.

CLX.

1. Wið þam fefore þe þy feorðan dæge on man becymeþ
5 genim þysse wyrte seaw [þe man] delfinion 7 oþrum naman (. . .)
nemneþ wel gegaderod 7 þæt mid pipore gecnucud 7 gemencged,
7 ðæra pipercorna sy ofertæl, þæt ys þonne þy forman dæge an 7
þrittig 7 þy oðrum dæge seofontyne 7 ðy þryddan dæge þreotyne;
f. 67 gyf þu him þis syllest / toforan þære ge'nea'læcincge þæs fefores,
10 wundorlicre hrædnysse he byð alysed.

CLXI.

Ðeos wyrt þe man æcios 7 oþrum naman (. . .) nemneþ hafað
sæd gelic næddran heafde, 7 [heo] hafað lange leaf 7 stiþe, 7
heo manega stelan of hyre asendeþ, heo hafað þynne leaf 7 ða
15 hwonlice þyrnihte, 7 heo hafað betweox þam leafon brune blostman, 7 betweonan ðam blostmum heo hafað, swa we ær cwædon,
sæd gelic nædran heafde, 7 hyre wyrttruma ys gehwæde 7 sweart.

1. Wyþ nædrena slitas genim ðysse ylcan wyrte wyrtruman þe
we æcios nemdon, syle drincan on wine, hyt fremað ge ær ðam
20 slite ge æfter. Sé sylfa drenc eac swylce þæra lendena sár geliðigað
7 eac drige on breoston meolc gegearwað. Soðlice an miht ys
þysse wyrte 7 þæs wyrttruman 7 þæs sædes.

CLXII.

1. Ðeos wyrt þe man centimorbia 7 oðrum naman (. . .) nemneþ
25 byþ cenned on beganum stowum 7 on stænigum 7 þæt on dunum

MS V

1 framigendlic] fragendlic B.   3 *title om.* VBH.   4 fefore] f'f'ere H
þy] *om.* H.   5 þe man] *from* B 117v/17a, *om.* V   delfinion] dælfinion H.
5–6 7 . . . nemneþ] *om.* H.   7 forman] feorþan H.   8 oðrum] oðrum
(r *alt. from* y) H   þreotyne] þreottene B.   9 him] *om.* H   syllest] sylest
H   genealæcincge] -læcnunge B, -læci'nc'ge H.   11 *title om.* VBH.
12 7 . . . nemneþ] *om.* H.   13 heo] *from* B, he V.   16 heo hafað] *om.* H.
18 nædrena] nædran H.   20 geliðigað] geþigoð H 85/5.   23 *title om.*
VBH.   24 7 . . . nemneþ] *om.* H.

MS O

2 attra] *second* a *alt. from* u.   3 *no trace of a title in red.*   7 ecios]
erios ecios (*first word, in which* ci *interlined above* ri, *exp.*).

lifr(e), þat sylfe ys fangenlice læcedom on wine ȝeþ(iȝ)ed aȝeon ealle attra.

CLX.

f. 14/19

1. (Contra febrim) (. . .) þa (ma)n delfinion (. . .) (m)id (pi)per(e)
(. . .).

5

CLXI. (. . .)

f. 12/2

þeos wyrt þæt (m)an ecios hætaþ ha(f)a(ð) lange leaf 7 stiþe 7 þinne, 7
heo hafað maneȝe (s)telan 7 betyx ðan leafan brune blosman 7 betyx þan
blosman sæd ȝelic næddran heafedan, 7 hyra wyrtruma his ȝehwæde 7
swert.

10

1. Wið næddra slite nim þisse wyrt wyrtrume þe we ecios nemdon,
sile drincan on wine, hit fremeð ȝe ær þan slite ȝe after. Se sylfa drenc
eac swylcæ ðæra lendena sar ȝeliþeȝað 7 eac driȝe on breostum meoluc
ȝearwað. S(oð)lice (. . .) (m)ih(t) þisse wyrt 7 þas wyrtru(man) (7) (þ)as
sædes.

15

CLXII *om*. O.

CLX. Herba delfion

A f. 75/5

1. Huius sucus collectus et cum piperis granis impartitus, id est xxi die
prima, secunda die xvii, tertia die xiii, hoc si ante accessionem dederis
quartanario, mira celeritate liberabitur.

CLXI. Herba hechios

A f. 70v/32

quod capiti vipereo habeat semen ipsius simile, folia habet longa,
aspera (. . .), caules multos emittit et tenues cum floribus inter folia
purpureis, inter quos semen capiti vipereo simile; radix parva et nigra.

1. Quae trita et cum vino pota contra serpentium morsus prodest, vel
ante vel postea. Eadem potio etiam lumborum dolores sedat, lac siccis
uberibus subministrat. Una autem vis est et herbae et radicis et seminis.

CLXII. Herba centimorbia

A f. 75/12

1. Nascitur locis cultis et petrosis, hoc est montuosis et laetis, de uno

7 on wynsumum stowum; 7 heo of anre tyrf manega bogas asendeþ,

f. 67v 7 heo is gehwædon leafun 7 sine/wealton 7 toslitenon, 7 heo
hafað þas mihte to lacnunge; gif hors on hricge oððe on þam
bogum awyrd sy 7 hyt open sy, genim þas wyrte ealle gedrigede
5 7 to swyðe smælon duste gecnucude, gescead to ðam sare, heo
hit gehæleþ; þu wundrast ðære gefremminge.

CLXIII.

Ðeos wyrt ðe man scordias 7 oðrum naman (. . .) nemneþ
hafaþ swæc swylce leac, 7 heo eac for þy scordios gecweden ys;
10 þeos wyrt byð cenned o'n' morum, 7 heo hafaþ leaf sinewealte,
7 ða bittere on byrgincge, 7 heo hafaþ feowerecgedne stelan 7
fealuwe blostman.

1. Wið þæs migðan astyrunge genim þas wyrte scordios swa
grene gecnucude 7 on wine geþigede oððe drigge on wine gewyl-
15 lede, syle drincan, heo þone migðan astyreþ.

2. Eac þæt sylfe fremað wið nædrena slitas 7 wið ealle attru
7 wið þæs magan sare, swa we ǽr cwædon, wið þæs migðan yrmðe.

3. Wið þa gerynnincge þæs worsmes ym ða breost genim þas
ylcan wyrte tyn penega gewihte mid hunige gemencged, syle
20 þicgean anne cuculere fulne, þa breost beoð afeormude.

4. Wið fotadle genim þas ylcan wyrte on ecede gecnucude
oððe on wætere, syle drincan, hyt fremað wel.

5. Wið niwe wunda genim þas ylcan wyrte sylfe gecnucude,
lege to ðam wundum, heo hy geþeodeþ; 7 eac heo mid hunige
25 gemencged ealde wunda afeormaþ 7 gehæleþ; 7 eac hyre dust
wexende flæsc wel gehnæceþ. /

CLXIV.

f. 62(!) 1. Ðeos wyrt þe man ami 7 oðrum naman miluium nemneþ
7 eac sume men (. . .) hatað hafað gecweme sæd to læcedome þæt

MS V

2 leafun] leafum B 118/25a, leafon H.   3 hors] hof'er' (f alt. from r) H.
5 swyðe] swiþon H   smælon] smalon (m alt. from w) B.   7 title om.
VBH.   8 scordias] scordios BH   7 oðrum naman] om. H.   9 7 heo eac]
om. H.   11 bittere] beoð biterre H.   16 nædrena] næddran B, nædran
H.   17 þæs] om. H 86/3.   18 worsmes] wormses B 118v/3a, H = B
ym] ymb BH.   20 þicgean] þicean H.   23 wunda] wun'd'a H.
26 gehnæceþ] gehneceþ H.   27 title om. VBH.   29 7 eac . . . hatað]
om. H.

CLXIII. Scordios

þeos wyrt þæt man scordios.

1, 2. —

3. (Ad pectus) Wið þa ȝerínníncge þæs wyrmses abota þa breost ním
þeos wyrte tyn peneȝa ȝewyhtæ mid huníȝe ȝemencged, syle dicȝean anne 5
cucelere fulne; þa breost afeormed.

4. (Ad morbum pedum) Wið fotadle cnuca þeos on ecede oþþer on /
wætere, sile drincan.

5. —

CLXIV. Aíní alias miluíum

1. (Contra motum uiscerum et urine difficultatem et contra ferarum 11
morsum et contra stipationem et contra maculas corporis) þeos wyrt ðe
man aíní 7 oðrum naman miluíum hata ð hafad ȝecweme sæd to læcedome

---

caespite multas [virgulas] emittit, foliis parvis et rotundis et scissis
. . .); eius virtus talis est ad medendum: eius herbae totius siccae pulvis
cribratus mollissime curat armora caballi si aperta habuerit, vel dorsum
læsum; miraberis bonum effectum.

CLXIII. De scordio

Scordium nascitur in palustribus locis. Folia habet (. . .) allium (. . .)
redolentia, astringentia gustuque amara, cauliculos quadrangulos, in
quibus flos rubicundus.

1, 2. Vim habet herba calefacientem, urinasque ciet. Recens trita
itemque arida, decocta in vino, adversus serpentium morsus venenaque
propinatur.

3. (. . .) binis drachmis ex hydromelite (. . .) pus crassius e pectore
expellit.

4. Valet et ad podagram ex aceto acri oblita vel ex aqua imposita.

5. Quin et vulnera conglutinat, vetera ulcera repurgat, et cum melle
ad cicatrices perducit. Sicca vero carnis luxuriem coercet.

CLXIV. De ammi

1. Ammi (. . .). Vulgo notum est semen minutum (. . .). Vim habet

on wine geseald byð, wel fremað wið þæs innoðes astyrunge 7 wið
earfoðlicnysse ðæs migðan 7 wið wildeora slitas, 7 eac hyt ða
monoðlican forð gecigeþ; 7 wið wommas þæs lichaman genim
þysse sylfan wyrte sæd mid hunige gecnucud, hyt afyrreð þa
5 wommas.

2. Wið ablæcnysse 7 æhiwnesse þæs lichaman do þæt sylfe:
þæt ys þæt ðu þone lichama(n) mid þam ylcan gesmyre, oððe
syle drincan, hyt þa æhiwnesse of genimeð.

CLXV. Bánwyrt

10 Ðeos wyrt þe man uiolam 7 oðrum naman banwyrt nemneð ys
ðreora cynna, þonne ys an brunbasuw 7 o(þ)er hwit, þridde is
geoluw; ðonne is seo geoluwe swaþeah swiþost læceon gecweme.

1. Wið þæs cwiðan sare 7 wið þone hætan genim þas ylcan
wyrte gecnucude 7 under gelede, heo hyne gelihteþ; eac swylce
15 heo ða monoðlican forþ gecigeþ.

2. Wiþ misenlice leahtras ðæs [bæcþearmes] þa ragadas hatað,
f. 62v þæt is swaþeah swiðost þæs blodes / utryne, genim þysse ylcan
wyrte leaf gecnucud(e) 7 to clyþan gemencgede, hy þa untrumnysse
e'a'lle gehæleþ.

20 3. þysse sylfæn wyrte leaf mid hunige gecnucude 7 gemencgede
þone cancor þæra toða gehæleð, of ðam foroft ða teþ fealleð.

MS V

2 wildeora] wilddeora B   eac] *om.* H.   4 þysse] þas H   sylfan]
om. B, ylcan H   wyrte] wyrtan B   gecnucud] cnucud H.   6 ablæcnysse]
æ- BH   æhiwnesse] æhiw'n'esse H.   7 þæt ðu] þæt sylfe þæt ðu H.
9 *title*: violam banwurt B, *om.* H 87/2.   12 geoluw] geola B 119/2a
swiþost] *om.* B.   16 misenlice] mistlice B, misen'lice' H   bæcþearmes]
from B, -þearmas V   ragadas] *id.* H (*first a alt. from* u)   hatað] hateð H.
18 gemencgede] geworhte B.   20 þysse] isse B   sylfæn] æ *alt. from* e V
leaf] *om.* H   gemencgede] gemængede 7 B.   21 fealleð] gefealleð B,
feallað H.

MS O

3 ȝecnucod] ȝe me cnucod (me *exp.*).   6 sylfe] sysf sylfe (sysf *exp.*
and struck out).   8 *title*: in black, framed in red.   13 hateð] *followed by*
cnuca þara wyrt leaf (*exp.*).

þæt on wyne ʒesæld byþ, fremað þaes innoðes astirunge 7 wið earfornysse
þæs miʒþan 7 wyð wyldeora slitas, 7 eac hít þa monoþlican forð ʒeciʒeð;
7 wyþ wommas ðas lichaman ʒením þisse wirte sæd mid huníʒe ʒecnucod,
hit afírþeð ða wommas.

2. (Contra deco(lo)rationem corporis) Wið æblæcnisse 7 æhiwnysse   5
þæs lichaman do þæt sylfe: þæt ys þæt þu ðone lichaman mid þam ylcan
ʒesmyru, odðer sylle dríncan, hyt þa æhywnyssa of ʒenymeð.

CLXV. De viola   f. 41v/1

þeos wyrt þæt man violam 7 oþrum nama banwurt nemned, heo ys
þreora cunna: þa on ys brunbasup 7 oþer hwít, þridde ys ʒeoluw; þanne 10
is þeo ʒeoluwe swaþeah swyþest læcon ʒecweme.

1. —

2. Wið missenlice leahtras þæs bæcþearmes þa radagas hateð, þæt ys
swaþeah swyþost þas blodas utrune, cnuca þisse wyrt leaf, 7 to clyþan
ʒemencgede hi þa untrumnysse healle ʒehæled.   15

3. Hure sylfe leaf mid huníʒe ʒecnucode 7 ʒemencgede þane cancor
þara toþa ʒehæled þur hwan þa teð oft feallad.

---

hoc (. . .) calefacientem, urentem et exsiccantem; valet ad tormina,
urinae difficultatem ac venenatorum morsus, ex vino bibitum. Ciet
quoque menstrua. Sugillata sub oculis cum melle impositum tollit.

2. Sed et potu ac illitu cuti pallorem conciliat.

CLXV. Herba viola aurosa   A f. 75/19

Cuius genera sunt tria: purpureum, album, et mellinum, sed mellinum
maxime medicinae aptum est.

1. Haec decocta et supersessa dolores et fervores matricis relevat,
menstrua etiam provocat.

2. Folia eius tunsa et ceroto mixta ragadas curant.   Ca

3. Eadem folia cum melle mixta cancri dentium, quo dentes decidunt, p. 531/17b
sanat.

4. Wyþ ða monoðlican to astyrigenne genim þysse ylcan wyrte sædes tyn penega gewihte on wine gecnucud 7 gedruncen oððe mid hunige gecnucud 7 to ðam gecyndelican lime geled, hyt þa monoð-lican astyreþ 7 þæt tudder of þam cwiðan gelædeþ.

5   5. Wið miltan sare genim þysse ylcan wyrte wyrttruman on ecede gecnucudne, lege to ðære miltan, hit fremaþ.

CLXVI. [Viola purpurea]

1. Wi(ð) niwe wundela 7 eac wið ealde g(e)nim þysse wyrte leaf þe m(an) uiola purpurea 7 oðrum na(ma)n (. . .) nemneþ 7 rysle,
10 (æg)þres gelice mycel, lege to ðam wund(um), scearplice hyt hy gehæleð; 7 eac geswel 7 ealle yfele gegaderunga hyt tolyseð.

2. Wiþ ðæs magan heardnysse genim þysse ylcan wyrte blost-man on hunige gemencgede 7 mid swiðe godon wine gewesede, þæs magan heardnys byð geliðigad.

15 ## CLXVII.

Ðeos wyrt þe man zamalentition 7 oþrum naman (. . .) nemneþ byð cenned on stænigum stowum 7 on dunum.

1. Wið ealle wundela genim þas wyrte zamalentition wel mid /
f. 71(!) rysle gecnucude butan sealte, lege to ðam wundum, ealle heo hy
20 gehæleþ.

2. Eft wið cancorwunda genim þas ylcan wyrte zamalentition gedrigede 7 to swyþe smalon duste gecnucude, lege to ðam wun-dum, ealne ʻþoneʼ bite þæs cancres heo afeormað.

MS V

1 astyrigenne] astyrgynne H.   3 gecyndelican] cyndelican H
geled] gelæd H.   6 gecnucudne] gecnucude H.   7 title: from B,
om. VH.   9 7 . . . nemneþ] om H 88/1   rysle] sile B.   13 gemencgede]
gemencged H.   14 geliðigad] -od BH.   15 title om. VBH.
16 7 . . . nemneþ] om. H.   18 wyrte] wyre H.   19 gecnucude]
gecnude H.   22 gecnucude] gecnude H.

MS O

4 in addition to title: Item Item de viola (black).   6 níwe] for níwe (for
exp.).   7 purpurea nemned] nemned purpurea, marked for reversal.
8 gehaleð] le gehaleð (le exp.).

4. —

5. Wið miltan sare cnuca þissa wyrt wurtrume mid ecede, leʒe to þara miltan, hit helped wel.

CLXVI. Viola purpurea   f. 41/1

1. (Ad omnem plagam et omnem inflationem et omnem malam col-   5
lectionem in corpore) Wið níwe wunda 7 eac wið ealde ním þara wyrt
leaf þæt man víola purpurea nemned 7 risles æʒres ʒelice mycel, leʒe to
þara wunda, scearplice hit hi ʒehaleð; 7 eac ʒeswel 7 ealle ʒegaderunga hit
toliseð.

2. (Ad stomachi duritiam) Wið þas mæʒen heardnesse nim þisse wyrt 10
leaf 7 blostman 7 huniʒe ʒemegged 7 mid swyðe gode wíne ʒewesede;
þæs mæʒe heardnesse byð ʒeliþegod.

CLXVII. Zima lentition   f. 44/18

þeos wyrt þæt man zíma lentítion byð cenned on staniʒum stowum 7
on dunum.   15

1. (Ad omnem plagam et cancram) Wið ealle wunda laʒe ʒ ením ` 7 ´ wyl
þeos wyrt mid risle ʒecnucode buton sealte, leʒe to þan wunda, ealle heo
hi ʒehæleð.

2. Eft wyð cancor þeos wyrt ʒedriʒede 7 to smale duste ʒecnucade,
leʒe to þan wunda, ealne þane bíte þæs cancores heo afeormað.   20

---

4. Semen ipsius dragmas ii cum vino tritum et potum vel cum melle
tritum genitalibus appositum menstrua movet, foetus matricibus deicit.

5. Radices cum aceto tritae et spleni superpositae.

CLXVI. Herba [viola] purpurea   Har
                                                                         f. 57/25

1. Purpureae violae folia cum axungia pari pondere contusa vulnera
recentia et pristina efficacissime sanant, tumores quoque et omnes collectiones dissolvunt.

2. Flores ipsius in melle missi et macerati cum vino optimo mixti
stomachi ardorem sedant.

CLXVII. Herba zamalentition   Har
                                                                        f. 57v/1

Nascitur locis petrosis.

1. Haec herba trita cum axungia bene sine sale et vulneribus apposita
omne vulnus sanat.

2. Item ad vulnera cancerosa herba zamalentition sicca et in pulverem
mollissimum redacta omnia vulnera cancerosa expurgat.

CLXVIII.

Ðeos wyrt ðe man ancusa 7 oðrum naman (. . .) nemneþ byð
cenned on beganum stowum 7 on smeþum, 7 ðas wyrte ðu scealt
niman on ðam monþe ðe man Martius hateþ; ðysse wyrte [syndon]
5 twa cynrenu, an is ðe Affrica`ni´ barbatam nemnað, (oðer ys t)o
læcedomum swyþe gec(ore)n, 7 ðeos byð cenned fyrmest on ðam
lande ðe man Persa hateþ, 7 heo ys scearpon leafon 7 þyrnihtum
butan stelan.

1. Wið forbærnednysse genim þysse wyrte wyrttruman ancusa
10 on ele gesodene 7 wið wex gemencgedne ðam gemete þe þu
plaster oþþe clyþan wyrce, lege to þam bærnytte, wundorlice hyt
gehæleþ.

CLXIX. [Pulicaris herba]

Ðeos wyrt ys psillios g(e)cweden for ðam þe heo (haf)að sæd
15 swylce flean, þanon hy man eac on Leden pulicarem nemneð, 7 hy
f. 71v eac sume men / (. . .) (nemnað), heo hafað gehwæde leaf (7 ru)he,
7 heo hafað (s)telan 7 ðone o(n) b(og)um geþ(u)fne, 7 heo ys drige
ge(c)yn(de) 7 tyddre, 7 heo byð cenned on beganum stowum.

1. Wið cyrnlu 7 wið ealle yfele gegaderunga genim þysse wyrte
20 sædes gecnucudes an elefæt ful 7 twegen bollan fulle wæteres,
mencg tosomne, syle drincan; nim þonne of ðam sylfan sæde,
wyrc [plaster], lege to ðam sare, hyt byþ gehæled.

2. Wið heafudsare do þæt sylfe mid rosan wose 7 mid wætere
gewesed.

MS V

1 *title om.* VBH.   2 7 . . . nemneþ] *om.* H.   3 7²] *om.* H.
4 on . . . man] monðe H   syndon] *from* B, syndo V.   5 Affrica`ni´]
Africâ H.   11 oþþe] oðð B 119v/29b.   13 Pulicaris . . . alysed
(p. 216/7)] *one folio missing* B   *title: from modern gl. in* H 89/6, coliandre VH.
15 Leden] Læden H.   15–16 7 . . . nemnað] *om.* H.   16 hafað]
`hæfð´ H   ruhe] ruge H.   17 hafað] hæfað H.   18 gecynde] gecynd H.
20 sædes gecnucudes] sæd gecnucude H.   21 of] `of´ H.   22 plaster]
from H, blaster V   byþ] *om.* H.

MS O

13 adríȝre] *also* adriȝere *in o.m.*   14 beȝanum] bea beȝanum (bea *exp.*).
16 an elefæt ful] on ele an elefæt f ful (on ele *and single* f *exp.*).

CLXVIII. Ancura   f. 5/21

þeos wyrt þa man ancura nemneð, þu þeos wyrt scealt níman on þan
monðe þe Martius hateð. þisse wyrte sindeþ twa cynne: an is þe offri-
cum barbatum nemnað, oþer ys to lacedomum syyðe ȝecoren, 7 þeos
byð cenned fyrmest on þan londa se Persa hæteð, 7 heo scearpon leafon 5
7 þirnihte butan stelan.

  1. (Ad ustionem; contra arsuram) Wið forbærdnysse / ȝením þisse wirte f. 5v
wurtrume, ancura hatte, on ele ȝesodone 7 wiþ wex ȝemencged þam
ȝemete þe þu plaster odðer clyþam wyrce, leȝe to þan baernette, wunderlice
hit ȝehæleð.   10

CLXIX. Psillios   pulicaria   f. 31v/12

þeos wyrt þæt man cweden psillios for he hafad sæd swylce flean, 7 þi
summe men hi pulicarem hata(ð), 7 heo his of adríȝre cunde, 7 heo biþ
cenned on beȝanum stowe.

  1. (Wis curnle 7 elle vfele ȝeȝaderunga) Wid curnlu 7 wid ealle ufele 15
ȝeȝaderunga nim þisse wyrte sæd ȝecnude an elefæt ful 7 tweȝen bollen
fulle wæteres, meng togadere, sile drincan; þat sar byð ȝeliþegad.

  2. (Ad capitis dolorem) Wið heafodsare do þat silfe mid rosan wosa 7
mid wætere wel ȝewesed 7 ȝemenged.

CLXVIII. Herba ancusa   A f. 75v/10

Nascitur locis cultis et planis, legis eam mense Martio; ancusae genera
sunt duo: unum quod Afri barbatam dicunt; est et altera, quae maxime
medicamini apta est; haec in terra pressa nascitur, foliis spinosis, sine
caule.

  1. Facit ad combusturas: herbae anchusae radix in oleo decocta et
[ceroto facto], induces combusturis, mirifice prodest et sanat (. . .).

CLXIX. Herba psillios   A f. 68/28

Dicta eo quod semen pulicis habeat (. . .), Latine herbam pulicarem
vocant; folia habet parva, hirsuta, caulem ramosum; ipsa omnis arida et
fragilis (. . .); nascitur locis cultis (. . .).

  1. Huius seminis acetabulum plenum teritur et in aquae cotulis
duobus, id est heminis, mittitur et cum aqua cum biberit pro implastro
corpori impositum curat parotidas et omnes collectiones,

  2. capitis autem dolores cum oleo roseo et aqua.

CLXX.

Ðeos wyrt þe man cynosbatus 7 oðrum naman (. . .) nemneþ, ðonne hy man of ðam stelan genimeþ, heo bið þam goman stið 7 wiðerræde for mete geþiged, ac heo swaþeah ða breost afeormað, 5 7 swa hwylce þincg swa syndon afore oððe bitere, ðeah hy þam magan derien, hi swaþeah ðære miltan wel fremað; þysse ylcan wyrte blostma gedruncen swa þone man gelacnað þæt he þurh ðone [innoð 7 þurh ðone] migþan forð gelæded bið; 7 he eac blodrynas áfeormaþ.

10   1. Eft wið miltan sare genim þysse ylcan wyrte wyrttruman of ðære rinde wel afeormadne, lege to ðære miltan, hyt bið hyre nytlic 7 fremgendlic; 7 se þe þysne læcedom þolaþ, he sceal upweard licgean þy læs he úngeþyldig ða strengþe þysre lacnunge ongite. /

f. 70(!) ## CLXXI.

16   Ðeos wyrt ðe man aglaofotis 7 oðrum naman (. . .) nemneþ scineð on nihte swa blæse, 7 heo mæg wið manega untrumnyssa.

   1. Wið þone fefor ðe þy ðriddæn 7 ðy feorðan dæge on man becymeþ genim þysse ylcan wyrte seaw aglaofotis mid rosenan ele 20 gemencged, smyre þone seocan, untweolice þu hyne alysest.

   2. Gy`f´ hwa hreohnysse on rewytte þolige genime ðas ylcan wyrte for rycels onælede, seo hreohnys byð forboden.

   3. Wiþ hramman 7 wið bifunge genime þas sylfan wyrte, hæbbe mid him, gif hy þonne hwa mid (him bere)þ ealle yfelu hyne (on- 25 dræda)ð.

MS V

1 *title om.* V, *modern gl.* wilde eglantine H.   2 7 oðrum naman] *om.* H. 3 goman] gemun H.   7 blostma] blostman H   gedruncen] gedru'n´cen H   þone] ðane H 90/1.   8 innoð . . . ðone] *from* H, *om.* V.   12 fremgendlic] framgendlíc H.   15 *title om.* VH.   16 7 . . . nemneþ] *om.* H. 17 scineð] heo scineð H   blæse] blyse H.   18 Wið] ið H   ðriddæn 7 ðy] *om.* H   ðriddæn] æ *alt. from* e V.   20 alysest] alesest H. 21 Gy`f´] Gið H   rewytte] nyrewytte H   genime] genim H.   23 hæbbe] habbe H.

MS O

6 hreohnysse] hreoþ he hreohnysse (hreoþ he *underlined*).

CLXX om. O.

CLXXI. De aglafota   Angl. foxes gloua   f. 5v/4

þeos wyrt þe man aglaofotis þæt hís foxes gloua, heo scineð on nihte
swa blæse, 7 heo mæʒ wið maneʒa untrumnesse.

1. —   5

2. Gif hwa on rewette hreohnysse þolie ʒením þas ylcan wyrte for
recels onælede, seo hreohnysse byþ forboden.

3. (Contra cancram et tremorem ualet; hanc herbam habentem omnia
mala fugiunt) Wið hramman 7 wyð bifunge ʒením`e´ ða wyrte man 7
habbe mid hym. Gif hy hwa þanne mid hym bereð, ealla yfele híne   10
ondrædað.

CLXX. Herba cinosbatos   A f. 75v/17

Huius bacae exemptae de medio lanugine — obstat faucibus — pro cibo
sumptae purgant toracem [et quaecumque] acria vel acidula sunt, quae
stomacho obsunt; lieni autem, quod est spleni, aptae; flos eius potus ita
medetur, ut per ventrem et urinam deducat et sanguinolenta purgat.

1. Radices etiam de cortice impositas lieni commodum est super-
ponere; supinus autem ligandus est laborans, ne vim medicamenti
impatiens remedia discutiat.

CLXXI. (See Note)

CLXXII. Wudubend

1. Wið miltan sare genim þysse wyrte wyrttruman þe man capparis 7 oþrum naman wudubend hateð, cnuca to duste 7 gewyrc to clyþan, lege to ðære miltan, he hy adrygeð; ac swaþeah
5 gewrið þone man þy læs he þurh þæt sár ða lacnunge of him asceace; 7 æfter þrim tidum gelæd hyne to bæþe 7 hyne wel gebaþa, he byþ alysed. /

f. 70v   CLXXIII.

Ðeos wyrt þe man eringius 7 oþrum naman (. . .) nemneþ
10 hafað hnesce leaf þonne heo ærest acenned byþ, 7 ða beoð werede on swæce, 7 hi man þigeþ s`w´a oðre wyrta, syððan hy beoð scearpe 7 ðyrnihte, 7 ʻheoʼ hafað stelan hwitne oððe grenne, on ðæs heahnysse ufeweardre beoð acennede scearpe 7 þyrnyhte pilas, 7 heo hafað lancne wyrtruman 7 þone uteweardne sweartne, 7
15 sé bið godes swæces; þeos wyrt byþ cenned on feldon 7 on wiðer-rædon stowum.

1. Wið þæs migþan astyrunge genim þa(s) ylcan wyrte þe we eringius ne(md)un gecnucude, syle drin(can on) wine, na þæt (an) þæt heo þone migþan astyreþ, ác eac swylce ða moʻnoʼþlican 7
20 ðæs innoðes astyrunge 7 toðundenysse heo tolyseþ, 7 eac wið liferseocnysse 7 wið næddrena slitas heo wel fremað.

2. Eac swylce wið mænigfealde leahtras þæra innoða heo wel fremað geþiged mid þære wyrte sæde þe man olisatrum nemneþ.

3. Wið þæra breosta geswel genim ðas ylcan wyrte to clyþan
25 geworhte, lege to ðam breostan, ealle þa yfelan gegaderungæ onbutan þa breost heo tofereð.

MS V

1 *title*: wudubed H.   3 wudubend] -bed H.   4 gewyrc] wyrc
H 91/1   ac] eác H.   6 7¹] *om.* H.   8 *title om.* VH, *for* B
see t.n.   9 7 oþrum naman] *om.* H.   12 ðyrnihte] ðyrmíhte H.
13 7] *om.* B 120/24a.   14 lancne] langne B   uteweardne]
utewearʻdʼne H.   15 feldon] feldum H.   15–16 wiðerrædon] -rædum B.
19 þone] ʻðoʼne H.   20 toðundenysse] -enn- BH   eac] *om.* H.   22 wel]
om. H.   25 breostan] breostum H 92/3   gegaderungæ] -unga B, -unge H.

MS O

10 þa] þ (*no damage*).

CLXXII *om.* O.

CLXXIII. (. . .)

(. . .) (wy)rt þe man eringius hated (. . .) hnesce leaf þane heo ærest
byð acenned, (. . .) beoð werede on swæcce 7 hi man þiʒeð swa (oðr)e
wyrte.   5

1. —

2. þeos wyrt eringius wið mæniʒf(ealde l)eahtras þara innoþ heo wel
fremað ʒeþiʒed mid þara wyrt sæde þe man oleastrum (nem)ned.

3. Wið þæra brosta ʒ(e)swel ním þa wyrt to clyðan ʒeworuhte, leʒe to
ðan breostum, ealla [þa] yfelan ʒeʒaderunga abutan þan breost heo   10
toferað.

CLXXII. Herba cappara

1. Ad splenis dolorem radix capparae tunsa et cribrata et facta vice
cataplasmae et imposita splenem consumit, sed ligabis eum hominem,
ne prae dolore medicamentum excutiat, et post horas tres ducis eum qui
patitur in balneum et fac eum super solium sedere (. . .) et liberabitur.

CLXXIII. Herba erigion

Cuius folia in principio nascendi mollia et saporis blandi pro olere
sumuntur, postea spinosa fiunt, et habet caulem vel cianeum vel album
vel viridem in cuius summitate pilulae asperae spinosaeque nascuntur;
radix longa, forinsecus nigra, odoris boni; et in campis et in locis asperis
gignitur (. . .).

1. Quae tunsa et pota cum vino urinam movet et menstruam, tortiones
etiam ventris inflationesque dissolvit; facit etiam ad hepaticos et morsus
serpentium.

2. Ad multa praeterea intimo viscerum vitia cum semine oliastri
datur.

3. Haec tunsa et pro cataplasmate imposita omnes collectiones, tubera
tumoresque dissolvit.

4. Wið scorpiones stingc 7 wið ealra næddercynna slitas 7
eac wið wedehundes slite genim þas ylcan wyrte, wyrc to plastre,
lege to ðære wunde swa þæt seo wund swaþeah ærest mid iserne
geopenud sy, 7 syððan þærto geled swa þæt se seoca þone stenc ne
5 ongite; eac swylce þeos sylfe wyrt wið oman wel fremaþ on þas
ylcan wisan gemetegud, 7 eac heo fotadle geliðigað gyf hy man
æt frymþe to gelegeþ. /

CLXXIV.

Ðas wyrte man [philantropos] nemneþ, þæt ys on ure þeode
10 menlufigende, for ðy heo wyle hrædlice to ðam men geclyfian, 7
heo hafað sæd gelic mannes nafolan, þa man eac oþrum naman
clate nemneð, 7 heo of hyre manega bogas asendeþ, 7 þa lange 7
feowerecge, 7 ys stið on leafon, 7 heo hafað greatne stelan 7
hwite blostman, 7 heo hafað heard sæd 7 sinewealt 7 on middan
15 hol, swa we ær cwædon, þam gemete þe byð mannes nafla.

1. Wið nædrena slitas 7 wið [þara] wyrma ðe man spalangiones
hateþ genim þysse wyrte wos gecnucud on wine, syle drincan,
hyt fr(e)mað.

2. Wið earena sare genim þ(ysse) ylcan wyrte wos, drype on
20 þæt eare, hyt gehæleþ þæt sár.

CLXXV.

Ðeos wyrt þe man achillea 7 oðrum naman (. . .) nemneþ byþ
cenned on beganum stowum 7 neah wætere, 7 heo hafað geoluwe
blostman 7 hwite.

4. —

CLXXIV. Philant'r'opos   clate   f. 31v/22

þeos wyrt þat man philantropos, þat is on ure Ledene manluuiende,
for heo wile hradlice to þn manne clefian, 7 Engle hate(ð) clate.

1. (Ad serpentis morsum; contra spalangiones) Wið nædrane slite 7   5
wið þara wyrma þæt man spalangiones hæteð ním þisse wirte wos
ȝecnucod on wíne, sile drinca(n) / on wíne; hit fremeð.   f. 32

2. (Ad aurium dolorem) Wið earane sore ním þisse wyrte wos, dripe
on þat eare; hit ȝehaled þat sor.

CLXXV. De herba quae dicitur acylleia   f. 4v/1
Introduction and cure 1 om. O.   11

---

4. Mirificum praestabit auxilium adversus ictus scorpionum omnium-
que serpentium vel canis rabidi morsus, si prius vulnus ferro scindas et
implastrum istud apponas, [ita] tamen, ne aeger odorem eius accipiat;
haec temperata etiam ignem sacrum refrigerat; dolorem podagri, si in
initio accessionis ponatur, lenit dolorem.

CLXXIV. Herba aperina   Har f. 58/8

Aperina sive filantropos, quia hominibus inhaerescat, sive omphalo-
carpos, quod semen umbilico simile habet (. . .); ramos multos emittit
longos et tetragonos, aspera folia habet caulem cingentia (. . .), florem
album, semen durum et rotundum, in medio concavum in umbilici
modum.

1. Eius tritae sucus cum vino potatus contra spalangionum morsus et
viperarum remedio est.

2. Item sucus eius auribus instillatus dolores aurium curat.

CLXXV. Herba achillea   A f. 70v/1

Nascitur in locis cultis et sablosis, habet flores aurosos et subalbidos.

1. Wið niwe wunda genim þysse wyrte croppas gecnucude, lege to ðam wundum, heo þæt sár genimð 7 heo ða wunda geðeodeþ 7 þone blodryne gewrið. /

2. Gif wif of ðam gecyndelican limon þone flewsan þæs wætan þoligen genim þas ylcan wyrte gesodene, gelege under þam wifon sittendum, ealne þone wæ(t)an of hyre æþme heo gewrið.

3. (E)ac ðeos sylfe wy(r)t (o)n wætere ge(dru)ncen wið utsi(ht wel fremað).

Ð(eos wyrt is áchillea gecwe)d(en for þam þe is sæd þæt Achi)lle(s se ealdorman hyre gel)omlic(e brucan scolde wunda) to gel(acnigenne).

CLXXVI.

1. Wið hagol 7 hreohnysse to awendenne, gyf ðu þas wyrte ðe man ricinum 7 oðrum naman (. . .) nemneð on þinre æhte hafast oððe hyre sæd on þin hus (ahegs)t oððe (on swa) hwilcere sto(we swa) þu hy (hafast) oððe hyre sæd, heo awende(ð h)agoles h(reohn)ysse, 7 gyf þ(u hy) oððe hire (sæd) on scyp ah(ehst), to ðam wundo(rlic he)o is þæt he(o) ælce hreohny(sse) gesmylt(eþ); þas wyrte þu scealt niman þus cweþende: Herba ricinum, precor uti adsis meis incantationibus et auertas grandines, fulgora, et omnes tempestates, per nomen omnipotentis Dei qui te iussit nasci; þæt is ðonne on ure geþeode: wyrt ri`ci´num, ic bidde þæt þu ætsy minum sangum 7 þæt ðu awende hagolas 7 ligræsceas 7 ealle hreohnyssa, þurh naman ælmihtiges Godes se þe het beon acenned; 7 þu scealt clæne beon þonne þu ðas wyrte nimest. /

MS V

2 genimð 7 heo] 7 H.   3 geðeodeþ] geðedeð H.   4 gecyndelican] `ge´cyndelicon B.        5 þoligen] ðolige H.        6 æþme] æðme (e *alt. from* a) B 121/2a.        7 gedruncen] *om.* H.        8 fremað] fra H.        9 Ðeos wyrt] eos wyrt. Ðeos wyrt H    áchillea] áchillea`s´ (s *in later hand*) H.   9–10 for þam . . . Achilles] *om.* H.   10 ealdorman] aldor- H.   11 gelacnigenne] lacnigende H.   12 *title om.* VBH.   14 7 oðrum naman] *om.* H. 15 ahegst] ahehst H.   18 wundorlic] wundorlice H   hreohnysse] h`r´eoh- H.   22 þæt²] þet H 94/8.   23 ligræsceas] -resceas H. 24 þurh] þur H.

MS O

1 Gif] *preceded by* Gif wyf on ða manlice (*underlined and struck out*). 2 `flewsan´] *this word in o.m.,* fweawsan (*underlined and struck out*) *in text.* 10 yif] *preceded by erasure of one symbol.*   12 hwylcere] hyl hwylcere (hyl *exp.*)   þa þu] þa þa þu (*second þa exp.*).

2. (Ad morbum mulierum) Gif wyf on ða ʒecundelican límon þolian 'flewsan' ðæs wæten min þeos wyrt ʒesodene þæt man hataþ acylleia, leʒe under wyf sittenden, ealle þane wæte of hyre æþme heo ʒewyrð.

3. (Contra fluxum uentris) Eac þeos sylfe wyrt on wætere ʒedruncan wið utsiht wel fremeð.   5

Ðeos wyrt is acyllea ʒecwedon for þan is sæd þæt Acylles se ealderman hyre ʒelomlice brucen sceolde wunde to lacníʒende.

CLXXVI. De ricino   f. 34/1

1. (Contra fulguram et tonitrum et grandinem et tempestatem) Wiþ haʒol hreohnisse to awendenne yif þu þeos wyrt þæt man ricínum hatað 10 on þine hæte hafast oþer hyre sæd on þine huse ahehst oþþer on swa hwylcere stowe þa þu hy hafast oþþer hire sæd, heo awendeþ þa haloles hreohnysse, 7 ʒif þu hy oþþer hire sæd on scyp ahehst, to þan wunder-lice heo hys þæt heo ælce hreohnysse ʒesmulteð; þeos wyrt þu scealt niman þus cweðende: Herba ricinum, precor uti adsis meis incantati- 15 onibus, et auertas grandines, fulgora et omnes tempestates, per nomen omnipotentis Dei qui te iussit nasci; þat is on ure ʒeþeode: wyrt rícínum, ic bidde þat þu ætsi mínum sangun 7 þu awende hæʒolas 7 liʒræceas 7 helle hreonnysse, þur nama ealmihtiʒes Godes þe þe ðe het beon acenned; 7 þu scealt clæne beon þanne þu þeos nímest.   20

---

1. Coma eius tunditur et apposita novis vulneribus et dolorem tollit et eadem glutinat et profluvium sanguinis stringit.

2. Haec etiam matricibus mulierum sanguinem profundentibus praestat; si autem humoris profluvium mulieres ex [naturalibus patiuntur], haec herba decocta omnem humorem supersedentium mulierum solo vapore constringit.

3. Eademque aqua pota disentericos curat.

Achillea autem dicta est ideo, quod ea Achilles curandis vulneribus, usus frequentissime [fertur].

CLXXVI. (See Note)

f. 72(!) **CLXXVII. [Porrum nigrum]**

Ðeos wyrt ðe man po(ll)oten 7 oþrum naman porrum nigrum nemneþ 7 eac sume men (. . .) hatað ys þyrnihton stelan 7 swearton 7 rugum 7 bradran leafon þonne leac 7 sweartran, 7 þa syndon 5 stranges swæces, 7 hyre miht ys scearp.

1. Wið hundes slite genim þysse wyrte leaf mid sealte gecnucude, lege to þam wundum, hit hæleþ wundorlice.

2. Eft wið wunda genim þyssæ ylcan wyrte leaf mid hunige gecnucude, lege to þam wundum, ælce wunde hyt gehæleþ.

10 **CLXXVIII. Netele**

1. Wið (fo)rcillede wunda genim þysse wyrte [seaw] þe man urticam 7 oðrum naman netele nemneþ mid eledrosnum gemencged 7 sumne dæl sealtes ðærto gedon, lege to þære wunde, binnan þrim dagum heo biþ hal.

15 2. Wið geswel do þæt sylfe, þæt ys þonne þam ylcan gemete lege to þam geswelle, hyt bið gehæled.

3. Gyf ðonne ænig dæl þæs lichaman geslegen sy genim þas ylcan wyrte urticam gecnucude, lege [to] þære wunde, heo byð gehæled.

20 4. Wið li(þ)a sare, gyf hy of hwylc(um) belimpe oððe of cyle oþ(þe) o(f) ænigum þincge gesarg(a)de (beoð), genim þysse ylcan wyrt(e s)e(a)w 7 eles efenmycel t(ogæ)dere gewylled, do þonne þærto þær hit swiðost derige, binnan þrim dagon ðu hyne gehælst.

5. Wið fule wunda 7 forr(otud)e genim þas ylcan wyrte urticam 25 gecnucude 7 þærto sumne dæl sealtes, gewrið to þære wunde, binnan þrym dagon heo biþ hal.

MS V

    1 *title*: *from* B 121v/t.m.a, *om.* VH.   2 polloten] *id.* B (*between* o *and* t *one letter erased*)   oþrum] 'o'þrum H.   3 nemneþ . . . men] *om.* H þyrnihton] þærnihtan H   swearton] sweartum B.   4 bradran] brad'r'an BH.   6 sealte] 's'ealte H.   8 þyssæ] þisse BH.   9 hyt] he H. 10 *title*: urticam B, *om.* H.   11 seaw] *from* B, *om.* V.   14 heo] he H. 18 to] *from* B, *om.* V   heo] he H 95/11.   23 dagon] dagum B   gehælst] gelacnast H.   26 dagon] dagum B   heo] hit B, he H.

MS O

    10 leȝe] 3 *alt. from* g.

CLXXVII. De porro quod polloton dicitur Grece   f. 32/3

þeos wyrt þat man polloten 7 oþrum nama porrum nigrum.

1. (Ad canis morsum) Wið hundes slite ním þisse wirte leaf mid sealte ȝecnucode, leȝe to þan wunda, hit hæleð wunderlice.

2. (Ad plagam) Eft wið wunda ním þissa wyrte leaf mid huníȝe 5 ȝecnucode, leȝe to þan wunda; ælce wunde hit ȝehæld.

CLXXVIII. De vrtíca   f. 43v/7

1. (Wyd cillende wunde) Wið forcillede wunda ním þisse wyrte seaw þæt man u'r'ticam 7 Engle netele hatað mid eledrosnun ȝemenged 7 sum dæl sealtes þarto ȝedon, leȝe to þara wunda; bínnen þrím dæȝe he 10 byð hal.

2. (Contra inflaturam) Wið ȝeswel do þæt silfe, þæt is þanne ðam ylican ȝemete leȝe to þan ȝeswelle; hit byð ȝehæled.

3. (Ad uulnus et plagam) Gif ání dæl þas lichames ȝesleȝen sy cnuca þa wyrt, leȝe to þara wunda; heo byð ȝehaled.   15

4. (Ad morbum neruorum) Wið liþa sare, ȝif hi of hwylcum belimpe odðer of cule oþþer of æniȝe þinge ȝesarȝode beon, ním þisse wyrt seaw 7 eles efenmucel togadere ȝewylled, do þanne þarto þar hit swiþost deriȝe; binnan þrim dæȝe þu híne ȝehælest.

5. (Ad plagam fetante(m) et putridam) Wið fule wunda 7 forrotude 20 cnuca þeos wyrt 7 þarto sum dæl sealtes, ȝewriþ to þara wunda, binne þrím dæȝe heo byð hal.

CLXXVII. Herba balloten   L f. 41v/13

Alio nomine porrum nigrum Graeci vocant (. . .). Angulosis caulibus nigris, hirsutis foliis vestientibus, maioribus quam porrum et nigrioribus, grave olentibus, vis eius efficax est.

1. Adversus canis morsum cum sale foliis tritis imposita mire sanat.

2. Item ad condilomata coctum in cinere folio oleris purgat et sordida cum melle persanat.

CLXXVIII. Herba urtica   L f. 31/13

1. Ad vulnera quae sunt a frigore facta herbae urticae sucus, conteris simul cum faecibus olei et addito salis pusillum et super vulnus imponito; vulnera quae fuerint a frigore facta intra triduo sanabis.

2. Idem si tumor fuerit eodem modo superimponito, sanabis.

3. Si aliqua pars corporis ictu percussa fuerit herbam urticam conterito et apponito vulneri, sanabis.

4. Ad articulorum dolorem si forte a frigore aut ab aliqua re doluerint herbae urticae sucum conteres et oleum tantumdem calefactum in eo loco qui dolebit imponis, per triduo sanabis.

5. —

6. Wið wifes flewsan genim þas ylcan wyrte on mortere wel gepunude oðþæt heo wel liþi sy, geyc þonne þærtó sumne dæl

f. 72v huniges, nim syþþan / wæte wull(e), 7 þa we(l get)æsede, smyre ðonne þa gewea(l)d mid þam læcedome 7 syþþan (h)yne þam wife

5 gesyle, þæt heo hyne hyre under gelecge, þy sylfan dæge hyt þone flewsan beluceð.

7. Wið þæt þu cyle ne þolige genim þas ylcan wyrte urticam on ele gesodene, smyre ðonne þærmid þa handa 7 ealne þone lichaman, ne ongitst ðu þone cile on eallum þinum lichaman.

10 CLXXIX.

1. Ðeos wyrt þe man priapisci 7 oðrum naman uicaperuica nemneð to manegum þingon wel fremað, þæt ys þonne ærest ongean deofolseocnyssa 7 wið nædran 7 wið wildeor 7 wið attru 7 wið gehwylce behatu 7 wið andan 7 wið ogan 7 þæt ðu gife hæbbe;

15 7 gif ðu þas wyrte mid þe hafast ðu bist gesælig 7 symle gecweme; ðas wyrte þu scealt niman þus cweþende:

Te precor ui`c´aperuica multis utilitatibus habenda ut uenias ad me hilaris florens cum tuis uirtutibus, ut ea mihi prestes, ut tutus et felix sim semper a uenenis et ab iracundia inlesus. þæt

20 ys þonne on ure geþeode, ic bidde þe, uica peruica, manegum nytlicnyssum to hæbbenne, þæt ðu glæd tó me cume mid þinum mægenum blowende, þæt ðu me gegearwie þæt ic sy gescyld 7 symle gesælig 7 ungedered fram attrum 7 fram yrsunge; ðonne ðu þas wyrt niman wylt ðu scealt beon clæne wið æghwylce un-

25 clænnysse, 7 ðu hy scealt niman þonne se mona bið nigon nihta [eald 7 endlyfon nihta] 7 ðreo`t´tyne nyhta 7 ðrittig nihta 7 ðonne he byð anre nihte eald. /

MS V

2 liþi] liþig B, liðe H.   5 hyne hyre under] hine under B 122/2a, under hyre H.   8 ðonne] om. BH.   9 on . . . lichaman] om. H 96/6.
10 title om. VBH.   14 gehwylce] hwylce H.   15 gecweme] cwæme H.
16 ðas] þa H.   19 tutus] t'u´tus H.   25 hy] om. H.   26 eald . . .
nihta] from B, om. V   endlyfon] ænlufon H 97/1   ðreo`t´tyne] þreottene B
7 ðrittig nihta] om. H.

MS O

3 þa hunda] preceded by þane lichama oþþer (exp.).   11 ʒyfe] li ʒyfe (li exp.)
þeos] preceded by þ + another symbol (exp.).   13 cweþende] cwe / cweþende.

6. —

7. (Contra frigus corporis) Wið þæt þu cule ne þolie ním þeos wyrt on
ele ӡesodene, smure þarmíd þa hunda oþþer eal þana lichama, / ne onӡyst   f. 44
þu cule on ealle þine lichama.

CLXXIX. De vica pervíca quod priaprissi dicitur   ·   f. 32/10

1. (Ad demoniacos; ad morsum serpentis et contra feras et contra 6
uenenum, contra odium et inuidiam et ut habeas gratiam et felix sit et
placens) þeos wyrt þat man priaprissi 7 oþrum naman uíca peruica nemneð
to maneӡum þinge wel fremeð, þat is þanne ærest onӡean deofelseocnessa
7 wið nadran 7 wið wyldeor 7 wið attru 7 wyð ӡehwylce behatu 7 wið   10
andan 7 wið oӡan 7 þat þu ӡyfe hæbbe; 7 ӡif þu mid þe þeos wyrt
hæbbe þu byst ӡesæliӡ 7 simble ӡecweman; þas wyrt þu scelt niman þus
cweþende:

Te precor uica peruíca multis utilitatibus habenda ut uenias ad me
hylaris florens cum tuis uirtutibus, ut ea mihi prestes, ut tutus et felix   15
sím semper a uenénis et ab iracundia inlesus. þæt ys on ure ӡeþeode:
Ic bidde þe, uica peruica, maneӡum nytlicnyssum to hæbbenne, þat þu
glæd to me cume mid þinum mæӡenun blowende, þæt þu me ӡearwie
þæt hic sy ӡescyld 7 symble tosæliӡ 7 unӡederod fram attru / 7 fran   f. 32v
yrsunge. þanne þu þeos wyrt níme wult þu scealt b'e'on clane wið   20
æӡhwile unclanasse, 7 þu scealt hi níman þanne þe mona byð neoӡa
nihta eald 7 enlufon nihta eald 7 þanne he byð anre niht eald.

---

6. Ad profluvium mulierum herbam urticam terito in mortario donec
lenis fiat, adicies mellis modicum, deinde lanam sucidam bene carpito et
intinge in medicamento et da, supponas mulieri, eodem die profluvium
praecludit (. . .).

7. —

CLXXIX. Herba vica pervica   L f. 37v/1

1. Ad multas res facit et adversus daemonia et serpentes sive ad bestias
et adversus venena sive ad compromissos, ad actos, ad negotia, ad
rationes et ambitu a vi gratia aut adversus invidiam, adversus terrores;
hanc herbam tecum si habueris felix et gratiosus eris semper; legis eam
sic dicens: te precor, vica pervica, multis utilitatibus, ut ea mihi praestes,
ut totus felix sim semper et a venenis et ab iracundia; leges eam mundus
ab omnibus, nona, undecima, tricesima, tertia decima tricesimaque et
prima luna.

f. 73 CLXXX.

Ðeos wyrt ðe man litospermon 7 oðrum naman [sunnancorn]
nemneð byð cenned in Italia, 7 seo fyrmeste in Creta, 7 heo hafað
maran leaf ðonne rude, 7 ða rihte, 7 on ðære hehnysse heo hafað
5 stanas hwite 7 sinewealte swylce meregrotu on pysna mycelnysse, 7
ða beoð on stanes heardnysse 7 eac swylce hy togædere geclifigen,
7 hy beoð innan hole 7 ðonne þæt sæd þæron innan.

1. Wið þæt stanas on blædran wexen 7 wið þæt man gemigan ne
mæge genim of ðysum stanum fif penega gewihte, syle drincan on
10 wine, [hit] ða stanas tobrycð 7 ðone migþan forð gelædeþ.

CLXXXI.

Ðeos wyrt þe man staui(s)agria 7 oðrum naman (. . .) nemneð
hafað leaf swylce wingeard 7 rihte stelan, 7 heo hafað sæd on
grenum coddum on ðære mycele þe pysan, 7 þæt (b)yð þreohyrne 7
15 hyt byþ a(fo)r 7 sweart, byð swaþeah innan hwit 7 biterre on
byrgincge.

1. Wið þone yfelan wætan þæs lichaman genim þysse wyrte
sædes fiftyne corn gecnucude on liðan beore, syle drincan, hyt
f. 73v þone lichaman ðurh spiwðan afeormað; 7 æfter ðam / þe he ðone
20 dren(c g)edruncan (haf)að he sceal ga(n) 7 hyne (styr)ian ær ðam
þe (h)e hyne [aspiwe, 7 þonne he hine] (spi)wan onginneþ he
(s)ceal (ge)lomli(ce) liðne wætan beores (þi)cgean, ði læs seo
strengð þære wyrte þa goman bærne 7 forðylme.

2. Wið scruf 7 wið sceb genim þysse sylfan wyrte sæd 7 rosan,
25 cnuca t(ó)somne, lege to ðam (s)curfe, he byð gehæled.

MS V

1 title om. VBH.   2 litospermon] -spernion H   7 . . . sunnancorn]
om. H   sunnancorn] emended from sund'corn' (in later hand) V, space B 122v/
17a (see note).   4 maran . . . hafað] om. H   hehnysse] hyh- B.
5 meregrotu] -grotan H.   6 geclifigen] clifien H   10 hit] from B,
om. V   tobrycð] tobrytð H   migþan] migðan (ð alt. from a) H   gelædeþ]
alædeð B.   11 title om VBH.   12 stauisagria] stamsagria H
7 oðrum naman] om. H.   13 wingeard] w'i'ngeard H.   17 wætan] gl. flā
(= fluida?) H.   18 fiftyne] -tene BH.   19 7] om. H   ðam] þon
B 123/1a.   20 drenc] drænc (æ alt. from a) H 98/1   gedruncan]
gedruncen BH   hyne] om B.   21 aspiwe . . . hine] from B, om. V.
22 seo] o crowded in later V.   24 scruf] scurf BH   sceb] scæb B
þysse sylfan] þas ylcan H   7 rosan . . . sæd (p. 228/2)] om. H.

CLXXX *om.* O.

CLXXXI. Stauisagria   f. 39v/1

þeoþ wyrt þæt man stauisagria nemneð. þeos wyrt hafeð sæd on grene
codde þe micele seo pysan, 7 hi byð þreohyrne 7 afor, 7 hit byð sweart,
byð swaþeah inne hyit 7 byter on byrȝincge.   5

1. (Wyd þan ufele wates sæs lichames) Wið þan yfele wæte sæs licha-
mæs ním þisse wyrt sædes fiftíne corn ȝecnucode on liþe beorre, syle
drincan, hit þane lichama þur spyþan afearmað, 7 after þam þe he þane
drenc ȝedruncan habbe he seal gan 7 hine stíríen ar þan he híne aspywe,
7 þanne he híne aspiwe ongynne he sceal ȝelomlice liþne wæte beores 10
ðicȝean, þe læs seo strengþe dære wirt ȝoman bærne 7 forþylmíe.

2. (Ad scabiem et pruriginem) Wid scurf 7 wyþ seeb ním þisse wyrte
sæd 7 rosan, cnuca tosomne, leȝe to þan scurfe, he byð ȝehæled.

CLXXX. Herba litospermon   L f. 42/18

Foliis duplo maioribus quam ruta (. . .), et in earum cacuminibus
lapillos candore et rotunditate margaritarum, magnitudine ciceris, duritia
vere lapidea, ipsi (. . .) adhaereant, cavernulas habent et intus semen;
nascitur in Italia, sed laudatissimum in Creta (. . .).

1. Dragmae pondere pota in vino albo cauculos frangit pellique
constat, stranguiriam discutit.

CLXXXI. Herba stafisagria   A f. 70v/11

Folia habet veluti vitis agrestis, caules rectos mittit, semen in folliculis
viridibus habens in modum ciceris, trigonum, asperum, fuscum, intus
sane album, gustu amarum.

1. Eius grana xv cum aqua mulsa trita et pota corpus humoribus per
vomitum purgat, si post potum prius deambulet, quam vomat; in ipso
autem vomitu assidue aqua mulsa sorberi debet, ne vis herbae fauces
inurat et praefocet.

2. Praeterea semen ipsius tritum cum portulaca et oleo phthiriasin et
prurigines et scabiem sanat, si corporibus infricetur.

3. Wið toþa (sare) 7 toðreomena genim þysse ylc(a)n wyrte sæd, seoð on ecede, healde þonne on his muð of ðam ecede lange hwile, ðæra toða sár 7 ðæra toðreomena 7 ealle þæs muðes forrotudnyssa beoð gelacnude.

5 CLXXXII.

1. Ðeos wyrt ðe man gorgonion 7 oðrum (naman) (. . .) nemneþ byð ce(n)n(ed o)n diglon stowum (7 on wæto)n; be (þyss)e wyrte is sæd þæt hy(re) wyrttruma sy gea(nlicud þæ)re n(ædran) heafde ðe man g(or)gon nemneð, 7 ða telgran habbað, þæs ðe eac is sæd, 10 ægðer ge eagan ge nosa ge næddrena hiw.

Eac se wyrttruma gehwylcne man him geanlicað, hwilon of goldes hiwe, hwilon on seolfres, 7 þonne ðu þas wyrte mid hyre wyrttruman niman wylle, ðonne warna þu þæt hy na sunne bescine, ðy læs hyre hiw 7 hyre miht sy awend þurh ðære sunnan 15 beorhtnysse; forceorf hy þonne mid anum wogan 7 swyþe heardon iserne; 7 se þe hy ceorfan wylle, ðonne sy he fram awend; for ðy hit nys alyfed þæt man hyre wyrtruman ánwealhne ‘ge’seon mote. Se þe þas wyrte mid him hafað, æghwylce yfele fotswaðu him ongean cumende he forbugeþ; ge forðon se yfela man hyne for- 20 cyrreþ oððe him onbugeþ. /

f. 69(!) CLXXXIII.

1. Ðeos wyrt þe man milotis 7 oðrum naman (. . .) nemneð byð cenned on beganum stowum 7 on wætum; þas wyrte þu scealt niman on wanigendum monan, on ðam monþe þe man Augustus 25 hateð, genim þonne þone wyrttruman þysse wyrte 7 gewrið to anum hefelþræde 7 ahoh to ðinum swyran, þy geare ne ongitst

MS V

5 *title om.* VBH. 6 gorgonion] *id.* H (*erasure after first* g) 7 oðrum naman] *om.* H. 7 diglon] diglum BH wæton] wætum B 10 nosa] nosan B. 11 of] on B. 12 on] of BH. 13 na] nan H sunne] sunne ne BH. 15 forceorf] ceorf B, 7 forceorf H. 16 awend] gewænd H 99/4. 17 ánwealhne] anweahne H. 19 ongean cumende] ongeande H. 21 *title om.* VB, *for* H *see t.n.* 22 7 oðrum naman] *om.* H. 24 Augustus] Agustus B 123v/17a, H = B. 25 wyrttruman] wyrttruma H. 26 hefel- þræde] hefeld- BH swyran] sweorán H ongitst] ongist H.

MS O

8 ȝiare] a *alt. from* r ongitst] *between* on *and* gitst *erasure of four exp.* symbols.

3. —

CLXXXII *om.* O.

CLXXXIII. De herba que dicitur melotis   f. 23v/13

1. (Haec erba collo hominis filo suspensa seruat hominem a cecitate oculorum et a dolore neruorum) þeos wyrt þæt man milotis byð cenned on bean(um) (. . .) 7 on wætum; þeos wyrt þu scealt níme on waniȝende mona on Augustus monþe; nim þane þisse wyrt wyrtrume 7 ȝewyrþ to ane hefelbræde 7 ahoh to ðinum syran; þe ȝiare ne ongitst þu dimnysse

---

3. Si dentibus diu conteratur, humores deducit [et crebro] ipsum semen in aceto coquitur; ipso dentium dolores et vitia gingivarum, omnes oris dolores et putredines curantur.

CLXXXII. Herba gorgonion   W f. 64/1

1. Haec herba nascitur in locis secretis et humidis; radix eius dicitur gorgonis capite similaris, nam et colorem et nasum et serpentium figuram radicula eius habet.

Haec hominem vis, modo aurum, modo argentum, similem; ergo qui eam legunt solem posse faciunt ne splendore eius ad solem oculorum aciem vertit et sacrum factum eam falcato id est dure dare eam fano praecidunt adversi quia fas non radicem eius videre; hanc ergo qui secum habuerit quaecumque vestigia contravenienti diffugiente taliam idem partem homo maius sedavit ille.

CLXXXIII. (*See Note*)

þu dymnysse þinra eagena, oððe gif heo þe belimpeð heo hrædlice
geswiceð, 7 þu byst hal; þes læcecræft ys afandud.

2. Wið sina togunge genim þysse ylcan wyrte wos, smyre
þærmid, hy beoð geliðegude; eac ys be þysse wyrte sæd þæt heo
on geare twigea blowe.

CLXXXIV.

Ðeos wyrt þe man bulbus 7 oþrum naman (. . .) nemneþ ys
twegea cynna, þonne ys þeos read 7 wið þæs magan s(a)re
fremgendlic; þonne ys oðer byterre on byrgincge, seo ys scillodes
gecweden, eac þam magan nytlicre, ægþer hafað strang mægen, 7
hy to mete geþigede mycelon ðone lichaman gestrangiað.

1. Wiþ geswel 7 wið fotadle 7 wið gehwylce gederednyssa genim
þas wyrte sylfe gecnucude oððe mid hunige gemencgede, lege to
ðam sare þe man þonne beþurfe. /

2. Wið wæterseocnysse genim þas ylcan wyrte, swa we ær
cwædon, gecnucude, lege to þam innoðe; eac hy mid hunige
gecnucude hunda slitas gelacniað; 7 hy eac swylce mid pipere
[gemængede] 7 to gelede, hy þæs lichaman swat gewriðaþ; 7
eac swa some hy þæs magan sáre geliðigað.

3. Wið wundela þe þurh hy sylfe acennede beoð genim þyssa
wyrta wyrtruman gecnucude mid ele 7 mid hwætenan meluwe 7
mid sapan ðam gemete þe þu clyðan wyrce, lege to ðam wundum;
eac hyt áfeormaþ ðone leahtor þe Grecas hostopyturas hatað,

MS V

2 7] *om.* H þes] þæs ðæs H. 4 ys . . . sæd] is sæd be þisse
wyrte BH. 5 twigea] tuwa B, twiwa H. 6 *title om.* VBH.
7 7 oþrum naman] *om.* H 100/1. 9 fremgendlic] framgedlic H. byterre]
byte`r´re H. 10 mægen] gen H. 12 wið[1]] *om.* H gedered-
nyssa] gedreced- B, gegaderunge H. 13 lege] le H. 15 ylcan] *om.* H.
16 gecnucude] gecnude H. 17 gelacniað] gelacnað H. 18 gemængede]
from B 124/2a, gencgede V. 19 sáre] sar BH. 20–1 þyssa wyrta] þisse
wirte BH. 21 hwætenan] hwætenum B. 21–2 hwætenan . . . mid] *om.* H.

MS O

4 ʒeþegode] ʒe god þegode (god *exp.*) heo] an heo (an *exp.*). 7 on
byrʒínc] *these words also in b.m.* 8 mæʒan] maʒen mæʒan (*first word*
exp., *third letter alt. from* t) micelon] micelon / celon (*second* celon *exp.*).
17 wundun] wundundû (dû *exp.*). 18 `7 eac´] *these words in o.m.*, 7 eac
(*exp.*) *in text.*

on þinum eæʒe; ʒyf heo þe límpeð heo hrædlice ʒeswyceþ, 7 þu byst hal; þes læcecræft hís afondon.

2. Wið syna toʒunge ním þisse wyrte wos, smure þærmíd; hi beoð ʒeþegode. Eac ys sæd be þisse wyrt þæt heo on ʒeare twigea boge.

CLXXXIV. De bulbo f. 8v/28

þeos wyrt þe man bubbus nemneð is twera cynna; þanne is þe oðer 6
bitere on byrʒínc, / seo is scillodes ʒecweþen; eac þam maʒan nytlicˋrˊe, f. 10(!)
æʒþer hafeð strang mæʒan; 7 hi to mete ʒeþiʒede micelon ðane lichaman
ʒestrangiað.

1. (Contra inflaturam et apost(ema) et dolores pedum et omnes malas 10
collectiones) Wið ʒeˋsˊwel 7 wið fotadle 7 wið ʒegæderednyssæ ʒením
þeos wyrt sylfe ʒecnucode oðe mid huníʒe ʒemegged, leʒe to ðan sare þe
man ðonne beþurfe.

2. —

3. (Contra scabiem) Wið wundela þe þurþ he suffe acennede beoð 15
cnuc þisse wyrte wurtruma mid ele 7 mid fætune meluwe 7 mid sapan
þan ʒemete þe þu clyþam wyrce, leʒe to þam wundun. Eac heo afeormað
þane leahtor ða Grecas hostopituras hætað, þat is scurf þas heafdes, ˋ7 eacˊ

CLXXXIV. Herba bulbus rufus A f. 71v/21

Stomacho convenit; est et alter gusto amaro, qui scillodes vocatur, et utilior est stomacho; utrique virtutem habent thermanticam (. . .); esca huiuscemodi magna corporis (. . .).

1. Trita vel sola [vel] cum melle luxationes, podagram vel læsuras aliquas (. . .) apposita curat.

2. Hydropicorum etiam ventri superponitur, morsibus etiam canum cum melle trita medetur; cum pipere mixta præcordiis admota sudorem restringit, dolores etiam stomachi sedat.

3. Cum nitro asso trita pytiras id est furfures capitis et achoras, id

þæt ys scurf þæs heafdes, 7 eac þone þe hy achoras nemnað, þæt ys
sceb se foroft þæt heafod fexe bereafað; eæc swylce mid ecede oððe
mid hunige gecnucude hy of þam andwlitan nebcorn afeormaþ.

4. Eac swa some on ecede geþigede hy þæra innoða [toþun-
5 dennesse] 7 toborstennysse gehæleð.

Be þysse wyrte ys sæd þæt heo of dracan blode acenned beon
sceolde on ufeweardum muntum on þiccon bearwum.

CLXXXV. [Cucurbita]

Ðeos wyrt þe man colocynthisagria, þæt ys cucurbita agrestis
10 þe man eac frigillam nemneþ, heo ealswa oðer cyrfætte wið þa
eorðann hyre telgran tobrædeþ, 7 [heo] hafað leaf cucumere
gelice 7 toslitene, 7 heo hafaþ wæstm sinewealtne 7 byterne, se ys
to nymenne to þam timan þonne he æfter his grennysse fealwað.

1. Wið innoðes astyrunge genim þyses wæstmes hnescnysse
15 innewearde butan þam cyrnlun twegea penega gewihte on liðan
beore gecnucude, syle drincan, hyt astyreþ þone innoð.

MS V

1 achoras] a'c'horas H.   2 sceb] scæb B   eæc] eac B, eác H 101/2.
3 hunige] hunig B   andwlitan] anwlitan H.   4–5 toþundennesse] *from* B,
toðunnysse V.   7 ufeweardum] ufonweardon H   on] 7 on H.   8 *title*:
from B, *om.* VH.   9 man] ma B   colocynthisagria] colocythi sagria H.
10 þe] þa BH   frigillam] frigillum H   cyrfætte] cyrfette BH.   11 eorðann]
eorðan BH   telgran] telgra B   tobrædeþ] tobredeð B   heo] *from* B, he V.
12 sinewealtne] -wealne H.   13 nymenne] nímene H.   15 cyrnlun]
cyrnlum H.

MS O

3 anwiten] a *alt. from* n.   4 ȝeþiȝede] þ *alt. from* ȝ.

þane þe hi achoras nemneð, þæt is sceb se foroft þæt heafod wexe
bereafaþ, eac sylce mid ecede oðöer mid huníȝe ȝecnucode hi of þa
anwiten nebcorn afeormað.

4. Eac swa same on ecede ȝeþiȝede hy þara innoþa toþundenysse 7
tobor`s´tennysse ȝehæleð.   5

Bi þisse wyrt is sæd þæt heo of dracan blode acenned beon sceolde on
uwe`a´rden mute on þiccen bærwum.

CLXXXV *om.* O.

---

est scabiem quae caput capillo despoliat, abstergent; cum melle lentigines e facie purgant (. . .).

4. Cum aceto comesta internorum viscerum vel tensuras vel ruptiones
sanat.

(*Last sentence not in Latin*)

CLXXXV. Herba colocintiosagria   A f. 72v/15

[Colocintisagria], id est cucurbita agrestis, quam Afri gelilam vocant
et similiter ut cucumis vel cucurbita per terram flagella tendit, folia habens
cucumeris similia et scissa, fructum habet rotundum (. . .), amarum,
qui eo tempore colligendus est quo ex viriditate pallescit.

1. Huius intestina mollities a semine separata, tertia parte dragmae, id
est scripulo uno, cum aqua mulsa trita et hausta ventrem deducit (. . .).

I.

1. SAGAÐ ÐÆT ÆGYPta cyning, Idpartus wæs haten,
Octauiano þam casere his freonde hælo bodade þyssum wordum
þus cweðende: Monegum bisenum ic eom gewis þinra mægena
5 7 snytro, 7 hwæþere ic wene þæt þu næfre to ðus mycles mægnes
læcedomum become swylcum swa ic gefregn ða we fram Æscolupio
ferdon. Ic þæt þa for ðinre cyððe 7 þe weorðne wiste þyses to
gewitanne, þæt ys be wylddeora læcecræftum, swa þæt wel gesæd ys.

2. Sum fyþerfete nyten is þæt we nemnað taxonem, þæt ys broc
10 on Englisc. Gefoh þæt deor 7 him þonne of cwicum þa téþ ádó þa
þe he mæste hæbbe 7 þus cweð: On naman þæs ælmihtigan Godes
ic þe ofslea 7 þe þine teþ of abeate; 7 þonne hy syððan on linenum
hrægle bewind, 7 on golde oþþe on seolfre bewyrc, þæt hio ne
mægen þinum lice æthrinan. Hafa mid þe, ðonne ne sceþþeð
15 þe ne tungol ne hagol ne strang st'o'rm né yfel man ne wolberendes
áwiht; ne þe æniges yfeles onhrine dereþ; oððe gyf hwæt yfeles
bið, hraþe hyt byð tosliten, swa wæs Abdias gyrdels þæs witegan.

3. Nim þonne þone swyþran fot þone furðran ðissum wordum
7 þus cweþ: On naman þæs lifigendan Godes ic þe nime to læce-
20 dome. þonne on swa hwylcum geflite oððe gefeohte swa ðu bist
sigefæst; 7 þu þæt gedigest gif þu ðone fot mid þe hafast.

MS V

1 title om. VBH.   2 SAGAÐ] 'her' SAG'A'Ð H 101v/15   ÆGYP/ta]
ÆGYPTA B 124v/2a, EGYPta H.   4 Monegum] Mongum B.   6 swylcum
swa] swylce H 102/8   gefregn] gefreng B, gefrægn H.   8 wyld-
deora] wyldeora B, willddeora H.   10 ádó] of ado B.   11 þæs
ælmihtigan Godes] ælmihtiges G'od'es H.   12 ofslea] of aslea B   syððan]
sy'ð'þan H.   13 hrægle] claðe H   bewind . . . golde] om. H   hio] hi B.
14 mægen] magon B   ne] 'ne' H   sceþþeð] scæððeð B.   16 þe]
þ'e' H   onhrine] onryne B, anryne H   dereþ] ne dereþ H   gyf] gif
þe H.   20–1 bist sigefæst] bist 'symle' sygefæ'st' H 103/4.

MS O

3 bysnum] bysnum bysnum (first word stained and exp.).   7 fuferfete]
Sum fuferfete / Sum nyten ys (first two words struck out and first Sum also exp.).
10 on linnenon hræȝele] gl. in lineo panno.   12 tungol] tungo / tungol
(tungo exp.), gl. tonitrum.   13 ne yfel man] gl. videlicet malus homo.
15 furþran] for furþran (for exp.).

I.

1. þe Egypta ʽkingʼ þe Idpartus wæs hatan Octauiano þan casere hys
frunde hælo bodede þis wordum þus cweþende: Mæneȝa bysnum ic eom
ȝewysȝra 7 læcedomes 7 become on þusse we fram Æscolupio ferdon.
Ic þæt þa for þinre cyððe 7 þe wurde wyste þis to ȝewitenne, þæt is be 5
wyldeora læcecræftef.

2. Sum [fuferfete] nyten ys þæt man nemned taxonem, þæt ys brocc
on Englis. Gefoh þat deor 7 him of cwicun þa teþ ado þa þe he mæste
habban, 7 þus cweð: On nama þæs ælmihtiȝon Godes ic þe ofslean 7
þe þine teþ of abeʽaʹte. 7 þanne hy siþþan on linnenon hræȝele biwind, 10
7 on golde oþþer on seolfre bewyrc, þæt hy ne mæȝen þine lice æthrínan.
Hafe hy mid þe, þanne ne sceþþes þe ne tungol ne haȝol ne strang storm
ne yfel man ne wolberende awyt; ne þe aniȝes yfeles onhríne dered;
oþþer ȝir hwæt yfeles byd tosliten swa / wæs Abbias gyrdels þæs witigan.

3. Nim þanne þane swyrðanan fot ðone furþran þissun worde 7 þus 15
cwed: On nama þas leuíende Godes ic þe níme to lacedome. þanne on
ȝehwylce ȝeflíte oþþer ȝefeohte swa þu byst sylefæst; 7 þu þæt ȝediȝest,
ȝif þu þane fot mid þe hafast.

MS L

I. De taxone [quem Latini melem dicunt]

1. Idpartus rex Aegyptiorum Octavio suo salutem. Plurimis exemplis
experti sumus virtutes tuas et prudentiam, et tamen arbitror numquam
incidisse tantae virtutis remedium quod ab Escolapio quoque expergimus
nostrum expertus sum. Igitur industriae tuae cognationis dignum iudi-
cavi bestiam quadrupedem quam nos taxonem appellamus, quidam etiam
[melem] dicunt.

2. Hunc apprehendis et vivo dentes exime quos maximos habuerit et
ita dicis: In nomine Omnipotentis decollo te; et dentes pertundes; et de
lino brachium ligabis in auro aut in argento sicut corpus tangat; ita neque
sidus neque caniculae [aut] tempestas neque homo malus neque pesti-
lentiae neque incursus mali [tibi] nocere poterunt; aut si quid fuerit mali,
statim disrumpitur sicut sonum audias.

3. Pedem quoque eius dextrum priorem [his] verbis tollis: In nomine
Dei [vivi] tollo te ad remedium; et in quacumque contentione vel in
pugna fueris, victor evadis, dum pedem eius tecum habes.

4. Mid his gelynde smyre þa hors þa þe syn on feofre oþþe on
ænigre adle, hio him fram ahyldeþ 7 lifes tid him ofer byð; 7
þeah hyt mycel adl sy, hraþe heo onweg gewiteþ. /

f. 75v   5. Meng hys blod wyþ lytlum sealte horsum 7 mulum 7
5   ælcum fiþerfetum neate þe on wole winnen oþþe on ænigum
yfle, do þurh horn on muð æfter þæs deores mihte, 7 efne ymb
þreo niht hy beoð hale.

6. His brægen geseoð on þrim sestrum eles on niwon croccan
oðþæt þrydda dæl sy bewe'a'llen, fætelsa 7 heald hyt. Gif h'w'a
10   sy on heafodwræce, æfter bæþe smyre mid on þrim nyhtum, he
byð gehæled, 7 swa eac þa fet; 7 þeah man sy on hwylcre
ungewendendlicre adle 7 unhalwendlicre, seo wise hine hæleð 7
lacnað.

7. Nim his lifre, todæl, 7 [bedelf] æt þam ymbhwyrftum þinra
15   landgemæra 7 þinra burhstaðola, 7 þa heortan æt þinum burh-
geatum behele; þonne þu 7 þine beoð alysde hale to feranne 7 ham
to cyrrenne, eall wol byþ aweg astyred; 7 þæt ær gedon wæs naht
sceþþeð; 7 byþ lytel frecne fram fyre.

8. Cuþ ys eac þæt his hyd is bryce hundum 7 eallum fiþerfetum
20   nytenum wið woles gewinne on to donne. Hafa þære [hyde]
fellsticceo on þinum sceon; ne gefelest þu gewin on þinum fotu(m).

9. Ðu halgusta casere, ic wille þæt ðu gelyfe þæt þis wilddeor
well fremað, gif þu þinum clænsungdagum, þær þu færest geond
eorðan ymbhwyrft, hys flæsc gesoden etest 7 þigest, hyt byþ god þe
25   7 þinum weorudum.

MS V

1 feofre] fefore B.   3 hraþe] hr'a'eðe H.   5 winnen] wunien H.
6 7] *om.* H.   8 sestrum] systres B   niwon] niwum B.   10 mid . . .
nyhtum] mid oþrum nihterne H.   12 ungewendendlicre] ungewended- H
unhalwendlicre] unhalwænd- H.   14 bedelf] *from* B, bedealf V.
15 heortan] heorte B 125/8a.   16 behele] behela B   feranne] farenne B.
18 sceþþeð] scæððeð BH   frecne] fræcne BH   fyre] fere H 104/7.   19 is
bryce] 'i's H   eallum] ealdum H.   20 nytenum] ny't'enum H   hyde]
from B, *om.* V.   21 fellsticceo] felstticce B, fell sticced H.   22 wilddeor]
wildeor BH.   23 færest] ferest H.   24 flæsc] flæs B   hyt] 7 hit H.
25 weorudum] werudum B, weorudum till H.

MS O

6 æfter] æf æfter (æf *stained and exp.*)   efne embe] efne a embe (a *exp.*).
17 ys brice] ys byi brice (byi *struck out and underlined*).

4. Mid his ȝelynde smure ða hors þe sinde on fefore oþþer on æníȝe
adle; heo fram ahyldeþ 7 life`s´ tyd hym ofer byð; 7 þeah hit mícel adle
sy raðe heo aweȝ ȝewyteþ.

5. Meng his blod wið litel sealte horsa 7 mule 7 alcen fuwerfæte
neate þe on wole winnon oþþer on æniȝun yfele; do ðurh horn on muþe   5
æfter þas deores mihte; 7 efne embe ðreo niht hy beoð hæle.

6. His braȝen ȝeseoð on þrym sestrum eles on níwen croccen to ðat
þryddan dæl si bewealled; fætelsa 7 heald hyt. Gif hwa si on heafodwræce, æfter baðe smyre mid þam on þrym nyhtum, he byð ȝehæled,
eac þa fet. 7 þeah man sy on hwylcere unȝewendedlicre adle 7 unhal-   10
wenlicre, seo wysa hyne hæleð 7 læcned.

7. Ním hys lifre 7 todæl 7 bedelf æt þan ymbhwyrftum línra land-
ȝemare æt / þínun burhstaþela; 7 þe heortan æt ðínum burgatun behele;   f. 45v
þanne þu 7 þíne beoð alisede hale to ȝefarenne 7 hale to cumende; eal
wol byð areȝ 7 astyred; 7 þæt ær ȝedon wæs naht ne sceþþes; 7 byð litel   15
frecne fram fyre.

8. Cuþ eac þæt his hid ys brice hundun 7 eallum fuwerfæte nítennum
wid woles ȝewínne `on´ to donne. Hafa hara hyde fel sacceo on þínum
seon; ne ȝefelest þu ȝewín þine fotun.

9. Ðu halgusta casere, ic wylle þæt þu ȝelífe þæt þis wyldeor wel   20
fremeð, ȝif þine clænsungdæȝes, þar þu fæst ȝeond eorþan embehwyrft,
his flæsc ȝesoden etest 7 þiȝest, hyt byd god þe 7 þíne weredun till.

MS L

4. Adipe quoque eius equum aegrum perungues, statim ei febres
declinant, dumtaxat sibi vita superest (. . .); quod si maior morbus fuerit,
celerius recedit.

5. Et sanguinem cum sale minuto commixtum equis et mulabus et
quaecumque quadrupedia videbuntur pestilentia laborare per triduum
per cornum deicito, prout fuerit magnitudo pecorum.

6. Cerebrum eius coque in oleo sestariis iii in olla rude, donec tertia
pars decoxerit, reliquum percola. Et si quis capitis dolore vel pedum
vexatur, caput a balneo curet per triduum, idem et pedes emendabis;
etiam comitiali morbo laborantes, et quod insanabile videtur, remediabit.

7. Item iocinera eius circa fines orbis tuae aut circa fundus obrues
secundum terminos; ceteram autem partem iocineris et cor ad portam
obrues qua tui ire et redire solent; omnis pestilentia amota erit, etiam
[quod] factum erat nihil nocebit; etiam ab igne minus erit periculum.

8. Item quod omnibus notum est pellem eius circumdari canibus ne
pestilentia laborent; etiam omnibus quadrupedibus proderit. Ex ea
pelle pellicula in calceis habeto, pedibus non laborabis.

9. Volo credas, sacratissime imperator, hunc bestiolum prodesse si
castimonialis diebus usus fueris; carnem eius quoque, ex eo orbem tuum
lustrabis et exercitibus proderis.

10. Gif hwam hwæt yfeles gedon bið, þæt he ne mæge hys wynlusta brucan, seoðe þonne his sceallan on yrnendum wylle-wætere 7 on hunige, 7 ðicge þonne fæstende þry dagas, sona he bið gebeted.

5   II.

1. Wið blodes flewsan, þonne eallum mannum sy seofontyne nihta eald mona, æfter sunnan setlgange ær monan upryne cyme to þam treowe þe man hateþ morbeam, 7 of ðam nim æppel mid þinre wynstran handa, mid twam fingrum, þæt is mid þuman 7
10 mid hringfingre, hwitne æppel þe þonne gyt ne readige, ahefe hyne þonne upp, 7 upp aris, he bið brice to þam uferan dæle þæs lichaman. Eft do hyne adune 7 onlut, he bið behefe to ðam neoð-ran dæle þæs lichoman. Ær ðon þu þysne æppel nime, cweð
f. 76 þonne þas word: Aps, aps, aps, / sparare rose prospasam emor-
15 ragiam pantosani opum æmesstanes. þonne þu þas word gecweden hæbbe genim þone æppel 7 hine þonne bewind on weolcreadum godwebbe 7 seoð þonne eft mid sceate oþres godwebbes, 7 beheald þæt þes læcedom ne hrine ne wæteres ne eorðan. þonne neadþearf sy 7 se ufera dæl 'þæs' lichoman on ænigum sare oððe
20 on earfeþum geswince, wrið on þone andwlitan, gyf hyt sy on þam neoðran dæle, wrið on þa wambe.

2. Wið wifes flewsan, genim þone camb þe heo ana hyre heafod mid cemde, 7 nænig man ær mid cemde ne æfter cembe. Under ðam treowe morbeame cembe þær hyre feax, þæt þær on þam
25 cambe geþolige, gesomnige, 7 aho on up standende twig þæs

MS V

5 *title om.* VBH.   9 mid twam] 7 mid twam H 105/2   þuman] his þuman H.   10 hringfingre] his hringfingre H.   11 þæs] 'to' þam H. 12–13 neoðran] nyðeran B, næoðeran H.   13 Ær ðon] Er þonne H   þysne] sysne H.   15 æmes/stanes] æmestanes B, æmestates H   þonne] þon H. 16 weolcreadum] wolc- BH.   17 sceate] s'c'eate H.   18 þes] ðæs H hrine] othrine H.   19 ufera] yfera H.   20 earfeþum] ea'r'feþum H gyf] gis H.   21 neoðran] nyþeran B.   22 flewsan] flew/'san' H. 23 nænig] mænig H   cembe] cæmde B 125v/1a.

MS O

9 byþ bryce] byþ by bryce (by *struck out and exp.*).   21 aho on] aho u(p) on (*second word exp.*).

10. Gif hwam hwæt hifeles ȝedon byð, þæt he ne maȝe his wiflusta brucan, seoðe þanne his sceallan on hyrnende willewætera 7 on huníȝe, 7 þícȝe þanne fæstende þri dæȝes; sona he byð ȝebeted.

II.

1. Wid blodes flewsan, þanne mona sy seofontyne nyhta eald, æfter 5 sunna setlgange, ær mona upryne cume, þanne cume to þan treowe þa man hætað morbeam, 7 of þan ním æppel mid þinre wynstran handa, mid twam fingran, þæt ys mid þuman 7 mid hríngfingrum hwítne æppel þe þanne ȝyt ne readíȝe. Ahefe hyne þanne upp, 7 up arís; he byþ bryce to þan uferan dæle þæs lichaman. Eft do híne ætdun 7 onlut; he byð behefe 10 to ðan nyþeran dæle þas lichaman. Ær þan þu þisne æppel nyme, cweþ þane þus word: Ic níme þe et cetera. / Ðane þu þas word ȝecweden f. 46 habbe, ȝením þane æppel 7 hyne ȝewínd on 'seolc' readum godewebbe, 7 loca þæt þes laecedon ne hrine wæteres ne eorþan. þanne neadþearf sy 7 se ufera dæl þæs lichamas on æniȝun sare oþþer on ærfodum ȝeswince, 15 wyrþ 'on' þane anwlitan. Gif hyt si on þan nyþeran dæle, wriþ on þa wambe.

2. (Ad fluxum mulieris) Wið wifef flewsan níme þane comb þa heo ane hyre heafad míd cembe 7 na mare ær mid cemde ne after mid ne cembde. Æt under þan treowe morbeame cembe þær hyre fex þat þar on 20 þan combe ȝeþoliȝe, ȝesomne 7 aho on up standende twi þæs morbeames;

MS L

10. Item si quid malefactum fuerit et non potuerit rebus veneriis uti, testiculum eius in melle coquat et ex aqua fontana quae sit perennis et ieiunus per triduum edat, emendabit.

II. [De moro]

1. Ad profluvium sanguinis: omni homini luna septimadecima post occasum solis ante ortum lunae venis ad arborem mori et ex ea pomum tollis manu sinistra digitis pollice et anulari, pomum autem album quod necdum coepit rubescere; elatum quidem et susum versus resurges; ad superiorem partem corporis profuturum. Demersum vero et declinatum, ad inferiorem partem corporis necessarium. Hoc autem pomum tenes digitis suprascriptis, antequam departas dicis ter verba haec: Aps, aps, aps, rar eroseprospasane, moragian pontosani Hopum aemestanes. Haec f. 18v verba cum dixeris auferis pomum, et cum abstuleris involvis cocco galatico, atque idem coctum involvis infinitio et ligabis lino vere purpureo; observabis autem ne hoc remedium aqua tangat aut terra; alligabis cum necesse fuerit, si superior pars laboraverit in fronte ligabis, si inferior in [ventre].

2. Ad profluvium mulieris, de pectine unde sola pectinat capillos suos ita ut nulla pectinaverit ante eam nec post eam pectinet; sub arbore mori pectinentur ei capilli, qui [adhaeserint] in pectine collecti in ramum

morbeames, 7 eft ymb hwyle clæne him to gesomnige 7 gehealde, þæt hyre bið læcedom þære ðe hyre heafod þær cembeþ.

3. Eft gif heo wylle þæt ðæt hyre blodryne cyme to, cembe eft hyre heafod under morbeame, 7 þæt feax þe on þam cambe
5 cleofige, somnige 7 do on anne telgran ðe sy adune gecyrred, 7 gesamnige eft, þæt hyre byþ læcedom.

4. Gyf ðu wylle þæt wif sy geclænsod þe næfre mihte clene beon, wyrc hyre sealfe of þam feaxe, 7 hit æthwego adrig, 7 do ón hyre lic, þonne byþ heo geclænsod.

10 III.

1. Wiþ nædran slite heortes horn hafað mægen ælcne wætan to adrigenne; for þam his man bruceþ on eagsealfe.

2. Wiþ heafodsare heortes hornes axan fif penega gewæge drinc, nim anne sester wines 7 twegen wæteres, nim þæs æghwylce
15 dæge scen`c´ fulne 7 drince, þes drenc eac wambe sar gehaþerað.

3. Wiþ toþa wagunge heortes horn gebærned 7 gecnucod þa teð getrymeþ, gif his man wislice bruceð. /

f. 76v   4. Wið wifes flewsan heortes horn to duste gebeaten 7 drince on wine, sona him byþ sel.

20 5. Wið wyrmas to cwellenne heortes horn gebærnedne drince on hatum wætere, þa wyrmas he ácwelleð 7 út aweorpeþ.

MS V

1 7¹] om. H 106/6.   2 cembeþ] cæm H.   5 cleofige] clyfige B
somnige] som H.   6 gesamnige] gesanige H.   7 clene] clæne BH.
10 title om. VBH.   12 eagsealfe] æg- H.   14 sester] ses/ster H.
15 þes] þæs H.   18 7] om. H 107/6.   19 him] hyre B.   20 cwel-
lenne] acwellenne H.   21 aweorpeþ] awyrpeð B.

MS O

13 dæʒ] dæʒ dæʒ (first word exp.).   19 acwellaþ] followed by a and one other
symbol, underlined and exp.

7 eft embe hwile clane hím to ȝesomne 7 ȝehealde; þæt hyre byþ læcedom
þare þe hyre heafod þare cembeð.

3. —

4. Gif þu wylle þæt wif ȝeclansod sy þe næfre ne mihte clansod byon,
wyrc hyre sealfe of þan fexe 7 hyt æthweȝa adriȝ, 7 do on hyre lic; þanne 5
byð heo ȝeclænsod.

III. Medicina de cervo

1. (Contra serpentes et contra omnem humorem aquaticum) Wyþ
nærdran slite h`e´ortes horn hæfeð mæȝen 7 eac ælcne wætan to adriȝenne;
for þan man hys bruced on eahsylfe.   10

2. (Ad dolorem capitis) Wið heafod/sare heortes hornes axan fif f. 46v
peniȝe ȝewæȝe drinc mid ane sester wines 7 tweȝen wæteres; ním ðæs
æȝhylce dæȝ scenc fulne 7 drince; þes drenc eac wambe sar ȝehaþeraþ.

3. Wið toþa waȝuga hortes horn ȝebarned 7 ȝecnucad þa teþ ȝetrymeð
ȝif his man wislice brucad.   15

4. Wið wifes flesan heortes horn to duste ȝebeaten 7 ȝedrucan on wine,
sona hym byð sel.

5. Wið wyrmas to acwellen hortes horn ȝebernede drinc on haten
watere; þa wurmas he acwellaþ 7 ut awyrfþ.

MS L

arboris ipsius mori qui [sursum] versus respicit erectus, legentur eidem
ramo ab ea quae pectinabit caput eius et remediat.

3. Rursum si voluerit ut eidem veniat sanguis, similiter sub arbore
mori pectinet capillos et purgamenta capillorum legat in ramo qui deor-
sum versus respicit et remediasti.

4. Ut mulier purgetur quae numquam potuerat purgari, porrum terat
et ex [eo] collirium faciat et modice subsiccet et [mittat] sibi in corpus,
purgabitur.

III. De cervo

1. Ad omnes homines: cornus cervinus habet vim omnes humores
siccandi, et ideo ex eo in colliriis ocularibus utuntur.

2. Ad capitis dolorem cinerem corni cervini dragmam i cum vini
sextario et aquae duobus bibat; etiam et ventris dolorem arcet.

3. Dentes si laxi fuerint, cornus combustus tritus dentes qui moventur
confirmat, si ex eo pro dentifrictio utatur.

4. Ad profluvium mulieris cornus cervinus tunsus, cum vino mixto
bibat, sanabitur.

5. Ad lumbricos necandos cornus cervinus combustus, in aqua calida
bibat, lumbricos necat et eiciet.

6. Nædran eac to acwellanne nim þæs hornes acxan 7 stred þær
hi syn, hi fleoð sona onweg.

7. Wið wifa earfodnyssum, þas uncyste Grecas hataŏ hystem
cepnizam, heortes hornes þæs smælestan dustes bruce þry dagas
5 on wines drince, gif he fefor'i'g sy drince þonne on wearmum
wætere, þæt bið god læcecræft.

8. Wiþ miltan sare heortes horn gebærnedne þicge on geswettum drince; he þa miltan adrigeð 7 þæt sar onweg afyrreþ.

9. Wið teter heortes horn gebærnedne meng wið eced, smyre
10 mid þam, hrædlice him cymeþ bot.

10. Eft wið teter of andwlitan tó donne heortes horn gebærnedne
meng wið ele, smyre, 7 þonne þæt bedrugud sy, eft þu hit geniwa;
do þis on sunnan upgange, hrædlice hit hæleþ.

11. Eft wið þam ylcan heortes horn gebærnedne nigon penega
15 gewæge do þærtó 7 geswyrfes of seolfre syx peninga gewæge;
gemeng 7 gegnid swiþe wel, 7 gewyrc to clyþan 7 smyre mid, hyt
hæleþ wel þæt sár.

12. Wið cyrnlu, patella, þæt ys heortes heagospind, gif þu
hafast mid þe, né arisað þe cyrnlu, 7 þa þe ǽr arison, mid hys
20 æthrine hy onweg gewitað.

13. Wifgemanan tó aweccanne nim heortes sceallan, dryg, wyrc
to duste, dó hys dæl on wines drinc; þæt awecceþ wifgemanan
lust.

[14. Wið þæt ilce nim heortes scytel 7 cnoca to duste, do on
25 wines drync, hit hæleð þæt ilce.]

MS V

1 acxan] axan BH.   3 earfodnyssum] earfoð- BH   hystem] hystæm H.
4 cepnizam] cepnizan BH.   6 þæt] hyt H.   7–8 geswettum]
geswættum H.   8 afyrreþ] gefyrreð B.   9 horn] hor H.   10 mid
þam] ðærmid H.   12 7] om. H   bedrugud] bedruncen B 126/4a.
15 geswyrfes] geswearfes B,   gl. litargirum H.   16 gemeng] gemæcg B
gegnid] gnid B.   18, 19 cyrnlu] cyrulu H 108/7, 10.   22 awecceþ]
aweceð H.   24–5 from B, om. V.   25 hæleð] 'hæ'læð H.

MS O

1 Nædran] Næ / Nædran (first Næ struck out).   4 ʒebærnede] ʒe brand br
bærnede (bra exp., nd br underlined).   9 bedruwod] bedrupod / druwod
eft] est eft (est exp.).   13 on] one on (one underlined).   14 wifʒemanen]
preceded by exp. s.

6. Nædran eac to acwellannením þas hornes axan 7 stred þar hi sínde;
hy fleoþ sona aweз.

7. —

8. Wið miltan sare hortes horn зebærnede þícзe on swete drence; he
þa míltan adriзed 7 þat sar onweз afyrred.   5

9. Wið teter hortes horn зebærned meng wið ecede, smíre mid þan,
hrædlice hym cymed bot.

10. Eft wið teter of anwlitan to do heortes horn зebærnedne meng
wið ele 7 smíre; þanne þæt bedruwod si, eft þu hyt зenywa; / do þis ar f. 47
sunnan upgange, hradlice hyt hæled.   10

11, 12. —

13. (Ad libidinem excitandam) Wið зemanan to aweccenne ním heortes
sceallen, driз, wyrc to duste, do his dæl on wínes drinc, þæt awecceð
wifзemanen lust.

14. (Item ad idem) Wið þæt ylce ním heortes scytel 7 cnuca to duste, 15
do on wínes drinc, hit haleð þat ylce.

MS L

6. Ad serpentes necandos cornum cervinum combure ubi fuerint f. 19
serpentes, effugat eas.

7. Mulier si a vulva offocatur, quod [nequissimum] vitium Graece
hystem cepnizan dicitur, corni cervini pulverem per triduum pulveri
potui cum vino dato, si febricitat in aqua calida, miraberis effectum.

8. Ad splenis dolorem (. . .) cornum cervinum combustum, et ex oximelli datur potui, splenem siccat et dolorem tollit.

9. Ad impetigines sanandos cornum cervinum combustum, cum aceto
tritum, mirifice sanat.

10. Ad impetigines de facie tollendas cornum cervinum combustum,
in sole faciem line et detersa, subinde renova, sed hoc sub ortu solis facias,
mire sanat.

11. Ad tetriginum dolores cornum cervinum combustum dragmas iii,
adiecta spuma argenti dragmas ii, et ceroto macerato mixtum, intertrigines dolentes mire sanat.

12. Ad inguina quae exeunt et surgunt, patella cervina, hoc est genu,
si tecum habeas, non surgunt inguina, et qui ante surrexerunt eadem
tacta recedunt.

13. Ad concubitum excitandum testiculum cervinum siccum, aliquam
partem potui cum vino dato, tritum, concubitum excitat.

14. Item moium eius tritum et potui sumptum idem facit ad quod
supra.

15. Wið nædran bite heortes gecyndlimu drig to duste 7 gedo rosan dust þærto þreora peninga gewæge on drince 7 þicge on dæge, scearplice se drenc hæleþ nædran bite.

16. Wið stede 7 for gebinde heortes hǽr beoð swiðe gode mid to smeocanne wifmannum. /

17. Wið wifes geeacnunge ban bið funden on heortes heortan, hwilum on hrife, þæt (y)lce hyt gegearwað; gif ðu þæt bán on wif-mannes earm ahehst, gewriðest scea`r´plice, hræþe heo geeacnað.

18. Wið innoþa wræce 7 gif gebind men byþ, heortes mearh gemylted syle him on wearmum wætere, hrædlice hyt hæleþ.

19. Wið nædrena afligenge heortes mearh gebærned oðþæt hyt smeoce oþþe þu hit mid þe hæbbe, hit afligeþ ða nædran.

20. Wið laðum lælum 7 wommum heortes smeoro gemylted 7 mid [ostorscillum] gecnucud 7 gemenged 7 to sealfe gedon 7 on geseted, wundorlice hyt hæleþ.

IV.

1. Wið wifa earfoðnyssum þe on heora inwerdlicum stowum earfeþu þrowiað, foxes leoþu 7 his smeoru mid ealdon ele 7 mid tyrwan wyrc him to sealfe, do on wifa stowe, hraþe hit þa earfeþu gehæleþ.

2. Wið heafodsare, þam gelice þe hyt her bufan gecweden ys, smyre þæt heafod, hyt hæleþ wundorlice.

3. Wið earena sare, eft gelice þon þe her bufan gecweden is, genim þa ylcan sealfe hluttre, drype on þæt eare, wundorlice hyt hæleþ.

MS V

1 gecyndlimu] -leomo H.   3 dæge] dæge 7 H.   5 smeocanne]
smeo`can/ne´ H.   7 hwilum] whilum H   þæt ylce] þylce H.
8 ahehst] ahohst H   hræþe] hraðe BH   geeacnað] getacnað H 109/2.
9 gif] om. H.   11 nædrena] nædran H   mearh] mearg H.
13 wommum] wonnum H   gemylted] gemyl H.   14 ostorscillum]
from B, stor- V.   15 geseted] gesette H.   16 title om. VBH.
17 heora] hyra B 126/6a   inwerdlicum] inweard- H.   18 leoþu] liðu H.
19 þa] om. B.   21 gecweden ys] cweð H.   23 þon] om. H.

MS O

2 in addition to title De Vulpe in o.m.

15–20. —

IV. Medicina de vulpe

1. Wið wifa earfodnyssa þe on hure inwerdlicum stowum earfeðu þrowiaþ foxes liþu 7 his smeru mid ealden ele 7 mid tyrwan wyrc hím to sealfe; do an wifa stowe, raðe hyt þa earfeþu ʒehæleð.   5

2. Wið heafodece, þan ʒelice þe hit her before ʒecweden is, ním þat ylcan 7 smure þat heafod, hyt hæled wunderlice.

3. Wið earane sare eft ním þa ylcan sealfe hlutre, drupe on þat eare; wunderlice hyt hæled.

MS L

15. Ad serpentium morsus. Natura cervina sicca et cum rosa sicca dragma i in sorbitione oboli sumpta, idem potatus viperarum morsus efficacissime curat.

16. Ad stranguiriam vel aborsum pili cervini, ex his suffumigaberis, mulier sanabitur.

17. Ut mulier concipiat, ossicula similiter inveniuntur in corde cervi f. 19v aut in pube eius quae idem praestant; nam si brachio eum ossiculum suspendas, efficacissime mulier concipit.

18. Ad intestinorum dolorem et si torminata fuerint, medulla cervina remissa, potui dabis in aqua calida, mire sanat.

19. Ad serpentes fugandos medulla cervina incensa, et de ea suffumigabis [aut] tecum habeas, [et effugat] serpentes.

20. Ad perniones sevum eius combustum simul cum ostrea testa minuta commixta et factum quasi malagma impone, mire sanat.

IV. De vulpe

1. Ad mulieres quae in locis inferioribus suffocationem patiuntur, articulamenta vulpis in oleo veteri una cum bitumine pro cataplasma supposita, mulieribus suffocationem sanat.

2. Ad alopitias sanandas simili modo ut supra illitum capiti, mire sanat.

3. Ad aurium dolorem simili modo ut supra [instillato in aures], mire sanat.

4. Wið miltan sare foxes lungen on hattre æscan gesoden 7
ær gecnucud 7 to drence gedon, þa miltan hyt wundorlice gehæleþ;
swa deþ hys lifer þæt ylce.

5. Wið weartan genim foxes sceallan, gegnid swiþe oft þærmid
5 þa weartan, hraþe hyt hy tobreceþ 7 onweg adeþ.

6. Wið nearwre sworetunge foxes lungen gesoden 7 on geswettum wine gedon 7 geseald, wundorlice hit hæleþ.

7. Wið sare cyrnlu foxes sceallan genim 7 gnid mid gelome,
hraþe hi beoð hale.

10 8. Wið gomena sare foxes sina genim 7 on hunige gewæt 7
gnid mid þa goman swiþe oft; sona him byþ sel þæs broces.

f. 77v   9. Wið heafodece genim foxes ge/cynd, ymfoh þæt heafod
utan, hraþe þæs heafodes sár byþ aweg afyrred.

10. To wifþingum foxes tægles se ytemæsta dæl on earm
15 áhangen, þu gelyfest þæt þis sy to wifþingum on bysmær gedon.

11. Wið liþadle genim cwicenne fox 7 seoð þæt þa ban ane beon
læfed, astige þærin gelomlice, 7 in oþer bæð, do he swa swiþe
oft; wundorlice hit hæleþ, 7 æghwylce geare [þisne] fultum he
him sceal gegearwian; 7 ele do þærto ðonne he hine seoðe, 7
20 his þyssum gemete to þearfe bruce.

12. Wið earena sare genim foxes geallan, menc wið ele, drype
on þa earan, hyt wel gehæleþ.

13. Wið eagena dymnysse genim foxes geallan gemencged mid
doran hunige 7 on eagan gedon, hyt hæleþ.

MS V

1 lungen] lucgen B   gesoden] gesodone B.   6 nearwre] nearwe B
7] om. H 110/9.   8 Wið sare cyrnlu] 'W'ið sa`re cy´relu H.   10 gomena]
gemena H.   12 ymfoh] ymb- BH.   14 ytemæsta] ytemesta BH.
15 on bysmær] on bismer B, abysmer H.   16 cwicenne] cwicne H.
17 astige] 7 stige H   7] om. H.   18 æghwylce] æghwyl H   þisne] from
B, þys V.   21 genim] nim H.   22 þa earan] þæt eare H.   24 on
eagan gedon] on þa eagon do B.

MS O

5 tobrycþ] to by brycþ (by exp.).   14 wifþingun] preceded by exp. ti.

4. (Ad splenis (. . .)ndos) Wið miltan sare foxes lungane on hæte
æsca ȝebræde 7 ȝecnucod 7 to drence ȝedon, þa miltan hit wunderlice
ȝehæleð; swa deþ his lifer þæt ylcan.

5. (Ad verucas) Wið wircan ním foxes sceallen, ȝecníd swiþe oft
þarmid þa weartan; hraþe hyt hi tobrycþ 7 áȝedeþ.   5

6. (Wið nearwe sworetunge) Wið nearwe sworetunga foxes lungane
ȝesoden 7 on swetan / wíne ȝedon 7 ȝeseald, wundelice hit haled.   f. 47v

7. Wið sare curnlu foxes sceallen ȝením 7 ȝegnid mid ȝelome, hraðe
hy byd hæle.

8. Wid gomane sara foxæs sína ȝením 7 on huníȝe ȝewæt 7 gnid mid   10
þarn goman swiþe oft; sona hym byd sel þas broces.

9. —

10. To wifþingun foxes tæȝeles se ytemesta dæl on hermen ahangen;
þu lifest þæt þis sy to wifþingun on besmer ȝedon.

11. —   15

12. Wið eara sare ním foxes geallan, mencg

13. mid dore huníȝe 7 on eaȝen ȝedon; hít hælþ.

MS L

4. Ad splenis dolorem pulmo vulpis in cinere calido coctus, (. . .) tritus
potui datur, splenem mirifice sanat. Iecur autem ut supra potui datum
mire sanat.

5. Ad parotidas testiculum vulpis, saepius ex hoc parotidas confricato,
dissolvit eas.

6. Ad suspirium pulmo vulpis, ex vino nigro ut supra potui datum, mire
sanat.

7. Ad inguinum dolorem testiculum vulpis ut supra, si saepius con-
fricaverit, cito sanat.

8. Ad faucium dolorem vel tumorem renes vulpis in melle, saepius
fauces tumentes confrica.

9. Ad capitis dolorem natura vulpis circumaddita capitis dolorem
statim tollet.

10. Ad coitum summa pars caudae vulpis in brachio suspensa, irrita-   f. 20
mentum ad coitum credat.

11. Ad morbum articulorum vulpes viva in vaso amplo decocta, ut
sola ossa relinquantur, mire sanat si saepius in aqua tamquam in vaso
descenderit, debet autem quod inanis hoc adiutorium uti; si quis voluerit,
idem praestat si oleum ubi decocta fuerit, si quis illo modo hoc opus
utatur.

12. Ad aurium dolorem fel vulpis in aurem cum oleo stillatur, mire
sanat.

13. Ad caliginem oculorum fel vulpis cum melle attico commixtum,
oculi inuncti mire sanantur.

14. Wið earena sare genim foxes gelynde gemylted, drype on þa earan, him cymð god hæl.

15. Wið fotwræce, gif se innera dæl þæs sceos byþ fixenhyd, 7 gyf hit sy fotadl, smyre mid ele þa fet, hy habbaþ þæs þe leohtran gang.

5 V.

1. Wið oferslæpe haran brægen on wine geseald to drence, wundorlice hyt beteþ.

2. Wiþ eagena sare haran lungen on geseted 7 þærto gewriþen, þæt sár byþ gehæled.

10 3. Wið fotswylum 7 sceþþum haran lungen ufan on 7 neoþan to gewriþen, wundorlice þa gongas beoð gehælede.

4. Ðam wifum þe him hyra beorðor losie, haran heortan adrige 7 wyrc to duste, 7 þriddan dæl recelses dustes, syle drincan seofon dagas on scirum wine.

15 5. þam þonne þe hyt oft oðfealleþ, þritig daga ge on wine ge on wyrtunge.

6. Ðonne þam wifum þe æfter beorþre on sumum stowum swincen, þæt ylce dó to drence fæstendum on wearmum wætere, sona hyt byþ gehæled.

f. 78 7. Wið eagena dymnysse haran geallan wið hunig gemencged / 7
21 mid gesmyre(d), þa eagan gebeorhtigeaþ.

8. Ðam mannum þe [swinglunge] þrowiað, haran lungen 7 seo lifer somod gemencged 7 feower penega gewæge myrran 7 ðreora [befores] 7 anes huniges, þis sceal beon awylled on godum ecede,
25 7 syþþan mid geswetton wine gewesed; 7 æfter þam drince sona hyt hæleþ.

MS V

4 gang] fet B.   5 title om. VBH.   10 sceþþum] scæððum BH
neoþan] niðon B 127/17a.   11 gehælede] gehæled H.   12 hyra] heora
H.   13 7¹] hy H.   15 þam] Ðam þe H   þritig] xxx H.   18 þæt
ylce] þæt / þæt ylce H.   20 hunig] hunige B.   22 swinglunge] from
B, swinclunge V, swinclunge H 112/5.   24 befores] from B, beores (erasure
between e and o) V   þis] 'þis' H.   25 geswetton] geswettum H   7²] om. H.
26 hæleþ] bið gehæled H.

MS O

4 smíre] smil smíre (smil exp.).   7 ȝewryþan] ȝew'r'yl wryþan (w'r'yl
underlined twice).   16 Ðon] Ða Ðon (Ða exp.).

14. Wið earane sara ním foxes ȝelínde, ȝedrupe 7 ȝemylted on þan eare, hím cymð god hæle.

15. Wid fota wˈrˈæce, ȝif se ínra dæl þæs sceos byð fixenhyd, 7 ȝif hít fotadl, smíre mid ele þa fet, hy habbað þæs þe leohtran gang.

V. Medicina de lepore   5

1. Wið oferslæpe hara braȝen ȝeseald to drince, wunderlice hyt beteð.

2. Wið eaȝena sare hara lungane on ȝesetted 7 þærto ȝewryþan, wunderlice þat sar byð ȝehæled.

3. Wid fotswulan 7 sceþþum hara lungun ufan 7 neoþan to ȝewriþen; wundorlice þa gangas beoð ȝehælede.   10

4. þan wyfam þe hím hyra beorðor losie, haran heortan adríȝe 7 wyrc to duste, 7 þriddan dæl receles dustes, syle drincan seofan dæȝes on scírum wíne.

5. þam þonne he hit oft oþfealleð, þritiȝ dæȝe ȝe on wíne ȝe on wyrtunge.   15

6. Ðon þam wifum þe after / beorðre on sumum stowum swíncon, f. 48 þæt ylce do to drencȝe fastínde on wˈeˈarme wætere; sona hit byð ȝehæled.

7. Wið eaȝena dímnesse hara ȝeallen wid huni ȝemenged 7 mid ȝesmired; þa eaȝene ȝebeorhtiȝed.

8. —   20

MS L

14. Ad aurium dolorem adipem vulpis remissum, instillatum, mire sanat.

15. Ad pedum dolorem de vulpina pelle interior pars calciamentorum fiat et podager ex eo oleo unguat pedes, leviores habebit accessiones.

V. [De medicamentis leporinis]

1. Ad submeiulos cerebrum leporis ex vino potui datum mire emendat.

2. Ad oculorum dolores leporis pulmo suppositus et alligatus dolores sanat.

3. Ad perniones vel si pedes laesi fuerint, leporis pulmo impositus supra pedes mire sanat, si sub accessionem ei suspendas.

4. Ad locosas mulieres leporis cor siccum et potui datum mire sanat.

5. Ad caducos leporis cor siccum, deradito partem tertiam turis mannam tritam ex vino albo, dato bibere per dies septem, his vero qui saepius cadunt diebus xxx; potio decocta in dies debet crescere et pondere vino.

6. Ad eas mulieres quae post partum a quibusdam locis laborant, idem supra aqua calida potui dato ieiunae, sanabitur.

7. Ad caliginem oculorum leporis fel cum melle mixtum et inunctum, ad claritatem oculi perveniunt.

8. Ad eos qui vertiginem patiuntur, fel leporis simul et iocinera f. 20v mustelae commixtum dragmas tres, castorei dragma una, myrrae dragmas quattuor, ex aceto musso dragmam i, ex melle aut ex passo bibant, sanabuntur.

9. Wið blædran sare haran sina gedrygede 7 mid sealte gebrædde 7 gehyrste sceaf on his drinc, wundorlice hyt hæleþ.

10. Wið attorcoppan bite haran sina gegyre 7 him syle þicgan, eac hyt is æltæwe gyf hi mon hreawe swylgeþ; eac wið wlættan hi 5 beoð gode gesodene.

11. Wiþ feallendum feaxe haran wambe seoð oþþe bræd on pannan on godum ele, smyre þæt feax 7 þæt heafod, þonne nimeþ þæt feax to, 7 seo sealf genydeð þæt hyt weaxeþ.

12. To þan þæt wif cenne wæpned cild, haran hrif gedryged 7 10 gesceafen oððe gegniden on drinc drincen butu; gif þæt wif ana hyt drinceþ, ðonne cenð heo androginem; ne byþ þæt to nahte, naþer ne wer ne wif.

13. Eft to þam ylcan haran sceallan wife æfter hyre clænsunge syle on wine drincan, þonne cenð heo wæpned cild.

15 14. Wíf to geeácnigenne haran cyslybb feower penega gewæge syle on wine drincan þam wife of wife, 7 þam were of were, 7 þonne don hyra gemanan, 7 æfter þon hy forhæbben; þonne hraþe geeacnað heo, 7 for mete heo sceal sume hwyle swamma brucan 7 for bæð smyrenysse, wundorlice heo geeacnaþ.

20 15. Wið scorpiones bite 7 nædran slite haran cyslyb geseald on wines drince, þæt wel gehæleþ.

16. Wið þæt cildum butan sare teð wexen, haran brægen gesoden, gnid gelome mid þa toðreoman, hi beoð clæne 7 unsare.

17. Wið wambe wræce genim haran helan, ber on þinum 25 hedclaþe, wundorlice hit hæleð. /

MS V

1 blædran] brædran H   7 mid sealte] *om.* H.   2 gebrædde] gebræded H
sceaf] scearfa B   drinc] drince B.   3 þicgan] ðincgan H.   4 swylgeþ]
swelgeð B.   11 cenð] cænneð B.   12 naþer] nawðer H.   15 Wíf] 'G'if
H 113/5   geeácnigenne] geeacnenne H.   17 forhæbben] forhabban
B 127v/10a.   18 mete] met B.   19 smyrenysse] smyrnysse H.
23 toðreoman] teð- H.   24 wræce] wrece H   helan] hælan BH.

MS O

4 feallendum fexe] fexe feallendum, *marked for reversal.*   5 sm'y´re] y
interlined above exp. e.   7 hrif] ri hrif (ri *exp.*).   8 hit] hit / hyt.
9 naþer] naþer to (to *exp.*).   10 clænsunge] æ *alt. from* a.   15 hedclaðe]
d *alt. from* o.

9. Wið blædran sara hara syna ჳedríჳede

10. 7 hím sile ðícჳean; eac hít hys ealtewa ჳif hi man hreawe swelჳeð. Eac wið w`l´æten hi beoð gode ჳesodene.

11. Wið feallendum fexe hara wamba seod oþþer bræd on pannum on gode ele, sm`y´re þæt fex 7 þæt heafod; þanne nímed þæt fex to, 7 seo 5 sealfe ჳenydeð þæt hít wexeð.

12. To þan þæt wyf cenne wæpned cyld, hara hrif ჳedriჳed 7 ჳesceawen odðer ჳecníden on drinc drincen butu, ჳyf þæt wif ane hit drinceð, þanne cenþ heo androჳinem; ne byð þæt to nahte, naþer ne wer ne wif.

13. Eft to þan ylcan hara sceallan wife afte hyre clænsunge sile on wíne 10 drincan; þan cenþ heo wæpned cyld.

14, 15. —

16. Wið þæt cyldum butan sare teþ wexan hara bræჳen ჳesodan, ჳegnid lelome mid þa teþreaman; hi byð clane 7 unsare.

17. Wið wambe wyæce nin haran helan, ber on þíne hedclaðe, wunder- 15 lice hit hæled.

MS L

9. Ad calculos leporis renes siccos in sale coctos, [derasos] in potione, mire sanant.

10. Ad araneorum morsus renes eius, fulicis etiam bestiae, qui ab araneis laborant sic crudos gluttiant, sanabuntur; nausiosis etiam hii cocti dantur.

11. Ad capillos fluentes leporis ventriculum coctum in sartagine, admixto oleo mirtino, impone capiti; capillos fluentes continet et cogit crescere.

12. Ut mulier masculum pariat, leporis vulvam siccam derasam in potionem tritam bibant utrique; si autem sola mulier biberit, androgyne nascitur, hoc est nec masculus nec femina.

13. Item et quod supra, testiculum leporis mulieri post purgationem in vinum potui dato, masculum pariet.

14. [Item ut concipiat foemina] leporis coagulum dragmas quattuor in potionem dato cum vino, feminae de femina, [masculo de] masculo, et statim faciant coitum, et post abstineat se, statim concipit, et pro cibo fungis utatur et a balneo unctionibus utatur, mire concipit.

15. Ad scorpionum et serpentium morsus coagulum leporis cum vino potui datum sanat.

16. Ut infantibus dentes sine dolore exeant, cerebrum leporis coctum, si ex eo gingivas infantibus defrices, sanae efficiuntur.

17. Ad ventris dolores talum leporis tolle et in ventrali portato, mire sanat.

f. 78v   18. Wið eagena sare haran lifer gesoden ys god on wine to drincenne, 7 mid þam broþe ða eagan to beþianne.

19. Ðam manum þe fram þære teoþan tide ne geseoð, þæs ylcan drinces smyc heora eagan onfon, 7 mid þam broþe recen, 7 þa lifre wæten 7 gniden 7 mid smyrwen.

20. Wið blodryne gebærned haran lifer 7 gegniden 7 on gestreded hraþe hyt gestilleþ.

VI.

1. Wið blodryne of nebbe firginbuccan, þæt ys wudubucca oððe gat, þæs lifer gebryted wið ecede 7 on næsþyrl bestungen, wundorlice hraþe hyt ðone blodryne gestilleþ.

2. To eagena beorhtnysse wudubuccan gealla gemencged wið feldbeona hunige 7 on gesmyred, seo beorhtnys him to cymð.

3. þæt ylce m(æ)g wið gomena sare, gemeng þone geallan 7 hunig tosomne, hrin þa goman mid, hyt hælð.

4. To eallum uncystum þe on gomum beoð acenned, wudugate geallan mid feldbeona hunige gemenged, þær sceal eac gelice awegen myrre 7 pipor 7 croh, seoð eall on wine oþþæt hyt sy wel to sealfe geworht; smyre þonne þa saran goman mid daga gehwylce oðþæt hy haligen.

5. Wið eagena dymnesse wudugate geallan 7 lytel wines meng tosomne, smyre mid ðriwa, þonne beoð hi gehælede.

6. Wið dropfagum andwlatan wudubucan geallan oððe gate gemencged wið wætere 7 on gesmyred, hraþe hit gelacnað.

MS V

1–2 on wine to drincenne] on wine gedruncen B, on windrince H.
3 manum] mannum BH.   5 smyrwen] *above the* w *an interlined* g V,
smyrigen B, smerwen H 114/1.   8 *title om.* VBH.   10 lifer] lifre B.
12 gealla] geallan H.   14 gemeng] gemæg H.   18 seoð eall on wine]
7 seoð eal tosomne H.   20 gehwylce] gehwilcne B 128/7a   hy] hyt H.
22 gehælede] hale H.   24 gelacnað] H *ends here* 114v/18.

18. Wið eaȝene sare haran lifer ȝesoden ys god on wine to drincanne 7 mid þan broðe þa eaȝen to beþíenne.

19. —

20. Wið blodrune ȝebærned haran lifer 7 ȝegníden, 7 on ȝestreded raðe hít ȝestyllæð. /   5

VI. Medicina de hirco et capra   f. 48v

1. (Ad sanguinem de naribus sistendum) Wið blodryne of nebbe firȝínbuccan, þæt ys wudebucca odðer gat, þæs lifer ȝebrited wið ecede 7 on nosþurlo ȝestungen, wunderlice raðe hyt þat blodrune ȝestilleð.

2. (Ad oculos) To eaȝena beorhnesse wudebuccan ȝealle ȝemenged wiþ   10 fealdbeona huníȝe 7 on ȝesmered; seo beornysse hym to cumed.

3. þæt ylca mæȝ wyþ ȝomena sare, ȝemengc þane ȝealle 7 huniȝ tosomne, hrín þa ȝoman mid, hit hæled.

4. —

5. (Ad oculos) Wid eaȝena dímnysse wudugate ȝeallan 7 lítel wines   15 meng tosomne, smyra mid þriwa, þanne beoð hí ȝehæled.

6. (Wiþ dropfaȝum) Wid dropfaȝum 7wlatan wudubucca ȝealle odðer gate ȝemenged wið wætere 7 on ȝesmyred, raðe hit ȝelacnað.

MS L

18. Ad oculorum dolores iecur contritum ex vino dato, bibat cum   f. 21 aqua calida sed mera, tum in fervore sanabitur.

19. Item hi qui ab hora decima non vident, [huius] potionis vaporem oculi excipiant, et ex eadem aqua oculos foveant, et iecur edant et ex liquefacto inunguantur.

20. Ad sanguinem fluentem iecur combustum et aspersum sanguinem fluentem statuet.

VI. De capra silvatica

1. Ad sanguinem de naribus nimium profluentem iecur caprae silvaticae contritum et ex aceto in naribus offultum mire statuet.

2. Ad oculorum claritatem fel caprae silvaticae cum melle attico commixtum, ungues, claritatem praestat.

3. Ad faucium dolores simili modo ut supra sed eodem melle cum felle caprae fauces tange, mire sanat.

4. Ad vitia omnia quae in faucibus nascuntur, fel caprae cum melle attico, adiecta murra et pipere et croco aequis ponderibus, simul omnia coquis in vino donec contrahitur, ex eo fauces cotidie tange donec sanescat.

5. Ad caliginem oculorum fel caprae silvaticae dragma una et modicum vini cum melle ut possit teri, inungue, sanabitur.

6. Ad ustionem in facie fel caprae silvaticae cum aqua mixtum, illitum   f. 21v in faciem ustam a sole, sanat.

7. Wið nebcorn þe wexað on þam andwlatan, smyre mid gate geallan, ealle þa nebcorn he of þam andwlitan aclænsað 7 ealne þone wom he geðynnað.

8. Wið earena sare 7 swege wudugate gealla mid neowum ele oðða æppeles seawe wlæc gemencged 7 on þa earan gedon, hyt hæleþ./

f. 79   9. Wið toþece wudugate geallan mencg wið ele, smyre mid swyþe gelome, þonne beoð hi hale.

10. Wið herðbylges sare oððe wunde fyregate geallan meng wið hunig, do to þam sare, hit hæleþ wel.

11. To wifes willan, þæs buccan geallan meng wið recels 7 wið netelan sæd; smyre þone teors mid ær foran to þæs restgemanan; þæt wif [onfehð] þæs willan on ðam hæmede.

12. þy læs cild sy hreosende, þæt is fylleseoc, oþþe scinlac mete, fyregate brægen teoh þurh gyldenne hring, syle þam cilde swelgan ær þam hyt meolc onbyrge, hyt byþ gehæled.

VII.

1. Wið homum nim gate horn 7 lege to fyre, þæt he byrne on fyrle, do þonne of þa scylle on niwe fæt, cnuca hyt þonne swiþe wið scearpum ecede; do on þa homan oþþæt hy hale syn.

2. To slæpe gate horn under heafod geled, weccan he on slæpe gecyrreþ.

3. Wið cyrnla sare smeoc þone man mid gate hærum, hraþe he byþ þæs sares hal.

MS V

2 he] heo B.   4 neowum] nywum B.   9 herðbylges] hyrð- B.
13 onfehð] *from* B, onfeh V.   16 hyt byþ gehæled] *om.* B.   17 *title
om.* VB.   21 gate] gæte B   weccan] wæccan B   slæpe] slæp B.

MS O

5 wudugate] *above this word* oþþer fire.   9 recels] rise recels (rise
exp.).   12 hreosende] hres hreosende (hres *exp.*).   17 níwe] wíne níwe
(wíne *struck out and underlined*).

7. Wið nebcorn þa wexaþ on anwlytan smyre mid gate gealle; ealle þa nebcorn he of þan anwlytan aclænsað 7 ealle þane wom he ȝeþínnaþ.

8. (Ad oculos) Wið earena sar 7 sweȝe wudugate ȝealle míd niwum ele oðð er aeppes siwe wlæc ȝemenged 7 on þa earan ȝedon; hyt hæled.

9. (Ad dolorem dentium) Wið top/ece wudugate geallen meng þyd ele,   f. 49
smyre mid swiðe ȝelome; þanne beoð hy hale.   6

10. Wið herþbuliȝes sare oððer wunde wudegete ȝellen meng wyð huníȝ, do to þan sare, hyt hæled wel.

11. To wifef willan þæs buccan ȝeallen meng wið recels 7 wið netelan   10
sæd, smyre þane terþ mid æt foran to þas resteȝemanan; þæt wif onfeahþ
þæs willan on þan hamede.

12. þi læs cild sy hreosende, þæt ys filleseoc, oþþer scínlac mete, firegate braȝen teoþ þurþ gyldene hring, syle ðan cilde swelȝan ær þan hit meoluc bruca 7 shuca; hyt byð ȝehæled.

VII. (*No separate chapter in* O)   15

1. Wið oman ním gate horn 7 leȝe to fyre, þæt he byrne on fyre; do þanne of þa scille on níwe fæt; cnuca hy þane swiþe wið scearpun ecede, do on ða oman fort hy hæl sy.

2. To slæpe gate horn under heafed ȝeled; wæccen he on slæp ȝecyrreð.

3. —   20

MS L

7. Ad lentigines in facie fel caprae silvaticae custo illitum, lentigines de facie purgat et omnes maculas extenuat.

8. Ad auricularum sonitum fel caprae silvaticae cum rosaceo aut suco porri tepefactum auriculis infunde, mire sanat.

9. Ad dentium dolores fel caprae silvaticae cum rosacio idem ut supra sanat.

10. Ad veretri exulcerationem fel caprae silvaticae mixtum cum melle aut suco rubi appositum mire sanat.

11. Ad voluptatem feminae fel mixtum cum urticae semine et turae, veretrum linito ante concubitum, voluntatem percipit femina in coitu.

12. Ne infans caducus sit aut fantasma experiatur, cerebrum caprae silvaticae [per] anulum aureum traiectum, si dederis infanti gluttire antequam lac ducat, sanus erit.

VII. De capra domestica

1. Ad ignem sacrum cornu caprae contra focum teneto, eversato crustas, excuties in vaso rude donec consumetur, deinde conteris cum aceto [acerrimo] et inducis, ignis sacrum sanabitur.

2. Ad somnum [cornu caprinum] capiti suppositum vigilias in somnum convertit.

3. Ad inguinum dolores ex pilis caprae suffumigabis eum cui inguine   f. 22
dolet, sanabitur.

4. Wið blodryne of nosum adryg gate blod 7 gnid to duste, do on þæt næsþyrl, hyt wiðstandeþ.

5. Wið eagena hætan 7 stice niwe gate cyse, ofer geseted mid þa eagbræwas, him byþ hrædlice bot.

6. Wið heafodece niwe gate cyse þærto gewriþen, hyt hæleþ.

7. Wið fotadle gate cyse niwe on gelegd þæt sár geliðegað.

8. Wið nædran slite sceaf gate horn on þry scenceas; 7 þare ylcan gate meolc wið wine gemencgede on þry siþas drince; syllice hyt þæt attor tosceadeþ.

f. 79v   9. Wið innoðes flewsan gate horn / gesceafen 7 wið hunige ge-
11 mencged 7 [gegniden] 7 æfter þam geþiged, þære wambe flewsan he forþryceð.

10. Wið [hreofle] 7 wið toflogen lic genim þæt wæter þe innan gæt byþ 7 heo hwilum ut geoteð, menge þone wætan wið hunige 7
15 sealte, 7 symle on æfenne his heafod 7 his lic mid þy þwea 7 gnide.

11. Wið innoðes heardnysse swa hwæt swa he [ete] menge wið þone wætan, 7 þone ylcan drince wið þæs innoðes heardnysse, þæt seo getogene wamb sy alysed; swa he má drinceð, swa hyt furðor clænsað.

20   12. Wið þone wætan do him eac [þæt he] drince gate blod, wel þæt hyne hæleð.

13. Gif innoð þinde, nim gate blod mid hyre smeorwe, 7 berene gryta gemeng, 7 on wambe utan gewrið, wundorlice hyt hælþ.

14. Wið ælces cynnes næddran bite gate smeoro 7 hyre tord 7
25 weax mylt 7 gemeng tosomne, wyrc swa hit man gehal forswelgan mæge, onfo se þe him ðearf sy, þonne bið he gehæled.

15. [Se] man se þe him seo wæteradl, gæten smeoro geþyd to poslum swelge, 7 drince mid ceald wæter, 7 somod swelge, 7 drince æfter þam gate blod, hym byþ hræd bot.

MS V

2 næsþyrl] nos- B.   9 hyt] *om.* B   tosceadeþ] toscaceð B 128v/18a.
11 gegniden] *from* B, gecweden V.   12 forþryceð] forþricceð B.
13 hreofle] *emended from* hreofe VB, *see note.*   14 wið] mid B.   16 ete]
from B, *om.* V.   20 þæt he] *from* O, *om.* VB, *see note*   drince] drincan
B.   22 þinde, nim gate] nim gate þinde V, *marked for reversal.*   25 gehal]
hal B.   27 Se] *from* B, þe V.   28 mid . . . drince] *om.* B.

MS O

14 ȝewryd] ȝe wy wryd.

4. Wið blodríne of nose adriȝd gate blod 7 gníd to duste, do on þæt nosþrul; hit wiðstandeþ.

5. Wið eaȝene hæte 7 wið stice niwe gate cuse, ofer ȝesedet mid þa eaȝebræwas, / hym byþ hrædlice bote.   f. 49v

6. Wið heafodece niwe gate cuse þarto ȝewriþen, hit hæled.   5

7. Wið fotadle niwe gate cuse on ȝeled; þæt sar ȝeliþegaþ.

8–10. —

11. Wid ínnoþes heardnysse swa hwæt swa he eta menge wiþ þane wætan 7 þone ylcan drincan wið þæs innoþes heardnysse, þæt seo toȝene wambe sy alysed; swa he drinceð, swa hít furþur clænsad.   10

12. Wið þane wætan do hím eac þæt he drince gate blod; wel þæt hine hæleð.

13. Gif ínnoþ þínde, ním gate blod mid hire smeruwe, 7 berena grutta gemeng 7 on wambe utan ȝewryd; wundelice hít hæleð.

14–16. —   15

MS L

4. Ad sanguinem de naribus qui fluit infricato, sanguinem deprimet.

5. Ad fervores vel punctiones oculorum caseus caprae recens oculis superpositus mire subvenit.

6. Ad capitis dolores caseus simili modo ut supra fronti impositus mire sanat.

7. Ad podagram caseus simili modo pedibus superimpositus mire sedat.

8. Ad serpentium morsus de cornu caprae pulvis cum origano et cum lacte eiusdem caprae cum vino cyatis tribus bibat, mire venenum discutit.

9. Ad ventris fluxum cornu caprae rasum, simul in melle mixtum et spiratum meditatum ventris fluxum reprimet.

10. Ad peduclosos simili modo ut supra, aqua quae in capra est paulatim effunditur, (. . .) misceatur cum melle et sale, ex eo corpus eius et caput sero fricetur.

11. Ad ventris duritiam idem ut supra bibitur et ventrem strictum solvit, et si plus biberit, purgat.

12. Ad humores sanguinis caprae potus remediat.

13. Ad torminosos caprae sanguis cum resina et polenta mixtus et ventri suppositus mire sanat.

14. Ad omnium serpentium morsus sevum caprae admixta sandaria et ceroto, et illo compositum in sorbitionem accipiat, sanabitur.

15. Ad ydropicos caprae sevum in sorbitionem coniectum, sed super-bibet aquam frigidam, sorbent simul et lotium caprae, mirifice sanat.

16. [Drince] eft buccan micgan 7 ete nardes ear 7 wælwyrte moran, selost ys se micga, þæt he sy oftost mid feded.

17. Wið earena sare gate micgan do on þæt eare, þæt sár geliðigað, gif þær wyrms inne bið, hyt þæt út awyrpð.

18. Wið cyrnlu gate tord menge wið hunige, smyre mid, sona bið sel.

19. Wið þeohwræce gate tord cned swyþe, þæt hyt sy swylce sealf, 7 smyre mid þa þeoh, sona hy beoð hale.

20. Wið liþa sare nim gate tord, meng wið scearpum ecede, 7 smyre mid; wel hyt hæleþ; 7 smeoce mid hæþe 7 þæt ylce on wine drince.

21. Wið cancre gate tord gemenged wið hunige 7 on þa wunde gedón, hraþe hyt hæleþ.

22. Wið swylas gate tord, smyre mid þa swylas, hyt hy todrifð 7 gehæleþ 7 gedeþ þæt hy eft ne arisað.

23. Wið sina getoge gate tord meng wið ecede 7 smyre mid þæt sár, hyt hælþ.

24. Wið springum gate tord meng wið hunige, smyre 7 on gelege, eac þa springas þe beoð on mannes innoðe ácenned hy`t´ todrifeþ. /

f. 80   25. Gate geallan on wine gedruncen wifa halan him of adeþ 7 hi gehæleþ.

VIII.

1. Wiþ wearras 7 wið swylas blacu rammes wul on wætere gedyfed 7 æfter þam on ele 7 syþþan aled on þa saran stowe; þæt sar heo onweg afyrreþ, 7 gyf hyt bið mid gereced, þa toslitenan wunda heo forþrycceþ.

MS V

1 Drince] *from* B, rince V.   2 micga] migga B.   10 smeoce] smoca
B 129/3a.   18 springum] springas B.   23 *title om.* VB.   25 syþþan]
siðð B.

MS O

3 tord] to tord (to *stained and exp.*).   4 swiþe] mid swiþe (mid *exp.*).
sealf] sealff sealf (sealff *exp.*).   15–16 7 æfter] 7 es / 7 æfter (es *exp.*).

17. Wið earane sare gate migga do on þæt eare; þæt sar ȝeliþegad; ȝif þar wurmas ínne beoð, hi þæt ut awirph.

18. Wið cyrnlu gate tord meng wid huniȝe; smura mid; sona byd sel.

19. Wið þeoþwrace gate tord cned swiþe, þæt hit sy swylce sealf, 7 smyre míd þa þeoh; sona hi byþ hal.   5

20, 21. —

22. Wið swylas gate tord, smyre mid þa swylas; hit hi todrifd 7 ȝehæled 7 ȝedeþ þæt hi eft ne arisaþ.

23. Wið syna ȝetoȝe gate tord meng wið ecede 7 smire mid, þæt sar byd ȝehæled.   10

24. —

25. Gate ȝealla on wíne ȝedruncen wifa halan hím of adeþ 7 hy ȝehælþ.

VIII. Medicina ariete

1. Wið wearras 7 wið swulas blac rammes wulon on wæte ȝedifed 7 15 æfter þan on ele 7 sidðan aled on þæt sara stowe; þæt sar heo onweȝ afyrred; 7 ȝyf hít byð mid ȝereced, / þa toslitena wunda heo forþricceð.   f. 50

MS L

16. [Item] hircinum lotium si eminam biberit et spicanardi et ebulum   f. 22v cynna vari, melius est lotium, si idem pasti fuerint.

17. Ad aurium dolorem lotium caprae missum in auribus dolorem sedat, [si cum] mulso misceat, et si pus habeat, eiciet.

18. Ad parotidas caprae stercus cum melle commixtum mire sanat.

19. Ad femorum dolores gummen caprae si stercori commisceas et factum quasi malagma, femora unguis, mire sanat.

20. Ad morbum articulorum stercus caprae cum aceto acerrimo mixtum sanat. Idem colicis pro fomento positum aut ex aceto potatum sanat.

21. Ad cancerosos stercus caprae cum melle mixtum et vulneri appositum sanat.

22. Ad luxum, idem stercus facit ad luxum et tumores discutit et non patitur postmodum consurgere.

23. Ad nervorum contractionem idem stercus caprae mixtum cum aceto et superillitum mire sanat et confirmat.

24. Ad carbunculos idem stercus cum melle commixtum et superpositum carbunculos qui in ventre nascuntur discutit.

25. Ad secundas eiciendas caprae secundas ex vino potas, mulierum secundas eiciunt.

VIII. De ariete

1. Ad locorum dolores lana arietis nigra tincta in aqua, deinde in oleo, superposita locis dolorem tollit et effumigata et prolapsa vulnera reprimet.

2. þa wearras 7 ða swylas þe beoð on mannes handum oððe on
oþrum limum oððe ymb þone utgang smyre mid þam wætan þe
drype of [healfsodenre] rammes lungenne, hraþe heo hy onweg
afyrreð.

5   3. Wið wundspringum [on] anwlatan rammes lungen smel
tocorfen 7 to þam sare geled, sona hyt gehælþ.

4. Wið scurfuɲ rammes smeoru, 7 meng ðærto sot 7 sealt 7
sand, 7 hyt wulla onweg; 7 æfter smyre, hyt byþ eft liðre.

IX.

10   1. Wið ælc sar bares brægen gesoden 7 to drence [geworht] on
wine, ealle sár hyt geliðegaþ.

2. Wið hærþena sare 7 teorses bares brægen meng wið hunig
7 wrið on, wundorlice hyt hæleþ.

3. Wið nædran bite bares brægen gesoden 7 gemencged wið
15 hunig, wundorlice hyt gehæleþ.

4. Eft wið sarum 7 gewundedum fotum bares lungen gebeaten
swiðe smale 7 wið hunig gemenged 7 to sealfe gedon, hraþe
heo þæt sár gehæleþ.

5. Wið innoðes flewsan niwe bares lifre wyrc to drence on
20 wine 7 þonne drince, sona him bið sel. /

f. 80v   6. Oras onweg to adonne nim bares lifre 7 swetre apuldre
rinde, wyl tosomne on wine gemenged 7 drince, hraðe hy fleoð
onweg fram him.

7. Gif earan syn innan sare 7 þær wyrms sy, on dó þa ylcan
25 sealfe, heo ys swyþe god to þam.

MS V

3 healfsodenre] healf- *from* B, ealf- V.   5 on] *emended from* 7 VB
smel] smæl B.   9 *title om.* VB.   10 geworht] *from* B, geworh
V.   12 hærþena] hyrðena B.   14 nædran] næddrena B 129v/10a.
21 adonne] 'a'donne B.   24 wyrms] worms B.

MS O

6 rammes] *preceded by exp.* n.   9 braȝen] bla braȝen (bla *exp.*).
11 tearse] a *alt. from* u.   16 flewsa] flew flewsa (*the incomplete word, in*
which w *resembles* þ, *exp.*).

2. þa wearres 7 swa swylas ðe beoþ on manes handum oþþer on oþrum líme oþþer embe þana utgang smure mid þan wætan þe druppe of healfe sodene rammes lungene; raðe heo hiȝ onweȝ afirreð.

3. Wið wundsprínȝum on anwlítan rammes lungane smæl tocorfan 7 to ðan sare ȝeled; sona hít ȝehaleð.

4. Wið scurfum rammes smeru ním, 7 meng to sot 7 sealt 7 sand, 7 hit willa onweȝ; 7 after smyre, hit byd eft liþere.

IX. Medicina de apro

1. Wið ælc sar bares braȝen ȝesoden 7 to drence ȝeworht on wíne, ealle sar hit ȝeliþegaþ.

2. Wið herþena sare 7 tearse bares braȝen meng wið huníȝ 7 wryþ on, wunderlice hít hæled.

3, 4. —

5. Wið inneþes flewsan nife bares lifere

6. 7 swetre apuldure rínde wul tosomne on wíne ȝemenged 7 drince, raðe se flewsa fram hym ȝewiteð.

7. Gif earan sín ínnan sara 7 þar wu`r´m sy, on do þa ylcan sealfe, heo ys swiðe god to þam.

MS L

2. Ad clauculos et cauculos liquor arietis qui de pulmonibus concoquis stilla, superpositus clauculos qui in manibus nascuntur aut in veretris illitus tollit.

3. Ad livores et suggellationes pulmo arietis concisus minutatim et impositus statim sanat et nigras cicatrices ad candorem perducit et calciamentis laesos sanat.

4. Ad scabias sevum arietis, scabiam ungue cum admixta sandaria et subinde rade, hoc ad perniones facit, sed cum alumine mixtum.

IX. De verre sive apro

1. Ad omnes dolores cerebrum [apri coctum] et potatum cum vino omnes dolores sedat.

2. Ad veretri dolores cerebrum coctum ex melle impositum mire sanat.

3. Ad serpentium morsus cerebrum coctum ex melle mire sanat.

4. Ad pedes exulceratos a calciamentis pulmo eius cum melle commixtus, ut malagma in pedibus superimpone, sanabuntur.

5. Ad ventris fluxum iecur verris recens ex vino potatum mire stringit.

6. Ad flegmata solvenda iecur eius in cortice mali Punici potatum flegmata solvet.

7. Ad aures purulentas iecur eius ut supra infusum et auribus stillatum mire sanat.

8. Weres wylla to gefremmanne nime bares geallan 7 smyre mid þone teors 7 þa hærþan, þonne hafað he mycelne lust.

9. Wið fylleseocum men bares sceallan wyrc to drence on wine oððe on wætere; se [drync] hyne gehæleþ.

5 10. (W)ið spiwþan 7 wlættan 7 hnap(punge) genim bares gelynde 7 seoð on þrim sestrum wæteres oþþæt se dridda dæl sy beweallen, do þærto bares fam 7 drince, he byþ hal; 7 he sylf wundrað 7 weneþ þæt hyt sy oþer læcedom þæt he dranc.

11. Wið stede 7 wið blæddran sare genim eoferes blædran mid 10 þam mi`c´gan, ahefe upp 7 abid oþþæt se wæta of aflogen sy, seoð syððan, 7 syle etan þam þe earfoþo þrowie, wundorlice hit gehæleþ.

12. þam þe under hy migað, bares blædre gebræded 7 ʽgeʼseald to etanne, þa unhæle heo gehælþ.

15 13. Wið homum bares scearn 7 swefel gegniden on wine, 7 gelome drince, þa homan hyt beteþ.

X.

1. Wiþ deofulseocnysse 7 wið yfelre gesihðe wulfes flæsc wel getawod 7 gesoden syle etan ðam þe þearf sy; þa scinlac þe him 20 ær ætywdon, ne geunstillað hy hine.

2. To slæpe [wulfes] heafod lege under þone pyle, se unhala slæpeþ.

3. Gif þu gesyxt wulfes spor ær þonne hyne, ne gesceþþeð he þe, gif ðu hafast mid þe wulfes hrycghær 7 tæglhær þa ytemæstan on 25 siðfæte, butan fyrhtu þu ðone sið gefremest, ác se wulf sorgað ymbe sið.

MS V

2 hærþan] hyrðan· B.   4 drync] *from* B, dren V.   6 sestrum] systres B.   10 aflogen] aflowen B.   16 beteþ] gebeteð B.   17 *title om.* VB.   21 wulfes] *from* B 130/6a, ʽhundesʼ (*in a different hand*) V. 23 gesyxt] gesihst B   gesceþþeð] scæððeð B.   24 ytemæstan] ytemestan B. 26 sið] his sið B.

_____

MS O

15 deofolseocnesse] deolfolseocnesse (*first* l *exp.*).

8. Weres willan to ʒefremmenne nyme bares ʒeallan 7 smíra mid þane tears 7 þa herðan; þane hafað he micelne lust.

9. (Ad caducos) Wið fylleseocum men bares ʒeallen wirc to drence on wíne oþþer on wætere; se drenc hine ʒehaled.

10. Wid spiwan 7 w'l'ætan 7 / nappunge ním bæres ʒelínde 7 seoð on þrím sesterum wæteres fort þæt þrindan dæl beo weallen, þarto bares fam 7 drince; he byð hæl; 7 he sylf wundraþ 7 weneþ þæt hit sy oþer læcedom þæt he drínce. f. 50v
6

11. —

12. þam þe under hy miʒað bares blædre ʒebræded 7 ʒeseald to etanne; þa unhæle heo ʒehæled. 10

13. Wið oman bæres scearn 7 swefel ʒegníde on wíne 7 ʒelome drínce, þa oman hyt ʒebeteþ.

X. Medina lupo

1. (Ad demoníacos) Wið deofolseocnesse 7 wið yfele ʒesihþe fulfes flæsc wel ʒetawod 7 ʒesoden syle etan þam þe þearf sy; þa scínlac þa hym ær ætiwdan, ne ʒeunstillaþ hy híne. 15

2. To slæpe fulfes heafod leʒe under þane pule; se unhala slæped.

3. —

MS L

8. Ad voluptatem viri fel verrinum, vir sibi veretrum si linuerit, magnam capit voluntatem.

9. Ad caducos testiculos verris ex aqua aut ex vino pota, remediabis.

10. Ad vomitum et somnum spuma verris adiecto adipe in eminis tribus ad tertias decoctum et datum, sanabitur, ita ut his qui biberit alios putet remedio esse eis.

11. Ad stranguiriam et vesicae dolores vesica apri cum suo lotio infusa, si suspenderis et passa fuerit donec aquaticus humor [affluat], et discoctum dederis manducare his qui patiuntur, mire sanantur.

12. Ad submeiulos vesica assa verris, dato manducare submeiulis, sanantur.

13. Ad coxios stercus agrestis [apri et] sulfur colatum et eminam vini picati potum coxios emendat.

X. De lupo

1. Ad daemoniacos vel umbrosos carnem lupi conditam qui ederit, a daemonibus vel umbris quae per fantasma apparent non tam inquietantur.

2. Ad somnum caput lupi suppositum sub pulvino, dormiet aeger.

3. Ne lupus te noceat, lupus cuius prior vestigia prospexeris tibi ipse non nocet, quod si ille te ante notaverit, caudae summam partem si habueris tecum in itinere, sine metu [iter] conficies; eadem ratione lupus ipse sollicitat. f. 24

4. Eagwræc onweg to donne genim wulfes swyþre eage 7 hyt
f. 81 tosting 7 gewrið to ðam eagon, hit ge/wanad þæt sar, gyf hyt
gelomlice þærmid gesmyred byþ.

5. Wið miltwræce cwices hundes milte abred of, wyrc to
drence on wine, syle drincan, hyt hæleþ. Sume nimað hwelpes
inylfe 7 wriðaþ on.

6. Wið wiþerweard hær onweg tó adonne, gif þu nimest wulfes
mearh 7 smyrest mid hraðe ða stowe þe þa hær beoð of [apullod],
ne geþafað seo smyrung þæt hy eft wexen.

7. Se wifman se þe hæbbe dead bearn on innoðe, gif he drinceð
wylfene meolc mid wine 7 hunige gemenged gelice efne, sona
hyt hælð.

8. Biccean meolc, gif ðu gelome cilda toðreoman mid smyrest
7 æthrinest, butan sare hy wexað.

9. Wearras 7 weartan onweg to donne nim wulle 7 wæt mid
biccean hlonde, wrið on þa weartan 7 on þa wearras, hraþe hi
beoð awege.

10. þam mannum þe magon hwon gehyran, hundes gelynde 7
wermodes seaw mid ealdum ele gemylt, dryp on þæt eare, hyt þa
deafan gebeteþ.

11. Wið wedes hundes slite nim þa wyrmas þe beoð under
wedehundes tungan, snið onweg, ymb læd utan fictreow, syle þam
þe tosliten sy, he bið sona hal.

12. Wið fefore nim blæces hundes deades þone swyþran foten-
sceancan, hoh on earm, he tosceaceð þone fefor.

13. Warna ðe þæt ðu ne mige þær se hund gemah, sume men
secgað þæt þær oncyrre mannes lichama, þæt he 'ne' mæge, þonne
he cymeþ to his wife, hyre mid gerestan.

14. Scinseocum men wyrc drenc of hwites hundes þoste on
bitere lege, wundorlice hyt hæleþ.

MS V

2 gewanad] -að B.   6 inylfe] milte B.   8 apullod] *from* B, awullud V.
11 hunige] mid hunige B.   13 toðreoman] -hréoman B.   21 wedes
hundes] wedehundes B.   24 Wið] ið B.   24-5 fotensceancan]
fotscancan B.

MS O

1 on'weʒ] *in text* weʒ *stained and underlined,* weʒ *in o.m.*

4. Eahhræc on'weʒ' to done ʒením fulfes swyrþre eaʒe 7 hyt tosting 7 wryþ to þan eaʒon; hit ʒewanaþ þæt sar, ʒif hyt ʒelomelice þarmid ʒesmyred byð.

5, 6. —

7. Se wifman þat habbæ dead bearn on innoþe, ʒif heo drinced ful-   5 fune meoluc mid wíne ʒemenged ʒelice efne, sona hyt haleð. /

8–18. —

___

MS L

4. Ad glaucomata oculus (. . .) dexter confricatur et illitus glaucoma extenuat et linitur si ante punctus fuerit.

5. Ad splenem canis vivi splenem exemptum et potatum cum vino, sanat; quidam incisum fissumque catulum supra splenem ponunt.

6. Ad pilos contrarios laccanicus lupi evulsos pilos non patitur recrescere, si statim locum linieris unde sublati sunt.

7. Ad mulieres quae mortuum in utero habent lac lupi catuli eiciet mortuum, si continuo biberit cum melle et vino pari mensura.

8. Ad dentes infantium lacte canino si assidue infantibus gingivas tangas, dentes eis sine dolore crescunt.

9. Ad callos et verrucas tollendas lotium caninum lutum factum, in lana collectum mire callos et verrucas tollit.

10. Ad eos qui minus audiunt adipem caninum naturaliter cum absinthii suco et oleo veteri remissos stillato in aures, surdos emendat.

11. Ad·canis rabidi morsus vermes qui sub lingua canis rabiosi inveniuntur excisos et circa arbores fici perlatos et datos, qui ab eo morsus fuerit sanabitur.

12. Ad febres anfimerimas coxa dextra canis mortui nigri brachio suspensa discutit febres.

13. Ne super canis lotium mingat, super urinam canis qui minxerit, quidam aiunt eum in corpore converti nec [posse] eum, cum venerit femina, comburi.

14. Ad caducos stercus canis albi potatum ex cinere de lexiva caducos mire sanat.

15. Hnite 7 wyrmas onweg to donne ðe on cildum beoð, bærn
hundes ðost 7 gnid smale, mengc wið hunige 7 smyre mid; seo
[sealf] adeþ ða wyrmas onweg; nim eac þæt græs þær hund ge-
driteþ, cnuca, wrið on, hraðe hyt hælð.

5 16. Wið wæteradle nim drigne hundes þost, wyrc to drence, he
hæleð wæterseoce.

17. Dweorg onweg to donne, hwites hundes þost gecnucadne to
duste 7 [gemænged] wið meolowe 7 [to] cicle abacen syle etan þam
f. 81v untruman / men ær þær tide hys tocymes, [swa] on dæge swa on
10 nihte swæþer hyt sy, his [togang] bið ðearle strang; 7 æfter þam
he lytlað 7 onweg gewiteþ.

18. Wið wæteradle hundes spiwþan lege 7 wrið on þam innoðe,
þurh þone utgang seo wæteradl ut afloweð.

XI.

15 1. Ða þe scinlac þrowien etan leon flæsc, ne þrowiað hy ofer
þæt ænig scinlac.

2. Wið earena sare nim leon gelynde, mylt on scylle, drype on
þæt eare, sona him byþ sel.

3. Wið ælcum sare gemylted leon gelynde 7 þærmid gesmyred,
20 ælc sar hyt geliðigað.

4. Wið sina 7 wið cneowa leoða sarum nim leon gelynde 7
heortes mearg, mylt 7 gemeng tosomne, smyre mid þæt sár ðæs
lichoman, sona hyt byþ hal.

XII.

25 1. Wið næddrena eardunge 7 aflygennysse fearres horn gebærnedne to acsan stred þær nædran eardien, hy fleoð onweg.

MS V

3 sealf] from B, self V   nim] genim B.   4 hraðe] hræðe B.
7 Dweorg] Dweorh B 130v/9a.   8 gemænged] from B, gemengen V
to] from B, om. V.   9 þær] þare B   swa] from B, wswa V.   10 swæþer]
swahwaþer B   togang] emended from togan VB.   14 title om. VB.
17 drype] drip B.   22 mearg] mearh B.   24 title om. V.
25 Wið . . . hundes (p. 272/6)] one folio missing B.

MS O

5 cneowa] cweo / cneowa.   9 'a'flyʒennysse] preceded by exp. afy.

XI.   f. 51

1. þa þe scinlac ðrowíon ete leones flæsc; ne ðrowiad hy ofer þæt scínlac.

2, 3. —

4. (Ad neruos et ad genua) Wið sína 7 wið cneowa liþe sare ním leon 5 ȝelinde 7 heortes merurh; mylt 7 meng tosomne; smíre míd þæt sar þæs lichames; sona hyt byð hal.

XII.

1. (Ad serpentes fugandas) Wið nardran eardunge 7 `a´flyȝennysse fearres horn ȝebarnedne to axan stred þær neardran eardien; hy fleoð 10 aweȝ.

MS L

15. Ad tineas infantibus stercus canis combustum et cum melle illitum f. 24v tineas tollit.

16. Ad ydropicos stercus canis siccum et in potionem aspersum ydropicos sanat.

17. Ad verrucas tollendas stercus canis albi tunsum cum farina, turtulam factam ante hora accessionis dato aegro, manducet et sanatur; si autem nocte ad eum accedunt, simili ratione dato ante accessionem, vehemens fit accessio, deinde minuitur et recedet.

18. Ad ydropicos vomitum canis ydropico super ventrem impone, loco incipit per secessum aquam emittere.

XI. De leone

1. Ad eos qui fantasma patiuntur carnem leonis manducent, fantasma non patiuntur.

2. Ad aurium dolorem adipem leonis remissum in strigile, ex eo in aures stillato, sanabitur.

3. Ad omnem dolorem adipem leonis remissum, statim mixtum omnem dolorem sedat.

4. Ad nervorum et geniculorum dolores adipem leonis cum medulla cervina et lactuca teres et commisces, tunc demum perungues corpus, sanabitur.

XII. De tauro   f. 25

1. Ad serpentes fugandos tauri cornum comburis eo loco ubi serpentes sunt, et fugiunt omnes.

2. Wommas of andwlatan to donne, smyre mid fearres blode, ealle þa wommas hyt of genimeþ.

3. Fearres geallan wið eagena þystru 7 genipe meng wið feld-beona hunig, do on þa eagan, wundorlice hyt gehæleþ.

5 4. Wambe to astyrigenne nim fearres geallan, somna on wulle, wrið under þæt setl neoðan, sona he þa wambe onlyseþ; do þæt ylce cildum ofer ðone nafolan, he weorpeþ ut þa wyrmas.

. 5. Wið earena sare fearres geallan meng wið hunige 7 drype on ða earan, sona him byþ sel.

f. 82 6. Wið cyrnlu ðe beoþ on mannes / andwlatan, smyre mid
11 fearres geallan, sona he byþ clæne.

7. Wið apan bite oððe mannes smyre mid fearres geallan, sona heo bið hal.

8. Wið ælce heardnysse fearres smeru mylt wið tyrwan 7 lege
15 on; ealle þa sár 7 þæt hearde hyt geliðigað 7 gehnesceaþ.

9. Wiþ fortogonysse fearremearg on gehættum wine drince, þæt beteþ.

10. Wið ælcum sare drince fearres gor on hatum wætere, sona hyt hælþ.

20 11. Wiþ bryce fearres gor wearm lege on þone bryce, syþþan him bið sel.

12. Wið wæteres bryne oððe fyres bærn fearres gor 7 scead þæron.

13. Gyf þu wylle don beorhtne andwlitan, nim fearres scytel,
25 cnuca 7 bryt 7 gnid swiðe smale on eced, smyre mid þone andwlatan, ðonne byð he beorht.

14. Wifgemanan to donne nim drige fearres sceallan, wyrc to dust(e), oððe elcor gnid on win, 7 drince gelome, he bið þy gearwra to wifþingum.

2. —

3. (Ad caliginem oculorum) Ferres ȝellan wið eaȝena þystru 7 ȝenipe meng wið feldbeona hunía; do on þa eaȝean, wunderlice hit ȝehaled.

4–11. —

12. (Contra combustionem ignis vel aquae) Wið wæteres bríne oþþer fíres bærn fearres gor 7 sced þæron.   5

13. —

14. (Ad coitum excitandum) Wið ȝemanen to done ním driȝe ferres scellan, wyrc to duste, odðer ælcor gníd on wíne, 7 drince ȝelome, he byþ þe ȝearra 7 þa h`r´ædra to fifþingumd.   10

MS L

2. Ad maculas de facie tollendas sanguis tauri illitus omnes maculas de facie tollit.

3. Ad suffusionem vel caliginem oculorum fel taurinum cum mulsa et melle attico inungues et sanabis mire.

4. Ad ventrem solvendum fel taurinum in lana collectum et suppositum ano ventrem solvit. Idem facit et infantibus super umbilicum positum, lumbricos proiciunt.

5. Ad auricularum dolores fel taurinum mulsum, infusum et auribus stillatum mire sanat.

6. Ad lentigines quae in facie nascuntur fel tauri illitum in faciem lentigines purgat.

7. Ad morsum simii et hominis fel tauri illitum super morsum persanat.

8. Ad omnem duritiam sevum tauri cum resina et creta Cimolia impone, omnem duritiam discutit.

9. Ad torminosos medulla tauri in vino macerata et pota emendat.

10. Ad omnes dolores fimum tauri cum aqua calida potatum mire sanat.

11. Ad alopicias fimum calidum tauri alopicis imponito.

12. Ad combusturas fimum tauri combustum et aspersum igne aut aqua ferventi combustum sanat.   f. 25v

13. Ut splendidam faciem facias, mugium tauri in aceto maceratum et contritum, illitum, splendidam faciem facit.

14. Ad coitum faciendum testiculum tauri aridum cum vino potui dato, ad concubitum paratior erit.

XIII.

1. Wið gehwylce wommas of lichoman onweg to nimenne genim ylpenban mid hunige gecnucud 7 to geled; wundorlice hyt þa wommas of genimeð.

5 2. Eft wið wommas of andwlatan to donne, gyf wifman mid þam sylfan duste dæghwamlice hyre andwlatan smyreð, heo þa wommas afeormaþ.

XIV.

1. Wið ealle sar, gyf þu on foreweardon sumera þigest hwylcne
f. 82v hwelp na þonne gyt geseondne, / ne ongitest þu ænig sár.

11 2. Wið fortogenysse drince hundes blod, hyt hæleþ wundorlice.

3. Wið geswel þæra gecyndlima hundes heafodpanne gecnucud 7 to gelegd, wundorlice heo hæleþ.

4. Wið cynelice adle wedehundes heafod gecnucud 7 mid wine
15 gemenged to drence, hyt hæleþ.

5. Wið cancorwund hundes heafod to acxan gebærned 7 on ges`t´reded, hit þa cancorwunda gehæleþ.

6. Wið [scurfedum] næglum gebærned hundes heafod 7 seo acxe þærón gedón, þa ungerisnu hyt onweg afyrreþ.

20 7. Wid wedehundes slite hundes heafod gebærned to acxan 7 þæron gedon, eall þæt attor 7 þa fulnysse hyt ut awyrpeð 7 þa wedendan bitas gehæleþ.

8. Eft, wedehundes heafod 7 his lifer gesoden 7 geseald to etanne þam þe tosliten bið, wundorlice hyt hyne gehæleþ.

25 9. To gehwylcum bryce hundes brægen aled on wulle 7 on þæt tobrocene to gewriþen feowertyne dagas, þonne byþ hyt fæste gebatod, 7 þær byð þearf to fæstere gewriðennysse.

10. Wið eagwræce 7 stice tobrec hundes heafod; gif þæt swyþre eage ace nim þæt swyþre eage; gif þæt wynstre eage ace nim
30 þæt wynstre, 7 wrið utan ón, hyt hæleþ wel.

MS V

1, 8 title om. V.   18 scurfedum] emended from scurfendu V, see note.

MS O

3 ylpenban] ylpen struck out in pale red ink, gl. ebur   7] 7 / 7.

XIII.

1. (Ad maculas corporis tollendas) Wyþ ȝehwilce wommas of lichama onweȝ to nímen ȝením ylpenban mid huníȝe ȝecnucod 7 to ȝeled, wunderlice hit þa womas of ȝenímeþ.

2. —

XIV. De canibus

1. Wyþ ealle sar, ȝyf þu on forewearde sumera þiȝest hwylce help na þonne ȝít ȝesodena, ne ongyst þu æníȝ sar.

2–12. —

MS L

XIII. De elefanto

1. Ad maculas tollendas ebur elefanti cum melle contritum et impositum mire maculas tollit.

2. Ad plagas de facie tollendas ebur elefanti, mulier de eodem pulvere si cottidie faciem suam fricaverit, plagas mundabit.

XIV. De cane

1. Ad omnem dolorem adhuc non videntem catellum conditum prima aetate si edas, nullum sentis dolorem.

2. Ad torminosos sanguinem canis bibant, mire sanantur.

3. Ad tumores testiculorum calvaria canis trita et imposita mire sanat.

4. Ad morbum regium canis rabiosi caput contusum et commixtum, potui cum vino datum mire sanat.

5. Ad vulnera cancerosa canis non rabidi [caput] combustum et cinis eius aspersum cancerosa vulnera sanat.

6. Ad [pterygia] quae nascuntur, caput canis ustum cinisque eius appositum [pterygia] quae nascuntur in digitis urit et cicatricem tollit.

7. Ad canis rabidi morsum caput canis ustum et appositum ragadiorum et omnem spurcitiam et eos qui cane rabioso morsi fuerint persanat.

8. Item ad canis rabidi morsum caput canis rabiosi et iecur coctum dato ei qui morsus est, mire sanat.

9. Ad aliquam fracturam cerebrum canis illitum et in lana impositum et subinde suffundatur fracturis diebus quattuordecim, [solidat. Fractura] autem debebit solida alligatione uti.

10. Ad glaucomata oculorum calvaria canis, findite, si dexter oculus glaucomatis laborat, in dexteriorem partem specellum dimittitur, si sinister, sinistrum.

11. Wið toþwræce hundes tuxas bærn to acxan, hæt scenc fulne wines, do þæt dust on, 7 drince, 7 do swa gelome, þa teþ beoð hale.

12. Wið toþreomena geswelle hundes tux gebærned 7 gegniden
5 7 seted on, he wel hæleþ.

13. Wið þæt teþ wexen buton sare, hundes tux gebærned 7 smale gegniden 7 on gedon toþreomena swylas gedwæsceað.

14. Wið hunda reðnysse 7 wiðerrædnysse, se þe hafað hundes heortan mid him, ne beoð ongean hine hundas cene.

MS V

8 hunda] *this word partly erased* B 130a/4a   reðnysse] hreð- B.

13. (Ad dentes) Wið þæt teþ wexon butan sare, hundes tux ʒeberned 7 smale ʒegnidon 7 on ʒedeon toðreomera swylas ʒedwæsceþ.

14. —

MS L

11. Ad dentium dolores dentem canis combure et cinerem eius in vini emina decoque et ex eo gargarizet et sanabitur.

12. Ad tumores gingivarum dens canis combustus et contritus gingivis (. . .) impositus sanat.

13. Ut dentes sine dolore crescant dens canis combustus et cum melle tritus gingivas reprimet (. . .).

14. Ne canes sint molesti, cor canis si quis secum habuerit, canes ei f. 26v molesti non erunt.

TEXTUAL NOTES

TEXTUAL NOTES TO MS V

Page	Folio	
1/1	12/1a–2a	*INCIPIUNT*: *T* written above *N*; *CAPITA*: second *A* written above *T*.
1/17	12/18a	*druncen*: manuscript has *druc*, with an unusual sign above *c*; the contraction was necessary because the last two words of the preceding item were written at the end of this half-line.
6/11	13/1b	*wærhbræde*: the vowel of the second syllable, which looks like *ei*, is probably an unsuccessful alteration of *e* to *æ*.
18/4	15v/28a	Cure 1 of XCIX comes directly after cure 3 of XCVIII; also in B.
26/6	17v/8a	After the title, in a later hand: *Se unbrade þistel he hauat þislece hauod.*
30/1	20/3a	*wyrt*: see description of MS V, p. xv n. 3.
46/25	23v/28a	In the same hand that wrote the corresponding note in MS H ≠ *Harl. 585 D*, to indicate that H begins here.
56/12	25v/15b	The first cure of XII comes directly after the last cure of XI; there is no space for an illustration; cf. B and O.
56/13	25v/17b	*mugwyrt*: the *u* has an unusual shape with a slanting left leg; probably the scribe first started a *y*.
64/17	28/20a	In addition to the usual triangular signes de renvoi there is an interlined *ð* in line 20a and an *h* with a crossed upstroke in b.m.
86/10	34/16a	*ipirus*: the word could also be read *jipirus*.
96/2	36v/7b	Between *blostm(an)* and *sunne* there cannot have been more than two short words. The scribe mistook the first *blostman* in the sentence for the second.
100/13	38/8a	The last three words of this cure, of which nothing can be seen in the manuscript owing to damage, have been placed in round brackets because there was originally enough space for them on the folio.
112/9	41/19b	*ad serpentis morsum*: the OE name of the

Page	Folio	
		herb, *wad*, may have been mutilated to *ad* in an earlier text of *OEH*, after which *serpentis morsum*, from the Latin title of the following cure, was added; cf. BH.
118/14	43/27a	In addition to the titles printed: *feuger* in a later hand.
152/13	52/1b	It is impossible to see whether the ungrammatical *þe*, found in BH, was also in V, because this part of the text is completely gone.
158/6	53v/14b	The words *id est Canuere* in a later hand.
158/14	54/10a	*Ruta*, in a later hand, in frame.
160/8	54/b.m. b	In addition to the titles printed: *Seofenleafe* in a later hand.
176/19	59/8b	In addition to the title printed, in the hand which has written the OE titles: *lauer*. Cf. B, and see BTS (*Add.*) s.v. *lawer*.
208/7	62/1b	*mid*: *m* on erased *o*, preceded by erased *d*; the scribe first wrote *do*, confusing the two instances of *lichaman* in this cure.
238/23	76/18a	Above this line in a sixteenth-century hand *Richerd Hollond thys boke*; on this page also some later pen-trials.
240/14	76/24b	*æghwylce*: *c* dotted.
244/8	77/5a	*scea`r´plice*: *r* interlined between *e* and *a*.
248/15	77v/24b	*þritig*: MS *xxx*, with superscript *tig*.
250/15	78/6b	*Wif*: manuscript has a red *G* in the space reserved for initials, a black *W* added between *G* and *i*, a black line under *G*. Cf. t.n. to this place in H, and t.n. to p. 268/27 in V.
252/14	78v/1b	*þæt*: *þ* in black, in a different hand, a little to the right of the space for initials.
254/15	79/16a	*hring*: *g* dotted.
266/9	81v/1a	*tocymes, swa*: MS *tocymeswswa*. The scribe mistook the final *s* in *tocymes* for the initial *s* of *swa* and discovered his error after having written his first *w*, then added *swa* and did not erase the first *w*.
268/27	82/29a	*Wifgemanan*: manuscript has a red initial *G* underlined in black, a black *W* inserted between *G* and *i*. Cf. t.n. to p. 250/15 in V.

TEXTUAL NOTES TO MS B

Page	Folio	
20/19	72/23b	In chs. CXX–CXXIII the cures are in the hand that wrote the titles in this part.
30/1	74/t.m. a	Here in a later hand *saluz maund a frere water de breouuode / cente cincquante millers.*
44/13	77/1b	*beowurt*: this is the name of herb VII.
50/21	78v/t.m. b	Here *ueneria (f)ac(i)e(s)*.
56/11	79v/21b	The first cure of ch. XII comes immediately after the last cure of ch. XI; no space has been left for an illustration; cf. V and O.
58/18	80v/t.m.	Here, in a crude later hand, part of an alphabet.
72/24	84/31b	*Wið* (*Wiþ* V): initial not coloured by rubricator; only a black *W* vaguely discernible.
86/15	87a/22a	After *hræce*, in a late hand not found elsewhere in the text, *omnis homo*.
90/16	87bv/t.m.	Here, in a crude later hand, three alphabet trials.
90/22	87bv/8b, 9b	Here, in a later hand, *teter* ($2 \times$).
112/9	93v/2b	*wad* in inner margin crowded in, in a later hand, after *hatað*.
112/10	93v/7b	B is the only manuscript which has a new title here; probably the writer of the titles did not realize that the space left open was meant for a drawing of a snake.
112/17	93v/31b	*Wið*: see textual note to 72/24.
124/17	97/30b	*sar* imperfectly erased. Cockayne, p. 188 n. 17, suggests it was done because it 'was not a good answer to *ece*'.
124/18	97v	In the a-column, above ch. LXXXVI, in a crude later hand, an alphabet; then *atque ∴ est. amen aue maria gracia plena dominus tecum benedicta tu in mulieribus atque benedictus fructus uentris tui amen. in manus tuas commendo spiritum meum redemisti me domine deus.* Note that the main part of cure LXXXVI. 4 is on the corresponding lines in the b-column.
128/1	98/1b	Above ch. LXXXIX, in a later hand, *O maria*.
140/16	101/29a	*wyrt 'þ'e*: the correct construction *wyrte* altered into an incorrect one; again in 142/2 (f. 101/25b).

Page	Folio	
140/16	101/b.m. a	Here added in a later hand *þas wyrt þe man nep*.
142/22	101v/14a	In the space for illustration, in the same crude hand as on f. 97v, *pater noster qui es in ecussan*.
146/9	102v/25a	There is a space for an illustration above this cure, and *spalongion* in 'title-hand'; cf. V, and note to C. 4.
152/14	104v/25a	There is a space for an illustration above this cure, and *bulbum* in 'title-hand'; cf. V, which has a drawing of a snake here.
184/10	113/22a	*yð*: this truncated word follows immediately after the preceding cure in the same line; cf. H.
184/22	113/13b	Under this cure, very pale, *contra pulices*.
188/2	114/1a	No space for illustration.
190/1	114v/15a	In o.m., in a later hand, (. . .)*ocche*.
194/14	115/t.m. a	Here in a modern hand *a folio missing*.
216/8	120/t.m. a	Here in a modern hand *a folio missing*.
216/8	120/13a	Here in a later hand *asatrescehere*.
222/9	121v/b.m. a	Here in a later hand *amen dico uobis semper omnia*.
232/8	124/11b	The title, very pale, is in the hand which wrote the early titles.
258/21	129/20a	*wine*: on the left of the *w*, attached to it, an incomplete *g*: the scribe was about to forget the word *wine* and started on *gedruncen*.
264/4–6	130/20a–24a	This cure is marked by short horizontal lines, in different ink, at the beginning and at the end, to indicate that it does not belong here; perhaps they were added by Junius. See description of MS B, p. xxiii.
264/12	130/3b	Under this cure a short horizontal line, in different ink, to indicate that the cures taken from the wolf end here.
266/12	130v/19a	To the right of this line, in a later hand, *natus*.
266/13	130v/22a	In the space under this line, in a later hand, three words: the first illegible, then *domino suo*.
272/6	130a/t.m. a	Here in a modern hand *a folio missing*.

TEXTUAL NOTES TO MS H

4/14	116/13	Above this line: *Si quis devotus defectusque fuerit in suis nuptiis*.

Page	Folio	
10/2, 3	124/18	The scribe first omitted the cure of XLV and the title of XLVI and crowded them in afterwards.
46/25	1/t.m.	In a modern hand *Liber Humfredi Wanley*, and in the same hand that wrote the corresponding note in MS V ≠ *Vitell. C III fo. 19b*.
48/9	1/13, 14	Above these two lines two interlined words erased, probably both *hennebelle*.
48/19	1v/16, 17	*simphoniacam* preceded by a caret mark and followed by a cross; also a caret mark between *hy* and *lege*. In b.m. a cross followed by *beþe þarmid* in a later hand. There was obviously some uncertainty concerning the place where this unwarranted addition was to be inserted.
50/11	2v/4	*gehæled*: after this word, in a later hand *herba uiperina in v. folio huius libelli*.
54/19	18/b.m.	Three names written under each other: *clifwyrt, foxes glofe, cawyrt*; to the right *idem*.
60/1	21r	In t.m. and o.m.: *Succus radicis dracontee loca cancrosa optime curat. Radix cum uino data uel cum melle contrita uentrem deducit. Radix uero eius plus operatiua est, purgat enim uiscera et extenuat. perungues etiam glutinosos humores et ad uulnera maliciosa optimum medicamentum est quod purgat et mundat fortiter.*
62/12	22/13–14	Here interlined and in o.m.: *Radix orbicularis uino mixto et bibita in modico drachmas iii hictericos purgat si loco calido et cooperti fuerint ut sudare possint. Quo sudore inuenies coleram rubram deponere.*
62/17	22r	In b.m.: *Vires habet acres et calefactorias, proicit consumendo et extenuat et eueniat. Nam succus eius emoroidas clausas aperit et laxat et educit uiolenter, sicut succus eius in floco lane susceptus et ano appositus stercora educit.*
68/9	25/8	*hit þa hwitnysse*: *it þa hwit* on erasure, *nysse* preceded by an imperfectly erased *n*.
74/11	28/14	*þæs*, at end of line, followed by an erased *m*.
84/15	33v/12	*Wið 'ni'we wunda*: the scribe first wrote *Wið wun*, then interlined *ni*, altered the first minim of *u* into *e*, made a wynn of the second minim of *u* and the first of *n*, used

Page	Folio	
		the second minim of *n* for a new *u* and added *nda*.
88/23	36/18	*þrum*: the initial *W* of this cure (line 16) has two circular decorations, the second of which may have been regarded as *o* of *oþrum*.
90/26	37v/9	*hræca`n´*: *n* interlined above *a*; the unexpunged letter following *a* is an *n* imperfectly altered into *ð*.
94/9	39/12	*Gyf swylas* on erasure of *Ðeos wyrt*, probably the beginning of the following chapter.
110/5	47v/2	*oþrumman*: second minim of *u* used as first minim of *m*.
110/15	47v	In b.m.: *Hec herba tam laudabilis est ut in tiriaca potionem mittatur sed si eam tecum portaveris nulla mala te contingant. Hec herba mirabilis est testantibus auctoribus.*
114/1	49/8	*feldwyrt*: the whole word in large uncials, except *e* which is an enlarged minuscule, and *d* which is a small minuscule inserted above the horizontal part of *L*.
116/3 ff.	3/3 ff.	On this folio a 'captious reader' has been at work. In *þær tosomne*, *ær to* is struck out, in *ærenum* a *þ* is interlined after *r*, in the sentence starting with *Eac* there are dividing lines between several words; all these emendations in pale ink.
128/15	9v/9	*þonne*: manuscript has *o* with swung dash and also *nn*; second *n* altered from *e*.
130/3	10/11	Here in o.m. *sy Achilles*.
136/24	14v/1	*wundorlic* followed by erased *e*.
140/4	16/4	*fæstende*: *æ* unsuccessfully altered from *e*.
144/5	17v/16	*wyrte*: between *r* and *t* an imperfectly erased *e*.
144/7	50/1	H goes here from f. 17 to f. 50; see the description of MS H; in t.m. of f. 50: *XI, XCVII* (2×), and *ribbe*.
144/15	50/15	*anræde*: probably altered from *andweard* as a 'better' reading of Latin *praesens*.
162/3	59v/14	The scribe telescopes two sentences into one. There is a caret mark between *n* and *a* of *corna*, and a vertical line after this word. In o.m., in a later hand: *wið watersecnesse*.
162/6	59v/15	*wines* followed by a caret mark; above it, in a later hand: *xxx cornes*.

Page	Folio	
164/13	61/12	Here added: *In Hibernia succum eius pro lacrimo uendunt. Iste eius lacrimus i.e. succus omnibus c(ur)is ocolorum oppitulatur.*
166/7	62/6	*7 on wætum*: the scribe first wrote *7 on un* (repeating the preceding phrase), discovered his mistake, erased *on*, altered *u* into *o*, and probably forgot to insert *na*.
182/23	72v/3	Above the first four words a gloss *Cornla fetida magno oed*(. . .).
182/24	72v/5	In o.m. *anetum*.
184/10	73/8	*ið*: no space reserved for *W*; cf. t.n. to B 184/10.
184/21	73v/7	*flean*: between *e* and *a* erasure of *ws*.
184/22	73v/10	*flean*: between *e* and *a* erasure of *w*.
190/1	76/17	Here, in a hand not found elsewhere in the text, a gloss *Cestiros*.
190/9	76v/14	*þingc*: *g* altered from *c*.
196/23	80v/14	*wætum* followed by erasure of *edc*.
214/21	90v/6	The scribe wrote the first five words of the next cure (one complete line), then altered *Wið* into *Gið*, leaving the *ð* unchanged, and *hramman* into *hwa hreohn*, he erased *7 wið bifunge*, leaving the final *e* partly unerased, and wrote *ysse on ny*, thus changing *rewytte* into *nyrewytte*.
222/1	94/14	Before this chapter the first part of cure 1 of CLXXVIII: *Wið . . . ne te'le nemneð*. It is repeated in its proper place.
228/21	99/13	Here in o.m. a gloss *mellilotis emanaretus*.
234/2	101v/15	*E* of *EGYPta* shows erasure of *A* on the left.
234/9	102/14	In o.m., in a later hand: *De taxone*.
234/21	103/5	*sygefæ'st' 7*: the scribe wrote *sygest*, then altered *st* into *fæ* and interlined new *st* above *7*.
236/19	104/7–8	*hys hyd 'i's hundum*: probably the scribe first wrote *hys* at the end of line 7, then went on with the first two letters of *bryce* at the beginning of line 8, mistaking *hys* for *ys*. He then discovered his error, wrote *hyd* after *hys* at the end of line 7, erased *br*, wrote low *s* on the place where *r* had been erased, interlined *i* before this *s*, and after all this forgot to write *bryce*.
240/11	106v/6, 7	In o.m., in two different later hands: *De cervo* (2×).
244/5	108v/11–12	*smeo'can/ne'*: *smeo* at the end of line 11, *can* interlined here, *ne* in o.m. of line 12.

Page	Folio	
244/16	109/16, 17	In o.m., in two different later hands: *De Wulpe* and *De uulpe*.
244/17	109/b.m.	Here: *testiculus eius dexter (. . .)utus et tritus et in potu supersparsus amoris est potus mulieribus datus et sinister viris.*
246/8	110/11	*sa`re cy'relu*: manuscript has *sarelu*, *re* interlined above *a*, *cy* interlined above *e*.
250/15	113/5	`*G'if*: *G* at end of line, in o.m., *if* at beginning of same line. Cf. t.n. to this place in V.
252/8	114/5	In o.m., in a later hand: *capra siluatica*.

TEXTUAL NOTES TO MS O

33/21	6v/1	The marginal title occurs twice in t.m.
39/7	25v/20	In o.m. *ad* and one illegible symbol, probably the beginning of a discarded marginal title.
43/8	26v/10	The marginal title, which is three lines lower but is connected with the cure by its frame, runs: *in homine. nota. contra omnem morbum cotitianum.*
45/6	27/1	The marginal title occurs twice in t.m.
51/14	43/1	The words *hæleð . . . todrifð*, with which f. 43 opens, are also found in b.m. of f. 42v.
53/14	27/14	In o.m. *Aristologi(a).*
55/18	1/1	Here in t.m. and in line 1, in a modern hand, *A Saxon Herball, 6258 b*, written on faded red title, of which *De* is still visible.
63/17	24v, 25r	*Ad morbum splenis* is written twice: on f. 24v and on f. 25r.
65/11	27r, 27v	*bu/tera ʒeliðeʒe, leʒe*: in b.m. of f. 27r also *tera ʒeliliðeʒa; leʒe.*
67/3	1/20	*Ið*: capital *I* (black), a very vague black *W* in i.m.
69/17	19v	In b.m., in black: *h(ierib)ulbum.*
71/16	10/21	In o.m., in a modern hand, *eganne dryb.*
81/10	10v/26	*Wið*: no red initial, black *w* in o.m.
81/13	10v/b.m.	The last part of cure 1, *lifer . . . sylfe*, is in b.m. This chapter was probably continued on a leaf that is now lost.
85/21	17/5	Here: *hic sequitur ꝓꝓ.*
89/8	8/2	In o.m. *talis erat in exem(plo).*
89/9	8/3	In o.m. *wilde deor.*

Page	Folio	
95/9	39v/17	*Temolum* (39v/17) comes before *saxifraga* (39v/22). The scribe restores the alphabetical order by marking *temolum* B, *saxifraga* A in both margins. In o.m. also *super* between B and A.
95/15	14v/1	Folio 14v begins in the second paragraph of *Sigelweorfa*. The end of f. 14r is illegible; on f. 14v the illegible part between *hæfð* and *hure* occupies a space of at most twenty letters.
97/12	15v, 19v	See description of MS O, p. xxxiv.
111/3	8/22	This version of *peristerion* is found under the letter *b* for *berbena*.
	28v/5	On this folio, under the letter *p*, there is the following reference: *Peristerion. þeos wyrt þat man peristerion 7 oþrum naman berbenam, 7 cetera; quaere (. . .) in tractatu de B.*
	29v/1	This folio, an inserted leaf, has the chapter in the following form: *Peristerio verbena idem est. Habet colorem columbe. Vnde quidam eam columbinam uocant. Gif hwa mid him þeos wyrt haueþ ne mæȝ he of hunde beon beborcan. Wið ealle attre sule drincan þisse wyrte dusti, id est puluerem; ealle attre he todrifð. Eac man seggeð þæt þrias to hera cræftum hure brucon. Valet contra latratum canum. Valet puluis eius potatus contra omnem uenenum. Dicunt quidam quod magi circa hanc herbam insaniunt* (*seggeð* is preceded by expunged *se* plus one letter).
121/2	18/1	Above this cure a sentence in black (very pale) framed in red, of which only one word, *nenneð*, is legible.
123/2	28v/8	No title, but line arrangement as usual for a new chapter.
125/4	32v/29	The marginal title occurs in two places: in o.m. and in b.m.
129/2	20/1	This folio begins with cure 9 of *millefolium*; the beginning of the chapter was probably on one of the lost leaves; see description of MS O, p. xxxvi. In t.m. the words *het haȝende*, perhaps a corruption of the end of cure 8.
135/10	33v/10	In text, after this cure: *Ad pediculos rutam cum oleo tere et inungete et peribunt.*

Page	Folio	
135/13	33v/14	In text, after this cure: *Wid earane amplius: verte socculam.*
135/19	21v/8	In text, after this cure: *haec herba ualet ad uermes in aure et leprosis.*
137/21	28v/b.m.	Here *pollegium dweror₃ dwosle.*
145/8	37v/10	There are two more versions of this chapter in O:
	35v/1	This folio, an inserted leaf, has the following version: *Saxifragiam sundcon. (Ad petras in uesica) þeos wyrt þæt man saxifragiam 7 Engle sundcorn nemneð. Gif stanes on bladran wexan cnuca þa wyrt, mencg mid wine 7 sile drincan, 7 þan fefer₃indan on wætere; swa anwerd heo his, 7 afondon ys þæt heo þi ylca dæ₃e þa stannes forbyrced 7 hy ut atyhð 7 þane man hæleð.*
	39v/22	*Saxifraga sundcorn. (Ad lapides in uesica; ad febres) þeos wyr þæt man saxifragam 7 oþrum naman sundcorn hateð. Wið þa stanes þe on bladran wexan cnuca þeos wyrt on wine, sile drincan, 7 þan feferrenda on wætere; þeos wyrt ðæs þat ys sæd of þan þe hi afondede, þæt heo þa ylca dæ₃e þa stanes forbricð 7 hit ut tyhð 7 þane man hæled (tyhð* in last sentence preceded by expunged *as).*
153/2	38/8	In o.m. *mentastrum.*
155/11	11v/24	The sentence *þeos wyrt byð cenned,* etc., is at the end of cure 2.
157/5	11v/26	Chapter CXV was probably continued on a leaf that is now lost.
161/14	22/3	The title follows the cure.
165/14	15, 19	See description of MS O, p. xxxiv.
169/1	8v/3	Here, in faded red ink *hic d(. . .).*
177/14	23v/10–12	In o.m. *hoc debet scribi infra in capitulo de s.* Probably the scribe originally intended to enter this chapter under the letter *l* of *laber* and discovered his failure to do so when he had almost got to the end of the letter *m.*
189/1	15v, 19v	See description of MS O, p. xxxiv.
191/1	3v/12	In o.m. *subtus,* probably to indicate that *aizon* should have come after *acantaleace* (CLIII, f. 3v/19).
193/10	40v/18	*De felle* is to the left of *ðan ₃e`a'llan.*
193/18	40v/25	In o.m. *exitat libid(inem).*
211/18	44/23	In o.m., red framed in red, *Ad (. . .).*

Page	Folio	
213/3	5/24	In o.m. again *offricum barbatum.*
213/7	5r, 5v	*Ad ustionem* is on f. 5r, *contra arsuram* on f. 5v.
225/5	32/b.m.	Here *priaprissi. uica peruica. satureon, id est Anglice hrefenes leac. in* (. . .) *folios(is).*
227/3	39v/3	The sentence *þeos wyrt hafeð*, etc., comes at the end of cure 1.
233/1	10/12	In o.m. *in fronte.*
235/2	44v/t.m.	Here *explicit de medicinis herbarum. Incipit de singulis feris medicamentum.*
235/2	44v/2	*king* is in o.m., with *rex* above it and below it. There are two symbols resembling *r* above *Egypta*, probably referring to *rex.*
237/17–19	45v/6–9	In o.m. *De lepore medicina*, based upon the corrupt OE text.
239/5	45v/17	In o.m., in red, very pale: *Contra fluxum sanguinis.*
239/12	46/1–2	The text *Ðane þu*, etc., starts on line 2; on line 1 *p*(. . .) *verba N*(. . .).
241/8	46/25	In b.m., in addition to the marginal title: *Valet. A*(. . .) *aquaticum.*
255/3	48v/20	The marginal title *Ad oculos* is exactly to the left of cure 8.
261/8	50/10	The title is followed by a word in red, of which only the first letter, *b*, is legible.
261/11	50/13	In o.m. a gloss *culli et veretri.*
267/2	50v, 51r	In b.m. of f. 50v *þa þe scinlac ðrowyon eta leones flæs*; in the right half of f. 51/1, in addition to the text, *þe ðe scinlac þrowion.*

EXPLANATORY NOTES

Preliminary remarks:

A For 'explanatory notes', read 'explanatory notes and commentary'.

B Numbered notes (bold figs.) refer to cures, and in the case of *MdQ* I and II to paragraphs; notes not preceded by a number refer to titles or to the introductory parts of chapters.

C In OE words the symbol ð is replaced by þ; in non-English plant names in the OE texts the voiced labio-dental fricative is printed *v*.

D Quotations from other manuscripts and from Ackermann and Humelberg are understood to be from the parallel places in these texts, unless stated otherwise.

E The arrangement of the plant names which are found in the titles and chapter introductions in *OEH* and which are listed under the chapter numbers is as follows:

1. The official botanical names, wherever possible followed by references to authorities giving them as equivalents of the names in E2, E3, and E4.

2. The non-English plant names as found in
   (*a*) the printed text of MS V, unless stated otherwise;
   (*b*) the Latin text used as parallel;
   (*c*) Pliny; if Pliny is mentioned, the plant names occur in the *Index of Plants* at the end of Volume VII of the Loeb edition (pp. 485–546), where full references can be found.

3. The OE names as found in the printed text of MS V, unless stated otherwise; relevant parallels in *DP* and/or *LHG* are added.

4. The usual Modern English names as given by *OED* and/or Grieve.

F Names of other plants in *OEH* are dealt with in accordance with the system described in E, in notes to the cures where they (first) occur.

G Appendix I contains alphabetical lists of the plant names described in E1, E2 (*a*), E3, and E4.

H Parallels of cures in *OEH* which are in Pliny can be found via the *Index of Plants* mentioned in E2 (*c*); other parallels have been listed in Appendix II.

I All chapter numbers in *MdQ* are preceded by *M*, chapter numbers I–XIV in *OEH* are preceded by *OEH* whenever this is necessary to avoid confusion.

I

1. *Stachys officinalis* (L.) Trevir. (= *Betonica officinalis* L.) (Bi., Co.)
2. betonica V; vettonica Vo = Pl.

3. betonice, biscopwyrt (*DP* 57 se leasse bisceop-vyrt)
4. betony, wood betony

The only occurrence of the name *biscopwyrt* in *OEH* is in the title in the table of contents (only partly legible in V), and it is probably an error. See BT(S) s.v. *bisc(e)opwyrt*, Bi. s.vv. *biscopwyrt* and *betonica*, Fö., p. 130 n. 5. As Bierbaumer (ii. 13, i. 19) points out, *biscopwyrt* occurs several times in *La* and *Lb* in enumerations together with *betonice* to denote two different plants. The usual meaning of *biscopwyrt* is *Althaea officinalis*, 'marsh mallow'. Cf. also *LHG* 199 and 227: *betonica i.e. atterlaþe*, and note to *LHG* 199.

Vettonica: the herb is said to have been first discovered by the Vettones, a Lusitanian tribe; see Pl. xxv. 84.

1 In the table of contents this item is mentioned as the first cure; it is in fact a fragment of the dedicatory letter which introduces the *De herba vettonica liber*.

1 Cf. Humelberg's emendation after *ambulationes*: 'a maleficio et periculis, et loca sancta et busta etiam a visibus metuendis tuetur et defendit, et omni rei sancta est'.

1 *Busta*: (Hum.) 'i.e. caemiteria et loca ubi mortui sepeliuntur. Olim enim bustum proprie dicebatur locus in quo mortuus combustus ac sepultus erat, nunc vero dicitur sepulchrum quamvis non uratur corpus'.

1 *Sine ferro*: for the taboo against iron see G. and S., pp. 36–7.

10 *Vino Amineo*: (Hum.) 'vino optimo quale est Amineum, i.e. Phalernum'.

11 *Twega trymessa wæge*: conflation of the two measures in the Latin text.

11 *Cruditas*: 'an overloading, repletion of the stomach'.

16 *Perfrictio*: 'catching cold'.

19 *Forþat heo heardie* O: *forþat* probably assimilated from *fort þat*; see note to *M* I. 6.

20 *Quiatos duo/þreo full*: MS L has *quiatos iii.*

21 *Veretri/innoþes*: *veretrum* confused with *venter*.

29 *Fotadl* is usually a rendering of *podagra* in the Latin texts, meaning 'gout'. See also the note to *morbus regius*, LXXXVII. 1, and cf. *La* 170/19: 'Wiþ þære miclan siendan fotadle, þære þe læceas hataþ podagre; seo adl biþ aswollen 7 heo sihþ wursme 7 gilstre 7 seonuwa fortogene 7 þa tan scrinceþ up.'

II

1. *Plantago maior* L. (Bi., Co.)
2. arniglosa, plantago V; arnoglossa, plantago Vo; plantago Pl.
3. wegbræde, wægbræde
4. greater plantain, waybread

2 *Blacu* for *wlacu* (cf. Latin *tepefacito*): clearly a mistake made by a copyist who wrote from dictation.

2 *Mid mycelre wlatunge*: probably due to an association of *fomentando* with *vomendo*.

10 *Ligula*: 'a spoonful'; according to Humelberg a *ligula* is the eighth part of a *cyathus*.

15 *Secundæ*: 'the afterbirth, secundine'. The Anglo-Saxon translator thought of the quartan and tertian fevers in cures 12 and 14.

19 *Parotis*: 'a tumour near the ear, a parotis'. See *Peri Didaxeon* 11/32: 'Ad parotidas, þæt ys to þan sare þe abutan þa earan wycst, þæt man nemneþ on ure geþeode healsgund.'

19 The alteration in V of *wes* into *wesc* is remarkable. B and O have *wes*, and in the other three places where V has the imp. *gewæsc, gewesc*, the parallels in BHO are *gewes*. Here and in XX. 5 there is no Latin parallel, in XII. 2 there is a form of *subigere*, in XCIV. 2 a form of *macerare*: the verb *gewesan* therefore seems more appropriate.

III

1. *Potentilla reptans* L. (Bi., Co.)
2. pentafolium V, pentafilon V, quinquefolium H; pentafilos, quinque-folium Vo; pentapetes, pentaphyllon, quinquefolium Pl.
3. fifleafe
4. cinquefoil, fiveleaf

3 *Arteria*: 'the windpipe'.

4 *Circumscribere*: (Hum.) 'est rei alicui lineam quandam circumducere quemadmodum facere solent cacodaemonum coniuratores'.

9 *De ligno in ligno*: (Ack.) 'cum ligneo nempe pistillo in ligneo vase'.

IV

1. *Verbena officinalis* L. (Bi., Co.)
2. vermenaca V; hierabotana, verminac(i)a Vo; vermenaca Pl.
3. æscþrote, æscþrotu (*DP* 60 eascvyrt)
4. vervain, verbena

2 *Struma*: 'a scrofulous tumour, struma'.

3 *Induratae venae*: (Hum.) 'quod fit ubi corpora et venae ac alimenti vasa et conceptacula calore aut frigore desiccantur et torrefiunt, adeo ut contrahantur et indurentur ... quorum causa parum aut nihil alimenti in corpus digeri et transire potest et illud alere'.

4 The translator did not see the correlation between *robusto*, which he left untranslated, and *ceteris*.

5 *Cauculos*, read *calculos*. *Calculosus*: 'afflicted with calculus or stone'.

8 *Spalangiones*: probably a corrupted form of φαλάγγιον, a kind of venomous spider, *Lathrodectes tredecimguttatus*, 'malmignatte'. See also note to C. 4.

8 *Forþ þæt hit hal siȝ* O: *forþ* probably assimilated from *fort* 'until'; see note to *M* I. 6.

9 It is evident that the last part of this cure, from *7 lege* to *þære wunde*, is an incorrect rendering of the Latin version. But the Latin scribes, too, had problems, as appears from the version of Ha: *si sic esse coeperint, periculo sublato* (H. and S. emend into *periculi sublati*) *signum est*. The OE was apparently translated from a version in which a form of the verb *tollere* occurred.

V

1. *Hyoscyamus niger* L. (Bi., Co.)
2. symphoniaca, jusquiamum V; symfoniaca, yosciamus Vo; hyoscyamus Pl.
3. hennebelle, belone
4. henbane

4 *Gesar*: Co. prints *gesar*, but in his *Additions and Corrections* after p. cv alters it into *ge sar*, which makes no sense and is not supported by the manuscripts. *Gesar* is probably an error, caused by the neighbouring *geswell*, and should be deleted from BTS:

5 *Pectinem/breost*. *Pecten* can mean 'the hair of the pubes'; the Latin version (A and Ha agree with Vo) may be the correct one. H. and S. give a variant from a thirteenth-century manuscript: *ad pectoris mulierum dolorem*.

VI

1. *Polygonum bistorta* L. (Bi., Co.)
2. viperina V = Vo
3. nædderwyrt, nædrewyrt
4. adderwort, bistort, snakeweed

Bitterre on byrgingce, with the adjective in the dsgf., an idiom which occurs several times in *OEH*, also *weredre on byrginge*; see Glossary s.v. *byrging*.

VII

1. *Acorus calamus* L. (Co.)
2. veneria V; acorum, veneria Vo; acoron, acorum Pl.
3. beowyrt (*DP* 331 smerovyrt)
4. sweet flag

Bi. interprets this herb as *Melissa officinalis* L., 'lemon-balm, balm-mint', on account of its use in antiquity as food for bees. But there can be little doubt that the drawings in V and Vo represent *Acorus calamus*.

7 on mædum: not in the Latin manuscripts consulted; the *Editio Princeps* has *et pratum*.

1 *Examinare*: 'to form swarms, to swarm'.

VIII

1. *Alchemilla vulgaris* L. (Bi., Co.)
2. pes leonis V; leontipodium, pedeleonis Vo
3. leonfot
4. lady's mantle, lion's foot

1 *Devotus*: 'bewitched'; *defixus*: 'bound with a knot', referring to the fixation of a person by witchcraft, which was characteristic of Mediterranean magic; for this, and also for the taboo on looking back, see G. and S., pp. 35–6.

Cis: G. and S. (p. 35) emend this word into *cist*, 'a chosen one', i.e. devoted by malign powers. *Cist* in this meaning is not found in BT(S).

IX

1. *Ranunculus sceleratus* L. (Bi., Co.)
2. scelerata V; botracion, scelerata Vo; batrachion Pl.
3. clufþunge, clufþung (*DP* 64 clufthunge vel thung)
4. celery-leaved crowfoot

Vo has *botracion* in the title only; *scelerata* is one of the fifteen synonyms. The end of the introduction is puzzling. The scribe of O replaced it by a simpler statement.

1 *Ulcera chironia*: (Hum.) 'hoc est, ulcera antiqua et immedicabilia quae . . . si curari et sanari debent, medico peritissimo indigent, qualis fuit Chiron'. Cf. Co., p. 121 note a: 'By Celsus (v. xxviii. 5) ulcus chironium is defined as "quod et magnum est, et habet oras duras, callosas, tumentes".' See also notes to XIII. 2 and XXIII. 1.

X

1. *Ranunculus acer* L., or *Ranunculus bulbosus* L. (Bi. both, Co. only R. acer)
2. batracion V; botracion, botracion statice Vo; botracion Pl.
3. clufwyrt
4. buttercup, upright meadow crowfoot, *or* bulbous buttercup

1 *On Octobre foreweardum*: not an accurate translation of the Latin text, which refers to the first part of the sign of the Scorpion.

XI

1. *Artemisia vulgaris* L. (Bi, Co.)
2. artemesia V; artemisia, artemisia monoclonos Vo; artemisia Pl.
3. mucgwyrt, mugcwyrt
4. mugwort

XII

1. *Artemisia dracunculus* L. (Bi., Co.)
2. artemesia tagantes V; artemisia, artemisia tagantes Vo
3. mucgwyrt, mugwyrt
4. tarragon

The Latin texts agree in having three separate chapters, with illustrations, for the three types of *Artemisia*. In the four OE manuscripts the arrangement of the text clearly shows that originally chs. XI and XII were treated as one single chapter: after cure 2 of ch. XI, MS V has no illustration and no title, B has no space for an illustration, and the twelfth-century title is found in a small space left open at the end of ch. XI, H has no enlarged capital (a practice otherwise consistently followed) for the first cure of ch. XII, and O has no new title. Surprisingly, in the table of contents of V the entire ch. XI (not XII) is left out. From the numbering in B and H and from the added titles in these manuscripts it appears that afterwards the arrangement of the Latin texts was observed.

1 This cure is translated inaccurately, perhaps because the translator did not understand the word *scripula*, for *scrupula* (one scrupulum is $\frac{1}{18}$ uncia).

2 *Gewæsc*: see note to II. 19.

XIII

1. *Artemisia pontica* L. (Bi., Co.)
2. artemesia leptefilos V; artemisia, artemisia leptafillos Vo
3. mucgwyrt, mugwyrt
4. Roman wormwood

2 *Cironi centauro*: (Hum.) 'Chiron centaurus Saturni et Phyllirae filius fuit, qui cum argonautis navigavit, quorum medicus fuit: medicinam et herbarum vires invenit, a quo medicinam didicit Aesculapius.'

XIV

1. *Rumex obtusifolius* L. (Bi., Co.)
2. lapatium V = Vo; lapathum Pl.
3. docce, doccæ, docca, doccoe
4. common wayside dock

XV

1. *Dracunculus vulgaris* Schott (= *Arum dracunculus* L.) (Bi., Co.)
2. dracontea V = Vo; dracontium, dracontion Pl.
3. dracentse
4. dragon, dragon-wort

XVI

1. *Orchis* L. (Bi., Co.)
2. satyrion, priapisci V = Vo; satyrion, satyrios Pl.
3. hræfnes leac, hreafnes leac, refnes leac
4. orchis, wild orchid

2 *Lippitudo*: 'blearedness, inflammation of the eyes'.

XVII

1. *Gentiana lutea* L.
2. gentiana V = Vo = Pl.
3. feldwyrt (*DP* 186 eorthnutu vel feldvirt)
4. felwort, gentian

Bi. has *Gentiana amarella* L., 'autumn gentian'. *Gentiana lutea* is the more common species. Co. has *Erythraea pulcella* Sw., which belongs to the same order of plants.

Gemelli montes: (Hum./Ack.) 'Per montes Gemellos intelligo Alpes, et qui his subiacent, subalpinos a Plinio vocatos.'

Scapus: 'stem, stalk, trunk'. But cf. Hum.: 'Scapus dicitur siliqua et vasculum in quo semen continetur, ut fabae, papaveris et similium.'

XVIII

1. *Cyclamen europaeum* L. (Bi.)
2. orbicularis V; cyclaminos, orbicularis Vo; cyclaminus, -os, -on Pl.
3. slite (*DP* 118 eortheppel vel slite vel attorlathe)
4. sowbread, cyclamen

Co. has *Cyclamen hederaefolium* Ait.

1 *Ad caput deplendum*: (Ack.) 'ad pituitam e capite deducendam'. The translator confused *deplere* with *depilare*.

2 *Collurium* = *collyrium*: 'a tent, pessary, suppository'.

2 *Heortece*: here probably the equivalent of 'heartburn, cardialgy'. See the quotation from Humelberg at LXXXIX. 3.

3 *Wundrasp*: see Cpb., p. 193 n. 5; perhaps also assimilation to *þære*.

XIX

1. *Polygonum aviculare* L. (Bi., Co.)
2. proserpinaca V; poligonus, proserpin(ac)a Vo; proserpinaca, polygonon Pl.
3. unfortredde, unfortrædde
4. knotgrass

3 Vo has *qui lac non habent*; the other Latin texts have *quae lac habent*.

XX

1. *Aristolochia rotunda* L. (Bi.), *Aristolochia clematitis* L. (Co.)
2. aristolochia V; aristolacia, aristolacia rotunda Vo; aristolochia Pl.
3. smerowyrt
4. heartwort, birthwort

4 *Ad frigore exustos*: cf. Q. Serenus 1039:

> Sunt diversa quidem mala frigoris atque caloris,
> Sed tamen amborum simili nocet ulcere virus:
> Illa quoque usta putes quae sunt nive laesa rigente.

Also Virgil, *Georgics*, i. 93:

> Ne tenues pluviae rapidive potentia solis
> Acrior, aut boreae penetrabilis frigus adurat.

5 *Gewesc*: see note to II. 19.

6 *Contristatus*: (Ack.) 'in stuporem datus'.

7 *Cum cypero/cypressum*: *Cyperus*, from Greek κύπειρος, κύπερος, is an aromatic marsh plant. *Cyperus longus* L. is the sweet cyperus or English galingale, having aromatic and astringent roots. The substance referred to by the compiler of *HA* must be a product of a herb belonging to this order. The word was apparently misinterpreted by the translator as being a form of *cypressus*, the tree. In XXII. 1 *cyprinum oleum* is mistranslated *of cypresso þam treowcynne . . . ele(s)*. Greek κύπρινος is 'oil or ointment made from the flower of the κύπρος, henna (*Lawsonia inermis* L.)'. See Grieve s.v. *henna*: 'The Egyptians are said to have prepared both an oil and an ointment from the flowers for making the limbs supple.' Co. (p. 119 n. c and p. 179 n. d) translates *oleum cyprinum* 'oil of

privet'; cf. *OED* s.v. *privet*[1] 3: 'Egyptian privet, the henna of the East.'
In LXXVI. 2 *ele of cypro* is a correct translation of *(cum) oleo cyprino*.
See also Bi. s.v. *cypresse*.

XXI

1. *Nasturtium officinale* R.Br., or *Lepidum sativum* L. (Bi. both, Co.
   only *N.o.*)
2. nasturcium, narstucium V; nasturcium Vo; nasturtium Pl.
3. cærse (*DP* 248 vilde cerse; *LHG* 1056 leac cherse; see also note)
4. watercress, *or* gardencress

  1 *Ad caput deplendum*: see note to XVIII. 1.
  3 *Cruditas*: see note to I. 11.
  4 *Lumentum*: 'a mixture of bean-meal and rice kneaded together, used
by the Roman ladies for preserving the smoothness of their skin'.

XXII

1. *Colchicum autumnale* L. (Bi., Co.)
2. hieribulbum V; hierobulbum, hierobulbus Ca
3. greate wyrt
4. meadow saffron

  Locis sordidis: (Hum.) 'i.e., locis non cultis'.
  1 *Of cypresso*: see note to XX. 7.
  1 *Innopes*: mistranslation of *uteris* (verb).
  2 *Lentigo*: 'a freckly eruption, freckles, lentigo'.

XXIII

1. *Convallaria maialis* L. (Bi., Co.)
2. apollinaris V = Ca = Pl.
3. glofwyrt
4. lily of the valley

  1 *Ad vulnera cyronia* (*chironia* Ha)/*Wiþ handa sare*: see note to IX. 1;
in this cure the translator must have associated *c(h)ironia* with χείρ.

  Ad ranatum, untranslated, is probably a corruption of *ad aranearum
morsus*, a variant found in a thirteenth-century manuscript; see H. and S.

  Gehæt butan smice: the Latin *sine fumo* refers to a certain way of preparing wine; see Co., p. 121 n. b: 'The interpreter did not know that
the Romans evaporated some watery particles of the must before fer-
mentation.'

XXIV

1. *Anthemis nobilis* L. (Bi., Co.)
2. camemelon V = Ca; chamaemelon Pl.
3. mageþe
4. common camomile

XXV

1. *Teucrium chamaedris* L., or *Medicago maculata* Sibth.
2. c(h)amedris V; camedris Ca; chamaedrys Pl.
3. heortclæfre (*LHG* 315 camedris i.e. heortleure)
4. common or wall germander, *or* spotted medick

Although *camedris* is identified with *heortclæfre* in *LHG* 315 and parallel glosses (see note to *LHG* 315), it is more likely that in this chapter the Latin and the OE texts deal with two different plants. Cf. Co., p. 17 n. 1: 'The Hellenic is *Germander, Teucrium C.*, the English is *Medicago maculata.*' *Medicago maculata* is 'spotted medick', which resembles *Melilotus officinalis*. Bi., who mentions *Teucrium chamaedris* and *Melilotus officinalis* as possible equivalents of *heortclæfre*, adds 'fraglich' to both plants. The drawings in the Latin texts show some resemblance with *Teucrium chamaedris*, a plant belonging to the order of the labiatae; the illustration in V, which is not helpful, certainly does not represent a clover-like plant. *Medicago maculata* has been suggested as the alternative in this chapter, because it is likely that the plant in CLXXXIII is meant to be *Melilotus officinalis*.

Heort- is probably from *heorot*, not from *heorte*; cf. *OED* s.v. *hart clover*, quot. 1664: 'Harts Claver, because Deer delight to feed upon it.'

1 *Convellere* can mean 'wrench, dislocate'. Possibly the cure is meant for those who have dislocated or broken limbs. For other meanings of *convulsus* and *ruptus* see note to LX. 2.

1 *De ligno in ligno*: see note to III. 9.

3 *Paragoria = paregoria*: 'alleviation, ease'.

XXVI

1. *Dipsacus silvester* Huds. (Bi., Co.)
2. chameaeleæ, chameæleæ V; camelea Ca; chamaeleon Pl.
3. wulfes camb
4. wild teasel

XXVII

1. *Ajuga chamaepitys* Schreb. (= *Teucrium chamaepitys* L.) (Bi., Cb.)
2. chamepithys V; camepytium, camepytis, camepitis Ca; chamaepitys Pl.
3. henep (*LHG* 267 cammipidis i.e. pinus terrae)
4. ground-pine

The meaning 'ground-pine' is not in BT(S).

2 *Strofus*: 'twisting of the bowels'.

XXVIII

1. *Ranunculus ficaria* L.
2. chamedafne V = Ca; chamaedaphne Pl.
3. hræfnes fot, hrefnes fot, ræfnes fot (*DP* 84 leoth-vyrt vel hrafnes-fot)
4. lesser celandine, figwort, pilewort

Bi. does not add *ficaria*; Co., p. 125 n. a: 'Ravens foot is *Ranunculus ficaria*. Chamaedafne is *Ruscus racemosus*. A ranunculus, but not ficaria, is drawn in MS V, a Ruscus in MS G [= Ha].'

XXIX

1. *Viburnum lantana* L.
2. ostriago V; hostriago Ca
3. liþwyrt, lyþwyrt
4. wayfaring-tree

It is difficult to identify this plant; cf. L. and S. s.v. *ostriago*: 'a plant, otherwise unknown'. The identification with *Sambucus ebulus* (Bi., Co., Hunger) is not supported here by the drawings in V, Ca, and Ha, whereas the illustrations in XCIII are fair representations of *Sambucus ebulus*. Bi.[1] s.v. *liþwyrt* mentions as a second possibility *Viburnum lantana*; see his discussion of the name.

XXX

1. *Cochlearia anglica* L., or *Rumex hydrolapathum* L. (Co., only *Cochl. angl.*)
2. brittanica, brittanice, bryttanica V; brittanica Ca; britannica Pl.
3. hæwenhydele, heawenhnydelu (*DP* 68 vihtmeres-vyrt vel heaven hnidele; *LHG* 228 brittannica i.e. henephydele, *LHG* 236 brittanica i.e. cusselopa)
4. scurvy-grass, *or* great water-dock

Bi. does not identify the plant; Co.'s reason for identifying it with *Cochlearia anglica* is probably that it is known as an anti-scorbutic; cf. Grieve, p. 419: 'Boerhaave recommended it to be given in scurvy'. For the sense *Rumex hydrolapathum* see Grieve, p. 260: 'It is interesting to find that Turner identifies the *Herba Britannica* of Dioscorides and Pliny (famed for having cured the soldiers of Julius Caesar of scurvy in the Rhine country) with *Polygonum bistorta*, which he observed plenti-fully in Friesland, the scene of Pliny's observations. This herb is held by modern authorities to be *Rumex aquaticus* (Great Water Dock).'

2 *Oscedo*: 1. 'an inclination to yawn'; 2. 'a sore in the mouth of children, aphthae'.

XXXI

1. *Lactuca scariola* L. (Bi., Co.)
2. lactuca silvatica V = Ca; lactuca Pl.
3. wudulectric
4. prickly lettuce

Cf. CXIV; little difference between the two.

1 *Tangere/hreppan*: the *Editio Princeps* has *delinire*, H. and S. print *tingere*.

XXXII

1. *Agrimonia eupatoria* L. (Bi., Co.)
2. argimonia, agrimonia V; argimonia Ca; argemonia Pl.
3. garclife (*DP* 16 garcliue oththe clifvyrt)
4. agrimony

1 *Tale* renders Latin *suggellationes*. The original meaning of the Latin word is 'bruise, livid spot, black and blue mark'. It is also used figuratively in the sense 'evil-speaking, calumny, vituperation'. This is the usual meaning of OE *tal*; see BT(S). In this context the word probably means 'fault, defect', a sense not recorded in BT(S).

6 The end of the Latin cure is corrupt. Ca has *corrumpet*; cf. also other variants in H. and S.

XXXIII

1. *Asphodelus ramosus* L. (Bi., Co.)
2. astularegia V; asfodulus (*gl.* astula regia) Ca; asphodelus, hastula regia Pl.
3. wudurofe (*DP* 48 vude-roue vel bare-popig)
4. asphodel, king's spear

For a discussion of the plant name *wudurofe* see note to LIII.

XXXIV

1. *Rumex acetosa* L. (Bi., Co.)
2. lapatium V; oxilapatium Ca; oxylapathon Pl.
3. wududocce
4. sorrel

XXXV

1. *Blackstonia perfoliata* (L.) Huds. (Bi., Co.)
2. centauria maior V = Ca; centaurium maius Pl.
3. eorþgealla, curmelle, curmelle seo mare (*DP* 107 eorth-gella vel hyrdvyrt vel curmelle)
4. yellow centaury, yellow-wort

1 *Angle*: this form occurs 4× in V (*Ængle/Engle* 4×), 3× in B (*Ængle/ Engle* 5×); it is not found in H and O. Like the other two words, *Angle* here denotes 'English' rather than 'Angles'.

1 *Curmelle seo mare* and (in the next chapter) *curmelle seo læssæ*: from these instances it can be concluded that plant names in the phrase *þe Grecas* etc./*man* etc. . . . *nemnaþ/nemneþ* are treated as nominatives.

XXXVI

1. *Centaurium umbellatum* Gilibert (Bi., Co.)
2. centauria minor, febrifuga V; centauria minor Ca; centaurium minus Pl.
3. feferfuge, curmelle seo læsse (læssæ)
4. common or lesser centaury

3 Manipulus: 'a handful, bunch'.

3 *Congius/ambur*: a *congius* is 3.48 litres; for *ambur*, see Harmer, p. 74: 'The amber seems originally to have been an adaptation of the Roman *amphora*, which was equivalent to about six gallons' (27 litres).

4 For the translation of *ad auriginem* see note to LXXXVII. 1.

6 The words *wiþ syna togunge . . . þriddan dæle* have no parallel in the Latin version. In all the Latin manuscripts cure 5 comes before cure 4. When the translator discovered that *her beforan* in cure 6 no longer referred to cure 4 but to cure 5, he hastened to warn his readers that *her beforan* only meant that the same herb was to be taken, and that it did not apply to the dosage mentioned in cure 5.

XXXVII

1. *Beta vulgaris* L. (Bi., Co.)
2. personacia V; prosepis, personacia Ca
3. bete, boete
4. beet, beetroot

It is doubtful whether the plant described in the Latin texts is *Beta vulgaris*. The drawings in Ca, Ha, Vo do not show any resemblance with a beetroot, and the Latin plant name *personata* (L. and S.) means 'a kind of large burdock'. Co., p. 136 (margin), also seems to have his doubts: 'personaca, however, otherwise'. But the drawing in V does show some resemblance with a beetroot, and in MS Bodley 130 *Personata* is glossed *bete*.

3 *Nitrum*: 'native mineral alkali, native soda, natron'.

3 *Picula*: 'a little pitch'.

XXXVIII

1. *Fragaria vesca* L. (Bi.; Co. has only *Fragaria*)
2. fraga V = Ca = Pl.
3. strea(w)berge, streowberie (*DP* 163 stravberian vel mersc-mealeve)
4. wild strawberry

   1 In Ca cures 1 and 2 are almost identical.
   2 *Suspiriosus*: 'breathing with difficulty, asthmatic'.

XXXIX

1. *Althaea officinalis* L. (Bi., Co.)
2. hibiscus V; altea, ibiscum Ca; hibiscus Pl.
3. merscmeal(u)we
4. marsh-mallow

   2 Equivalents of *wyllecærse*:

1. *Trigonella foenum graecum* L. (Bi., Co.)
2. fenum graecum Ca = Pl.
4. fenugreek

   Co., p. 141, translates the OE word 'cress from a spring', but states in note b that *foenum græcum* is *Trigonella*.

XL

1. *Equisetum* L. (Co.)
2. ip(p)irus, æquiseia V; hyppirum (*gl.* equiseia) Ca; hippuris, equisaetis, -um Pl.
3. —— (*DP* 208 ippirus, equiseia vel toscan-leac; *LHG* 838 ipirum i.e. equisetiam, equi cauda)
4. horsetail

The corrupted form in -*seia* is also found in Ha.

XLI

1. *Malva silvestris* L. (Bi., Co.)
2. malva er(r)atica, malfa err., malve erratice V; malva erratica Ca; malva Pl.
3. hocleaf (*DP* 228 hoc-leaf vel geormen-leaf)
4. common mallow

   1 *In congio/sester ful oþþe mare*. A *congius* (3.48 litres) is much more than a sester, which is 0.58 litre.

XLII

1. *Cynoglossum officinale* L. (Bi., Co.), or *Lycopsis arvensis* L. (Gunther)
2. buglossa, lingua bubula V; buglossa, bovis lingua Ca; lingua bubula Pl.
3. hundes tunge (glofwyrt)
4. hound's-tongue, dog's-tongue, *or* bugloss

There is much uncertainty about the identity of this plant; cf. the following entries in *DP*:

> 69 buglosse   foxes-gloue (Von Lindheim adds: = *Digitalis purpurea* L.)
> 71 buglossan   glofwyrt vel hundes-tunga
> 221 lingua bobule   oxan-tunge (cf. Wright–Wülcker 593, 4 *lingua bovis*: oxtunge)

See also BTS (*Add.*) s.v. *hundes tunge*. For *glofwyrt* as an erroneously used synonym of *hundes tunge*, see Bi. s.v. *glofwyrt*.

   2 *Suspirationes* is probably an error. Vo has *duritias* in the text, *suppurationes* in the table of contents.

XLIII

1. *Urginea maritima* (L.) Bak. (= *Scilla maritima* L.) (Bi., Co.)
2. bulbiscil(l)it(t)ica, bulbiscillitici V; bulbiscillitici, scilla Ca
3. glædene
4. sea-onion, squill

   Co. in the table of contents has *Iris pseudacorus*; the drawings do not support this.
   2 *Perniones*: 'chilblains'.
   3 *Paronichias*: see *OED* s.vv. *paronychia, agnail*.

XLIV

1. *Cotyledon umbilicus* L. (Co.)
2. cotiledon, cotulidonus, umbilicum, umbilicus Veneris V; cotuledon, cotulidon Ca; cotyledon Pl.
3. ——
4. wall pennywort, navelwort

XLV

1. *Panicum crus galli* L. (Bi., Co.)
2. gallicrus V = Ca
3. attorlaþe
4. cockspur-grass

XLVI

1. *Marrubium vulgare* L. (Bi., Co.)
2. prassion, marubium, marabium V; prassion, marrubium Ca; marrubium, prasion Pl.
3. harehune
4. horehound, hoarhound

   3 Equivalents of *elehtre*:

1. *Lupinus* L. (Bi.)
2. lupinus Ca = Pl.
4. lupine

   4 *Condyloma*: 'a swelling in the parts about the anus'.
   7 *Extensio*: 'a swelling, tumour'.

XLVII

1. *Sparganium emersum* Rehmann (= *Sparganium simplex* Huds.) (Co.)
2. xifion V; xyfion, xifion Ca; xiphion Pl.
3. foxes fot
4. unbranched bur-reed

Bi.[3] rejects *Sparganium emersum* on several grounds. His suggestion that *foxes fot* may be a misinterpretation of *adiPES VULPINUS* is not supported by the Latin manuscripts. Only A, f. 37, has *adipes vulpis*, clearly as two separate words.

   1 *Amylum*: literally 'not ground at the mill', hence 'of the finest meal'.

XLVIII

1. *Callitriche verna* L., or *Asplenium trichomanes* L. (Bi. both, Co. only *Call. v.*)
2. gallitricus V; gallitricum Ca; callitrichon Pl.
3. wæterwyrt
4. water starwort, *or* common maidenhair

   MSS BH have *callitricum*.

XLIX

1. *Pinguicula vulgaris* L.
2. temolus V; etmolum Ca; moly Pl.
3. singrene, syngrene
4. butterwort

Both Bi. and Co. have *Sempervivum tectorum*. But see Co.'s note a, p. 153: 'the flowering stem and flower are given as very slender, and solitary, so that one thinks of "Pinguicula vulgaris" '. It is more probable that the herb in CXXV is *Sempervivum tectorum*.

Equivalents of *leac*:

1. *Allium* L. (Bi.)
2. caepa Vo; cepa, caepa Pl.
4. leek

L

1. *Hypochoeris glabra* L. (Bi.)
2. æliotrophus, vertamnus V; eliotropis, eliotropum Ca
3. sigelhweorfa, sigelwearfa
4. cat's-ear

Bi., who mentions five possible equivalents of *sigelhweorfa*, regards *Hypochoeris glabra* as the most likely candidate for the plant described in this chapter, and rejects *Achillea tomentosa* L., which is suggested by Co. and Stracke (note to *LHG* 542).

LI

1. *Rubia tinctorum* L. (Bi., Co.)
2. gryas V; grias Ca
3. mædere, mæderu
4. madder

LII

1. *Trifolium procumbens* L. (Bi., Co.)
2. politricus V; politricum Ca; polytrichon Pl.
3. hymele
4. hop-trefoil, yellow clover

LIII

1. *Asperula odorata* L. (Bi.)
2. malochinagria, -agrea, astularegia V; astula regia Ca
3. wudu(h)rofe (*LHG* 155 astula regia i.e. wuderoue i.e. malacinagria i.e. musga)
4. (sweet) woodruff

Co. has *Asphodelus ramosus*, as in XXXIII.

Wudu(h)rofe is probably a fusion of *wudurife* and *wudurofe*. *Wudurife*, meaning *Asperula odorata*, is found in *Lb* 20/22. Bi.[1], s.vv. *wudurofe* and *hegerife*, shows that *wudurife* can be plausibly regarded as the original form of the name indicating the plant in this chapter. *Wudurofe* is probably the original name for *Asphodelus ramosus* (see XXXIII), *-rofe* meaning 'tuber' (cf. German *Rübe*). It may be assumed that the two words were confused and that the form with *o* was eventually used for both plants; in that case it is difficult to ascertain the quantity of the *o*. The variant *-hrofe*, for which there is no satisfactory explanation, is found three times in VH (only in this chapter), as against fifteen occurrences of *-rofe* (*-roue*, *-roua*) in VBH.

LIV

1. *Papaver somniferum* L. (Bi., Co.)
2. metoria, moetorias, papaver album V; papaver Ca = Pl.
3. (hwit) popig
4. opium poppy

    1 *Epiphora*: 'a persistent flow of tears' (Li. and S.).
    2 *Emigraneum*: (Hum.) 'Hemicraneus sive hemicrania, cum in sinistra dextrave capitis parte dolor sit.'

LV

1. *Oenanthe pimpinellifolia* Sprengel (Co.)
2. oen(n)antes V; oenantes Ca; oenanthe Pl.
3. ——
4. dropwort

LVI

1. *Campanula trachelium* L. (Bi., Co.), or *Narcissus poeticus* L. (Gunther)
2. narcisus V; narcissus Ca = Pl.
3. halswyrt
4. throatwort, nettle-leaved bellflower, *or* narcissus

LVII

1. *Asplenium ceterach* L., or *Phyllitis scolopendrium* (L.) Newm. (= *Scolopendrium vulgare* Sm.) (Bi., both)
2. splenion, teuerion V; splenion Ca = Pl.
3. brunewyrt
4. finger-fern, spleenwort, *or* hart's-tongue

    Co. in contents: 'usually *Scrofularia aquatica*', in text: '*Ceterach officinarum*'.

    1 Equivalents of *hysope*:
1. *Hyssopus officinalis* L. (Bi.)
2. ysopus Ca; hys(s)opum Pl.
4. hyssop

LVIII

1. *Teucrium scorodonia* L., or *Teucrium polium* L. (Co., only *Teucrium p.*)
2. polion V = Ca

3. ——
4. sage-leaved germander, wood-sage, *or* hulwort, cat-thyme, poly germander

It is impossible to say which of the two herbs is described here and which in CLI. Cf. L. and S. s.v. *polion, polium*: 'a strong-smelling plant, perhaps the poley-germander, *Teucrium polium* L.'; Li. and S. s.v. πόλιον: 'hulwort, *Teucrium polium*'. *OED* s.v. *hulwort* quotes Miller 1884, who equates *Teucrium polium* to cat-thyme, hulwort and poly germander, and Gerarde 1597, who says that hulwort is polium. See also *DP* 278: polion—peonia.

1 *Pilula*: (Hum.) 'Per pilulam intelligit capitulum ipsum, quod in corymbi et pilae figuram habet.'

LIX

1. *Ruscus aculeatus* L. (Bi., Co.)
2. victoriole, victoriola V; victoriola Ca
3. cneowholen
4. butcher's broom, knee-holly

1 For *dropa*, see *OED* s.v. *drop* sb. 11, and Bonser, pp. 407–8.

LX

1. *Symphytum officinale* L. (Bi., Co.)
2. confirma V; symphitum, confirma Ca; symphytum Pl.
3. galluc
4. comfrey

2 *Convulsus*, according to Humelberg, means 'spastic' in this cure. He continues: 'Rupti vero sunt quibus in carnosa parte citra vulnerationem facta est divisio, quam rhegma nominant Graeci.' But in his note to XXV. 1 he gives a very different definition of *ruptus*: 'Ruptos vocat, qui alio nomine herniosi et ramicosi . . . dicuntur.'

3 *Oxygarum*: 'a sauce of vinegar and garum'. *Garum* is a rich sauce, made of small fish.

LXI

1. *Stellaria media* Cyrill. (Co.)
2. asterion V = Ca; aster Pl.
3. ——
4. chickweed

For the choice of *Stellaria media* see Co., p. 165 n. a.
There is no support in the Latin texts for the synonym *sauina* in O.

LXII

1. *Trifolium arvense* L. (Bi., Co.)
2. leporis pes, pes leporis V; leporis pes Ca
3. haran hig(e), haran hyge
4. hare's-foot clover

LXIII

1. *Dictamnus albus* L. (Co., *Diptamnus alba*)
2. dictamnus V; diptamnum Ca; dictamnum Pl.
3. ——
4. white dittany

  5 Equivalents of *æpelferpincwyrt*:

1. *Stellaria holostea* L. (Bi.)
2. agrimonia Ha; argemonia Pl.
4. stitchwort

   See Bi. s.v. *æpelferpingwyrt* for the relation between this herb and *garclife* (XXXII).

  5 Equivalents of *hindehælepe*:

1. *Eupatorium cannabinum* L. (Bi.)
2. ambrosia Ha = Pl.
4. water hemp, hemp agrimony

LXIV

1. *Calendula officinalis* L. (Gunther), or *Heliotropium europaeum* L. (Co.)
2. solago maior, helioscorpion V; solago maior Ca; helioscopion Pl.
3. ——
4. marigold, *or* white heliotrope

   It is impossible to say which of the two herbs is described here and which in CXXXVII.

LXV

1. *Croton tinctoria* Juss. (= *Croton tinctorium* L.) (Co.)
2. solago minor, æliotropion V; solago minor Ca; heliotropium Pl.
3. ——
4. croton

LXVI

1. *Paeonia officinalis* L. (Bi. (without *officinalis*), Co.)
2. peonia, pionia V; peonia Ca; paeonia Pl.
3. peonie
4. peony

   Coccel is a mistranslation of *granum cocci*, 'cochineal grain'.

LXVII

1. *Aquilegia vulgaris* L.
2. peristereon, berbena, columbina V; peristereon Ca; peristereos Pl.
3. berbene (H only)
4. columbine

   Bi. and Co. give *Verbena officinalis* as the equivalent of berbene. The names *peristereon* and *columbina* and the explicit reference to pigeons indicate that *Aquilegia vulgaris* is meant; cf. *OED* s.v. *columbine* sb. 2. *Verbena officinalis* is described in IV.

LXVIII

1. *Bryonia* L. (Bi.)
2. bryonia, brionia V; brionia Ca; bryonia Pl.
3. hymele
4. bryony

Co. identifies this plant as *Humulus lupulus* L., 'hops'. See also Bonser, pp. 359–60.

LXIX

1. *Nymfaea alba* L. (Co.)
2. nymfete V; nymfea Ca; nymphaea Pl.
3. —— (*DP* 251 nimphea collon-croh vel sigel-hveorua)
4. white water-lily

Collon-croh (in *DP* 251): 'water-lily'.

LXX

1. *Trifolium pratense* L. (Bi., Co.)
2. crision, crisyon V; crysion Ca
3. clæfre
4. clover, trefoil

1 *Goman*, in all the recorded instances in *OEH* and *MdQ*, is a translation of *fauces*. The general meaning of *fauces* is 'throat'; cf. L. and S. s.v. *fauces*: 'the upper part of the throat, from the root of the tongue to the entrance of the gullet, the pharynx, throat, gullet', *OED* s.v. *fauces* 1: 'Anat. The cavity at the back of the mouth, from which the larynx and pharynx open out.'

LXXI

1. *Isatis tinctoria* L. (Bi., Co.)
2. is(s)atis, ysatis, aluta V; ysatis Ca; isatis Pl.
3. wad (B only)
4. woad

Ad serpentis morsum in the OE text: see the textual note to V, f. 41/19b. It is remarkable that this mistake is also found in B and H.

LXXII

1. *Teucrium scordium* L. (Co., in contents)
2. scordea V; scordeon Ca; scordion Pl.
3. ——
4. water germander

Co., in margin of text, has *Teucrium scorodonia* with a question mark.
3 *þæs þriddan dæges fefor* is the most plausible reading; cf. II. 12 and XLII. 1.

LXXIII

1. *Verbascum thapsus* L. (Bi., Co.)
2. verbascus V; verbascum Ca = Pl.
3. feltwyrt (feldwyrt)
4. great mullein

Feldwyrt is clearly wrong. *Feldwyrt* is 'gentian'; see XVII. See also Co. ii (orig. edn.), 383: 'The reading feldwyrt is a mistake, the felty leaves give it the name, whence it is also called in German Wollkraut; mullein is also supposed to be woollen.'

LXXIV

1. *Centaurea calcitrapa* L.
2. heraclea V = Ca
3. ──
4. star-thistle

The identification is based upon a gloss *calcetreppe* in MS Bodley 130; see Co., p. 177 n. a.

LXXV

1. *Chelidonium maius* L. (Bi., Co.)
2. celidonia, cælidonia V; celidonia Ca; chelidonia Pl.
3. cyleþenie
4. greater celandine

    1, 2 *Mel atticum*: see note to *M* IV. 13.

LXXVI

1. *Atropa belladonna* L., or *Solanum nigrum* L. (Bi. both, Co. *Solanum nigrum, Solanum dulcamara*)
2. solate, solata, solsequia V; solata Ca
3. solosece (*LHG* 1322 solata i.e. solsece)
4. deadly nightshade, *or* black nightshade

    2 *Ele of cypro*: see note to XX. 7.

LXXVII

1. *Senecio vulgaris* L. (Bi., Co.)
2. senecio V; senecion Ca; senecio, erigeron Pl.
3. grundeswylige
4. common groundsel

LXXVIII

1. *Filix* L.
2. filix, felix V; filix Ca; felix, filix Pl.
3. fearn, fern
4. fern

    Bi.: 'eine Fern-art', Co.: '*Aspidium, Polypodium*, etc.'

1 For *æþelferþincgwyrt* see note to LXIII. 5.

2 The word *aesculus* denotes the winter or Italian oak, *Quercus farnetto* Ten.; see Bi. s.v. *becen*.

LXXIX

1. *Agropyrum repens* (L.) P.B. (= *Triticum repens* L.) (Bi., Co.)
2. gramen V = Ca = Pl.
3. cwice
4. quitch, couch-grass

LXXX

1. *Iris pseudacorus* L. (Bi., Co.)
2. gladiolus, gladiolum V; gladiolum Ca; gladiolus Pl.
3. glædene
4. yellow flag, gladdon

   3 *Praecordia*: 'the entrails, the stomach'.

LXXXI

1. *Rosmarinus officinalis* L. (Bi., Co.)
2. rosmarinum, rosmarim V; rosmarinum Ca = Pl.
3. boþen (*DP* 290 sundeav vel bothen vel feld-medere)
4. rosemary

   4 Equivalents of *nard*:

1. *Nardostachys jatamansi* L. (Bi.)
2. spica nardi Ca
4. nard, spikenard

It would seem that the two recorded forms of *nard* in *OEH*, *nardis* gsg. here and *nardo* dsg. in CXXXII. 2, hardly justify its inclusion in an OE glossary. See, however, *nardes ear* in *MdQ* VII. 16, and two more instances of *nardes* gsg. recorded in BT.

4 There are more ingredients in the Latin version than in the OE: a little cardamom (see *OED* s.v. *amomum*) and two dates. The translator confused *palmula* and *palma*.

LXXXII

1. *Daucus carota* L., or *Pastinaca sativa* L. (Bi. both, Co. both, in contents)
2. pastinaca silvatica, p—e s—e V; pastinaca silvatica Ca; pastinaca Pl.
3. feldmoru
4. wild carrot, *or* wild parsnip

LXXXIII

1. *Parietaria officinalis* L. (Bi., Co.)
2. perdicalis V = Ca; perdicium Pl.
3. dolhrune
4. pellitory of the wall

LXXXIV

1. *Mercurialis perennis* L., or *Sinapis arvensis* L. (Bi. both, Co. *Merc. p.* only)
2. mercurialis V = Ca = Pl.
3. cedelc (*DP* 237 cedelc vel merce)
4. mercury, *or* field-mustard, charlock, kedlock

LXXXV

1. *Polypodium vulgare* L. (Bi., Co.)
2. radiolum, radiola V; radiolum Ca; polypodium Pl.
3. eforfearn (*DP* 287 eofer-fearn vel brun-vyrt)
4. polypody

LXXXVI

1. *Anthriscus silvestris* Hoffm. (Bi.)
2. sparagi (agrestis), spurgia agrestis V; sparagus (agrestis) Ca; asparagus Pl.
3. wuducerfilla, wuduceruille
4. wild chervil

Co.: '*Asparagus acutifolius*'.

4 *Devotare*: 'to bewitch'; *lustrare*: 'to purify by means of a propitiatory offering'.

LXXXVII

1. *Juniperus sabina* L. (Bi., Co.)
2. sabina, savina V; savina Ca; sabina Pl.
3. sauine, safinæ
4. savine

1 *Morbus regius/cynelic adl/king's evil*, usually interpreted as a disease curable by a king or through the agency of a king. The identity of king's evil varied in different periods. For the classical meaning of *morbus regius* see Du Cange, v. 518: 'morbus regius: icterus recentioribus, antiquioribus lepra'. *Icterus* is from Greek ἴκτερος, 'jaundice'. For *aurugo* (not *aurigo*, as in our texts), see Isidorus, *Origines*, iv. 8. 13: 'aurugo, quam quidam regium, quidam arquatum morbum vocant'. Jaundice is a disease in which the skin turns to the yellow colour of the rainbow (*arquus*).

In the *Herbarium* and the *Medicina de Quadrupedibus* we find the following instances in which the words *morbus regius*, *aurigo*, and *ictericus* occur:

XXXVI. 4 Ad auriginem—Wiþ sina togunge
LXXXVII. 1 Ad morbum regium quod est auriginem—Wiþ þa cynelican adle þe man aurignem nemneþ, þæt ys on ure geþeode þæra syna getoh 7 fota geswel
CXVIII. 1 Ad pedum dolorem vel auriginosos—Wiþ fotadle

CXLI. 2	ictericis—Wyþ æwyrdlan þæs lichoman þe cymeþ of togotennysse þæs eallan
CXLIII. 1	morbum regium—þa cynelican adle
CXLVI. 2	ictericis—wiþ þæs eallan togotenysse
M XIV. 4	Ad morbum regium—Wiþ cynelice adle

From these instances it appears that *ictericus* is interpreted by the Anglo-Saxon translator as jaundice. *Morbus regius* and *aurigo* are associated with a foot disease, probably gout. Cf. Geldner (i. 6), who mentions the word *Herrenkrankheit* as a popular name for gout. The later meaning of king's evil, 'scrofula', is not found in these texts. For a detailed discussion of the term *king's evil*, see Bonser, ch. XVIII; for *fotadl*, see also note to I. 29.

LXXXVIII

1. *Antirrhinum orontium* L. (Bi., Co.)
2. canis caput, c. capud V; canis caput, c. cerebrum Ca; antirrhinum Pl.
3. hundes heafod
4. small snapdragon, calves'-snout

LXXXIX

1. *Rubus fruticosus* L. (Bi., Co.)
2. erusti V; erustum, rustum, rubus Ca; rubus Pl.
3. bremel
4. bramble, blackberry

   1, 2 *Cima* = *cyma*: 'a young sprout of a cabbage'.

   3 *Cardiacus*, cf. Hum.: 'Cardiaca passio, uti Galenus in Isagoge tradit, appellatio est, non quia in corde malum sit, sed quoniam antiqui καρδίαν stomachum appellabant.' But in this cure the reference to *mamilla sinistra* seems to contradict his statement.

   4 *Mora*, plural of *morum*, 'berry of the bramble'; the translator thought of *mora*, 'delay'.

XC

1. *Achillea millefolium* L. (Bi., Co.)
2. millefolium, mylle-, milli-, achylleos V; millefolium Ca = Pl.
3. gearwe
4. milfoil, common yarrow

   Telephos, son of Heracles and Auge, was first wounded by Achilles, afterwards cured by the rust of Achilles' lance (see Pl. xxv. 42). The name is *Elephos* in A, Ca, Ha, and Har, *Melephos* in Slo and Vi; the correct form *Telephos* is in the *Editio Princeps*.

   9 The combination of hardened veins with faulty digestion is also found in IV. 3; see note to that cure.

XCI

1. *Ruta graveolens* L. (Bi., Co.)
2. ruta V; ruta (hortensis) Ca; ruta Pl.

3. rude, rute
4. rue

2 *Inflatio*: 'a swelling or puffing up, inflation, flatulence'.
3 *Sulfur vivum*: (Hum.) 'dicitur quod ignem non expertum est'.
5 *Litargum*: cf. Celsus, iii. 20. 1: 'In hoc [morbo] marcor et inexpugnabilis paene dormiendi necessitas. Lethargum Graeci nominarunt.'

XCII

1. *Mentha longifolia* (L.) Huds. (= *Mentha silvestris* L.) (Bi., Co.)
2. mentastrus V; mentastrum Ca = Pl.
3. horsminte (B only), minte (H only)
4. horse-mint

1 *Brocminte* in O is probably not correct; cf. CVII.
2 The words *hreofl, hreofla* (*hreof*), found here and in CX. 3, CXLVI. 4 and *M* VII. 10, occur frequently in religious texts as equivalents of λέπρα, λεπρός, used as comprehensive terms for various skin diseases. See also the following examples:

(a) Wright–Wülcker 162, 9: *Ulcerosus*, hreofla; ibid. 374, 22: *Callosi*, hreofe oþþe wearrihte; ibid. 389, 31: *Elephantinosa*, sio hreoflice.
(b) Bede, v. 2 (ed. Miller, p. 388/17): 'swæ micle hreofle 7 scyrf', translating 'scabiem tantam et furfures' (ed. Plummer, p. 283).
(c) *Pastoral Care* XI (ed. Sweet, p. 71/4): 'Ðonne bi þam sceabbe suiþe ryhte sio hreofl getacnaþ þæt wohhæmed', rendering 'per [scabiem] recte luxuria designatur' (*Liber Regulae Pastoralis*, i, ch. xi).
(d) *Lacnunga* 178/12: 'Wiþ poccum 7 sceapa hreoflan': 'against pox and scab of sheep'.

In the B-version of the Latin parallel to *M* VII. 10 the word *pediculosus* is preceded by a corrupted form of *phthiriasis*: see Ca 540/6a: *ptirias*, A 58/30: *ptyrias*, Harley 1585, 71v/16a: *tyrias*, Bodley 130, 89v/18: *turias*. *Pediculosis* and *phthiriasis* denote a condition of the body in which lice multiply in swellings of the skin. See also Ælfric's description of King Herod's *wæterseocnyss*, which was accompanied by a similar condition (Whitelock XIV/144).

Apparently the words *hreofl, hreofla* (*hreof*) in our texts are used in connection with different skin diseases, and consequently can only be interpreted in general terms like 'scabbiness', 'itching', 'rash'.

For detailed discussions of the words *hreofl, hreofla, hreof*, and their derivatives, see Geldner, ii. 36–40; W. Bonser, 'Anglo-Saxon Medical Nomenclature', *English and Germanic Studies* (University of Birmingham), iv (1951–2); A. Hille, 'Exit Middle English micclelic, "multitude", Enter þe miccle lic, "leprosy"', *English Studies*, 50 (1969), 284–90. For the complicated semantic development of the words *elephantiasis* and *leprosy*, see H. A. Skinner, *The Origin of Medical Terms*, 2nd edn. (Baltimore, 1961), pp. 157, 249.

XCIII

1. *Sambucus ebulus* L. (Bi., Co.)
2. ebulus V; ebulum Ca = Pl.
3. wealwyrt, wælwyrt, ellenwyrt
4. dwarf elder, danewort, wallwort

2 For other instances of the magic use of the numbers *three* and *nine*, see *Lb* 34/20, 36/3, 36/5, 43/18, 88/19.

2 *Ne respicias*: for the taboo on looking back, see G. and S., pp. 35–6.

XCIV

1. *Mentha pulegium* L. (Bi., Co.)
2. pollegium, pollegion, polleium V; puleium Ca = Pl.
3. dweorgedwosle, -dweosle, polleie (*DP* 277 hyllvyrt vel dveorge-
   dveosle)
4. pennyroyal

The first element of the OE plant name *dweorgedwosle* is probably used in the sense '(intermittent) fever'; cf. *Peri Didaxeon*, 31/14: '7 hwile he riþaþ [*hriþian* 'to shake, quake, have a fever'], swylce he on dueorge sy'. For a discussion of the word *dweorg*, the role played by dwarfs in Anglo-Saxon magic, and the interpretation 'fever', see Storms, pp. 168 ff. For a different interpretation of the plant name, see Bi.[1], p. 49.

Bleo(h) is 'colour' and translates *coloribus*. But Ha has *maximis aestatis caloribus*, which makes more sense in this context.

2 *Gewæsc*: see note to II. 19.

6 *Codas*: Pl. xx. 13 has *surculi*, 'twigs'.

XCV

1. *Nepeta cataria* L. (Bi., Co.)
2. nepitamon, neptamnus, mente orinon V; nepeta (montana) Ca; nepeta Pl.
3. nepte
4. catmint

XCVI

1. *Peucedanum officinale* L. (Bi., Co.)
2. peucedanum, peucedana V; peucedanum Ca = Pl.
3. cammoc
4. hog's fennel, sulphurwort

XCVII

1. *Inula helenium* L. (Bi., Co.)
2. hinnula campana V; innula campana Ca; inula Pl.
3. sperewyrt (*LHG* 786 hinnulacampana i.e. horsellen)
4. elecampane

1 Equivalents of *eorþnafla*:

1. *Asparagus officinalis* L. (Bi., Co.)
2. sparagus Ca; asparagus Pl.
4. asparagus

XCVIII

1. *Plantago lanceolata* L. (Bi., Co.)
2. cynoglossa, arnoglossa V; cynoglossa, lingua canis Ca; cynoglossos Pl.
3. ribbe
4. ribwort, narrow-leaved plantain

XCIX

1. *Saxifraga granulata* L. (Bi., Co.)
2. saxifraga, saxifragia V; saxifraga Ca; (saxifragum Pl.)
3. sundcorn
4. saxifrage

Pl. equates *saxifragum* with *adiantum*, a sort of fern. The illustrations in our texts are clearly of *Saxifraga granulata*.

1 *Cauculosus*: see note to IV. 5.

C

1. *Glechoma hederaceum* L. (Bi., Co.)
2. hedera, hedera nigra, hedera terrestris V; hedera (nigra) Ca; hedera Pl.
3. eorþifig, eorþyfig
4. ground-ivy, ale-hoof

2 Equivalents of *rose*:

1. *Rosa* L. (Bi.)
2. ——
4. rose

3 *Diurnis diebus*: (Hum.) 'i.e. singulis et tempore matutino circa auroram dum adhuc a cibo vacuus est stomachus'.

4 *Spalangiones* in the OE text: this Latin word is not naturalized: in all the instances where it occurs in V (see Glossary) it has Latin or pseudo-Latin endings. It is probably used to denote a kind of spider that is unknown in England; see note to IV. 8. The common OE word for spider, *attorcoppe*, is found as an equivalent of *araneus* in IV. 8 (Vo: 'Ad morsus araneorum quos Graeci spalangiones vocant' / V: 'Wiþ attorcoppan bite') and in *M* V. 10. In the places where the Latin text has *spalangio* only, the word is found untranslated in the OE version, but always with a further qualification: in C. 4, CXXXIX. 3, CLXXIV. 1 it is combined with *wyrm*, in CXXXV. 4, CXLVII. 3 (and XC. 13, where no Latin parallel cure has been found) with *nædder(cynn)*. In Wright–Wülcker 121, 28 we find the gloss '*loppe*, fleonde næddre, vel attorcoppe'. The association of spiders with flying also appears from the drawings in our texts, all of which show winged creatures. The earliest drawing, representing two *spalangiones*, is found in Ca, at C. 4; V has a similar but more elaborate illustration in the same place, and also one at IV. 8, where the word *attorcoppe* is added; at CXXXV. 4 this manuscript has a drawing of a *spalangio* being attacked by a scorpion. Reproductions of the drawings at C. 4 can be found in G. and S., p. 75; their suggestion that the creatures are bees is based on the erroneous association of the plant name *ap(p)ium* with the drawings.

CI

1. *Thymus serpillum* L. (Bi.)
2. serpillum, serpillus V; serpullum Ca; serpyllum Pl.
3. organe, organa
4. wild thyme

   Co. has *Origanum vulgare*, as for CXXIV.
   1 *Gebærned*: a mistranslation of *frictum*.
   3 For *æscþrotu* as a translation of *ancusa* see Bi.[1] s.v. *æscþrotu*; for *ancusa* see CLXVIII.
   3 *Spuma argenti*: 'silver-spume, litharge of silver'.
   3 *Cera pumica = c. punica = c. poenica*: 'exceedingly white wax'.
   3 *Semunciam/healfes pundes ʒewihte*: A has *semilibra*.

CII

1. *Artemisia absinthium* L. (Bi., Co.)
2. absinthius, absynthius V; absynthium Ca; absinthium Pl.
3. wermod
4. wormwood, absinth
   2 Equivalents of *ele(c)htre*: see XLVI. 3.

CIII

1. *Salvia officinalis* L. (Bi., Co.)
2. salvia, salfia V; salvia Ca; salvia, elelisphacus Pl.
3. saluie, salfie
4. sage

CIV

1. *Coriandrum sativum* L. (Bi., Co.)
2. coliandra, coliandrum V; coliandrum Ca; coriandrum Pl.
3. cel(l)endre, coliandre
4. coriander

CV

1. *Portulaca sativa* L., or *Portulaca oleracea* L. (Co., *P. sativa* only)
2. porclaca V; porcacla Ca; porcillaca Pl.
3. ——
4. golden purslane, *or* green purslane

CVI

1. *Anthriscus cerefolium* (L.) Hoffm. (Bi., Co.)
2. cerefolium, cerefolia V; cerefolium Ca
3. cerfille, cearfille (*DP* 112 cerfille vel hynne-leac)
4. chervil

CVII

1. *Mentha aquatica* L., or *Mentha hirsuta* L. (Bi. *M.a.* only, Co. *M.h.* only)
2. sisimbrium, sisimbrius V; sisimbrum Ca; sisymbrium Pl.
3. brocminte
4. water-mint, *or* brook-mint

CVIII

1. *Smyrnium olus atrum* L. (Co.)
2. olisatrum, olisatra V; olixatrum Ca; olusatrum Pl.
3. ——— (*LHG* 1087 olisatra i.e. alexandrum)
4. alexanders, horse-parsley

For occurrences of alexandr(i)e in *Lb* see Bi.[1] s.v. *alexandria*.

CIX

1. *Lilium* L. (Bi.)
2. lilium V = Ca = Pl.
3. lilie
4. lily

The 'Latin' name *erinion*, found in BO, is probably a corruption of *crinion*, cf. κρίνον 'lily'.
   1 The Anglo-Saxon translator misinterprets *bulbum* and adds *halswyrt*, a name used for several plants, from which it is impossible to choose here; see Bi. s.v. *healswyrt*.

CX

1. *Euphorbia lathyris* Sprengel (Bi., Co.)
2. titymallos calatites, titi-, tyty-, -mallus, lacterida V; titimallo salatite Ca; tithymalis, -us Pl.
3. ———
4. caper-spurge

Calatites and *salatite* are corruptions of γαλακτίτης = L. *lacterida*. Cf. this chapter with CXIII. Both deal with plants that secrete a milky juice; there is no agreement as to which plant is described here and which in CXIII. See Bi. s.v. *giþcorn*, esp. Anm. 3.
   3 *Hreoflan*: see note to XCII. 2.
   3 *Tyrwe* here, and in CLII. 1, is a translation of L. *resina*.

CXI

1. *Sonchus oleraceus* L. (Bi., *Sonchus* spec.)

2. carduum silvaticum, c—us s—us V; cardum silvaticum Ca; carduus Pl.
3. wuduþistel
4. sow-thistle

Co.: '*Cnicus lanceolatus*, or perhaps *Cnicus palustris*.'
1 *Mearune*: probably confusion of *mearu* and *mearg* (L. *medulla*).

CXII

1. *Lupinus albus* L. (Co., *Lupinus luteus*)
2. lupinum montanum, lapinum m. V; lupinum montanum Ca; lupinus Pl.
3. —— (*LHG* 904 lupinum i.e. montanum)
4. white lupine

The OE equivalent of lupine, *elehtre*, occurs in XLVI. 3 and in CII. 2.

CXIII

1. *Daphne laureola* L. (Bi., Co.)
2. lactirida, lactyrida, lactyride V; laterida, latyrida Ca
3. giþcorn, gyþcorn (*DP* 210 gythcorn vel libcorn)
4. spurge laurel

See note to CX.

CXIV

1. *Lactuca virosa* L.
2. lactuca (leporina) V; lactuca leporina Ca; lactuca Pl.
3. —— (*LHG* 891 lactuca leporina i.e. cucumeris)
4. wild lettuce

Co.: '*Prenanthes muralis*'.
Cf. XXXI: little difference between the two.

CXV

1. *Cucumis sativus* L. (Bi.)
2. cucumis silvaticus, cucumeris silvatica V; cucumis silvaticus, siciden agria Ca; cucumis Pl.
3. hwerhwette
4. cucumber

Co.: '*Cucumis . . . Momordica elaterium* ("squirting cucumber") is probably meant by the drawing, MS V.'

CXVI

1. *Cannabis sativa* L. (Bi., Co.)
2. cannave silvatica, cannane silvatica, canuere V; cannabum silvaticum, c—is s—a Ca; cannabis Pl.
3. henep
4. hemp

CXVII

1. *Ruta montana* Mill. (Bi., Co.)
2. ruta montana, r. silvatica V; ruta montana, r. silvatica, piganum agrion Ca; ruta Pl.
3. rude
4. wild rue

   1 *Roscidus*: 'full of dew, wet with dew, dewy'.

CXVIII

1. *Potentilla tormentilla* Sibth. (Bi., Co.)
2. eptafilon, septifolium V; eptafillon, septemfolium Ca
3. seofenleafe, seofonleafe
4. tormentil

   Sablosis et cultis: thus Ha; the *Editio Princeps* has the same order as V.
   1 *Fotadl*: see notes to I. 29 and LXXXVII. 1.

CXIX

1. *Calamintha clinopodium* Benth., or *Viscum album* L. (Bi.[3], only *Viscum album*)
2. ocimus V; ocimum Ca = Pl.
3. mistel (*LHG* 1123 ocimum i.e. basilicum herba)
4. wild basil, missel, *or* mistletoe

   1 Equivalents of *wyrtriw*:
1. *Myrica gale* L. (Bi.)
2. ——
4. myrtle

CXX

1. *Apium graveolens* L. (Bi., Co.)
2. ap(p)ium V; appium Ca; apium Pl.
3. merce
4. wild celery, march

CXXI

1. *Hedera helix* L. (Bi., Co.)
2. hedera, hedera crysocantes V; hedera crisocantes Ca; hedera Pl.
3. ifig, yfig
4. ivy

CXXII

1. *Mentha arvensis* L. (Bi., Co.)
2. menta V = Ca = Pl.
3. minte
4. mint, field-mint, corn-mint

1 *Ignis sacer*: in our texts it has the following OE equivalents:
(*h*)*oman* in CXXXIX. 1, CXLIV. 1, CLXXIII. 4, *M* VII. 1 (2×);
teter 7 pypylgende lic in CXXII. 1;
berstende lic in CXLVII. 1.

Teter is also found as an equivalent of *impetigo*, in XLVI. 6 (2×), *M* III. 9, *M* III. 10; *pypelgende lic* occurs as an equivalent of *herpeta, quae se papulis rubris per corpus ostendit*, in CXLIV. 2.

CXXIII

1. *Anethum graveolens* L. (Bi., Co.)
2. an(n)etum V; anetum Ca = Pl.
3. dile, dyle
4. dill, anet

CXXIV

1. *Origanum vulgare* L., or *Origanum majorana* L. (Bi. both, Co. Orig. *v.* only)
2. origanum V = Ca = Pl.
3. organe (*LHG* 1089 origanum i.e. organe vel wurmele i.e. pulegium)
4. wild marjoram, *or* sweet marjoram

For other glosses of *origanum*, see Stracke's note to *LHG* 1089.
1 Ca has only cure 2; cure 1 in Ha and A is not a parallel of cure 1 in V.
1 For *dropa*, see note to LIX. 1.

CXXV

1. *Sempervivum tectorum* L. (Bi., Co.)
2. sempervivus V; sempervivum Ca
3. sinfulle
4. houseleek, sengreen

For the names of this plant in O, see *LHG* 192 and note.

CXXVI

1. *Foeniculum vulgare* Mill. (Bi.)
2. fenuculus, feniculus V; feniculum Ca = Pl.
3. finul, finol
4. fennel
   2 For *eorþnafola*, see note to XCVII. 1

CXXVII

1. *Galega officinalis* L.
2. erifion V = Ca
3. liþwyrt, lyþwyrt
4. goat's rue

Bi. s.v. *lipwyrt* has *Sambucus ebulus* and *Ruta graveolens*, but has doubts about the latter. *Sambucus ebulus* is described in XCIII, *Ruta graveolens* in XCI. Co. has *Sambucus ebulus*, only in the table of contents. The description of *Galega officinalis* in Grieve (p. 696) corresponds with the drawings in our texts; the name *erifion* (ἔριφος 'young goat') is a striking parallel to *goat's rue*.

CXXVIII

1. *Fraxinus excelsior* L.
2. sinfitus albus V; symfitum (album) Ca; symphytum Pl.
3. halswyrt
4. common ash

The drawings in V, Ca, and Ha show very different plants, and do not resemble a *symphytum*. For *Symphytum officinale* see LX. Bi. s.v. *healswyrt* has four possible candidates, but adds 'fraglich' to each of them. Co. (p. 241 n. a): '*Symphytum officinale* is not what the figure means, which shows *Fraxinus excelsior*.' Cf. Grieve, p. 66: 'Ash bark . . . is said to be valuable as an antiperiodic.'

CXXIX

1. *Petroselinum sativum* Hoffm. (= *Apium petroselinum* L.) (Bi., Co.)
2. petroselinum, -silinum, triannis V; petroselinum Ca = Pl.
3. petersilie
4. parsley

Wætersilie O is not found anywhere else; it must be a corruption of *petersilie*.

CXXX

1. *Brassica napus* L. (Bi., Co.)
2. brassica (silvatica) V; brassica silvatica Ca; brassica Pl.
3. caul, cawel (*LHG* 210 brassica i.e. caulis siluatica i.e. wilde caule)
4. colewort, rape

CXXXI

1. *Ocimum basilicum* L. (Bi.)
2. basilisca V = Ca
3. nædderwyrt
4. sweet basil

Co., p. 242 margin: 'The figure in MS V . . . shows a *Matricaria*, a *Tanacetum*, or a *Pyrethrum parthenium*.'

CXXXII

1. *Atropa mandragora* L. (Co.)
2. mandragora, mandregara V; mandragora Ca; mandragoras Pl.
3. ——
4. mandrake

For the mandrake and its role in ancient and medieval medicine, see Bonser, pp. 328–33.

CXXXIII

1. *Agrostemma coronaria* L. (Bi., Co.)
2. lyc(h)anis (lich-) stefanice (steph-) V; licanis stefanotice Har; lychnis Pl.
3. læcewyrt
4. campion, ragged robin

λυχνίς: 'rose campion'; στεφανωτικός = *coronaria*, 'used for making garlands'.

CXXXIV

1. *Arctium lappa* L. (Co.)
2. action V; action(um) L; lappa Pl.
3. ——
4. burdock

Equivalents of *cyrfætte*:

1. *Cucurbita* L. (Bi.)
2. cucurbita L = Pl.
4. gourd

Duobus digitis/twegea fæþma: the OE measure is undoubtedly the correct one. A *digitus* is less than an inch, a *fæþm* is 18 inches; the burdock is a tall plant.

Equivalents of *þistel*:

1. *Carduus arvensis* Sm. (Bi.[1])
2. carduus L = Pl.
4. thistle

CXXXV

1. *Artemisia abrotanum* L. (Bi., Co.)
2. abrotanum, -us V; abrotanum Har.
3. suþernewuda
4. southernwood

   5 *Melacidoniam*: μῆλα κυδώνια, 'quinces'.

CXXXVI

1. *Sium latifolium* L.
2. sion, laber V; syon Har; laver, sion, sium Pl.
3. ——
4. water-parsnip

CXXXVII

1. *Heliotropium europaeum* L. (Bi., Co.), or *Calendula officinalis* L. (Gunther)

2. eliotropus, -os V; eliotropus masculus L; heliotropium Pl.
3. sigilhweorfa
4. white heliotrope, *or* marigold

It is impossible to say which of the two herbs is described here and which in LXIV.

2 *Nytrum*: here probably 'salt'; cf. *LHG* 1062: 'nitrum i.e. sal'.

CXXXVIII

1. *Anagallis arvensis* L. (Co.)
2. spreritis V = A; anagallis Pl.
3. ——
4. scarlet pimpernel

For *spreritis* and its possible development from σπυρῖτις or from σφαιρῖτις, see Co., p. 257 n. a.

Mirrae: A has *murteum*, 'of the myrtle'. Both myrtle and myrrh are used in perfumery.

CXXXIX

1. *Sedum acre* L.
2. aizos minor, ayzos minor V; aizos minor A; aïzoum minus Pl.
3. ——
4. common stonecrop, wallpepper

Co.: '*Sempervivum sediforme*'.

The leaves, which are long according to V and A, are round in the Greek version of Dioscorides (iv. 90).

CXL

1. *Veratrum album* L. (Bi., Co.)
2. elleborum album, elleborus albus V; elleborum album L; helleborum Pl.
3. tunsin(c)gwyrt, wedeberge
4. white hellebore

Wedeberge refers to mental disorders (*wede*, 'mad') which had been associated with this herb since antiquity; see Pauly–Wissowa s.v. *Helleborus*, and see Erika von Erhardt-Siebold, 'The Hellebore in Anglo-Saxon Pharmacy', *Englische Studien* 71 (1936), 161–70.

CXLI

1. *Chrysanthemum segetum* L., or *Chrysanthemum leucanthemum* L.
2. buoptalmon V; buotthalmon A; bu(o)phthalmus Pl.
3. —— (*DP* 70 bucstalmum   hvit megethe)
4. corn-marigold, yellow ox-eye, *or* ox-eye daisy, marguerite

With regard to Co.'s suggestion *Anthemis valentina* L. and the gloss in *DP*, cf. *OED* s.v. *ox-eye* 3: 'sometimes also (app. by confusion) applied to species of *Anthemis* with yellow or white flowers resembling these [i.e. *Chrysanthemum segetum* and *Chrysanthemum leucanthemum*].'

Iuxta moenia civitatum/wiþ Meoniam þa ceastre: in his description of *buphthalmus* Pliny (xxv. 82) uses the expression *circa oppida nascens*; he also mentions a Scythian variety *circa Maeotim nascens*. *Maeotis* is 'the Sea of Azov'. In the extant Latin versions of the *Liber medicinae ex herbis femininis* we do not find a geographical name. Although it is not impossible that the OE version was translated from a Latin exemplar which contained a corrupted form of *Maeotis*, it is more likely that *Meonia* is simply a mistranslation of *moenia*.

2 For *ictericis* and its OE translation, see note to LXXXVII. 1.

CXLII

1. *Ulex europaeus* L. (Bi., Co.)
2. tribulus V; tribulosa A; tribulus Pl.
3. gorst
4. gorse, furze, whin

CXLIII

1. *Inula conyza* DC. (= *Conyza squarrosa* L.), or *Inula pulicaria* L.
2. coniza, conize V; coniza A
3. ——
4. ploughman's spikenard, *or* fleabane

    Co.: '*Inula viscosa*'.
    1 For *cynelic adl*, see note to LXXXVII. 1.

CXLIV

1. *Datura stramonium* L.
2. trycnos manicos, tricnos manicos V; strignos, manicos A; strychnos Pl.
3. foxes glofa (*DP* 327 trycnosmanicos   foxes-gloua; *LHG* 1446 tricnos-manicos i.e. foxes gloue)
4. thorn-apple

The Greek plant name στρύχνος means 'nightshade'. The thorn-apple belongs to the order of the *Solanaceae*. Cf. Co., p. 267 n. b: 'Strychnos manikos is . . . not an English plant, and certainly not foxglove. The leechdoms recorded here seem derived from what Dioskorides says of the στρύχνος κηπαῖος: namely, τὰ φύλλα καταπλασσόμενα ἁρμόζει πρὸς ἐρυσιπέλατα καὶ ἔρπητας; and so on of κεφαλαλγία and στόμαχος καυσούμενος and ὠταλγία (iv. 71).' The sedative effect of drugs containing *Datura stramonium* is generally recognized; see Grieve, pp. 802–7. Foxglove or *Digitalis purpurea* L. has an entirely different effect: it stimulates the action of the heart; see Grieve, pp. 322–6. It seems therefore unlikely that the herb in this chapter is *Digitalis purpurea*. Cf. also *OED* s.vv. *thorn-apple, foxglove*, and the notes to *DP* 327 and *LHG* 1334.

3 *Parotis*: see the first note to II. 19.

CXLV

1. *Glycyrrhiza glabra* L.

2. glycyrida V; glycyriza A; glycyrrhiza Pl.
3. ——
4. liquorice

Co.: '*Glycyrrhiza glandulifera*'.

CXLVI

1. *Saponaria officinalis* L. (Co.)
2. strutius V; strutios A; strutheum Pl.
3. ——
4. soapwort

Byscupwyrt O does not find any support elsewhere.
2 For *wiþ þæs eallan togotenysse*, see note to LXXXVII. 1.
3 Equivalents of *lubastice*:

1. *Levisticum officinale* Koch (= *Ligusticum levisticum* L.) (Bi.)
2. panax A; panaces, panax, ligusticum Pl.
4. lovage

Cf. *DP* 225: 'lubestica luuestice', and *LHG* 1162: 'panaca i.e. radix luuestici'. See also *OED* s.vv. *lovage* and *panace*.
3 For *capparis*, see CLXXII.
4 For *hreoflan*, see note to XCII. 2.

CXLVII

1. *Sedum telephium* L. (Co.)
2. aizon V; aizonos Ca; aizum Pl.
3. ——
4. orpine, livelong

For the names of this plant in O, see *LHG* 192 and note.
1 For *berstende lic*, see note to CXXII. 1.

CXLVIII

1. *Sambucus nigra* L. (Bi., Co.)
2. samsuchon V; samsucum A; sampsuchum Pl.
3. ellen (*LHG* 1302 samsucon i.e. ellenwurt)
4. elder

1 *Unmihticnyss* VH is probably a corruption of *unmihtilicnyss*, which is found in the corresponding title in the table of contents.

CXLIX

1. *Lavandula stoechas* L. (Co.)
2. stecas V; sticas A; stoechas Pl.
3. ——
4. French lavender

CL

1. *Capsella bursa-pastoris* (L.) Med.
2. thyaspis V; thlaspi A = Pl.

3. ——
4. shepherd's purse

CLI

1. *Teucrium polium* L., or *Teucrium scorodonia* L.
2. polios, omnimorbia V; polium Dio. iii. 124 = Pl.
3. ——
4. hulwort, cat-thyme, poly germander, *or* sage-leaved germander, wood-sage

It is impossible to say which of the two herbs is described here and which in LVIII. See also note to LVIII.

CLII

1. *Hypericum perforatum* L.
2. hypericon, corion V; hypericon A = Pl.
3. ——
4. St. John's-wort

Co.: '*Hypericum coris*'.
1 For *cymen* see CLV.
1 Equivalents of *bere*:

1. *Hordeum vulgare* L. (Bi.)
2. hordeum A
4. barley

1 For *tyrwe* see second note to CX. 3.

CLIII

1. *Echinops sphaerocephalus* L.
2. acantaleuce, acantaleuca V; hecinum A; echinopus Pl.
3. —— (*DP* 9 acantaleuca   smel-thistel)
4. ball-thistle, globe-thistle

Mearwran B/*mealuwran* V: the form in V may be regarded as an early link in the relation between OE *mearu* and Modern English *mellow*; see *OED* s.v. *mellow* (adj.).
4 The Latin of the last sentence is obscure. A has *eadem* and *effugat*. Kästner emends *quam* into *quidam*, *homines* into *omnem*.

CLIV

1. *Acanthus mollis* L. (Bi.), or *Onopordon acanthium* L. (Co.)
2. acanton V; acantum A; acanthion Pl.
3. beowyrt
4. bear's breech, brank-ursine, *or* Scotch thistle, woolly thistle

CLV

1. *Carum carvi* L., or *Cuminum cyminum* L. (Bi. both, Co. *Cuminum cym.* only)
2. quim(m)inon V; cyminum A; cuminum Pl.

3. cymen
4. caraway, *or* cummin

See also Bi.[1] s.v. *cymen*.

CLVI

1. *Carlina acaulis* L. (Co., and three other suggestions)
2. camelleon alba V = A
3. wulfes tæsl
4. carline thistle, wolf's-thistle

Dipsacus silvester (Bi., Co.) is the herb identified in XXVI. The medicinal properties of *camelleon alba* are very similar to those of *Carlina acaulis* in modern herbals; cf. Flück, p. 167.

CLVII

1. *Scolymus cardunculus* L.
2. scolimbos, scolymbos V; scolimos A; scolymus Pl.
3. —— (*DP* 312 scolimbos se unbrade thistel) (Cf. textual note to V, f. 17v/8a)
4. artichoke

Co.: '*Skolymos Hispanicus*'.

CLVIII

1. *Iris germanica* L. (Co., also *Iris florentina*)
2. iris Illyrica, iris Yllyrica V; iris (illyrida) Dio. i. 1
3. ——
4. blue iris, German iris

1 *And to hnesce* probably means 'and if the patient is too weak'.

CLIX

1. *Urginea maritima* (L.) Bak. (= *Scilla maritima* L.)
2. elleborum album, elleborus albus V
3. ——
4. sea-onion, squill

Co., p. 287 n. a: 'The drawing in MS V has some resemblance to *Veratrum album*, but is *Scilla*.' *Veratrum album* is described in CXL, *Scilla* in XLIII. The cure in this chapter is not found in any of the Latin texts consulted.

CLX

1. *Delphinium consolida* L. (Co.)
2. delfinion V; delfion A
3. —— (*DP* 144 delfinion fugeles-vise)
4. larkspur

CLXI

1. *Echium vulgare* L.
2. æcios, acios V; hechios A; echium Pl.
3. —— (*DP* 152 ecios   haranspeccel (manuscript has -sveccel; see von Lindheim's note))
4. viper's bugloss

   Co.: '*Echium rubrum*'.

CLXII

1. *Lysimachia nummularia* L. (Co.)
2. centimorbia V = A
3. ——
4. moneywort

CLXIII

1. *Epimedium alpinum* L. (Co., p. 291 n. b)
2. scordios, scordias V; scordium Dio. iii. 125 = Pl.
3. ——
4. barrenwort

CLXIV

1. *Ammi maius* L.
2. ami, milvium V; ammi Dio. iii. 70; ami Pl.
3. ——
4. bishop's weed, bishop-weed

   Co: '*Ammi copticum*'.

CLXV

1. *Viola tricolor* L. (Bi.)
2. viola V; viola aurosa A; viola Pl.
3. banwyrt (*DP* 334 viola   cleafre vel banvyrt)
4. heartsease, wild pansy

   Co.: '*Viola lutea* L.'
   2 *Ragadas*: Cf. Celsus, VI. xviii. 7 (De ani morbis): 'Ac primum in eo saepe, et quidem pluribus locis, cutis scinditur; ῥαγάδια Graeci vocant.'
   3–5 The last three cures in this chapter have no parallels in A and Har.

CLXVI

1. *Viola odorata* L. (Co.)
2. viola purpurea V = Har
3. ——
4. sweet violet

CLXVII

1. ──
2. zamalentition V = Har
3. ──
4. ──

CLXVIII

1. *Anchusa tinctoria* L. (Co.)
2. ancusa V = A = Pl.
3. ──
4. alkanet

Perhaps *Anchusa officinalis* L. is meant; see *OED* s.v. *alkanet*.

CLXIX

1. *Plantago psyllium* L. (Co.)
2. psillios, pulicaris V; psillios A; psyllion Pl.
3. coliandre, *wrongly*
4. fleawort, fleaseed

The title *coliandre* in the text of VH is clearly wrong; this was realized by the glossator in H who added *Pulicaris herba*.

CLXX

1. *Rosa canina* L., or *Rosa rubiginosa* L.
2. cynosbatus V; cinosbatos A; cynosbatus Pl.
3. ──
4. dog-rose, *or* sweet-briar, eglantine

Dioscorides' observation (i. 123) 'θάμνος ἐστί, δενδρώδης' is more applicable to the dog rose than to the evergreen rose mentioned by Co.

1 The meaning of the last clause in the Latin cure is: 'lest, being unable to endure the potency of the medicine, he should scatter the remedy'. The obscurity of the OE version is due to a misinterpretation of *impatiens*.

CLXXI

1. *Helianthus annuus* L.
2. aglaofotis V; aglaophotis Pl.
3. ──
4. sunflower

This chapter is not found in any of the Latin texts consulted. *Aglaofotis* occurs in the Latin texts as one of the synonyms of *peonia* (LXVI); Co. suggests that the plant in this chapter is *Paeonia officinalis*. On account of the name *aglaofotis*, meaning 'splendidly bright', I would suggest *Helianthus annuus*. The drawing, although 'monstrous' (Co.), may represent a sunflower. Cf. Pl. xxiv. 160: 'Aglaophotim herbam, quae admiratione hominum propter eximium colorem acceperit nomen';

and Bonser, p. 328, who mentions instances of orange and yellow flowers emitting luminous radiations at twilight.

Foxes gloua in O does not find any support elsewhere.

CLXXII

1. *Capparis spinosa* L. (Co.)
2. capparis V; cappara A; capparis Pl.
3. wudubend, *wrongly*
4. caper

There must have been confusion of *capparis* with *caprifolium*, which is *Lonicera periclymenum* L., 'woodbine'. See Bi.'s commentary s.v. *wudubend*.

CLXXIII

1. *Eryngium maritimum* L., or *Eryngium campestre* L.
2. eringius, eryngius V; erigion A
3. ——
4. sea-holly, eryngo, *or* field eryngo

It is impossible to say which of the two herbs is described here and which in CLXXXII. Co.: '*Eryngium*, various species'.

3 *þæra breosta*: not taken from the Latin text.

CLXXIV

1. *Galium aparine* L. (Bi., Co.)
2. philantropos V; aperina, filantropos Har; philanthropos, aparine Pl.
3. clate
4. cleavers, clivers, goosegrass

Menlufigende: cf. Pl. xxiv. 176: 'Philanthropon herbam Graeci appellant nasute, quoniam vestibus adhaerescat.'

CLXXV

1. *Achillea ptarmica* L.
2. achillea V = A = Pl.
3. —— (*DP* 11 achillea collo-croch)
4. sneezewort

Co. has five varieties of *Achillea*, but not *ptarmica*.

CLXXVI

1. *Ricinus communis* L. (Co.)
2. ricinus V = Pl.
3. ——
4. castor-oil plant

Not found in any of the Latin texts consulted. Co.'s Modern English equivalent is 'Croton oil plant'; this is incorrect. See Bonser, p. 309 n. 2.

CLXXVII

1. *Ballota nigra* L. (Co.)
2. polloten, porrum nigrum V; balloten L; ballote, porrum nigrum Pl.
3. —— (*DP* 279 polloten   crave-lec)
4. black horehound

   The association with leek (*porrum*), also in *DP*, is due to a mistranslation from Greek into Latin: confusion of πράσιον 'horehound' with πράσον 'leek'.

CLXXVIII

1. *Urtica dioica* L. (Bi.[1]), or *Urtica urens* L. (Co.)
2. urtica V = L = Pl.
3. netele
4. common nettle, greater nettle, *or* lesser nettle

   Singer (Introduction to reprint of Co., p. xlv): *netele* = *Urtica dioica*.

CLXXIX

1. *Vinca maior* L. (Co.)
2. priapisci, vicapervica V; vica pervica L = Pl.
3. —— (*DP* 338 vica pervica   tvileafa)
4. greater periwinkle

CLXXX

1. *Lithospermum officinale* L. (Bi., Co.)
2. litospermon V = L; lithospermon Pl.
3. (sunnancorn) (*LHG* 897 litosperimon i.e. suncorn)
4. common gromwell

   Sundcorn in V is clearly a later insertion, and it is not correct; *corn* had to be interlined because there was not enough space. The emendation into *sunnancorn* is given by Co. (*Additions and Corrections*, after p. cv). See also Bi. s.vv. *sundcorn*, esp. Anm. 3 and 4, and *sunnancorn*.

CLXXXI

1. *Delphinium stafis agria* L. (Co.)
2. stavisagria V; stafisagria A; staphis Pl.
3. ——
4. stavesacre, lousewort

CLXXXII

1. *Eryngium campestre* L., or *Eryngium maritimum* L. (Co., *Eryngium m.* only)
2. gorgonion V = W
3. ——
4. field eryngo, *or* sea-holly, eryngo

   See CLXXIII, and cf. Li. and S.: 'Γοργόνιον = ἠρύγγη'. The illustrator emphasizes the association of this plant with a gorgon: it has a tuberous root with a face drawn in it, and with a number of snake-like sprouts issuing from it. The very corrupt version of W is not helpful.

CLXXXIII

1. *Melilotus officinalis* L. (Co.)
2. milotis V; melilotos Pl.
3. ——
4. melilot

Not found in any of the Latin texts consulted.

CLXXXIV

1. *Allium cepa* L., or *Dioscorea alata* L.
2. bulbus V; bulbus rufus A; bulbus Pl.
3. ——
4. onion, *or* red, white or winged yam

Βολβός: 'onion'. Co., in contents, has *Dioscorea alata*, with a question mark, in text 'Hyacinthus comosus (Sibthorp), otherwise *Muscari comosum*'.

3 *Hostopyturas*: the Greek word πίτυρον 'bran, scurf, dandruff', is recognizable; ἀχώρ: 'scurf, dandruff'.

CLXXXV

1. *Cucumis colocynthis* L. (Co.)
2. colocynthisagria, cucurbita (agrestis), frigilla V; colocintiosagria A; colocynthis Pl.
3. —— (*LHG* 347 coloquintisagria i.e. cucurbita et frigilla)
4. colocynth, bitter-gourd

Cucumere: in all the instances in *OEH* where plant names are found in combination with *gelic*, they are OE; the form *cucumere* can therefore be regarded as the dative sg. of the naturalized plant name *cucumer*, a synonym of *hwerhwette*; seè CXV.

M I

1 For the textual problems of the Latin version of the *Liber de taxone* and the problems regarding the identity of the writer and of the person addressed, see pp. lxiii f.

1 *Sagaþ* as an equivalent of a plural in the Latin texts. In the conjugation of the verb *secgan* confusion of singular and plural is occasionally found; see Cpb., p. 339 n. 1, who mentions a Northumbrian plural *sægas*.

1 *Monegum . . . wel gesæd ys*: it is hardly surprising that the OE text is difficult to understand: all the extant Latin versions are very corrupt. In VBH the sentence *Monegum . . . ferdon* is grammatically correct: *ferdon* is probably a rendering of *expergimus*, which form, whatever its meaning may be, was associated with *pergere*. As Cockayne (p. 326 n. 19) points out, the sentence *Ic . . . ys* would be intelligible, or at any rate grammatically correct, if a verb form like *sende, write* were supplied after

Ic. We can recognize *cognationis* in *cyþþe*, *dignum* in *weorþne* (but *dignum* has not the same function as *weorþne*). The final phrase *swa þæt wel gesæd ys* in VBH may be a 'translation' of *quam melem dicunt* (MS Ha has *mele*), through association with *melius*. L has *maledicunt*.

2 *Hagol*: the equivalent of this word is not found in LHa. In some of the texts containing the B-version the word *grando* does occur.

2 *Sicut sonum audias* LHa/*swa wæs Abdias gyrdels* VBHO: a very interesting case of mistranslation. Confusion of *u/v* and *b* in Latin is not unusual; see M. Leumann, *Lateinische Laut- und Formenlehre* (München, 1963), p. 130. 2; it is therefore possible that the exemplar of the OE text had *abdias*. The translator associated this with the name of the prophet Obadiah; he probably regarded the form *abdias* as a genitive. *Sonum* could not mean *sound* in this context, but another solution was available: it could be a 'mis-spelling' of *zonam*. The translator, who a few lines earlier had written *on linenum hrægle*, remembered an Old Testament account of a prophet and his linen girdle, and wrote down his version of *sicut sonum abdias*. He made the mistake, however, of confusing Obadiah with Jeremiah; see Jer. 13: 1–11.

3 *þu bist* VBHO should have been written twice.

3 *Sylefæst* O: a corruption of *symle sygefæst*; see the variant in H.

6 *To þat þryddan dæl si bewealled* O, also *M* IX. 10 *fort þæt þrindan dæl beo weallen* O: two phrases showing a remarkable parallelism: *dæl* is undoubtedly the subject, but this masculine nominative is preceded by *þat/þæt* and an inflected adjective. Perhaps *þat* was written here because VBH have *oþþæt*. *To* can only be regarded as a conjunction. It is not recorded in this function in OE; in ME the use of *to* as a conjunction is characteristic of the north-east Midlands; see *OED* s.v. *to*, C 1. Cf. *Sir Orfeo*, ed. A. J. Bliss, MS Ashmole 61, lines 63–4: 'Sche slepe welle fer after þe non, / To þe undryn-tyde wer gon.' *Fort* is not recorded in OE; it occurs in ME as a conjunction meaning *until*; cf. *MED* s.v. *forto*. The use of the inflected adjective in both phrases may indicate that the scribe had his doubts about the conjunctive function of *to* and *fort*. Cf. also *forþat* in *OEH* I. 19 and *forþ þæt* in *OEH* IV. 8, which may have been assimilated from *fort þat/þæt*; here *þat/þæt* must be regarded as part of the conjunction.

6 *Æfter bæþe* belongs to the main clause; cf. B, which in this sentence has stops after *heafodwræce*, *mid*, *nihtum*, and *gehæled*, not after *bæþe*.

7 The Latin could be rendered thus: 'Likewise you will bury parts of his liver round the boundaries of your land, or round the land along the boundaries.' H. and S. print *urbis* for *orbis* (without a footnote), thus justifying *tuae*, but both L and Ha clearly show an *o*. In manuscripts A, Slo, Harley 1585, and Ashmole 1462 we find *urbis*. If the Anglo-Saxon translator had used a Latin text containing *urbis*, he would not have produced the obscure version which is evidently the result of his failure to deal with the word *orbis*. Cf. also *M* I. 9, where *orbem* is rendered by *eorþan ymbhwyrft*.

The accusative *fines* has been rendered by the genitive *landgemæra*, and the genitive *orbis tuae* by *æt þam ymbhwyrftum*. The scribe of O must have been puzzled by this sentence, and therefore wrote *æt þinun burhstaþela*, thus making *burhstaþela* independent of *ymbhwyrftum*.

For *ymbhwyrftum* Cockayne has 'turnings round'. BT, s.v. *ymbhwyrft*, V, gives 'bend', mentioning this place, the only instance. It gives an intelligible Modern English translation, but it is doubtful whether this is what the Anglo-Saxon translator, with the Latin original in front of him, had in mind. A more plausible rendering would be 'circuit', 'circum-ference'; cf. BT s.v. *ymbhwyrft*, III, where the word occurs in four quotations as an equivalent of Latin *circuitus*.

9 *Lustrare* means 'purify through a sacrifice'. The OE version contracts the two Latin sentences into one, wrongly.

M II

For this chapter L is the only early source in Latin. In the Junius transcript (Bodleian Library, MS Junius 58) of B this marginal note is added: 'Haec aliunde videntur in hoc opusculum transflata, cum non pertineant ad medicinam quae petitur ex quadrupedibus.' H. and S. do not print this part of the text.

1 The magic formula is emended by Cockayne(p. 333) into: '$\H{a}\psi$, $\H{a}\psi$, $\H{a}\psi$, ὡς φάρμακον αἴρω σε πρὸς πᾶσαν αἱμορραγίαν παντὸς αἵματος πᾶν τε αἱμοσταγές'. Cockayne reads *temesstanes* in V, which is not likely to be correct: *æ* does resemble the sequence *te*, but in this manuscript there is more space between *t* and *e* than between the two elements of *æ*.

2 *Ana* can be regarded either as an extension of the masculine weak form of the adjective *an* to the feminine, cf. Cpb. 683, or as an adverb meaning 'only' rather than 'alone'. See also Pope, glossary, p. 824, s.v. *ana*.

2 Both the Latin and the OE version are corrupt, but the mistakes in L are not reflected in the OE text. *Adhaeserint* has been emended from *quia/eserint* (no damage), *sursum* from *iussu*. In the OE version *clæne* is a mistranslation, through association with *purus*, of the word *purgamenta*, which in Latin was probably originally found in combination with *legentur*; cf. *purgamenta capillorum legat* in *M* II. 3. It is strange that in that place the translation is correct.

Him to (*gesomnige*) should be translated 'from it', sc. the twig. For instances of the preposition *to* in this sense, see BT s.v. *to*, I (5) (h). In their editions of the OE version both Cockayne and Delcourt emend the passage. Cockayne (p. 332) substitutes *hi* for *him*, Delcourt (p. 6) has *hit*. But in all the four manuscripts the word is unmistakably *him*.

M III

7 Hum., p. 12: 'Vulvam vocat Sextus . . . non muliebre pudendum, . . . sed uterum et muliebres locos atque vas ipsum quo foetus continetur, et [quod] hodie matrix appellatur.'

7 *Hystem cepnizam* is a corruption of ὑστερικὴ πνίξ: 'suffocation of the womb'; the term is found in Hum. on pp. 6, 11, and 12; Junius in his transcript of B (Bodleian Library, MS Junius 58) has a marginal note here:

'ὑστερικὴ πνίξ, strangulatus vulvae, praefocatio matricis'. The cure is not in the B-version.

7 *Nequissimum*: in L the word comes after *pulverem*, in Ha after *quod*.

8 *Oxymel*: (Hum.) '. . . est acetum mulsum'.

11 *Tetriginum*: the word appears as *intertrigines* in MS Ca and in MS Harley 1585. Hum., p. 12: 'Intertrigines sunt, quae Plinius nunc attrita nunc confricata membra vocat, malum quod fit atterentibus in itinere pedes calceis, aut confricatis equitatione aut alia causa foeminibus et aliis partibus.'

11 *Spuma argenti*: see note to CI. 3.

12 *Heagospind*: either the OE version is a correct rendering of a corrupt Latin text, cf. Ha *genuinum*, or it is the result of *genu* having been misread, and wrongly translated, as *gena*. The explanation *hoc est*, etc., is not found in the B-version.

14 This recipe is not in V. *Moium* (= *mugium* M XII. 13) means 'penis' (see Souter). The Anglo-Saxon translator did not know the word, mistranslated it and also misinterpreted the last clause, thus giving the cure the appearance of being out of place in the context. The scribe of V, copying from an OE exemplar, realized this and omitted the cure.

15 The *rosa* in this cure is not mentioned in any other Latin manuscript. It is perhaps a corruption of the verb form *deraseris*; cf. MS Har: 'Cervi naturam siccatam si deraseris dragmam i . . .', and *M* V. 9, where L has *darosos*, Ha *derasos*. See also the parallel in Pliny.

15 *In sorbitione oboli*: cf. MS Har: 'in sorbitione in ovo', MS Harley 1585: 'in ovo sorbili'.

16 *Stranguiria/stede*. The Anglo-Saxon translator may have used the word *stede* in the sense 'strangury', as suggested in BT (IV c), and we may believe that the context enabled him to guess what kind of ailment was meant, but the use of the vague word *stede* by a man who otherwise shows no inclination to euphemize may also indicate that he did not know the exact meaning of *stranguiria*.

17 This is an erroneous combination of two cures which have effects exactly opposite to each other. Cf. MS A:

(*a*) 'Ad conceptum, ut mulier concipiat. Lapis qui in vulva aut in ventriculo invenitur, filacterium est; praegnanti vero efficit ut partum perferat, eo [quod] ratio colligit velocissimum esse illud animal nec tamen aborsum facere. Ut supra simili ratione ossicula inveniuntur aut in corde aut in vulva, quae idem praestant.'

(*b*) 'Ut mulier non concipiat. Idem ossum inventum in brachio suspensum efficit ne mulier concipiat.'

In MS Ha there are in the margin, in a later hand, the words *Ut mulier non concipiat*, to be added after *praestant*. Moreover, an interlinear gloss has been added to the phrase *efficacissime mulier concipiet*, so that it reads *efficit ne mulier concipiat*.

The words *similiter* and *idem* in L are reminiscent of the original version.

19 In L the verb form *fugat* is found after *simul* in cure 20.

M IV

1 *Loca inferiora*: the translator confused the second word with *interiora*; the expression is apparently used to denote 'womb', 'genitals'. See also *M* V. 6, and note to *M* VIII. 1.

2 *Alopitias*. It is not without significance that the word is used in this chapter (ἀλώπηξ: 'fox'). For the meaning in classical Latin see L. and S. s.v. *alopecia*: 'a disease common among foxes, in which the hair falls off'.

For a detailed discussion of the meaning of the word in the Middle Ages, see Curry, pp. 37–47, also Bowden, pp. 263–4. It appears to be a kind of leprosy, and it is probable that Chaucer's Summoner, who was 'saucefleem' (*CT*, A 625), suffered from this disease. One of the symptoms was falling hair, caused by ulcers or rashes; cf. Wright–Wülcker 113, 30: '*alopecia*, feaxfallung'.

As a translation of *alopitias*, 'ulcers on the head' is undoubtedly more accurate than 'headache', but it remains to be seen if the Anglo-Saxon translator meant this when he wrote *heafodsare*. He obviously did not know the word: in *M* XII. 11 it is translated *bryce*. In the cure in this chapter the word *capiti* directed him to the head, and he confidently wrote down his translation *heafodsare*, leaving it to his readers to find out what kind of *sar* the cure was meant for. *Heafodece* in O can of course only mean 'headache'.

5 *Parotidas*: see note to *OEH* II. 19. The translations *uncuþe blædran* in *OEH* II. 19 and *cyrnlu* in *M* VII. 18 are better than *weartan* in this cure.

8 *Fauces/goman*: see note to LXX. 1.

8 *þam* O is a mistake for *þa*, *mid* having been misinterpreted.

11 There is no equivalent of this puzzling prescription in any other manuscript of the text. In Ha there is a marginal sign beside the passage, probably indicating that it is unintelligible. Hum. (p. 31) prints: 'Vulpis viva in amplo vase decocta donec ossa relinquat, mire sanat, si saepius in aquam in vase quis descenderit. Idem praestat oleum ubi decocta fuerit. Si quis hoc aut illo modo vult, utatur.' H. and S. (p. 240) emend *quod inanis* into *quotannis*, which corresponds with the OE version.

13 *Mel atticum/doran hunig*. The Latin term is also found in LXXV. 1, 2, where its OE equivalent is merely *hunig*, and in *M* VI. 2, *M* VI. 4, and *M* XII. 3, where it is *feldbeona hunig*. *Atticus* is not connected with Attica, as Hum. suggests, but with *attacus*. In Li. and S. ἄττακος is translated 'a kind of locust'. In late Latin, however, *attacus/atticus* can mean 'bumble-bee, wild bee'. For exact references, see Du Cange s.v. *atticus*, Diefenbach and *Mittellateinisches Wörterbuch* s.v. *attacus*, BT(S) s.vv. *dora* and *feld-beo*.

15 *Fotadl*: see note to *OEH* I. 29

15 *Accessiones*: the word means 'attacks', not 'going'.

M V

1 The word *submeiulos*, mistranslated here, occurs with its correct equivalent in *M* IX. 12.

3 Two cures telescoped. The first cure runs from *Ad* to *sanat*: this

version is found in MS A, the second cure does not occur in that manuscript. MS Ca has the two original cures:

(a) 'Ad pernionem et pedes laesos. Idem pulmo affert remedium.'
(b) 'Ad quartanas frigorum sanandas. Leporis viventis cor sublatum
et quartanariis collo vel brachio suspensum [emendat].'

4, 5 These two cures are arranged differently in LHa and in the OE
texts. Cf. the version of MS Harley 1585:

(a) 'Ad loca mulierum. Leporis cordis sicci partem terciam radas et
cum thuris manna teras et in vino albo patienti potum tribuas per
septem dies; emendat.'
(b) 'Contra caducos. Leporis cor siccum accipe et ipsum derade et his
qui saepius cadunt dabis bibere usque in tricesimo die. Luna autem
crescente potio debet condiri ex vino cotidie; sanabitur mirifice.'

The word *wyrtunge* is very probably a reflection of Latin *condiri*, found
in the B-version. On the other hand, *luna crescente*, which is found in all
the important manuscripts containing the B-version, has no equivalent
in the OE texts.

5 *Caducos*: (Hum.) 'id est, comiciales [epileptics]'.

5 *Turis manna*: (Hum.) 'est thuris pollin et pulvis. Plinius concussu
elisas thuris micas esse dicit'.

7 *Gebeorhtigeaþ* is the plural of the present indicative of the intransitive
verb *gebeorhtian* 'to become bright'. BT gives the word only as a transitive verb, with quotations where it corresponds with Latin *clarificare*;
BTS quotes this passage and also adds the qualification 'transitive',
following Cockayne. This cannot be correct: the preceding part of the
sentence contains no nominative plural, so that *gebeorhtigeaþ* must have
þa eagan for its subject. See also MS L.

10 In the manuscripts containing the B-version this cure does not
refer to spiders. Cf. MS Harley 1585: 'Ad nefreticos qui a renibus
laborant. Leporis renes si crudi deglutiantur nefreticos emendant, si
caveat dum transglutit ne dentem tangat. Quidam nolunt illos crudos
sumere, eodem modo cocti edentur.'

It is not impossible that *a renibus* was misinterpreted as a form of
aranea by the copyist or the scribe who was dictated to, but the reference
to the *fulix* remains inexplicable.

14 *Item ut concipiat foemina* is a later gloss in Ha. Both L and Ha open
this cure with *Ad auricularum dolores*, which is clearly an error.
Among the manuscripts of class B there is disagreement as to whether
the cure promotes or prevents conception: in MS Har the cure has the
incipit *Mulier ut non concipiat*, whereas MS Harley 1585 has *Ad mulierem
quae non concipit ut concipiat*.

The therapy recommended by the texts containing the B-version is
very different from that of LHa. In MS Harley 1585 we read: 'Leporis
coaguli si acceperit dragmas quatuor in potione, masculus de masculo,
femina de femina, et post cubitum abstinere se debet ab omni acrimonio
et a fungis et a cibis et ab unctionibus inter initia.' MS Har is practically

identical, but gives the patient a better chance to survive by leaving out the words *et a cibis*.

19 *Fram þære teoþan tide*: the tenth hour in the system of the 'hours inequal': about two hours before sunset.

20 There are differences as to where ch. V ends. In L and in the OE manuscripts this is the last cure of the hare, but the last time the animal is mentioned in L is in cure 17. In the original version ch. VI began with a cure following V. 17 (not included in this edition because the OE texts omit it); this arrangement is found in the B-texts; see also Pliny's parallel to cure 19, which contains the words *sanguine hircino*.

M VI

Capra silvatica. For the animal in this chapter L and Ha have *capra silvatica* 13/12×, *capra* 2/3×; in Ha there is a marginal gloss *caprea* in V. 18. In the OE texts we find combinations of *wudu* or *fyre/fire/firgin* with *gat* or *bucca*, and the simplicia *gat* and *bucca*. The OE words are discussed by Jordan, *Säugetiernamen*, pp. 133–42. The compounds with *wudu* are mentioned under *bucca* and *gat* and translated 'Waldbock, Waldgeiß, wilde Ziege'; all the instances recorded are from *MdQ*. The compounds with *firgin*, *fyre* (*fiergen* 'mountain, hill') are mentioned in a separate section. *Firginbucca* is recorded only once (the place in this text is mentioned); for *fyregat* the two instances in *MdQ* are mentioned, and in all the other seven instances recorded by Jordan the word is found in glossaries as a translation of *ibex*. According to Jordan the word *fyregat* is 'eine allgemeine Bezeichnung für die Horntiere des Hochgebirgs, unter der man nach den Glossaren zunächst den Steinbock (Ibex), aber auch Gemse und wilde Ziege verstehen möchte'. This statement needs some qualification. The illustrations showing this animal and the *capra domestica* of the following chapter all represent horned animals, except in Ha, where for the *capra silvatica* there is a drawing of an antlered animal whose build is more like that of a roe than of a goat. None of the drawings of the animal resembles a chamois with its typical horns; the horns in the drawings often do resemble those of an ibex, but the ibex is not the only variety of goat possessing long crooked horns. Moreover, the word *ibex* is not used in any of the Latin manuscripts containing this text, and Pliny and Marcellus in their parallel cures only use the words *capra* (*silvatica*) and *hircus* with their derivatives. Taking this into account, one can only follow in the footsteps of the Anglo-Saxon translator and use terms that are equally vague as his: 'mountain-buck/goat' and 'wild buck/goat'.

M VII

1 *Ignis sacer*: see note to CXXII. 1

10 *Hreofle* is an emendation from *hreofe*. *Hreof* is an adjective meaning 'rough, scabby, leprous'. The repetition of *wiþ* indicates that *hreofe* is not to be connected with *lic*, and from this we may conclude that the word is meant to be a noun denoting the disease rather than an adjective denoting the persons or bodies afflicted with the disease.

For the interpretation of these words see also note to XCII. 2.

12 *Do him . . . drince* V; *do him . . . drincan* B; *do him . . . þæt he drince* O: of these three constructions those in VB are ungrammatical. There is no reason to regard *him* as an accusative: the distinction *hine/him* is observed consistently in the OE texts. The version in O could be regarded as a variant of a construction of which instances are given in *OED* s.v. *do* 21, and in BTS and BTS (*Add.*) s.v. *don* III. 2b. Cf. also Chaucer *CT*, A 4254: 'That makes me that I ga nat aright.'

14 In the Latin versions of the cure the patient is not made to swallow *gate tord*. Probably the OE version is a combination of two different cures; cf. Pl. xxviii. 153: 'Fimo quoque caprarum in aceto decocto illini ictus serpentium placet.'

15, 16 The title of cure 15 belongs to cure 16; cf. MS Ca: 'Ad ventrem stringendum. Caprinum sebum in sorbitionem collectum ventrem cludet, sed supersorbere debeat aquam frigidam.' Then follows a cure that is not found in LHa, and after this: 'Ad idropicos. Hircinum lotium, si ex eo eminam des bibere . . .'

15 The form *seo* is probably the subj. sg. of *beon*; cf. Charter 45 (Surrey) in Sweet, *Oldest English Texts*; but it is possible that in this case there is fusion of the verb form *sy* with the pronoun *seo*.

16 *Cynna 'vari* (*cuma vari* Ha): perhaps a corruption of *cymarum*; cf. Diefenbach s.v. *cymarum*: 'Holunderknopf'. Humelberg prints *cum aruerit*, and quotes Pl. xxviii. 232: 'Hydropicis auxiliatur urina vesicae caprae paulatim data in potus. Efficacius quae inaruerit in vesica sua.' See also Ca: 'Quidam lotium in ipsa vesica sua siccant.'

17 *Mulsum*: cf. *Lb* 61/3: 'Drince mulsa, þæt is gemilscede drincan.'

17 *Wurmas* O: it is remarkable that here and in *M* IX. 7 the scribe of O mistakes *wyrms* for *wurm(as)*, while in *OEH* the three instances of *worsm* in VBH are rendered by *wyrms*.

18 *Parotidas*: see first note to *OEH* II. 19.

M VIII

1, 2 In the OE text the title of cure 1 belongs to cure 2.

1 *Loci* in LHa is *vulva* in Pliny, *veretrum* in Marcellus. For the second part of this cure, after *oleo*, cf. Ca: '. . . et supposita locis dolorem tollit. Suffumigatam autem prolapsam matricem locis suis reprimet.' In LHa *vulva* is confused with *vulnus*.

2 *Ad clauculos et cauculos*: the B-text has only one word: *Ad callos* (MS Wrocław III F 19), 'callosities'. Pliny refers to *verendorum formicationes*, 'itchings of the pudenda'; Humelberg emends *clauculos* into *claviculos* and comments: 'Claviculi e verrucarum genere sunt.' For *cauculi* see note to *OEH* IV. 5.

2 *In manibus*: not in the B-text, which has *in veretro*, corresponding with the parallels in Pliny and Marcellus.

2 The form *(h)ealfsodenre* could be a reflection of *inassati* or *assatur*, not recorded in any of the Latin texts of *MdQ*, but found in Pliny and Marcellus.

3 *Suggellationes*: (Hum.) '. . . nihil aliud sunt quam livores'.

4 There is no equivalent in LHa for OE *sot 7 sealt 7 sand*. Perhaps *sot* is an unsuccessful attempt to translate *cinere pumicis*, found in the parallel in Pliny, *pum-* having been associated with *fum-*.

M IX

6 *In cortice mali Punici*: 'in the peel of a pomegranate'; *swetre apuldre rinde*: 'the bark of a sweet apple tree (pomegranate tree?)'. In LHa the fruit (*malum*) is meant, not the tree (*malus* f.).

10 *Spiwan* O must be regarded as a corruption of *spiwþan*. There is a noun *spiwe* m., of which the accusative/dative singular would be *spiwe*. The possibility of *spiwan* being an infinitive can be excluded: the idiom does not occur in OE; see Visser 976.

10 *Fort þæt þrindan dæl* O: see note to *M* I. 6.

11 *Stranguiria/stede*: see note to *M* III. 16.

13 *Coxios*: Hum. emends this into *coxendicos*, which he explains thus: 'Coxendici dicuntur quos Graeco vocabulo ischiadicos appellamus.'

M X

3 The two different situations as described in LHa are not reflected in the OE version, probably because the cure in the exemplar of the Anglo-Saxon translator was equally corrupt as L, or worse.

5 Something has gone wrong with the division of the chapters containing cures of the wolf and of the dog (X and XIV). V and L are parallel: they have a chapter on the wolf, containing cures of the wolf and the dog, then chapters on the lion, the bull, and the elephant, and finally a chapter on the dog containing more cures of the dog. B and O show the same arrangement, but B has lost a leaf and O has many omissions throughout. Ha has a different arrangement: a chapter on the wolf, containing cures of the wolf, immediately followed by a chapter on the dog, containing two more cures of the wolf and twenty-seven of the dog, and then the chapters on the lion, the bull, and the elephant. Junius, in his transcript of MS B (Bodleian Library, MS Junius 58), places cure 5 of ch. X between cures 10 and 11, and the last two cures of ch. XIV, which are the only cures that remain of this chapter in B (f. 130a begins at *tux* in cure 13; Junius opens this cure with *Hundes* and then follows the text), between cures 9 and 10 of ch. X.

6 *Pili contrarii*: according to Hum. 'eyelashes irritating the eyes'.

6 *Laccanicus*: an interlined *s* in Ha changes *canicus* into *canis*. The addition of *lupi* does not simplify the interpretation of the cure; the rendering *wulfes mearh* in VB is not justified by any of the extant parallels in the Latin B-version.

7 *Wylfene*: it is difficult to say whether this is the genitive singular of the noun *wylfen* or the accusative singular feminine of the adjective *wylfen*. Cf. BT *wylfen(n)* f. 'a she-wolf', with this place quoted, and *wylfen* adj. 'wolfish, fierce'. But in BTS s.v. *wylfen* adj. we find the quotation *þa grægan, wylfenan harnesse*; here the word has the more neutral meaning '(characteristic) of a wolf'. Cf. BT *gæten*: 'of or pertaining to goats', with the instance in this text, *M* VII. 15, quoted.

9 The healing powers of wool are described in Pl. xxix. 29–38.

15 *Nim eac*, etc. This addition in VB is not found in any of the Latin texts.

17 In the Latin version of this cure, which is only found in L, the title is clearly that of a different recipe. The OE version was either taken from an exemplar which had the correct title, or it was provided with the correct title by the translator.

17 *Dweorg*: see note to XCIV.

17 *Togang*: see BT s.v. *togang*, where this place in Cockayne is quoted (but 10 should be 17), with the addition that the manuscript reading *togan* should be read *togang*.

M XI

1 *Leon* VB: the form is the regular genitive singular of the noun *leo*; *leones* O is the genitive singular of a noun *leon*, not recorded in BT(S) and *MED*; it may have come into use as a back-formation of the genitive plural of the noun *leo*. Cf. *OED* s.v. *lion*.

2 *Strigile*: cf. Ackermann: '. . . fistula, qua loco cuipiam aliquid infunditur'.

M XII

8 *Creta Cimolia*: 'chalk from the island of Cimolus'.

11 *Alopicias/bryce*: see note to *M* IV. 2.

13 There seems to be uncertainty among the Latin texts containing this cure as to the meaning of *mugium* (*muium* Ha). MS Harley 1585 has *mugium*, MS Slo *mugitum* (!), while in MS A a space has been left between *Taurinum* and *aceto*. H. and S. print *muium* for the B-version, with a textual variant *fimum* from MS Vi. Humelberg prints *Membrum*, Ackermann *fimus*. It is possible that the cure was confused with Pl. xxviii. 184: 'Fimo taurino malas rubescere aiunt', and that the Anglo-Saxon translator, not knowing the word *mugium* (see *M* III. 14 and note), rendered it by *scytel*.

M XIV

4 *Morbus regius/cynelic adl*: see note to LXXXVII. 1.

5 *Cancorwund*: an irregular form, probably an accusative plural corresponding to *vulnera cancerosa* LHa.

6 *Pterygia*: Humelberg's emendation of *iphter(eg)ia* L/*hyptergia* Ha. See the *British Medical Dictionary*, s.v. *pterygium unguis*: 'abnormal adhesion of the cuticle to the finger nail'. The word was misinterpreted by the translator.

6 *Scurfedum*: emended from *scurfendu* V. The insertion of *-n-* in this form is to be regarded as an error. See Wright, *OEG* 624, Quirk and Wrenn 172, for examples of the suffix *-ed(e)* in adjectives denoting the presence of the thing expressed by the corresponding nouns. Instances of *scurfed(e)* are found in *Lb* 6/1 and 45/21 and in *Peri Didaxeon* 29/14.

9 *Solidat. Fractura*: Humelberg's emendation of *solida autem fractura* L.

12, 13 The two cures are confused in LHa and in the OE version. Cf. MS A:

(*a*) 'Ad gingivas reprimendas. Canis dentes combustos et pisatos cum melle dentifricium uti sunt.'

(*b*) 'Ad dentes infantum. Caninus dens combustus et contritus et appositus gingivis infantum efficit ut dentes sine dolore crescant.'

BIBLIOGRAPHY

Editions of texts are to be found under the name of the (first) editor. Abbreviations and short titles used as references in this book are added in square brackets; in most other cases the works included in this Bibliography are referred to by the full surname(s) of the author(s) or editor(s).

Ackermann, J. C. G., *Parabilium Medicamentorum Scriptores Antiqui, Sexti Placiti Papyriensis de medicamentis ex animalibus liber, Lucii Apuleii de medicaminibus herbarum liber* (Norimbergae et Altorfii, 1788). [Ack.]

Ælfric, *see* Needham, Pope.

Alfred, *see* Endter, Sweet.

Beccaria, A., *I codici di medicina del periodo presalernitano (secoli ix, x e xi)* (Roma, 1956).

Bede, *see* Miller, Plummer.

Berberich, H., *Das Herbarium Apuleii nach einer früh-mittelenglischen Fassung*. Anglistische Forschungen, Heft 5 (Heidelberg, 1901; repr. Amsterdam, 1966).

Berendes, J., *Die Pharmacie bei den alten Culturvölkern*, 2 vols. (Halle, 1891).

Bernard, E., *Catalogi librorum manuscriptorum Angliae et Hiberniae in unum collecti* (Oxford, 1697).

Bierbaumer, Peter, *Der botanische Wortschatz des Altenglischen*. I. Teil: *Das Lǣcebōc*. Grazer Beiträge zur englischen Philologie, 1 (Bern/ Frankfurt am Main, 1975). [Bi.¹]

—— *Der botanische Wortschatz des Altenglischen*. II. Teil: *Lācnunga, Herbarium Apuleii, Peri Didaxeon*. Grazer Beiträge zur englischen Philologie, 2 (Bern/Frankfurt am Main/München, 1976). [Bi.]

—— *Der botanische Wortschatz des Altenglischen*. III. Teil: *Der botanische Wortschatz in altenglischen Glossen*. Grazer Beiträge zur englischen Philologie, 3 (Frankfurt am Main/Bern/Las Vegas, 1979). [Bi.³]

Bliss, A. J., *Sir Orfeo* (Oxford, 1954; 2nd edn., Oxford, 1966).

Bonser, W., *The Medical Background of Anglo-Saxon England* (London, 1963).

Bosworth, J., and T. N. Toller, *An Anglo-Saxon Dictionary* (Oxford, 1898) (a); *Supplement*, by T. N. Toller (Oxford, 1921) (b); *Enlarged Addenda and Corrigenda*, by A. Campbell (Oxford, 1972) (c). [Abbreviations: BT = a; BTS = b; BT(S) = a and b; BTS (*Add.*) = c].

Bowden, Muriel, *A Commentary on the General Prologue to the Canterbury Tales* (New York, 1948; 2nd edn., London, 1967).

The British Medical Dictionary, ed. Sir Arthur S. MacNalty (London, etc., 1961).

Britten, J., and R. Holland, *A Dictionary of English Plant-names* (London, 1886; repr. Vaduz, 1965).

Bülbring, K. D., *Altenglisches Elementarbuch*. I. Teil: *Lautlehre* (Heidelberg, 1902).

Campbell, A., *Old English Grammar* (Oxford, 1959; corrected repr. 1962). [Cpb.]

Catalogue of the Additional Manuscripts (*Nos. 6666–10018*), no date, in BL.

A Catalogue of the Harleian Manuscripts in the British Museum, 4 vols. (London, 1808–12). [Cat. Harl.]

Celsus, *see* Spencer.

Cockayne, (Th.) O., *Leechdoms, Wortcunning and Starcraft of Early England*, 3 vols. (London, 1864–6; rev. edn., with a new introd. by Ch. Singer, London, 1961). [Co., Cockayne; references are to vol. i of the original edition, unless stated otherwise.]

Curry, W. C., *Chaucer and the Medieval Sciences* (New York, 1926, 2nd edn., 1960).

Delcourt, J., *Medicina de Quadrupedibus, an early ME Version*. Anglistische Forschungen, Heft 40 (Heidelberg, 1914).

Diefenbach, L., *Glossarium Latino-Germanicum Mediae et Infimae Aetatis*, new edn. (Darmstadt, 1968).

Diels, H. A., *Die Handschriften der antiken Ärzte*, 3 vols. (Berlin, 1905–8; repr. in one vol., Leipzig, 1970).

Diepgen, Paul, 'Zur Tradition des Pseudoapuleius', *Janus*, 29 (1925), 55–70 and 140–60.

Dioscorides, *see* Sprengel.

Du Cange, C., *Glossarium mediae et infimae latinitatis* (Niort, 1883–7).

Editio Princeps, *see* p. lxi.

Endter, W., *König Alfred der Große: Bearbeitung der Soliloquien des Augustinus* (Hamburg, 1922).

Flom, G. T., 'On the Old English Herbal of Apuleius, Vitellius C III', *Journal of English and Germanic Philology*, 11 (1941), 29–37.

Flora Europaea, several editors, 3 vols. (Cambridge, 1964–72).

Flück, Hans, *Petit guide panoramique des herbes médicinales*, 2me éd., (Neuchâtel/Paris, 1975).

Förster, M., 'Die altenglische Glossenhandschrift Plantinus 32 (Antwerpen) und Additional 32246 (London)', *Anglia*, 29 (1917), 94–161. [Fö.]

Galen, *see* Kühn.

Geldner, J., *Untersuchungen zu altenglischen Krankheitsnamen*, 1. Teil (Würzburg, 1906; 2. und 3. Teil, Augsburg, 1907–8).

Giacosa, P., *Magistri Salernitani nondum editi* (Torino, 1901).

Grattan, J. H. G., and C. Singer, *Anglo-Saxon Magic and Medicine* (London, 1952). [G. and S.] Contains *Lacnunga* on pp. 96–205 [*La*].

Grieve, Mrs M., *A Modern Herbal*, edited and introduced by Mrs C. F. Leyel (London, 1931; repr. 1974).

Gunther, R. W. Th., *The Herbal of Apuleius Barbarus* (Oxford, 1925). A facsimile edition of MS Bodley 130.

Harmer, F. E., *Select English Historical Documents of the 9th and 10th Centuries* (Cambridge, 1914).

Heusinkveld, A. H., and E. J. Bashe, *A Bibliographical Guide to Old English*. University of Iowa Humanistic Studies, iv (1931).

Hilbelink, A. J. G., *Cotton MS Vitellius C III of the Herbarium Apuleii* (diss.) (Amsterdam, 1930).

Howald, E., and H. E. Sigerist, *Antonii Musae de herba vettonica liber. Pseudoapulei herbarius. Anonymi de taxone liber. Sexti Placiti liber medicinae ex animalibus etc.* Corpus Medicorum Latinorum, iv (Leipzig/Berlin, 1927). [H. and S.]

Humelberg, G., *Ant. Musae de Herba Vetonica Liber I, L. Apulei de Medicaminibus Herbarum Liber I* (Isinae, 1537). [Hum.]

—— *Sextus philosophus Platonicus de medicina animalium bestiarum, pecorum, et avium* (Isinae, 1539). [Hum.]

Hunger, F. W. T., *The Herbal of Pseudo-Apuleius* (Leiden, 1935).

Hurter, H., *Gregorius I Magnus, Liber Regulae Pastoralis* (Oeniponti (Innsbruck), 1872). [*Liber Regulae Pastoralis*]

Inguanez, M., *Codicum Casinensium manuscriptorum catalogus*, i (Montecassino, 1915).

Isidorus, *see* Lindsay.

Jones, *see* Rackham.

Jordan, R., *Die altenglischen Säugetiernamen*. Anglistische Forschungen, Heft 12 (Heidelberg, 1903). [Jordan *Säugetiernamen*]

—— *Eigentümlichkeiten des anglischen Wortschatzes*. Anglistische Forschungen, Heft 17 (Heidelberg, 1906). [Jordan *Eigent.*]

—— *Handbuch der mittelenglischen Grammatik*, 1. Teil: *Lautlehre*, 2. Auflage (Heidelberg, 1934). [Jordan *MEG*]

Jost, K., *Wulfstanstudien*. Schweizer anglistische Arbeiten, 23. Band (Bern, 1950).

Kästner, H. F., 'Pseudo-Dioscoridis de Herbis Femininis', *Hermes*, 31 (1896), 578–636, and 32 (1897), 160.

Ker, N. R., *Catalogue of Manuscripts containing Anglo-Saxon* (Oxford, 1957).

Kühn, C. G., *Claudii Galeni Opera Omnia*. Medicorum Graecorum Opera quae Exstant, vols. 1–18 (Lipsiae, 1821–30). [Galen]

Lacnunga, *see* Grattan.

Læceboc, *see* Leonhardi, *also* Wright, C. E.

Lawn, B., *The Salernitan Questions* (Oxford, 1963).

Leonhardi, G., *Kleinere angelsächsische Denkmäler I*. Bibliothek der angelsächsischen Prosa, Band VI (Hamburg, 1905). Contains *Læceboc* on pp. 1–109 [*Lb*].

Lewis, C. T., and C. Short, *A Latin Dictionary* (Oxford, 1879). [L. and S.]

Liber Regulae Pastoralis, *see* Hurter.

Liddell, H. G., and R. Scott, *A Greek–English Lexicon*, new edn. revised and augmented by Sir Henry Stuart Jones (Oxford, 1940). [Li. and S.]

Liebermann, F., *Die Gesetze der Angelsachsen*, 3 vols. (Halle, 1903–16; repr. 1960).

Lindheim, B. von, *Das Durhamer Pflanzenglossar* (Bochum–Langendreer, 1941; repr. New York/London, 1967). [*DP*]

Lindsay, W. M., *Isidorus Hispalensis, Etymologiarum sive Originum libri XX* (Oxford, 1911; repr. Oxford, etc., 1957). [Isidorus *Origines*]

Löweneck, M., *Peri Didaxeon*. Erlanger Beiträge, Heft 12 (Erlangen, 1896).

Madan, F., H. H. E. Craster, and N. Denholm-Young, *A Summary Catalogue of Western Manuscripts in the Bodleian Library at Oxford* (Oxford, 1937–53).

Mancini, A., *Studi Italiani di filologia classica VIII* (Firenze, 1900).

Marcellus, *see* Niedermann.

Meyier, K. A. de, *Codices Vossiani Latini, pars II, codices in quarto* (Leiden, 1975).

Middle English Dictionary, edited by H. Kurath *et al.* (Michigan, 1952–). [*MED*]

Miller, T., *The Old English Version of Bede's Ecclesiastical History of the English People*. EETS os 95, 96, 110, 111 (1890–8; repr. 1959–63).

Mittellateinisches Wörterbuch, edited by Paul Lehmann *et al.* (München, 1959–).

Moorat, S. A. J., *Catalogue of Western Manuscripts on Medicine and Science in the Wellcome Historical Medical Library*, i (London, 1962).

Napier, A. S., *History of the Holy Rood-tree*. EETS os 103 (1894).

Needham, G. I., *Ælfric: Lives of Three English Saints*. Methuen's Old English Library (London, 1966)

Niedermann, M., *Marcelli de Medicamentis Liber*. Corpus Medicorum Latinorum, v (Leipzig/Berlin, 1916). [Ma.]

Oxford Classical Dictionary, edited by N. G. L. Hammond and H. H. Scullard, 2nd edn. (Oxford, 1970).

Oxford English Dictionary (Oxford, 1933). [*OED*]

Paulys Real-Encyclopädie der classischen Altertumswissenschaft, edited by Georg Wissowa *et al.* (Stuttgart, 1894–1970).

Peri Didaxeon, *see* Löweneck.

Planta, J., *A Catalogue of the Manuscripts in the Cottonian Library deposited in the British Museum* (London, 1802).

Pliny, *see* Rackham.

Plummer, C., *Venerabilis Baedae Opera Historica*, 2 vols. (Oxford, 1896; repr. 1946).

Pope, J. C., *Homilies of Ælfric, A Supplementary Collection*. EETS os 259, 260 (1967–8).

Quirk, R., and C. L. Wrenn, *An Old English Grammar*. Methuen's Old English Library (London, 1955; 2nd edn. 1957; repr. 1977).

Rackham, H., W. H. S. Jones, and D. E. Eichholz, *Pliny, Natural History, with an English Translation*. The Loeb Classical Library, 10 vols. (London, 1947–63). [Pl.]

Rauh, Hildegard, *Der Wortschatz der altenglischen Uebersetzungen des Matthaeus-Evangeliums untersucht auf seine dialektische und zeitliche Gebundenheit* (diss.) (Berlin, 1936).

Renwick, W. L., and H. Orton, *The Beginnings of English Literature to Skelton 1509*. Introductions to English Literature, i, 3rd edn. (London, 1966).

Riddle, J. M., 'Dioscorides', in *Catalogus Translationum et Commentariorum*, iv. 1–143 edited by F. Edward Cranz and Paul O. Kristeller (Washington DC, 1980).

Schanz, M., C. Hosius, and G. Krüger, *Geschichte der römischen Litteratur*, IV. Teil, Band 2 (München, 1920). [Schanz–Hosius]

Schaubert, Else von, *Vorkommen, gebietsmäßige Verbreitung und Herkunft altenglischer Partizipialkonstruktionen in Nominativ und Akkusativ* (Paderborn, 1954).

Scherer, G., *Zur Geographie und Chronologie des angelsächsischen Wortschatzes* (diss.) (Berlin, 1928).

Schlemilch, W., *Beiträge zur Sprache und Orthographie spätaltenglischer Sprachdenkmäler der Uebergangszeit 1000–1200*. Studien zur englischen Philologie, 34 (Halle, 1914; repr. Tübingen, 1973).

Serenus, *see* Vollmer.

Sievers, E., *Altenglische Grammatik nach der Angelsächsischen Grammatik von Eduard Sievers*, neubearbeitet von Karl Brunner, 3. Auflage (Tübingen, 1965). [SB]

Singer, C., 'The Herbal in Antiquity', *Journal of Hellenic Studies*, 47 (1927), 1–52.

Sisam, C., and K. Sisam, *The Salisbury Psalter*. EETS os 242 (1959). [Sisam *Psalter*]

Sisam, K., *Studies in the History of Old English Literature* (Oxford, 1953). [Sisam *Studies*]

Smith, Th., *Catalogus librorum manuscriptorum Bibliothecae Cottonianae* (Oxford, 1696).

Souter, A., *A Glossary to Later Latin to 600 A.D.* (Oxford, 1949).

Spencer, W. G., *Celsus, De Medicina, with an English Translation*, 3 vols. (London/Cambridge Massachusetts, 1948–53).

Sprengel, C., *Pedanii Dioscoridis Anazarbei De Materia Medica Libri Quinque*. Medicorum Graecorum Opera quae Exstant, xxv (Lipsiae, 1829). [Dio.]

Steinmeyer, E., and E. Sievers, *Die althochdeutschen Glossen*, Band IV (Berlin, 1898).

Storms, G., *Anglo-Saxon Magic* (diss.) ('s-Gravenhage, 1948).

Stracke, J. Richard, *The Laud Herbal Glossary* (Amsterdam, 1974). [*LHG*]

Sweet, H., *King Alfred's West Saxon Version of Gregory's Pastoral Care*. EETS os 45, 50 (1871–2; repr. 1958).

—— *The Oldest English Texts*. EETS os 83 (1885, repr. 1966).

Talbot, Ch. H., 'Medico-Historical Introduction', in *Kommentarband*, 11–35, published together with *Medicina Antiqua, Facsimile Vol. XXVII: Codex Vindobonensis 93 der österreichischen Nationalbibliothek* (Graz, 1972).

Thorndike, L., *A History of Magic and Experimental Science During the First Thirteen Centuries of Our Era*, i, 2nd printing with corrections (New York, 1929).

Visser, F. Th., *An Historical Syntax of the English Language*, i–iii (Leiden, 1963–73).

Voigts, Linda E., *The Old English Herbal in Cotton Vitellius C III: Studies* (diss.) (Missouri, 1973). [Voigts, *OE Herbal*]

—— 'A New Look at a Manuscript containing the Old English Translation of the *Herbarium Apulei*', *Manuscripta*, 20 (1976), 40–60. [Voigts, 'A New Look']

—— 'One Anglo-Saxon View of the Classical Gods', *Studies in Iconography*, 3 (1977), 3–16.

—— 'The Significance of the Name "Apuleius" to the *Herbarium Apulei*', *Bull. Hist. Medicine*, 52 (1978), 214–27.

Vollmer, F., *Quinti Sereni Liber Medicinalis*. Corpus Medicorum Latinorum, vol. ii, fasc. 3 (Leipzig/Berlin, 1916). [Q. Serenus]

Vriend, H. J. de, *The Old English Medicina de Quadrupedibus* (diss.) (Tilburg, 1972).

Wanley, H., *Humphredi Wanleii Librorum Vett. Septentrionalium . . . Catalogus. Liber Alter* in vol. iii of *Linguarum Vett. Septentrionalium Thesaurus*, by George Hickes (Oxford, 1705; repr. Hildesheim, 1970).

Wells, J. E., *A Manual of the Writings in Middle English 1050–1400*, with nine supplements (New Haven, 1916–52).

Whitelock, Dorothy, *Sweet's Anglo-Saxon Reader in Prose and Verse*, rev. edn. (Oxford, 1967).

Wildhagen, K., *Der Psalter des Eadwine von Canterbury*. Morsbach-Studien, Heft XIII (Halle, 1905).

Wright, C. E., *Bald's Leechbook*. Early English MSS in Facsimile, v (Copenhagen, 1955). [Wright, *Bald's Leechbook*]

Wright, J., *An English Dialect Dictionary*, i–vi (London/New York, 1898–1905). [Wright *Dial. Dict.*]

—— and E. M. Wright, *Old English Grammar*, 3rd edn. (Oxford, 1925; repr. 1950). [Wright *OEG*]

Wright, T., and R. P. Wülcker, *Anglo-Saxon and Old English Vocabularies*, 2nd edn. (London 1884). [Wright–Wülcker]

Zupko, R. E., *British Weights & Measures, A History from Antiquity to the Seventeenth Century* (Madison/London, 1977). [Zupko *W. & M.*]

—— *A Dictionary of English Weights and Measures, from Anglo-Saxon Times to the Nineteenth Century* (Madison/London, 1968). [Zupko *Dict.*]

GLOSSARY

I. GENERAL REMARKS

1. The glossary is based upon the printed text of V; it also contains a small number of words which are found only in B, H, or O. Nouns and adjectives are entered in the form of the nominative singular (masculine); irregular inflected forms are also mentioned. All the recorded forms of pronouns and verbs are included in the glossary; they are found under the nominative singular masculine and infinitive respectively.

2. Of each recorded word, and of each recorded form of pronouns and verbs, up to five instances are mentioned; if a word or form occurs more than five times, 'etc.' is added after the fifth reference; the references are to pages and lines in the printed text of V. Names of plants which are found in the titles and described in the openings of chapters are referred to by the chapter numbers; page/line references are added whenever these names are also found in other chapters. There are no references to places in the table of contents, unless a word or form is exclusively found in that part of V.

3. All words beginning with the prefix *ge-* are listed according to their unprefixed forms. The prefix is added to the lemma in brackets whenever a word occurs both with and without it, but in verbs *ge-* is not added if the only form in which it occurs is the past participle. In a few cases, where the semantic difference is important, there are separate lemmas for forms with and without *ge-*.

4. If a word is found as a simplex and as the second element of a compound or a derivative, the simplex is followed by cross-references to all the compounds or derivatives in which it occurs. If a word is recorded only as the second element in two or more different compounds or derivatives, each of these is provided with a cross-reference or with cross-references.

5. The grammatical abbreviations are the usual ones; see Cpb., p. xiv. For other abbreviations see the List of Abbreviations on p. ix.

II. SPELLING

1. The symbol *æ* is treated as a separate letter between *a* and *b*.

2. If a word is recorded both with *i* and with *y*, it is entered in the form in which it occurs most frequently in V; the variant spelling is recorded under the same lemma. There are no cross-references.

3. The symbol *ð* is replaced by *þ*, which is treated as a separate letter between *t* and *u*.

4. With regard to the quantity of the vowel in words like *cild*, *næd(d)re*, the usual convention is followed (see Cpb. 283 n. 4, 285 n. 1).

5. If a word occurs only in an unusual spelling, the regular form is placed immediately after it in quotation marks and brackets.

III. VERBS

1. The class of a strong verb is indicated by an arabic numeral, of a weak verb by a roman numeral. The subdivisions of class 7 are in accordance with Cpb. 745.

2. The case governed by a verb is mentioned if it is not exclusively the accusative.

3. Finite verb forms not described as pret. are forms of the present tense; finite verb forms not described as subj. or imp. are forms of the indicative; finite verb forms described as imp. are forms of the imperative singular.

4. In the present and preterite indicative singular the three persons are specified by the numerals 1, 2, and 3.

A

abacan 6 bake. *pp.* abacen 266/8.

abēatan 7b beat, knock. *1 sg.* abēate 234/12.

abīdan 1 wait. *imp.* abīd 262/10.

ablǣcnyss *f.* paleness 208/6.

ablendan I stop, prevent spreading (*of cancer*). *inf.* ablendan 44/7.

abrecan 4 break. *pp.* abrocen 1/19.

abrēdan 3 snatch. *subj. sg.* abrēde 170/21; *imp.* abrēd 264/4; *pp.* abrōden 170/24.

abūtan, abūton (I) *adv.* around, about 64/16. (II) *prep. w. a., d.* around, about 34/26, 44/17, 58/3, 62/22, 68/20, etc. [Cf. onbūtan.]

ac *conj.* but 52/3, 54/1, 114/17, 168/10, 170/16, etc.

acan 6 ache. *subj. sg.* ace 38/2, 44/1, 146/19, 270/29; *subj. pl.* acen 36/18, 42/14. [The verb is impersonal in 44/1.]

acennan I generate, produce. *pp.* acenned 60/3, 74/9, 12, 86/7, 100/10, etc.

aclǣnsian II (*a*) cleanse, purify. *3 sg.* aclǣnsaþ 60/23; *pp.* aclǣnsod 56/23. (*b*) remove by cleansing. *3 sg.* aclǣnsaþ 254/2.

acōlian II grow cold. *pp.* acōlod 130/10.

acse *see* acxe.

acwellan I kill, destroy. *inf.* tō acwellanne 242/1; *3 sg.* acwelleþ

48/17, 178/8, 186/6, 240/21; *pp.* acweald 134/21.

acxe, axe, ahse, acse, æsce *f.* ash(es) 58/25, 92/9, 104/2, 116/3, 240/13, etc.

ādl *f.* disease, sickness 90/3, 108/25, 134/8, 142/9, 236/2, etc.; *apl.* ādlu 182/20; cynelic ～ the king's evil 126/10, 186/8, 270/14. [See note to LXXXVII. 1, and cf. fōt-～, lifer-～, liþ-～, lungen-～, wæter-～.]

ādlian II be ill. *pres. p.* ādliġende 120/19, 20.

adōn *anom. vb.* remove, take away (*with* fram, of, onweġ, ūt). *inf.* tō adōnne 260/21, 264/7; *3 sg.* adēþ 56/26, 92/2, 106/24, 246/5, 258/21, etc.; *imp.* adō 234/10.

adrīfan 1 drive away. *3 sg.* adrīfþ 78/8.

adrīgan, adrȳgan I dry (up). *inf.* tō adrīġenne 240/12; *3 sg.* adrīġeþ, adrȳġeþ 216/4, 242/8, *imp.* adrīg, adrȳg 240/8, 256/1, adrīġe 248/12.

adūne *adv.* down, downwards 238/12, 240/5.

afandian II *w. g.* try, test. *pret. pl.* afandedon 144/16; *pp.* afandud 230/2.

afǣran I terrify. *pp.* afǣred 104/10.

afeormian II cleanse, purge, purify. *3 sg.* afeormaþ 70/3, 76/9, 104/3,

118/7, 124/5, etc., **afeormeþ** 66/10;
pp. **afeormud** 122/15, 124/16,
156/11, **afeormad** 214/11.

afeormung *f.* cleansing, purging
122/13.

Affricani *mpl.* Africans 212/5.

aflēogan 2 fly away. *pp.* **aflogen**
262/10. [Probably an error, cf.
aflōwen B.]

aflīgan, aflȳgan, aflīan I expel, put
to flight. *inf.* **aflīan** 142/5; **tō**
aflīgenne 25/12; *3 sg.* **aflīgeþ**,
aflȳgeþ 84/7, 114/17, 176/8, 186/4,
194/12, etc., **aflīgþ** 48/17, 56/3,
66/7.

aflīgeng *f.* expulsion 244/11.

aflōwan 7f flow away. *3 sg.* **aflōweþ**
266/13; *pp.* **aflōwen** 263/10 (B
only).

aflȳgennyss *f.* expulsion 266/25.

afor *adj.* acid, sour 214/5, 226/15.

afyrman I cleanse, purify. *3 sg.*
afyrmeþ 169/13 (**afyrreþ** BH, *see*
Latin).

afyrran I remove. *3 sg.* **afyrreþ**
200/12, 208/4, 242/8, 258/26,
260/4, etc.; *pp.* **afyrred** 249/13.

Agustus, Agustes *see* **Augustus.**

agyfan 5 give. *3 sg.* **agyfþ** 184/2; *pp.*
agyfen 82/14.

aheardian II harden. *pp.* **aheardod**
40/4, 130/18.

ahebban 6 lift up, raise. *3 sg.* **ahefþ**
108/24; *imp.* **ahefe** 42/24, 238/10,
262/10; *pp.* **ahafen** 106/19.

ahlȳtrian I make clear, purify. *pp.*
ahlȳtred 146/15.

ahōn 7d hang. *inf.* **ahōn** 200/23;
2 sg. **ahēhst** 220/17, 244/8, **ahēgst**
220/15; *3 sg.* **ahēhþ** 169/19; *subj.*
sg. **ahō** 238/25; *imp.* **ahōh** 62/22,
228/26; *pp.* **ahangen** 58/8, 104/17,
246/15.

ahryssan I shake. *imp.* **ahryse** 30/8.

ahse *see* **acxe.**

ahwǣnan I vex, trouble. *pp.* a-
hwǣned 66/19.

ahyldan I (*a*) incline. *pres.* *p.*
ahyldende 192/15. (*b*) turn away
(*intr.*) *3 sg.* **ahyldeþ** 236/2.

aīdlian II annul, get rid of. *pp.*
aīdlud 162/7.

alecgan I lay. *3 sg.* **alegþ** 48/7,

108/24; *pp.* **alēd** 178/15, 258/25,
270/25.

alȳfan I permit. *pp.* **alȳfed** 228/17.

alȳsan I (*a*) relieve. *2 sg.* **alȳsest**
214/20; *3 sg.* **alȳseþ** 144/6, 184/18,
194/9; *pp.* **alȳsed** 204/10, 216/7,
256/18. (*b*) release, allow (to go)
pp. **alȳsed** 236/16.

ambur *f.?* (*a measure of capacity*)
82/17. [See p. lxxxiii and note to
XXXVI. 3.]

amearcian II describe, give particulars of. *3 pret. sg.* **amearcode**
108/19.

amerian I purify, refine. *pp.* **amered**
150/21.

amigdal *m.* almond 58/6, 80/3.

ampulle *f.* bottle, flask 78/1, 175/2.

ān [Forms regular, except *asgm.*
ǣnne (3 ×), **āne** (1 ×) as against
ānne (24 ×).] (I) *pron. adj.* (*a*) a
certain, one, a 54/14, 58/7, 64/16,
78/1, 89/30, etc. (*b*) *following a*
noun or pronoun alone, only 46/4,
246/16; **nā þæt ~ þæt** not only
106/16, 172/15, 216/18. [See also
āna.] (*c*) *correlative with* **ōþer,**
þridda (the) one 168/10, 208/11,
212/5. (II) *num.* one 30/23, 34/1, 9,
13, 18, etc.; **~ 7 ~** one by one
34/23.

āna *indecl. adj.* alone, only 238/22,
250/10.

anǣlan *see* **onǣlan.**

anbyrgan *see* **onbyrgan.**

and (*in the MS always* 7) *conj.* and
30/3, 5, 6, 7, 8, etc.

anda *m.* enmity, envy 224/14.

andwealcan 7c roll. *imp.* **andwealc**
175/1.

andweard *adj.* effective, active (*Latin*
praesens) 144/15.

andweardnyss *f.* efficacy (*Latin*
praesentia) 106/17.

andwlata, andwlita *m.* face 30/18,
98/20, 116/10, 134/10, 144/25,
etc., **anwlata** 260/5.

anginn *n.* beginning 190/19.

Angle *see* **Engle.**

animan 4 take away. *3 sg.* **animþ**
50/9, 112/18, 21, **animeþ** 48/20,
50/3; *pp.* **anumen** 46/24.

(ge)ānlīcian II (*a*) compare. *pp.*

geānlīcud 228/8. (b) make like.
3 sg. geānlīcaþ 228/11.

ānrǣd adj. constant, resolute, prompt
144/15 (H only).

anwealh adj. whole, entire 202/18,
228/17.

anwlata see andwlata.

anȳdan I (with fram, ūt) expel. 3 sg.
anȳdeþ 136/5, 138/28, 172/26,
192/20; pp. anȳd(d) 186/16. [Cf.
genȳdan.]

apa m. ape, monkey 268/12.

Aprēlis m. April 50/20, 54/16.

apulder f. apple-tree 260/21.

apullian II pull, pluck. pp. apullod
264/8.

ār f. help, service. tō gōdre āre
cuman be of good service 38/30.

arǣcan I reach. inf. arǣcan 170/21.

arǣran I raise up, restore health of.
3 sg. arǣrþ 92/3.

argang ('earsgang', arsgang') m.
anus 38/16.

arīsan 1 arise. pl. arīsaþ 242/19,
258/15; imp. arīs 238/11; pret. pl.
arison 242/19.

asceacan 6 shake (off). subj. sg.
asceace 216/6.

asendan I (a) discharge from the
body. inf. asendan 52/8; 3 sg.
asendeþ 106/8. (b) emit, send
forth. subj. sg. asende 182/4. (c)
produce. 3 sg. asendeþ 178/15,
180/5, 194/4, 204/14, 206/1.

asettan I place, impose. naman on
~ give a name. 3 sg. pret. asette
70/7.

aspīwan 1 spit out. 3 sg. aspīweþ
36/3; subj. sg. aspīwe 226/21.

astīgan 1 descend, go. subj. sg.
astīge 246/17.

astyrian I (a) move, stir up. inf. tō
astyrigenne 74/2, 210/1, 268/5;
3 sg. astyreþ 74/4, 156/12, 186/7,
192/22, 194/21, etc. (b) (with aweg)
remove. pp. astyred 236/17.

astyrung f. motion (of the bowels),
passing (of urine) 176/26, 190/20,
196/10, 198/1, 202/7, etc.

atēon 2 draw. 3 sg. atȳhþ 54/9,
60/14, 68/10, 94/4, 124/4, etc.;
pp. atogen 46/24, 88/26.

āttor n. poison 36/1, 3, 50/19, 60/12,

66/4, etc. [Always -tt- except 1 ×
ātru 110/11.]

āttorcoppe f. spider 46/12, 13,
250/3.

āttorlāþe f. cockspur-grass XLV.

āttorþigen f. taking of poison 1/26,
12/9.

atȳwan see ætȳwan.

aþindan 3 swell, inflate. pp. aþunden
38/7.

aþundenyss ('aþundennyss') f.
swelling 17/13.

Augustus m. August 50/25, 72/7,
104/16, 228/24, Agustus 44/11,
Agustes 30/7.

aweallan 7c be hot, become hot. pp.
aweallen 142/10.

aweccan I bring about, arouse. inf.
tō aweccanne 242/21; 3 sg.
awecceþ 242/22.

aweg, awege see onweg.

awegan 5 weigh. pp. awegen 252/18.

awendan I (a) turn away, avert. inf.
tō awendenne 220/13; 3 sg.
awendeþ 56/5, 220/16; subj. sg.
awende 220/23; pp. awend 228/
16. (b) change. pp. awend 228/14.

aweorpan 3 cast, throw. 3 sg.
aweorpeþ 240/21, awyrpeþ
156/4, 270/21, awyrpþ 82/30,
258/4.

āwiht pron. anything 234/16.

awrītan 1 write (down), record. pp.
awriten, awryten 68/6, 96/6.

awyllan I boil. pp. awylled 34/22,
38/23, 248/24.

awyrdan I injure. pp. awyrd 206/4.

axe see acxe.

Æ

æcer m. field 50/14.

ǣdre, ǣddre f. (a) vein 44/21, 130/
18. [See note to XC. 9.] (b) kidney
126/3, 160/21, 188/6.

ǣfen(n) mn. evening 178/26, 256/15.

ǣfre adv. ever 182/11.

æfter (I) adv. afterwards 238/23,
260/8. [Cf. þǣr-~.] (II) prep. w. d.
(a) after (temporal) 30/14, 40/28,
64/17, 132/1, 11, etc.; ~ þon adv.
afterwards 250/17; ~ þām þe
conj. after 226/19. (b) according to
96/2, 236/6.

æftra *adj. comp.* second 40/17.

æfþanca *m.* spite, ill will 126/5.

ǣghwǣr *adv.* everywhere 36/16, 86/20.

ǣghwæþer *pron.* each of two 136/24.

ǣghwylc *pron. adj.* each, every, all 36/7, 42/1, 12, 82/17, 86/7, etc.

ǣgþer *pron. adj.* each of two, both 84/16, 90/13, 140/12, 172/13, 210/ 10, etc.; ~ ge . . . ge both . . . and 98/5, 150/15, 228/10.

Ægypte *mpl.* Egyptians 234/2.

ǣhīwness *f.* paleness, discoloration 208/6, 8.

ǣht *f.* possession 220/14.

ǣlc *pron. adj.* each, every, all 42/10, 62/25, 76/3, 96/19, 128/12, etc.

ælmihtig *adj.* almighty 220/24, 234/11.

æltǣwe, ælteowe *adj.* excellent 36/27, 250/4.

ǣne *adv.* once 136/16.

Ængle *see* Engle.

ǣnig *pron. adj.* any 58/9, 114/5, 8, 17, 126/5, etc.

ǣnne *see* ān.

æppel, æpl *m.* (*a*) apple 160/22, 254/5. (*b*) fruit 238/8. (*c*) (apple-) dumpling 174/17.

ǣr (I) *adj.* early. *comp.* ǣrra former 48/13. [See also ǣrnemergen.] (II) *adv.* earlier, previously 46/23, 74/11, 23, 76/24, 82/5. [See also ǣrest.] (III) *conj.* before 40/9, 64/14². (IV) *prep. w. d. instr.* 64/14¹, 18, 70/14, 74/13, 238/7, etc.; ~ þām (þe) *conj.* before 136/7, 226/20, 254/16; ~ þon *conj.* before 40/16, 238/13.

ǣren *adj.* (made of) brass 116/4.

ǣrest, ǣrost *adv. sup.* first 32/26, 58/15, 70/6, 116/8, 146/1, etc.

ǣrnemergen *m.* dawn, daybreak 118/5, 154/18. [For a discussion of this word see Pope, note to XIII. 193.]

ǣrost *see* ǣrest.

æsce *see* acxe.

æscþrote, æscþrotu *f.* (*a*) vervain, verbena IV. (*b*) alkanet 148/2.

æt *prep. w. d.* (*a*) at, by, near 236/14, 15. (*b*) (*with* cyrre, sǣle) at, on 146/2, 3, 4, 5, 6. [Cf. þǣr-~.]

ætbēon *anom. vb.* be present at. *subj. sg.* ætsȳ 220/23.

ætflēon 2 flee away, escape. *subj. sg.* ætflēo 170/12; *subj. pl.* ætflēon 52/1.

æthrīnan 1 *w. a., d.* touch. *inf.* æthrīnan 234/14; *2 sg.* ǣthrīnest 264/14; *subj. sg.* æthrīne 170/16.

æthrine *m.* touch 60/6, 62/7, 242/20. [Cf. onhrine.]

æthwego *adv.* a little, somewhat 240/8.

ǣtrig, ǣttrig *adj.* poisonous 48/13, 94/5.

ætstandan 6 stand still, stop. *3 sg.* ætstandeþ 102/24, ætstent 116/ 23; *pp.* ætstanden 52/5, æt-standene ǣdran hardened veins 44/21.

ætȳwan, atȳwan 1 appear. *3 sg.* atȳweþ 76/4; *pret. pl.* ætȳwdon 262/20.

æþelferþinc(g)wyrt *f.* stitchwort 108/1, 118/17.

ǣþm *m.* vapour, smell 220/6.

ǣwyrdla *m.* damage, injury 184/1.

B

bacan 6 bake. *pp.* gebacen 88/19. [Cf. a-~, ofenbacen.]

bān *n.* bone 60/15, 94/3, 5, 96/17, 168/22, etc. [Cf. ylpen-~.]

bānbryce *m.* fracture of a bone *or* bones 60/13, 96/16.

bānece *m.* pain in the thigh(-bone), sciatica 96/16, 176/1. [Cf. hype-~.]

bānwyrt *f.* heartsease, wild pansy CLXV, 194/18.

bār *m.* boar 170/4, 260/10, 12, 14, 16, etc.

batian II heal, get better. *3 sg.* bataþ 38/11, 40/6; *pp.* gebatod 270/27.

gebaþian II wash. *imp.* gebaþa 216/6.

bæcþearm *m.* rectum, anus 208/16.

bærnan I burn (*tr.*) *subj. sg.* bærne 226/23; *imp.* bærn 88/3, 92/8, 162/18, 266/1, 268/22, etc.; *pp.* gebærned 146/25, 240/16, 20, 242/7, 9, etc. [Cf. for-~.]

bærnet(t), bærnyt(t) *n.* (*a*) burn 148/6, 212/11. (*b*) burning 158/12.

bærwas *see* **bearu.**

bæþ *n.* bath 98/4, 124/22, 140/13, 164/21, 216/6, etc.

be *prep. w. d.* (*a*) about, concerning 42/1, 110/22, 136/11, 156/16, 228/7, etc.; ~ **þām þe** concerning how, of how 13/10. (*b*) by, according to 68/22, 72/15, 76/8, 90/13, 92/5, etc.

bēan *f.* bean 102/2, 166/8.

bēanen *adj.* made of beans, bean- 198/16.

bearg, bearh *m.* barrow-pig 44/8.

bearn *n.* child 264/10.

bearu *m.* grove, wood. *npl.* **bærwas** 60/4 (**bearwas** BH).

bēatan 7b beat, cut up. *pp.* **gebēaten** 240/18, 260/16. [Cf. **a-~.**]

bēcen *adj.* beech- 118/19.

beclȳsan I close. *pl.* **beclȳsaþ** 96/4.

becuman 4 (*a*) come. *3 sg.* **becymeþ** 172/8. (*b*) (*with* **on** *and a.*) come upon. *3 sg.* **becymþ** 112/19, **becymeþ** 40/14, 138/13, 144/4, 172/8, 194/23, etc. (*c*) (*with* **tō** *and d.*) come upon, find. *pret. subj. sg.* **becōme** 234/6. (*d*) **tō frēcnysse** ~ *w. d.* endanger. *3 sg.* **becymþ** 158/3.

bedelfan 3 bury. *imp.* **bedelf** 236/14.

bedrincan 3 absorb. *pp.* **bedruncen** 242/12 (B *only*).

bedrūgian II dry up. *pp.* **bedrūgud** 242/12.

befealdan 7c fold. enfold. *inf.* **befealdan** 200/22; *imp.* **befeald** 58/24, 138/14.

befeallan 7c fall. *subj. sg.* **befealle** 82/15.

befor *m.* (beaver,) castoreum 248/24.

beforan *see* **hēr.**

begalan 6 enchant, lay under a spell. *3 sg.* **begaleþ** 126/6; *subj. sg.* **begale** 15/9.

begān *anom. vb.* cultivate. *pp.* **begān** 48/10, 50/23, 60/20, 62/14, 64/3, etc.

begēotan 2 wet, besprinkle. *imp.* **begēot** 134/10, 142/12, 190/11.

begyrdan I gird. *3 sg.* **begyrdeþ** 132/13; *imp.* **begyrd** 84/6.

behabban III surround. *pp.* **behæfd** 198/24.

behāt *n.* promise, threat 224/14.

behealdan 7c take heed, beware. *imp.* **beheald** 238/18.

behēfe *adj.* suitable, useful 238/12.

behelian I, II hide. *imp.* **behele** 236/16.

belīfan 1 remain, be left. *3 sg.* **belīfeþ** 168/22.

belimp *n.* event, accident 222/20.

belimpan 3 befall, happen. *3 sg.* **belimpeþ** 230/1.

belone *f.* henbane V.

belūcan 2 stop. *3 sg.* **belūceþ** 224/6.

bēo *f.* bee 52/1.

bēon *anom. vb.* (*a*) be. *inf.* **bēon** 32/26, 46/15, 60/3, 74/13, 88/26, etc.; *1 sg.* **eom** 234/4; *2 sg.* **bist, byst** 224/15, 230/2, 234/20; *3 sg.* **biþ, byþ** 30/2, 6, 32/18, 19, 34/3, etc., **is, ys** 38/30, 40/9, 12, 18, 48/6, etc.; *pl.* **bēoþ** 52/2, 60/4, 64/11, 68/17, 74/9, etc., **sindon, syndon** 156/11, 168/10, 186/3, 212/4, 214/5, etc.; *subj. sg.* **bēo** 30/20, 46/16, 48/4, 104/15, 122/14, etc., **sȳ** 30/11, 32/20, 34/4, 12, 36/14, etc., **sēo** 256/27 (*see note to M VII.* 15); *subj. pl.* **bēon** 48/17, 100/25, 134/20, 246/16, **sȳn, sīen** 36/10, 46/20, 50/4, 106/10, 118/1, etc.; *pret. 3 sg.* **wæs** 108/16, 114/25, 234/2, 17, 236/17; *pret. pl.* **wǣron** 202/16, **wǣran** 128/23; *pret. subj. sg.* **wǣre** 96/18, 100/19, 182/21; *negative form 3 sg.* **nys** 168/9, 228/ 17. [Cf. **æt-~.**] (*b*) *auxiliary of tense* have. *subj. sg.* **bēo** 30/21.

bēor *m.* beer 30/13, 34/14, 36/19, 22, 56/7.

beorc *f.* barking 12/19.

beorcan 3 bark at. *pp.* **borcen** 110/9.

beorg *m.* hill, mound 58/4, 64/4, 74/7, 90/11, 122/9, etc.

beorht *adj.* bright, splendid 268/24, 26; *sup.* **beorhtust** 94/16.

beorhte *adv.* clearly. *comp.* **beorhtor** 76/18.

gebeorhtian II become bright. *pl.* **gebeorhtigeaþ** 248/21.

beorhtnys(s), beorhtness *f.* brightness, clearness 76/20, 82/14, 228/15, 252/12, 13.

beorþor *n.* (*a*) embryo, foetus 248/12.
(*b*) childbirth 248/17.

bēowyrt *f.* (*a*) sweet flag VII. (*b*)
bear's breech, brank-ursine, *or*
Scotch thistle, woolly thistle CLIV.

bera *m.* bear 148/5.

beran 4 bear, carry. *2 sg.* byrst
154/20; *3 sg.* byrþ 112/6, 114/7,
162/3, bereþ 132/14, 214/24;
subj. sg. bere 44/5; *imp.* ber
250/24. [Cf. for-∼, wōlberende.]

berbēne *f.* (H *only*) columbine
110/4.

bere *m.* barley 194/19.

berēafian II despoil, deprive. *3 sg.*
berēafaþ 232/2.

berēcan I cause to smoke. *imp.*
berēc 58/24.

beren *adj.* of barley 188/27, 256/22.

berie, berge *f.* berry 104/13, 120/11,
144/21, 194/18. [Cf. strēaw-∼,
wēde-∼, wīn-∼.]

berstan 3 burst. *inf.* berstan 190/23;
subj. sg. berste 130/13; *pres. p.*
berstende (līc) with sores or
rashes breaking out 190/8. [Cf.
tō-∼.]

bescīnan 1 shine upon. *subj. sg.*
bescīne 228/13.

besēon 5 (*refl.*) look, look around.
subj. sg. besēo 52/17; *imp.* beseoh
136/12.

besēoþan 2 boil down. *pp.* besoden
36/25.

besingan 3 enchant. *imp.* besing
136/9.

besprengan I besprinkle. *imp.*
besprengc 126/7.

bestingan 3 push, thrust. *pp.*
bestungen 252/10.

beswīcan 1 deceive. *pp.* beswycen
170/24.

bet *adv. comp.* better 130/21.

(ge)bētan I heal, cure. *2 sg.* gebētst
68/12, 88/2; *3 sg.* (ge)bēteþ 248/7,
262/16, 264/20, 268/17, gebēt
134/7, 152/11; *pp.* gebēted 238/4,
gebēt 66/23, 146/8.

bēte, bœte *f.* beet, beetroot XXXVII.

betonice *f.* betony, wood betony I,
142/6.

betweoh *prep. w. d.* between, among
104/8.

betwēonan *prep. w. d.* between,
among 178/16, 204/16.

betweox *prep. w. d.* between, among
204/15.

(ge)beþian II, beþþan I wash. *inf.*
tō beþianne 252/2; *subj. sg.*
beþige 122/12; *imp.* (ge)beþa
30/16, 126/23, 148/23, 162/19,
beþe 40/24, 84/9, 122/20; *pp.*
gebeþod 116/8, gebeþed 128/15.

beþurfan *pret. pr.* need. *subj. sg.*
beþurfe 30/10, 230/14.

beweallan 7c boil away. *pp.*
beweallen 236/9, 262/6.

bewindan 3 bind, wrap. *3 sg.*
bewindeþ 138/16; *imp.* bewind
234/13, 238/16.

bewrītan 1 mark round. *subj. sg.*
bewrīte 170/3; *imp.* bewrīt 42/23,
64/16, 170/12, 15.

bewyrcan I work, adorn. *imp.*
bewyrc 234/13.

bicce *f.* bitch 264/13, 16.

biddan 5 pray, beg. *1 sg.* bidde
220/22, 224/20.

bifung *f.* trembling, tremor 58/10, 12,
214/23.

gebind *n.* constipation 244/4, 9.

(ge)bindan 3 bind, tie. *subj. sg.*
binde 38/3, 130/14; *imp.* (ge)bind
38/29, 42/25, 46/6, 50/8, 56/17.
[Cf. un-∼.]

binnan, bynnan *prep. w. d.* within
52/7, 54/8, 58/7, 64/7, 86/24, etc.

biscopwyrt *f.* betony I. [See note
to I.]

bisen *f.* example 234/4.

bite *m.* (*a*) bite 46/13, 244/1, 3,
250/3, 20, etc. (*b*) acute pain
210/23.

biter, bitter *adj.* bitter 50/15, 62/7,
174/27, 182/4, 6, etc. [See also
byrging.]

biternyss *f.* bitterness 192/19.

blæc *adj.* black 38/6, 182/15, 258/24,
264/24.

blǣdre, blǣddre *f.* (*a*) bladder
46/1, 56/12, 86/21, 120/2, 124/19,
etc.; *nsg.* blǣdder 138/26. (*b*)
pustule, pimple 42/1.

blǣse *f.* torch, lamp 214/17.

blēoh *n.* colour 96/14, 136/25,
174/14, 178/2, 200/19.

blind *adj.* (*of a wound*) not outwardly visible 48/2.

blōd *n.* blood 32/23, 42/27, 44/21, 60/3, 64/4, etc.; blōde ūt yrnan have a discharge of blood 38/16.

blōdgyte *m.* bleeding 42/29.

blōdrēad *adj.* blood-red 168/13.

blōdryne *m.* (*a*) bleeding 32/3, 116/21, 198/18, 214/9, 220/3, etc. (*b*) flux of blood, menses 240/3.

blōstma *m.* flower, blossom 96/2, 116/2, 128/11, 136/23, 162/25; *asg.* blōsþman 58/4; *npl.* blōsman 96/3.

blōwan 7f bloom, blossom. *3 sg.* blēwþ 52/4, 102/3; *pl.* blōwaþ 136/25; *subj. sg.* blōwe 230/5; *pres. p.* blōwende 166/7, 224/22.

bōc *f.* book 108/18.

bodian II announce; hǣlo ~ send greetings. *pret. 3 sg.* bodade 234/3.

bœte *see* bēte.

bōg, bōh *m.* (*a*) branch, twig, sprout 88/11, 13, 174/4, 24, 178/15, etc. (*b*) shoulder 206/4.

boga *m.* bow 200/18.

bolla *m.* bowl, cup, cupful 212/20.

bōt *f.* recovery 36/27, 242/10, 256/4, 29; tō bōte cuman bring recovery 34/27.

boþen *mn.* rosemary LXXXI, 192/6.

brād *adj.* broad 178/1; *comp.* brādra 222/4.

gebrǣceo *f.* coughing, catarrh 164/3, 6, 14.

(ge)brǣdan I roast. *subj. sg.* gebrǣde 104/2; *imp.* brǣd 250/6; *pp.* gebrǣded 250/2, 262/13.

brægen *n.* brain 236/8, 248/6, 250/22, 254/15, 260/12, etc.

brēaþ *adj.* brittle 182/2.

brecan 4 break. *pp.* gebrocen 34/4. [Cf. a-~, for-~, tō-~.]

brēgan I frighten. *pp.* brēged 114/8.

brēmel *m.* bramble, blackberry LXXXIX.

brēost *n.* (*a*) breast (*Latin* mamilla) 50/4, 5, 120/10, 158/9, 10, etc. (*b*) breast, chest (*Latin* pectus) 140/1.

(ge)bringan 3 *and* I bring, (*with* fram) remove. *inf.* bringan 202/2; *subj. sg.* gebrincge 174/8.

brīw *m.* brew, pottage 182/15.

broc *m.* badger 234/9.

broc *n.* affliction, disease 246/11.

brōc *m.* brook 68/6.

brōcminte *f.* water-mint, *or* brook-mint CVII.

broþ *n.* broth 252/2, 4.

brūcan 2 *w. g.* (*a*) use, have (bæþes ~). *inf.* brūcan 220/10; *3 sg.* brūceþ 240/12, 17; *subj. sg.* brūce 78/2, 124/22, 164/21, 246/20; *subj. pl.* brūcen 110/12; *imp.* brūc 30/10. (*b*) enjoy. *inf.* brūcan 238/2. (*c*) consume, eat, take. *inf.* brūcan 250/18; *subj. sg.* brūce 242/4.

brūn *adj.* brown 136/23, 198/23, 204/15.

brūnbasu(w) *adj.* dark purple 208/11.

brūnewyrt *f.* finger-fern, spleenwort, *or* hart's-tongue LVII.

bryce *m.* fracture 268/20, 270/25. [Cf. bān-~, hēafod-~.]

brӯce *m.* use, service 76/6.

brӯce, brīce *adj.* useful 236/19, 238/11.

bryne *m.* burn 268/22. [Cf. gund-~.]

(ge)brӯtan I crush, pound. *inf.* brӯtan 78/7; *2 sg.* (ge)brӯtest 58/4, 178/16; *imp.* (ge)brӯt 30/17, 146/26, 268/25; *pp.* gebrӯted 252/10.

bucca *m.* buck 254/11, 258/1. [Cf. firgin-~, wudu-~.]

bufan *adv.* above 244/21, 23.

burhgeat *n.* gate of a fortified place 236/15.

burhstaþol *m.* foundation of the wall of a fortified place 236/15.

būtan, būton *prep.* (*a*) *w. d.* without 03/7, 40/5, 21, 42/15, 44/8, etc. (*b*) *w. a.* except 168/22; būton þæt *conj.* except that 192/7; būton þonne *conj.* except when 52/4.

butere *f.* butter 46/26, 64/12, 108/2, 130/6, 11, etc.

būtū *pron. adj.* both 172/16, 250/10.

bӯgan I bend. *pp.* gebӯged 182/2.

byrgen *f.* grave, burial place 74/7, 180/4.

byrging, byring *f.* taste 50/15, 60/7, 174/27, 182/5, 6, etc.;

bitter(r)e, weredre on ~**e** bitter, sweet to the taste.

byr(i)gan I taste. *imp.* **byrig** 30/10. [Cf. **onbyrgan.**]

byrnan 3 burn (*intr.*). *subj. sg.* **byrne** 254/18.

byrþþinen *f.* midwife 162/23.

bysgian II trouble, vex. *pp.* **gebysgod** 38/20.

bysmær *mfn.* mockery, insult 246/15.

C

cald *see* **ceald.**

camb *m.* comb 238/22, 25, 240/4. [See also **wulfes** ~.]

cammoc *mn.* hog's fennel, sulphurwort XCVI.

cancer, cancor *m.* (*a*) cancer 44/7, 78/11, 80/19, 84/8, 122/19, etc. (*b*) canker, gangrenous stomatitis 208/21.

cancorwund *f.* wound made by cancer 210/21, 270/16, 17.

cāsere *m.* emperor 234/3, 236/22.

cāul, cāwel *m.* colewort, rape CXXX, 58/24.

cænnan *see* **cennan.**

cærse *f.* watercress, *or* gardencress XXI, 166/5, 178/7. [Cf. **wylle-** ~.]

ceald, cald *adj.* cold 124/22, 23, 256/28.

cearfille *see* **cerfille.**

ceaster *f.* city, town 182/26.

cedelc *f.?* mercury, *or* field-mustard, charlock, kedlock LXXXIV.

gecēlan I cool, quench. *inf.* **gecēlan** 90/6.

celendre, cellendre, coliandre *f.* coriander CIV, 98/3, 164/11.

cemban I comb. *3 sg.* **cembeþ** 240/2; *subj. sg.* **cembe** 238/23, 24, 240/3; *pret. 3 sg.* **cemde** 238/23.

cēne *adj.* aggressive 272/9.

cennan, cænnan I generate, produce, give birth to. *inf.* **cennan** 150/6, 186/12; *3 sg.* **cenþ** 250/11, 14; *subj. sg.* **cenne** 250/9; *subj. pl.* **cennen** 122/10, **cennan** 14/21; *pp.* **cenned** 30/2, 44/15, 50/14, 23, 52/11, etc., **cened** 122/18, **cænned** 154/12. [Cf. **a-** ~.]

cenning *f.* birth (*Latin* partus) 186/13.

ceorfan 3 cut. *inf.* **ceorfan** 78/22, 228/16. [Cf. **for-** ~, **tō-** ~.]

cerfille, cearfille *f.* chervil CVI. [Cf. **wudu-** ~.]

cicel ('cycel') *m.* small cake 266/8.

(ge)cīgan I call, name. *3 sg.* **gecīgeþ** 208/3, 15; *pp.* **gecīged** 100/23.

cild, cyld *n.* child 66/19, 72/18, 138/18, 156/5, 158/1, etc. [Plural without r.]

cīs *adj.* fastidious; under an evil spell 52/12. [See note to VIII. 1.]

clām *m.* poultice 40/6.

clāte *f.* cleavers, clivers, goosegrass CLXXIV.

clāþ *m.* cloth 58/7, 84/10, 86/30, 92/24, 102/12, etc. [Cf. **hed-** ~.]

clǣfre *f.* clover, trefoil LXX.

clǣne *adj.* clean 30/3, 58/7, 74/13, 84/20, 102/12, etc., **clēne** 240/7. [Cf. **un-** ~.]

clǣnsian II purge, purify. *3 sg.* **clǣnsaþ** 36/16, 38/12, 42/18, 21, 256/19; *subj. sg.* **clǣnsie** 170/3; *pp.* **geclǣnsod** 240/7, 9. [Cf. **a-** ~.]

clǣnsung *f.* purging 250/13.

clǣnsungdæg *m.* day for purging 236/23.

clēne *see* **clǣne.**

cleofian II adhere, stick. *subj. sg.* **cleofige** 240/5.

geclifian, (ge)clyfian II adhere, stick. *inf.* **geclyfian** 218/10; *3 sg.* **geclifaþ** 80/23; *subj. sg.* **clyfie** 30/8; *subj. pl.* **geclifigen** 226/6; *pret. 3 sg.* **geclyfude** 100/21.

clufþunge *f.*, **clufþung** *m.* (*a*) celery-leaved crowfoot IX. (*b*) *wrong for* **clufwyrt** 154/5.

clufwyrt *f.* buttercup, upright meadow crowfoot, *or* bulbous buttercup X.

clyþa *m.* poultice 36/15, 44/9, 58/6, 60/14, 70/11, etc.

cnapa *m.* boy 150/9.

gecnāwan 7e know. *inf.* **gecnāwan** 52/4.

cnedan 5 knead. *imp.* **cned** 258/7.

cnēo *n.* knee 48/18, 122/22, 266/21; *apl.* **cnēwu** 122/20.

cnēowholen *mn.* butcher's broom, knee-holly LIX.

cnēwu *see* cnēo.

(ge)cnīd *see* (ge)gnīdan.

(ge)cnucian, cnocian II pound.
subj. sg. cnucie 138/22, cnucige
34/2, 96/20; *imp.* (ge)cnuca 32/4,
36/12, 15, 25, 38/20, etc., cnoca
180/9, 242/24; *pp.* gecnucud
78/23, 25, 82/9, 100/3, 108/8, etc.,
gecnucod 46/14, 240/16, gecnu-
cad 266/7, gecnocod 140/21.

cnyttan I tie, bind. *imp.* cnyte
150/7.

coccel *m.* corn cockle 108/21. [See
note to LXVI.]

codd *m.* (bean-)pod, husk 226/14.

cōl *adj.* cool, cold 32/24, 164/22,
176/7, 178/18, 186/14.

cōlian II become cool, become cold.
inf. cōlian 138/8; *3 sg.* cōlaþ
38/21. [Cf. a-∼.]

coliandre *see* celendre.

gecoren *adj.* excellent, suitable 212/6.
[The word is a pure adjective,
preceded by swȳþe.]

corn *n.* (a) grain, seed 46/19, 20, 21,
22, 98/3, etc. [Cf. pipor-∼.] (b)
berry 162/3, 5.

cræft *m.* craft; power 110/12. [Cf.
lǣce-∼.]

cræftig *adj.* skilful, powerful 44/6.

crocca *m.* earthenware pot 164/19,
236/8.

croh *m.* saffron 160/13, 252/18.

crop(p) *m.* (a) flower-head, umbel
154/8, 14, 194/5, 198/23. (b) sprout,
shoot 128/5, 150/19, 166/26. (c)
berry 116/20, 146/1.

cruma *m.* crumb, crumbs 80/11.

cuculer, cuceler *m.* spoon, spoonful
42/18, 44/27, 72/17, 18, 130/24, etc.

cucumer *m.*? cucumber 232/11.
[See note to CLXXXV.]

culfre *f.* pigeon, dove 110/6.

cuman 4 come. *inf.* cuman 106/23;
2 sg. cymst 170/10; *3 sg.* cymeþ
34/27, 40/17, 44/4, 130/15, 154/21,
etc., cymþ 30/24, 248/2, 252/13;
subj. sg. cume 38/30, 40/10, 16,
44/6, 124/23, etc., cyme 238/7,
240/3; *pres. p.* cumende 228/19;
tō āre ∼ be of service 38/30; tō
bōte ∼ bring recovery 34/27,
44/4; tō freme ∼ be beneficial

40/10; tō gōde ∼ be beneficial
44/6. [Cf. be-∼, ofer-∼.]

cumul *n.* glandular swelling 202/17.

cunnan *pret. pr.* know. *pl.* cunnun
104/12; *subj. sg.* cunne 136/22.

curmelle *f.* centaury XXXV,
XXXVI.

cūþ *adj.* known 236/19. [Cf. un-∼.]

cwellan I kill. *inf.* tō cwellenne
240/20; *3 sg.* cwelþ 92/7, 148/18,
184/22. [Cf. a-∼.]

gecwēme *adj.* (a) fit, convenient
180/26, 206/29, 208/12, 224/15.
(b) agreeable 186/1.

gecwēmlīce *adv.* conveniently 78/12.

cweþan 5 (a) say. *pl.* cweþaþ 44/6;
subj. sg. cweþe 70/16; *imp.* cweþ
64/16, 136/8, 234/11, 238/13;
pres. p. cweþende 220/19, 224/16,
234/4; *pret. pl.* cwǣdon 72/5,
74/11, 23, 76/24, 82/28, etc.,
cwǣdan 90/1, cwǣdun 100/7; *pp.*
gecweden 168/11, 238/15, 244/21,
23. (b) call, name. *pl.* cweþaþ
98/15; *pp.* gecweden 162/3, 168/
18, 190/2, 200/17, 19, etc., cweden
134/9.

cwice *mf.* quitch, couch-grass
LXXIX.

cwician II become sensitive, recover
feeling. *3 sg.* cwicaþ 130/12.

cwicu, cwycu *adj.* living 190/3,
234/10, 246/16, 264/4.

cwiþa *m.* womb 94/19, 186/11,
208/13, 210/4.

cyle, cile *m.* cold, chill 66/12, 158/12,
190/15, 222/20, 224/7, etc.

cyleþenie *f.* greater celandine LXXV.

cymen *n.* caraway, *or* cummin CLV,
138/2, 194/16.

cyn(n) *n.* kind 38/11, 56/14, 136/22,
168/9, 11, etc. [Cf. nǣdder-∼,
trēow-∼.]

gecynd *f.* (a) nature, kind 164/3,
192/17, 200/24, 212/18. (b) genitals
246/12.

gecyndelic *adj.* (a) natural 44/22,
184/2, 202/12. (b) sexual 194/22,
210/3, 220/4; þā gecyndelicu the
genitals 186/13. [See also sǣd.]

gecyndlimu *npl.* genitals 244/1,
270/12.

cynelic *see* ādl.

cyning *m.* king 234/2.

cynren *n.* kind, species 212/5.

cypressus cypress 66/22, 68/23. [See note to XX. 7.]

cyprus henna 116/18. [See note to XX. 7.]

cyrfætte *f.* gourd 174/11, 232/10.

cyrnel *n.* (*a*) glandular swelling 44/16, 19, 58/21, 25, 26, etc. (*b*) pimple, freckle 268/10. (*c*) kernel 174/16, 232/15.

cyrr *m.* turn, time 146/3, 4, 5.

(ge)cyrran I (*a*) turn, return. *inf.* tō cyrrenne 236/17; *pp.* gecyrred 240/5. (*b*) turn, change (*tr.*) *3 sg.* gecyrreþ 254/22. [Cf. for-⁓, on-⁓.]

cȳse *m.* cheese 256/3, 5, 6.

cȳslyb(b) *m.* rennet, curdled milk 250/15, 20.

cystel *f.*? chestnut 60/7.

cȳþ *m.* sprout, root 138/19.

cȳþþu *f.* information 234/7.

D

dæg *m.* day 40/14, 17, 52/7, 56/18, 58/7, etc.; *locative* dæg 44/26, 128/8, 136/16; ǣlces ⁓es daily, quotidian 42/10; þæs þriddan, fēorþan ⁓es fefer tertian, quartan fever 40/7, 88/9, 112/21. [Cf. clǣnsung-⁓.]

dæghwāmlic *adj.* quotidian, daily 112/21.

dæghwāmlīce *adv.* daily 112/19, 146/6, 270/6.

dǣl *m.* part, portion 30/16, 24, 32/4, 8, 36/14, etc.; be sumum ⁓e in some part 182/2; sume, sumon ⁓e somewhat 88/15, 192/7, 196/6.

dǣlmēlum *adv.* little by little 134/2.

dēad *adj.* dead 264/10, 24.

dēadboren *adj.* still-born 106/5, 138/18.

dēadspring *m.* malignant ulcer, carbuncle 44/16, 52/24, 126/18, 134/16.

dēaf *adj.* deaf 264/20.

(ge)dēcan I smear, daub. *imp.* (ge)dēc 92/24, 118/20.

delfan 3 dig. *inf.* delfan 170/16, 17. [Cf. be-⁓.]

dēofulsēocnyss, dēofolsēocnyss *f.* devil-sickness, being possessed by demons 56/3, 66/8, 172/17, 224/13, 262/18.

dēop *adj.* deep 72/23.

dēor *n.* animal 234/10, 236/6. [Cf. wild-⁓.]

gederednyss *f.* injury 230/12.

derian I *w. d.* injure, harm, do harm. *inf.* derian 58/9, 168/16; *3 sg.* dereþ 96/20, 114/8, 146/22, 234/16; *pl.* deriaþ 112/6, 180/17, dereþ 198/5; *subj. sg.* derige 92/2, 106/7, 140/3, 14, 156/5, etc.; *subj. pl.* derigen 94/9, 148/15, 156/1, 178/6, dergen 82/27, 108/11, 200/1, derien 214/6; *pres. p.* dergende 94/4. [Cf. ungedered.]

dīc *f.* ditch 52/11, 58/3.

gedīgan I do well in, come successfully out of. *2 sg.* gedīgest 234/21.

dīgol *adj.* dark, shady 228/7, dīhgol 84/20.

dile, dyle *m.* dill, anet CXXIII.

dimmian, dymmian II be dim. *pres. p.* dimgende, dymgende 82/13, 116/1.

docce (-a, -æ, -œ) *f.* common wayside dock XIV, 88/16. [Cf. wudu-⁓.]

dolh *n.* (*a*) scar 54/18, 60/23; *dpl.* dolchum 54/19. (*b*) wound 132/20. (*c*) sore, ulcer 158/17, 162/13.

dolhrūne *f.* pellitory of the wall LXXXIII.

(ge)dōn *anom. vb.* (*a*) do, perform. *inf.* tō dōnne 268/27; *3 sg.* dēþ 126/13, 246/3; *subj. sg.* dō 246/17, 272/2²; *subj. pl.* dōn 250/17; *imp.* dō 36/5, 80/18, 82/27, 222/15; *pret. 2 sg.* dydest 46/23; *pp.* gedōn 150/10, 236/17, 238/1, 246/15. (*b*) put, place; (*with* tō, þǣrtō) add, apply. *inf.* tō dōnne 236/20; *subj. sg.* dō 102/12, 240/5, 246/19; *imp.* dō 32/6, 38/10, 23, 42/3, 11, etc.; *pp.* gedōn 86/29, 222/13, 246/7, 24, 254/5, etc. (*c*) (*with* of, onweg) remove, take (away). *inf.* tō dōnne 242/11, 264/1, 15, 266/1, 7, etc.; *subj. sg.* gedō 148/11; *imp.* dō 254/19. [Cf. a-⁓.] (*d*) make. *inf.* dōn

268/24; *2 sg.* **gedēst** 66/20; *3 sg.*
gedēþ 54/20; *imp.* **dō** 30/21, 58/23,
248/18; *pp.* **gedōn** 244/14, 246/2,
260/17. (*e*) (*with* þæt-*clause*) make,
cause to *w. acc. and inf.*, bring
about. *3 sg.* **gedēþ** 80/23, 98/5,
258/15; *imp.* (ge)**dō** 36/9, 38/6,
256/20. (*f*) produce. *3 sg.* **dēþ**
102/13, 194/22.

dora *m.* bumble-bee, wild bee 246/24.
[See note to *M* IV. 13.]

draca *m.* dragon 60/3, 8, 232/6.

dracentse *f.* dragon, dragon-wort
XV, 66/22.

dreccan I vex, afflict. *pp.* **gedreht**
56/25.

drenc, drinc, drync *m.* drink,
potion; drinking 30/14, 50/5, 62/6,
72/12, 110/17, etc.

drīfan I drive out, expel. *3 sg.* **drīfþ**
54/8. [Cf. a-~, tō-~.]

(ge)**drīgan**, (ge)**drȳgan** I dry (up).
inf. **gedrīgean** 182/8; *3 sg.*
gedrīgeþ 200/6; *imp.* **drīg, drȳg**
30/8, 42/2, 130/23, 242/21, 244/1,
(ge)**drīge**, (ge)**drȳge** 62/10, 66/6,
76/4, 88/23, 94/1, etc.; *pp.* **ge-**
drīged, gedrȳged 108/13, 182/8,
190/22, 198/2, 200/23, etc.,
gedrīgid 126/6. [Cf. a-~.]

drīge, drȳge, drīgge *adj.* dry 74/22,
78/6, 13, 188/2, 204/21, etc.

drinc, drync *see* drenc.

(ge)**drincan** 3 drink. *inf.* **drincan**
30/23, 32/17, 36/20, 38/17, 40/8,
etc.; **tō drincenne** 252/1; *3 sg.*
drinceþ 250/11, 256/18, 264/10;
subj. sg. **drince** 34/6, 10, 14, 36/3,
38/24, etc.; *subj. pl.* **drincen** 250/
10; *imp.* (ge)**drinc** 32/12, 34/18,
36/6, 26, 240/14; *pret. 3 sg.* **dranc**
262/8; *pp.* **gedruncen** 84/24,
184/19, 188/9, 192/18, 194/21, etc.,
gedruncan 226/20. [Cf. be-~.]

gedrītan I drop excrement. *3 sg.*
gedrīteþ 266/3.

dropa *m.* gout 102/16, 19, 164/4.
[See note to LIX. 1.]

dropfāh *adj.* spotted 168/12, 252/23.

druncen *adj.* drunk 32/26.

drȳ *m.* magician, sorcerer 110/11.

drȳpan I (*a*) (*tr.*) drop, drip. *imp.*
drȳpe 30/21, 48/16, 64/21, 116/18,

124/9, etc., **drȳp** 264/19. (*b*) (*intr.*)
drop, drip. *subj. sg.* **drȳpe** 260/3.

dugan *pret. pr.* be of use, be good.
3 sg. **dēah** 30/4, 42/12, 130/25;
subj. sg. **dyge** 40/19.

dūn *f.* hill, mountain 60/19, 62/6,
70/20, 74/8, 84/20, etc.

dūnland *n.* hilly *or* mountainous
land 30/3, 62/14, 66/3.

durran *pret. pr.* dare. *subj. sg.* **dyrre**
114/12.

duru *f.* door 58/8.

dūst *n.* powder, dust 30/10, 12, 38/18,
42/2, 44/27, etc.

gedwǣscan I efface, remove. *3 sg.*
gedwǣsceaþ 272/7.

dweorg *m.* dwarf; fever 266/7. [See
note to XCIV.]

dweorgedw(e)osle *f.* pennyroyal
XCIV, 150/20, 200/3.

dwīnan I get rid of swelling. *3 sg.*
dwīneþ 38/14. [Cf. for-~.]

dȳfan I dip. *pp.* **gedȳfed** 258/25.

dymnys(s), dymness *f.* dimness
30/22, 24, 76/17, 21, 114/19, etc.

dyppan I dip *imp.* **dype** 78/6, 13,
116/22.

E

ēac *adv.* also 34/27, 36/6, 44/11, 29,
46/4, etc., **ēc** 196/19, **ēæc** 232/2;
~ **swylce** likewise, also 66/7,
70/22, 184/16, 19, 186/6, etc.

geēacnian II (*a*) conceive. *3 sg.*
geēacnaþ 244/8, 250/19. (*b*) make
pregnant. *inf.* **tō geēacnigenne**
250/15.

geēacnung *f.* (*a*) conception 244/6.
(*b*) parturition 150/10.

ēagbrǣw *m.* eyelid 256/4.

ēage *n.* eye 30/15, 16, 17, 32/1, 2,
etc., *gpl.* **ēgena** 30/22.

ēagsealf *f.* eye-salve 240/12.

ēagwræc *m.* pain in the eyes 264/1,
270/28.

eal *adv.* altogether, exactly 182/4,25.

eald *adj.* old 32/7, 11, 15, 44/8, 58/3,
etc.; *comp.* **yldra** 168/4.

ealdor *m.* (*a*) prince, chief 108/17.
(*b*) authority 86/6, 108/18, 114/12.

ealdorman *m.* prince, chief 114/4,
128/21, 220/10.

eall *pron. adj. and subst.* all, entire;

everything 42/19, 44/9, 46/10, 58/12, 60/10, etc. [See also **mid ealle** s.v. **mid**.]

ealla *m.* gall, bile 184/2, 188/19. [Cf. **ġealla**.]

ealo *n.* ale 38/11; *dsg.* **ealoþ** 40/18, 82/16.

ealswā (I) *adv.* just as, just like 158/26, 170/11, 232/10. (II) *conj.* as 82/27.

ēar *see* **nardes ēar**.

eardian II dwell, live. *subj. pl.* **eardien** 266/26.

eardung *f.* dwelling, living 266/25.

ēare *n.* ear 30/19, 21, 48/15, 16, 64/20, etc.

earfeþe, earfoþ *n.* trouble, difficulty 130/26, 238/20, 244/18, 20, 262/11.

earfoþlic *adj.* painful 60/21.

earfoþlīce, earfuþlīce *adv.* with difficulty 122/10, 130/8, 176/1.

earfoþlicnyss *f.* difficulty, pain; ~ þæs miġþan strangury 186/7, 200/7, 208/2.

earfoþnyss *f.* trouble, difficulty 132/5, 244/17, **earfodnyss** 242/3.

earm *m.* arm 244/8, 246/14, 264/25.

earn *m.* eagle 76/17.

ēaþelīce *adv.* easily 34/16, 202/1; *sup.* **ēaþelīcost** 78/7, 172/19.

ēæc, ēc *see* **ēac**.

ece *m.* pain 42/20, 22, 26, 194/25. [Cf. **bān-**~, **hēafod-**~, **heort-**~, **hypebān-**~, **lenden-**~, **tōþ-**~.]

eced *mn.* vinegar 32/8, 38/23, 40/24, 54/19, 56/17, etc.

ġeefenlǣcan I be like, resemble. *subj. sg.* **ġeefenlǣce** 200/19.

efenlīce *adv.* calmly 64/22.

efenmycel *n.* just as much 84/16, 94/2, 222/22.

efne (I) *adv.* just, exactly 264/11. (II) *interj.* behold, indeed 236/6.

eforfearn *n.* polypody LXXXV.

eft *adv.* afterwards; again 30/21, 36/8, 38/13, 16, 44/19, etc.

eftsōna *adv.* soon afterwards 56/23.

ēġe *see* **ēaġe**.

egeslic *adj.* terrible, terrifying 30/5.

eġlan I, **eġlian** II trouble, vex. *3 sg.* **eġleþ** 2/22, 17/6, 25/16; *subj. sg.* **eġliġe** 16/8; *subj. pl.* **eġlen** 40/1.

ehteoþa *adj.* eighth 146/5.

elcor *adv.* else, otherwise 268/28.

ele *m.* oil 56/20, 26, 58/6, 11, 64/9, etc.

elechtre *see* **elehtre**.

eledrōsna *plf.* lees of oil, oil-dregs 222/12.

elefæt *n.* oil-jar (*a measure of capacity*) 212/20. [See p. lxxxiii.]

elehtre *f.* lupine 92/5, **elechtre** 148/16.

ellen *n.* elder CXLVIII, 58/4.

ellenwyrt *f.* dwarf elder, danewort, wallwort XCIII.

eln *f.* ell 190/3; *gpl.* **elne** 196/5.

ende *m.* end 170/19.

endebyrdnyss *f.* row, series 124/13.

endlufon, endlyfon *num.* eleven 144/21, 146/3, 150/7, 224/26.

Engle *mpl.* the English 74/3, 18, 88/7, 100/17, **Angle** 80/16, 90/24, 94/23, 112/8, **Ængle** 98/9. [See note to XXXV. 1.]

Englisc. *adj.* English 234/10.

eofor *m.* wild boar 262/9.

eornlīce *adv.* diligently 126/15. [Cf. **ġeornlīce**.]

eorþe *f.* (*a*) earth, ground 42/25, 170/17, 178/15, 192/15, 232/11, etc. (*b*) the earth, the world 236/24.

eorþġealla *m.* yellow centaury, yellow-wort XXXV.

eorþīfiġ, eorþȳfiġ *n.* ground-ivy, ale-hoof C.

eorþnaf(o)la *m.* asparagus 142/15, 164/19.

etan 5 eat. *inf.* **etan** 46/22, 56/22, 104/14, 106/23, 116/20, etc.; **tō etanne** 262/14, 270/23; *2 sg.* **etest** 236/24; *3 sg.* **yt** 54/1, 5; *pl.* **etaþ** 100/25; *subj. sg.* **ete** 34/23, 38/14, 27, 140/2, 158/5, etc.; *subj. pl.* **etan** 266/15; *imp.* **et** 42/6, 11; *pp.* **ġeeten** 188/8, **ġeetan** 138/10.

F

fām *n.* foam 262/7.

fandian II *w. g.* test, try. *inf.* **fandian** 54/3. [Cf. **a-**~.]

faran 6 go. *2 sg.* **færest** 236/23. [Cf. **tō-**~.]

fæc *n.* period, space of time 64/8.

fæġer *adj.* beautiful 124/14.

fǣmne *f.* virgin 94/9.

fæst *adj.* (*a*) solid, firm 66/3, 70/20, 82/4, 90/18. (*b*) constipated 32/20, 76/7. (*c*) (*of hair*) firm, not falling out 94/13. (*d*) firm, tight 270/27. [Cf. **sige-**∼.]

fæstan III fast. *pres. p.* **fæstende** not having eaten or drunk 30/23, 52/22, 64/7, 84/12, 86/25, etc.

fæste *adv.* firmly 40/3, 270/26.

fæstnys(s) *f.* constipation 104/19, 22.

fæt *n.* vessel 70/22, 116/4, 158/19, 21, 22, etc.

fætelsian II put in a vessel. *imp.* **fætelsa** 236/9.

fætt *adj.* fat 176/29, 180/6, 186/2, 190/4.

fæþm *m.* ell, cubit 174/12. [See p. lxxxiv.]

fēaġe *see* **fēawe.**

feallan 7c fall, fall out. *inf.* **feallan** 138/12; *pl.* **fealleþ** 208/21; *subj. sg.* **fealle** 62/15, 68/2, 94/12; *pres. p.* **feallende** 250/6. [Cf. **be-**∼, **oþ-**∼.]

fealu *adj.* reddish yellow 206/12.

fealwian II grow yellow. *3 sg.* **fealwaþ** 232/13.

fearn, fern *n.* fern LXXVIII, 124/12. [Cf. **efor-**∼.]

fearr *m.* bull 170/5, 266/25, 268/1, 3, 5, etc.

fearremearġ *n.* bull's marrow 268/16.

fēawe *adj.* few, a few 54/12, 114/11, 138/27; *dpl.* **fēaġum** 54/8.

feax, fex *n.* hair 62/15, 68/2, 4, 94/12, 13, etc.

febriġ *adj.* feverish 36/21. [Cf. **feforiġ.**]

fēdan I feed. *pp.* **fēded** 258/2.

fefer, fefor *m.* fever 40/7, 9, 14, 16, 17, etc., **feofor** 236/1.

feferfuge *f.* common centaury, lesser centaury XXXVI.

feferian, feforian II be feverish, suffer from fever. *pres. p.* **feferġende** 84/7, 144/15, **feforġende** 152/5, 156/19, **feferġinde** 72/11.

feforiġ *adj.* feverish 242/5. [Cf. **febriġ, unfeferiġ.**]

fela *indecl. w. partitive g.* many, much 92/5, 136/21, 166/6.

gefēlan I feel. *2 sg.* **gefēlest** 236/21.

feld *m.* field 52/11, 54/12, 86/3, 102/22, 184/7, etc.

feldbēo *f.* bumble-bee, wild bee 252/13, 17, 268/3. [See note to *M* IV. 13.]

feldmoru *f.* wild carrot, *or* wild parsnip LXXXII.

feldwyrt *f.* felwort, gentian XVII.

fellsticce *n.* piece of skin 236/21.

feltwyrt *f.* great mullein LXXIII.

feofor *see* **fefor.**

ġefeoht *n.* fight 234/20.

feormian II cleanse, purge, purify. *inf.* **tō feormienne** 24/1; *3 sg.* **feormaþ** 54/1; *imp.* **feorma** 148/5. [Cf. **a-**∼.]

fēorþa *adj.* fourth 40/7, 88/10, 124/21, 144/4, 146/3, etc.

fēower *num.* four 34/5, 23, 36/2, 88/13, 96/15, etc.

fēowerecġe *adj.* four-edged 218/13.

fēowerecġede *adj.* four-edged 206/11.

fēowertiġ *num.* forty 194/26.

fēowertȳne *num.* fourteen 270/26.

fēran I go, travel. *inf.* **fēran** 114/15; **tō fēranne** 236/16; *pret. pl.* **fērdon** 234/7.

fern *see* **fearn.**

feþer *f.* feather 162/11.

fex *see* **feax.**

fexede *adj.* having hair, hairy 174/25.

fīctrēow *n.* fig-tree 264/22.

fīf *num.* five 44/27, 52/13, 58/7, 62/20, 72/17, etc.

fīflēafe *f.* cinquefoil, fiveleaf III.

fīfta *adj.* fifth 118/21, 146/3.

fīftȳne *num.* fifteen 146/4, 226/18.

filgan I follow. *subj. sg.* **filiġe** 150/12.

findan 3 find. *inf.* **findan** 58/14, 70/6, 82/5, 94/17, 128/21, etc.; *2 sg.* **findest** 36/26; *pret. 3 sg. or pret. subj. sg.* **funde** 15/24; *pp.* **funden** 52/3, 100/19, 108/16, 19, 244/6. [Cf. **on-**∼.]

finger *m.* finger 32/5, 42/24, 158/22, 178/16, 190/5, etc.; *gsg.* **fincres** 190/4. [Cf. **hring-**∼.]

finul, finol *m.* fennel CXXVI, 142/16, 182/24.

firġinbucca *m.* mountain buck 252/9. [See note to *M* VI.]

fiþerfēte, fyþerfēte *adj.* four-footed 234/9, 236/5, 19.

fixenhȳd *f.* skin of a fox 248/3.

flān *f.* arrow 106/22, 24.

flǣsc *n.* flesh 80/23, 206/26, 236/24, 262/18, 266/15.

flēa *m.* flea 184/21, 22, 186/6, 212/15.

flēah *n.* white speck in the eye, albugo 70/16.

flēon 2 (*a*) flee, depart. *pl.* flēoþ 242/2, 260/22, 266/26. (*b*) fly. *inf.* flēon 76/17. [Cf. æt-∼, for-∼, tō-∼.]

flēwsa *m.* flux, flowing 96/10, 98/11, 102/23, 24, 128/5, etc.

geflit *n.* strife, contest 234/20.

flōwan 7f flow. *subj. sg.* flōwe 132/24. [Cf. a-∼, tō-∼.]

gefōn 7d catch. *imp.* gefōh 234/10. [Cf. onfōn, ymbfōn.]

for *prep.* (*a*) *w. a. d.* (1) for, on account of, for the sake of 146/19, 156/17, 182/11, 194/16, 202/2, etc.; (2) for (*expr. prevention*), against 244/4; ∼ þām *adv.* for that reason, therefore 240/12; ∼ þām þe *conj.* because 76/3, 212/14, 220/9. (*b*) *w. a.* (*marking substitution*) for, as, instead of 214/22, 250/18, 19. (*c*) *w. instr.* ∼ þȳ, ∼ þī *adv.* for that reason, therefore 100/22, 128/ 23, 156/18, 158/4, 170/14, etc.; ∼ þȳ *conj.* for, because 180/26, 200/23, 218/10, 228/16; ∼ þȳ þe *conj.* because 162/3, 200/18.

foran *adv.* in advance 202/11; ∼ tō *prep. w. g.* before (*temporal*) 254/12.

forbærnan I burn (*tr.*). *pp.* for-bærned 44/5, 116/11, 148/1.

forbærnednyss *f.* burn, injury by burning 190/9, 212/9.

forbēodan 2 prevent, restrain. *3 sg.* forbȳt 56/4, 90/8; *pp.* forboden 214/22.

forberan 4 retain (in the body). *pp.* forboren 46/14.

forbrecan 4 break (to pieces). *3 sg.* forbrycþ 144/17; *pp.* forbrocen 94/3.

forbūgan 2 avoid. *3 sg.* forbūgeþ 228/19.

forceorfan 3 cut up. *subj. sg.* for-ceorfe 136/7; *imp.* forceorf 136/ 10, 228/15.

forcilled *adj.* chilled 222/11.

forcyrran I turn about. *3 sg.* for-cyrreþ 228/19.

fordwīnan 1 vanish, disappear. *3 sg.* fordwīneþ 38/8.

foresprecen *adj.* aforesaid 172/23.

foreweard *adj.* early 54/17, 270/9.

forflēon 2 flee from. *inf.* forflēon 170/14.

forhabban III (*a*) (*refl.*) restrain oneself. *subj. sg.* forhæbbe 158/4. (*b*) abstain, be abstinent. *subj. pl.* forhæbben 250/17.

forlǣtan 7e (*a*) leave, abandon. *3 sg.* forlǣteþ 52/23; *pp.* forlǣten 202/16. (*b*) let go, void. *3 sg.* forlǣteþ 72/19.(*c*) dismiss, remove. *pp.* forlǣten 140/8.

forma *adj. sup.* first 168/16, 204/7.

forne *adv.* in front 62/22.

forniman 4 (*a*) take away. *3 sg.* fornimeþ 178/10, 192/22, for-nimþ 54/20, 78/21; *pp.* fornumen 68/17. (*b*) consume. *subj. sg.* for-nime 54/3; *pret. 3 sg.* fornam 100/22. (*c*) heal. *3 sg.* fornimeþ 194/13.

foroft *adv.* very often 182/7, 208/21, 232/2.

forrotian II putrefy. *pp.* forrotud 222/24.

forrotudnyss *f.* putrefaction 184/10, 190/8, 228/3.

forscrincan 3 shrink up, dry up. *3 sg.* forscrincþ 168/19.

forsettan I stop up, block. *imp.* forsete 116/22.

forswelgan 3 swallow up. *inf.* forswelgan 256/25.

fort (þæt) *conj.* (O *only*) until 263/6. [See note to *M* I. 6.]

fortogenyss, fortogonyss ('-to-gennyss') *f.* cramp, colic 268/16, 270/11.

forþ *adv.* (*a*) away 46/5, 52/8, 110/16, 188/19, 23, etc. (*b*) forth 208/3, 15.

forþat *conj.* (O *only*) until 35/14. [See note to I. 19.]

forþindan 3 swell. *pp.* forþunden 132/18.

forþon *adv.* even, indeed 106/18, 228/19.

forþryccan I (*a*) suppress, stop. *3 sg.*

forþryceþ 256/12. (b) close by pressing. *3 sg.* forþrycceþ 258/27.

forþ þæt *conj.* (O *only*) until 47/12. [See note to IV. 8.]

forþylman I, forþilmian II choke, suffocate. *pl.* forþilmiaþ 182/7; *subj. sg.* forþylme 226/23.

forweaxan 7c swell. *pp.* forweaxen 38/13, forwexen 86/11, 98/7, 110/19.

forwundian II wound, injure. *pp.* forwundud 2/14.

fōt *m.* foot, paw 36/26, 40/12, 23, 24, 50/7, etc. [See also hræfnes ∼, lēon-∼, foxes ∼.]

fōtādl *f.* foot-disease, gout 36/24, 40/11, 56/21, 72/4, 86/4, etc. [See note to I. 29.]

fōtensceanca ('fōtsceanca') *m.* shank, leg from knee downwards 264/24.

fōtswæþ *n.* foot-print, track 228/18.

fōtswyle *m.* foot-swelling 248/10.

fōtwræc *m.* pain of the feet 248/3.

fox *m.* fox 92/23, 244/18, 246/1, 4, 6, etc.

foxes fōt *m.* unbranched bur-reed XLVII.

foxes glōfa *m.* thorn-apple CXLIV.

fram (I) *adv.* away 56/26, 92/2, 186/16, 228/16. (II) *prep. w. d.* (a) from (*local and temporal*) 138/11, 234/6, 236/2, 18, 252/3, etc. (b) by (*indicating agent of action*) 100/23, 104/11, 108/16, 19, 162/22, etc. (c) from (*expr. protection against*) 132/14.

framian II benefit, be of advantage. *3 sg.* framaþ 62/6, 188/18.

framigendlic *adj.* beneficial 204/1.

Francland *n.* country of the Franks 166/3.

fræcenyss *see* frēcnyss.

gefrætewian II adorn. *pp.* gefrætewud 96/15.

frēcenfull *adj.* harmful, dangerous 182/7.

frēcenyss *see* frēcnyss.

frēcne *n.* danger 236/18.

frēcnys(s) *f.* danger 46/24, 76/9, 82/15, 106/9, 158/4, fræcenyss 184/18, frēcenyss 128/12; tō ∼e becuman *w. d.* endanger 158/3.

gefregn *see* gefrignan.

fremful *adj.* beneficial 94/17, 170/9.

fremfulnyss *f.* beneficial effect, usefulness 98/10, 104/5, 118/25, 164/7

fremgendlic *adj.* beneficial 214/12 230/9.

fremian II benefit, be of advantage *3 sg.* fremaþ 44/18, 28, 62/11, 18 64/19, etc.; *subj. sg.* fremige 76/13 78/14, fremie 132/4; *pret. 3 sg* fremade 114/13.

gefremman I perform, do. *inf.* tō gefremmanne 262/1; *2 sg.* gefremest 262/25; *3 sg.* gefremeþ 186/13.

gefremmin(c)g *f.* effect 62/21 74/24, 206/6, gefremincg 108/3.

fremu *f.* benefit; tō freme cuman *w. d.* benefit 40/10, 130/15.

frēond *m.* friend 234/3.

gefrignan 3 hear, learn. *pret. 1 sg* gefregn 234/6.

gefriþian II shelter. *pp.* gefriþed 30/3

frymþu *f.* beginning 218/7.

fuht *adj.* moist, damp 52/21, 86/3 96/24.

fūl *adj.* dirty, foul 68/20, 200/11 222/24.

ful(l) *n.* cup, cupful 32/12, 15, 25 34/11, 15, etc.

ful(l) *adj.* full 32/12, 15, 25, 34/9, 11 etc.

fullīce *adv.* fully 64/15.

fūlnyss *f.* foulness, filth 184/10 270/21.

fūlstincende *adj.* foul-stinking 200/13.

fultum *m.* help, succour 246/18.

furþor, furþur *adv.* further 80/20 256/19.

furþra *adj. comp.* fore, front 234/18.

fyllesēoc *adj.* epileptic 186/8, 254/14 262/3.

fyllesēocnyss *f.* epilepsy 104/13.

fyllu *f.* fullness; tō fylles as a full dose 38/24. [See BT s.v. tō II (5).]

fȳr *n.* fire 236/18, 254/18, 268/22.

fyregāt *f.* mountain goat 254/9, 15 [See note to M VI.]

fyrhtu *f.* fear 262/25.

fyrlu *f.* distance 254/19.

fyrmest *adj. sup.* first, most importan 226/3.

fyrmest, fyrmust *adv. sup.* originally 96/14, 108/17, 166/3, 182/26, 212/6.

fyrst *m.* space of time, period 32/22.

G

gegaderian II gather. *3 sg.* **gegaderaþ** 144/22; *pp.* **gegaderod** 108/22, 204/6.

gegaderung *f.* gathering, collection of diseased matter 86/7, 158/11, 164/9, 188/28, 192/21, etc.

galluc *m.* comfrey LX.

(ge)gān *anom. vb.* go, walk, come. *inf.* **gān** 110/16, 114/12, 226/20; *pl.* **gāþ** 80/22; *subj. sg.* **gā** 52/17; *imp.* **gā** 64/15, 17; *subj. pret. sg.* **gēode** 184/4. [Cf. be-∼.]

gang, gong *m.* going, (power of) walking 34/8, 248/4, 11. [Cf. setl-∼, tō-∼, up-∼, ūt-∼.]

gangan 7d go. *3 sg.* **gangeþ** 96/4; *subj. sg.* **gange** 98/4, 154/19.

gāt, *dsg.* **gǣt** *f.* goat 32/24, 252/10, 23, 254/1, 18, etc. [Cf. fyre-∼, wudu-∼.]

gārclife *f.* agrimony XXXII.

gǣt *see* **gāt.**

gǣten *adj.* of goats 68/22, 116/12, 120/11, 256/27.

ge *conj. in combinations* **ge . . . ge, ge . . . 7** both . . . and 30/4, 36/6, 50/2, 68/24, 132/4, etc.

gē *adv.* yes, indeed 228/19.

gealla *m.* gall, bile 192/19, 246/21, 23, 248/20, 252/12, etc. [Cf. ealla.]

gēan *prp. w. a.* against 62/22. [Cf. on-∼.]

gēancyme *m.* encounter, meeting 114/9, 154/17.

gēar *n.* year 136/18, 228/26, 230/5, 246/18.

gearu *adj.* ready. *comp.* **gearwra** 268/29.

gearwe *f.* milfoil, common yarrow XC.

gegearwian II (a) bring about, establish. *3 sg.* **gegearwaþ** 72/6, 188/11, 244/7; *subj. sg.* **gegearwie** 224/22. (b) provide. *3 sg.* **gegearwaþ** 200/14, 204/21. (c) prepare. *inf.* **gegearwian** 246/19.

geolu(w) *adj.* yellow 174/5, 178/16, 182/25, 208/12, 218/23.

geond *prep. w. a.* throughout 236/23.

geong *adj.* young 72/16, 118/18, 120/7; *comp.* **gingra** 72/17.

geornlīce *adv.* diligently 170/16. [Cf. eornlice.]

gēotan 2 pour. *3 sg.* **gēoteþ** 256/14; *imp.* **gēot** 146/15, 172/10. [Cf. be-∼.]

gicþa *m.* itch, itching 68/8, 120/21, 138/7, 9, 148/20, etc.

gif *conj.* if 30/11, 32/20, 26, 34/1, 4, etc.

gifu *f.* grace 224/14.

gind *prep. w. a.* throughout, over 192/16.

gindstrēdan I strew about, scatter. *pp.* **gindstrēd** 176/8, 186/4.

gingra *see* **geong.**

giþcorn, gyþcorn *n.* spurge laurel CXIII.

gegladian II appease, comfort. *3 sg.* **gegladaþ** 188/19.

glæd *adj.* glad, cheerful 224/21; *comp.* **glædra** 66/20.

glædene *f.* (a) sea-onion, squill XLIII. (b) yellow flag, gladdon LXXX, 200/20.

glæsen *adj.* made of glass 78/1, 158/19.

glǣwlīce ('glēawlīce'), *adv.* prudently, well 64/22.

glōfwyrt *f.* (a) lily of the valley XXIII. (b) hound's-tongue, dog's-tongue, *or* bugloss XLII. [See note to XLII.]

gnæt(t) *m.* gnat 186/6.

(ge)gnīdan I rub. *subj. sg.* **gnīde** 256/15; *subj. pl.* **gnīden** 252/5; *imp.* **(ge)gnīd** 30/12, 32/11, 14, 34/26, 36/5, etc., **(ge)cnīd** 36/9, 40/8, 15; *pp.* **gegniden** 124/3, 144/21, 250/10, 252/6, 256/11, etc.

God *m.* God 220/24, 234/11.

gōd (I) *adj.* good 38/30, 44/28, 64/6, 82/16, 96/8, etc.; *comp.* **sēlra** 120/11, 138/26; *sup.* **sēlest** 58/26, **sēlost** 258/2, **sēlust** 76/23. (II) *subst. n.* good, benefit; **tō ∼e cuman** be good for 44/6.

godcundnyss *f.* divine quality 96/1.

(ge)gōdian II (a) (tr.) do good. 3 sg. gegōdaþ 32/2. (b) (intr.) get better, improve. pl. gōdiaþ 36/23.

godwebb n. fine cloth, purple 238/17.

gold n. gold 124/14, 162/3, 168/11, 170/3, 228/12, etc.

gōman mpl. throat, pharynx 112/4, 6, 184/10, 12, 214/3, etc. [See note to LXX. 1.]

gong see gang.

gor n. dung 54/7, 268/18, 20, 22.

gorst m. gorse, furze, whin CXLII.

gōs f. goose 68/9.

græs n. grass 266/3.

grēat adj. (a) large, big 174/12, 24, 218/13. (b) coarse(-grained) 84/14.

grēate wyrt f. meadow saffron XXII.

grēatnyss f. thickness 190/4, 196/5.

Grēca wrong for Crēta Crete 108/18.

Grēcas mpl. the Greeks 74/2, 17, 76/10, 80/15, 86/12, etc.

grēne adj. green 60/7, 74/18, 22, 76/11, 78/5, etc.; sup. grēnost 30/20.

grēnnyss f. greenness 232/13.

gripa m. handful, bunch 82/16, 122/2, 158/25, 164/18, 178/24, etc.

gegrīpan 1 grasp. inf. gegrīpan 158/22.

grōwan 7f grow. 3 sg. grēwþ 52/4.

grundeswylige f. common groundsel LXXVII.

gryta fpl. grits, coarse meal 256/23.

gundbryne m. burning of foul matter, purulent inflammation 132/2.

gylden adj. made of gold, golden 64/16, 168/12, 14, 254/15.

gyrdels m. girdle 234/17.

gegyrwan 1 prepare. imp. gegyre 250/3.

gyst m. yeast 68/16.

gȳt adv. yet 238/10, 270/10.

H

habban III (I) notional verb have, keep. inf. habban 44/22, 56/24; tō hæbbenne 224/21 (passive meaning); 2 sg. hafast 220/14, 16, 224/15, 234/21, 242/19, etc.; 3 sg. hæfþ 46/10, 48/13, 56/4, 58/4, 66/13, etc., hafaþ 108/25, 110/8, 112/7, 136/23, 166/4, etc.; pl. habbaþ 44/21, 136/24, 172/23,

176/17, 182/6, etc.; subj. sg. hæbbe 56/2, 88/10, 104/16, 114, 15, 172/26, etc.; imp. hafa 42/6, 234/14, 236/20; neg. form subj. sg. næbbe 74/22, 78/6. [Cf. be-∼ for-∼, ge-∼.] (II) auxiliary of tense have (a) w. object and inflected pp.: subj. sg. hæbbe 30/7, 34/21 (b) w. object and uninflected pp. 3 sg. hafaþ 226/20; pl. habbaþ 64/22, 96/6; subj. sg. hæbbe 86/29, 238/16.

gehabban III keep. inf. gehabban 34/20.

hagol m. hail 220/13, 16, 23, 234/15

hāl adj. sound, healthy 32/21, 25 34/3, 38/19, 40/22, etc. [Cf. un-∼.]

gehāl adj. whole, entire 46/19 256/25.

hala m. afterbirth 258/21.

hālian II recover, get well, hea (intr.). inf. hālian 190/23; 3 sg hālaþ 30/14, 38/21, 40/28, 42/4 16, etc.; subj. pl. hāligen 252/20.

hālig adj. holy 30/6, 60/5; sup hālgusta 236/22.

halswyrt f. (a) throatwort, nettle leaved bellflower, or narcissus LVI (b) common ash CXXVIII. (c wrong for Latin bulbus 152/15 [See note to CIX. 1.]

hālwende adj. healing, salutary 184 20, 200/14; comp. hālwendra 168/5.

hām adv. home(wards) 236/16.

hand f. hand 54/4, 56/1, 70/8, 12 136/7, etc.

handfull f. handful 122/3.

hangian II hang (intr.) subj. sg hangie 62/22.

hara m. hare 156/16, 248/6, 8, 10 12, etc.

haran hig(e), haran hyge m. hare's-foot clover LXII.

hārēhūne f. horehound, hoarhoun XLVI, 148/16.

hāt adj. hot 30/13, 34/23, 46/2 56/14, 58/24, etc.

hātan 7a name, call. 3 sg. hāte 104/16, 106/3, 110/7, 132/8, 134/8 etc., hātaþ 126/22; pl. hāta 48/10, 60/22, 80/17, 82/3, 88/7 etc., hāteþ 112/9, 142/24, 166/19 *pp.* **hāten** 234/2; *pass. sg.* **hātte** (O *only*) 213/8.

hātian II become hot. *3 sg.* **hātaþ** 132/12; *pres. p.* **hātigende** 130/17. [Referring to the beginning of the healing process of a wound.]

hātung *f.* inflammation 40/20.

gehaþerian II restrain. *3 sg.* **gehaþeraþ** 240/15.

hægþorn *m.* common hawthorn 84/16.

hǣl *f.* health 248/2.

(ge)hǣlan I heal, cure. *inf.* **(ge)hǣlan** 36/7, 66/11, 78/12, 128/24, 158/27; **tō gehǣlenne** 80/22; *2 sg.* **gehǣlst** 122/22, 160/20, 222/23, **gehǣlest** 120/20; *3 sg.* **(ge)hǣlþ** 32/8, 44/20, 24, 46/3, 48/23, etc., **(ge)hǣleþ** 70/23, 78/24, 26, 84/5, 86/25, etc.; *pl.* **gehǣlaþ** 128/13; *subj. sg.* **gehǣle** 86/14, 96/11; *pret. 3 sg.* **gehǣlde** 128/22; *pp.* **gehǣled** 50/11, 54/17, 56/23, 62/23, 80/4, etc. [Cf. **þurh-~**.]

hǣlo *f.* health 36/27, 66/10, 72/6, 124/23, 144/17; **~ bodian** send greetings 234/3. [Cf. **un-~**.]

hǣmed *n.* coitus 254/13.

hǣr *n.* hair 244/4, 254/23, 264/7, 8. [Cf. **hrycg-~**, **tægl-~**.]

hǣr *adv.* see **hēr**.

hǣrþan *pl.* testicles 260/12, 262/2.

hǣtan I heat. *imp.* **hǣt** 272/1; *pp.* **gehǣt(t)** 70/10, 268/16.

hǣte, hǣtu *f.* (*a*) heat 36/21, 38/20, 146/19, 156/17, 184/8; *asg.* **þone hǣtan** 208/13. (*b*) inflammation 186/26, 190/8, 192/1, 198/15, 256/3.

hǣþ *mn.* heather 258/10.

hǣwen *adj.* purple, flax-blue 174/3, 192/16.

hǣwenhydele, hēawenhnydelu *f.* scurvy-grass, *or* great water-dock XXX.

hē *pron.* he (*etc.*). *nsgm.* **hē** 32/25, 34/11, 20, 21, 36/3, etc.; *nsgf.* **hēo, hīo** 30/2, 4, 19, 32/2, 36/11, etc., **hȳ** 232/3, 4; *nasgn.* **hit, hyt** 30/13, 20, 21, 24, 32/6, etc.; *asgm.* **hine, hyne** 30/4, 34/12, 21, 52/15, 17², etc., *refl.* 52/17¹; *asgf.* **hī, hȳ** 30/6,

7, 9, 12, 32/4, etc., **hig** 108/25; *gsgmn.* **his, hys** 30/4, 32/12, 23, 34/20, 36/18, etc.; *gdsgf.* **hyre** 30/8, 10, 42/5, 46/10, 50/5, etc.; *dsgm.* **him, hym** 32/15, 17, 34/4, 7, 15, etc., *refl.* 56/1, 2; *napl.* **hȳ** 30/17, 40/25, 46/2, 21, 48/17, etc.; *npl.* **hīo** 234/13; *apl.* **hig** 96/2, *refl.* **hȳ** 262/13; *gpl.* **heora** 44/22, 58/14, 110/12, 114/25, 168/9, etc., **hyra** 248/12, 250/17; *dpl.* **him, hym** 52/3, 114/25, 136/24, 174/8, 248/12, etc.

hēafod *n.* head 30/11, 14, 38/2, 4, 42/23, etc.; *dsg.* **hēfde** 46/6. [See also **hundes ~**.]

hēafodbryce *m.* fracture of the skull 94/1.

hēafodece *m.* headache 116/9, 124/15, 126/15, 132/6, 134/13, etc.

hēafodpanne *f.* skull 270/12.

hēafodsār *n.* (*a*) headache 46/6, 144/24, 240/13. (*b*) rashes or ulcers on the head 68/8, 212/23, 244/21.

hēafodwrǣc *m.* headache 236/10.

heagospind *n.* cheek 242/18.

hēah *adj.* high 60/19.

hēahnyss, hēhnyss *f.* highest point, top 216/13, 226/4.

(ge)healdan 7c keep, preserve. *inf.* **gehealdan** 44/22, 76/4; **tō gehealdenne** 76/3; *3 sg.* **gehealdeþ** 196/15; *pl.* **healdaþ** 82/7; *subj. sg.* **(ge)healde** 48/22, 74/19, 120/18, 126/2, 150/9, etc.; *imp.* **(ge)heald** 76/5, 154/20, 236/9. [Cf. **be-~**.]

healf *adj.* half 66/17, 82/18, 86/23, 25, 136/18, etc.; **ōþer ~** one and a half 158/25.

healfsoden *adj.* half-boiled 260/3.

hēalic *adj.* remarkable, intense 50/11, 78/2, 100/18.

hēalīce *adv.* remarkably 44/18, 100/5, 126/17, 142/12, 148/24, etc.; *sup.* **hēalīcost** 114/13.

hēalyde ('hēalede') *adj.* suffering from rupture or hydrocele 118/18.

heard *adj.* hard 60/19, 90/21, 182/5, 218/14, 228/15; *comp.* **heardra** 174/11.

heardian II harden, be hard. *subj. sg.* **heardige** 34/18, 40/6. [Cf. **a-~**].

heardnyss *f.* (*a*) hardness, callosity

182/28, 188/28, 226/6, 268/14.
(b) constipation 124/2, 4, 156/10,
256/16, 17. (c) *a mistranslation of
Latin* ardor 210/12, 14.

hēawenhnydelu *see* hǣwenhydele.

hedclāþ *m.* cloak, overcoat 250/25.

hefelīce *adv.* vehemently, violently
56/21, 90/23, 25.

hefelþrǣd *m.* thread for weaving
228/26.

hefig *adj.* (a) heavy, unpleasant 186/2,
194/5; (b) burdensome, grievous
172/24, 182/19; *sup.* hefegust
172/12.

hefiglic *adj.* vehement, violent 38/20.

hege *m.* hedge 154/24, 158/8; *dpl.*
heogan 68/20.

hēhnyss *see* hēahnyss.

hēla *m.* heel 250/24.

helpan 3 *w. d.* help. *inf.* helpan
172/3; *3 sg.* helpeþ 76/2, 176/6,
186/9, 196/17; *imp.* help 172/4.

gehende *adj.* near 106/18.

henep *m.* (a) ground-pine XXVII,
72/15. (b) hemp CXVI.

henfugol *m.* hen 46/21.

hennebelle *f.* henbane V.

hēo *see* hē.

heofon *m.* sky 104/9.

heofonlic *adj.* heavenly, celestial;
~ boga rainbow 200/18.

heogan *see* hege.

heora *see* hē.

heor(o)t *m.* deer, hart 142/7, 170/4,
240/11, 13, 16, etc.

heortclǣfre *f.* common germander,
wall germander, *or* spotted medick
XXV, 72/15.

heorte *f.* heart 140/1, 236/15, 244/6,
248/12, 272/9.

heortece *m.* (a) pain in the heart
128/9. (b) heartburn, cardialgy 62/18.

heorten *adj.* of a hart *or* deer 148/5.

heorþbacen *adj.* baked on the hearth
90/20.

hēr *adv.* here; ~ beforan earlier in
this chapter, above 72/5 (hǣr V,
alt. from ǣr), 82/27, 88/14, 100/7,
162/23, etc.; ~ wiþæftan later in
this chapter, below 96/5.

herian I praise. *pp.* gehered 102/4.

herigendlic *adj.* laudable 110/17
(herigindlic V).

herþbylg *m.* scrotum 254/9.

hig *see* hē.

hig(e) *see* haran hig(e).

him/hym *see* hē.

hindehǣleþe *f.* water hemp, hemp
agrimony 108/2.

hine/hyne, hīo, his/hys, hit/hyt *see*
hē.

hīw *n.* (a) colour 48/12, 184/3, 228/
12, 14. (b) form, appearance 228/10

hīwcūþ *adj.* familiar 110/6.

hlāf *m.* bread 80/11, 88/18, 90/4, 20
160/25, etc.

hlēapan 7b leap; *in combinatio*
tosomne ~ close too quickly (*of c*
wound). *inf.* hlēapan 132/10.

hlēor *n.* cheek 40/27.

hlihhan 6 laugh. *pres. p.* hlihhend
52/22.

hlond *n.* urine 264/16.

hlūttor *adj.* pure, clear 244/24.

hnappung *f.* dozing, drowsiness
262/5.

gehnǣcan I restrain, check. *3 sg*
gehnǣceþ 190/18, 206/26.

gehnehsod *see* (ge)hnescian.

hnesce *adj.* (a) soft, tender 40/27
50/14, 60/6, 62/7, 146/20, etc. (b
weak, lacking in energy 202/2.

(ge)hnescian II become or make soft
3 sg. hnescaþ 40/6, gehnesceaþ
268/15; *pp.* gehnehsod 46/20.

hnescnyss *f.* soft part 232/14.

hnitu *f.* nit 266/1.

hnutu *f.* nut, fruit 174/17.

hoclēaf *n.* common mallow XLI.

hof *n.* house, home 172/24.

hofer *m.* (H *only*) hump, swelling 206/3

hol *adj.* hollow 218/15, 226/7.

hōman *see* ōman.

(ge)hōn 7d hang (*tr.*). *imp.* (ge)hōþ
52/2, 64/18, 264/25. [Cf. a-~.]

horn *m.* horn (a) (*class noun*) 76/4
236/6. (b) (*material noun*) 170/4, 5
240/11, 13, 16, etc.

hors *n.* horse 206/3, 236/1, 4.

horsminte *f.* (B *only*) horse-mint
XCII.

horu *n.* filth, pus 54/1.

hrāca *m.* coughing; what is coughed
up 100/8, 188/16, 202/1.

hramma *m.* spasm, cramp 140/3
196/16, 214/23.

hraþe *adv.* quickly, immediately 30/14, 34/27, 40/28, 88/26, 170/12, **hræþe** 36/23, **raþe** 32/25; *sup.* **hraþost** *see* **swā** (III).

hrǣcan I cough, cough up, spit. *subj. sg.* **hrǣce** 86/15, 90/23, 100/6, 174/15, 196/7, etc., **rǣce** 9/10, 11/11; *subj. pl.* **hrǣcen** 90/26.

hrǣd *adj.* quick, prompt 256/29.

hrǣdlīce *adv.* quickly, immediately 46/4, 17, 48/6, 62/23, 66/10, etc.

hrǣdnyss *f.* quickness, rapidity 62/24, 204/10.

hrǣfnes fōt *m.* lesser celandine, fig-wort, pilewort XXVIII, 72/14. [Also **hrefnes ~, ræfnes ~.**]

hrǣfnes lēac *n.* orchis, wild orchid XVI. [Also **hreafnes ~, refnes ~.**]

hrǣgel *n.* garment 234/13.

hræþe *see* hraþe.

hreafnes lēac *see* hrǣfnes lēac.

hrēaw, hrǣw *adj.* raw 176/23, 250/4.

hrefnes fōt *see* hrǣfnes fōt.

hrēodbedd *n.* reed-bed 52/11.

hrēofl *f.*, hrēofla *m.* scabbiness, itching, rash 134/22, 154/8, 188/25, 26, 256/13. [See note to XCII. 2.]

hrēohnys(s) *f.* roughness (of the weather), tempest 214/21, 22, 220/13, 16, 18, etc.

hrēosan 2 fall. *pres. p.* hrēosende 254/14.

hreppan I touch. *inf.* hreppan 76/19; *3 sg.* hrepeþ 168/21.

hricg *m.* back 206/3.

hrif *n.* womb 244/7, 250/9.

hrīnan 1 *w. a. or g.* touch. *subj. sg.* hrīne 238/18; *imp.* hrīn 252/15. [Cf. æt-~.]

hring *m.* ring 64/16, 254/15.

hringfinger *m.* ring-finger 238/10.

hrōf *m.* roof 90/11, 116/26.

hrycghǣr *n.* hair of the back 262/24.

hū *adv.* how 172/7, 10.

hund *m.* dog, hound 90/19, 110/9, 170/19, 20, 222/6, etc. [Cf. **wēde-~.**]

hundes hēafod *n.* small snapdragon, calves'-snout LXXXVIII.

hundes tunge *f.* hound's-tongue, dog's-tongue, *or* bugloss XLII.

hungrig *adj.* hungry 170/20.

hunig *n.* honey 34/13, 17, 22, 44/24, 46/16, etc.

huntoþ *m.* hunting 106/21.

hūs *n.* house 52/15, 56/4, 58/8, 9, 74/7, etc.

hūsstede *m.* site of a building, ruin 96/24, 124/13.

hwā *pron.* someone, anyone, **hwæt** something, anything. *nsgm.* **hwā** 52/5, 12, 56/1, 21, 25, etc.; *nsgn.* **hwæt** 54/1, 94/4, 162/22, 234/16, 238/1; *dsgm.* **hwām** 66/21, 238/1; **swā hwæt swā** *n., a.* whatever 46/4, 168/17, 19, 21, 256/16.

gehwā *pron.* everyone. *nsgm.* gehwā 158/4.

gehwār *see* gehwǣr.

gehwǣde *adj.* small, slight 174/26, 178/14, 180/4, 5, 182/1, etc.

hwǣr *adv.* somewhere 38/19; swā ~ swā wherever 48/18, 106/17, 19.

gehwǣr *adv.* everywhere 44/15, 64/3, gehwār 94/23.

hwæt *see* hwā.

hwǣten *adj.* wheaten, of wheat 46/19, 132/17, 230/21.

gehwæþer (I) *pron.* each of two things. *asgn.* gehwæþer 36/6. (II) *adv.* in each (of two) case(s) 30/4.

hwæþere *adv.* however, yet 234/5.

hwelp *m.* whelp, young dog 264/5, 270/10.

hwēne *adv.* somewhat, a little 64/14.

hwerhwette *f.* cucumber CXV.

hwīl, hwȳl *f.* while, (space of) time 118/21, 158/24, 228/3, 240/1, 250/18; þā ~e þe *conj.* while 136/10, 178/26.

hwīlon, hwīlum *adv.* (*a*) sometimes 190/6, 228/11, 12, 244/7, 256/14. (*b*) once, at some time past 100/20.

hwīt *adj.* white 96/14, 136/23, 198/24, 208/11, 216/12, etc.; *comp.* hwīt(t)ra 48/13, 196/4.

hwītness *f.* whiteness 68/9.

hwōn *adv.* somewhat, a little 194/5, 18; *used subst.* little 264/18.

hwōnlīce *adv.* slightly, a little 182/4, 204/15.

hwylc (I) *pron. adj.* some, any. *nsgmfn.* hwylc 36/1, 14, 66/19,

80/9, 106/5, etc.; *asgm.* **hwylcne** 36/4, 74/19, 270/9; *asgf.* **hwylce** 172/24; *gsgmn.* **hwylces** 40/4, 58/8; *dsgmn.* **hwylcum** 40/7, 88/9, 130/18, 140/3, 222/20; *dsgm.* **hwylcon** 172/3; *dsgf.* **hwylcre** 236/11; *apl.* **hwylce** 78/22; **swā ∼** whichever 62/23; **swā ∼ . . . swā** whichever 46/9, 52/21, 130/25, 214/5, 220/15, etc. (II) *pron. subst.* someone, anyone *dsg.* **hwylcum** 40/26.

ġehwylc *pron. adj.* every, each; all. *asgm.* **ġehwylcne** 228/11; *asgf.* **ġewhylce** 180/18; *dsgm.* **ġehwylcum** 270/25; *instr. sgm.* **ġehwylce** 252/20; *apl.* **ġehwylce** 182/27, 198/4, 224/14, 230/12, 270/2; *dpl.* **ġehwylcum** 182/10.

ġehwyrfan I turn. *3 sg.* **ġehwyrfeþ** 138/27.

hȳ *see* **hē.**

hȳd *f.* skin 236/19, 20. [Cf. **fixen-∼.**]

hȳf *f.* hive 52/2.

hymele *f.* (a) hop-trefoil, yellow clover LII. (b) bryony LXVIII.

hypebānece *m.* sciatica 110/1. [Cf. **bānece.**]

hyra *see* **hē.**

ġehȳran I hear. *inf.* **ġehȳran** 144/7, 146/17, 264/18.

hyrde *m.* shepherd 104/11, 108/19, 22.

hyre *see* **hē.**

hysope, ysope *f.* hyssop 102/1, 3, 178/7.

ġehȳwlǣcan I colour. *pp.* **ġehȳwlǣht** 184/3.

I

ic *pron.* I 132/4, 220/22, 224/20, 234/4, 5, etc.

īce ('ȳce') *f.* frog, toad 88/17.

ifiġ, ȳfiġ *n.* ivy CXXI.

īgland *n.* island 106/3.

in *prep.* (a) *w. a.* into 246/17. [Cf. **þǣr-∼.**] (b) *w. d.?* in, of 190/5.

incund *adj.* internal 132/5.

innan (I) *adv.* inside, internally 34/4, 12, 36/16, 40/1, 42/22, etc. (II) *prep. w. d.* in, inside 256/13.

innancund *adj.* internal 42/12.

innaþ *see* **innoþ.**

inne *adv.* inside 56/4, 258/4.

innera *adj. comp.* inner 248/3.

inneweard *adj.* interior, the inward part of 88/24, 90/2, 232/15.

inneweard, inneweardes *adv.* internally, inside 38/11, 42/10.

innoþ *m.* (a) intestines 32/18, 20, 34/25, 38/10, 56/6, etc., **innaþ** 34/15. (b) womb 106/5, 264/10. (c) belly, abdomen 142/21.

intō *prep. w. d.* into 184/22.

inwerdlic *adj.* interior, inward 244/17.

inwyrm *m.* intestinal worm 2/18.

inylfe *n.* intestines 264/6.

īsern *n.* iron, tool *or* weapon made of iron 30/7, 78/25, 106/10, 118/4, 128/22, etc.

Itali *mpl.* the Italians 86/12.

Iulius *m.* July 60/16, 74/14.

L

(ġe)lācnian II (a) heal, cure. *inf.* **tō ġelācnienne** 136/11, **tō ġelācniġenne** 220/11; *2 sg.* **ġelācnast** 88/12, **ġelācnust** 152/6; *3 sg.* **(ġe)lācnaþ** 156/18, 186/7, 202/9, 204/1, 214/7, etc.; *pl.* **ġelācniaþ** 230/17; *pp.* **ġelācnud** 104/17, 146/18, 178/27, 182/20, 188/26, etc. (b) dress (a wound) *imp.* **lācna** 132/22.

lācnung *f.* (a) medicine, medicament 56/4, 58/15, 92/25, 162/21, 214/13, etc. (b) healing 146/12.

lanc *see* **lang.**

land *n.* (a) land, field, ground 44/15, 48/11, 54/12, 60/20, 70/20, etc. (b) country 60/5, 68/6, 200/20, 212/7.

landġemǣre *n.* boundary 236/15.

lang *adj.* long 114/15, 174/3, 12, 180/6, 182/5, etc., **lanc** 196/5, 216/14.

lange *adv.* long 42/6, 154/20, **langæ** 202/15; *comp.* **lenġc** 54/2.

langnyss *f.* length 182/9.

lāþ (I) *n.* annoyance, grief 32/18, 74/11. (II) *adj.* hateful, harmful 244/13.

lawertrēow *n.* laurel 112/18.

lǣce *m.* physician, doctor 66/11, 70/7, 208/12.

lǣcecræft *m.* medicine, remedy 230/2, 234/8, 242/6.

lǣcedōm *m.* (*a*) medicine, remedy 40/13, 64/17, 78/2, 96/5, 116/4, etc. (*b*) healing power 58/14, 136/21, 182/9.

lǣcewyrt *f.* campion, ragged robin CXXXIII.

(ge)lǣdan I lead, carry, take. *3 sg.* gelǣdeþ 46/5, 66/10, 144/17, 172/16, 188/19, etc.; *imp.* (ge)lǣd 52/15, 216/6, 264/22; *pp.* gelǣded 214/8.

lǣfan I leave. *pp.* lǣfed 246/17.

lǣl *f.* bruise, weal 148/11, 196/12, 244/13.

lændenbrǣde *see* lendenbrǣde.

lǣngu *see* lengu.

lǣs *adv.* less; *in conj.* þȳ ~, þī ~ lest 54/2, 170/12, 214/13, 216/5, 226/22, etc.

lǣssa, lǣst *see* lȳtel (I).

lǣtan 7e let, leave. *imp.* lǣt 40/28, 82/17. [Cf. for-~.]

lēac *n.* leek 94/18, 180/24, 206/9, 222/4. [See also hræfnes ~.]

lēaf *n.* leaf 30/17, 19, 40/11, 42/5, 46/10, etc. [Cf. hoc-~.]

leahtor *m.* disease, malady, disorder 58/12, 78/12, 188/8, 9, 208/16, etc.

(ge)lecgan I lay, place. *3 sg.* gelegeþ 194/22, 218/7, gelegþ 174/7; *subj. sg.* (ge)lecge 34/2, 96/21, 170/5, 224/5; *imp.* (ge)lege 30/17, 34/26, 36/6, 13, 16, etc.; *pp.* gelegd 256/6, 270/13, gelēd 186/11, 210/3, 218/4, 230/18, 254/21, etc., gelǣd 78/26, 96/18. [Cf. a-~.]

Leden *n.* Latin 50/22, 200/19, 212/15.

lēh ('lēah') *f.* lye 264/30.

lendenbrǣde *f.* loin 1/13, lænden-brǣde 32/13.

lendenece *m.* pain in the loins 17/15.

lendenu *npl.* loins 36/18, 23, 118/11, 12, 140/11, etc.

lengc *see* lange.

lengu, lencgu *f.* length 190/5, 192/14.

lēo *m.* lion 266/15, 17, 19, 21.

lēoht *adj.* light, comfortable; *comp.* lēohtra 248/4.

lēohtfæt *n.* lantern, lamp 108/21, 170/11.

lēohtian II become light; be relieved. *3 sg.* lēohtaþ 34/6.

lēonfōt *m.* lady's mantle, lion's foot VIII.

leoþu *see* liþ.

gelettan I hinder, obstruct. *3 sg.* gelet 46/4.

libban III live. *pres. p.* lifigende 234/19.

līc *n.* body 54/20, 68/11, 162/9, 186/23, 190/8, etc. [See also ōþer.]

gelīc *adj.* (*a*) similar, like 54/20, 88/13, 102/1, 2, 108/21, etc. (*b*) equal (*referring to quantity*) 68/22.

gelīce *adv.* (*a*) similarly, in the same way, *often in combinations* þām ~ þe, ~ þon þe 60/14, 74/20, 88/13, 19, 100/12, etc. (*b*) equally (*referring to quantity*) 72/15, 90/13, 92/5, 140/12, 148/16. (*c*) in equal portions 252/17, 264/11.

licgan 5 lie. *inf.* licgan 40/28, licgean 214/13; *subj. sg.* licge 54/2; *pres. p.* ligcgende 108/24.

līchoma, līchama *m.* body 30/4, 34/4, 7, 38/19, 21, etc.

gelīcian II please, be pleasing to. *3 sg.* gelīcaþ 52/3.

gelīcnyss *f.* likeness, resemblance 166/4, 182/9, 194/16.

līf *n.* life 52/22, 236/2.

lifer *f.* liver 44/26, 80/6, 188/5, 204/1, 236/14, etc.

liferādl *f.* disease of the liver 80/15.

lifersār *n.* pain in the liver 158/25.

lifersēoc *adj.* suffering from a liver complaint 164/5.

lifersēocnyss *f.* disease of the liver 72/9, 122/1, 188/16, 202/24, 216/21.

ligræsc *m.* flash of lightning 220/23.

gelīhtan I relieve. *3 sg.* gelīhteþ 208/14. [Cf. onlīhtan.]

lilie *f.* lily CIX.

lim *n.* (*a*) limb 260/2. (*b*) (*with* gecyndelic) organ 194/22, 210/3, 220/4. [Cf. gecyndlimu.]

gelimpan 3 happen. *pret. 3 sg.* gelamp 100/20. [Cf. belimpan.]

linen *adj.* of linen 110/2, 116/22, 166/29, 200/22, 234/12.

līnsǣd *n.* linseed 86/8.

liþ *n.* limb; joint 68/21, 25, 90/1,

92/8, 128/14, etc.; *pl.* leoþu 42/14, 244/18, 266/21.

liþādl *f.* gout 246/16.

liþe *adj.* (*a*) light, mild 100/18, 120/8, 182/18, 188/18, 22, etc. (*b*) soft, smooth; *comp.* līþra 260/8.

liþelīce *adv.* gently 110/16, 116/3.

līþian II abate, become less. *pres. p.* līþigende 32/18.

līþig *adj.* soft 224/2 (B *only,* līþi V, līþe H).

gelīþigian, gelīþegian II (*a*) assuage, relieve. *3 sg.* gelīþigaþ 100/7, 126/24, 128/16, 138/6, 17, etc., gelīþegaþ 56/7, 72/6, 94/20, 98/21, 118/9, etc.; *pp.* gelīþigod 164/23, 176/15, gelīþigud 180/12, gelīþigad 192/3, 210/14. (*b*) make soft. *3 sg.* gelīþigaþ 268/15; *imp.* gelīþga 64/12; *pp.* gelīþigod 182/18, gelīþegod 80/5. (*c*) soothe, calm. *pp.* gelīþigud 230/4.

liþung *f.* relief 62/25.

liþwyrt, lyþwyrt *f.* (*a*) wayfaring-tree XXIX. (*b*) goat's rue CXXVII.

lōcian II (O *only*) take heed. *imp.* lōca 239/14.

gelōgian II put, place. *subj. sg.* gelōgige 78/1.

gelōme *adv.* often 246/8, 250/23, 254/8, 262/16, 264/13, etc.

gelōmlīce *adv.* often 64/10, 66/18, 132/25, 138/23, 220/10, etc.

losian II be lost, perish. *subj. sg.* losie 248/12.

lubastice *f.* lovage 188/21.

gelūcan 2 close, heal. *3 sg.* gelȳcþ 60/23. [Cf. belūcan.]

lufian II appreciate. *inf.* tō lufigenne 180/26.

lungen *f.* lung 246/1, 6, 248/8, 10, 22, etc.

lungenādl *f.* lung disease 50/10, 92/15, 166/9, 198/4.

lust *m.* desire 242/23, 262/2. [Cf. wyn-~.]

gelȳfan I believe. *inf.* tō gelȳfenne 38/30, 40/18; *2 sg.* gelȳfest 246/15; *subj. sg.* gelȳfe 236/22; *pp.* gelȳfed 76/12, 78/14, 86/13, 96/11, 120/8, etc. [Cf. alȳfan.]

gelynd *f.,* gelynde *n.* fat 236/1, 248/1, 262/5, 264/18, 266/17, etc.

lȳtel, lītel (I) *adj.* (*a*) small, little 34/22, 72/18; *comp.* læssa 88/15, 184/25, 186/1, 17, læssæ 82/3; *sup.* læst 42/24. (*b*) little, a little (*quantity*) 236/4, 18. (II) *subst. n.* a little (*quantity*) 42/3, 252/21.

lȳtlian, lītlian II become less. *3 sg.* lȳtlaþ 266/11; *pres. p.* lȳtliende, lītliende 42/22, 26.

M

mā *indecl. comp.* (I) *subst. n.* more 158/27, 164/21, 256/18. (II) *adv.* more, rather 174/25.

maga *m.* stomach 38/12, 58/5, 92/1, 2, 102/16, etc.

magan *pret. pr.* (*a*) can, be able. *2 sg.* meaht 36/7, 52/12, 17, miht 158/27; *3 sg.* mæg 44/22, 52/4, 7, 58/9, 62/25, etc.; *pl.* magon 44/23, 66/11, 264/18; *subj. sg.* mæge 32/5, 34/20, 52/5, 56/12, 24, etc., mege 4/12; *subj. pl.* mægen 106/23, 234/14; *pret. 3 sg.* mihte 240/7. (*b*) avail, have power. *3 sg.* mæg 214/17, 252/14.

mageþe *f.* common camomile XXIV.

man(n), mon(n), *dsg., npl.* men (I) *subst. m.* man 30/4, 11, 32/20, 21, 23, etc. (II) *pron.* one 30/2, 34/12, 20, 38/13, 16, etc.

gemāna *m.* coitus 250/17. [Cf. rest-~, wīf-~.]

gemang (I) *adv.* together 174/15. (II) *prep. w. a., d.* among, together with 110/15.

manig, monig *adj.* many 44/29, 124/22, 136/21, 178/14, 180/4, etc.

māra *see* mycel.

marma *m.* marble 96/14.

Martius *m.* March 212/4.

mǣd *f.* meadow 30/3, 50/24, 60/20, 94/24, 102/22, etc.

mǣdere, mǣderu *f.* madder LI.

mǣgden *n.* girl 150/9.

mǣgen *n.* power, strength 48/14, 56/24, 58/14, 166/12, 170/13, etc.

mǣgþhād *f.* virginity 150/9.

gemǣnelic *adj.* common, usual; natural 192/19.

mǣngc, gemǣnged *see* (ge)-mengan.

mænigfeald *adj.* manifold, various 190/7, 216/22.

mǣre *adj.* glorious, famous 108/18, 170/8, 13.

mæssedæg *m.* (O *only*) festival day 45/19.

mǣst *see* **mycel.**

mearh, mearg *n.* marrow 142/7, 244/9, 11, 264/8, 266/22. [Cf. **fearre-~.**]

mearu *adj.* tender, delicate, soft 128/3, 6, 136/4, 148/13, 154/14; *comp.* **mearwra** 196/4.

melc *adj.* giving milk 64/11.

melu, meolu *n.* meal, flour 86/9, 100/12, 188/25, 27, 190/6, etc.

men *see* **man(n).**

(ge)mengan I mix, mingle. *3 sg.* **gemencgeaþ** 110/17; *subj. sg.* **gemencge** 192/11, **gemengce** 78/1; *imp.* (ge)meng 32/4, 42/2, 94/2, 104/4, 198/13, etc., (ge)-mencg 44/1, 8, 24, 28, 46/22, etc., (ge)mengc 50/18, 54/19, 56/7, 70/2, 82/18, etc., menc 246/21, mængc 180/12, menge 256/14, 16, 258/5; *pp.* gemenged 58/23, 102/18, 190/11, 244/14, 252/17, etc., gemencged 58/11, 76/23, 98/12, 126/16, 168/2, etc., ge-mengced 68/24, 84/23, 116/2, 15, 134/19, gemengcged 160/13, ge-mænged 198/19, 230/18, 266/8.

menlufigend *adj.* 'men-loving' (*translating* filantropos) 218/10.

meolc *f.* (a) milk 32/24, 120/11, 178/25, 204/21, 254/16, etc. (b) juice, sap 114/24, 154/5, 170/1.

meolu *see* **melu.**

merce *m.* wild celery, march CXX, 142/15, 164/18, 166/4.

meregrot *n.* pearl 226/5.

mergen *see* **morgen.**

merscmeal(u)we *f.* marsh-mallow XXXIX.

gemet *n.* (a) manner, way 46/3, 23, 48/7, 16, 58/6, etc. (b) measure, quantity 202/10.

mētan I (a) meet (with), encounter. *subj. sg.* **mēte** 254/15. (b) find. *pp.* **gemēt** 100/25, 108/22.

mete *m.* food 34/16, 20, 110/15, 130/18, 170/20, etc.

gemetegian II temper, prepare. *pp.* **gemetegud** 202/14, 218/6.

micg *m.* midge, mosquito 186/6.

micga *m.* urine 258/1, 2, 3, 262/10.

micgþa, micþa *see* **migþa.**

mid (I) *adv.* with, with it, with them 42/3², 66/20, 236/10, 244/4, 250/23, etc. (II) *prep. w. d., instr.* (a) with, together with 30/9¹, 32/5, 36/10, 11, 38/6, etc. (b) with, by (*referring to agent*) 66/12. (c) *in combination* ~ **ealle** altogether 30/9. [Cf. **þǣr-~.**]

mid(d) *adj.* mid-, middle of 118/5, 180/25.

midde *f.* middle 198/22, 218/14.

middesumor *m.* midsummer 44/26.

midrif ('midhrif') *n.* midriff, diaphragm 44/1.

(ge)mīgan I urinate. *inf.* **gemīgan** 52/5, 56/12, 100/2, 120/2, 130/8, etc.; *pl.* **mīgaþ** 262/13; *subj. sg.* **mīge** 264/26; *pret. 3 sg.* **gemāh** 264/26.

migþa, micgþa, micþa *m.* (passing of) urine 46/4, 52/5, 7, 72/19, 88/26, etc. [See also **earfoþlic-nyss.**]

miht *f.* power 76/2, 8, 104/12, 136/25, 170/22, etc.

mihtelīce *adv.* strongly 152/10.

milte *f.* spleen, milt 62/19, 23, 78/20, 21, 80/18, etc.; *dsg.* **milten** 100/25; *asg.* **milte** 264/4.

miltsēoc *adj.* having a spleen-disease 194/11.

miltwræc *m.* pain in the spleen 264/4.

mīn *pron. adj.* my 220/23.

minte *f.* (a) mint, field-mint, corn-mint CXXII. (b) (H *only*) horse-mint XCII.

misboren *adj.* misshapen, born prematurely 158/1.

misenlic *adj.* various 208/16.

misenlicnyss *f.* variety, diversity 200/17.

mistel *f.* wild basil, missel, *or* mistletoe CXIX, 178/1.

mōd *n.* mind 142/10.

mon(n) *see* **man(n).**

mōna *m.* moon 52/15, 54/16, 104/14, 224/25, 228/24, etc.

mōnaþ, mōnþ *m.* month 30/7, 44/11, 50/19, 24, 54/16, etc.

mōnoþlic *adj.* used as subst. *pl. in* þā ~an the menses 192/22, 194/21, 202/15, 208/3, 15, etc.

mōnoþsēoc *adj.* lunatic 54/14, 102/9, 108/23.

mōnoþsēocnyss *f.* lunacy 108/23.

mōnþ *see* **mōnaþ.**

mōr *m.* moor 102/22, 206/10.

mōrbēam *m.* mulberry tree 238/8, 24, 240/1, 4.

more *f.* root 258/2.

morgen *m.* morning 44/2; *dsg.* **mergen** 178/26. [See also **ǣrnemergen.**]

mortere *m.* mortar (*bowl*) 86/30, 148/4, 150/20, 224/1.

mōtan *pret. pr.* may. *subj. sg.* **mōte** 228/17.

mucgwyrt, mugcwyrt, mugwyrt *f.* (*a*) mugwort XI. (*b*) tarragon XII. (*c*) Roman wormwood XIII.

mūl *m.* mule 236/4.

munt *m.* mountain 60/4, 106/3, 166/3, 232/7.

muntland *n.* mountainous country 102/4.

mūþ *m.* mouth 32/23, 42/5, 20, 22, 48/22, etc.

mycel, micel (I) *adj.* (*a*) great, large 36/21, 38/6, 40/10, 56/24, 104/5, etc.; *comp.* **māra** 80/16, 174/11, 182/5, 184/25, 186/2, etc.; *sup.* **mǣst** 76/20, 136/25, 234/11. (*b*) much 34/8, 192/6, 202/1. (*c*) strong, intense 174/27. (II) *subst. n.* much, a great quantity 32/5, 56/2, 66/11, 72/15, 82/21, etc.; *comp.* **māre** 58/23, 86/24.

mycelnyss *f.* size 108/20, 226/5.

mycelu *f.* size 94/18, 226/14.

mycelum, mycelon, myclum, miclum *adv.* greatly, much 44/29, 62/11, 84/24, 118/9, 136/17, etc.

(ge)myltan I (*a*) melt. *imp.* (ge)mylt 256/25, 264/19, 266/17, 22, 268/14; *pp.* **gemylted** 244/10, 13, 248/1, 266/19. (*b*) digest. *inf.* **gemyltan** 130/18; *subj. sg.* **gemylte** 34/16.

myrre *f.* myrrh 178/17, 248/23, 252/18.

myxen *f.* dunghill 58/20, 114/3.

N

nā *adv.* not, not at all 46/4, 52/17, 56/2, 124/22, 136/12, etc.; ~ þæt ān þæt . . . ac not only . . . but 106/16, 172/15.

naf(o)la *m.* navel 40/3, 82/27, 92/4, 7, 108/11, etc. [Cf. **eorþ-~.**]

nāht (I) *pron.* nothing; tō ~e as nothing 250/11. (II) *adv.* not (at all) 66/11, 236/17.

nālæs *adv.* (*a*) not (at all), by no means 36/22. (*b*) ~ . . . ēac swylce not only . . . also 66/7.

nama *m.* name 44/14, 48/9, 50/13, 52/10, 20, etc.

nān *pron. adj. and subst.* no; none 154/17, 168/16.

nānwiht *pron.* nothing 30/8, 154/20, 168/22.

nard *m.* nard, spikenard; *gsg.* **nardis** 122/2; *dsg.* **nardo** 172/10. [See note to LXXXI. 4.]

nardes ēar *n.* spikenard 258/1.

nāþer *adv.*; *in combination* ~ ne . . . ne neither . . . nor 250/12.

næbbe *see* **habban.**

nǣddercyn(n) *n.* kind of serpent 132/8, 15, 168/16, 24, 174/6, etc.

nǣdderwyrt, nǣdrewyrt *f.* (*a*) adderwort, bistort, snakeweed VI. (*b*) sweet basil CXXXI.

nǣddre, nǣdre *f.* serpent, snake, adder 36/4, 7, 8, 38/25, 26, etc.; **nēddre** 140/18, 142/3.

nǣfre *adv.* never 52/3, 108/25, 112/6, 234/5, 240/7.

nægl *m.* nail 270/18.

nǣnig *pron. adj.* not any 32/18, 238/23.

næsþyrl *n.* nostril 32/6, 62/16, 66/9, 10, 116/22, etc., **næsþurl** 6/7.

ne (I) *adv.* not 30/8, 32/19, 34/20, 44/21, 22, etc. (II) *conj.* nor 52/3²; ne . . . ne neither . . . nor 234/15.

nēadþearf *f.* need 238/19.

nēah (I) *adv.* nearly, almost 178/1. (II) *prep. w. d.* near 150/10, 156/23, 178/15, 218/23.

genēalǣcan I approach. *inf.* **genēalǣcean** 178/19; *3 sg.* **genēalǣceþ** 108/25.

genēalǣcing *f.* approach, access 204/9.

nēalīce *adv., in combination* þonne ～ just about when 136/25.

nearu *adj.* narrow, difficult 246/6.

nēat *n.* animal 236/5.

neb(b) *n.* nose 42/1, 3, 70/1, 252/9.

nebcorn *n.* pimple 70/1, 3, 232/3, 254/1, 2.

nēddre *see* nǣddre.

nellan *see* willan.

(ge)nemnan I name, call. *3 sg.* nemneþ 30/2, 44/15, 50/14, 23, 25, etc.; *pl.* nemnaþ 74/3, 80/16, 86/12, 88/6, 90/3, etc., nemneþ 9/23; *pret. 3 sg.* genemnede 58/17; *pret. pl.* nemdon 52/2, 13, 58/3, 13, 70/21, etc., nemdun 68/22, 98/12, 102/10, 106/6, 118/2, etc., nendun 140/19, 158/18; *pp.* genemned 128/23, 156/18, 168/17, 20, 178/11, nemned 100/24.

nēod *f.* necessity; necessary evacuation of the bowels 172/3, 192/20.

neoþan *adv.* beneath, below 248/10. [See also **under** *prep.*]

neoþeweard *adv.* below 60/8.

neoþra *adj. comp.* lower 238/13, 21.

nēowe *see* nīwe.

nepte *f.* catmint XCV.

netele *f.* common nettle, greater nettle, *or* lesser nettle CLXXVIII, 158/13, 254/12.

nigon *num.* nine 40/28, 64/7, 98/3, 136/8, 146/3, etc.

nigontȳne *num.* nineteen 146/5.

nigoþa *adj.* ninth 146/5.

nihstig *see* nistig.

niht, nyht *f.* (*a*) night 32/12, 15, 21, 34/6, 10, etc. (*b*) night, day (*in calculating time*) 32/22, 40/28, 224/25, 26, 27, etc.

nihterne *adv.* (H *only*) by night 236/10.

nihtgenga *m.* goblin, evil spirit 30/5.

(ge)niman, nyman 4 take, take away. *inf.* (ge)niman 30/6, 32/5, 50/19, 24, 60/16, etc., nimen 64/4; tō nymenne, tō nimenne 232/13, 270/2; *1 sg.* nime 234/19; *2 sg.* nimest 220/25, 264/7; *3 sg.* (ge)nimeþ 58/12, 102/3, 160/14, 208/8, 214/3, etc., genimþ 56/10,

62/3, 64/10, 68/24, 78/19, etc.; *pl.* nimaþ 264/5; *subj. sg.* (ge)nime 32/26, 34/1, 5, 9, 36/1, etc.; *imp.* (ge)nim 30/11, 12, 15, 17, 19, etc.; *pp.* genumen 30/7; nimeþ . . . tō (*of hair*) holds on, does not fall out 250/7. [Cf. a-～, for-～.]

genip *n.* mistiness, dimness 268/3.

nistig, nihstig *adj.* fasting, not having eaten or drunk 32/12, 15, 21, 34/6, 10, etc.

nīwe *adj.* new 46/25, 56/7, 80/21, 84/15, 88/3, etc.; *dsgm.* nēowum 254/4.

(ge)nīwian II renew. *subj. sg.* nīwie 128/8; *imp.* genīwa 242/12.

nosu *f.* (*a*) nose 66/21, 68/3, 228/10. (*b*) *in pl.* nosa nostrils 32/3, 40/26, 42/27, 116/21, 132/24, etc.

nū *adv.* now 82/6, 100/7, 162/23.

genȳdan I compel. *3 sg.* genȳdeþ 250/8. [Cf. anȳdan.]

nyllan *see* willan.

nyrwyt(t), nyrwet(t) *n.* shortness of breath, asthma 84/24, 88/18, 164/5, 14, 176/1, etc.

nys *see* bēon.

nytan, nytende *see* witan.

nȳten *n.* animal 234/9, 236/20.

nytlic *adj.* useful, beneficial 136/24, 214/12; *comp.* nytlicra 230/10. [Cf. un-～.]

nytlīce *adv.* usefully, profitably 180/15, 19, 188/4, 194/11, 198/13, etc.

nytlicnyss *f.* useful quality 224/21. [Cf. un-～.]

nytrum *n.* (*here probably*) salt 178/7. [See note to CXXXVII. 2.]

nyþer *adv.* downwards 192/14.

O

October *m.* October 54/16.

of (I) *adv.* off, away 30/24, 46/24, 48/20, 50/3, 9, etc. (II) *prep. w. d.* (*a*) (away) from, (out) of 32/3, 38/3, 42/24, 27, 52/17, etc. (*b*) by means of, with 30/16, 220/6. [Cf. þǣr-～.]

ofenbacen *adj.* baked in an oven 80/11.

ōfer *m.* bank, shore 152/22.

ofer (I) *adv.* (*a*) over 256/3. (*b*) left over 236/2. (II) *prep. w. a.* (*a*) over, on 30/17, 50/8, 58/8, 25, 68/15, etc. (*b*) after 266/15.

ofercuman 4 overcome. *imp.* ofercum 136/9.

ofergytulnys(s) *f.* forgetfulness 134/9.

oferslǣp *m.* oversleeping 248/6.

oferswīþan I overcome. *3 sg.* oferswīþ 66/5.

ofertǣl *n.* odd number 204/7.

ofertogennyss *f.* (*of the eyes*) condition of being covered with a film; albugo 114/19.

ofslēan 6 kill. *1 sg.* ofslēa 234/12; *3 sg.* ofslyhþ, ofslihþ 106/17, 108/14.

ofsteppan 6 tread on. *3 sg.* ofstepþ 94/5.

ofstlīce *adv.* speedily, quickly 78/8.

oft *adv.* often 246/4, 11, 18, 248/15; *sup.* oftust, oftost 108/22, 258/2. [Cf. for-∼.]

ōga *m.* terror 114/8, 224/14.

ōman *pl.* erysipelas 180/8, 186/20, 218/5, hōman 254/18, 20, 262/15, 16. [See note to CXXII. 1.]

on (I) *adv.* on, in, thereon, therein 34/1, 3, 42/9, 46/14, 48/17, etc. (II) *prep.* (*a*) *w. a.* on, into, onto, unto, in 30/18, 21, 32/6, 34/2, 36/6, etc.; ∼ Englisc in English 234/10; ∼ bysmǣr in mockery 246/15; ∼ þrȳ sīþas three times 256/8. (*b*) *w. d.* on, in, upon, at 30/2, 3, 7, 9, 13, etc. (*c*) *w. instr.* (ǣfen, dæg, mergen) on, in 44/26, 118/4, 136/16, 154/18, 178/25, etc. [Cf. þǣr-∼.]

onǣlan, anǣlan I kindle, set fire to. *3 sg.* anǣleþ 168/18; *pp.* onǣled 176/9, 186/4, 194/12, 214/22.

onbæc *adv.* back(wards) 52/17.

onbūgan 2 submit, yield. *3 sg.* onbūgeþ 228/20.

onbūtan (I) *adv.* about, around 88/23, 138/16, 170/5. (II) *prep. w. a., d.* about, around 54/15, 64/18, 102/12, 112/20, 116/26, etc. [Cf. abūtan.]

onbyrgan, anbyrgan I taste, take. *subj. sg.* onbyrge 32/26, 254/16, anbyrge 32/20; *pp.* onbyrged 76/6.

onbyrging *f.* tasting, taking 82/23.

oncyrran I change. *subj. sg.* oncyrre 264/27.

ondrǣdan 7e (*a*) *w. refl. d. pron. and acc. obj.* fear. *inf.* ondrǣdan 13/15; *3 sg.* ondrǣdeþ 114/17; *subj. sg.* ondrǣde 154/17. (*b*) *w. acc. obj. only* fear. *pl.* ondrǣdaþ 214/24; *pret. 3 sg.* ondrēd 114/6.

onfindan 3 find out. *pret. pl.* onfundun 114/24; *pp.* onfunden 64/22.

ongeflogen *adj.* attacked with disease 42/14.

onfōn 7d *w. a., g.* take, receive. *3 sg.* onfēhþ 76/19, 254/13; *subj. sg.* onfō 256/26; *subj. pl.* onfōn 252/4; *pret. 3 sg.* onfēng 182/26.

onforan *prep. w. d.* before 52/15.

onfundelnyss *f.* (*a*) experience, proof 102/13. (*b*) proved efficacy 86/6.

ongēan *prep. w. a., d.* against 146/21, 154/21, 174/6, 176/18, 184/20, etc.

onginnan 3 begin. *inf.* onginnan 56/1; *3 sg.* onginneþ 226/21; *subj. sg.* onginne 64/15.

ongitan, ongytan 5 perceive, feel. *2 sg.* ongitst, ongytst 64/8, 78/2, 98/10, 100/19, 104/5, ongitest, ongytest 118/25, 270/10, ongist 170/10; *3 sg.* ongit, ongyt 56/2, 62/24, 124/24; *subj. sg.* ongite 46/24, 214/14 (*see note to CLXX. 1*), 218/5.

onhrine *m.* touch, contact 234/16. [Cf. æthrine.]

onlīhtan I make clear. *3 sg.* onlīht 32/2.

onlūtan 2 bend down. *imp.* onlūt 238/12.

onmiddan *prep. w. d.* in the middle of 172/25.

onsendan I send, give. *2 sg.* onsenst 98/23.

onsundrum *adv.* separately 182/12.

onweg, aweg *adv.* away 38/7, 42/18, 132/7, 150/11, 236/3, etc., awege 264/17.

open *adj.* open 132/20, 206/4.

(ge)openian II (*tr. and intr.*) open, become open. *inf.* openian 48/4; *3 sg.* geopenaþ 78/24, 118/6; *pl.*

ġeopeniaþ 96/4; *pp.* ġeopenud 46/15, 48/4, 218/4.

ōras *pl.* (*sg.* (h)orh *m.*) phlegm, rheum 260/21.

organe *f.*, organa *m.*? (*a*) wild thyme CI. (*b*) wild marjoram, *or* sweet marjoram CXXIV, 200/3.

orþanc *mn.* device, artifice 54/3.

ostorscill *f.* oyster-shell 244/14.

ōþer *adj.* (*a*) other 44/14, 29, 46/22, 48/9, 12, etc.; ~ . . . ~ the one . . . the other 184/25; þām ōþrum līce to the rest of the body 54/20. (*b*) second 204/8; ~ healf one and a half 158/25.

oþfeallan 7c fall off, fall out. *3 sg.* oþfealleþ 248/15.

oþstandan 6 stop. *3 sg.* oþstandeþ 42/28.

oþstillan I stop. *pp.* oþstilled 38/17.

oþþæt *conj.* until 34/18, 36/24, 46/16, 19, 48/6, etc.; oþþet 200/23.

oþþe *conj.* or 32/8, 34/4, 8, 12, 25, etc.

ōxn *f.* armpit 200/11.

P

panne *f.* pan 250/7. [Cf. hēafod-~.]

pening (*gpl. mostly* peneġa) penny, pennyweight 66/17, 82/25, 172/14, 18, 174/16, etc.

peonie *f.* peony LXVI.

petersilie *f.* parsley CXXIX.

pīl *m.* prickle 216/13.

pīntrȳwen *adj.* of the pine-tree 174/16.

pipor, piper *m.* pepper 84/23, 114/22, 140/12, 204/6, 230/17, etc.

piporcorn, pipercorn *n.* pepper-corn 32/11, 14, 98/3, 204/7.

plaster *n.* plaster 190/25, 212/11, 22, 218/2.

polleie *f.* pennyroyal XCIV, 68/12.

popiġ *n.*? opium poppy LIV, 150/21.

ġepos *n.* cold in the head 90/23.

posel *m.* pill 256/20.

posling *m.* pill 34/23.

prica *m.* point, spot 124/14.

pund *m.* pound (*weight*) 68/23, 70/10, 86/22, 148/4.

(ġe)punian II pound. *imp.* ġepuna 148/3; *pp.* ġepunud 114/22, 166/24, 224/2.

pyle *m.* pillow 156/20, 262/21.

pypelian II be *or* grow pimply. *pres. p.* pypelġende, pypylġende 162/9, 186/23.

pyse *f.* pea 182/9, 16, 226/5, 14.

R

rā *m.* roebuck 106/21.

rād *f.* riding 34/8.

ramm *m.* ram 76/4, 258/24, 260/3, 5, 7.

raþe *see* hraþe.

rǣcan *see* hrǣcan.

ræfnes fōt *see* hræfnes fōt.

rǣġe *f.* roe 106/22.

rængcwyrm *see* rengwyrm.

rēad *adj.* red 36/9, 54/15, 96/15, 136/23, 166/5, etc. [Cf. weolc-~, wolcen-~.]

rēadian II be red, become red. *subj. sg.* rēadiġe 238/10.

rēcan I steam. *subj. pl.* rēcen 252/4; *pp.* ġerēced 258/26. [Cf. be-~.]

rēcels, rȳcels *n.* frankincense 214/22, 248/13, 254/11.

refnes lēac *see* hræfnes lēac.

rengwyrm *m.* (intestinal) worm 92/4, 142/20, 148/15, 150/2, rængc-wyrm 108/11.

rēocan 2 smell, reek. *3 sg.* rȳcþ 182/3.

ġerestan I (*a*) (*refl.*) rest, lie. *subj. sg.* ġereste 158/23. (*b*) (*non-refl.*) rest, lie. *inf.* ġerestan 264/28.

restgemāna *m.* coitus 254/12.

rēþnyss *f.* fierceness 272/8.

rēwytt *n.* rowing 214/21.

ribbe *f.* ribwort, narrow-leaved plantain XCVIII.

riht *adj.* straight 182/2, 226/4, 13.

rind *f.* bark, rind 160/21, 214/11, 260/22.

Rōmāne *pl.* the Romans 88/6, 94/22, 112/8.

rose *f.* rose 144/24, 148/3, 160/17, 180/11, 186/29, etc.

rosen *adj.* of roses 214/19.

rūde, rūte *f.* (*a*) rue XCI, 122/3, 170/1, 194/16, 226/4. (II) wild rue CXVII.

rūġ, rūh *adj.* rough, hairy 178/1, 212/16, 222/4.

rūme *adv.* amply, plentifully 200/4.

rūmian II become free from encumbrance. *3 sg.* rūmaþ 34/15.

rūte *see* rūde.

rȳcels *see* rēcels.

gerȳman I clear away. *3 sg.* gerȳmþ 46/5.

ryne *m.* (*a*) course, orbit 96/3, 104/15. (*b*) running, flowing 44/22. [Cf. blōd-⁓, un-⁓, up-⁓, ūt-⁓.]

gerynnincg *f.* coagulation, thickening 206/18.

rysel, rysle *m.* fat 44/8, 58/22, 86/5, 26, 90/19, etc.

S

safinæ *see* sauine.

salf *see* sealf.

salfie, saluie *f.* sage CIII.

same *see* some.

gesamnian *see* (ge)somnian.

sand *n.* sand 260/8.

sandig *adj.* sandy 48/11, 54/12, 23, 58/20, 60/20, etc.

sang *m.* song, singing 220/23.

sāpe *f.* soap 84/9, 230/22.

sār (I) *subst. n.* pain, sore, soreness 30/15, 19, 32/9, 10, 13, etc. [Cf. hēafod-⁓, lifer-⁓; for gesār see note to V. 4.] (II) *adj.* sore, painful 34/4, 36/14, 38/2, 5, 50/4, etc. [Cf. un-⁓.]

sārgian II make painful. *pp.* gesārgad 222/21.

sārnyss *f.* pain 68/11, 13, 114/19, 154/16, 190/8.

sauine, safinæ *f.* savine LXXXVII.

sāwan 7e sow. *pp.* sāwen 68/5.

sāwol *f.* soul 30/4.

sǣ *f.* sea 156/23.

sǣd *n.* seed 38/18, 42/2, 68/9, 88/11, 13, etc.; gecyndelic ⁓ semen 202/12. [Cf. līn-⁓.]

sǣl *m.* time, occasion 146/2, 6.

gesǣlig *adj.* happy 224/15, 23.

gescapu *see* gesceapu.

scænc *see* scenc.

sceab *see* sceb.

scead *n.* shade 30/9, 200/23.

(ge)sceādan 7a scatter, sprinkle. *imp.* (ge)sceād 38/19, 206/5, 268/22. [Cf. tō-⁓.]

sceafan 6 scrape. *imp.* sceaf 256/7; *pp.* gesceafen 250/10, 256/10.

sceallan *pl.* testicles (of an animal) 238/2, 242/21, 246/4, 8, 250/13, etc.

sceanca *m.* shank of a leg 48/18, 80/2, 194/25. [Cf. fōten-⁓.]

gesc(e)apu *npl.* genitals 138/7, 148/20, 21, 162/17.

scearfian II scrape, shred. *imp.* scearfa 30/12, 38/8.

scearflian II scrape. *imp.* scearfla 122/2.

scearn *n.* dung 262/15.

scearp *adj.* sharp 254/20, 258/9.

scearplīce *adv.* (*a*) efficaciously 76/5, 96/11, 114/12, 142/17, 152/19, etc. (*b*) firmly 244/8.

scearpnumul *adj.* efficacious 80/21, 94/6; *comp.* scearpnumulra 168/5.

scearpnyss *f.* keenness 32/2.

scēat *m.* piece (of cloth) 238/17.

sceatt *m.* (BO *only*) portion 88/25.

sceaþa *m.* robber 114/17.

sceb *m.* scab 92/12, 226/24, 232/2, sceab 29/15.

scenc *m.* cup, cupful 44/28, 62/11, 19, 76/12, 78/16, etc., scænc 70/9.

scēōh *m.* shoe 236/21, 248/3.

(ge)sceþþan 6 *w. d.* injure, harm. *3 sg.* (ge)sceþþeþ 234/14, 236/18, 262/23.

sceþþu *f.* injury 248/10.

scīnan 1 shine. *3 sg.* scīneþ 104/9, 108/20, 170/11, 214/17; *pl.* scīnaþ 124/14; *subj. sg.* scīne 168/11. [Cf. be-⁓.]

scīnlāc *n.* apparition, phantom 104/10, 254/14, 262/19, 266/15, 16.

scīnsēoc *adj.* haunted by apparitions 264/29.

scip, scyp *n.* ship 138/21, 220/17.

scīr *adj.* pure, clear 248/14.

scorpio(n), scorpius *m.* scorpion 38/28, 29, 108/5, 174/6, 7, etc.

scrincan 3 wither, fade, shrink. *pl.* scrincaþ 136/26. [Cf. for-⁓.]

scruf *see* scurf.

sculan *pret. pr.* must, shall, be destined to. *2 sg.* scealt 30/6, 44/11, 50/19, 24, 60/15, etc.; *3 sg.* sceal 46/15, 48/4, 68/4, 88/26, 110/15, etc.; þær sceal ... awegen there must be weighed out 252/17; *pl.* sculon 106/20, sceolon 134/21, 182/18; *subj. sg.* scyle 170/23,

172/4; *pret. 3 sg.* sc(e)olde *in combination* ys sǣd þæt . . . (*inf.*) sc(e)olde is said to have (*pp.*) 58/14, 60/3, 70/6, 82/4, 114/4, etc.

scurf *m.* scurf 68/8, 10, 226/25, 232/1, 260/7, scruf 92/14, 226/24.

scurfed(e) *adj.* scaly 270/18.

scyldan I protect. *3 sg.* scyldeþ 30/5; *pp.* gescylded 132/14, gescyld 224/22.

scyll *f.* (*a*) shell, shell-shaped dish 266/17. [Cf. ostor-~.] (*b*) integument, outer covering 254/19.

scyllincg *m.* (*weight*) 166/21. [See p. lxxxii f.]

scytel *m.* dung 242/24, 268/24.

sē, se (I) *pron. adj.* this, that; the. *nsgm.* sē, se 32/21, 34/3, 4, 7, 15, etc.; *nsgf.* sēo, sīo 30/6, 24, 38/7, 14, 46/15, etc.; *nasgn.* þæt 30/14, 20, 21, 36/3, 26, etc.; *asgm.* þone 30/18, 24, 34/2, 36/16, 38/12, etc., þæne 46/4, 70/7, 134/10, 142/20, 170/19, etc.; *asgf.* þā 30/11, 32/1, 3, 7, 34/18, etc.; *gsgmn.* þæs 30/4, 24, 32/18, 34/24, 36/10, etc.; *gdsgf.* þǣre 30/15, 19, 22, 32/10, 16, etc., þāre 32/13, 36/18, 96/2, 100/13, 256/7; *gsgf.* þǣræ 30/17; *dsgmn.* þām 30/14, 16, 38/3, 40/14, 42/24, etc.; *dsgf.* þǣr 266/9; *dsgn.* þan 132/8; *instr. sgmn.* þȳ 36/11, 40/14, 17, 56/17, 86/5, etc.; *napl.* þā 30/16, 17, 32/6, 36/26, 38/12, etc.; *gpl.* þǣra 32/2, 8, 36/23, 48/16, 50/1, etc., þāra 48/23, 50/3, 58/10, 140/11, etc.; *dpl.* þām 36/10, 54/7, 78/8, 90/14, 118/2, etc. (II) *pron. subst.* (*a*) (*in deictic/ anaphoric function*) this, that. *nsgf.* sēo 30/3; *nasgn.* þæt 34/27, 40/12, 18, 44/6², 46/4, etc.; *gsgmn.* þæs 240/14, 252/10; *dsgmn.* þām 40/29, 238/8, 240/12, 242/10, 256/11, etc.; *instr. sgn.* þȳ 256/15; *npl.* þā 124/14. (*b*)(*functioning as antecedent to a relative clause*) that, the one. *nsgm.* sē 104/9, 114/15, 170/2; *dsgm.* þām 262/11, 19, 264/22, 270/24; *dsgf.* þǣre 240/2; *napl.* þā 84/15, 172/23, 234/10², 236/1², 242/19, etc.; *dpl.* þām 248/15,

262/13. (*c*) (*after an antecedent to introduce a relative clause*) that, who, which. *nsgm.* sē 58/15; *nsgf.* sēo 88/15; *nasgn.* þæt 76/10, 206/29, 234/9, 262/8²; *asgf.* þā 152/15²; *dsgm.* þām 128/25; *apl.* þā 208/16. (*d*) (*as an 'independent relative' pronoun*) what; that which. *nsgn.* þæt 236/17, 238/24. (*e*) (*instr., with comparative*) the. þȳ 76/18², 268/28, þē, þe 50/6, 66/ 20. (*f*) (*in adverbial and conjunctional phrases*) nā þæt ān þæt *see* ān ; þæs þe *w. comp.* (so much) the 248/4; þæs þe (*marking agreement*) according to what, as 94/16, 100/24, 174/7, 228/9; þām gelīce þe *see* gelīce ; æfter þām þe *see* æfter ; be þām þe *see* be ; tō þām swȳþe *see* swȳþe ; tō þām . . . þæt *see* tō (IV); tōforan þām þe *see* tōforan ; *instr.* þȳ/þī, þon/ þan *in combinations, see* æfter, for, lǣs, gelīce, tō (IV), wiþ.

sealf *f.* ointment, salve 240/8, 244/14, 19, 24, 250/8, etc., salf 62/17. [Cf. ēag-~.]

sealt *n.* salt 32/4, 40/5, 21, 42/3, 15, etc.

sēaw *n.* juice, sap 38/5, 10, 17, 40/1, 8, etc.

secgan III say. *3 sg.* sægþ 94/16, 100/24, 104/10, 110/11, sagaþ 234/2 (*see note to* M I. 1.); *pl.* secg(e)aþ 174/7, 264/27, sæcgeaþ 102/1; *pret. pl.* sǣdon 176/18, sǣdun 114/13; *pp.* (ge)sǣd 58/13, 60/3, 70/6, 76/17, 82/4, etc.

sēl *adv. comp.*, used as predicative adj. *in* him/hyre biþ ~ he/she/they will be better 50/6, 56/18, 96/17, 114/25, 240/19, etc.

seldon *adv.* seldom 52/3.

sēlest *see* gōd.

self *see* sylf.

sēlost, sēlra, sēlust *see* gōd.

sēo *see* sē. [For sēo 256/27 *see* note to M VII. 15.]

sēoc *adj.* sick, ill, diseased; *used subst.* the patient 110/22, 214/20, 218/4. [Cf. fylle-~, lifer-~, milt-~, mōnoþ-~, scīn-~, wæter-~.]

sēocnys(s) *f.* sickness 88/26. [Cf. lifer-∼, wæter-∼.]

seofenlēafe, seofonlēafe *f.* tormentil CXVIII.

seofon *num.* seven 144/20, 162/7, 164/21, 166/5, 172/14, etc., seofan 124/22, seofone 146/2, seofeone 128/6.

seofontȳne *num.* seventeen 146/5, 204/8, 238/6.

seofoþa *adj.* seventh 146/4.

seolfor *n.* silver 148/2, 170/3, 228/12, 234/13, 242/15.

sēon 1 trickle, flow. *pp.* ġesiġen 124/8.

ġesēon 5 (*a*) see, behold. *inf.* ġesēon 76/18, 228/17; *2 sg.* ġesyxt 262/23; *3 sg.* ġesihþ, ġesyhþ 104/10, 168/17, 19, 21; *pl.* ġesēoþ 252/3; *subj. sg.* ġesēo 104/10, 170/11, 18, 24, 172/24, etc.; *pres. p.* ġesēonde 270/10. (*b*) (*in passive constr.*) seem. *pp.* ġesewen 174/25. [Cf. be-sēon.]

(ġe)sēoþan 2 boil, cook. *subj. sg.* sēoþe 52/6, 86/16, 238/2, 246/19; *imp.* (ġe)sēoþ 30/15, 32/11, 34/10, 18, 36/24, etc.; *pp.* ġesoden 86/29, 122/14, 132/20, 146/28, 154/9, etc. [Cf. be-∼, healfsoden, unġesoden.]

sester *m.* sextarius (*a measure of capacity*) 66/17, 82/18, 86/23, 136/16, 158/26, etc.

ġesetednyss *f.* medical preparation 114/13.

setl *n.* anus 148/22, 23, 268/6.

setlġang *m.* setting (of the sun) 238/7.

(ġe)settan I (*a*) place, put. *imp.* sete 40/12; *pp.* ġeseted 190/6, 244/15, 248/8, ofer ġeseted covered over 256/3, seted 272/5. (*b*) make, prepare. *pret. 3 sg.* ġesette 58/16. (*c*) diminish, become less, abate. *3 sg.* ġeset 172/15; *pres. p.* settende 32/18. [Cf. a-∼, for-∼.]

sex ('seax') *n.* knife 136/10.

shūca *see* sūcan.

sīde, sȳde *f.* side 32/10, 64/9, 76/10, 86/28, 168/1, etc.

ġesīgan 1 sink, set. *inf.* ġesīgan 64/15; *3 sg.* ġesihþ 96/3.

sigefæst *adj.* victorious 234/21.

sigelhweorfa, sigilhweorfa, sigelwearfa *m.* (*a*) cat's-ear L. (*b*) white heliotrope, *or* marigold CXXXVII.

ġesiġen *see* sēon 1.

sigilhweorfa *see* sigelhweorfa.

ġesihþ *f.* (*a*) eyesight 82/12. (*b*) aspect 170/9. (*c*) vision, apparition 30/5, 262/18.

sinetrundæl *adj.* round, globular 58/24.

sinewealt, synewealt *adj.* round 32/6, 94/18, 178/2, 194/18, 198/23, etc.

sinfulle *f.* houseleek, sengreen CXXV.

singallīce *adv.* continually 160/3.

singrēne, syngrēne *f.* butterwort XLIX.

sinu, synu *f.* nerve; sinew 40/11, 12, 56/19, 58/10, 82/20, etc.

sīo *see* sē.

(ġe)sittan 5 (*a*) sit. *pl.* sittaþ 42/2; *pres. p.* sittende 186/10, 220/6. (*b*) settle; develop. *inf.* ġesittan 34/1, 3; *subj. sg.* ġesitte 130/13.

sīþ, sȳþ *m.* (*a*) journey 40/23, 56/3, 262/25, 26. (*b*) time, occasion 256/8; *apl.* sīþan 136/8.

sīþfæt *m.* journey 56/1, 262/25.

sixta *adj.* sixth 146/3.

slāpan, slǣpan 7e sleep. *inf.* slāpan 172/5; *3 sg.* slǣpeþ 262/22.

slǣp, slēp *m.* sleep 98/23, 172/8, 202/7, 254/21, 262/21. [Cf. ofer-∼.]

slǣpan *see* slāpan.

slǣpbǣre *adj.* soporific 200/24.

slǣplēast *f.* sleeplessness 98/22.

slēan 6 strike, smite. *pp.* ġeslegen 118/4, 128/22, 222/17. [Cf. of-∼.]

slege *m.* stroke, blow 78/25.

slēp *see* slǣp.

slite *mf.* sowbread, cyclamen XVIII.

slite *m.* bite, sting 36/7, 8, 12, 38/26, 29, etc.

smale *adv.* small, finely 30/12, 34/26, 36/5, 13, 15, etc., smǣle 202/3.

smǣl *adj.* small, fine 72/2, 16, 74/3, 96/8, 100/18, etc., smel 260/5; *comp.* smǣlra 174/14; *sup.* smǣlest 242/4.

smǣle *adv.* see smale.

smælþearmas *mpl.* intestines 38/12.

smed(e)ma *m.* fine flour 92/22, 180/9, 182/17, 186/24.

smel *see* smæl.

smēocan 2 smoke. *inf.* tō smēocanne 244/5; *subj. sg.* smēoce 244/12, 258/10; *imp.* smēoc 254/23.

smeoro, smeoru(w), smero, smeru *n.* fat, grease 34/2, 40/5, 21, 42/2, 15, etc.

smerowyrt *f.* heartwort, birthwort XX.

smēþe *adj.* flat, smooth 44/15, 212/3. [Cf. un-~.]

smēþian II become smooth. *3 sg.* smēþaþ 42/4.

smīc, smӯc *m.* smoke, vapour 64/6, 70/10, 76/23, 86/16, 182/4, etc.

smocian II smoke, fumigate. *imp.* smoca 66/7, 20.

gesmyltan I appease, smooth. *3 sg.* gesmylteþ 220/18.

smyrenyss *f.* ointment 250/19.

smyrung *f.* ointment, rubbing 264/9.

(ge)smyrwan I smear, rub, apply ointment to. *2 sg.* smyrest 264/8, 13; *3 sg.* smyreþ 270/6; *subj. sg.* gesmyre 208/7, smyrige 70/17, 138/22; *subj. pl.* smyrwen 252/5; *imp.* smyre, smire 36/10, 26, 40/24, 42/3, 28, etc., smyra 78/7, 82/11, 90/2, 94/13, 102/10, etc.; *pret. pl.* smyredon 114/25; *pp.* gesmyred 134/7, 248/21, 252/13, 24, 264/3, etc.

snaca *m.* snake 94/5.

snīþan I cut. *imp.* snīþ 264/22.

snytro *f.* wisdom 234/5.

sogoþa *m.* hiccup, heartburn 132/1, 5.

sōlosēce *f.* deadly nightshade, *or* black nightshade LXXVI.

som . . . som *conj.* whether . . . or 106/10.

some, same *adv., in combination* swa ~ similarly, likewise 44/29, 48/17, 60/20, 80/23, 82/13, etc.

(ge)somnian, gesamnian II collect, gather. *subj. sg.* (ge)somnige 238/25, 240/1, 5, gesamnige 240/6; *imp.* somna 268/5; *pp.* gesomnud 76/23.

somod *adv.* together 248/23, 256/28.

sōna *adv.* immediately, forthwith, quickly 32/18, 34/3, 11, 15, 36/11, etc.; ~ swā *conj.* as soon as 150/10, 170/24.

sorgian II grieve, be anxious. *3 sg.* sorgaþ 262/25.

sōt *n.* soot 260/7.

sōþlīce *adv.* truly, indeed 106/13, 168/18, 182/19, 202/14, 204/21, etc.

spalangio, spalangius *m.* kind of poisonous spider 132/8, 146/9, 176/10, 180/13, 190/12. [See notes to IV. 8 and C. 4.]

sperewyrt *f.* elecampane XCVII.

spīwan I spit; bring up, vomit. *inf.* spīwan 226/21; *subj. sg.* spīwe 34/20, 64/5. [Cf. a-~.]

spīwþa *m.* vomit(ing) 192/20, 226/19, 262/5, 266/12.

spor *n.* track 262/23.

sprengan I scatter, sprinkle. *imp.* sprengc 184/22. [Cf. be-~.]

spring *m.* carbuncle; boil 34/1, 3, 182/28, 190/21, 258/18, etc. [Cf. dēad-~, wund-~.]

stān *m.* stone 46/1, 104/8, 136/2, 138/24, 28, etc.

standan 6 stand. *inf.* standan 82/17; *pl.* standaþ 74/8; *pres. p.* standende 238/25; *pp.* gestanden 30/20. [Cf. æt-~, oþ-~, wiþ-~.]

stānig *see* stǣnig.

stæf *m.* staff 170/17.

stæla *see* stela.

stǣnig *adj.* stony, rocky 180/3, 196/3, 24, 204/25, 210/17, etc., stānig 54/23, 60/6, 124/12.

stǣniht *adj.* stony, rocky 144/12, 148/9.

stede *m.* (*a*) place 34/2. (*b*) (*translating Latin stranguiria*) strangury 244/4, 262/9. [See note to M III. 16.]

stela *m.* stalk, stem 98/17, 102/1, 122/3, 160/2, 166/6, etc., stæla 96/15.

stenc *m.* (I) smell, odour 106/18, 200/11, 218/4. (II) *see* steng.

gestence *adj.* fragrant, having a strong smell 198/25, 200/22.

steng *m.* stake, cudgel, pole 78/25, stenc 106/10.

steorra *m.* star 104/9.

stēran I perfume, fumigate. *imp.*
stēr 52/16, 138/14.

sticca *m.* spoon, spoonful 62/20.

stice *m.* pricking 256/3, 270/28.

gestillan I stop. *3 sg.* gestilleþ
252/7, 11. [Cf. oþstillan, geun-
stillan.]

(ge)stincan 3 smell. *pl.* gestincaþ
106/20; *subj. pl.* stincen 138/19,
146/14. [Cf. fūlstincende.]

stincg, sting, stingc *m.* sting 108/5,
174/6, 190/24, 25, 218/1.

stīþ *adj.* (*a*) stiff, strong 204/13,
218/13; *comp.* stīþ(e)ra 48/12,
192/7. (*b*) strong, violent 182/14;
sup. stīþust 66/6. (*c*) sharp, harsh
98/12, 214/3.

stīþnyss, stīþness *f.* hardness,
stiffness 80/9, 86/9, 92/17.

storm *m.* storm, tempest 234/15.

stōw *f.* place 30/3, 50/23, 52/21,
54/23, 58/20, etc.

strang *adj.* strong 48/22, 64/6, 82/4,
86/16, 112/1, etc.; *sup.* strengost
200/20.

gestrangian II strengthen; comfort. *3 sg.* gestrangaþ 80/17; *pl.*
gestrangiaþ 230/11; *pp.* gestrangod 146/8.

stranglīce *adv.* strongly, vigorously
176/8.

strēa(w)berge, strēowberie *f.* wild
strawberry XXXVIII.

strēdan I scatter, strew. *imp.* strēd
242/1, 266/26; *pp.* gestrēded
252/6, 270/17, gestrēd 194/12.

strengost *see* strang.

strengþ(u) *f.* strength, power 66/13,
106/16, 168/23, 182/11, 200/6, etc.,
strencþ(u) 6/5, strenþ(u) 66/4,5.

strēowberie *see* strēa(w)berge.

styrian I move, stir. *inf.* styrian
226/20; tō styrigenne 76/7. [Cf.
a-~.]

styrung *f.* motion 62/17. [Cf. a-~.]

sūcan 2 suck. *subj. sg.* (O only) shūca
255/14.

sum (I) *pron. adj.* some 32/4, 38/10,
46/21, 48/10, 60/22, etc. (II) *pron.
subst. in pl.* sume some people
102/1, 264/5.

sumor, sumur *m.* summer 64/4,
156/16, 180/25, 270/9.

sundcorn *n.* saxifrage XCIX.

sunnancorn *n.* common gromwell
CLXXX.

sunne *f.* sun 64/14, 18, 70/14, 74/14,
96/3, etc.

sūpan 2 drink. *inf.* sūpan 40/2,
42/18, 21, 126/2, 132/4, etc.; *subj.
sg.* sūpe 48/22; *imp.* sūp 42/11.

sūþernewuda ('-wudu') *m.* southernwood CXXXV.

swā (I) *adv.* so, thus 32/15, 36/7,
38/23, 40/5, 46/19, etc. (II) *conj.*
(*a*) as 74/11, 76/24, 78/7, 86/24,
90/1, etc. (*b*) so that 138/19,
170/16. (III) *in combinations* ~ . . .
~ (1) so . . . as 32/5, 82/21; (2)
according as . . . so 256/18; (3)
either . . . or 266/9; ~ . . . hraþost
as quickly . . . as 106/23; ~ þæt
conj. so that 44/21, 56/23, 58/22,
62/22, 80/22, etc. [See also hwā,
hwǣr, hwylc, some.]

swamm *m.* mushroom 250/18.

swāt *n.* sweating 230/18.

swāþēah *adv.* however, nevertheless
56/13, 90/13, 164/22, 182/11, 18,
etc.

swæc(c) *m.* smell, flavour 58/4, 60/7,
106/20, 142/5, 178/17, etc.

swǣtan I sweat. *subj. sg.* swǣte
29/25.

swǣþer *pron. subst.* whichever (of
two) 266/10.

sweart *adj.* black, dark 48/12, 54/18,
94/18, 194/19, 204/17, etc.

swefel *m.* sulphur 134/3, 162/11,
262/15.

swefn *n.* dream 30/6.

swēg *m.* sound; ringing in the ears
254/4.

swelgan 3 swallow. *inf.* swelgan
254/16; *3 sg.* swylgeþ 250/4;
subj. sg. swelge 74/20, 256/28.
[Cf. for-~.]

geswel(l) *n.* swelling, tumour 32/9,
46/14, 48/3, 18, 19, etc.

sweltan 3 die. *inf.* sweltan 106/20.

swencan I afflict, torment. *pp.* geswenced 56/21.

swētan I sweeten. *pp.* geswētt 34/10,
80/7, 86/12, 92/6, 148/17, etc.

swēte *adj.* sweet 260/21.

(ge)swīcan 1 (*a*) *w. g.* desist, cease.

3 sg. **geswīceþ** 120/12, 230/2; *pl.*
geswīcaþ 58/11. (*b*) depart, go
away. *pl.* **swīcaþ** 52/3. [Cf. **be-~.**]
swīn *n.* swine, pig 100/24.
(ge)swincan 3 labour, suffer. *subj.*
sg. **geswince** 238/20; *subj. pl.*
swincen 248/18.
swīnen, swȳnen *adj.* of swine; pig's
54/7, 66/13, 80/10, 90/12, 98/2.
swinglung *f.* giddiness 248/22.
swīþ *adj.* strong; *sup.* **swīþost**
200/20. [See also **swȳþra.**]
swīþlic, swȳþlic *adj.* excessive,
violent, vehement 32/3, 150/14,
156/17, 164/3, 182/6, etc.
sworetung *f.* (difficult) breathing
246/6.
swylc *pron. subst. and adj.* such
162/22, 234/6; **~ . . . ~** such . . .
as 104/11.
swylce, swilce (I) *adv.* like 58/4,
60/7, 8, 98/2, 104/9, etc. [See also
ēac ~.] (II) *conj.* as if 96/17,
166/28, 168/12, 13, 174/25, etc.
swylcnyss *f.* quality 182/13.
swyle *m.* swelling, tumour 54/6, 7,
68/14, 15, 90/12, etc. [Cf. **fōt-~.**]
geswync *n.* hardship, fatigue; **nā**
mycel tō ~e not much hardship
56/2.
swȳra *m.* neck 36/14, 16, 38/3, 44/17,
54/15, etc.
geswyrf *n.* filings 148/2, 242/15.
swȳþe, swīþe *adv.* very, very much,
strongly 30/6, 9, 12, 14, 32/25,
etc.; **tō þām ~** to that degree
174/6; *sup.* **swȳþost, swīþost,**
swīþust (*a*) mainly, chiefly 60/4,
102/4, 108/19, 208/12, 17. (*b*) most
strongly 138/19, 140/14.
swȳþlīce *adv.* strongly, greatly 82/10.
swȳþra *adj. comp.* (stronger,) right
172/12, 234/18, 264/1, 24, 270/28,
etc. [See also **swīþ.**]
syde *m.* decoction 196/13.
syfeþa *m. or fpl.* bran 198/10.
gesȳgan I soak. *3 sg.* **gesȳgþ** 80/24.
sylf, self (*a*) *adj.* same 30/17, 38/20,
40/2, 44/19, 50/10, etc. (*b*) *pron.*
himself *etc.* 76/8, 78/6, 96/4, 108/
24, 128/10, etc.
sylfwylles *adv.* spontaneously 202/12.
syllan I give. *inf.* **syllan** 58/15, 70/7,

114/4, 182/12; *2 sg.* **sylst** 112/1,
syllest 204/9; *subj. sg.* **sylle** 52/7,
202/4; *imp.* **syle** 30/23, 32/1, 15,
17, 36/19, etc. (**gesyle** 1 ×, 224/5);
pret. 3 sg. **sealde** 13/10; *pp.*
geseald 174/5, 186/8, 208/1, 246/
7, 248/6, etc.
syllīce *adv.* wonderfully 256/9.
symle *adv.* always 38/24, 190/3,
224/15, 23, 256/15.
synderlic *adj.* exceptionally good
116/4.
synderlīce *adv.* exclusively, especially 116/6.
syndrige *adv.* separately 94/10.
syþþan, siþþan (I) *adv.* afterwards,
then 44/23, 48/2, 56/17, 70/2, 17,
etc. (II) *conj.* after, when 30/20,
46/15, 48/4, 86/29.
syx, six *num.* six 68/22, 92/22, 202/
26, 242/15.
gesyxt *see* **gesēon** 5.

T

tācn *n.* sign; constellation 104/15.
tāl *f.* fault, defect 78/8. [See note to
XXXII. 1.]
tāwian II prepare. *pp.* **getāwod**
262/19.
tægl *m.* tail 246/14.
tæglhǣr *n.* hair of the tail 262/24.
tǣlan I blame, deride. *pp.* **tǣled**
104/11.
tǣsan I tease (wool). *pp.* **getǣsed**
224/3.
tǣsl *see* **wulfes ~.**
tealgor *f.* twig, branch 114/7.
telgra *m.* twig, branch 132/19,
194/4, 17, 228/9, 232/11, etc.
getenge *adj.* oppressing, afflicting;
in combination **bēon ~** afflict 40/7,
132/1.
tēon 2 (*a*) draw. *imp.* **tēoh** 254/15.
[Cf. **a-~.**] (*b*) constipate. *pp.*
getogen 256/18.
tēorian II tire, fatigue. *pp.* **getēorud**
156/17, **getēorad** 34/9, **getēored**
1/21.
teors *m.* penis 254/12, 260/12, 262/2.
tēoþa *adj.* tenth 146/6, 252/3.
teter *m.* ringworm 92/12, 14, 162/9,
242/9, 11.
tēþ *see* **tōþ.**

tīd *f.* (*a*) hour 40/9, 54/8, 114/11, 216/6, 252/3. (*b*) time 236/2, 266/9. [Cf. **winter-~**.]

tīdre, tȳddre *adj.* fragile, tender 182/3, 212/18.

till *adj.* (HO *only*) good, serviceable 236/25, 237/22.

tīma *m.* time 76/3, 138/15, 232/13; *dsg.* **tīmam** 178/19.

tit(t) *m.* nipple 64/11, 128/10.

tō (I) *adv.* (*a*) to, on (somebody, something) 40/17, 42/3, 78/26, 96/18, 106/23, etc. (*b*) too (much) 32/20, 42/27, 202/2. (II) *prep. w. d.* (*a*) to, on, for, at 30/9, 12, 16, 32/8, 34/27, etc. (*b*) with, in addition to 44/1. [Cf. **þǣr-~**.] (*c*) as, as a 74/9, 11, 230/10. (*d*) according to 246/20. (*e*) from 240/1. [See note to *M* II. 2.] (III) *conj.* (O *only*) until 237/7. [See note to *M* I. 6.] (IV) *in combinations* **foran ~** *see* **foran**; **~ fylles** *see* **fyllu**; **~ þām swȳþe** *see* **swȳþe**; **~ þām . . . þæt** so . . . that 110/16, 114/11², 220/17; **~ þan þæt** *conj.* in order that 250/9; **~ þȳ þæt** *conj.* in order that 76/18, 82/14.

tōberstan 3, *in pp.* **tōborsten** (*a*) ruptured 104/1. (*b*) with sores *or* rashes breaking out 190/21.

tōborstennyss *f.* rupture 232/5.

tōblāwan 7e blow upon. *3 sg.* **tōblǣwþ** 168/18.

tōbrǣdan I expand. *3 sg.* **tōbrǣdeþ** 166/6, 232/11; *pl.* **tōbrǣdaþ** 96/5.

tōbrecan 4 break (to pieces), destroy. *3 sg.* **tōbricþ, tōbrycþ** 144/22, 226/10, **tōbreceþ** 246/5; *imp.* **tōbrec** 270/28; *pp.* **tōbrocen** 30/11, 60/15, 182/3, 270/26.

tōbrȳsan I bruise. *pp.* **tōbrȳsed** 70/21.

tōceorfan 3 cut up. *inf.* **tōceorfan** 182/9; *pp.* **tōcorfen** 260/6.

tōcyme *m.* approach, arrival 266/9.

tōdǣlan I divide. *imp.* **tōdǣl** 236/14; *pp.* **tōdǣled** 192/14.

tōdrǣfan I expel. *3 sg.* **tōdrǣfþ** (BH) 72/3, 82/24 (-**drēf**- V).

tōdrīfan 1 expel, dispel. *3 sg.* **tōdrīfþ** 50/19, 64/13, 110/11, 258/14, **tōdrīfeþ** 258/20.

tōfaran 6 go away, disappear. *3 sg.* **tōfærþ** 68/13, 72/13, 92/11, 128/10.

tōferian I expel, disperse. *3 sg.* **tōfereþ** 60/12, 64/21, 78/17, 86/9, 90/14.

tōflēogan 2, *in pp.* **tōflogen** covered with rashes 256/13.

tōflēon 2 be dispersed. *3 sg.* **tōflīhþ** (BH) 124/9 (-**flȳþ** V).

tōflōwan 7f be destroyed. *3 sg.* **tōflēwþ** 168/21.

tōforan *prep. w. d.* before 138/15, 170/20, 204/9; **~ þām þe** *conj.* before 102/11.

tōgang *m.* access, attack 266/10. [See note to *M* X. 17.]

tōgædere *adv.* together 80/22, 23, 86/29, 198/10, 222/22, **tōgædre** 188/26.

getog *see* **getoh.**

tōgotennyss *f.* effusion 184/1, **tōgotenyss** 188/19.

togung *f.* spasm 82/20, 28, 172/16, 21.

getoh, getog *n.* spasm 258/16.

tōlǣteness ('**tōlǣtennyss**') *f.* despair 182/21.

tōlȳsan I reduce, remove (pains, swellings) (*rendering Latin* (dis)-solvere). *3 sg.* **tōlȳseþ** 188/23, 24, 210/11, 216/20; *pl.* **tōlȳsaþ** 182/27.

tord *n.* turd 256/24, 258/5, 7, 9, 12, etc.

tornīge ('**torenīge**') *adj.* blear-eyed 62/1, 98/15.

tōsceacan 6 drive out, expel. *3 sg.* **tōsceaceþ** 264/25.

tōsceādan 7a scatter. *3 sg.* **tōsceādeþ** 256/9.

tōslītan 1 (*a*) bite. *subj. sg.* **tōslīte** 36/4, 42/8; *pp.* **tōsliten** 264/23. (*b*) destroy. *3 sg.* **tōslīt** 88/20; *pp.* **tōsliten** 234/17. (*c*) tear open, lacerate. *pp.* **tōsliten** 258/26. (*d*) *in pp.* **tōsliten** serrated (*of leaves*) 206/2, 232/12.

tōslūpan 2 be dissipated *or* dispelled. *3 sg.* **tōslȳpeþ** 104/22; *pl.* **tōslūpaþ** 186/27.

tōsomne *adv.* together 32/14, 34/24, 36/3, 42/6, 44/9, etc.

tōstingan 3 pierce, perforate. *imp.* **tōsting** 264/2.

tōþ, *napl.* tēþ *m.* tooth 32/9, 48/21, 23, 76/1, 120/17, etc.

tōþece *m.* toothache 32/7, 116/20, 120/16, 126/1, 130/1, etc.

tōþindan 3 swell. *pp.* tōþunden 46/20, 64/11.

tōþrēoman *mpl.* gums 228/1, 3, 250/23, 264/13, 272/4.

tōþundennyss, tōþundenness *f.* swollenness, swelling 64/13, 134/1, 140/5, 198/15, 17, etc., tōþun-denyss 216/20.

tōþwræc *m.* toothache 272/1.

tremes(s) *see* trymes(s).

trēow *n.* tree 118/19, 238/8, 24. [Cf. fīc-∼.]

trēowcyn(n) *n.* kind of tree 68/23.

trum *adj.* strong, able to resist 46/11, 168/24, 200/21. [Cf. un-∼.]

trymes(s), tremes(s) *mf.*, try-mes(s)e *f.* (*weight*) 30/13, 23, 32/10, 14, 16, etc. [See p. lxxxiii.]

getrymman I make (teeth) stay firmly. *3 sg.* getrymeþ 142/19, 240/17.

trȳwen *adj.* wooden 70/22, 150/20, 158/21.

tuddur, tudder *n.* embryo, foetus 106/5, 8, 210/4.

tunge *f.* tongue 42/20, 90/7, 264/22. [See also hundes ∼.]

tungol *n.* star 234/15.

tunsin(c)gwyrt *f.* white hellebore CXL.

turf *f.* tussock; *dsg.* tyrf 206/1.

tuwa *adv.* twice 148/17. [See also twie.]

tux *n.* (canine *or* molar) tooth 170/4, 272/1, 4, 6.

twā, twēgen *num.* two 30/13, 32/5, 16, 34/13, 19, etc.

twentig *num.* twenty 146/6, 162/5.

twie, twigea *adv.* twice 92/6, 230/5.

twig. *n.* twig 48/1, 98/2, 102/1, 132/9, 138/14, etc.

twigea *see* twie.

tȳddernyss *f.* weakness 42/10.

tȳdrian II become weak. *subj. pl.* tȳdrien 40/23.

tȳn *num.* ten 66/16, 82/25, 182/11, 202/3, 206/19.

tȳran I run with tears. *pres. p.* tȳrende 32/1.

tyrf *see* turf.

tyrwe *f.* (*a*) resin 154/8, 194/20, 268/14. (*b*) tar 244/19.

þ

þā (I) *adv.* then 234/7. (II) *conj.* when 114/5, 234/6. (III) *pron. see* sē.

geþafian II allow, permit. *3 sg.* geþafaþ 80/20, 264/9; *imp.* geþafa 54/1.

þām *see* sē.

þanon, þanun *adv.* thence 70/7, 82/6, 102/2, 110/6, 136/12, etc.

þāra, þāre; þāron *see* sē; þǣron.

þās *see* þes.

þǣne *see* sē.

þǣr (I) *adv.* there 48/17, 54/1, 96/18, 116/3, 134/20, etc. (II) *conj.* where 40/6, 60/4, 80/4, 92/13, 118/18, etc. (III) *pron. see* sē.

þǣra, þǣræ *see* sē.

þǣræfter *adv.* after it 150/12.

þǣræt *adv.* in it, on it 36/27, 54/2.

þǣre *see* sē.

þǣrin *adv.* into it 246/17.

þǣrmid *adv.* with it 36/26, 40/24, 50/6, 52/15, 58/11, etc.

þǣrof *adv.* of it, from it, with it 34/23, 74/20, 92/24, 132/6, 136/15.

þǣron *adv.* on it, on them, in them 38/20, 40/28, 42/15, 138/28, 268/23, etc., þāron 138/24.

þǣrto *adv.* to it, to them 32/4, 11, 40/3, 44/20, 46/15, etc.

þæs, þæt *pron. see* sē.

þæt *conj.* (*a*) (*introducing a noun clause*) that 34/16, 36/9, 38/6, 7², 30, etc. (*b*) (*introducing an adverbial clause of purpose, result, manner*) (so) that, (in order) that, (in such a way) that 30/8, 32/18, 122/11, 158/4, 170/13, etc. [See also oþ-∼, swā (III), tō (IV), wiþ.]

þē *see* þū.

þe (I) *indecl. relative particle* who, which, that 30/2, 24, 34/3, 40/14, 17, etc. (II) *as an enclitic element in conjunctions, see* be, gelīce, sē (IIf), þēah, wiþ.

þēah (I) *adv.* however, yet 128/7. (II) *conj.* (also ∼ þe) although, even if; if 48/17, 74/19, 118/1, 134/20, 136/21, etc., þēh 102/11.

þearf *f.* need 54/2, 78/2, 82/18, 22, 158/27, etc. [Cf. nēad-~.]

þearle *adv.* very much, exceedingly; hard 30/9, 34/14, 36/6, 72/2, 86/23, etc.

þearm *m.* entrail, intestine 100/20, 130/22. [Cf. bæc-~, smæl-~as.]

þēh *see* þēah.

þencan I (*a*) think. *imp.* þenc 136/11. (*b*) intend. *2 sg.* þencst 136/11.

geþēod *n.* language 50/22, 100/23, 126/11, 22, 128/20, þēod 218/9.

geþēodan I join together, heal. *3 sg.* geþēodeþ 206/24, 220/3.

þēodscipe *m.* people 110/6.

þēoh *n.* thigh 36/18, 23, 50/2, 56/16, 140/11, etc.

þēohwræc *m.* pain in the thighs 258/7.

þēos *see* þes.

þes (I) *pron. adj.* this, that. *nsgm.* þes 230/2, 238/18; *nsgf.* þēos 30/2, 44/14, 48/9, 50/13, 22, etc.; *nasgn.* þis, þys 80/18, 90/21, 236/22; *asgm.* þysne, þisne 182/8, 214/12, 238/13, 246/18; *asgf.* þās 32/20, 40/17, 42/8, 46/9, 50/17, etc.; *gsgmn.* þys(s)es, þisses 54/3, 182/10, 232/14; *gdsgf.* þysse, þisse 48/12, 15, 52/6, 13, 56/22, etc.; *gsgf.* þysre 214/13, þyssæ 56/13; *dsgn.* þyssum 48/6, 172/4, 246/20; *napl.* þās 48/14, 58/13, 16, 82/5, 190/9, etc.; *gpl.* þyssa, þissa 72/15, 92/5, 168/16, 186/2, 17, etc.; *dpl.* þys(s)um, þis(s)um 58/15, 96/5, 180/10, 226/9, 234/3, etc. (II) *pron. subst.* this, that. *nsgf.* þēos 168/21; *asgn.* þis, þys 58/26, 76/23, 98/4, 116/4, 134/20, etc.; *gsgn.* þys(s)es 98/10, 234/7.

þicce *adj.* thick, dense 166/28, 232/ 7.

(ge)þicgan I partake of, eat, take. *inf.* þicgan 250/3, þicgean, þycgean 72/16, 78/20, 110/15, 23, 112/1, etc., þiggean 92/16, þigccean 32/2; *2 sg.* þigest 236/24, 270/9; *3 sg.* þigeþ, þygeþ 62/24, 158/3, 216/11, þigþ 52/22; *subj. sg.* (ge)þicge, (ge)þycge 34/24,

36/1, 38/11, 100/7, 104/2, etc.; *imp.* þyge, þige 30/13, 34/27, 38/6; *pp.* geþiged, geþyged 34/21, 88/16, 144/3, 150/16, 198/5, etc.

þicnyss, þycnyss *f.* thickness 74/23, 202/2.

þigen *f.* (*a*) what has been eaten, food 44/22. (*b*) partaking of 92/10.

þīn (I) *pron. adj.* your 34/16, 36/14, 42/6, 54/4, 224/9, etc. (II) *pron. subst.* yours 236/16.

þincan I (*a*) seem. *subj. sg.* þince 78/23; *pp.* geþūht 200/18. (*b*) seem good *or* fit. *subj. sg.* þince 64/25.

geþind *n.* swelling 92/8.

þindan 3 swell. *subj. sg.* þinde 256/22. [Cf. a-~, for-~, tō-~.]

þing *n.* thing 102/14, 182/10, 190/9, 224/12, þincg 74/11, 170/23, 176/18, 222/21, þingc 64/8, 74/ 9, 78/22, 100/19; **on eallum þingum, þingon** on all accounts, in all respects 108/3, 176/17. [Cf wīf-~.]

þiss-, þyss- *see* þes.

þistel *m.* thistle 174/13. [Cf. wudu-~.]

(ge)þolian II (*a*) suffer, undergo. *3 sg.* þolaþ 102/13, 214/12; *subj. sg.* þolie 140/1, þolige 138/21, 202/1, 214/21, 224/7; *subj. pl.* þoligen 102/10, 220/5; *pres. p.* þoligende 144/14, 152/4, þolegende 124/4. (*b*) remain, be left (over). *subj. sg.* geþolige 238/25.

þon, þone *see* sē.

þonne (I) *adv.* (*a*) then 30/8, 10[1], 12, 13, 14, etc. (*b*) however, on the other hand 104/21, 106/7, 182/5, 248/15. (II) *conj.* (*a*) when 30/7, 10[2], 19, 34/21, 52/16, etc. (*b*) (*after a comparative*) than 54/2, 58/23, 262/23.

þost *m.* excrement 264/29, 266/2, 5, 7.

þræd *m.* thread 54/15, 150/8. [Cf. hefel-~.]

þrēo *see* þrȳ.

þrēohyrne *adj.* triangular 226/14.

þrēot(t)ȳne *num.* thirteen 146/4, 150/7, 204/8, 224/26.

þridda, þrydda *adj.* third 30/16, 32/8, 36/25, 40/14, 52/6, etc.

þrīt(t)iġ *num.* thirty 224/26, 248/15.

þriwa *adv.* three times 42/23, 92/6, 128/6, 136/8, 148/18, etc.

þrote, þrotu *f.* throat 36/14, 42/20.

þrōwian II suffer (from). *pl.* þrō-wiaþ 244/18, 248/22, 266/15; *subj. sg.* þrōwie 262/11; *subj. pl.* þrōwien 266/15; *pres. p.* þrōwi-ende 36/21.

þrȳ, þrēo *num.* three 32/10, 12, 14, 15, 21, etc.

þū *pron.* thou, you. *n.* þū 30/6, 7, 10, 32/5, 34/12, etc.; *ad.* þē 36/14, 78/22, 154/21, 172/3, 220/24, etc., *refl.* þē 136/12, 154/17, 234/14, 21, 242/19, etc.

ġeþūf *adj.* luxuriant, bushy 174/3, 4, 178/14, 212/17; *comp.* ġeþūfra 196/5.

þūma *m.* thumb 42/24, 238/9.

þunwong *f.* temple (of the head) 98/19, 126/17, 144/25, 146/29, 162/26.

þurh *prep. w. a.* through (*local and causal*) 32/23, 38/16, 46/20, 72/18, 76/19, etc.; ~ hit self, ~ hy selfe, ~ hy sylfe (*Latin* per se) by itself, unmixed 76/8, 78/5, 128/9, 140/7, 150/15.

þurhhǣlan I heal thoroughly. *3 sg.* þurhhǣleþ 74/12.

þurst *m.* thirst 90/6, 8, 188/7.

þus *adv.* thus, so 30/6, 52/17, 100/19, 234/4, 5, etc.

þwǣnan I soften. *inf.* þwǣnan 38/22.

þwēan 6 wash. *subj. sg.* þwēa 70/2, 256/15; *imp.* þweah 52/15, 158/2, 162/20, þweh 92/13.

þwīnan 1 become less swollen. *pl.* þwīneþ 40/24.

þȳfel *m.* plant 52/14.

þȳ *see* sē.

þȳn I press, squeeze. *pp.* ġeþȳd 256/27.

þynne *adj.* thin 54/13, 192/15, 204/14.

ġeþynnian II diminish (*tr.*). *3 sg.* ġeþynnaþ 254/3.

þynnyss *f.* weakness 82/12.

þyrniht, þyrnyht *adj.* thorny 198/22, 23, 204/15, 216/12, 13, etc.

þyrstan I be thirsty. *pres. p.* þyrs-tende 188/7.

þȳstru *f.* dimness 268/3.

U

ufan *adv.* above 248/10.

ufera *adj. comp.* upper 238/11, 19.

ufeweard, ufewerd *adj.* (*a*) upper part of 60/4, 94/1, 154/14, 174/4, 13, etc. (*b*) (*used as subst.*) on ufewe(a)rdum at the top 192/16, 194/4.

unbeġān *adj.* uncultivated 158/16, 166/6.

unbindan 3 (*a*) release, free. *inf.* unbindan 52/13, 18; *pp.* unbunden 126/8. (*b*) untie, unbind. *subj. sg.* unbinde 88/1.

unclǣne *adj.* not clean, impure 170/13.

uncūþ *adj.* unknown, strange 42/1, 130/13.

uncyst *f.* disease 242/3, 252/16.

under (I) *adv.* under (it, etc.) 186/10, 194/22, 208/14, 224/5. (II) *prep.* (*a*) *w. a.* under (*direction*) 90/7, 156/20, 254/21, 262/13, 21; ~ ... neoþan under(neath) 268/6. (*b*) *w. d.* under (*position*) 220/5, 238/23, 264/21.

ungedered *adj.* uninjured 224/23.

unfeferiġ *adj.* free from fever 104/21.

unfortredde, unfortrædde *f.* knot-grass XIX.

unhāl *adj.* unsound, sick 34/12, 262/21.

unhālwendlic *adj.* incurable 236/12.

unhǣlo *f.* disease, infirmity 42/12, 262/14.

ungehēafdud *adj.* not come to a head (*of a swelling*) 48/3.

unhȳre *adj.* dreadful, monstrous 30/5.

unlācniġendlic *adj.* incurable 182/19.

unmihticnyss *see* unmihtilicnyss.

unmihtiġness *f.* weakness 174/8.

unmihtilicnyss *f.* impossibility, in-ability 24/27, 190/20. [See note to CXLVIII. 1.]

unnytlic *adj.* useless 180/7, 186/3.

unnytlicnyss *f.* uselessness 144/7, 146/16.

ungerisene *n.* inconvenience 270/19.

unryne *m.* diarrhoea 112/2.

unsār *adj.* free from pain 250/23.

unsmēþe *adj.* rough 102/8, 104/8.

un(ge)soden *adj.* not boiled *or* cooked 48/5, 132/21.

ġeunstillan I disturb. *pl.* ġeunstillaþ 262/20.

ungesylt *adj.* unsalted 90/13.

untrum *adj.* weak, sick 174/18, 266/9; *comp.* **untrumra** 72/17.

untrumnyss *f.* illness, disease; weakness 44/24, 29, 46/1, 3, 52/8, etc.

untwēolīce *adv.* undoubtedly 214/20.

ungeþyldiġ *adj.* impatient 214/13. [See note to CLXX. 1.]

ungewendendlic *adj.* unchanging; chronic 236/12.

unwēriġ *adj.* not tired 34/11.

up, upp *adv.* up, upwards 32/23, 42/24, 96/4, 108/24, 154/19, etc.

upgang *m.* rising 64/14, 18, 70/14, 74/14, 242/13.

uppan *prep. w. a.* upon 100/21.

upryne *m.* rising 238/7.

upweard *adv.* upwards; ~ **licġean** lie on one's back 214/13.

ūre *pron. adj.* our 50/22, 100/23, 114/12, 126/11, 22, etc.

ūt *adv.* out 38/16, 42/27, 46/24, 52/15, 17, etc.

ūtan *adv.* (on the) outside 36/17, 246/13, 256/23, 270/30. [See also **ymb.**]

ūtene *adv.* outside, externally 64/23.

ūteweard *adj.* outer part of 120/3, 216/14.

ūtgang *m.* anus 260/2, 266/13.

ūtryne *m.* running out, flux 208/17.

ūtsiht *f.* diarrhoea, dysentery 64/24, 176/25, 180/16, 182/16, 190/14, etc.

W

wād *n.* (B *only*) woad 112/9.

wāg *m.* wall 68/7, 74/7, 116/26, 180/3.

wagian II move, be loose. *subj. pl.* **wagegen** 76/1.

wagung *f.* looseness 142/18, 240/16.

gewald *see* **geweald.**

wamb, womb *f.* stomach, belly 32/16, 34/26, 38/5, 7, 8, etc.

(ge)wanian II (*a*) lessen, diminish

(*tr.*). *3 sg.* **gewanaþ** 30/24, 46/7, 128/4, 264/2. (*b*) wane. *pres. p.* **wanigende** 104/14, 228/24.

wanwegende, wanwæġende *adj.* waning 52/14, 54/15.

warnian II take warning, beware. *imp.* **warna** 228/13, 264/26.

(ge)wǣcan I (*a*) weaken, afflict. *3 sg.* **gewǣceþ** 106/22; *pp.* **gewǣht** 66/12. (*b*) weaken, lessen. *3 sg.* **gewǣceþ** 102/19.

wæġbrǣde *see* **wegbrǣde.**

(ge)wǣġe *n.* weight 30/13, 23, 32/11, 14, 17, etc.

wælwyrt *see* **wealwyrt.**

wǣndan *see* **wendan.**

wǣpen *n.* weapon 106/22.

wǣpned *adj.* male 250/9, 14.

wǣrhbrǣde *see* **weargbrǣde.**

gewǣscan, (ge)wescan ('wascan') 6 wash. *imp.* **gewǣsc** 56/17, 138/5, **(ge)wesc** 42/3, 66/17. [See note to II. 19.]

wǣstm *m.* fruit 98/18, 158/3, 12, 170/5, 232/12, etc.

wǣt *adj.* wet, moist 44/15, 152/22, 166/7, 176/21, 196/23, etc.

wǣta *m.* (*a*) liquid, fluid 34/24, 46/20, 84/15, 124/23, 136/18, etc. (*b*) (evil) humour 256/20.

(ge)wǣtan I moisten. *inf.* **wǣtan** 76/19; *subj. pl.* **wǣten** 252/5; *imp.* **(ge)wǣt** 246/10, 264/15.

wǣter *n.* water 30/16, 20, 23, 32/17, 21, etc. [Cf. **wylle-~**.]

wǣterādl *f.* dropsy 256/27, 266/5, 12, 13.

wǣteriġ *adj.* watery 52/21.

wǣtersēoc *adj.* dropsical 90/6, 136/17, 190/19, 200/6, 266/6.

wǣtersēocnyss *f.* dropsy 72/14, 88/22, 136/14, 162/5, 190/17.

wǣterwyrt *f.* water starwort, *or* common maidenhair XLVIII.

wē *pron.* we 52/1, 13, 58/2, 13, 64/21, etc.

geweald *n.* (*a*) genitals. *dsg.* **gewealde** 58/21, 150/10, **wealde** 5/10; *apl.* **geweald** 224/4; *gpl.* **gewealda** 50/1, **gewalda** 50/3. (*b*) power 172/1.

weall *m.* wall 122/18, 190/6.

weallan 7c (*a*) flow. *subj. sg.* **wealle**

32/23. (b) boil, be hot. *pres. p.*
weallende 116/3, 138/8. [Cf. **a-~,**
be-~.]

wealwyrt, wælwyrt *f.* dwarf elder,
danewort, wallwort XCIII, 258/1.

weargbrǣde *f.* sore, ulcer 40/26,
weargebrǣde 2/26, **wærhbrǣde**
66/21.

wearm *adj.* warm 30/21, 32/15, 17,
21, 36/22, etc.

wearmian II become warm. *3 sg.*
wearmaþ 130/12.

wearr *m.* callosity, piece of hard
skin 258/24, 260/1, 264/15, 16.

wearte *f.* wart 54/6, 7, 68/16, 78/18,
19, etc.

weax, wex *n.* wax 148/4, 212/10,
256/25.

weaxan, wexan 7c grow, wax. *inf.*
weaxen 68/7, **wexen** 68/4; *3 sg.*
weaxeþ 250/8, **wexeþ** 98/5, 200/
20, **wyxþ** 60/6, **wihst** 48/10; *pl.*
weaxaþ 46/1, 194/17, **wexaþ**
254/1, 264/14, **weaxeþ** 138/28,
wexeþ 58/21; *subj. sg.* **weaxe**
40/26, **wexe** 66/21, 80/20, 84/8;
subj. pl. **wexen** 70/1, 136/2, 138/24,
144/13, 19, etc.; *pres. p.* **wexende**
206/26; *pp.* **gewexen** 118/19. [Cf.
for-~.]

wecce ('wæcce') *f.* waking 254/21.

wēdan I be furious, rage. *pres. p.*
wēdende 270/22.

wēde *adj.* mad 264/21.

wēdeberge *f.* white hellebore CXL.

wēdehund *m.* mad dog 36/12, 42/8,
46/18, 84/13, 132/16, etc., **wōdenhund** 2/3.

weg *m.* road 90/18, 114/15, 16,
122/18, 132/14, etc.

wegbrǣde, wǣgbrǣde *f.* greater
plantain, waybread II.

wel(l) *adv.* (a) well 38/12, 56/17, 20,
58/6, 23, etc. (b) quite, very 180/6,
190/4.

wēn *f.* hope, expectation 40/9.

wēnan I (a) think. *1 sg.* **wēne** 132/4,
234/5; *2 sg.* **wēnst** 56/23; *3 sg.*
wēneþ 262/8. (b) *w. g.* expect.
subj. sg. **wēne** 40/9.

wendan, wǣndan I turn. *pl.* **wǣn-
daþ** 96/3; *subj. sg.* **wende** 136/12;
pp. **gewend** 118/21. [Cf. **a-~.**]

weolcrēad *adj.* purple 238/16. [See
also **wolcenrēad.**]

weorc *n.* work, action 114/5.

weornian II fade. *pl.* **weorniaþ**
136/26.

(ge)weorpan, (ge)wurpan 3 cast,
throw. *3 sg.* **weorpeþ** 268/7; *imp.*
(ge)wurp 46/21, 170/20; *pret. 3
sg.* **gewearp** 100/21. [Cf. **a-~.**]

weorþ *adj.* worthy, deserving 234/7.

weorþan 3 become. *subj. sg.* **weorþe**
34/8; *pp.* **geworden** 64/25.

weorud *n.* army 236/25.

wer *m.* man, male 98/5, 136/22, 23,
176/17, 250/12, etc.

wered *adj.* sweet 60/6, 194/5, 216/10.
[See also **byrging.**]

wermōd *m.* wormwood, absinth CII,
92/5, 138/22, 156/6, 264/19.

(ge)wēsan I soak, macerate. *imp.*
(ge)wēs (BH *only*) 42/3, 56/17, 66/
17, 138/5 (*see note to* II. 19); *pp.*
gewēsed 134/10, 144/25, 158/13,
188/10, 210/13, etc.

(ge)wescan *see* **(ge)wæscan.**

wex, wexan *see* **weax, weaxan.**

ġewhylc *see* **ġehwylc.**

wīd *adj.* wide 80/22.

wīf *n.* woman, female; wife 50/4,
64/11, 72/17, 90/12, 98/5, etc.

wīfman(n) *m.* woman 70/1, 122/10,
162/22, 244/5, 7, etc.

wīfgemāna *m.* coitus 242/21, 22,
268/27.

wīfþing *n.* coitus 246/14, 15,
268/29.

wihst *see* **weaxan.**

(ge)wiht *n.* weight 62/11, 68/23,
70/11, 72/15, 78/16, etc.

wildēor, wilddēor, wylddēor *n.*
wild beast 114/8, 136/9, 208/2,
224/13, 234/8, etc.

willa, wylla *m.* desire; pleasure
254/11, 13, 262/1.

willan, wyllan *anom. vb.* wish, want.
1 sg. **wille** 236/22; *2 sg.* **wylt**
224/24; *3 sg.* **wyle** 170/14, 218/10;
subj. sg. **wille, wylle** 34/1, 16,
38/22, 44/7, 54/4, etc.; *subj. pl.*
wyllon 106/23; *pret. 3 sg.* **wolde**
34/3; *negative forms subj. sg.* **nelle**
46/22, 130/19, **nylle** 16/6.

wīn *n.* wine 32/8, 15, 34/6, 10, 24, etc.

gewin(n) *n.* suffering, pain 236/20, 21.

wīnberie *f.* grape 198/16.

wind *m.* wind 106/19.

wīngeard *m.* vine 226/13.

winnan 3 suffer. *subj. pl.* winnen 236/5.

winter *m.* winter 76/3.

wintertīd *f.* winter time 90/15.

gewis *adj.* (*a*) certain 116/5. (*b*) *w. g.* acquainted with 234/4.

wīse *f.* stalk with leaves, plant 84/18.

wīse *f.* manner, method 168/4, 218/6, 236/12.

wīslīce *adv.* wisely 240/17.

gewis(s)līce *adv.* with certainty, certainly 40/13, 128/4, 134/23.

witan *pret. pr.* know. *pret. 1 sg.* wiste 234/7; *negative form pres. p.* nytende 104/10, 156/20.

gewitan *pret. pr.* get to know, learn. *inf.* tō gewitanne 234/7.

gewītan 1 (*a*) depart, go. *3 sg.* gewīteþ 38/3, 7, 202/13, 236/3, 266/11; *pl.* gewītaþ 242/20. (*b*) die. gewīteþ 168/20.

witega *m.* prophet 234/17.

gewitlēast *f.* madness, insanity 172/17, gewitlǣst 17/20, gewitlēst 142/10.

witodlīce *adv.* truly, certainly, indeed 58/13, 64/23, 66/11, 76/5, 82/13, etc.

wiþ, wyþ *prep.* (*a*) against, (as a cure *or* remedy) for (a disease, a patient) *w. a.* 30/15, 19, 32/1, 3, 44/16, etc.; *w. d.* 30/5, 32/10, 13, 16, 34/25, etc.; *w. instr.* 40/17. (*b*) with *w. a.* 34/2, 40/5, 12, 42/2, 56/7, etc.; *w. d.* 236/4, 252/10, 12, 24, 254/20, etc. (*c*) (*local*) against, next to, near *w. a.* 68/7, 74/8, 90/18, 122/18, 154/12, etc. (*d*) *in combinations* ~ . . . tō *w. inf.* in order to 76/7, 240/20, 242/11, 264/7, 270/2, etc.; ~ þæt (*in affirmative phrases*) (1) (in order) that not, lest 64/5, 66/12, 21, 68/2, 82/27, etc., (2) (in order) that 148/11, 150/6, 250/22, 272/6; ~ þæt (*in negative phrases*) (1) (in order) that not, lest 52/1, 146/19, 154/17, 224/7, (2) (in order) that 56/12, 90/6, 160/1, 188/13; ~

þæt þæt (in order) that not, lest 62/15; ~ þon þe (in order) that not, lest 32/23, 38/13, 16; ~ þon þe . . . (man) ne (mæge) . . . 7 (he spīwe) in order that . . . and lest 34/20.

wiþæftan *see* hēr.

wiþerrǣde *adj.* disagreeable, rough 158/8, 198/22, 214/4, 216/15.

wiþerrǣdnyss *f.* ferocity 272/8.

wiþerweard *adj.* rebellious 264/7.

wiþrian II resist, act against. *3 sg.* wiþrǣþ 88/17.

wiþstandan 6 act as a preventive. *3 sg.* wiþstandeþ 256/2.

wlātian II (*impersonal*) feel nausea. *3 sg.* wlātige 34/12.

wlātung *f.* nausea 38/6.

wlæc *adj.* lukewarm 116/18, 124/9, 132/4, 142/16, 254/5.

gewlæht *see* wleccan.

wlætta *m.* nausea 138/6, 21, 250/4, 262/5.

wleccan 1 make lukewarm. *pp.* gewleht 120/12, 128/4, gewlæht 64/20, 144/9.

wōdenhund *see* wēdehund.

wōh *adj.* crooked 228/15.

wōl *m.* pestilence 236/5, 17, 20.

wōlberende *adj.* pestilential 234/15.

wolcenrēad *adj.* purple 170/2. [See also weolcrēad.]

womb *see* wamb.

wom(m) *m.* (*a*) spot, stain 208/3, 5, 244/13, 268/1, 2, etc. (*b*) impurity 254/3.

word *n.* word 234/3, 238/14, 15.

worsm, worms *n.* pus, matter 27/1, 54/8, 174/15, 206/18. [See also wyrms.]

wōs *n.* moisture, juice 30/20, 36/26, 38/23, 42/11, 70/17, etc.

wōsig *adj.* juicy 180/6, 190/4, 196/11.

wrǣc *m.* pain 244/9, 250/24. [Cf. ēag-~, fōt-~, hēafod-~, milt-~, tōþ-~, þeoh-~.]

wrīd *m.* shoot, stalk 148/2, 154/1.

(ge)wringan 3 wring, press out. *imp.* (ge)wring 30/20, 40/2, 27, 42/17, 72/23, etc.; *pp.* gewrungen 116/2, 192/18, gewrungan 112/18.

(ge)wrīþan 1 (*a*) fasten, tie. *2 sg.* gewrīþest 244/8; *pl.* wrīþaþ 264/6; *subj. sg.* gewrīþe 102/12;

imp. (**ge**)**wrīþ** 40/3, 44/17, 50/2, 54/4, 14, etc.; *pp.* **gewriþen** 138/11, 248/8, 11, 256/5, 270/26. (*b*) keep under control; staunch. *3 sg.* **gewrīþ** 86/17, 98/13, 112/2, 132/26, 166/16, etc.; *pl.* **gewrī-þaþ** 230/18.

gewriþennyss *f.* binding up 270/27.

wudubend *f.*? (*mistranslation of Latin* capparis) caper CLXXII. [See note to CLXXII.]

wudubucca *m.* wild buck 252/9, 12, **wudubuca** 252/23. [See note to *M* VI.]

wuduceruille, wuducerfilla *f.* wild chervil LXXXVI.

wududocce *f.* sorrel XXXIV.

wudugāt *f.* wild goat 252/16, 21, 254/4, 7. [See note to *M* VI.]

wuduhrofe *see* **wudurofe.**

wudulectric *m.* prickly lettuce XXXI.

wudurofe *f.* (*a*) asphodel, king's spear XXXIII. (*b*) (*also* **wuduhrofe**) (sweet) woodruff LIII.

wuduþistel *m.* sow-thistle CXI.

wulf *m.* wolf 262/18, 21, 23, 24, 25.

wulfes camb *m.* wild teasel XXVI, 196/4.

wulfes tǣsl *f.* carline thistle, wolf's-thistle CLVI.

wul(l) *f.* wool 40/27, 138/14, 186/13, 224/3, 258/24, etc.

wullian II wipe with wool. *imp.* **wulla** 260/8.

gewun *adj.* usual 110/17.

wund *f.* wound 36/6, 11, 13, 38/19, 40/20, etc. [Cf. **cancor-**~.]

wundel *f.* wound 46/25, 52/24, 60/21, 72/21, 78/11, etc.

wundian II wound. *pp.* **gewundud** 38/18, 128/23, **gewunded** 260/16. [Cf. **for-**~.]

wundorlic, wundurlic *adj.* wonderful, wondrous 46/3, 48/16, 62/24, 64/8, 76/2, etc.

wundorlīce, wundurlīce *adv.* wonderfully, wondrously 32/8, 44/20, 50/9, 18, 52/8, etc.

wundrian II *w. g.* wonder (at). *2 sg.* **wundrast** 92/25, 108/3, 164/7, 166/11, 172/7, etc., **wundrasþ**

62/20 (*see note to* XVIII. 3); *3 sg.* **wundraþ** 262/7.

wundrum *adv.* wonderfully, wondrously 38/12.

wundrung *f.* wondering, astonishment 50/11.

wundspring *m.* ulcerous wound 260/5.

gewunelic *adj.* customary, usual 192/10.

wunian II remain. *pres. p.* **wungynd** 52/2.

(**ge**)**wurpan** *see* (**ge**)**weorpan.**

gewyldan I subdue. *3 sg.* **gewyldeþ** 164/4.

wylfen *f.* she-wolf 264/11. [See note to *M* X. 7.]

wyll *m.* spring, fountain 68/6.

(**ge**)**wyllan** I boil. *subj. sg.* **wylle** 34/14, 36/3; *imp.* (**ge**)**wyl(l)** 30/20, 23, 32/7, 14, 17, etc.; *pp.* **gewylled** 86/24, 140/6, 152/10, 190/18, 198/10, etc., **gewyld** 56/20, 112/17. [Cf. **a-**~.]

wyllecærse *f.* fenugreek 86/8.

wyllewæter *n.* spring-water 126/7, 238/2.

wynlust *m.* sexual pleasure 238/2.

wynstra *adj.* left 128/10, 150/9, 172/13, 238/9, 270/29, etc.

wynsum *adj.* pleasant 196/23, 206/1.

(**ge**)**wyrcan** I (*a*) work, make, produce. *pl.* **gewyrceaþ** 84/15; *subj. sg.* **wyrce** 58/6, 60/14, 70/11, 80/12, 88/19, etc.; *imp.* (**ge**)**wyrc** 30/9, 32/6, 34/22, 36/15, 40/5, etc.; *pp.* **geworht** 130/3, 174/20, 182/27, 186/5, 192/2, etc. (*b*) gather, obtain (*Latin* legere). *inf.* **gewyrcean** 44/11. [Cf. **be-**~.]

wyrm *m.* worm; serpent 40/1, 48/17, 82/27, 29, 92/7, etc. [Cf. **in-**~, **reng-**~.]

(**ge**)**wyrman** I warm. *inf.* **tō gewyrmenne** 66/14; *imp.* (**ge**)**wyrm** 48/15, 60/11, 116/18.

wyrms *n.* pus, matter 258/4, 260/24. [See also **worsm.**]

wyrt *f.* herb, plant, wort 30/2, 6, 11, 15, 17, etc.; *nsg.* **wyrte** 188/5, 192/13. [Cf. **æþelferþinc(g)-**~ and the compounds in I, VI, VII, X, XI, XII, XIII, XVII, XX,

XXII, XXIII, XXIX, XLII,
XLVIII, LVI, LVII, LXXIII,
XCIII, XCVII, CXXVII,
CXXVIII, CXXXI, CXXXIII,
CXL, CLIV, CLXV.]

wyrtbedd *n.* bed *or* plot planted with
herbs, garden-bed 50/23, 120/15.

wyrtrīw *n.* myrtle 160/17.

wyrtrȳwen *adj.* of a myrtle 162/21.

wyrt(t)ruma *m.* root 30/9, 15, 46/10,
52/14, 58/8, etc.

wyrtūn ('wyrttūn') *m.* garden 48/11,
184/7.

wyrtung *f.* preparation seasoned with
herbs 248/16.

wyrtwala *m.* root 38/3, 29, 42/6, 21,
44/17, etc.

wyxþ *see* weaxan.

Y

ge̅ycan I add. *imp.* ge̅yc 224/2.

yfel (I) *adj.* bad, wicked, evil 56/4,
5, 114/5, 8, 136/9, etc. (II) *subst.*
n. (*a*) evil 214/24, 234/16, 238/1.
(*b*) disease, complaint 54/8, 68/13,
86/14, 102/10, 13, etc.

yfeldǣde *adj.* evil-doing 126/5.

yfele *adv.* ill, badly 146/14.

yfelnyss *f.* wickedness, badness
172/24.

ylca, ilca *adj.* same 30/11, 15, 19,
22, 32/1, etc.

yldincg, yldingc *f.* delay 62/2,
120/17, 128/12, 156/3, 164/22.

yldra *see* eald.

ylpenbān *n.* ivory 170/4, 270/3.

ylpenbānen *adj.* made of ivory
170/17.

ymb, ymbe *prep. w. a.* (*a*) around,
about (*local*) 82/27, 108/11, 142/20,
148/15, 150/2, etc., **ym** 206/18.
(*b*) after (*temporal*) 236/6, 240/1.
(*c*) about, concerning 262/26. (*d*) *in
combination* **ymb . . . ūtan** *prep.
w. a.* around 264/22.

ymbhwyrft *m.* (*a*) circuit, circum-
ference 236/14. [See note to *M* I.
7.] (*b*) extent, expanse 236/24.

ymfōn ('ymbfōn') 7c surround, en-
wrap. *imp.* **ymfōh** 246/12.

yndse, yntse *f.* ounce 34/14, 18,
68/22, 24, 92/22, etc.

yrmþ(u) *f.* misery, distress 206/17.

yrnan 3 run, flow. *subj. sg.* **yrne**
38/16, 42/27; *pres. p.* **yrnende**
238/2. [See also **blōd**.]

yrsung *f.* anger 224/23.

ysope *see* hysope.

ȳtemǣst ('ȳtemest') *adj. sup.* ex-
treme 246/14, 262/24.

APPENDIX I

THIS Appendix consists of four alphabetical lists containing plant names as described in the preliminary remarks to the Explanatory Notes E1, E2 (*a*), E3, and E4. The Glossary contains a number of OE plant names which do not answer to this description; they are mentioned here with the numbers of the chapters where they (first) occur: *æþelferþinc(g)wyrt* 63, *berbene* 67, *bere* 152, *cucumer* 185, *cyrfætte* 134, *ele(c)htre* 46, *eorþna-f(o)la* 97, *hindehæleþe* 63, *hysope* 57, *leac* 49, *lubastice* 146, *nard* 81, *rose* 100, *þistel* 134, *wad* 71, *wyllecærse* 39, *wyrtriw* 119. Further information about the nomenclature of these plants is given in the corresponding notes. See also note to 172 for *wudubend*.

For practical reasons arabic numbers are used to refer to the chapters, in OE words the symbol *ð* is replaced by *þ*, and in Latin words the voiced labiodental fricative is printed *v*.

1. INDEX OF OFFICIAL BOTANICAL NAMES

2. INDEX OF NON-ENGLISH PLANT NAMES

3. INDEX OF OLD ENGLISH PLANT NAMES

4. INDEX OF MODERN ENGLISH PLANT NAMES[1]

[1] The plant names in this list which consist of more than one single word are arranged according to the first letter of the first element, whether this is a separate word or the first element of a compound.

APPENDIX II

THE list in this Appendix contains a number of relevant parallel cures, to be found in:

(a) *Læceboc*, page/line references;

(b) *Lacnunga*, page/line references;

(c) Pliny (*MdQ* only; for parallels of cures in *OEH* see Explanatory Notes, Preliminary Remarks, E2 (*c*)), book and section references;

(d) Q. Serenus, author of a compilation of medicinal recipes known as *Liber Medicinalis* (third century), line references;

(e) Marcellus Empiricus Burdigalensis, author of a compilation of medicinal recipes known as *Liber de Medicamentis* (fifth century), a work 'chiefly noteworthy as marking the depth of futility to which "medicine" descended' (see Bonser, pp. 39 f.), chapter and section references.

I.
1 : Ma. xx/106
4 : Ma. ix/75
7 : Ma. x/57
8 : *Lb* 16/22
9 : *Lb* 20/23
10 : *Lb* 20/31, *La* 168/5
11 : Ma. xxviii/64
13 : *Lb* 17/9, *La* 166/9
17 : *Lb* 45/35
25 : *Lb* 44/4
29 : *La* 170/16, Ma. xxxvi/8

II.
10 : *Lb* 37/18
17 : *Lb* 21/35

III.
7 : *Lb* 34/9

IV.
4 : Ma. xxii/35
6 : Ma. i/46

V.
1 : *Lb* 13/19

XI.
Intr. : *Lb* 46/20

XIII.
2 : *Lb* 21/28

XVIII.
3 : Ma. xxiii/26

XIX.
5 : Ma. ix/21, ix/81

XXI.
2 : Ma. iv/16
3 : Ma. xx/79
4 : Ma. xv/78

XXX.
1, 2 : Ma. xi/16

XXXII.
1 : Ma. viii/163

XXXV.
1a : Ma. xxii/32

XXXVI.
2 : Ma. viii/91

XLIII.
2 : Ma. xxxiv/23

XLVI.
1 : *Lb* 96/13, Q. Serenus 298

LXXIII.
2 : Ma. xxxvi/6

LXXV.
1, 2 : *Lb* 9/8

LXXVII.
　4b: Ma. xxxvi/9
LXXX.
　2: *Lb* 75/37
LXXXII.
　1: *Lb* 100/26
LXXXIV.
　1: Q. Serenus 515
LXXXVI.
　2: Ma. xii/39
　3: Ma. xxvi/49
LXXXVII.
　3: *La* 164/19
LXXXVIII.
　1: Ma. viii/32
LXXXIX.
　1: Ma. ix/85
XCI.
　1: Ma. x/38
　2: *Lb* 109/1, Ma. xx/64
　3: Ma. xx/60
　7: *Lb* 6/26, Q. Serenus 99
XCII.
　1: Q. Serenus 167
　2: Q. Serenus 134, Ma. xix/21
XCIV.
　2: *Lb* 56/8, *La* 180/6, Ma. xx/20
　3: *La* 172/4
　4: *Lb* 109/5
　11: *Lb* 109/3, *La* 180/6
XCVII.
　2: Ma. xii/39
C.
　3: Ma. xxiii/60
　6: Ma. x/59
　8: Ma. i/79
CI.
　2: Ma. i/75
CIII.
　1: *Lb* 22/12
CIV.
　1: Q. Serenus 570
　2: *Lb* 100/28

CVII.
　1: Ma. xxvi/61
CXI.
　1: *Lb* 109/8
CXIII.
　1: *Lb* 109/10
CXVII.
　3: *Lb* 65/1, Ma. xxii/1
CXIX.
　1: Ma. i/74
CXXVI.
　1: *La* 166/5, Ma. xvi/21
CXXX.
　2: *Lb* 20/28
CXXXVII.
　3: Ma. xix/64
CLXXVIII.
　7: *Lb* 46/3
M III.
　1: Pl. xxviii/167
　2: *Lb* 7/17, Pl. xxviii/166
　3: Pl. xxviii/178, Ma. xii/8
　4: Pl. xxviii/246
　5: *Lb* 37/25, Pl. xxviii/211
　6: Pl. xxviii/149
　8: Pl. xxviii/200
　10: Pl. xxviii/187
　15: Pl. xxviii/150
　17: Pl. xxviii/247
　19: Pl. xxviii/150
M IV.
　2: Pl. xxviii/165
　3: Pl. xxviii/176
　4: Pl. xxviii/201
　5: Pl. xxviii/177, Ma. xv/74
　6: Pl. xxviii/197, Ma. xvii/2
　9: Pl. xxviii/166
　11: Pl. xxviii/220
　13: *La* 98/10
　14: Pl. xxviii/176
M V.
　1: Pl. xxviii/215, Ma. xxvi/125,
　　Q. Serenus 587
　2: Pl. xxviii/172

3: Pl. xxviii/221, Ma. xxxiv/29
4, 5: Pl. xxviii/224–5
7: *Lb* 10/7
9: Pl. xxviii/213
10: Pl. xxviii/199, Ma. xxvi/19
11: Pl. xxviii/166
12: Pl. xxviii/248
15: Pl. xxviii/154
16: Pl. xxviii/259
17: Pl. xxviii/199, Ma. xxviii/21
19: Pl. xxviii/170

M VI.
1: Pl. xxviii/240
2: *Lb* 10/3, Pl. xxviii/171
3, 4: Pl. xxviii/189, Ma. xv/27
6, 7: Pl. xxviii/187–8
8: *Lb* 13/24, Pl. xxviii/176
10: Pl. xxviii/214, Ma. xxxiii/41
12: Pl. xxviii/259

M VII.
4: Ma. x/44
5: Pl. xxviii/169, Ma. viii/40
8: Pl. xxviii/152
13: Pl. xxviii/206
16: Pl. xxviii/232
17: *Lb* 13/25, Pl. xxviii/176, Ma. ix/105
18: Ma. xv/76
22: *Lb* 22/38
23: *Lb* 21/22, Ma. xxxv/20, xxxv/28
25: Pl. xxviii/255

M VIII.
1: Pl. xxix/32, Ma. xxiii/56
2: Pl. xxx/72, xxx/113, Ma. xxxii/39
3: Pl. xxx/28, xxx/120
4: Pl. xxx/108, Ma. xxxiv/14

M IX.
2: Pl. xxviii/213, Ma. xxxiii/37
3: Pl. xxviii/152
5: Pl. xxviii/202, Ma. xxvii/96
7: Pl. xxviii/173, Ma. ix/99
8: Pl. xxviii/261
9: Pl. xxviii/224
11: Pl. xxviii/212, Ma. xxvi/73, xxvi/102
12: *Lb* 28/4, Pl. xxviii/215
13: Ma. xxv/41

M X.
3: Pl. viii/80
5: Pl. xxx/51, Ma. xxiii/47, xxiii/48
9: Pl. xxx/81, Ma. xix/65
10: Pl. xxix/133, Ma. ix/21
11: Pl. xxix/100
13: Pl. xxix/102, xxx/143
18: Pl. xxx/105

M XII.
4: Pl. xxviii/203, Ma. xxviii/17
5: *Lb* 13/28, Pl. xxviii/173, Q. Serenus 171, 174
9: Pl. xxviii/205

M XIII.
1: Pl. xxviii/88

M XIV.
1: Pl. xxix/58, Q. Serenus 439
3: Ma. xxiii/40
5: *Lb* 100/22, Pl. xxx/114
6: Pl. xxx/111
7, 8: Pl. xxix/98
9: Pl. xxx/119
10: Pl. xxix/117, Ma. viii/142
11: Pl. xxx/21
13: Pl. xxx/22
14: Pl. xxix/99